THE FINANCIAL AND ECONOMIC CRISES AND THEIR IMPACT ON HEALTH AND SOCIAL WELL-BEING

Edited by

Vicente Navarro and Carles Muntaner

POLICY, POLITICS, HEALTH AND MEDICINE SERIES
Vicente Navarro, Series Editor

Routledge
Taylor & Francis Group

LONDON AND NEW YORK

First published 2014 by Baywood Publishing Company, Inc.

Published 2017 by Routledge
2 Park Square, Milton Park, Abingdon, Oxon OX14 4RN
711 Third Avenue, New York, NY 10017, USA

Routledge is an imprint of the Taylor & Francis Group, an informa business

Copyright © 2014 by Taylor & Francis

Library of Congress Catalog Number: 2014008221
ISBN 13: 978-0-89503-878-4 (hbk)
ISBN 13: 978-0-89503-879-1 (pbk)

Library of Congress Cataloging-in-Publication Data

The financial and economic crises and their impact on health and social
well-being / edited by Vicente Navarro and Carles Muntaner.
    p. ; cm. -- (Policy, politics, health and medicine series)
    The contributions in this volume, articles selected from the
International Journal of Health Services, contrast explicitly with
conventional approaches to population health and offer new insights and
results that advance a critical understanding of public health.
    Includes bibliographical references.
    ISBN 978-0-89503-878-4 (cloth : alk. paper) -- ISBN 978-0-89503-879-1
(pbk. : alk. paper) -- ISBN 978-0-89503-880-7 (e-pub) -- ISBN
978-0-89503-881-4 (e-pdf)
    I. Navarro, Vicente, editor. II. Muntaner, Carles, 1957- editor. III.
International journal of health services. Contained in (work): IV.
Series: Policy, politics, health, and medicine series (Unnumbered)
    [DNLM: 1. Health Policy--Collected Works. 2. Public Health--
economics--Collected Works. 3. Social Determinants of Health--Collected
Works. 4. Socioeconomic Factors--Collected Works. WA 530.1]
    RA410.5
    362.1068'1--dc23

2014008221

Credit line: INDUSTRIAL WORKERS OF THE WORLD: "*Pyramid of Capitalist System,
issued by Nedeljkovich, Brashick and Kuharich, Cleveland: The International Publishing
Co., 1911.*" Used with permission.

Contents

Introduction

Vicente Navarro and Carles Muntaner

Most parts of the globalized world are facing economic crises and political turmoil not seen since the Great Depression of the 1930s and 1940s. Daily reports of the current global recession are as predictable as they are discouraging: "Economy Expected to Show Sluggish Growth" (1); "Eurozone Unemployment Rate Remains at Record High 12.2 Per Cent" (2); "Britain Reels as Austerity Cuts Begin" (3). Now and again, bleak economic forecasts are interrupted by the promise of economic recovery; however, these promises have proved to be overly optimistic: "Hopes for Faster Global Growth Dashed" (4). Moreover, the ongoing crisis has triggered new or has exacerbated existing health problems, including, for example, increasing rates of intravenous drug use, HIV/AIDS, and suicides, as well as falling fertility rates (5–7). Clearly, the global recession has had negative effects on the larger economy as a whole and on the health of individuals as a population. The proverbial light at the end of the tunnel seems farther away than ever, especially since the so-called Troika—the European Commission, the European Central Bank, and the International Monetary Fund—has prescribed that debt-ridden nations should follow a harsh regimen of austerity measures, prioritizing debt over people, rather than stimulus measures, which protect people during economically vulnerable times.

Explanations for why the economic crisis occurred in the first place and how to solve the crisis are abundant. Not surprisingly, most explanations implicate the failings of individuals and financial interest groups in causing the crisis (e.g., individuals with poor credit and insufficient incomes took on too much personal debt and created a housing bubble). Dominant explanations also favor neoliberal solutions to encourage economic recovery (e.g., cost-cutting policies that scale back social spending, reduce the size of governments, and privatize public goods). Placing the onus on individuals and dismantling welfare states have the injurious effects of overlooking unequal power relations, accepting the status quo, and shifting the balance of political power toward the right and its preference for fiscal conservatism.

1

Rather than the current crisis being viewed as a direct consequence of unequal political and economic relations, the Great Recession is often understood as a normal, temporary glitch of an otherwise workable system. In more concrete terms, this line of thinking contends that capitalist relations, banking institutions, multinational corporations, and sovereign governments are interrelated parts that, in theory, effectively and efficiently work together to promote economic growth, maximize worker productivity, and generate global levels of financial prosperity. In practice, however, the contradictions and consequences of this social system have been known for decades and made crystal-clear in recent years during the economic crisis. On the one hand, welfare capitalism is charged with the task of regulating financial activities and providing social protections to the unemployed, disabled, and elderly, for example. Democratically elected state governments are expected to organize the distribution and redistribution of economic resources by legislating rules of exchange between the state, market, and family. On the other hand, these rules of exchange and social protections are now expected to undergo necessary self-corrections that overwhelmingly favor the interests of business and markets over the interests of families and workers. As a result, the global recession has reframed the interactions between the state and the market in a way that empowers the latter. Through generous corporate bailouts, weaker labor unions, and strengthened ties with pro-market political parties, business has been able to *increase* its economic power, political influence, and cultural dominance during the downs of the Great Recession.

Given that most attention is paid to figuring out the motivations and behaviors of individuals and interest groups, our understanding of how economic, political, and ideological contexts contributed to the crisis in the first place and how these contexts exacerbate the negative consequences of the crisis remains at best limited and at worst detrimental. Possessing a limited focus comes at a tremendous intellectual and public health cost—researchers remain largely ignorant of how economic crises occur, why crises occur with some regularity, and, perhaps most important for our discussion, what the health consequences of capitalist relations are that create economic cycles of "booms and busts." These questions should challenge public health researchers to explicitly consider solutions, strategies, and interventions that bring about desired change that, in turn, improves health and reduces health inequalities.

Taken together, our central argument is that the current global recession should serve as a clarion call for fellow public health researchers to think more critically about population health and health inequalities. Thinking critically involves developing a better understanding of how economic, political, and cultural forms of power are unequally distributed in capitalist societies, and how these unequal power relations affect the well-being of populations. The underlying claims are that economic and political events do not unfold in vacuums, are not randomly distributed, and reflect the ongoing social struggle between more powerful and less powerful actors over valuable resources. From a social conflict perspective, economic and political events mirror unequal distributions of power and, in particular, the unequal distribution of social class relations, or capitalist versus working-class power. Although a consideration of social class is forbidden (by some), forgotten (by others), and controversial (for most), structured relations between employers, managers, and workers persist as a defining feature of unequal power relations in capitalist societies and remain underexamined within the context of the current recession. Our position is three-fold: first, private-property rights allow some actors to own productive means; second, these rights empower owners to control the labor of workers to their own advantage; and third, private-property rights function as a primary determinant of unequal power relations and health outcomes.

An understanding of social class relations is essential to understanding the connections between the current economic crisis and population health, especially given that social class plays such a dominant role in generating and reproducing social inequalities at different levels and through different pathways. Examples of the power of social classes are plentiful: social class relations influence the ability of political parties to win elections (e.g., political lobbying and financing of election campaigns), shape popular views on the advantages or disadvantages of labor unions (e.g., increasing wages, job security, and class solidarity), and institutionalize the degree to which employer-worker relations are exploitative (e.g., adopting and enforcing occupational safety measures). Among the most prominent mechanisms by which social class relations affect health inequalities is through the production and reproduction of ideology. By influencing dominant value-generating systems such as schools, workplaces, and media outlets, dominant ideologies are often presented with ample justification as to why a certain approach is the only or best option for moving forward. Neoliberalism serves as a prime example. From the perspective of class ideology, neoliberalism argues that the current economic crisis was caused in large part by welfare state expansion. If welfare states are the problem, the ensuing logic claims that economic recovery requires a drastic restructuring and retrenchment of welfare state regulations, programs, and services. Neoliberalism encompasses a whole series of public interventions, also known as austerity policies, which reduce health-promoting resources provided through the welfare state (8, 9). Much like Thatcher's "there is no alternative" slogan during the 1980s, the current economic crisis has produced its own neoliberal mantra: austerity is the panacea for all our economic woes.

Needless to say, social class relations alone do not fully or adequately explain the complex roots and consequences of the economic crisis. Other unequal power relations, including those related to gender (sexism), race/ethnicity (racism), and immigrant/migrant status (xenophobia), among other unjust inequalities, are important determinants of social inequalities in health. However, the key idea is that social class has generated, and continues to generate, avoidable inequalities in capitalist societies. In fact, these inequalities have increased dramatically during the current recession. Given this, any explanation of the current crisis requires incorporating a social class perspective so as to understand the modus operandi of the economic-financial-political system. A critical understanding of how class relations are produced and reproduced across time and place represents a logical starting point to unravel the complex links between the global recession, capitalist economies, business-worker relations, welfare states, population health, and health inequalities. To this end, the current volume provides a distinct perspective on how social class, as well as gender, race, and other inequalities, affects the well-being of capitalist societies experiencing economic crises and political turmoil.

The contributions in this volume—articles selected from the *International Journal of Health Services* (*IJHS*)—contrast explicitly with conventional approaches to population health and offer new insights and results that advance a critical understanding of public health. The chapters are organized around six themes. Part I applies a social-conflict perspective to better understand how political forces, processes, and institutions precede and give rise to social inequalities, economic instability, and population health. The need to politicize dominant (neoliberal) ideologies is emphasized, given its explanatory power to elucidate unequal power relations. Since social class affects well-being through several pathways and interventions, and interacts with welfare states to influence the characteristics and generosity of social protection policies, the next four parts focus on the health impacts of growing inequalities and economic decline on government services and transfers (Part II); labor markets and employment conditions (Part III); welfare states and regimes (Part IV); and social class relations (Part V). The volume concludes by presenting specific alternative proposals, analyzing some of the well-known studies that seek to move beyond conventional policy recommendations. Specifically, Part VI advocates for a more politically engaged approach to population health and presents alternative solutions for achieving egalitarian outcomes.

In several ways, the current crisis resembles a dense fog filled with perplexity and confusion. (How did it begin? What are its effects? How can we overcome the crisis?) In response, this volume provides a timely collection of the most germane studies and commentaries that effectively clear this fog of confusion and improve visibility (seeing the crisis through a critical perspective), increase understanding (considering the economic and political contexts of the crisis), and motivate action (curbing the power of business by mobilizing the power of leftist collective political actors). Taken together, these individual works reflect the *IJHS*' enduring commitment to publishing high-impact studies, inspiring fruitful debates, and advancing the discipline in new and critical ways. As always, the publishing goal of *IJHS*, as evidenced by this collection, is to offer the public health community a much-needed critical perspective on the determinants of population health and health inequalities in order to effect social change.

This introduction cannot conclude without thanking, for their editorial assistance, Edwin Ng at the University of Toronto, *IJHS* copyeditors Linda Strange and Amy Burroughs, and *IJHS* managing editors Paloma Navas and Colleen Boland, all of whom worked tirelessly to prepare this collection for publication.

REFERENCES

1. Wearden, G. *Guardian*, October 26, 2010. www.theguardian.com/business/2010/oct/26/economy-expected-to-show-sluggish-growth.
2. Baetz, J. Associated Press, October 31, 2013. www.foxnews.com/world/2013/10/31/eurozone-unemployment-rate-remains-at-record-high-122-percent-in.
3. Lyall, S. *New York Times*, August 9, 2010. www.nytimes.com/2010/08/10/world/europe/10britain.html.
4. Jones, C., Carnegy, H., and Politi, J. *Financial Times*, November 14, 2013.
5. De Vogli, R., Marmot, M., and Stuckler, D. Excess suicides and attempted suicides in Italy attributable to the great recession. *Journal of Epidemiology and Community Health* 67(4):378–379, 2013. www.ft.com/cms/s/0/8f178ee0-4c81-11e3-958f-00144feabdc0.html#axzz2lVfInHuo.
6. Malliori, M., et al. Financial crisis, austerity, and health in Europe. *Lancet* 382(9890): 392, 2013.
7. Michas, G., Papadopoulos, S., and Micha, R. Austerity in Greece not only kills but also curtails births and marriages. *BMJ* 347, 2013.
8. Stuckler, B. and Basu, S. *The Body Economic: Why Austerity Kills*. Penguin, UK, 2013.
9. Blyth, M. *Austerity: The History of a Dangerous Idea*. Oxford University Press, 2013.

PART I

The Causes of the Crisis

Edwin Ng

INTRODUCTION

This first part of the book revolves around two central questions: What explains the inequalities across and within nations? And what are the underlying causes of the most recent financial crisis? The answers to these questions have enormous implications for the health and well-being of populations and, by extension, reflect the extent to which welfare states institutionalize equality and intervene in market affairs.

Common explanations for growing inequalities are often based on modernization theories (e.g., inequalities reflect technological differences between countries), structural-functional paradigms (e.g., inequalities are natural, useful, and inevitable in the pursuit of innovation and economic growth), and systems of meritocracy (e.g., inequalities are no more than the sum of personal merit). Efforts to explain the most recent financial crisis are wide-ranging and include factors focused on the risk-taking behaviors of consumers (e.g., individuals overleveraged themselves), characteristics of the U.S. housing market (e.g., sub-prime lending, mortgage fraud, and predatory lending), and lack of government oversight (e.g., deregulation).

A notable omission from current explanations has been the undeniable importance of politics in shaping and influencing inequalities, on the one hand, and responding to the Great Recession, on the other. To these ends, the two chapters in Part I reorient our critical understanding of inequalities, financial

6

instability, welfare states, and population health toward a more politically informed paradigm. In Chapter 1, Navarro argues that the key driver of inequalities in capitalist economies is neoliberalism, or the political-economic ideology that skews toward private enterprise, big business, free markets, competitiveness, restructuring, and deficit reduction as governing priorities. Then, in Chapter 2, Navarro makes the compelling argument that political ideologies matter, and, in particular, the dominance of right-wing parties and their fiscal conservative agendas that preceded the collapse of financial markets and guided the resulting austerity policies. Intellectually, these two contributions add a much-needed critical understanding of how politics, power, and ideology determine the nature of welfare states, which, in turn, affect inequalities in population health.

CHAPTER 1

Neoliberalism as a Class Ideology; Or, the Political Causes of the Growth of Inequalities

Vicente Navarro

Neoliberalism is the dominant ideology permeating the public policies of many governments in developed and developing countries and of international agencies such as the World Bank, International Monetary Fund, World Trade Organization, and many technical agencies of the United Nations, including the World Health Organization. This ideology postulates that the reduction of state interventions in economic and social activities and the deregulation of labor and financial markets, as well as of commerce and investments, have liberated the enormous potential of capitalism to create an unprecedented era of social well-being in the world's population. This chapter questions each of the theses that support such ideology, presenting empirical information that challenges them. The author also describes how the application of these neoliberal policies has been responsible for a substantial growth of social inequalities within the countries where such policies have been applied, as well as among countries. The major beneficiaries of these policies are the dominant classes of both the developed and the developing countries, which have established worldwide class alliances that are primarily responsible for the promotion of neoliberalism.

*****

A trademark of our times is the dominance of *neoliberalism* in the major economic, political, and social forums of the developed capitalist countries and in the international agencies they influence—including the International Monetary Fund (IMF), the World Bank, the World Trade Organization (WTO), and the technical agencies of the United Nations, such as the World Health Organization (WHO), Food and Agriculture Organization, and UNICEF. Starting in the United States during the Carter administration, neoliberalism expanded its influence through the Reagan administration and, in the United Kingdom, the Thatcher administration, to become an international ideology. Neoliberalism holds to a theory (though not necessarily a practice) that posits the following:

1. The state (or what is wrongly referred to in popular parlance as "the government") needs to reduce its interventionism in economic and social activities.
2. Labor and financial markets need to be deregulated in order to liberate the enormous creative energy of the markets.
3. Commerce and investments need to be stimulated by eliminating borders and barriers to allow for the full mobility of labor, capital, goods, and services.

Following these three tenets, according to neoliberal authors, we have seen that the worldwide implementation of such practices has led to the development of a "new" process: a globalization of economic activity that has generated a period of enormous economic growth worldwide, associated with a new era of social progress. For the first time in history, we are told, we are witnessing a worldwide economy, in which states are losing power and are being replaced by a worldwide market centered in multinational corporations, which are the main units of economic activity in the world today.

This celebration of the process of globalization is also evident among some sectors of the left. Michael Hardt and Antonio Negri, in their widely cited *Empire* (1), celebrate the great creativity of what they consider to be a new era of capitalism. This new era, they claim, breaks with obsolete state structures and establishes a new international order, which they define as an imperialist order. They further postulate that this new imperialist order is maintained without any state dominating or being hegemonic in that order. Thus, they write (1, p. 39):

> We want to emphasize that the establishment of empire is a positive step towards the elimination of nostalgic activities based on previous power structures; we reject all political strategies that want to take us back to past situations such as the resurrection of the nation-state in order to protect the population from global capital. We believe that the new imperialist order is better than the previous system in the same way that Marx believed that capitalism was a mode of production and a type of society superior to the mode that it replaced. This point of view held by Marx was based on a healthy despisement of the parochial localism and rigid hierarchies that preceded the capitalist society, as well as on the recognition of the enormous potential for liberation that capitalism had.

Globalization (i.e., the internationalization of economic activity according to neoliberal tenets) becomes, in Hardt and Negri's position, an international system that is stimulating a worldwide activity that operates without any state or states leading or organizing it. Such an admiring and flattering view of globalization and neoliberalism explains the positive reviews that *Empire* has received from Emily Eakin, a book reviewer for the *New York Times,* and other mainstream critics, not known for sympathetic reviews of books that claim to derive their theoretical position from Marxism. Actually, Eakin describes *Empire* as the theoretical framework that the world needs to understand its reality.

Hardt and Negri celebrate and applaud, along with neoliberal authors, the expansion of globalization. Other left-wing authors, however, mourn rather than celebrate this expansion, regarding globalization as the cause of the world's growing inequalities and poverty. It is important to stress that even though the authors in this latter group—which includes, for example, Susan George and Eric Hobsbawm—lament globalization and criticize neoliberal thinking, they still share with neoliberal authors the basic assumptions of neoliberalism: that states are losing power in an international order in which the power of multinational corporations has replaced the power of states, operating within a global market that is responsible for the international order (which neoliberals applaud) or disorder (which some left-wing critics lament).

THE CONTRADICTION BETWEEN THEORY AND PRACTICE IN NEOLIBERALISM

Let's be clear right away that neoliberal *theory* is one thing and neoliberal *practice* another thing entirely. Most members of the Organization for Economic Cooperation and Development (OECD)—including the U.S. federal government—have seen state interventionism and state public expenditures *increase* during the past 30 years. My area of scholarship is public policy, and, as such, I study the nature of state interventions in many parts of the world. I can testify to the expansion of state intervention in most countries in the developed capitalist world. Even in the United States, Reagan's neoliberalism did not translate into a decline of the federal public sector. As a matter of fact, federal public expenditures increased under his mandate, from 21.6 to 23 percent of gross national product (GNP), as a consequence of a spectacular growth in military expenditures from 4.9 to 6.1 percent of GNP during the Reagan years (2). This growth in public expenditures was financed by an increase in the federal deficit (creating a burgeoning of the federal debt) and increase in taxes. As the supposedly anti-tax president, Reagan in fact increased taxes for a greater number of people (in peace time) than any other president in U.S. history. And he increased taxes not once, but twice (in 1982 and in 1983). In a demonstration of class power, he reduced the taxes of the top 20 percent (by income) of the population enormously, at the cost of increasing taxes for the majority of the population.

It is not accurate, therefore, to say that President Reagan reduced the role of the state in the United States by reducing the size of the public sector and lowering taxes. What Reagan (and Carter before him) did was dramatically change the nature of state intervention, such that it benefited even more the upper classes and the economic groups (such as military-related corporations) that financed his electoral campaigns. Reagan's policies were indeed class policies that hurt the majority of the nation's working class. Reagan was profoundly anti-labor, making cuts in social expenditures at an unprecedented level. It bears repeating that Reagan's policies were not liberal: they were Keynesian, based on large public expenditures and large federal deficits. Also, the federal government intervened very actively in the nation's industrial development (mainly, but not exclusively, through the Defense Department). As Caspar Weinberger (3), secretary of defense in the Reagan administration, once indicated (in response to criticisms by the Democratic Party that the U.S. government had abandoned the manufacturing sector), "Our Administration is the Administration that has a more advanced and extended industrial policy in the western world." He was right. No other Western government had such an extensive industrial policy. And today, the huge growth of the U.S. biomedical industry is to a large degree stimulated by an active state intervention. Indeed, the U.S. federal state is one of the most interventionist states in the Western world.

There exists very robust scientific evidence that the United States is not a liberal state (as it is constantly defined) and that the U.S. state is not reducing its key role in developing the national economy, including in the production and distribution of goods and services by large U.S. corporations—which, incidentally, are wrongly referred to as "multinationals" but are actually "transnationals." *This empirical evidence shows that the U.S. federal government's interventionism (in the economic, political, cultural, and security spheres) has increased over the past 30 years.* In the economic sphere, for example, protectionism has not declined. It has increased, with higher subsidies to the agricultural, military, aerospace, and biomedical sectors. In the social arena, public interventions to weaken social rights (and most particularly labor rights) have increased enormously (not only under Reagan, but also under Bush Senior, Clinton, and Bush Junior), and surveillance of the citizenry has increased exponentially. Again, there has been no diminution of federal interventionism in the United States, but rather an even more skewed class character to this intervention during the past 30 years.

Neoliberal narrative about the declining role of the state in people's lives is easily falsified by the facts. Indeed, as John Williamson, one of the intellectual architects of neoliberalism, once indicated, "We have to recognize that what the U.S. government promotes abroad, the U.S. government does not follow at home," adding that "the U.S. government promotes policies that are not followed in the U.S." (4, p. 213). It could not have been said better. In other words, if you want to understand U.S. public policies, look at what the U.S. government does, not what it says. This same situation occurs in the majority of developed capitalist countries. Their states have become more, not less, interventionist. The size of the state (measured by public expenditures per capita) has increased in most of these countries. Again, the empirical information on this point is strong. What has been happening is not a reduction of the state but rather a change in the nature of state intervention—further strengthening its class character.

DETERIORATION OF THE WORLD ECONOMIC AND
SOCIAL SITUATION

Another correction that needs to be made as a rebuttal to neoliberal dogma is that neoliberal public policies have been remarkably unsuccessful at achieving what they claim to be their aims: economic efficiency and social well-being. If we compare the period 1980–2000 (when neoliberalism reached its maximum expression)[1] with the immediately preceding period, 1960–1980, we can easily see that 1980–2000 was much less successful than 1960–1980 in most developed and developing capitalist countries. As Table 1 shows, the rate of growth and the rate of growth per capita in all developing (non-OECD) countries (excluding China) were much higher in 1960–1980 (5.5% and 3.2%) than in 1980–2000 (2.6% and 0.7%). Mark Weisbrot, Dean Baker, and David Rosnick (7) have documented that the improvement in quality-of-life and well-being indicators (infant mortality, rate of school enrollment, life expectancy, and others) increased faster in 1960–1980 than in 1980–2000 (when comparing countries at the same level of development at the starting year of each period). And as Table 2 shows, the annual rate of economic growth per capita in the developed capitalist countries was lower in 1980–2000 than in 1960–1980. But, what is also important to stress is that due to the larger annual economic growth per capita in the OECD countries than in the developing countries (except China), the difference in their rates of growth per capita has been increasing dramatically. This means, in practical terms, that income inequalities between these two types of countries have grown spectacularly, and particularly between the extremes (see Table 2). But, most important, inequalities have increased dramatically not only among but *within* countries, developed and developing alike. Adding both types of inequalities (among and within countries), we find that, as Branco Milanovic (8) has documented, the top 1 percent of the world population receives 57 percent of the world income, and the income difference between those at the top and those at the bottom has increased from 78 to 114 times.

It bears emphasizing that even though poverty has increased worldwide and within countries that are following neoliberal public policies, this does not mean

---

[1] The starting point of neoliberalism and of the growth in inequalities was July 1979, with Paul Volker's dramatic increase in interest rates that slowed down economic growth—plus the two oil shocks that particularly affected countries highly dependent on imported oil (see 5). Volker increased interest rates (thus creating a worldwide recession) as an anti–working class move to weaken labor in the United States and abroad. The rate increase also initiated, as Arrighi (6) noted, a flow of capital to the United States, making it very difficult for other countries, especially poor countries, to compete for the limited capital. The fact that petrol Euro dollars (which increased enormously with the oil shocks) were deposited in the United States made the scarcity of capital particularly hard for poor countries to adapt to. This is the time when the stagnation of the poor countries started. The countries most affected by these neoliberal public policies were the Latin American countries, which followed these policies extensively, and the African countries (the poorest of the poor), which saw extremely negative economic growth. In 2000, 24 African countries had a smaller GNP per capita than 25 years earlier.

Table 1

Economic growth, 1960–2000

	1960–1980	1980–2000
Rate of economic growth in developing countries (except China):		
Annual economic growth	5.5%	2.6%
Annual economic growth per capita	3.2%	0.7%
Rate of economic growth in China:		
Annual economic growth	4.5%	9.8%
Annual economic growth per capita	2.5%	8.4%

Sources: World Bank, *World Development Indicators,* 2001; R. Pollin, *Contours of Descent,* Verso, 2003, p. 131.

Table 2

I. Average annual rate of economic growth per capita in the OECD and developing countries

	1961–1980	1981–2000
(A) OECD countries	3.5%	2.0%
(B) Developing countries (except China)	3.2%	0.7%
Growth differential (A – B)	0.3%	1.3%

II. Growth in income inequalities, 1980–1998 (excluding China)

Income of richest 50% as share of poorest 50%	4% more unequal
Income of richest 20% as share of poorest 20%	8% more unequal
Income of richest 10% as share of poorest 10%	19% more unequal
Income of richest 1% as share of poorest 1%	77% more unequal

Sources: World Bank, *World Development Indicators,* 2001; R. Sutcliffe, *A More or Less Unequal World?* Political Economy Research Institute, 2003; R. Pollin, *Contours of Descent,* Verso, 2003, p. 133.

the rich within each country (including developing countries) have been adversely affected. As a matter of fact, the rich saw their incomes and their distance from the non-rich increase substantially. Class inequalities have increased greatly in most capitalist countries.

NEOLIBERALISM AS THE ROOT OF INEQUALITIES

In each of these countries, then, the income of those at the top has grown spectacularly as a result of state interventions. Consequently, we need to turn to some of the categories and concepts discarded by large sectors of the left: class structure, class power, class struggle, and their impact on the state. These scientific categories continue to be of key importance to understanding what is going on in each country. Let me clarify that a scientific concept can be very old but not antiquated. "Ancient" and "antiquated" are two different concepts. The law of gravity is very old but is not antiquated. Anyone who doubts this can test it by jumping from the tenth floor. There is a risk that some sectors of the left may pay an equally suicidal cost by ignoring scientific concepts such as class and class struggle simply because these are old concepts. We cannot understand the world (from the Iraq War to the rejection of the European Constitution) without acknowledging the existence of classes and class alliances, established worldwide between the dominant classes of the developed capitalist world and those of the developing capitalist world. *Neoliberalism is the ideology and practice of the dominant classes of the developed and developing worlds alike.*

But before we jump ahead, let's start with the situation in each country. Neoliberal ideology was the dominant classes' response to the considerable gains achieved by the working and peasant classes between the end of World War II and the mid-1970s. The huge increase in inequalities that has occurred since then is the direct result of the growth in income and well-being of the dominant classes, which is a consequence of class-determined public policies such as: (*a*) *deregulation of labor markets,* an anti–working class move; (*b*) *deregulation of financial markets,* which has greatly benefited financial capital, the hegemonic branch of capital in the period 1980–2005; (*c*) *deregulation of commerce in goods and services,* which has benefited the high-consumption population at the expense of laborers; (*d*) *reduction of social public expenditures,* which has hurt the working class; (*e*) *privatization of services,* which has benefited the top 20 percent of the population (by income) at the expense of the well-being of the working classes that use public services; (*f*) *promotion of individualism and consumerism,* hurting the culture of solidarity; (*g*) *development of a theoretical narrative and discourse that pays rhetorical homage to the markets,* but masks a clear alliance between transnationals and the state in which they are based; and (*h*) *promotion of an anti-interventionist discourse,* that is in clear conflict with the actual increased state interventionism, to promote the interests of the dominant classes and the economic units—the transnationals—that foster their interests. Each of these class-determined public policies requires a state action or intervention that conflicts with the interests of the working and other popular classes.

THE PRIMARY CONFLICT IN TODAY'S WORLD: NOT BETWEEN NORTH AND SOUTH BUT BETWEEN AN ALLIANCE OF DOMINANT CLASSES OF NORTH AND SOUTH AGAINST DOMINATED CLASSES OF NORTH AND SOUTH

It has become part of the conventional wisdom that the primary conflict in the world is between the rich North and the poor South. The North and the South, however, have classes with opposing interests that have established alliances at the international level. This situation became clear to me when I was advising President Allende in Chile. The fascist coup led by General Pinochet was not, as was widely reported, a coup imposed by the rich North (the United States) on the poor South (Chile). Those who brutally imposed the Pinochet regime were the dominant classes of Chile (bourgeoisie, petit bourgeoisie, and upper-middle professional classes), with the support not of the United States (U.S. society is not an aggregate of 240 million imperialists!) but of the Nixon administration (Nixon as spokesperson for the dominant classes of the United States)—which at that time was very unpopular in the United States, having sent the Army to put down the coalminers' strike in Appalachia.

A lack of awareness of the existence of classes often leads to condemnation of an entire country, frequently the United States. But, in fact, the U.S. working class is one of the first victims of U.S. imperialism. Some will say that the U.S. working class benefits from imperialism. Gasoline, for example, is very cheap (although increasingly less so) in the United States. It costs me $35 to fill my car in the United States and 52 euros to fill the same-model car in Europe. But, by contrast, public transportation in the United States is practically nonexistent in many regions. The working class of Baltimore (where the Johns Hopkins University is located), for example, would benefit much more from first-class public transportation (which it does not have) than dependency on a car, whatever the price of gasoline. And let's not forget that the energy and automobile industry interests have been major agents in opposing and destroying public transport systems in the United States. The U.S. working class is a victim of its nation's capitalist and imperialist system. It is not by chance that no other country in the developed capitalist world has such an underdeveloped welfare state as the United States. More than 100,000 people die in the United States every year due to a lack of public health care.

The tendency to look at the distribution of world power while ignoring class power within each country is also evident in the frequent criticism that the international organizations are controlled by the rich countries. It is frequently pointed out, for example, that the 10 percent of the world population living in the richest countries has 43 percent of the votes in the IMF, but it is not the 10 percent of the population living in the so-called rich countries that controls the IMF. It is the dominant classes of those rich countries that dominate the IMF, putting forward public policies that hurt the dominated classes of their own countries as well as those of other countries. The director of the IMF, for example, is Rodrigo Rato, who while Spain's minister of economy in the ultra-right government of José María Aznar (who partnered with Bush and Blair to support the Iraq War) carried out the brutal austerity policies that severely reduced the standard of living of the Spanish popular classes (9).

Let me also clarify another point. Much has been written about the conflict within the WTO between rich and poor countries. The governments of the rich countries, it is said, heavily subsidize their agriculture while raising protective barriers for industries such as textiles and foods that are vulnerable to products coming from the poor countries. While these obstacles to world trade do indeed adversely affect poor countries, it is wrong to assume that the solution is freer worldwide trade. Even without the barriers, the higher productivity of the rich countries would guarantee their success in world trade. What poor countries need to do is to change from export-oriented economies (the root of their problems) to domestic-oriented growth—a strategy that would require a major income redistribution and is thus resisted by the dominant classes of those (and of the rich) countries. It is extremely important to realize that most countries already have the resources (including capital) to break with their underdevelopment. Let me quote from an unlikely source. The *New York Times,* in the middle of the Malthusian highs (when population explosion was held to be the cause of world poverty), published a surprisingly candid assessment of the situation in Bangladesh, the poorest country in the world. In this extensive article, Ann Crittenden (10) touched directly on the root of the problem: the patterns of ownership of the production asset—the land:

> The root of the persistent malnutrition in the midst of relative plenty is the unequal distribution of land in Bangladesh. Few people are rich here by Western standards, but severe inequalities do exist and they are reflected in highly skewed land ownership. The wealthiest 16% of the rural population controls two thirds of the land and almost 60% of the population holds less than one acre of property.

Crittenden is not hopeful that the solution is technological. Quite to the contrary, technology can make things even worse:

> The new agricultural technologies being introduced have tended to favor large farmers, putting them in a better position to buy out their less fortunate neighbors.

Why does this situation persist? The answer is clear.

> Nevertheless, with the government dominated by landowners—about 75% of the members of the Parliament hold land—no one foresees any official support for fundamental changes in the system.

Let me add that in the U.S. State Department's classification of political regimes, Bangladesh is placed in the democratic column. Meanwhile, hunger and underweight are the primary causes of child mortality in Bangladesh. The hungry face of a child in Bangladesh has become the most common poster used by many charitable organizations to shame people in developed countries into sending money and food aid to Bangladesh. With what results?

Food aid officials in Bangladesh privately concede that only a fraction of the millions of tons of food aid sent to Bangladesh has reached the poor and hungry in the villages. The food is given to the Government, which in turn sells it at subsidized prices to the military, the police, and the middle class inhabitants of the cities.

The class structure of Bangladesh and the property relations that determine it are the causes of the enormous poverty. As Ann Crittenden concludes:

Bangladesh has enough land to provide an adequate diet for every man, woman and child in the country. The agricultural potential of this lush green land is such that even the inevitable population growth of the next 20 years could be fed easily by the resources of Bangladesh alone.

Most recently, Bangladesh has been much in the news as having undergone high economic growth due primarily to its exports in the world market. But that growth has been limited to a small, export-oriented sector of the economy and has left untouched the majority of the population. Malnutrition and hunger, meanwhile, have increased.

THE STATES AND CLASS ALLIANCES

In the establishment of class alliances, states play a key role. U.S. foreign policy, for example, is oriented toward supporting the dominant classes of the South (where, incidentally, 20 percent of the world's richest persons live). These alliances include, on many occasions, personal ties among members of the dominant classes. Examples are many—among them, the traditional support of the Bush family for the Middle East feudal regimes; Clinton's support for the United Arab Emirates (UAE), one of the major supporters of the Clinton Library in Arkansas and major donor to Clinton in speaking fees (up to a million dollars) and to causes favoring Clinton (11). The UAE is one of the world's most oppressively brutal regimes. The dominant classes deny citizenship to 85 percent of the working population (called "guest workers"). Needless to say, international agencies (heavily influenced by the U.S. and European governments) promote such alliances based on the neoliberal rhetoric of free markets. Cutting public social expenditures (including health expenditures), as advocated by the IMF and the World Bank, is part of the neoliberal public policies pushed by the dominant classes of the North and South at the expense of the well-being and quality of life of the dominated classes of both North and South. In all these examples, the states of the North and the South play a critical role.

Another example of alliances among dominant classes is the current promotion of for-profit health insurance by the Bush administration, both to the U.S. population and, increasingly, to the developing world. This is done with the advice and collaboration of conservative governments in Latin America on behalf of their dominant classes, which benefit from private insurance schemes that select clientele and exclude the popular classes. Those popular classes, in the United States and Latin America, profoundly dislike this push toward for-profit health care. (The movie *John Q* relates the hostility toward health insurance companies among the U.S. working class.) The fact that the dominant classes in the developed and developing countries share class interests does not mean they see eye-to-eye on everything. Of course not. They have major disagreements and conflicts (just as there are disagreements and conflicts among the different components of the dominant classes in each country). But these disagreements cannot conceal the commonality of their interests, as clearly exposed in the neoliberal focus (such as at Davos) and neoliberal instruments that have a hegemonic position (such as the *Economist* and the *Financial Times*).

IS THERE A DOMINANT STATE IN THE WORLD TODAY?

More than globalization, what we are witnessing in the world today is the *regionalization* of economic activities around a dominant state: North America around the United States, Europe around Germany, and Asia around Japan—and soon China. Thus there is a hierarchy of states within each region. In Europe, for example, the Spanish government is becoming dependent on public policies of the European Union, in which the German state predominates. This dependency creates an ambivalent situation. On the one hand, the states of the European Union chose to delegate major policies (such as monetary policies) to a higher institution (the European Central Bank, which is dominated by the German Central Bank). But this does not necessarily mean that the Spanish state loses power. "Losing power" means you had more power before, which is not necessarily the case. Spain, for example, is more powerful with the euro as currency than it was with the peseta. Indeed, Spain's President Zapatero would have paid a very high cost in his confrontation with Bush (in withdrawing Spanish troops from Iraq) if Spain still had the peseta as its national currency. Sharing sovereignty can increase power. On the other hand, the European government is frequently used by Europe's dominant classes as excuse and justification for unpopular policies that they want to implement (such as reducing public expenditures as a consequence of the European Stability Pact, which forces countries to maintain a central government deficit below 3 percent of GNP); these policies are presented as coming from European legislation rather than from any of the member states, thus diluting the responsibility of each government. Class alliances at the European level are manifested through the operation of E.U. institutions heavily committed to neoliberal ideology and public policies. The "no" vote on the proposed European Constitution was the response of the working classes of some member states to the European institutions that operate as alliances for Europe's dominant classes.

Within the hierarchy of states, some are dominant. The U.S. state has a dominant place that is maintained through a set of alliances with the dominant classes of other states. Neoliberal ideology provides the linkage among these classes. Needless to say, there are conflicts and tensions among them. But these tensions cannot outweigh the commonality of their class interests. Among the practices that unite them are aggressive policies against the working class and left-wing instruments. The 1980–2005 period was characterized by an aggressive campaign against left-wing parties that had been successful in the earlier, 1960–1980, period. During the "neoliberal" period, the alliance of the dominant classes has promoted multi-class religious movements that have used religion as a motivating force to stop socialism or communism. It was the administration of President Carter that began to support the religious fundamentalists in Afghanistan against the communist-led government. From Afghanistan to Iraq, Iran, the Palestinian Territories, and many other Arab countries, the dominant classes of the United States and Europe, through their governments, funded and supported the religious fundamentalists—often not only out of their own class interests, but out of their own religiosity. The "moral majority" in the United States was supposed to become the moral majority worldwide. These profoundly anti-left fundamentalist movements developed their own dynamics, channeling the enormous frustrations of the Arab masses with their oppressive, feudal regimes, to replace those regimes with equally oppressive religious theocracies, as has happened in many Arab countries.

But it is wrong to see the support by the dominant classes for the feudal regimes as simply a product of the Cold War. It was much more than that. It was a class response. The best evidence for this is that the support continued even after the collapse of the Soviet Union. The Cold War was an excuse and justification for carrying on the class struggle at the world level—as its continuation proves. Class war has indeed become an extremely active component of U.S. interventionism. It was the "shock therapy" pushed by Lawrence Summers and Jeffrey Sachs in Russia during the Clinton administration that led to the shortening of life expectancy in Russia, a consequence of the dramatic decline in the standard of living of the Russian popular classes. (That Sachs was asked to chair the WHO Commission on Macroeconomics and Health illustrates the enormous influence of neoliberalism. Another example of such influence is the WHO report on health systems performance, co-authored by Christopher Murray and Julio Frenk (12) and critiqued by Navarro (13).) The increased privatization of major public assets was part of that class war in Russia, as it has been in Iraq. The chief of the U.S. occupation in Iraq, Paul Bremer, fired half a million government workers, slashed business taxes, gave investors extraordinary new rights, and eliminated all import restrictions for all business except the oil industry. As Jeff Faux relates in *The Global Class Struggle* (14), the only laws from the brutal Iraqi dictatorship that the occupation did not supplant were those that were anti–labor union, including a restrictive collective-bargaining agreement that took away all workers' bonuses and food and housing subsidies. As the *Economist* (15) editorialized, "The occupation of Iraq is a capitalist's dream."

Recently, another version of the North-South divide appears in the writings of one of the most influential thinkers in the United States, the philosopher John Rawls, who divides the countries of the world into *decent* and *non-decent* countries. The decent countries (mostly located in the developed capitalist world) are those that have democratic rights and institutions, while the non-decent countries (mostly located in the developing capitalist world) are those that do not. After dividing the world into these two categories, Rawls concludes that the non-decent countries had better be ignored, although he admits "a moral responsibility to help poor countries that are prevented by poverty from organizing themselves as liberal or decent society." I find such positions and statements remarkable for their overwhelming ignorance of past and present international relations, as well as of the class relations in each of those countries. Rawls further confuses governments with countries (a confusion that occurs frequently in the assumption that the primary conflict is between North and South). What he calls non-decent countries (characterized by brutal and corrupt dictatorships) have classes; their dominant classes have not been ignored in activities cultivated and supported by the dominant classes of the decent countries, which have also hurt the quality of life and well-being of their own dominated classes. Also, in Rawls's so-called non-decent countries, there are class-based movements that endure enormous sacrifices, carrying out a heroic struggle for change, struggling constantly while handicapped and opposed by the dominant classes of the so-called decent countries. I find it remarkable (but predictable) that such an intellectual figure defines the moral compass of these indecent classes. The latest example of this indecency is the reported support of the U.S. and U.K. governments for the King of Nepal, in their concern to stop a mass revolt led by left-wing parties.

INEQUALITIES AMONG COUNTRIES AND THEIR SOCIAL CONSEQUENCES

That inequalities contribute to a lack of social solidarity and increase social pathology is well documented. Many people, including myself, have documented this reality (16). The scientific evidence supporting this position is overwhelming. In any given society, the greatest number of deaths would be prevented by reducing social inequalities. Michael Marmot studied the gradient of heart disease mortality among professionals at different authority levels, and he found that the higher the level of authority, the lower the heart disease mortality (17). He further showed that this mortality gradient could not be explained by diet, physical exercise, or cholesterol alone; these risk factors explained only a small part of the gradient. The most important factor was the position that people held within the social structure (in which class, gender, and race play key roles), the social distance between groups, and the differential control that people had over their own lives.

This enormously important scientific finding, which builds upon previous scholarly work, has many implications; one of them is that the major problem we face is not simply eliminating poverty but rather reducing inequality. The first is impossible to resolve without resolving the second. Another implication is that poverty is not just a matter of resources, as is wrongly assumed in World Bank reports that measure worldwide poverty by quantifying the number of people who live on a standardized U.S. dollar a day. The real problem, again, is not absolute resources but social distance and the different degrees of control over one's own resources. And this holds true in every society.

Let me elaborate. An unskilled, unemployed, young black person living in the ghetto area of Baltimore has more resources (he or she is likely to have a car, a mobile phone, a TV, and more square feet per household and more kitchen equipment) than a middle-class professional in Ghana, Africa. If the whole world were just a single society, the Baltimore youth would be middle class and the Ghana professional would be poor. And yet, the first has a much shorter life expectancy (45 years) than the second (62 years). How can that be, when the first has more resources than the second? The answer is clear. It is far more difficult to be poor in the United States (the sense of distance, frustration, powerlessness, and failure is much greater) than to be middle class in Ghana. The first is far below the median; the second is above the median.

Does the same mechanism operate in inequalities among countries? The answer is increasingly, yes. And the reason for adding "increasingly" is communication—with ever more globalized information systems and networks, more information is reaching the most remote areas of the world. And the social distance created by inequalities is becoming increasingly apparent, not only within but also among countries. Because this distance is more and more perceived as an outcome of exploitation, we are facing an enormous tension, comparable with that of the 19th and early 20th centuries, when class exploitation became the driving force for social mobilization. The key element for defining the future is through what channels that mobilization takes place. What we have seen is a huge mobilization, instigated and guided by an alliance of the dominant classes of the North and South, aimed at—as mentioned earlier—stimulating multi-class religious or nationalistic mobilizations that leave key class relations unchanged. We saw this phenomenon at the end of the 19th and beginning of the 20th centuries. Christian Democracy in Europe, for example, appears as the dominant classes' response to the threat of socialism and communism. The birth of Islamic fundamentalism was also stimulated for the same purposes.

The progressive alternative must be centered in alliances among the dominated classes and other dominated groups, with a political movement that must be built upon the process of struggle that takes place in each country. The struggle for better health in any country has to be part of that broader struggle to build a better world, emphasizing that another world—based on solidarity—is possible. But, to intervene in and change current reality, we have to understand it, with a critical evaluation of the conventional wisdom that reproduces neoliberalism worldwide—an evaluation that should be uncompromising in the sense that it should fear neither its own results nor conflict with the powers that be. In that respect, this evaluation should include the political analysis rarely seen in scholarly work. And here, I am concerned that the newly established WHO Commission on Social Determinants of Health (18) is not looking at the basis of the problems that determine poor health, problems that are rooted in class as well as in race and gender power relations and in the political instruments through which such power is exercised and reproduced. The political determinants of health need to be understood and acted upon, however uncomfortable or risky this may be. Such is the intention of this chapter.

REFERENCES

1. Hardt, M., and Negri, A. *Empire.* Harvard University Press, Cambridge, 2000.
2. Congressional Budget Office National Accounts 2003.
3. Weinberger, C. *Washington Post,* July 13, 1983.
4. Williamson, J. What Washington means by the policy reform. In *Latin America Adjustment: How Much Has Happened?* ed. J. Williamson. Institute for International Economics, Washington, DC, 1990.
5. Harvey, D. *A Brief History of Neoliberalism.* Oxford University Press, New York, 2005.
6. Arrighi, G. The African crisis: World systemic and regional aspects. *New Left Review,* May–June, 2002.
7. Weisbrot, M., Baker, D., and Rosnick, D. The scorecard on development: 25 years of diminished progress. *Int. J. Health Serv.* 36:211–234, 2006.
8. Milanovic, B. *Worlds Apart: Measuring International and Global Inequality.* Princeton University Press, Princeton, NJ, 2005.
9. Navarro, V. Who is Mr Rato? *CounterPunch,* June 2004.
10. Crittenden, A. *New York Times,* September 12, 1992.
11. *Financial Times,* March 4, 2006.
12. Murray, C., and Frenk, J. *World Health Report 2000: Health Systems—Improving Performance.* World Health Organization, Geneva, 2000.
13. Navarro, V. Assessment of the World Health Report 2000. *Lancet* 356:1598–1601, 2000.
14. Faux, J. *The Global Class Struggle.* Wiley, New York, 2006.
15. *Economist,* September 25, 2003.
16. Navarro, V. (ed.). *The Political Economy of Social Inequalities: Consequences for Health and Quality of Life.* Baywood, Amityville, NY, 2002.
17. Marmot, M. *The Status Syndrome: How Social Standing Affects Our Health and Longevity.* Owl Books, New York, 2005.
18. WHO Commission on Social Determinants of Health. *Towards a Conceptual Framework for Analysis and Action on Social Determinants of Health.* World Health Organization, Geneva, 2005.

CHAPTER 2

The Crisis and Fiscal Policies in the
Peripheral Countries of the Eurozone

Vicente Navarro

This chapter explains the political causes of the current financial crisis of the eurozone peripheral countries (Spain, Greece, Portugal, and Ireland) and how the crisis affects their welfare states. It examines how their profoundly conservative governments (dictatorships in Spain, Portugal, and Greece and authoritarian regime in Ireland) during the post–World War II period and the dominance of their states by right-wing forces have made these countries very vulnerable to the speculations of the financial markets.

*****

INTRODUCTION:
THE POLITICAL CONTEXT

To understand the situation in the countries at the periphery of the European Union—four countries within the eurozone, Portugal, Ireland, Greece, and Spain—we have to understand the political context they have in common. All of them were governed by fascist or fascist-like dictatorships (Spain, Portugal, and Greece) or by authoritarian right-wing regimes (Ireland) for most of the period from the late 1930s or early 1940s until the late 1970s. This history is usually ignored in analyses of these countries.

This shared history, however, has determined the nature of their states, a critical variable for understanding countries' economic behavior. Their states have been very repressive. Even today, these countries have the largest number of police per 10,000 individuals in the EU-15. Another shared characteristic is their very low level of state revenues and their highly regressive fiscal policies. The revenues to the state are much lower than the EU-15 average: approximately 34 percent of gross national product (GNP) in Spain, 37 percent in Greece, 39 percent in Portugal, and 34 percent in Ireland, compared with the EU-15 average of 44 percent, and compared with 54 percent in Sweden—the EU-15 country where the left has governed for the longest period. The low state revenues result from extremely regressive policies. The super-rich, rich, and high-income upper-middle classes in these countries do not pay taxes at the same level and intensity as those in most of the central and northern EU-15 countries—a consequence of a history of government by ultra-right-wing parties. Of course, progress has been made since the dictatorships ended. But the dominance of conservative forces in the political and civil lives of these countries explains why their state revenues are still so low.

As a result, the public sectors in Portugal, Ireland, Greece, and Spain are extremely underdeveloped. And their welfare states are poorly funded and very limited, including their public transfers (pensions) and public services (medical care, education, child care services, home care services, social services, and others). Indicators of this are many. One example is public social spending as percentage of GNP, which is lower in these countries than the EU-15 average (27%): Spain, 22.1 percent; Greece, 25.9 percent; Portugal, 24.3 percent; and Ireland, 22.1 percent (compared with Sweden, 29.3%). Another example is the percentage of the adult population working in public services of the welfare state—again, lower than the EU-15 average (15%): Spain, 9 percent; Greece, 11 percent; Portugal, 7 percent; and Ireland, 12 percent (compared with Sweden, 25%). In fact, Greece's percentage is three points higher, 14 percent, because it includes services for the military (which represents approximately 30 percent of public employees).

THE SPECIFICITY OF THE POLITICAL REGIMES

Thus, for these four countries, not enough attention has been paid in the economic literature to the consequences of being governed by ultra-conservative forces. The influence of such forces has been enormous. It is also important to emphasize that the conservative forces in these peripheral countries are different from those in northern and central EU-15 countries. They do not belong to democratic traditions, since they are the inheritors of either fascist or authoritarian regimes. Even today, after almost 30 years of democracy, such forces continue to be very influential in the four states, even when the states are governed by social democratic parties. As just one example, Spain's Supreme Court has taken Judge Baltasar Garzon, who used to be a member of the Court, to trial for daring to inquire about crimes committed by General Franco's fascist regime. It is not fully comprehended outside Spain just how influential the ultra-right-wing forces still are within the Spanish state. They dominate political culture in many different ways, including control of the major media. There are no major left or left-of-center media in Spain, or in the other countries in this group.

The domination of the state in these four countries by ultra-conservative forces has many consequences besides their low level of state revenues, their regressive fiscal policies, and their underdevelopment of the welfare state. Labor income, as percentage of national income, has declined since 1992, when policies were implemented (including by social democratic governments) in preparation for entering the eurozone. This income decline has occurred more rapidly in Portugal, Ireland, Greece, and Spain than the EU-15 average, and is particularly accentuated in Spain, with a decrease from 70 to 61 percent of national income—despite an increase in the percentage of working adult population.

As noted, a consequence of domination by conservative forces, considerably limiting the public reforms approved and implemented by social democratic governments from the early 1980s onward, is regressive fiscal policies. As a result of these policies, the impact of state interventions on income redistribution has been very limited. For example, in Spain, as late as 2009, the level of poverty (60% of median income) declined only 4 percentage points after implementation of state interventions (public social transfers): from 24 percent before to 20 percent after transfers. The EU-15 average decreased from 25 to 16 percent. Sweden's poverty rate fell from 27 to 13 percent. The decline in poverty rate resulting from public social transfers in Spain is the lowest in the EU-15. Another indicator of the limited redistributional impact of state interventions is that the Gini coefficients in all four countries are higher than the EU-15 average (29.2). Spain's Gini coefficient is 31.3, the same as Ireland's; Greece's is 34.3; and Portugal's is the highest, at 36.8.

HOW THE CRISIS HAS BEEN BUILDING UP

Another characteristic of this group of countries is the acceptance by the governing social democratic parties of most of the neoliberal policies pushed by the E.U. establishment. This acceptance has been generalized among the social democratic parties of the European Union. Actually, these parties were part of the consensus in developing neoliberal policies (usually referred to as the "Brussels consensus," the European version of the "Washington consensus"). As part of this consensus, both conservative-liberal and social democratic governing parties have been reducing taxes, particularly for the top income brackets. It was none other than Spain's socialist candidate in the 2004 election (and later prime minister), Jose Luis Rodriguez Zapatero, who promised to reduce taxes if elected, saying that lowering taxes was a cause to be promoted by the left. The major economic thinker of Spain's socialist party at that time was Jordi Sevilla, an economist who wrote in his book *The Future of Socialism* that "the left had to stop raising taxes and increasing public expenditures"—this said in the EU-15 country with the lowest state revenues and poorest welfare state.

The tax reductions over the past 15 years have led to a structural public deficit that was disguised by the fast economic growth created by the housing bubble, responsible for the banking–real estate–construction industry complex at the center of the bubble. When the bubble burst, and the economy came to a halt, the structural public deficit appeared in all its intensity. The public deficits in

Portugal, Ireland, Greece, and Spain were the result of declining state revenues, not expanding public expenditures. This is why the public policies of these governments are profoundly wrong. They have been cutting public spending, assuming, incorrectly, that the cause of public deficits was an exaggerated growth of public expenditures.

ARGUMENTS USED TO JUSTIFY CUTS IN PUBLIC EXPENDITURES

The slogan now being used to justify these cuts is: "The country has been living beyond its means." Major political figures in the four countries claim that their welfare states are larger than they can pay for. But the data show otherwise. In Spain, for example, the GNP per capita is 94 percent of the EU-15 average, but public social expenditure per capita is only 72 percent of the EU-15 average. If it were 94 percent, the Spanish state would have 66,000 million more euros than it does today. So, Spain has the resources. The problem is that the state does not collect them, because its fiscal policies are so regressive and fiscal fraud is widespread among high-income groups and economic and financial corporations. Actually, banking in Spain is the primary entity responsible for fiscal fraud. Mr. Botin, the country's major banker (president of Santander Bank, the third most profitable bank in the world, after two Chinese banks), was discovered this year to have 2,000 million euros in a Swiss bank account—not declared until two whistleblowers at the bank went to the press. Such fraud is general practice. The tax inspectors of Spain's Ministry of Economy estimate there are 88,600 million euros that the state does not collect because of tax fraud.

HOW AND WHY THE CRISIS AROSE

Before the financial crisis there was an economic crisis, largely the result of the decline in labor income as percentage of total national income. The neoliberal policies developed since the 1980s (accentuated over the past 15 years, and carried out by governments of various political persuasions, including social democratic, in Spain, Greece, and Portugal) have had a strong impact on income distribution, accelerating the concentration of income in the high income brackets. The decline of labor-derived income diminished the purchasing power of the popular classes, forcing them into debt in order to maintain their standard of living. And credit was relatively easy to obtain, because house values were rising and provided a means of borrowing from banks by putting up homes as security. The growth of the credit sector (and of financing) was based on the decline of labor income. But the decline of labor income was creating a major problem for demand and limited profitability in the economy.

With this limited profitability in the productive economy, the super-rich, rich, and upper-income middle class invested in sectors with higher returns, especially in real estate. The deregulation of banking (and deregulation of zoning laws) during the 1990s led to a real estate bubble, based on the complex of banking, real estate, and construction industries. In Spain, this complex was the main motor of economic growth and was supported by both central and local authorities, since local authorities were primarily funded by property taxes.

Stimulating the growth of housing construction was the influx of immigrants, with the immigrant population increasing from 4 to 10 percent of the population in only 10 years. Housing construction reached 10 percent of GNP, and this sector produced the most (but very low-paid) jobs. The Spanish "miracle" of job creation was based on large investments in a speculative sector of the economy. And it was funded with debt. This is the cause of the enormous private debt in Spain, which was facilitated by introduction of the euro—much more stable in the economy than the national currency it replaced. Introduction of the euro dramatically increased the size of the financial sector in the four peripheral eurozone countries. When the bubble burst, the whole credit economy came to a stop.

THE POLITICAL ORIGINS OF THE PUBLIC DEBT

In the four countries, there has been an alliance between the upper income brackets (the super-rich, rich, and upper middle class, whose taxes have been reduced in the past 15 years) and the banks, on the one hand, and the state, on the other. A fruit of this alliance was the reduction in taxes that created the structural public deficit, masked by the economic growth within the bubble.

The decline of revenues to the states (the consequence of tax cuts) forced the states to borrow from the banks, where the rich deposited the money saved due to reduced taxes. The indebtedness of the states and the need to borrow were clearly related to the reduction of taxes. When the economy came to a stop as the bubble burst, the structural public deficit became apparent. As a consequence, public deficits as percentage of GNP increased substantially in all four countries from 2007 to 2009. Spain went from a surplus of 1.9 percent of GNP in 2005 to a public deficit of 11.1 percent in 2009. Greece went from a deficit of 6.4 percent in 2007 to 15.4 percent in 2009, with Ireland moving from 0 to 14 percent in the same period. In all of them, rapid growth of the public deficit was based on the extremely regressive nature of state revenues. With most taxes based on labor income and consumption, when employment declined, unemployment grew, and consumption declined, the public deficit escalated dramatically.

SOLUTIONS THAT ARE NEVER CONSIDERED

The neoliberal response to this situation, which entails cuts in public expenditures, is making the situation worse because it reduces demand. The trade unions have accurately described neoliberalism as the ideology of banks and large employers. The major media support this doctrine, based more on faith than on evidence. At the root of the problem is class power and its realization through the state.

If Spain implemented the same fiscal policy as Sweden, the Spanish state would take in 200,000 million euros more than it now does. With those millions of euros, it could create 5 million new jobs (particularly in the underdeveloped welfare state services, such as the national health service, educational system, child care services, and other social services). If one in every four adults worked in such services (as occurs in Sweden), instead of one in every ten adults (as occurs now in Spain), Spain would create 5 million more jobs, eliminating unemployment: 5 million is more or less the number of people currently unemployed in Spain.

A second point is that the fiscal stimulus applied by most of the governments in this group of countries in 2008 was basically tax cuts and transfers. Only a minuscule part of the stimulus went to creating jobs (through investment by local authorities). Stimulating the economy through the creation of jobs has not occurred in any of these countries. Moreover, reduction of the deficit is achieved by cutting public expenditures, not by increasing taxes. The European Federation of Trade Unions has proposed alternative ways of reducing the deficit, primarily by increasing taxes (reversing the tax reductions of the past 15 years). Class power, however, is the most potent opposition to these alternative policies. A manufacturing worker in Spain pays taxes estimated at 74 percent of the taxes paid by a manufacturing worker in Sweden. The top 1 percent of income earners in Spain, however, pay only 20 percent of the taxes paid by the top 1 percent in Sweden. This is what explains the enormously regressive fiscal policy in the four peripheral EU-15 countries and the enormous resistance to change by their dominant classes.

The problem of the public debt is thus basically a political, not an economic or financial, one. The current situation is untenable because Europe's dominant classes and their allies, the E.U. leadership ("the troika": the European Council, European Commission, and European Central Bank), are trying to reduce the power of labor using the argument of "pressure from the financial markets"— the aim being to get labor to accept the huge sacrifices that the dominant classes have wanted for many years. In Spain, for example, the socialist government is cutting public social expenditures, which, besides adversely affecting economic growth and reducing level of demand, is hurting the popular classes. The parties to the left of the governing socialists have clearly shown that for each cut in public social expenditures, the government could obtain even larger revenues by selectively increasing taxes, which would not affect taxes for the majority of the population. Moreover, they have shown that the revenues obtained with those taxes could create jobs in the underdeveloped public sector, especially in the welfare state.

Another issue is that, at this time, no major force on the left has called for exit from the euro. An explanation for this is that Europe has always been a point of reference for progressive democratic forces. In Spain, for example, under the fascist dictatorship, Europe meant liberty, democracy, and the welfare state. The attraction of Europe is now waning, though not very rapidly. Because of this, most of the debate centers on correction of the fiscal regressiveness of the state and development of expansionary policies as a way of stimulating economic growth and job production. Sectors of the left in Spain believe this is not possible, pointing to the Mitterrand case as an example of how one country cannot follow expansionary policies. This needs to be shown as wrong, although expansionary policies at the European level would help a lot. This is unlikely to occur at this time, however, given the control of the major E.U. institutions by neoliberal dogma.

THE *INDIGNADOS* MOVEMENT

Meanwhile, a new movement has appeared that has surprised everyone. Initially led by the young unemployed, it has attracted enormous support from the majority of the population. Its primary focus is on denouncing the absence of democracy, in Spain and elsewhere in Europe, showing how governments are making decisions not mandated by the population. This movement is going to the root of the problem: the nature of democracy and who it is that democratic institutions are representing. Of course, in Spain, the government is worried about this movement—the *indignados*. The candidate of the governing socialist party, hoping to succeed Zapatero (the Spanish president with the least popular support during the democratic period), has called for increased taxation of bankers and the banks to help resolve the fiscal problems of the state. This is important because the proposal is a response to the public outrage directed at banking and the wealthy. The financial and industrial bourgeoisie are seen as using the "pressure of the financial markets" as a way of getting what they have always wanted: to weaken labor. And what is really threatening to the establishment is that all the polls show enormous sympathy for this popular movement, including among large sectors of the conservative parties. We'll see what happens next.

Acknowledgments — The work of Marta Tur, Miquel Campa Sole, and Maria Allwine in the preparation of this chapter is gratefully acknowledged.

PART II

The Crisis and Its Consequences for Welfare Services and Transfers

Edwin Ng

INTRODUCTION

In recent years, a growing body of social epidemiological work has focused on the health effects of political institutions such as welfare states and their services (e.g., health, education, and housing) and transfers (e.g., income maintenance programs) on population health and health inequalities (1–3). This relatively new focus on welfare states and regimes has raised central questions on the degree to which democratic governments in capitalist economies should institutionalize equality and promote population health through Keynesian economic policies (e.g., full-employment policies), universal welfare provision (e.g., supports from cradle to grave), and decommodification and defamilization mechanisms (e.g., easing the reliance of workers and families on private markets to meet human needs). Given the growth in inequalities across and within countries and the instability caused by the Great Recession, public health scholars have paid keen and critical attention to how welfare states and regimes have responded to such crises and how public policies, in turn, have shaped and influenced social inequalities and population health.

Reflective of this work, Part II includes four high-impact studies that range in content from health care reforms and comparative financing structures to social inequalities in health care utilization and welfare generosity in the form of income maintenance policies. In Chapter 3, Gelormino and coauthors undertake a critical review of the extant European literature to identify key mechanisms that connect health care and health inequalities within the context of economic globalization and welfare state reforms. In Chapter 4, considering recent major reforms of the British National Health Service, Reynolds and coauthors provide an informed and timely account of the potentially adverse consequences of moving away from the egalitarian principles (e.g., single-payer system) on which the NHS was founded and toward the neoliberal and managed care approach of the United States. In their comparative Canada-U.S. study (Chapter 5), Kaplan and colleagues explore the connections between elderly persons and visits to family physicians and specialists and find important between-country differences, depending on variations in burden of illness and socioeconomic status. Finally, Nelson (Chapter 6) focuses on inequality and welfare states by way of welfare generosity among European nations and, specifically, assesses whether minimum income protection levels have converged or diverged from 1990 to 2005. Taken together, these chapters provide new and important insights on how welfare states and regimes respond to and negotiate with external forces while striving to meet the health needs of their citizens.

REFERENCES

1. Beckfield, J., and Krieger, N. Epi + demos + cracy: Linking political systems and priorities to the magnitude of health inequities—Evidence, gaps, and a research agenda.*Epidemiologic Reviews* 31(1):152–177, 2009.
2. Brennenstuhl, S., Quesnel-Vallée, A., & McDonough, P. Welfare regimes, population health and health inequalities: A research synthesis. *Journal of Epidemiology and Community Health* 66(5):397–409, 2012.
3. Muntaner, C., Borrell, C., Ng, E., Chung, H., Espelt, A., Rodriguez-Sanz, M., . . . & O'Campo, P. Politics, welfare regimes, and population health: Controversies and evidence. *Sociology of Health & Illness* 33(6):946–964, 2011.

CHAPTER 3

The Effects of Health Care Reforms
on Health Inequalities:
A Review and Analysis of the
European Evidence Base

Elena Gelormino, Clare Bambra, Teresa Spadea,
Silvia Bellini, and Giuseppe Costa

Health care is widely considered to be an important determinant of health. The health care systems of Western Europe have recently experienced significant reforms, under pressure from economic globalization. Similarly, in Eastern Europe, health care reforms have been undertaken in response to the demands of the new market economy. Both of these changes may influence equality in health outcomes. This chapter aims to identify the mechanisms through which health care may affect inequalities. The authors conducted a literature review of the effects on health inequalities of European health care reforms. Particular reference was paid to interventions in the fields of financing and pooling, allocation, purchasing, and provision of services. The majority of studies were from Western Europe, and the outcomes most often examined were access to services or income distribution. Overall, the quality of research was poor, confirming the need to develop an appropriate impact assessment methodology. Few studies were related to pooling, allocation, or purchasing. For financing and purchasing, the studies showed that publicly funded universal health care reduces the impact of ill health on income distribution, while insurance systems can increase inequalities in access to care. Out-of-pocket payments increase inequalities in access to care and contribute to impoverishment. Decentralizing health services can lead to geographic inequalities in health care access. Nationalized, publicly funded health care systems are most effective at reducing inequalities in access and reducing the effects on health of income distribution.

*****

Health is considered an intrinsic human right, independent of socioeconomic status, gender, nationality, and ethnic origin. Many descriptive studies across Europe, however, show that poor health is often related to disadvantaged socioeconomic conditions and increases the probability of falling into poverty. The majority of socioeconomic health inequalities are socially determined (1). In Dahlgren and Whitehead's well-known "rainbow" model of the social determinants of health, health care is identified alongside housing, income, and so forth, as an important social determinant (2). But within the context of the developed welfare states of Western Europe, in which health care services are mostly universalistic and egalitarian, the role (if any) played by health care policies and interventions in determining health inequalities is not fully understood and, generally, the proportion of health inequalities explained by inadequate care has been evaluated as low (3).

Even though population health indicators have improved remarkably across Western Europe in the past few decades, the direction and size of socioeconomic health inequalities, particularly mortality, have remained unchanged. This suggests that the benefits of improvements in health care (and other social determinants of health) may not have been distributed evenly across the population and thus have not been able to redistribute the burden of mortality.

The political and economic evolution of the European continent has been dramatic since the end of the Cold War. Since 1989, the Eastern European countries have experienced extensive political, social, and economic upheaval. The welfare and health care systems have been rapidly reformed in order to adapt to the new liberal economic order. Moreover, in the same period, all over Europe, welfare states have faced the difficult challenge of reforming their health care systems in the face of the pressures of economic globalization. These changes suggest that the importance of health care as a determinant of health inequalities may be increasing across all of Europe.

Concerns about the new global macroeconomic order are forcing European health care systems to reform and change, but the traditional attention paid in Europe to human rights means that implementation of such reforms without decreasing equity is still considered extremely important. Thus it is the duty of public health researchers to pursue knowledge about effective interventions so as to inform decision-making and thus avoid worsening inequalities in health. Even if the direction of reform often depends on the public resources available rather than population health needs or income distribution, most of these reforms remain firmly within the parameters of a universalistic and egalitarian health care system. Newly introduced policies tend to change the way in which the system is financed and services are provided. It is therefore particularly important to ascertain which of the main elements of health care systems need to be safe-guarded during implementation of reforms, if equity is to be ensured.

As part of the E.U.-wide Eurothine project on inequalities in health (http://mgzlx4.erasmusmc.nl/eurothine), this study reviews recent primary research and review articles on health care policies and their impact on health inequalities.

This builds on previous evidence reviews, which were mainly focused on equity-oriented processes of care (4, 5).

Our review is informed by the theoretical frameworks proposed to identify the mechanisms through which health care may affect health inequalities, while also highlighting the entry points through which the main policies on the health care services reform agenda around Europe might interfere with such mechanisms.

The theoretical frameworks developed for the study of access to medical care (6) and inequalities in health care (7) have considered the role of characteristics of both the health system ("supply side") and population needs ("demand side"), sometimes at the global level (7). Our review is limited to the supply side and its role in determining inequalities in health care in advanced societies with market economies and democratic regimes. Inequalities in health outcomes may be influenced by inequalities in utilization of preventive care (reception and efficacy of health education and promotion messages; preventive attitude of general practitioners (GPs)), diagnosis (delay or inaccuracy of diagnosis; missed recognition or denial of symptoms and need; ability to "jump the queue"), and treatment (cultural sensitivity of pattern of care; failure to empower patients/families; access to appropriate care; lack of comprehensive social and health care networks). Some factors in health care may affect utilization: accessibility (geographic, legal, or information barriers), affordability (the service; the purchasing power of the individual), and quality and acceptability (professional training and practice; patient-professional interaction; compliance; continuity; appropriateness in supply organization). Some features of a health care system modify its accessibility, affordability, and quality—that is, financing and pooling, resource allocation, purchasing, and provision of services. These features were described by Kutzin (8), and we used them to search the literature for pathways of equity in health care. We also took into account that these pathways exist in a context where the prevailing welfare regime of a country and its variations in decentralization at the regional level may influence how the health care system is designed and managed.

We hypothesized that each of the steps that can generate inequalities in health care could be an entry point for a policy or intervention to tackle such inequalities. In terms of funding and pooling, a more progressive system could facilitate redistribution of resources and remove barriers to health care. In regulation of service supply, a socially selective allocation formula could address the investment and allocation of money, technologies, facilities, and professionals where the need is greatest. Similarly, positive discrimination could limit the socially unequal impact of waiting lists and co-payments. Finally, the provision of health care could be managed in a way that makes it more explicitly equity-oriented in each process of health care, through both problem finding (equity audit) and problem solving (proactive approaches). Adopting these strategies should make a health care system more accessible, more affordable, and higher-quality for everybody in each phase of care (prevention; identification of need; diagnosis; treatment; quality of care), and finally, should lead to more equality of outcomes in terms of both intermediate outcomes of utilization and longer-term health outcomes. This review assesses the ability of these kinds of policies to tackle socioeconomic inequalities in access to health care and in health outcomes.

Thus our intention is to clarify the pathways of organization and financing arrangements followed by the European health systems while supplying services to people, and the impact of these arrangements on equity in health care. Our framework builds on previous efforts on the economic, epidemiological, and public health side: by Aday (6) and her macro point of view; by the Donabedian (9) "triangle," which evaluated the components of health care (structure, process, and outcome), and the wider version recently proposed by De Maeseneer (10); by the World Health Organization in its 2000 report dedicated to health systems (11) and the 2007 report devoted to equity in health care systems (7); and, on the economic side, by Kutzin (8), disaggregating the components of health care in financing sources, resource allocation mechanisms, and associated organizational and institutional arrangements.

METHODS

Inclusion Criteria

In this literature review, we included only those studies relevant to the framework presented by Kutzin (8), and only if they were implemented within the geographic borders of Europe (E.U. or non-E.U. countries). We also included international comparative studies as long as they included at least one European country.

Studies that examined the impact of macro-level economic and political contexts and upstream interventions on health care provision and inequalities were also included. In terms of study design, we searched for all studies that included a formal observation related to a clearly identifiable intervention/ decision. We included both reviews and primary studies. In the literature search we considered an "intervention" as any act of planning within the health care system, classified according to the factors shaping the health care system: financing and pooling, allocation, purchasing, and provision of services (8). We were interested only in those studies that measured equity in terms of health status, access to services, or income distribution.

Search Strategy

The combination of intervention terms together with equity and health care terms provided the keywords for the search. The most frequently used Boolean combinations were: (health OR health services OR health care OR health system) AND (equity OR socioeconomic factors) AND (funding OR financing OR progressivity OR regressivity OR Kakwani OR pooling OR insurance OR provision OR supply).

We searched several electronic databases: Medline, CINAHL, Embase, Econlit, and PsychInfo. We selected all studies in English, Italian, French, and Spanish, for 1990–2007. In addition, we searched the Internet for gray literature on research foundations and government sites. However, no hand searching was performed.

Critical Appraisal

All studies on the health situation and access to health care services of any socioeconomic strata were included, but those that provided stratified analyses and comparisons of strata were treated as being of higher quality. These criteria were applied to both published and gray literature. No other criteria of exclusion were adopted.

RESULTS

Description of Studies

In terms of funding and regulation of service supply and demand, we found 45 articles and selected from these 29 primary studies; 11 studies were excluded because the intervention was not clearly identifiable, and 5 because they were non-empirical policy analyses. Three of the 29 studies were interrupted time series, seven were international comparisons, and 19 used a case study design (Table 1). The majority of the studies (23 studies) were from Western Europe, with only a few (6 studies) from Eastern Europe. Two of the studies were located through the gray literature searches. In terms of pathway of care (the way in which provision of service is rendered), our analysis included few studies exploring the role of equity audit in the daily activity of health services.

Synthesis

Due to the heterogeneity of data in the selected studies, meta-analysis and full data extraction were not deemed appropriate. For the same reason, we were unable to adopt any instrument to rank the internal and external validity of the studies. Given the variety of the European health systems, a specific activity is required to evaluate the external validity of each research study, which lies outside the scope of this review. We therefore identified the design of the studies and classified them according to Campbell (12). The same criterion was adopted by Stronks and Mackenbach (13) in a review that divided studies into observational, quasi-experimental, and experimental. We conducted a narrative synthesis, with the studies described according to the area of policy/intervention of the framework (8) to which they relate, adding macro-level studies that examined the impact of the social and political context. The characteristics of the studies are outlined in Table 1.

The Social and Political Context

Our review located four studies that provided information on two main aspects of context: the role of political ideology and commitment, and the impact of decentralization. We did not deal with other, wider topics among upstream phenomena (transition to market economy and welfare state) recently reviewed by Beckfield and Krieger (14).

An analysis of the role played by political ideologies in Europe in the period of full development of capitalism (1945–1980) in the social distribution of benefits in health care and health is provided by Navarro and Shi (15). The results of their study indicate that political traditions more committed to redistributive policies were generally more successful in improving the health of populations (infant mortality) and in having the highest coverage (total public medical care divided by population), the highest public health expenditure, and the lowest poverty rates. No information was available on the impact of political traditions on health inequalities.

The devolution of power and other political options that shape the distribution and exercise of power (among central government and regions; between parliaments and governments; between politics and bureaucracy) within a country potentially produce heterogeneity in welfare and health care provision. The study by Costa-i-Font (16) analyzed the situation in Spain after decentralization of the national health service, which started in 1981 and was completed in 2002. According to his results, devolution in health care does not seem to lead to interregional inequalities in health. However, in regions where the private sector plays a dominant role, higher social inequalities in health care can be identified. Interestingly, the health concentration index, following the procedure used by Kakwani and colleagues (17), reveals that Catalonia, followed by the INSALUD (the centralized network of health services) regions, has a higher mean concentration index than some other Spanish regions (such as Navarre, Andalusia, and the Basque Country), where the primary care reform (integrating primary care services into the public network from the end of the 1980s) was rapidly applied and the private sector has a significantly lower role (than in areas still under INSALUD in 1997 and in Catalonia), and the devolution includes fiscal accountability and higher expenditure (Navarre and the Basque Country).

The findings of Lopez-Casasnovas (18) support the view that Spain has decentralized the health system without significantly weakening social cohesion, at least when considering interregional inequalities. Studies estimating

Table 1

Characteristics of included studies

Study, year (reference)	Design	Intervention	Outcome	Results
Aspinall and Jacobson, 2005 (44)	XO; case study	Provision (equity audit)	Equity of care	Percentage of primary care trusts taking action against inequalities ≤20%
Aspray et al., 2006 (43)	XO; case study	Provision (equity audit)	Equity of care	Entry of patients in diabetes register: low SES, 3%; high SES, 11%
Bellanger and Mossé, 2005 (25)	XO; case study	Financing	Access to prevention services	Gap in life expectancy at age 35, blue- vs. white-collar, <6.5 yrs
Buchmueller et al., 2004 (29)	OXO; before-and-after study	Pooling	Access to care	Utilization of physician service: low SES vs. high SES, +2.1%
Burström, 2002 (39)	OOXOO; interrupted time series	Provision	Access to care	Forgone care trend (in low SES) from OR 0.94 (95% CI 0.7–1.27) to OR 1.65 (95% CI 1.22–2.22)
Costa-i-Font, 2005 (16)	XO; case study	Political configuration (decentralization)	Self-perceived health in different areas	Kakwani index: centralized system and high private provision, –0.020; less centralized and lower private provision, –0.015
Delcheva et al., 1997 (35)	XO; case study	Provision	Willingness to pay per income stratum	Percentage of people willing to pay: high SES, 80%; low SES, 43%

Donia Soflo et al., 2006 (40)	XO; case study	Provision	Financial burden of health expenditures	People below poverty line due to out-of-pocket expenses, 1.3%
Van Doorslaer et al., 1999 (23)[a]	X_1O, X_2O, X_nO; case studies compared	Financing	Income distribution (progressivity, horizontal inequity, and re-ranking)	Comparison among countries
Habicht et al., 2006 (36)	XOOO: case study with multiple observations	Provision	Financial burden of health expenditures	People below poverty line due to out-of-pocket expenses, 1% to 1.3%
Hakkinen, 2005 (19)	OOXOO; interrupted time series	Political configuration (decentralization)	Structural changes, user charges, inequalities in mortality	Out-of-pocket expenses after decentralization, from 13% to 20%
Hisao Endo, 2001 (26)	X_1O, X_2O, X_nO; case studies compared	Financing	1. Expenditure ratio (medical-related expenditure/pretax income) 2. Kakwani index (progressivity or regressivity of out-of-pocket burden)	Comparison among countries
Hurst, 2002 (42)	XO; case study	Financing and planning	Access to care	Consensus; no qualitative data
Iversen and Kopperud, 2005 (31)	XO; case study	Purchasing	Access to care	Specialist care: high education vs. low education, >43%

Table 1 (Cont'd.)

Study, year (reference)	Design	Intervention	Outcome	Results
Keskimaki, 2003 (38)	OOXOO; interrupted time series	Financing	Provision of services per income stratum	Cataract surgery: high income vs. low income, >18%
Liaropoulos and Tragakes, 1998 (28)	XO; case study	Provision	Financial burden of health expenditures	Trend of out-of-pocket over total health expenditures: from 2.68% to 3.43%
Lopez-Casasnovas et al., 2005 (18)	X_1O, X_2O, X_nO; case studies compared	Political configuration (decentralization)	1. Interregional equity in service provision 2. Interregional equity in health outcomes	Comparison among regions
Mackenbach, 2003 (21)	XO; case study	Financing	Access to care	Specialist care: low education, 36.2%; high education, 40.5%
Mastilica and Bozikov, 1999 (33)	XO; case study	Provision	Financial burden of health expenditure	Out-of-pocket (% of total health expenses): low-income, 17.3%; high-income, 23%
Mooney, 2002 (41)	XO; case study	Financing and planning	Access to care	Consensus; no quantitative data
Navarro and Shi, 2001 (15)	X_1O, X_2O, X_nO; case studies compared	Political configuration (regimen)	1. Welfare expenditures 2. Health outcome 3. Poverty	Comparison among national trends
Oliveira Duarte and Gouveia Pinto, 2005 (27)	XO; case study	Provision	Access to care	Kakwani national index, −0.0445

Study	Design	Allocation	Access to care	Results / Comparison
O'Loughlin, 2004 (30)[a]	XO; case study			Consensus; no quantitative data
Petrova et al., 2002 (37)	X_1O, X_2O, X_nO; case studies compared	Provision	Equity among administrative areas	Comparison among administrative areas
Schoen and Doty, 2004 (24)	X_1O, X_2O, X_nO; case studies compared	Financing and organization of health system	1. Self-reported income status 2. Self-reported health status 3. Insurance status 4. Race/ethnicity and education 5. Access to health care 6. Financial burden 7. Quality-of-care rating	Comparison among countries
Szende and Johr Culyer, 2006 (34)	XO; case study	Provision	Financial burden of health expenditure	Kakwani index: −0.38 for general practice; −0.39 for specialist care; −0.35 for hospital care
Voncina et al., 2007 (32)	XO; case study	Provision	Financial burden of health expenditure	Out-of-pocket (% of total health expenses, euros/yr): workers, 375.3; unemployed, 200.8; disabled, 362.4
Wagstaff and van Doorslaer, 1997 (20)	XO; case study	Financing	Income distribution	Kakwani national index: −0.05431
Wagstaff et al., 1999 (22)	X_1O, X_2O, X_nO; case studies compared	Financing	Income distribution	Comparison among countries

Note: X, intervention (subscripts indicating different interventions); O, observation; SES, socioeconomic status; OR, odds ratio; 95% CI, 95% confidence interval.
[a]Study with a strong methodological component.

intraregional inequalities are still scarce, even if geographic patterns of mortality highlight some spatial distribution of mortality linked to variations in social and environmental features. Health interview surveys from 1987 to 1997 show an increasing social equality in utilization of health care.

The Finnish reforms described by Hakkinen (19) have increased the autonomy of municipalities. The Finnish health system is now the most decentralized in the world. The state and the 432 municipalities impose different taxes and allocate the money to the National Health Insurance fund (state) and to services (municipalities). This two-tier financing system gives rise to increased health care expenses for households (the share paid by the household increased from 13% to 20%) and, as a result, the Finnish health care system has become slightly more regressive. The increase in user charges to patients and increased unemployment levels could also have increased inequalities in access to care; regarding the degree of inequity for visits to a doctor, about 3 to 4 percent of total visits need to be redistributed from the richer to the poorer part of the population in order to achieve equity (outpatient visits to health centers still follow a pro-poor distribution; public specialists' visits are in line with differences in need between income groups; private doctors' services and occupational care are concentrated among high-income groups).

Taken together, these three studies (16, 18, 19) suggest that decentralization challenges equity in health care and that it may provide an opportunity for more in-depth studies of the impact of welfare systems on inequalities in health care through regional comparisons. At this stage, the comparative studies at the national level do not provide definitive evidence.

Financing and Pooling

In comparison with other types of intervention, the research on equity is quite extensive in the area of health care financing. Our searches located 11 studies. Here, we consider only those interventions that affect the parts of financing prepaid by the population (individuals and corporate entities).

In 1997, Wagstaff and van Doorslaer (20) analyzed the financing arrangements of the Dutch health system (direct and indirect taxes, social insurance, private insurance, and direct payments). Progressivity, re-ranking, and horizontal equity were considered as financial outcomes. The study showed that the Dutch health care financing system was, at that time, regressive. This was mainly due to the duality of insurance payments (income-related payments for the lower half of the income distribution; non-income-related premiums for the higher income groups).

The health system of the Netherlands was also described by Mackenbach (21). He paid special attention to equality in access to care, and his study confirmed that a regressive financing system results in a situation of unfairness. In the Dutch system, the more vulnerable people are those who are on a lower income and are chronically sick; mainly due to out-of-pocket payments, the more severe the chronic disease, the greater the financial disadvantage.

An international comparative study by Wagstaff and coauthors (22) analyzed the financial arrangements of some European health systems and their impact on income redistribution. The authors concluded that direct taxes are a progressive means of raising revenue, although local income tax can reduce the progressivity of the system (e.g., in the Scandinavian countries). Indirect taxes are regressive, as is social insurance in some countries (when the high-earners are not, or not completely, involved). Private insurance is regressive where the bulk of the population relies on this. Out-of-pocket payments are a highly regressive means of revenue.

According to the findings of van Doorslaer and coauthors (23), public finance sources in health care tend to have small positive redistributive effects and result in less differential treatment, while private financing sources generally have larger negative redistributive effects.

The international survey by Schoen and Doty (24) of the United Kingdom, United States, Australia, Canada, and New Zealand measured various health care outcomes: access difficulties, waiting times, cost-related access problems, ratings of physicians, and quality of care. The study demonstrates that some health systems—those based on public financing through taxes—are better able to minimize financial barriers to access and quality of care among low-income adults. The only European country included in the analysis, the United Kingdom, ranked highest in terms of equality in access to care. Inequalities in the United States by income were much more pronounced than in any other country. Australia, Canada, and New Zealand were between these two extremes in terms of both income-related access differences and the extent to which having private supplemental insurance is associated with more positive access experiences.

The situation in France is described by Bellanger and Mossé (25). The authors acknowledge that the topic of health inequality has been less documented in France than in other countries, in part due to the greater importance attached to health system performance as a way of gaining egalitarianism. In spite of this health care focus, between 1980 and 2003 the public share in health care spending decreased from 79.4 to 75.5 percent and, concomitantly, the role of complementary private health insurance increased to 12.3 percent and the contribution of user charges to 10.9 percent (a much higher proportion than in most other European countries). The study suggests that there is now evidence that social and spatial inequalities in health are more pronounced in prevention than in access to care. Some indicators of equity have worsened, especially in the field of perinatal health and HIV infection.

The experience and economic methods of evaluation used in Europe were adopted in an unpublished Japanese study (26). It compares Germany, the United Kingdom, and the United States with Japan. The outcomes considered are the expenditure ratio (medical-related expenditure divided by pretax income) and the Kakwani index. The author classified the countries into several groups: those with high expenditure ratio and high Kakwani index (Germany), high expenditure ratio and low Kakwani index (United States), low expenditure ratio and high Kakwani index (United Kingdom), and low expenditure ratio and low Kakwani index (Japan). Countries with compulsory universal insurance systems have low expenditure ratios (United Kingdom). Germany has a high expenditure ratio because high-income earners are allowed to opt out of public health insurance. Here, as in the United Kingdom, where middle- to high-income groups can take out private medical insurance that allows them to receive services outside the National Health Service, private medical insurance is a luxury good and insurance premium expenditures are progressive (i.e., the Kakwani index is positive).

In the paper by Lopez-Casasnovas and coauthors (18) on the progressivity of Spain's funding system, around a quarter of total financing is through indirect taxation (regressive) and the remainder is through direct taxes. The combination of both sources shows that the financing system has become less progressive.

The study by Oliveira Duarte and Gouveia Pinto (27) analyzes the content and impact of policies designed to reform the Portuguese health system between 1979 and 2002. It shows that the trend in health is improved, but the reform did not affect equity and access, and an increased expenditure is in evidence. There are still inequalities between urban and rural coverage and between high- and low-income groups. The allowance of multiple coverage (public and private) has created a two-tier structure and implies inequalities in access and outcomes.

In Greece, the 1983 reform aimed to increase equity in financing through expansion of the role of the public sector (28). However, the rigid application of certain measures, the failure to design and implement other measures, and a growing dissatisfaction with public services combined to increase the private share of health care financing. The greatest portion of this increase involved out-of-pocket payments, which are the most regressive form of financing. The growing share of private insurance financing has also contributed to reducing equity. Low-income families seem to devote a larger share of their total expenditure to health than do middle- or high-income families. Private payments were considered an increasingly inequitable form of financing, hitting low-income families especially hard in 1993–94, probably because of the considerable burden of co-payments in pharmaceutical care.

We found only one study that examined pooling. "Pooling" refers to the accumulation of prepaid health care revenues on behalf of a population. In France, a study by Buchmueller and co-workers (29) described the findings of a national survey. It investigated the role of supplemental insurance in economic efficiency and equity. Supplemental insurance, which is very common in France but unequally distributed, can increase demand for health care and can reduce the ability of cost sharing to control utilization. In fact, there is a statistically significant difference between French adults with and without supplementary insurance in the probability of seeing a physician in a one-month period. The findings of this study are strong enough to conclude that because the public system covers the majority of the cost of outpatient care, the moral hazard effect of private insurance leads to higher public expenditures for medical care in general and in favor of higher-income groups.

We did not find any study on the pooling of health care fund mechanisms and the consequences for equity.

Allocation

"Allocation" of funding means the transfer of money from one level to the next (8). In an attempt to improve equity in the distribution of public funds, several countries have changed the basis for determining the size of their budgets so that resource flow more closely reflects population needs rather than historical patterns of utilization or infrastructure development. The evidence base in this area is very small. Our search identified only one study, by O'Loughlin (30). It examined whether the Irish allocation method, in which historical expenses are considered as the basis for calculation, is unfair in terms of equity. The study surveyed expert opinion (by the Delphy method). Panelists provided several reasons why the current method of resource allocation in Ireland is inequitable. The main suggestion centered around the development of a needs-based resource allocation formula. Potential obstacles identified included methodological difficulties, insufficient resources, and resistance from potential losers. We found no other studies that looked at the impact on inequalities in health care of different rules of allocation of funds, staffing, facilities, and technologies.

Purchasing

The terms "purchasing" and "provider payment" refer to contracting rules that can generate financial incentives for service providers to behave in certain ways (for instance, increasing or decreasing waiting lists). Again, there are few studies of this type of reform. We found only one, a Norwegian study that examined the type of contract in place between public insurance and private services. The study, by Iversen and Kopperud (31), found that after reforms to the rules governing the public purchase of private services, accessibility and socioeconomic variables played a larger role in determining the probability and number of visits to a private specialist (paid out-of-pocket or by private insurance). For example, having a university degree increased the probability of at least one private visit by 11 percentage points. The study also found that household income had a positive impact on the use of private specialists, although not on the use of hospital services. However, a link was found between the ratio of public GPs per resident and the probability of the use of private services: the higher the ratio, the lower the probability of a visit and the number of private visits. This was not the case for hospital outpatient department visits.

Provision of Services

The provision of services needs to be analyzed by taking into consideration the market structure (whether provision is competitive or monopolistic), the autonomy of managers, and the geographic distribution of services. In this subset of interventions, we also consider the mechanism of implicit or explicit rationing of the supply of services, operationalized by varying the amount of direct payment requests to patients when accessing services (e.g., out-of-pocket; formal and informal co-payments). These forms of cost sharing are a source of funding of health care, but following the criterion of Kutzin (which includes in the funding function only prepaid and pooled resources), we analyzed the available literature on cost sharing as mainly a way of controlling the demand and rationing the provision of services.

Six of the 11 included papers in this area were from Eastern European countries. They focus mainly on the impact of out-of-pocket payments (formal and informal). A study by Voncina and colleagues (32) describes developments in the Croatian health care financing system from 1999 to 2002. It suggests an overly strong bias toward private spending and an increase in its proportion of total health care expenditure. Using data from 2003, the authors found that retired people spent, on average, substantially more on services than did workers and farmers; disability pension recipients spent about the same as active contributors and workers; and the unemployed spent by far the lowest amount (yearly expenditure per insured person by the Croatian Institute for Health Insurance). This might indicate a certain degree of regressivity in the contribution of health care services.

The inequity of the Croatian system is also suggested in a study by Mastilica and Bozikov (33), which shows that the new legislation on delivery and financing of health care services in Croatia, adopted in 1993, increased the out-of-pocket payments for private care and co-payments for public care services. The study shows that distribution of out-of-pocket payments in Croatia is highly regressive, with a greater burden falling on lower-income people: lower-income groups were significantly more likely to report having out-of-pocket expenses for drugs, private medical care, private dentistry, and traditional drugs. They were also significantly more likely to report incurring expenses for gifts and gratuities to health care providers. And this group was more likely to receive a reduction in salary because of sickness absence.

In Hungary, the informal payment system operates within the national health care service. A study by Szende and Johr Culyer (34) found that the Kakwani progressivity index for Hungary has a negative value for all informal payments, indicating that this is a highly regressive feature of the system. The index was similar for access to GPs and outpatient and inpatient care, so individuals with a lower income paid proportionally more in informal payments at all levels of public health care. Some evidence was found that price discrimination may occur across age groups, favoring the elderly, who typically belong to the middle- rather than the lower-income groups.

In Bulgaria, Delcheva and colleagues (35) measured informal payments and the willingness of people to pay them; they found a popular willingness to pay that could be converted into formal co-payments. Of interest in this study is that people who tend to be advantaged by a situation of inequity due to the high impact of informal payments in Eastern Europe—that is, older people, those on lower incomes, and sick people—are those least likely to want to change the system. In the whole population, 65 percent stated that they were in favor of introducing official user fees for health services; this view was significantly less common among those over 65, those with low household incomes, and those describing their health as poor or bad.

In Estonia, Habicht and colleagues (36) analyzed the trend in out-of-pocket expenditure, the distribution of out-of-pocket payments across income groups, and the household financial burden of out-of-pocket payments after the social health insurance system was introduced in 1991. From 1995 to 2002, households spending more than 20 percent of their budget on health care increased from 3.4 to 7.4 percent; the lower the income, the more frequently households spent more than 20 percent. Over the same period, more households were pushed below the poverty line after paying for health services. In 1995, 1 percent of the population fell below the poverty line as a result of health care payments; this increased to 1.3 and 1.4 percent by 2001 and 2002, respectively. The popula- tion most at risk was low-income elderly patients, as they spent high amounts of money on medicines.

Studying the provision of drugs in two administrative areas of Bosnia- Herzegovina, Petrova and coauthors (37) found inequality in regulation, pricing, manufacturing, accessibility, and availability of drugs between the two areas (Federation of Bosnia Herzegovina and Republika Srpska). The authors suggest that this inequality could be due to the way in which licenses are issued to private pharmacies, even though the country is experiencing a lack of pharmacists and, consequently, less correct information is disseminated to patients about the correct use of drugs. In addition, government coverage of drug expenditures per capita is different in the two administrative areas, increasing geographic inequity in the country.

Keskimaki (38) studied the impact of Finland's health system reforms and the contemporary economic recession (which slashed more than 10% of gross domestic product and resulted in a 12% decrease in national health expenditure) on socioeconomic equity in the use of general hospital care in the late 1980s and the mid-1990s. Analyzing the provision of services per income stratum, the author found that the tendency in the late 1980s for high-income groups to receive more surgical care than lower-income groups with poorer health status seemed to have become more systematic and pronounced after the reforms, despite the considerable increase in supply of surgical procedures. Keskimaki suggests that some of the socioeconomic discrepancies in access to surgical care could be due to certain features of the Finnish health care system—namely, the high profile of the private sector in specialized ambulatory care and in the supply of some elective procedures.

In a study of the experience of market-oriented health care reform in Sweden, Burström (39) analyzed the change in funding (increased user fees) and in jurisdiction and provision of care (cuts in numbers of hospital beds; shorter hospital stays). The measures of distribution of health care utilization across income groups showed slight differences over time. The access to emergency care was higher in lower income groups in 1996–97 than in 1988–89. Furthermore, for the indicator "having needed but not sought medical care" in the past three months, the analysis also showed a change over time: in 1996–97, persons in the lowest income quintiles reported to a greater extent than in 1988–89 that they had needed but had not sought medical care in the past three months.

An unpublished study by Donia Soflo and colleagues (40) found that an increase in the amount of co-payments and out-of-pocket payments for private services in Italy during the 2000s led to the impoverishment of 1.3 percent of Italian households. This study also found that this trend was likely to increase in the future. The impact on income distribution was mainly through pharmaceutical expenses, as well as specialist and dental care.

We found two studies that reported the experience of a SWOT (strengths, weakness, opportunities, and threats) analysis of the Danish health system (41, 42). They concluded that all steps in financing and planning of health care showed a good level of equity, although there were some concerns about the provision of hospital services, because of waiting lists and the quality of relationships between patients and providers.

We found two reports on evaluation of the equity audit process. Aspray and co-workers (43) assessed the equity of care provision among frail British care-home residents with diabetes, by means of a rapid assessment method. If compared with national standards of care, disadvantages were evident: lack of recording in diabetes registers, higher rates of inappropriate glucose monitoring and secondary care, little evidence of coordinated eye screening, and staff in need of training in diabetes care. In the United Kingdom, Aspinall and Jacobson (44) surveyed primary care trusts and their experience with the health equity audit promoted by the National Health Service through a national-based survey in 2004, all trusts being mailed a questionnaire. The research shows only limited use of health equity audit as a tool for multisectoral use.

DISCUSSION

In this review we looked at five areas of importance in the contribution of health care to health inequalities: the social and political context, financing and pooling, allocation, purchasing, and the provision of services. We found few studies on the allocation of resources. Those that we did find were not substantive enough to be informative in policy development. Lack of research also extends to the purchasing mechanisms and their effect on equity of supply, as well as studies of pooling. We also found few studies that looked at health outcomes. However, we did locate a number of studies that examined the effects of health care financing and provision of health care services on inequalities in income and health care access (key social determinants of health).

The studies that looked into financing models, identifying the characteristics that produce or reduce inequalities in income distribution and access to care, show that public universal coverage (e.g., a national health care system such as the U.K. National Health Service) is able to reduce the impact of ill health on inequalities in income distribution, while other forms of coverage and multiple coverage (private and public insurance) can increase inequalities in access to care. Similarly, the studies of service provision show that if some services are not regularly provided by the national health system (e.g., dental care and some pharmaceuticals), the out-of-pocket payments imposed on citizens increase inequalities in access to care and contribute to impoverishment.

The review also highlights the importance to health care access (and resulting inequalities) of the wider social and political arenas. At the political level, the review highlights the potential risks of decentralization processes (including the risk of creating geographic inequalities in health within countries and among citizens). This topic has recently gained the attention of the World Health Organization (45).

The message of this evidence synthesis is therefore very clear: nationalized, publicly funded health systems are the most effective at reducing inequalities in access to medical services and in reducing the effects on health of income distribution.

Limitations of the Study

Due to the extensive nature of this field of research, some important topics could not be reviewed here. In general, the existing knowledge in this field seems fragmentary and often lacking in scientific validity. This confirms De Maeseneer and colleagues' diagram (10) showing the progressive reduction of research quality and quantity when passing from medical evidence, through contextual evidence, to policy evidence. In fact, many studies describe health systems in a generic manner, choosing indicators of effect that are nonspecific and not directly related to the interventions analyzed, and at best are focused on the utilization of health care, disregarding the impact on health outcomes. Health equity impact assessment of policies is scanty. We found equity-oriented planning acts by governments and local authorities, but seldom were they evaluated by a suitable research design. In fact, only three studies among those included in this review provide an analysis of historical trends (interrupted time series).

Lack of research literature in this area could also be explained by a strong publication bias—likely to be stronger in this field than others: economic and organizational arrangements are often considered to be of local interest, and studies are published in national scientific journals, in languages other than English, and may not be indexed by international databases.

Considering the quality of the research available, we had difficulties classifying study designs and forming opinions about their internal validity. This lack of methodological rigor is perhaps not surprising, however, given the barriers faced by those trying to conduct research on the effects of political and economic decisions. Moreover, the research is particularly poor in countries where the political interest is low, and the difficulty in designing a more appropriate impact evaluation study often seems to be related to poor interaction with decision makers. Proper strategies and methods for exchanging knowledge and experience between the policy arena and academia should be considered a must.

As highlighted by Judge (46), the quality of research in this field is poor and the impact on health equity evaluation using experimental or quasi-experimental methods or even natural experiments is still uncommon. Moreover, few countries have been studied, and very few have been studied properly and in a comprehensive way. For example, there is little research about health equity in the former Eastern bloc countries. We found no comparisons between these and Western countries (although hand-searching techniques might increase the likelihood of finding such studies). Similarly, the impact of being part of the European Union on health equity has not yet been investigated, and mostly unknown is the situation of the health systems of the satellite countries of the former Eastern bloc. For example, the only studies from Eastern Europe identified in this review related to out-of-pocket payments. Our findings will be useful given the importance of the introduction of the market in these countries and the correspondingly high risk of inequalities in access to health care and health status.

All these elements confirm the need to develop an appropriate impact assessment methodology, as well as the importance of providing scientific support to the countries of Eastern Europe and facilitating a better interaction among European scientific communities and between scientists and policymakers at all decision levels. This is essential if we are to be better able to ascertain and thus mitigate the effects of European countries' health care reforms on inequalities in health.

Acknowledgments — This study was partially funded by the European Commission through the Eurothine Project (Public Health Program, grant agreement 2003125), and by the Italian Ministry of Labor, Health, and Social Policy, through the National Center for the Prevention and Control of Diseases. We are grateful to colleagues in the Eurothine network for helpful comments during the project meetings.

REFERENCES

1. Marmot, M., and Wilkinson, R. *Social Determinants of Health.* Oxford University Press, Oxford, 2006.
2. Dahlgren, G., and Whitehead, M. *Policies and Strategies to Promote Social Equity.* Institute for the Futures Studies, Stockholm, 1991.
3. Stronks, K. The Netherlands. In *Reducing Inequalities in Health: A European Perspective.* Routledge, London, 2002.
4. Paterson, I., and Judge, K. Equality of access to health care. In *Reducing Inequalities in Health: A European Perspective.* Routledge, London, 2002.
5. Arblaster, L., et al. A systematic review of the effectiveness of health service interventions aimed at reducing inequality in health. *J. Health Serv. Res. Policy* 1:93–103, 1996.
6. Aday, L., and Andersen, R. A framework for the study of access to medical care. *Health Serv. Res.* 9(3):208–220, 1974.
7. Gilson, G., et al. *Challenging Inequity through Health Systems.* WHO Commission on Social Determinants of Health. World Health Organization, Geneva, 2007.
8. Kutzin, J. A descriptive framework for country-level analysis of health care financing arrangements. *Health Policy* 56:171–204, 2001.
9. Donabedian, A. The quality of care: How can it be assessed? *JAMA* 260:1743–1748, 1988.
10. De Maeseneer, J. M., et al. The need for research in primary care. *Lancet* 362: 1314–1319, 2003.
11. World Health Organization. *Health Systems: Improving Performance.* World Health Report. Geneva, 2000.
12. Campbell, S. *Experimental and Quasi-Experimental Designs for Research.* Rand McNally, Chicago, 1966.
13. Stronks, K., and Mackenbach, J. P. Evaluating the effect of policies and interventions to address inequalities in health: Lessons from a Dutch programme. *Eur. J. Public Health* 16:346–353, 2006.
14. Beckfield, J., and Krieger, N. E. Epi + demos + cracy: Linking political systems and priorities to the magnitude of health inequities—Evidence, gaps and a research agenda. *Epidemiol. Rev.*, Advance Access. June 9, 2009.
15. Navarro, V., and Shi, L. The political context of social inequalities and health. *Soc. Sci. Med.* 52:481–491, 2001.
16. Costa-i-Font, J. Inequalities in self reported health within Spanish regional health services: Devolution re-examined? *Int. J. Health Plann. Manage.* 20:41–52, 2005.
17. Kakwani, N., Wagstaff, A., and van Doorslaer, E. Socioeconomic inequalities in health measurement, computation and statistical inference. *J. Econ.* 77:87–103, 1999.

18. Lopez-Casasnovas, G., Costa-i-Font, J., and Planasa, I. Diversity and regional inequalities in the Spanish "system of health care services." *Health Econ.* 14:S221–235, 2005.
19. Hakkinen, U. The impact of changes in Finland's health care system. *Health Econ.* 14:S101–118, 2005.
20. Wagstaff, A., and van Doorslaer, E. Progressivity, horizontal equity and reranking in health care finance: A decomposition analysis for the Netherlands. *J. Health Econ.* 16:499–516, 1997.
21. Mackenbach, J. P. An analysis of the role of health care in reducing socioeconomic inequalities in health: The case of the Netherlands. *Int. J. Health Serv.* 33:523–541, 2003.
22. Wagstaff, A., et al. Equity in finance of health care: Some further international comparisons. *J. Health Econ.* 18:263–290, 1999.
23. Van Doorslaer, E., et al. The redistributive effect of health care finance in twelve OECD countries. *J. Health Econ.* 18:291–313, 1999.
24. Schoen, C., and Doty, M. F. Inequities in access to medical care in five countries: Findings from 2001 Commonwealth Fund International Health Policy Survey. *Health Policy* 67:309–322, 2004.
25. Bellanger, M. M., and Mossé, P. R. The search for the Holy Grail: Combining decentralized planning and contracting mechanisms in the French health care system. *Health Econ.* 14:119–132, 2005.
26. Hisao Endo. *The Out of Pocket Burden of Medical Expenses: An International Comparison and Time Series Analysis of Expenditure Ratios and the Kakwani Index.* Institute for Health Economics and Policy, Tokyo, 2001.
27. Oliveira Duarte, M., and Gouveia Pinto, C. Health care reform in Portugal: An evaluation of the NHS experience. *Health Econ.* 14:203–220, 2005.
28. Liaropoulos, L., and Tragakes, E. Public/private financing in Greek health care system: Implications for equity. *Health Policy* 43:153–169, 1998.
29. Buchmueller, T. C., et al. Access to physician services: Does supplemental insurance matter? Evidence from France. *Health Econ.* 13:669–687, 2004.
30. O'Loughlin, K. A. Equity in resource allocation in the Irish health service: A policy Delphy study. *Health Policy* 67:271–280, 2004.
31. Iversen, T., and Kopperud, G. S. Regulation versus practice: The impact of accessibility on the use of specialist health care in Norway. *Health Econ.* 14:1231–1238, 2005.
32. Voncina, L., Dzakula, A., and Mastilica, M. Health care funding reforms in Croatia: A case of mistaken priority. *Health Policy* 80:144–157, 2007.
33. Mastilica, M., and Bozikov, J. Out of pocket payments for health care in Croatia: Implications for equity. *Croat. Med. J.* 40:152–159, 1999.
34. Szende, A., and Johr Culyer, A. The inequity of informal payments for health care: The case of Hungary. *Health Policy* 75:262–271, 2006.
35. Delcheva, E., Balabanova, D., and McKee, M. Under-the-counter payments for health care: Evidence from Bulgaria. *Health Policy* 42:89–100, 1997.
36. Habicht, J., et al. Detecting changes in financial protection: Creating evidence for policy in Estonia. *Health Policy Plann.* 21:421–431, 2006.
37. Petrova, G. I., et al. Towards improving pharmaceutical equity in transition in Bosnia and Herzegovina. *J. Soc. Adm. Pharm.* 19:15–24, 2002.

38. Keskimaki, I. How did Finland economic recession in the early 1990s affect socioeconomic equity in the use of hospital care? *Soc. Sci. Med.* 56:1517–1530, 2003.
39. Burström, B. Increasing inequalities in health care utilisation across income groups in Sweden during the 1990s? *Health Policy* 62:117–129, 2002.
40. Donia Soflo, A., et al. *Rapporto CEIS Sanità.* Università degli Studi di Roma Tor Vergata, Rome, 2006.
41. Mooney, G. The Danish health care system: It ain't broke . . . so don't fix it. *Health Policy* 59:161–171, 2002.
42. Hurst, J. The Danish health care system from a British perspective. *Health Policy* 59:133–143, 2002.
43. Aspray, T. J., et al. Rapid assessment methods used for health equity audit: Diabetes mellitus among frail British care-home residents. *Public Health* 120:1042–1051, 2006.
44. Aspinall, P. J., and Jacobson, B. Managing health inequalities locally: A baseline survey of primary care trusts' experience with health equity audit in the implementation year. *Health Serv. Manage. Res.* 18:223–231, 2005.
45. Saltman, R., Bankauskaite, V., and Vrangbaek, K. *Decentralization in Health Care: Strategies and Outcomes.* Open University Press, Maidenhead, UK, 2007.
46. Judge, K. *Health Inequalities: A Challenge for Europe.* UK Presidency of the European Union. Brussels, 2006.

CHAPTER 4

Ditching the Single-Payer System in the National Health Service: How the English Department of Health is Learning the Wrong Lessons from the United States

Lucy Reynolds, Clare Gerada, and
Martin McKee

Reforms to the British National Health Service introduce major changes to how health care will be delivered. The core elements include the creation of new purchaser organizations, Clinical Commissioning Groups, which unlike their predecessors will be able to recruit and reject general practices and their patients without geographical restriction. The Clinical Commissioning Groups are to transition from statutory bodies to freestanding organizations, with most of their functions privatized and an increasingly privatized system of provision. In this chapter, we explore the likely consequences of these proposals, drawing in particular on the experience of managed care organizations in the United States, whose approach has influenced the English proposals extensively. We argue that the wrong lessons are being learned and the English reforms are likely to fundamentally undermine the principles on which the British National Health Service was founded.

*****

The British National Health Service (NHS) is moving into uncharted waters. Reforms that have been described by its chief executive, David Nicholson, as "so big you can see them from space" (1) are likely to have profound implications for how health care is delivered. Yet, as civil servants struggle to comprehend what the language in the Act actually means, it remains far from clear what these implications are. Guidance on interpretation has been extensively delayed and, in some cases, heavily qualified almost as soon as it is issued. This has occurred despite the fact that, quite remarkably, many elements of the bill were implemented even before it had passed into law, a seeming contempt that Parliament seems willing to tolerate.

The Health and Social Care Act (2) is permissive, making it possible for many things to be done differently, rather than prescriptive, setting out precisely how they will be done. In broad outline the Health Minister no longer will be responsible to Parliament for the provision of a comprehensive health service, as he has been since 1948. Money for health care will be given to an appointed autonomous body, the National Health Service Commissioning Board, which will allocate most of it to Clinical Commissioning Groups (CCGs) to purchase care in a marketplace. Originally seen as statutory public bodies led by general practitioners (GPs), guidance makes clear the intention that most of the CCGs' work will be undertaken by private corporations who will facilitate their transition to "freestanding enterprises." The CCGs have been portrayed as similar to Primary Care Trusts (PCTs), the statutory NHS bodies they will replace that purchase care for patients of general practices in a geographically defined population within a largely internal market of NHS providers. However, the CCGs are fundamentally different. Their link to a geographical area will be confined to purchasing those services, such as emergency ambulances, that must be provided on a geographical basis. It will be possible for individuals living anywhere in England to sign up with a particular CCG. However, crucially, the CCG will be able to decline to sign up general practitioners, and therefore their patients, in the area they are associated with. This practice already has been seen in the pre-legislation "pathfinder" CCGs. They have a powerful financial incentive to make these declinations where practices (and their patients) use higher than average amounts of hospital care.

Patients referred for secondary care will be treated by a combination of NHS and, increasingly, private for-profit and voluntary (non-profit) sector operators who will compete for available funds. Indeed, the NHS operating framework makes clear that CCGs will be expected to increase, year on year, the share of care delivered by private providers. The CCGs will have to manage their budgets carefully to avoid running out of money, but will be allowed to retain any surpluses. In the remainder of this chapter, we examine what this will mean in practice.

FINANCING COMMISSIONING

England's proposed new system will establish two new budgets for commissioning services not provided by GPs: one to cover financial and administration costs, at £25 (US$39) per patient registered with a GP per year, and the other to pay for referrals. The commissioning budget, which must cover needs assessment, development of care packages, contract management, and monitoring and evaluation, is substantially smaller than the corresponding amount available to the predecessor PCTs.

The workload involved is considerable. CCGs will need new administrative systems to handle individualized billing for standalone referrals, as well as systems for launching, judging, and administering competitive bids for larger-scale service provision. Even before the legislation was enacted, initial enthusiasts were starting to withdraw, citing pressure of work (3). In practice, as noted above, CCGs are being required to outsource commissioning support functions, although many are resisting. International health insurance companies and management consultancy firms have been lining up to take advantage of these outsourcing opportunities (4, 5), although given the limited budgets, some are now questioning whether this will yield adequate profits.

FINANCING REFERRALS

Patients can be referred to any provider that has registered with the statutory quality regulator, the Care Quality Commission (CQC), and been "accredited" under a process termed *Any Qualified Provider* to supply the service concerned (6). However, it is not clear whether the patient, GP or CCG will be able to select the provider; despite rhetoric on patient choice, it seems likely to be the CCG. Furthermore, quite what is meant by *Qualified* is at present unclear and is likely to change given evidence about significant recent failings by the CQC (7) that questions its ability to provide effective, affordable regulation in a complex market. The act contains no "fit and proper person test" for NHS providers.

The budget for referrals may not cover all of the care needed or generated by patients, as some of the pathfinder CCGs already have discovered (8). Random fluctuations in the number of patients needing particularly expensive treatment also can cause this problem, especially in smaller CCGs (because of their limited risk pool). Research published more than 20 years ago in the first wave of major NHS reforms, but now seemingly forgotten, drew on the experience of American HMOs (health maintenance organizations) and highlighted the risks associated with risk pools of less than about 250,000 (9), with more recent research identifying further problems (10). The pathfinder CCGs have some risk pools with as few as 14,000 patients (11).

CCGs thus will be forced to ration care. Because the legislation removes the Secretary of State's duty to provide a comprehensive health service, CCGs will be able to determine what services they provide as standard (that is, free at the point of use), with others left for private purchase by those patients who can afford it.

One approach to rationing that already is being implemented involves what has been termed the "Croydon" list (after the PCT in south London that first compiled it) (12, 13). This excludes some treatments of dubious merit, but also some therapies of proven effectiveness. These include hip replacements and cataract surgery (8), both straightforward, elective procedures that are prime targets for private hospitals. In some of the pathfinder CCGs and in existing PCTs that have anticipated the legislation, this rationing is being carried out by referral management systems, with health professionals (not always doctors) employed to decide from referral letters whether referrals recommended by GPs can be funded (14). Reductions in referrals will have consequences for secondary care providers, with patients being referred later, with worse morbidities. CCGs could be subject to legal action for "anti-competitive behavior" by any existing or potential provider that suspects they have favored a competitor, even where they do so to safeguard the viability of an existing NHS provider threatened by loss of specific services. Some are already being deluged with intimidating letters from major corporations, in effect warning them against giving contracts to smaller companies. This is a recipe for cherry-picking by profit-seeking providers, an arrangement facilitated by the government requirement that each patient be offered at least two alternative providers in addition to the local NHS hospital. Many of these incoming providers will be private firms willing to offer only the most profitable services.

Some NHS hospitals are especially vulnerable as they have inherited large debts as a consequence of participation in poor-value, public-private partnerships for capital funding, the now-notorious Private Finance Initiative (PFI) (15). They now must make repayments that rise with inflation using income that is falling in real terms. All will face considerable pressure to undertake additional fee-generating services, facilitated by the government's decision to remove a cap on private-patient income. The American experience has illustrated the scope for profiteering (16).

In addition to creating pressures for GPs to deny necessary care, the new system creates barriers to cooperation between primary and secondary care practitioners. The incentives embedded in the new system pit GPs against hospitals and other providers, with the latter trying to increase charges to cover their overheads and make profits, and the former trying to stop them in order to balance their own budgets. Five years ago, the Netherlands moved to competition among its insurance funds, with primary care doctors now finding that attempts to coordinate patient care result in sanctions from the Dutch Competition Authority (17). In theory, E.U. competition law is invoked to defend patients' interests, but in practice it is used against existing providers by companies wanting to enter the health care market (17).

LESSONS FROM THE UNITED STATES

The English reforms owe much to ideas imported from the United States, where programs such as the Harkness Fellowships have exposed a generation of policy advisors to emerging ideas in managed care. British observers have returned full of enthusiasm for American managed care organizations. Yet there are crucial reasons why this enthusiasm is misplaced.

First, the managed care model is an imperfect solution to a problem to which the NHS is not prone. This is the soaring cost of market-based provision of secondary and tertiary care, largely paid for on a fee-for-service basis, which encourages supplier-induced demand. This is rampant in the American system but not in the NHS, at least as long as the proposed market-based reform is not yet implemented.

Second, the NHS has risk-pooling across the whole population. In managed care organizations, however, individual risk profiles are calculated by an actuary on the basis of the medical history they declare, age, gender, and possibly other characteristics. This means the cost of health care coverage shoots up when the enrollee has been diagnosed with something, just at the time when ill health hits their earnings. Many people in the United Kingdom seem to be under the misapprehension that health insurance can be bought to cover the cost of all needed care, as a full replacement for NHS care. It cannot, because one can only insure risks and not certainties: if the managed care organization knows the enrollee has a pre-existing condition (because they have declared it), the premium they charge will increase so the organization will still turn a profit. If that care will certainly be needed, then the insurance premium must logically exceed what the managed care organization has to pay to purchase this care, so it is effectively uninsurable. In addition, in this model, clinically justified treatment is minimized so as to widen the profit margin between premiums received and treatment purchased by the managed care organization (18). If the pre-existing condition is not declared, so as to keep the premium at an affordable level, the managed care organization will be able to legally deny reimbursement or payment for any medical costs related to that condition.

Furthermore, managed care organizations have strong incentives to game the system by recruiting those least likely to need care, cherry-picking the healthiest clients through targeted advertising. In one case, an HMO subcontracting for Medicare targeted the healthiest people over age 65 by advertising their health insurance in advertisements painted on the floors of swimming pools (16). Managed care organizations also reduce claims by excluding high-cost subscribers: those who had become ill and started to make claims, or those known to be at high risk of disease.

Third, managed care organizations usually have shareholders, who expect to be paid for the use of their money. The NHS is funded from taxes. So, other things being equal, providing a service through a managed care organization will be more expensive because it is necessary to pay not only the costs of providing the service, but also a payment to investors. There is a misconception, frequently encouraged by British politicians, that the private sector is inherently more efficient than the public sector, which, it is frequently implied, is staffed by lazy incompetents. As the Archbishop of York recently noted: "For many years, it seems that our society has perpetuated the myth that the private sector is always more professional and more proficient than the public sector. This has never been my experience of public services, and I think this does a great disservice to the many people who devote their lives to working in the public sector to support others" (19). A shift to the managed care model will divert limited funds that otherwise would be available to provide necessary care.

Fourth, the NHS has managed, and CCGs will manage, the care pathway with the aim of controlling costs, resulting in some rationing of costly care. The difference is that in the past, this was based on objective, transparent assessments by the National Institute for Health and Clinical Excellence. In the future, care rationing will be much less transparent, based substantially on the decisions of CCG referral gateways, backed by their boards. Redress for perceived abuses will have to be through the courts, but since publicly funded legal aid relating to medical matters also is being withdrawn, most people may have no recourse against unfair decisions other than exercising their right to choose a different CCG the following year.

LOOKING AHEAD

The reforms do not specify an end point. Instead, they start a ball rolling to a destination that remains uncertain. There has already been rapid consolidation of CCGs, with more successful ones taking over those falling into financial difficulties. Newcomers to the market are likely to embark upon an acquisition effort with the kind of aggressive patient recruitment strategies seen in the United States. They also may adopt predatory pricing to drive competitors out of business or into their arms. The act legitimizes and protects such strategies through its "provider autonomy" provisions (Clause 4).

The implementation of CCGs will coincide with introduction of "personal care budgets" to be rolled out in 2012 (20). Although initially limited to those receiving long-term care, the budgets provide a basis for individuals to be given sums of money, adjusted in some way according to their expected health needs, to purchase a package of care from a CCG. In this way, their entitlement will shift from a defined benefit (comprehensive care) to a contribution defined by government. In due course, it is easy to envisage that a future government might announce that, because of an aging population, costly medical advances, and a limited budget, enrollees will be required to provide a supplemental payment to cover the full cost of their care. As noted above, it also seems likely that providers will impose additional charges.

A NATIONAL HEALTH SERVICE SERVING
HEALTH NOT WEALTH

The NHS works. It produces some of the best health results of any modern health care system (21, 22) and recently has achieved record-high approval ratings (23). It is a universal service, pooling risk across the whole population, ensuring equity in health care and a sound basis for maximizing public health through a caring, personalized service. GPs largely are paid by capitation, which creates financial incentives to keep patients alive, well, and pleased with their GP. In the present arrangement, there are no obstacles to cooperation with salaried hospital doctors, since GPs have no incentive to over-treat or over-charge for financial gain.

The NHS has its flaws, but reorganizing it along the lines of a poorly performing and costlier model is not the way to address them. This reform will move the NHS to a system loaded with perverse incentives and conflicts of interest, multiplication of administrative tasks, and avoidable risk that will exacerbate rather than address those flaws.

Over 60 years, the NHS has provided very good health care and security against catastrophic medical expenditure. It has achieved this while spending the second least amount among the 10 developed countries reviewed in the latest Commonwealth Fund Report, at the same time achieving the highest approval ratings from the public (23). Rather than implementing the failed American market-based model that prioritizes corporate profits over health outcomes, the government should learn the proper lessons from experience here and abroad and terminate the expensive and distracting experiment with market-based solutions. GPs should instead be focusing on patients' priorities: convenient access to high-quality care to meet their medical needs, coordinated by caring family doctors.

The managed care model is designed to deal with uncontrollable increases in costs of specialist care that exist within fragmented, privately-owned health systems. This is not, at present, a problem facing the NHS, but it will be with implementation of the proposals. The alternative is to draw back from a competition-based reorganization, instead investing in the universal, solidarity-based NHS that has safeguarded physical, mental, and economic health in England for three generations.

REFERENCES

1. United Kingdom Parliament. *Health and Social Care Bill*. 2010–2011 Session. www.publications.parliament.uk/pa/cm201011/cmpublic/health/110208/am/110208 s01.htm (accessed March 19, 2012).
2. United Kingdom Parliament. *Health and Social Care Act*. London, 2012.
3. GPs quit CCG roles as commissioning enthusiasts lose heart. *Pulse*. December 6, 2011. www.pulsetoday.co.uk/newsarticle-content/-/article_display_list/13150087/gps-quit-ccg-roles-as-commissioning-enthusiasts-lose-heart.
4. Leys, C., and Player, S. *The Plot Against the NHS*. Merlin, London, 2011.
5. Iacobucci, G. Dozens of consortia turn to McKinsey. *Pulse*. March 9, 2011. www.pulsetoday.co.uk/newsarticle-content/-/article_display_list/11054828/dozens-of-consortia-turn-to-mckinsey.
6. Reynolds, L., and McKee, M. "Any qualified provider" in the NHS reforms: But who will qualify? *The Lancet* 2011. doi:10.1016/S0140-6736.

7. Campbell, D. Care Quality Commission's leaders "lack the necessary skills." November 29, 2011. *The Guardian.* www.guardian.co.uk/society/2011/nov/29/care-quality-commission-leaders.

8. Quinn, I. Radical new gateways reject one in eight GP referrals. *Pulse.* February 23, 2011. www.pulsetoday.co.uk/newsarticle-content/-/article_display_list/11053620/radical-new-gateways-reject-one-in-eight-gp-referrals.

9. Scheffler, R. Adverse selection: The Achilles heel of the NHS reforms. *The Lancet* 333:950–952, 1989.

10. Bevan, G. Calculating target allocations for commissioning general practices in England. *Brit. Med. J.* 343, 2011. doi:10.1136/bmj.d6732.

11. Mathieson, S. A. DH launches smaller GP pathfinder groups. January 18, 2011. www.guardian.co.uk/healthcare-network/2011/jan/18/gp-commissioning-second-wave-david-cameron (accessed March 19, 2012).

12. Blogger, R. NHS "efficiency savings" achieved by cutting cataract and hip ops. April 27, 2011. www.falseeconomy.org.uk/blog/nhs-efficiency-savings-are-being<ach ieved-by-rationing-patient-healthcare (accessed March 19, 2012).

13. Audit Commission. Reducing spending on low clinical value treatments. Health Briefing April 2011. www.audit-commission.gov.uk/sitecollectiondocuments/downloads/20110414reducingexpenditure.pdf (accessed March 19, 2012).

14. Gateways using nurses to screen GP referrals. *Pulse.* August 10, 2011. www.pulsetoday.co.uk/main-content/-/article_display_list/12511567/gateways-using-nurses-to-screen-gp-referrals.

15. McKee, M., Edwards, N., and Atun, R. Public-private partnerships for hospitals. *Bull. World Health Org.* 84:890–896, 2006.

16. Woolhandler, S., and Himmelstein, D. U. Competition in a publicly funded healthcare system. *Brit. Med. J.* 335:1126, 2007. doi:10.1136.

17. Sheldon, T. Is competition law bad for patients? *Brit. Med. J.* 343:d4495, 2011.

18. Sullivan, K. On the "efficiency" of managed care plans. *Health Affairs* 19(4):139–148, 2000.

19. Sentamu, J. (The Archbishop of York). Health and Well-being, and the NHS. Presented at the Archbishop of York Symposium, Summer 2011. www.archbishopofyorksymposium.org/?p=264.

20. Department of Health. *Personal health budgets update: October 2011.* November 22, 2011. www.dh.gov.uk/health/2011/11/personal-health-budgets-update.

21. Davis, K., Schoen, C., and Stremikis, K. *Mirror mirror on the wall: How the performance of the U.S. health care system compares internationally, 2010 update.* The Commonwealth Fund, New York, 2010.

22. Pritchard, C., and Wallace, M. S. Comparing the USA, UK and 17 Western countries' efficiency and effectiveness in reducing mortality. *J. R. Soc. Med.* 2:60, 2011. doi:10.1258/shorts.2011.011076.

23. Thomson, S., et al. *International Profiles of Health Care Systems.* The Commonwealth Fund, Washington, D.C., 2011.

CHAPTER 5

Visits to Family Physicians or Specialists by Elderly Persons in Canada and the United States: An Exploratory Comparative Study

Mark S. Kaplan, Nathalie Huguet, David Feeny,
Bentson H. McFarland, and
Stacey S. Williams

The objective of this exploratory study was to compare elderly persons' likelihood of visiting a family doctor/general practitioner or a medical specialist and the association of that likelihood with socioeconomic factors and health-related quality of life (a measure of perceived need) in Canada and the United States. The data were obtained from the 2002–2003 Joint Canada/United States Survey of Health. The main dependent measure was whether respondents saw a medical specialist or a general practitioner during their last health care visit. U.S. patients in the highest household income group were more likely to have seen a specialist during their last health care visit, after adjusting for potential confounding factors. Further, visits to a specialist in Canada were determined by need rather than by household income. In Canada, likelihood of specialist visits by elderly persons is systematically related to the burden of illness (need) and not systematically related to income. In the United States, the opposite is the case. These results suggest that there may be important lessons from Canada on the organization of health care services.

*****

In industrialized countries, such as the United States and Canada, the health of elderly people is growing in importance as aging increases medical needs and expenditures. Roughly 29.8 million (80%) older adults in the United States (1) and 3.8 million (91%) in Canada (2) live with one or more chronic health conditions. A topic of considerable interest is the provision of medical care for this growing population of elderly people. Canada has emphasized primary care practice by maintaining approximately equal numbers of generalists and specialists. In contrast, less than one-third of U.S. physicians are engaged in primary care practice. Although elderly Canadians do not face financial barriers in access to primary health care, visits to specialist care services are limited because of waiting times and referral policy (3, 4). Conversely, elderly people in the United States are generally free to consult specialists. Several studies have indicated that high-quality primary care is effective in managing health problems before they are serious enough to require hospitalization or emergency services (5, 6). However, other studies have suggested that specialists are usually more knowledgeable about their areas of expertise and quicker to adopt new and effective treatments than are generalists (7). The optimal use of primary versus specialist care remains to be determined.

Comparisons among countries may provide opportunities for the United States to learn from other health care systems about how to organize care for older patients with complex needs (8). For example, international comparisons, such as those conducted by the Commonwealth Fund, have concluded that the United States could build on lessons learned from Canada and other industrialized countries to develop a comprehensive, coordinated, and equitable approach to the delivery of health care (9). However, international comparisons based on self-reported data have heretofore been difficult, because population surveys have generally used dissimilar methodologies and study designs. Moreover, few international studies have compared visits to generalists and specialists by older adults in Canada and the United States.

Health information recently collected from the United States and Canada presents a unique opportunity to compare visits to specialists by elderly persons. A comparative study of these two North American countries with similar population characteristics can show the impact of different health care systems on the use of specialist care services. In both countries, elderly people are covered under universal, comprehensive, publicly financed, and privately delivered health care. Canadian Medicare provides universal lifetime coverage through individuals' provincial health plans (10). In the United States, Medicare provides basic universal coverage to virtually all citizens aged 65 and older (with a few exceptions). Critics of the U.S. system have long argued that access to care is rationed by the ability to pay (11). However, few, if any, studies have directly compared visits to specialists by older adults in the two countries who are covered under the two universal health care systems. The Joint Canada/United States Survey of Health (JCUSH) provides a unique opportunity to examine the factors associated with visits to generalists and specialists by elderly persons. The purpose of the present study was to compare elderly persons' visits to family doctors/general practitioners (GPs) and specialist providers and the association of these visits with socioeconomic factors and health-related quality of life (a measure of perceived need) in Canada and the United States.

METHODS

Data Sources

The data were obtained from the JCUSH, a population health survey conducted jointly by Statistics Canada and the U.S. National Center for Health Statistics in 2002 and 2003. A detailed description of the survey is presented elsewhere (12). In brief, the JCUSH is the first collection of comprehensive, fully comparable data on health status, lifestyle behaviors, and other determinants of health and utilization of health care services, using a single questionnaire and a standard survey approach in the two countries. The JCUSH interviewed 3,505 Canadian and 5,183 U.S. non-institutionalized persons aged 18 and older. The elderly ($\geq$65 years) sample consisted of 755 Canadian and 1,151 U.S. individuals. The overall response rates for Canada and the United States were, respectively, 66 and 50 percent.

Measures

Health Care Services. The following question was used to assess whether respondents had visited a physician at least once in the past year: "In the past 12 months, not counting hospital visits, have you received any health care services from a family doctor or other physician?" Furthermore, whether the visit was to a GP or a specialist was ascertained with the question: "Thinking of the most recent time, was the care provided by a family doctor (general practitioner) or a medical specialist?"

Household Income. One independent variable of interest was household income, where income represented total household income from all sources, including wages, income from self-employment, dividends and interest, workers' compensation, retirement pensions, Old Age Security and Guaranteed Income Supplement, social assistance or welfare, child support, alimony, Social Security, and other sources. Quintiles were developed separately for each country using distributions of household income (12) and adjusted for the number of people living in the household. Due to small cell sizes, household income quintiles were combined into three groups: low (lowest and lower middle), middle, and high (upper middle and highest).

Health Status. The other independent variable of interest was health-related quality of life (HRQL), assessed with the Health Utilities Index Mark 3 (HUI3), a multidimensional measure of health-related quality of life that provides a description of the various effects of illnesses on daily life (for a fuller description of the HUI3, see 13, 14). Based on responses to 30 questions about eight attributes of functional health (vision, hearing, speech, ambulation, dexterity, cognition, emotion, and pain and discomfort), together with a valuation component, the HUI3 overall score generated for each individual has a theoretical range of 1.00 to –0.36. Perfect health is rated as 1.00, and dead as 0.00; negative scores reflect health states considered to be "worse than dead." A detailed description of HUI3's validity, reliability, and scoring procedures can be found elsewhere (13, 15–21).

Other Covariates. Other independent variables included gender, age, marital status, race (white vs. nonwhite), education (<12 years vs. ≥12 years), smoking status (never or former vs. current), functional status (limited vs. not limited), and chronic conditions ("Have you ever been told by a doctor or other health professional that you have . . . ?" with the following conditions—lasting, or expected to last, 6 months or more—included: asthma, arthritis, hypertension, chronic bronchitis, diabetes, heart disease, coronary heart disease, and heart attack). An examination of the association between HUI3 and number of chronic conditions revealed that these two variables were moderately correlated in both countries ($r = -0.33$; $p < .001$).

Analysis

Rates of visits to a GP and a specialist were estimated for each country. Bivariate analyses based on unadjusted logistic regression were performed to assess the factors associated with having visited a physician in the past 12 months and with having seen a specialist at the last visit. Multivariate logistic regression was then used to analyze the factors associated with physician visits in the past 12 months. Additional multivariate logistic regression models were estimated to analyze the factors associated with having seen a specialist at this visit. Adjusted odds ratios (AOR) and 95% confidence intervals (CI) were calculated. All independent variables were entered simultaneously in the logistic regression model. The analyses were conducted with SUDAAN (22) to adjust for the JCUSH complex sampling design (12).

RESULTS

Table 1 shows the distributions of the variables used in the study. Some notable differences ($p < .05$) were found in educational attainment, household income, functional status, smoking, and type of physician seen during the previous year. The prevalence of one or more chronic conditions was quite similar in the two elderly populations. Mean HUI3 scores indicating, on average, moderate disability (16) were also quite similar. Approximately the same proportion of elderly persons in Canada (78.8%) and the United States (81.6%) had seen a physician in the previous year. However, the U.S. respondents (25.6%) were significantly more likely (AOR = 1.55; 95% CI = 1.09–2.20) than their Canadian counterparts (16.4%) to have seen a specialist during their last visit.

Table 1

Characteristics of elderly respondents in the Joint Canada/United States
Survey of Health

	United States n = 1,151	Canada n = 755
Gender, %		
Men	42.8	43.8
Women	57.2	56.2
Age, mean (SE)	74 (0.19)	74 (0.24)
Marital status, %		
Married	60.1	60.9
Not married	39.9	39.1
Race, %		
White	87.6	87.1
Other	12.4	12.9
Education, %		
<12 years	21.9	46.1***
≥12 years	78.1	53.9
Household income, %		
Low	39.3	51.4
Middle	10.4	11.2
High	13.8	12.9**
Missing	36.6	24.6***
Chronic conditions, %		
0	26.5	27.2
1	30.7	35.3
2+	42.8	37.4
Health Utilities Index Mark 3 (HUI3), mean (SE)	0.78 (0.01)	0.79 (0.01)
Functional limitations, %		
Limited	56.9	51.4*
Not limited	43.1	48.6
Smoking status, %		
Current	9.2	12.2**
Former	52.8	55.9*
Never	38.1	31.9
Physician visit in the past 12 months, %		
Yes	81.6	78.8
No	18.4	21.2
Type of physician seen during the last visit, %		
General practitioner	74.4	83.6
Specialist	25.6	16.4***

Note: Numbers are unweighted; percentages and means are based on weighted numbers. HUI3 score ranges from 1.00 (perfect health) to –0.36 (worst possible health).

$*p < .05; **p < .01; ***p < .001$.

Table 2 examines the factors associated with having visited a physician in the past 12 months. For the United States, the results indicate that ≥12 years of education; middle, high, or missing income (relative to low income); HUI3 score; being female; and number of chronic conditions all were associated with a physician visit. For Canada, having seen a physician was correlated with number of chronic conditions and being a former smoker but not with other characteristics.

The multivariate logistic regression shows the factors associated with having seen a specialist during the most recent health care visit (Table 3). Unlike the United States, poorer HRQL (as measured by HUI3) was strongly associated with a visit to a specialist in Canada, when adjusted for all other variables in the model. In the United States, but not in Canada, higher income was related to a visit to a specialist for respondents who had seen a physician in the previous year. In fact, those in the highest U.S. income group were 1.74 (95% CI = 1.02–2.97) times more likely to have seen a specialist than those in the lowest income group. The association between number of chronic conditions and specialist services was statistically significant in the United States, but not in Canada.

DISCUSSION

In Canada, but not in the United States, visits to a specialist seem to be associated with need, as reflected by lower HRQL. Although visits to a specialist by elderly persons in Canada are more limited than in the United States, Canadian specialist services seem to be focused on patients in especially poor health. Conversely, in the United States, higher-income elderly persons who visit physicians were more likely than those with low incomes to consult a specialist. These results point to socioeconomic disparities in specialist visits in the United States.

The present results support and conflict with previous research. Finkelstein (23) showed that utilization of specialists by Ontario residents aged 40 to 79 was associated with poor self-rated health and was not associated with household income, after adjusting for potential confounders. In contrast, van Doorslaer and colleagues (24, 25), in a study of health care utilization among individuals aged 16 and older in 14 Organization for Economic Cooperation and Development countries, found that in Canada, higher-income individuals were more likely to see a specialist. Although van Doorslaer and coauthors' study seems to contradict the present results, it is important to note that their investigation did not focus specifically on older adults and failed to provide a clear definition of medical specialists.

Interpretations of the present findings should keep in mind some limitations. First, the survey response rate was relatively low in the United States, and there was a difference in response rates between the two countries. In spite of the lower response rate in the United States, the demographic profile of the elderly sample closely matches data obtained from the Census Bureau (26). Similarly, the

Table 2

Factors associated with having received health care services from a family doctor
or other physician at least once in the previous year

	United States n = 871 AOR (95% CI)	Canada n = 643 AOR (95% CI)
Gender		
Men	1.00	1.00
Women	1.75 (1.10–2.80)	1.46 (0.90–2.39)
Age	0.98 (0.94–1.01)	0.98 (0.95–1.02)
Marital status		
Married	1.00 (0.64–1.58)	0.68 (0.41–1.11)
Not married	1.00	1.00
Race		
White	1.33 (0.77–2.30)	1.30 (0.68–2.49)
Nonwhite	1.00	1.00
Education		
<12 years	1.00	1.00
≥12 years	2.07 (1.28–3.36)	1.27 (0.83–1.96)
Household income		
Low	1.00	1.00
Middle	2.78 (1.37–5.64)	1.39 (0.70–2.77)
High	2.18 (1.19–4.01)	2.02 (0.96–4.25)
Missing	1.80 (1.13–2.86)	1.18 (0.69–2.00)
Health Utilities Index Mark 3 (HUI3)	0.23 (0.08–0.65)	2.51 (0.91–6.92)
Functional limitations		
Limited	1.20 (0.78–1.84)	1.63 (0.99–2.68)
Not limited	1.00	1.00
Smoking status		
Current	0.83 (0.43–1.58)	1.29 (0.66–2.52)
Former	1.54 (0.99–2.39)	1.84 (1.12–3.03)
Never	1.00	1.00
Number of chronic conditions	1.19 (1.01–1.39)	1.54 (1.27–1.88)

Note: AOR, adjusted odds ratio; CI, confidence interval. HUI3 score ranges from 1.00 (perfect health) to –0.36 (worst possible health). Sample sizes reduced due to missing data.

demographic profile of the Canadian sample matches census data from Canada (27). Second, the data were self-reported without verification by independent sources and may be influenced by socially desirable responses and missing data (e.g., household income). Third, the JCUSH did not specifically probe for the use of services from a general internist. In the United States, much of primary care is provided by general internists, not GPs. Therefore, we may be overestimating the

Table 3

Factors associated with having seen a specialist during last health care visit

	United States n = 719 AOR (95% CI)	Canada n = 502 AOR (95% CI)
Gender		
Men	1.00	1.00
Women	1.78 (0.50–1.22)	0.86 (0.47–1.55)
Age	0.99 (0.96–1.03)	0.97 (0.92–1.02)
Marital status		
Married	1.35 (0.89–2.04)	0.72 (0.40–1.29)
Not married	1.00	1.00
Race		
White	1.23 (0.62–2.46)	1.00 (0.44–2.26)
Nonwhite	1.00	1.00
Education		
<12 years	1.00	1.00
≥12 years	1.62 (0.89–2.93)	1.72 (0.98–3.01)
Household income		
Low	1.00	1.00
Middle	1.44 (0.76–2.72)	0.82 (0.33–2.00)
High	1.74 (1.02–2.97)	1.51 (0.72–3.16)
Missing	1.30 (0.82–2.08)	077 (0.37–1.60)
Health Utilities Index Mark 3 (HUI3)	0.91 (0.39–2.10)	0.33 (0.12–0.91)
Functional limitations		
Limited	1.21 (0.79–1.86)	1.62 (0.89–2.96)
Not limited	1.00	1.00
Smoking status		
Current	0.46 (0.20–1.08)	1.29 (0.51–3.24)
Former	0.94 (0.60–1.45)	1.72 (0.88–3.37)
Never	1.00	1.00
Number of chronic conditions	1.26 (1.10–1.45)	1.03 (0.86–1.23)

Note: AOR, adjusted odds ratio; CI, confidence interval. HUI3 score ranges from 1.00 (perfect health) to –0.36 (worst possible health). Sample sizes reduced due to missing data.

use of specialists in the United States. Fourth, visits to primary care providers and specialists may differ by type of geographic area (especially urban vs. rural) (28). Although the JCUSH instrument did not include a question on the geography of health care services, participants were asked whether the location of the care provider was a barrier. Relatively few Canadians and U.S. participants reported that location of care was problematic (data not shown). Fifth, the cross-sectional nature of the study did not allow us to test for causal inferences, and the directionality of the effect cannot be inferred. However, it seems unlikely that, for example, visits to a specialist in the United States lead to higher income among older patients. Sixth, the small number of respondents aged 65 and older may have limited the statistical power to detect relationships. Finally, there is a potential for the effects of unobserved variables that were not available in the JCUSH database. However, unlike previous studies, a comparison between the two countries was possible because the JCUSH data collection followed identical procedures and dependent and independent variables were comparably measured in both countries.

The results of this study, using a carefully designed, large population-based survey, suggest that the probability of visiting a specialist is associated with need in Canada and with income in the United States. In Canada, the likelihood of visits to a specialist by elderly residents seems to be systematically related to the burden of illness (need) and not systematically related to household income. Furthermore, the lower probability of visits to a specialist in Canada suggests more efficient gatekeeping and disease-management functions by primary care providers. In the United States, unlike Canada, lower-income older adults face a lower probability of visiting a specialist, due in part to the increasing costs associated with out-of-pocket expenditures and privatized supplemental insurance in the Medicare program (29, 30). Our exploratory comparative analysis suggests that there may be important lessons from Canada for the United States concerning the equitable access to health care services.

Acknowledgment — This research was supported by a grant from the Retirement Research Foundation.

REFERENCES

1. Centers for Disease Control and Prevention and Merck Company Foundation. *The State of Aging and Health in America 2007*. Merck Company Foundation, Whitehouse Station, NJ, 2007.
2. Canadian Institutes of Health Research. CIHR Institute of Aging Strategic Plan 2006. www.cihr-irsc.gc.ca/e/34013.html (accessed August 10, 2007).
3. Iglehart, J. K. Revisiting the Canadian health care system. *N. Engl. J. Med.* 342: 2007–2019, 2000.
4. Health Statistics Division. *Access to Health Care Services in Canada*. Catalogue 82-575-XIE. Statistics Canada, Ottawa, 2005.
5. Starfield, B., Shi, L., and Macinko, J. Contribution of primary care to health systems and health. *Milbank Q.* 83:457–502, 2005.
6. Rothman, A. A., and Wagner, E. H. Chronic illness management: What is the role of primary care? *Ann. Intern. Med.* 138:256–261, 2003.
7. Harrold, L. R., Field, T. S., and Gurwitz, J. H. Knowledge, patterns of care, and outcomes of care for generalists and specialists. *J. Gen. Intern. Med.* 14:499–511, 1999.

8. Schoen, C., et al. Taking the pulse of health care systems: Experiences of patients with health problems in six countries. *Health Aff. (Millwood)* W5:509–525, 2005.

9. Huynh, P. T., et al. The U.S. health care divide: Disparities in primary care experiences by income findings from the Commonwealth Fund 2004 International Health Policy Survey. April 2006. www.cmwf.org/usr_doc/Huynh_UShltcaredivide_900.pdf (accessed August 10, 2007).

10. Health Canada. Canada's Health Care System at a Glance. www.hc-sc.gc.ca/ahc-asc/media/nr-cp/2002/2002_care-soinsbk5_e.html (accessed January 14, 2008).

11. Evans, R., and Roos, N. P. What is right about the Canadian health care system? *Milbank Q.* 77:393–399, 1999.

12. Statistics Canada, National Center for Health Statistics. Joint Canada/United States Survey of Health public use microdata file user guide. 2004. www.cdc.gov/nchs/about/major/nhis/jcush_mainpage.htm (accessed August 10, 2007).

13. Feeny, D. H., et al. Multi-attribute and single-attribute utility functions for the Health Utilities Index Mark 3 System. *Med. Care* 40:113–128, 2002.

14. Horsman, J., et al. The Health Utilities Index (HUI): Concepts, measurement properties and applications. *Health Qual. Life Outcomes* 1:1–13, 2003.

15. McDowell, I. *Measuring Health: A Guide to Rating Scales and Questionnaires.* Oxford University Press, New York, 2006.

16. Feeny, D., et al. Comparing directly measured standard gamble scores to HUI2 and HUI3 utility scores: Group and individual-level comparisons. *Soc. Sci. Med.* 58:799–809, 2004.

17. Grootendorst, P., Feeny, D. H., and Furlong, W. Health Utilities Index Mark 3: Evidence of construct validity for stroke and arthritis in a population health survey. *Med. Care* 38:290–299, 2000.

18. Wilkins, K. Predictors of death in seniors. *Health Rep.* 16:57–67, 2006.

19. Fisk, J. D., Brown, M. G., and Sketris, I. S. A comparison of health utility measures for the evaluation of multiple sclerosis treatments. *J. Neurol. Neurosurg. Psychiatry* 76:58–63, 2005.

20. Jones, C. A., Feeny, D. H., and Eng, K. Test-retest reliability of health utilities index scores: Evidence from hip fracture. *Int. J. Technol. Assess. Health Care* 21:393–398, 2005.

21. Marra, C. A., et al. Are indirect utility measures reliable and responsive in rheumatoid arthritis patients? *Qual. Life Res.* 14:1333–1344, 2005.

22. SUDAAN, Version 9.0.1. Research Triangle Institute, Research Triangle Park, NC.

23. Finkelstein, M. M. Do factors other than need determine utilization of physicians' services in Ontario? *CMAJ* 165(5):565–570, 2001.

24. van Doorslaer, E., Masseria, C., and Koolman, X. The OECD Health Equity Research Group: Inequalities in access to medical care by income in developed countries. *CMAJ* 174(2):177–183, 2006.

25. van Doorslaer, E., Koolman, X., and Puffer, F. Equity in the use of physician visits in OECD countries: Has equal treatment for equal need been achieved? In *Measuring Up: Improving Health Systems Performance in OECD Countries*, ed. OECD, pp. 225–248. OECD, Paris, 2002.

26. He, W., et al. *U.S. Census Bureau, Current Population Reports, P23-209, 65+ in the United States: 2005.* U.S. Government Printing Office, Washington, DC, 2005.

27. Statistics Canada. CANSIM Database, Using E-STAT (distributor). http://estat.statcan.ca (accessed January 30, 2008).
28. Arcury, T. A., et al. The effects of geography and spatial behavior on health care utilization among the residents of a rural region. *Health Serv. Res.* 40(1):135–155, 2005.
29. Eichner, J., and Vladeck, B. C. Medicare as a catalyst for reducing health disparities. *Health Aff. (Millwood)* 24:365–375, 2005.
30. Huguet, N., Kaplan, M. S., and Feeny, D. Socioeconomic status and health-related quality of life among elderly people: Results from the Joint Canada/United States Survey of Health. *Soc. Sci. Med.* 66:803–810, 2008.

CHAPTER 6

Minimum Income Protection and European Integration: Trends and Levels of Minimum Benefits in Comparative Perspective, 1990–2005

Kenneth Nelson

This chapter draws attention to the Europeanization of social policy and the development of minimum income protection in a large number of welfare democracies. The empirical analyses are based on unique institutional and comparative data on benefit levels from the Social Assistance and Minimum Income Protection Interim Dataset. *There is some evidence of convergence in benefit levels among the European countries in the new millennium, but there is no clear proof of universal ambitions to fight poverty or of the existence of a single European social model. There are still welfare frontrunners and those who lag behind in this regard, not only among industrial welfare democracies in general but also in Europe.*

*****

The issue of welfare state convergence has reappeared on the social policy research agenda in recent years. Several factors are assumed to create more or less universal policy responses throughout the industrialized world, usually in the form of the downsizing of redistributive budgets and the creation of more market- and work-friendly welfare states (1–8). One such factor is international demographic shifts, another is increased economic globalization. A third factor that has recently received greater attention is European integration and the role of the European Union. Since at least the mid-1980s European integration has featured a social dimension alongside the pursuit of a single European market. Although social policy is still the domain of national jurisdiction and not regulated by E.U. law, the social dimension of the integration process has fostered a discussion about a uniform European social model (9, 10). The content of this model is not established in any great detail, although it indicates institutional conformity rather than diversity (11).

The social dimension of European integration specifically concerns arrangements for poor and needy citizens, whereby each member state is advised to provide minimum income protection in accordance with various principles. These principles include, for example, universal coverage, differentiated benefit amounts, and formal indexation procedures (12, 13). With the announcement of the Open Method of Coordination (OMC) in 2000, the social dimension of European integration was further extended. The intention is not to impose policy harmonization via formal E.U. regulations, but rather to promote soft-policy coordination by means of peer pressure from other governments and the benchmarking of best practices (14–17). In the late 1990s the European Commission maintained that the strengthened social dimension of the integration process had resulted in policy convergence in minimum income protection across the community, for example in terms of guaranteed provisions and eligibility criteria (18). Referring to minimum income protection policies within the European Union, Threlfall (19) more recently concluded that "a free-mover can now count on receiving a reasonably similar amount of subsistence-level support in all states." Not only does this statement signal a belief in tendencies of convergence, it is also a strong argument for increasingly similar minimum income guarantees being adopted throughout the European Union. Hence, social policy is assumed both to become more alike and to guarantee citizens approximately the same levels of social protection.

While institutional convergence and conformity may characterize some aspects of minimum income protection, such as the emergence of national social assistance standards and the emphasis on workfare, there is less evidence of a convergence in benefit levels of the magnitude hinted at above. Although each member state is encouraged to develop minimum social benefits that are sufficient to cover essential needs, the European Union provides no detailed guidelines on the issue of adequacy. Questions related to benefit amounts are instead passed over to the OMC and processes of emulation, whereby policies conceived or implemented in one country are supposed to be voluntarily adopted in other countries. Since Threlfall fails to provide any systematic comparison of minimum income benefits actually guaranteed in the various E.U. member states, the statement above about a convergence in subsistence-level support still needs to be empirically justified.

The purpose of this study is to analyze the evolution of minimum income protection on a cross-national basis and to subject the above arguments about policy convergence and the Europeanization of social policy to empirical tests. The first question concerns changes in benefit levels and whether minimum income protection has become more similar across countries. The second question concerns the size of benefits and whether citizens are guaranteed similar levels of subsistence support across countries. The chapter also presents results from a unique and recently established institutional dataset on social policy in indus-trialized welfare democracies: the *Social Assistance and Minimum Income Protection Interim Dataset*. "Minimum income protection" refers to the entire benefit package provided to low-income households. In addition to means-tested social assistance, this benefit package also includes, for example, child allow-ances, housing benefits, and refundable tax credits. The study is ambitious not only in time but also in space. Besides tracing the year-by-year development of minimum income benefits in 13 European countries over 1990–2005 (Austria, Belgium, Denmark, Finland, France, Germany, Ireland, Italy, the Netherlands, Norway, Switzerland, Sweden, and the United Kingdom), I also include develop-ments in Australia, Canada, Japan, New Zealand, and the United States. The inclusion of countries outside Europe further strengthens the analysis since it is possible to distinguish specific European trends from more global convergence tendencies, resulting for example from the worldwide internationalization of trade and capital.

The chapter begins with a discussion of the resurgence of low-income targeting and minimum income protection in social policy; this is followed by a presenta-tion of the data. Subsequent sections are devoted to empirical analyses of social policy convergence and cross-country variability in benefit levels, and a con-cluding discussion.

THE RESURGENCE OF LOW-INCOME TARGETING

Despite substantial variation among countries in the design of social policy, there is also a degree of resemblance in the types of programs that have been developed. In this regard, policy conformity in the broad sense is not a new phenomenon. One common but not necessarily mutually excluding distinction is that between social insurance, child benefits, and minimum income protection (often equated with social assistance). Social insurance compensates workers for income losses during periods of work incapacity and is granted on the basis of citizenship, contributions, or occupational status. Child benefits are designed to assist households with the extra financial burden of having children and are often universal in character. Social assistance is activated when people cannot qualify for benefits from other programs or when these other provisions are insufficient for providing a certain income level. Social assistance is granted on the basis of need, and attached to receiving benefits is a means-test. Social assistance often enters the distributive process in the last stage.

The historical origins of social assistance go back farther than social insurance and child benefits. The means-test resembles the old poor-relief, the dominant form of social protection in the 19th century and earlier. A major change in recent years is that many countries have introduced or strengthened already-established work requirements as part of the contract for receiving assistance (20). Insofar as these elements of workfare are used as a means of reducing the number of claimants rather than to strengthen the human capital of recipients, it represents something of a return to the type of relief work or workhouses that were often characteristic of the old poor laws. Alongside these strong similarities in institutional design there are also clear differences between the modern and the historical forms of last-resort social programs for the poor and needy. Most important, the means-test for social assistance is less restrictive and the program is much less stigmatizing than the old poor-relief. Since the Second World War, social assistance has also increasingly become subject to national standards, and benefits are either partly or fully financed from general tax revenue. In most countries, citizens can also legally appeal against the system of benefits, which makes social assistance resemble the type of social rights discussed by Marshall (21). Although social assistance represents a more humane form of low-income targeting than did the old poor-relief, it is still often associated with stigma. This may reduce the take-up rate of benefits, with potential negative consequences for poverty alleviation.

The introduction and expansion of social insurance after the Second World War were followed by the widespread belief that the demand for social assistance and other forms of means-tested benefits would gradually diminish. This view is, for example, clearly expressed in the Beveridge Report, which laid out recommendations for a new social security system in the United Kingdom in the 1940s (22). Indeed, in most Western countries, expenditure on means-tested benefits went down during the expansion of the welfare state in the first immediate decades of the postwar period. Sweden is a striking example, where social assistance expenditure was reduced from 16 to 4 percent of total social expenditure after the introduction of universal child benefits and old-age pension in the late 1940s (23). In a few countries, however, mostly in the English-speaking welfare democracies, means-tested benefits have continued to play an important role throughout the postwar period. Here, the high prevalence of low-income targeting can be related both to insufficiencies in first-tier benefits and to political priorities. In the United Kingdom, for example, inadequate social insurance payments have forced recipients to supplement income with means-tested alternatives (24). In Australia and New Zealand, where most parts of the social security system are subject to various means- or income-tests, low-income targeting is used both to guarantee a certain minimum standard and as a means of restricting access to benefits by the well-off.

The general expectation that social insurance would make the need for social assistance redundant has not been realized, not even in countries where social assistance expenditure initially was substantially reduced. Instead the extent of means-tested benefits has increased. On average, spending on means-tested benefits rose by about 40 percent in the OECD (Organization for Economic Cooperation and Development) area over the period 1970–1980 (25). Figure 1

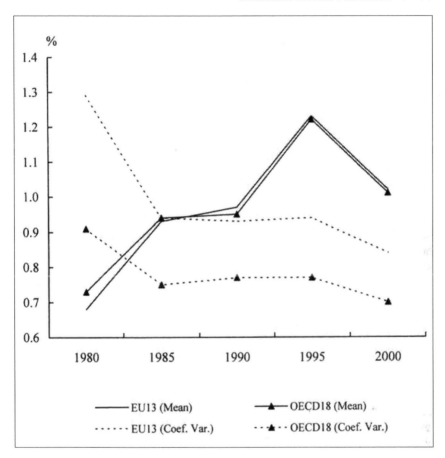

Figure 1. Changes in means-tested benefit expenditure as percentage of GDP in 18 OECD countries and in 13 E.U. countries, 1980–2001. *Note*: Coef. Var., coefficient of variation. *Source*: OECD Social Expenditure Database, 1980–2003.

shows changes in means-tested benefit expenditure as percentage of GDP (gross domestic product) for the period 1980–2001. Two averages are used: one for the 13 European countries (EU13) and another for the larger OECD group (OECD18, which includes the 5 non-European countries in addition to the EU13). The coefficient of variation is also shown. There are no substantial differences between the two groups of countries. Means-tested benefit expenditure continued to rise until the mid-1990s, after which it started to decline. It is difficult to judge whether spending will continue to decrease. Since low-income targeting is heralded by many observers to be the necessary policy response to the recent economic and demographic challenges faced by nearly all welfare democracies (26–29), it will not come as a surprise if means-testing continues to be an attractive way of redistributing income also in the predictable future.

The increased emphasis on low-income targeting also raises important questions in relation to policy convergence. As indicated by changes in the size of the coefficient of variation, the volume of means-tested expenditure is becoming more similar across countries. However, this development should not be confused with policy convergence and processes of institutional conformity. Increased reliance on low-income targeting does not necessarily involve strengthened protection against economic hardship and poverty for the needy. In Europe at least, the rise in means-tested benefit expenditure in the first half of the 1990s was mainly due to labor market transformations, especially increases in long-term unemployment (30). In order to explore whether countries have also become more similar in policy content we need information based on sources other than expenditure data. One alternative is to focus on social policy inputs rather than outputs and to assess the quality of benefits provided to low-income households.

THE SOCIAL ASSISTANCE AND MINIMUM INCOME PROTECTION INTERIM DATASET

Despite recognized validity problems (31–34), expenditure levels are still widely used as proxies for the institutional configuration of social policy.[1] In this chapter we follow a different and more sophisticated approach. Instead of levels of public spending, the empirical analyses are based on a new set of independent variables, which measure the quality rather than the quantity of social benefits. The focus is on social assistance and minimum income protection benefit levels. Data are from the *Social Assistance Minimum Income Protection Interim Dataset* (SaMip), which is under construction at the Swedish Institute for Social Research, Stockholm University (37). SaMip provides excellent opportunities to study the evolution of last-resort safety nets from a comparative perspective. Compared with similar studies and projects SaMip is unique, given the large number of countries covered and the long time period studied. It is also specifically designed for cross-national research purposes, which means that data have been assembled so as to be as comparable across nations as possible.

---

[1] There are at least three drawbacks to measuring welfare state organization in terms of social expenditure. First, social spending does not capture the essential elements of social citizenship, which includes social rights and correlated duties. Second, social expenditure is influenced by several factors more or less unrelated to the design of social policy. Third, expenditure statistics do not usually take into account taxation of benefits, although tax claw-backs on transfer income can be substantial (35, 36).

In its present state the dataset covers 18 countries, and data on entitlement levels have been collected for every year between 1990 and 2005. The variables included in the dataset are based on social assistance and minimum income protection regulations and legislation codified into empirical indicators. Benefit levels have been assessed on the basis of the type-case approach, in which social assistance and minimum income protection are computed for three household types: a single person, a lone-parent family, and a two-parent family with two children. Generally, social assistance and other means-tested benefits are not taxable. In cases where tax liability does exist, benefits are measured net of taxes. To facilitate cross-national comparisons, benefit amounts are expressed in purchasing power parities (PPPs) using U.S. dollars as the common denominator. Although PPPs have certain limitations and weaknesses, they are nevertheless more meaningful for cross-national comparisons of monetary values than are market exchange rates. PPPs are also widely used to compare the monetary value of social benefits cross-nationally (38–40).

Minimum income protection includes, besides social assistance payments, family benefits, housing benefits, and refundable tax credits. Social assistance includes *Special Benefit* (Australia), *Sozialhilfe* (Austria), *Minimex* (Belgium), *General Assistance* and *Ontario Works* (Canada), *Social Bistand* (Denmark), *Living Allowance* (Finland), *Revenue Minimum d'Insertion* (France), *Sozialhilfe* (Germany), *Supplementary Welfare Allowance* (Ireland), *Minimo Vitale* (Italy), *Public Assistance* (Japan), *Algemene Bijstand* (Netherlands), *Unemployment Assistance* (New Zealand), *Sosialhjelp* (Norway), *Socialbidrag* (Sweden), *Aide Sociale* (Switzerland), *Income Support* (United Kingdom), and *Food Stamps* as well as *Aid to Families with Dependent Children* and *Temporary Assistance to Needy Families* (United States). Where appropriate, housing benefits are established with reference to typical rent levels for the various household types in each particular country.

In most countries, the basic rates of social assistance are set at the national level. In a few countries, however, social assistance standards vary slightly regionally. This applies to Germany, where we use the average level of social assistance guaranteed by the provinces. In both Sweden (until 1998) and Switzerland, benefit rates are based on national guidelines issued by the Swedish National Board for Health and Welfare and the Conférence Suisse des Institutions d'Asistance Publique. In Austria and Canada, we use the benefit rates for Vienna and Ontario, while Aid to Families with Dependent Children and Temporary Assistance for Needy Families in the United States are for Michigan. For Finland and Japan, we use the highest rated bands for the different geographic areas. The Italian data should be interpreted with extra caution due to quite extensive regional and local differences in social assistance benefit rates. In some Italian municipalities there is still no minimum income protection scheme available for persons with low incomes. The Italian data reflect the rates in Milan.

TRENDS IN MINIMUM INCOME BENEFITS

The past 50 years have posed challenges to the welfare state that have had major consequences for social policy. Welfare states expanded in terms of both total expenditure and areas covered by social policy during the first three decades of the postwar period (41–43). The return of mass unemployment in a number of countries and increased economic internationalization since the mid-1970s generally put a halt to this development. In addition, decreasing fertility rates, aging populations, and adjustments to supranational organizations—such as the European Union, the OECD, and the World Bank—have triggered new policy responses in many countries (10, 44–46). Welfare states have added to this diversity of context by implementing differing degrees of cutbacks in social benefits and services (6, 47, 48). The development of minimum income protection in recent decades is no exception in this regard. Figure 2 shows changes in the level of minimum income protection for the years 1990–2005 as averages of EU13 and OECD18. The lines in this figure reflect an unweighted additive index comprising benefits for the three household types above, and benefits are standardized for both price and wage developments.

The trends in the European countries are almost identical with those of the OECD group. Although benefits seem to have kept up with prices, hence strengthening recipients' purchasing power, minimum income protection has been substantially eroded relative to wages. This finding indicates that the income position of recipient households has fallen behind the general income growth in society, thus placing beneficiaries in a more precarious position in the overall income distribution. Although it is difficult to establish any clear linkages between the various principles used in the year-to-year adjustment of benefits and the long-term development of minimum income protection, the above results demonstrate that most governments use some form of price movement to regularly adapt benefits in order to alleviate poverty. As long as wages continue to grow faster than prices, the strategy of indexing benefits to prices may not prove very successful in securing future living standards of the lowest income segments. However, the alternative adjustment mechanisms used in other countries may not always be preferable. In countries where benefits are linked to the development of wages, such as in Austria, Denmark, the Netherlands, and New Zealand, or to consumption, as in Germany, Finland, and Japan, benefit increases do not necessarily correspond to movements in average wages or changes in consumption patterns in the population as a whole. In Finland, for example, benefits are regularly adapted to changes in consumption patterns of the lowest income quintiles, while in the Netherlands they are adapted to changes in minimum wages. In addition, governments often bypass or make adjustments to the formal indexation procedures, for example in periods when social expenditure is growing rapidly (49). As a result, benefits often fail to keep up with general income growth in these particular countries. If indexation of minimum income

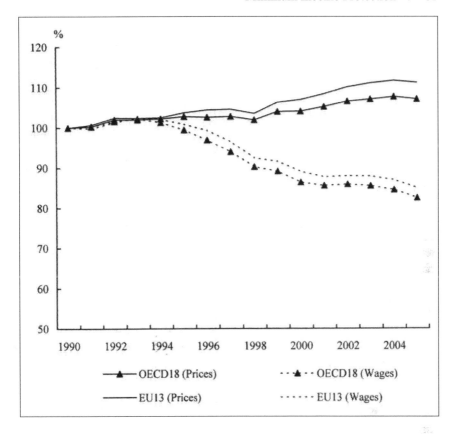

Figure 2. Changes in the level of minimum income protection standardized for price and wage development in 18 OECD countries and in 13 E.U. countries, 1990–2005. Averages of three typical household types: single person, lone-parent family, and two-parent family. Index 100 = 1990. *Source*: SaMip.

protection is to be a priority of the European Union as a means of securing the relative income position of recipient households, efforts should perhaps be made to encourage countries to establish a formal linkage of benefits to the overall development of wages rather than to prices or circumstances of the lowest income groups.

Despite the fact that minimum income protection has declined relative to wages, there is no clear trend of convergence in benefit levels across countries. Figure 3 shows how minimum income benefits vary across countries in terms of the coefficient of variation. The distribution of benefit levels is shown for each year during 1990–2005. The major difference between the European and the OECD countries appears at the end of the period. Since the turn of the new millennium

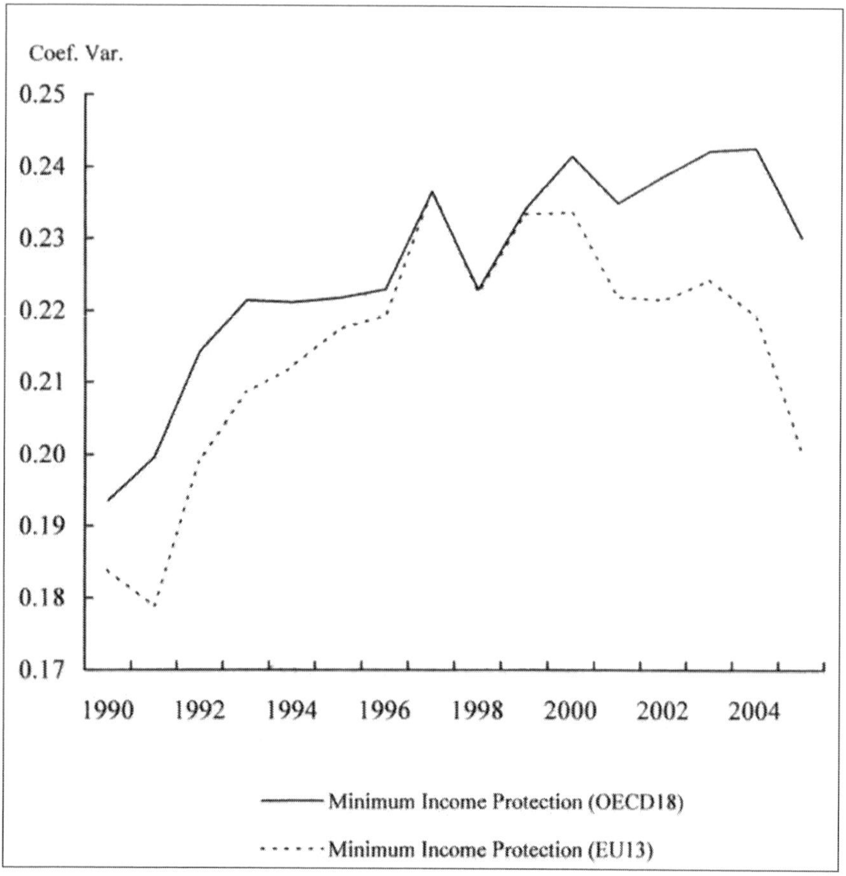

Figure 3. Cross-national variation in the level of minimum income protection in 18 OECD countries and 13 E.U. countries, 1990–2005. Averages of three typical household types: single person, lone-parent family, and two-parent family. *Note:* Benefits adjusted for purchasing power parities (PPPs); Coef. Var., coefficient of variation. *Source*: SaMip.

and the introduction of OMC the European countries demonstrate a stronger benefit convergence than the OECD group. Whether this development is the result of the social agenda of the European Union or is due to other circumstances in the European countries is of course difficult to assess here. In this regard it is interesting to note that increased spending on means-tested benefits does not necessarily coincide with tendencies of institutional assimilation. Although the volume of means-tested expenditure rose in most countries during much of the 1990s, benefit levels diverged almost continuously. When we add the social dimension of European integration to this process we would expect benefit convergence to appear earlier. It is also evident that countries continue to grant benefits according to different standards. In fact, countries differ more in this regard today than they did 15 years ago, which is somewhat at odds with the social agenda of the European Union and the intentions of the kind of soft coordination of social policy that has been emerging in Europe lately (50).

LEVELS OF MINIMUM INCOME PROTECTION

As noted above, the Europeanization of social policy concerns both changes in and levels of benefits. It is assumed that minimum income protection will become more similar across countries and that citizens in various countries are provided approximately the same benefit amounts. The previous section was largely devoted to the issue of social change; the size of benefits is addressed in more detail below. The discussion begins with a general assessment of benefit levels in the various countries and proceeds with more detailed analyses of benefit differentiation across household types.

Welfare Frontrunners and Welfare Laggards

Although there are some easily observable general trends in the development of minimum income protection during the last one and a half decades, quite substantial differences among countries in benefit standards are evident. This remains the case if the analysis is confined to the European countries alone. Hence, benefit convergence in the most recent years has not coincided with similar benefit amounts being adopted across countries. There are still welfare frontrunners and those who lag behind, both in Europe and elsewhere. Figure 4 shows minimum income protection for the single-person type-case household in PPPs and 2005 U.S. dollars for the years 1990 and 2005. The diagonal lines indicate countries where the development has been unusual.

In 1990 minimum income protection varied between US$13,212 (PPPs) in Norway and US$1,775 (PPPs) in the United States. In 2005, the most generous benefits were also found in Norway, where minimum income protection corresponded to US$15,876 (PPPs). Once again, the United States was the least generous country with benefit levels at US$1,728 (PPPs) in 2005.[2] The most generous benefits in 2005 were about nine times the size of the least generous

[2] Some caution should be exercised concerning data for Norway and the United States. The level of social assistance in Norway is based on expenditure statistics and includes both lump-sum payments and special needs supplements. The data for the single-person type-case in the United States include only Food Stamps; low-income households with children may also qualify for additional benefits, which slightly improve their economic situation. In some parts of the United States low-income households may receive various forms of general assistance, administered and financed locally; such local benefits are not taken into consideration in the SaMip.

1990		2005	
Nor	13212	Nor	15876
Swi	12272	Swi	12794
Den	10284	Den	11280
Swe	9979	Net	10080
Net	9686	Ger	9849
Fin	9481	Ire	9448
Ire	9073	Aus	9339
Ger	9063	Fin	9215
Aut	8625	Swe	9015
Can	8512	Jap	8784
Aus	8494	Aut	8483
Bel	8069	Bel	8023
Nzl	8037	UK	7875
Jap	7869	Ita	7695
UK	7354	Nzl	7304
Fra	7007	Fra	7118
Ita	6420	Can	5469
USA	1775	USA	1728

Figure 4. Minimum income protection for the single-person type-case household in 18 countries, 1990 and 2005. *Note*: PPPs and 2005 US$, yearly amounts. Aut, Austria; Aus, Australia. *Source*: SaMip.

benefits, which clearly indicates substantial cross-national variation. If one excludes the United States, the corresponding ratio is around three. In Europe, minimum income protection in the most generous country is about twice that of the least generous country. Although the range between the highest and lowest scores is greater among the OECD countries, it is nevertheless high enough among the European countries to reject any strong claims about conformity of benefit levels within the European Union. Some E.U. countries are still more generous than others. There is clearly no single European social model for minimum income benefit levels. Neither is it possible to distinguish any clear cross-national patterns or groups of countries that correspond neatly with previous attempts to cluster welfare states into certain institutional types (32).

The most striking pattern is that countries specifically devoted to targeted solutions to the poverty problem do not necessarily offer citizens the most generous benefits. This applies especially to the English-speaking countries, which are generally located in the lower half of the rankings presented in Figure 4. In 1990, Ireland was the only Anglo-Saxon country in the upper half of the rankings. During the 15 years covered by the analysis, minimum income protection in Australia improved relative to the other countries, and in 2005 Australia joined Ireland in the upper part of the rankings in Figure 4. It is also evident that minimum income protection in Canada was substantially curtailed between 1990 and 2005. This extraordinary development was mainly due to two factors; the first was the cap on cost-sharing under the Canada Assistance Plan in the wealthiest provinces in the early 1990s; the second was the introduction of the Canada Health and Social Transfer in the mid-1990s (51). Both these reforms had serious implications for governments' decisions concerning benefit levels. In 1995, for example, the conservative provincial government in Ontario cut the standard benefits for General Assistance by more than 20 percent for almost all recipients. This meant that Ontario ceased to be one of the leading Canadian provinces in the provision of minimum income protection (52).

Although cross-national variation in minimum income protection does not necessarily follow the same pattern as that observed for other social security schemes, the findings reported do not at least contradict previous claims about potential institutional relationships between minimum income protection policies and first-tier benefits, such as social insurance (53). The ranking of countries in Figure 4, especially the location of the English-speaking countries, seems to suggest that an excessive targeting of the redistributive budget to those with low incomes may hamper the development of generous minimum income benefits. The relationship is not perfect, which of course reflects the complex set of factors operating here.

In some countries minimum income protection has undergone particularly dramatic developments. In addition to Canada, as noted above, Sweden is also found in this group. The curtailment of benefits in Sweden is due to a complex set of factors involving both re-basing and down-rating of benefits, such as when the recommended norms of the Social Welfare Allowance were replaced by national guaranteed amounts in 1998 (51). The result of these exercises is a significant drop in the country ranking in Figure 4, from place four in 1990 to place nine in 2005. However, contrary to the situation in many other countries, unemployed persons in Sweden who have no previous work record and who are ineligible for income-related unemployment benefits often receive a basic unemployment benefit that guarantees a certain flat-rate amount. In many cases, these beneficiaries are better off than those receiving the means-tested Social Welfare Allowance considered in this analysis.

Other countries demonstrate the opposite trend. Between 1990 and 2005 the level of minimum income protection improved substantially in Australia, Germany, Italy, and Japan relative to the development in other countries. Since benefits in Italy and Japan were very low to start with, these two countries still figured in the cluster of welfare states providing medium to low minimum income protection levels in 2005. It should, again, be noted that the data for Italy must be interpreted with considerable caution due to extensive regional and local variations. In some parts of Italy there are still no minimum income protection policies in force, despite efforts by the European Union to recommend each member state to implement national social assistance schemes.

Implied Scales of Equivalence

One peculiarity of social assistance and minimum income protection, as opposed to first-tier benefits, is the sensitivity to economies of scale within households. Although social insurance in some countries may include specific supplements for children, lone parents, and adult dependents, this is more a rule than an exception in the area of minimum income protection. In most countries, the scale rates of social assistance vary by family type as well as by the number and ages of children. These institutional characteristics often apply for family benefits and income-tested housing allowances as well. Embodied in social assistance, and consequently also reflected in minimum income packages, are certain implied scales of equivalence, which reflect judgments made in each country about the treatment of families of different kinds. Insofar as these differences in standard benefits among families do not fully realize the particular needs of households of different types and sizes, it may or may not imply more deeply rooted inequalities, whereby particular family types are viewed and construed as less deserving or even as undeserving groups.

Two dimensions of minimum income protection are particularly worth exploring in more detail. The first aspect is the treatment of children, which is measured by relating the benefits available to the lone-parent type-case and the two-parent family with those granted to the single person. The second aspect is the longstanding and ongoing discussion of how welfare states differentiate between the needs of women and men (54–56).[3] It is more difficult to measure this gender dimension since few programs directly target women.[4] One alternative is to focus on the situation of lone parents, most of whom tend to be mothers.[5] The extent to which minimum income protection reflects gender-based inequalities is measured by relating the benefit package of the lone-parent type-case to that of the two-parent family.

[3] The discussion on how welfare states often reinforce and create gendered inequalities has not specifically concerned the formation of social assistance. Instead the focus has often been on first-tier benefits and how social insurance legislation is sometimes disadvantageous to women due to precarious positions in the labor market.

[4] Some countries (such as Ireland and Japan) have implemented programs specifically targeted at lone parents. These benefits are included in the minimum income benefit package for the lone-parent type-case household.

[5] A study of child benefit packages in 22 industrialized countries in 2002 revealed that over 80 percent of lone parents in each country were female (40). Lone parents also often tend to be overrepresented among welfare clients receiving social assistance and dependent on minimum income protection for their livelihood (57).

Figure 5 shows the results of plotting the child and gender dimensions of minimum income protection next to each other. Economies of scale within households are corrected for by using the square root equivalence scale.[6] The two indicators are remarkably stable over the years, and this comparison is confined to the situation in 2005. Benefits are not equally distributed across household types, but there is no clear indication that the European countries substantially differ from the non-European countries. Neither is there any overall pattern showing that countries systematically place one family type in a substantially more favorable or considerably less advantageous income position. In a few countries the differences across household types are of such magnitude that they can be expected to be reflected in income and poverty statistics. This applies for example to Australia, Austria, the Netherlands, and Norway, where the two types of households with children—hence the lone-parent type-case and the two-parent family—on average receive benefits that are more than 10 percentage points lower than those received by the single person. If we turn to the treatment of lone parents and the gender dimension, Australia, Denmark, Ireland, and Norway satisfy this criterion.

Even though several countries are located near the crossover point of 100 percent on both dimensions (Figure 5) it is nevertheless possible to distinguish certain groups of countries with some common characteristics. Here it should be remembered that this analysis is about the relative treatment of various household types within countries, not the extent to which minimum income protection satisfies the actual needs of particular households. The issue of adequacy is beyond the scope of this study. In Figure 5, countries located in the upper left corner (a) treat children generously but are less generous toward women. The majority of countries fall into this category, which includes Denmark, Ireland, Italy, Finland, Germany, Sweden, Switzerland, the United Kingdom, and the United States. In the upper right corner (b) we find Canada, Japan, and New Zealand, where minimum income protection is relatively helpful for women and children. Australia, Austria, and Norway are located in the lower left corner (c),

---

[6] The square root equivalence scale is the standard approach to correct for differences in household size in income distribution studies (58). This scale is also used by the Luxembourg Income Study and the OECD to compare income inequality and poverty across households and countries (59). Since different scales of equivalence may yield different results, however, one must interpret the results with caution (60). Compared with two other commonly used equivalence scales, the "old" and "modified" OECD scales, the square root scale assumes low to moderate economies of scale within households. Sometimes the two OECD scales may overestimate the degree of income sharing within households, which can produce biased results for certain family types (61). In the analysis below, both OECD scales produce somewhat lower values for the two-parent type-case, as does the "old" OECD scale for the lone-parent household; the "modified" OECD scale gives the lone-parent type-case slightly higher values. Compared with the square root scale, the OECD scales strengthen the income position of the lone-parent household vis à vis the two-parent family.

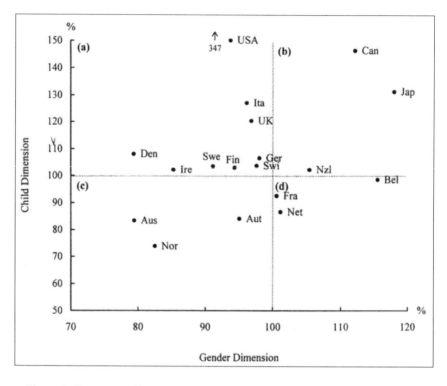

Figure 5. Treatment of lone-parent and two-parent families with children in minimum income protection (MIP) in 18 countries, 2005. Child dimension = [(MIP for the two-parent family / MIP for the single person) + (MIP for the lone parent / MIP for the single person)] / 2 * 100. Gender dimension = (MIP for the lone parent / MIP for the two-parent family) * 100. The square root scale is used to standardize benefits for differences in household size. *Note*: Aut, Austria; Aus, Australia. *Source*: SaMip.

where minimum income protection scores low on both the child and gender dimensions. Finally, the lower right corner (d) includes countries where minimum income protection treats women generously but children less so. Included in this group are Belgium, France, and the Netherlands.

DISCUSSION

The Europeanization of social policy involves at least two issues: the extent to which social policy is becoming more similar across E.U. member states and the degree to which European citizens enjoy approximately similar levels of social rights. The results presented in this study show that the social dimension of European integration has not necessarily resulted in policy convergence across member states. Despite E.U. recommendations in the early 1990s to reform parts of the system of minimum income protection, benefits continued to diverge among the European countries throughout the 1990s. In this regard trends in Europe do not differ from more global tendencies. To decide whether this result mainly reflects national differences in political priorities or is due to other factors, such as macro-economic performance, more detailed assessments of developments in each particular country are necessary. This type of analysis would involve a close focus on the intersection of economic and political global-ization processes and national party politics.

Since the new millennium and the introduction of OMC, the situation in Europe has begun to change and European countries are now showing more visible convergence tendencies in minimum income protection than the broader OECD group. Therefore we cannot entirely reject the social policy convergence hypothesis raised in connection with the development of the European Union. Nevertheless, it is important to emphasize that minimum income benefits still vary substantially across the European Union. Although benefits have declined relative to general income growth in most countries, it is not accurate to say that countries in the European Union have adopted uniform ambitions to fight poverty. Some member states still offer citizens more generous minimum income benefits than others. Despite convergence tendencies in recent years, benefit levels show wider variation across countries today than in the early 1990s.

An interesting question is whether the E.U. member states will continue to converge in the institutional formation of minimum income protection and whether this development will gradually cause the distance between welfare frontrunners and welfare latecomers in the European Union to more or less disappear. Proponents of the kind of soft coordination of social policy that has lately emerged in the European Union as a means to establish some form of European social agenda assume that this will be the case. However, the impact of, for example, the Open Method of Coordination, which is one of the means whereby the European Union attempts to influence national social policy systems, is still unclear. Perhaps it is too early to see any substantial effects of this integration process. It is therefore important to continue to look at how social policy in the various member states is formed and investigate whether national or local governments take into consideration policy recommendations at the European level and evidence on best practices when designing benefit scale rates. These studies should also look at developments in the transition countries of former communist Europe and southern Europe. However, such an enlargement of the empirical analyses is more easily said than done, since it would require placing much more effort into data collection and preparation.

One of the most important discussions in the comparative welfare state literature in recent decades has concerned the gendered dimensions of social policy, where it is argued that many social security programs fail to adequately satisfy the needs of women. This chapter has broadened this discussion beyond social insurance and concentrated on the formation of social assistance and minimum income protection. Here the European Union specifically encourages each member state to address the differentiated needs of households of different types and sizes. In most countries, lone parents (the majority of whom are women) and families with children are not treated substantially less generously than other household categories. In this regard, the European countries seem to fulfill one policy objective raised at the European level. However, this objective was already reached in 1990, before the European Union specifically became engaged in member states' organization of minimum income protection. Moreover, differentiated benefit amounts are not unique for the European countries; they are also found in welfare democracies outside Europe. These findings about the gendered dimension of benefit standards do not prove the superiority of minimum income protection over social insurance. In most countries, social insurance provides more generous benefits than minimum income protection, particularly in countries where insurance benefits are related to previous earnings. For this reason it is essential to continue the discussion about how social policy can be organized to better serve the needs of women and how processes in welfare state development can promote gender equality.

Although the empirical analysis presented in this chapter is an improvement compared with previous investigations on the evolution of social assistance and minimum income protection, there is a need for continued research in this policy area. An enlargement of the *Social Assistance and Minimum Income Protection Interim Dataset* to include developments in eastern and southern Europe is warranted. One should also emphasize that benefit levels, which have been the focus here, are not the only important feature for the organization of minimum income protection. Consideration should also be directed to how these schemes foster take-up of benefits and whether some population groups are excluded from assistance. The degree of discretion in connection with benefit administration should also be emphasized.

One general limitation of institutionally informed analyses of social security legislation is that they show how the systems should function, which is not necessarily the same as how the programs actually work. However, the most common alternatives to institutional data also have their weaknesses and limitations. The drawbacks of expenditure data have already been recognized and are not repeated here. Using micro-level census information on income to simulate benefit levels is associated with other and in some cases even more serious problems, such as the underestimation of social assistance in many countries, the absence of duration-level indicators, and the mix of institutional and outcome-related variables. In this regard, institutional data of the kind presented in this study are in many cases preferable.

Acknowledgments — I wish to thank Ingalill Montanari and Joakim Palme, who introduced me to and provided valuable expertise for the questions raised in this chapter. Gratitude also goes to Björn Halleröd, Olof Bäckman, and Anders Nilsson, who commented on an earlier draft of the manuscript.

This work has received financial support from the Swedish Research Council and the Swedish Council for Working Life and Social Research.

REFERENCES

1. Strange, S. Territory, state, authority and economy: A new realist ontology of global political economy. In *The New Realism: Perspectives on Multilateralism and World Order*, ed. R. W. Cox. Macmillan Press, Basingstoke, UK, 1997.

2. Kitschelt, H., et al. (eds.). *Continuity and Change in Contemporary Capitalism.* Cambridge University Press, Cambridge, 1999.

3. Bonoli, G., et al. (eds.). *European Welfare Futures: Towards a Theory of Retrenchment.* Polity Press, Cambridge, 2000.

4. Dunning, J. *Global Capitalism at Bay?* Routledge, London, 2000.

5. Scharpf, F. W., and Schmidt, V. A. (eds.). *Welfare and Work in the Open Economy, Vol II: Diverse Responses to Common Challenges.* Oxford University Press, Oxford, 2000.

6. Pierson, P. (ed.). *The New Politics of the Welfare State.* Oxford University Press, Oxford, 2001.

7. Esping-Andersen, G. *Why We Need a New Welfare State.* Oxford University Press, Oxford, 2002.

8. Rieger E., and Leibfried, S. *Limits to Globalization: Welfare States and the World Economy.* Polity, Cambridge, 2003.

9. Ebbinghaus, B. Does a European social model exist and can it survive? In *The Role of Employer Associations and Labour Unions in the EMU: Institutional Requirements for European Economic Policies,* ed. G. Huemer et al. Ashgate, Aldershot, UK, 1999.

10. Scharpf, F. W. The European social model: Coping with the challenges of diversity. *J. Common Market Stud.* 40(4):645–670, 2002.

11. Montanari, I., et al. Towards a European social model? Trends in social insurance among EU countries 1980–2000. *European Societies,* 2007, in press.

12. European Council. *Council Recommendation of 24 June 1992 on Common Criteria Concerning Sufficient Resources and Social Assistance in Social Protection.* 92/441/EEC. Brussels, 1992.

13. European Council. *Council Recommendation on the Convergence of Social Protection Objectives and Policies.* 92/442/EEC. Brussels, 1992.

14. Borrás, S., and Jacobsson, K. The Open Method of Co-ordination and new governance patterns in the EU. *J. Eur. Public Policy* 11(2):185–208, 2004.

15. Radaelli, C. M. *The Open Method of Coordination: A New Governance Architecture for the European Union?* Swedish Institute for European Policy Studies, Stockholm, 2003.

16. Wincott, D. Beyond social regulation? New instruments and/or a new agenda for social policy at Lisbon? *Public Adm.* 81(3):533–553, 2003.

17. Zeitlin, J., et al. (eds.). *The Open Method of Co-ordination in Action.* P.I.E.-Peter Lang S. A, Brussels, 2005.

18. European Commission. *Report on the Implementation of the Recommendation 92/441/EEC of 24 June 1992 on Common Criteria Concerning Sufficient Resources and Social Assistance in Social Protection Systems.* Commission Report to the Council, European Parliament, Economic and Social Committee, and Committee of the Regions. COM (98) 774 Final. Brussels, 1998.

19. Threlfall, M. European social integration: Harmonization, convergence and single social areas. *J. Eur. Soc. Policy* 13(2):130, 2003.

20. Lødemel, I., and Trickey, H. (eds.). *An Offer You Can't Refuse: Workfare in International Perspective.* Policy Press, Bristol, 2000.

21. Marshall, T. H. *Citizenship and Social Class and Other Essays.* Cambridge University Press, Cambridge, 1950.

22. Beveridge, W. *Social Insurance and Allied Services.* HMSO, London, 1942.

23. Korpi, W. Poverty, social assistance and social policy in postwar Sweden. *Acta Sociol.* 18(2–3):120–141,1975.

24. Stitt, S. *Poverty and Poor Relief: Concepts and Reality.* Avebury, Aldershot, UK, 1994.

25. Gordon, M. S. *Social Security Policies in Industrial Countries: A Comparative Analysis.* Cambridge University Press, Cambridge, 1988.

26. Freeman, R., et al. *Att reformera välfärdsstaten: Ett amerikanskt perspektiv på den svenska modellen.* NBER-rapporten 2. SNS Förlag, 2006.

27. Afonso, A., et al. Public sector efficiency: An international comparison. *Public Choice* 123:321–437, 2003.

28. Schuknecht, L., and Tanzi, V. *Public Sector Efficiency: An International Comparison.* Working Paper Series No. 242. European Central Bank, Frankfurt, 2003.

29. Schuknecht, L., and Tanzi, V. *Reforming Public Expenditure in Industrialised Countries: Are There Trade-offs?* Working Paper Series No. 435. European Central Bank, Frankfurt, 2006.

30. EUROSTAT. *The Social Situation in the European Union 2000.* European Communities, Luxembourg, 2000.

31. Esping-Andersen, G. The comparison of policy regimes: An introduction. In *Stagnation and Renewal in Social Policy,* ed. M. Rein et al. M. E. Sharpe, Armonk, NY, 1987.

32. Esping-Andersen, G. *The Three Worlds of Welfare Capitalism.* Polity Press, Cambridge, 1990.

33. Clayton, R., and Pontusson, J. Welfare-state retrenchment revisited: Entitlement cuts, public sector restructuring, and inegalitarian trends in advanced capitalist societies. *World Politics* 51:67–98, 1998.

34. Korpi, W., and Palme, J. The paradox of redistribution and strategies of equality: Welfare state institutions, inequality, and poverty in the western countries. *Am. Sociol. Rev.* 63(5):661–687, 1998.

35. Adema, W. *Net Social Expenditure, Ed. 2.* OECD Labour Market and Social Policy Occasional Papers No. 52. OECD, Paris, 2001.

36. Ferrarini, T., and Nelson, K. Taxation of social insurance and redistribution: A comparative analysis of ten welfare states. *J. Eur. Soc. Policy* 13(1):21–33, 2003.

37. Nelson, K. *The Social Assistance and Minimum Income Protection Interim Data-Set: Documentation.* Unpublished working paper. Swedish Institute for Social Research, Stockholm University, February 2007.

38. Eardley, T., et al. *Social Assistance in OECD Countries: Synthesis Report.* Department of Social Security Research Report No. 46. Stationery Office, London, 1996.
39. Kemp, P. A. *A Comparative Study of Housing Allowances.* Security Research Report No. 60. Stationery Office, London, 1997.
40. Bradshaw, J., and Finch, N. *A Comparison of Child Benefit Packages in 22 Countries.* Department for Work and Pensions Research Report No. 174. Corporate Document Services, Leeds, 2002.
41. Flora, P. *Growth to Limits: The Western European Welfare States since World War II, Vol. 4, Appendix: Synopses, Bibliographies, Tables.* de Gruyter, Berlin, 1987.
42. Pierson, C. *Beyond the Welfare State? The New Political Economy of Welfare.* Polity, Cambridge, 1991.
43. Huber, E., and Stephens, J. D. *Development and Crises of the Welfare State: Parties and Policies in Global Markets.* University of Chicago Press, Chicago, 2001.
44. Thomson, D. *Selfish Generations? How Welfare States Grow Old.* White Horse Press, Cambridge, 1996.
45. Scharpf, F. W., and Schmidt, V. A. (eds.). *Welfare and Work in the Open Economy, Vol II: Diverse Responses to Common Challenges.* Oxford University Press, Oxford, 2000.
46. Kotlikoff, L. J., and Burns. S. *The Coming Generational Storm: What You Need to Know about America's Economic Future.* MIT Press, Cambridge, MA, 2005.
47. Korpi, W., and Palme, J. New politics and class politics in the context of austerity and globalization: Welfare state regress in 18 countries 1975–1995. *Am. Polit. Sci. Rev.* 97(3):1–22, 2003.
48. Montanari, I., et al. Convergence pressures and responses: Recent social insurance development in modern welfare states. *Comp. Sociol.* 6(3):295–323, 2007.
49. Cantillon, B., et al. The Evolution of Minimum Income Protection in 15 European Countries 1992–2001. Unpublished working paper, Centrum voor Sociaal Beleid Herman Deleeck, Antwerp, 2004.
50. Chapon, S., and Euzéby, C. Towards a convergence of European social models? *Int. Soc. Security Rev.* 55(2):37–56, 2002.
51. Nelson, K. *Fighting Poverty: Comparative Studies on Social Insurance, Means-Tested Benefits and Income Redistribution.* Dissertation Series No. 60. Swedish Institute for Social Research, Stockholm, 2003.
52. National Council of Welfare. *Another Look at Welfare Reform.* Ottawa, 1997.
53. Nelson, K. The last resort: Determinants of the generosity of means-tested minimum income protection policies in welfare democracies. In *Welfare Politics Cross-Examined: Eclecticist Analytical Perspectives on Sweden and on the Developed World,* ed. E. Carroll and L. Ericsson. Aksel Atland Printers, Amsterdam, 2006.
54. Lewis, J. Gender and the development of welfare regimes. *J. Eur. Soc. Policy* 2(3):159–173, 1992.
55. Hobson, B. Solo mothers, social policy regimes and the logics of gender. In *Gendering Welfare States,* ed. D. Sainsbury. Sage, London, 1994.
56. Sainsbury, D. *Gender, Equality and Welfare States.* Cambridge University Press, Cambridge, 1996.
57. Ruspini, E. *Living on the Poverty Line: Lone Mothers in Belgium, Germany, Great Britain, Italy and Sweden.* MZES Working Papers 28. MZES, Mannheim, 1998.

58. Jesuit, D., et al. *Regional Poverty within the Rich Countries*. Luxembourg Income Study Working Paper No. 318. LIS, Luxembourg, 2002.

59. Förster, M., and Mira d'Ercole, M. *Income Distribution and Poverty in OECD Countries in the Second Half of the 1990s*. OECD Social Employment and Migration Working Papers No. 22. OECD, Paris, 2005.

60. Buhmann, B., et al. Equivalence scales, well-being, inequality, and poverty: Sensitivity estimates across ten countries using the Luxembourg Income Study (LIS) database. *Rev. Income Wealth* 34(2):115–142, 1988.

61. Smeeding, T., et al. Income distribution in European cities. In *Incomes and the Welfare State: Essays on Britain and Europe,* ed. A. Atkinson. Cambridge University Press, Cambridge, 1994.

PART III

The Crisis and Changes in the Labor Market

Edwin Ng

INTRODUCTION

True to form, sharp increases in global inequalities and declines in the global economy have had important implications for labor markets and employment conditions. The aftermath of these global crises are dire and well-documented, including, for example: the real gross domestic product of the United States contracted at the fastest pace seen since the 1950s; worldwide unemployment rates, for the first time, exceeded 200 million; and austerity policies have been implemented contrary to the interests of vulnerable individuals and families. Critical questions have been raised about the impact of these structural changes on the health and well-being of populations.

The chapters in Part III make these connections more concrete and focus on significant changes in the labor market and their impact on population health and health inequalities. Chung and colleagues (Chapter 7) propose a global labor market typology, consisting of core, semi-peripheral, and peripheral nations, to better understand and explain global variations in population health. Zhang (Chapter 8) evaluates the differential impact of private versus public employment on health status and the degree of health inequalities within employment sectors. Heymann and coauthors (Chapter 9) calculate and compare the financial support available to workers facing different kinds of health problems: a case of the flu that requires missing 5 days of work, and a cancer treatment that requires 50 days of absence. Quinlan and Bohle (Chapter 10) undertake a large review of international studies on the occupational health and safety effects of downsizing, restructuring, and job insecurity over the past two decades. Gould (Chapter 11) provides a timely and relevant analysis of how the share of non-elderly Americans covered by employer-sponsored health insurance plans has experienced rapid declines during the Great Recession. And finally, Holland and coauthors (Chapter 12) pose and address the pressing question of how macro-level contexts and policies affect the employment chances of chronically ill and disabled people. In all, these studies provide important bridges that directly and indirectly connect macro-level market forces with labor markets and employment conditions, which, in turn, shape and influence population health.

CHAPTER 7

Employment Relations and Global Health: A Typological Study of World Labor Markets

Haejoo Chung, Carles Muntaner, Joan Benach, and the EMCONET Network

In this study, the authors investigate the global labor market and employment relations, which are central building blocks of the welfare state; the aim is to propose a global typology of labor markets to explain global inequalities in population health. Countries are categorized into core (21), semi-peripheral (42), and peripheral (71) countries, based on gross national product per capita (Atlas method). Labor market–related variables and factors are then used to generate clusters of countries with principal components and cluster analysis methods. The authors then examine the relationship between the resulting clusters and health outcomes. The clusters of countries are largely geographically defined, each cluster with similar historical background and developmental strategy. However, there are interesting exceptions, which warrant further elaboration. The relationship between health outcomes and clusters largely follows the authors' expectations (except for communicable diseases): more egalitarian labor institutions have better health outcomes. The world system, then, can be divided according to different types of labor markets that are predictive of population health outcomes at each level of economic development. As is the case for health and social policies, variability in labor market characteristics is likely to reflect, in part, the relative strength of a country's political actors.

*****

In recent years there has been an increased interest in social determinants of health. With the aim of tackling "causes of causes," this field of research asks researchers to pay attention to determinants of health that go beyond medical care. The increasing interest culminated in the recent report published by the World Health Organization's Commission on Social Determinants of Health

97

(1). Among the various social determinants, employment relations deserves significant attention.

Work is one of the most fundamental aspects of human life. The recent wave of neoliberal reform has deeply affected work organization and employment relations around the globe. One of the most significant changes is the increase in flexible employment (2). In an increasingly deregulated labor market, the former model of production has broken down, "flexibility" has emerged as a core goal and value, and precarious jobs have increased (3). Precarious employment can be considered a multidimensional phenomenon, characterized by four main dimensions: high job insecurity, low wage level, lack of or limited social benefits, and powerlessness (2–4). All of these conditions have potential health implications.

Some authors have used several labor market indicators to understand the impacts of work on population health, but no attempt has yet been made to map the variety of labor market types around the globe and their population health consequences. In this study, we generate a labor market typology for 134 countries and determine its association with population health indicators.

CONCEPTUAL MODEL

In our politics–policy–health model, we start from power relations—namely, workers' bargaining power (Figure 1). As is well known from the literature, workers' bargaining power, measured by collective bargaining coverage and union density, roughly correlates with the type of welfare state regime (5). Union

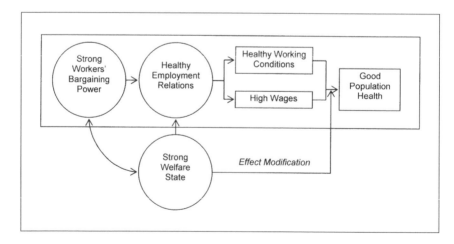

Figure 1. Model for the relationship between workers' bargaining power, welfare state, employment relations, and health outcome.

power is one of the two key factors, along with pro-egalitarian party power, in the power resources type of explanation for the establishment and expansion of welfare states (6–11). In the context of the post–World War II social environment, authors argued that bargaining power is greatest when unions are effectively organized to take advantage of a "permissive" economic environment—one in which employers have an enhanced "ability to pay" (12–20). While it is an abstract concept, bargaining power is embedded in labor institutions in various ways, such as average wage and benefit levels or control over the job process (3). The latter includes not only direct chemical, ergonomic, and psychological risk factors, but also labor standards, occupational health and safety regulations, and union protections, among other factors (3). The strong welfare state, a byproduct of strong bargaining power (6–11), also affects workers' health.

MEASURING THE LABOR MARKET

Our core concept, "workers' bargaining power," cannot be measured directly. Therefore, we needed to come up with other ways to quantify it. Here, we turn to the concept of "flexicurity." Flexicurity is defined as (21, 22):

> (1) a degree of job, employment, income and "combination" security that facilitates that labour market careers and biographies of workers with a relatively weak position and allows for enduring and high quality labour market participation and social inclusion, while at the same time providing (2) a degree of numerical (both external and internal), functional and wage flexibility that allows for labour markets' (and individual companies') timely and adequate adjustment to changing conditions in order to maintain and enhance competitiveness and productivity.

This concept combines an axis of (labor market) flexibility for the goals of economic performance, competitiveness, and growth (21, 23) with another axis of security to promote social policy to preserve social cohesion in societies (21).

The Organization for Economic Cooperation and Development (OECD) "Employment Protection Legislation (EPL) Index" (24) reflects the concept of "flexibility" well. "Employment Protection Legislation," in the context of employment protection, refers to "all types of employment protection measures, whether grounded primarily in legislation, court rulings, and collectively bargained condition of employment customary practice" (24). This definition serves well for our purpose, and the OECD also provides an overall index and separate indices for regular and temporary workers. This enables us to take into account the recent global change of an increasingly dual labor market, with a rise in precarious labor contracts (2, 3).

We did not have, however, the luxury of these types of well-developed indicators for the analysis of developing countries. For this reason, we decided to use labor market outcome indicators for our analysis of semi-peripheral and peripheral countries. What happens in the labor market when workers' bargaining power is low? We argue that wage level will correlate with the magnitude of workers' bargaining power. Also, with diminished bargaining power, we expect to see fewer workers' rights, resulting in greater gender inequities, more child workers, and coercion in the labor market. In brief, for low- and middle-income countries, we conceptualized the labor market by using two dimensions: inequality and poverty. The former concerns inequality among workers, especially in the gender dimension. The latter refers to poverty derived from wages.

Based on the line of reasoning outlined above, and the evidence reviewed, we hypothesize that workers' bargaining power positively correlates with population health. In wealthy (core) countries, workers' bargaining power is measured by union density and employment protection indicators; in middle- (semi-peripheral) and low-income (peripheral) countries, workers' bargaining power is measured by labor market inequality and poverty indicators.

METHODS: DATA AND ANALYSES

We used gross national product per capita (GNPpc) in 2000, generated through the World Bank's Atlas Method (adjusted for exchange rate), for the classification of countries based on their position in the world-system (25). Then we re-categorized countries on the basis of our knowledge and perception of position in the world-system. For example, oil-rich countries are categorized as core countries in the method of Babones (25), but their function as providers of oil does not qualify them as core countries, which usually dominate in high-value-added sectors such as finance and banking. East Asian countries, except for Japan, were also re-categorized as semi-peripheral, because of their relationship with the core.

For core countries, we used the mean EPL index for regular workers and temporary workers, for the years 2000–2003 (2000–2004 for Germany and Portugal), and union density (logarithmic) to generate clusters of labor markets. For semi-peripheral and peripheral countries, we constructed two labor market factor scores. The first labor market variable, inequality in the labor market (labeq), was generated with three standardized variables: estimated earned income ratio between male and female workers (incr1999, incr2003); labor force participation gap between female and male workers (lfp1997, lfp2003); and employment-to-population ratio (epr1997, epr2003). The second factor score measured poverty and income level in the labor market (labpov), also using three standardized variables measured twice: percentage of children in the labor market (chldl1997, chldl2003); percentage of workers that are poor (wkpr1997, wkpr2003); and average income level (aveinc1999, aveinc2003). Variables and sources are summarize in Table 1. The descriptive statistics of explanatory variables are given in Table 2.

Table 1

Labor market variables used in the typology of countries

Variables			Years	Source
Labor market variables	Core	Union density (logarithmic) EPL (Employment Protection Legislation) indices: • EPL index for regular workers • EPL index for temporary workers	Average of 2000–2003 (2000–2004 for Germany and Portugal)	Organization for Economic Cooperation and Development (OECD)
	Semi-periphery and periphery	Labor market inequality factor score (labeq) • Estimated earned income ratio between male and female workers (incr) • Labor force participation gap between female and male workers (lfp) • Employment-to-population ratio (epr) Labor market poverty factor score (labpov) • Percentage of children in labor market (chldl) • Percentage of workers that are poor (wkpr) • Average income level (aveinc)	1997 and 2003 (1999 and 2003 for incr and aveinc)	Key Indicators of Labour Market (KILM)
Health outcomes			2002 or 2004	WHO Statistics Information System (WHOSIS)

Table 2

Descriptive statistics of labor market variables by labor market cluster

| | Core | | | | | | Semi-periphery | | | | | | Periphery | | | | | |
| | Social democratic labor institutions (n = 6) | | Corporatist conservative labor institutions (n = 8) | | Liberal labor institutions (n = 7) | | Residual labor institutions (n = 16) | | Emerging labor institutions (n = 16) | | Informal labor markets (n = 10) | | Post-communist labor markets (n = 18) | | Less successful informal labor markets (n = 22) | | Insecure labor markets (n = 31) | |
Variables	Mean	S.D.	Mean	S.D.	Mean	S.D.	Mean	S.D.	Mean	S.D.	Mean	S.D.	Mean	S.D.	Mean	S.D.	Mean	S.D.
meplall	*2.11*	*0.38*	*2.69*	*0.66*	*0.93*	*0.41*												
meplreg	*2.05*	*0.50*	*2.83*	*0.63*	*1.22*	*0.51*												
mepltcm	*2.17*	*0.62*	*2.55*	*1.21*	*0.63*	*0.44*												
muden	*62.28*	*17.30*	*22.01*	*7.92*	*24.78*	*7.98*												
incr1999	*58.82*	*12.08*	*48.86*	*6.36*	*57.53*	*10.26*	59.12	6.70	38.01	6.99	34.99	15.32	61.80	8.39	35.42	6.51	60.07	9.41
incr2003	*64.68*	*12.02*	*48.86*	*7.55*	*65.64*	*14.54*	60.37	5.75	39.89	6.99	36.98	14.44	62.64	8.02	36.52	6.34	59.78	9.66
lfp1997	*−15.88*	*6.93*	*−22.28*	*4.63*	*−18.84*	*3.95*	−18.51	5.47	−35.04	6.13	−47.28	14.15	−16.18	9.55	−46.95	5.00	−20.05	10.59

lfp2003	-13.62	6.62	*-19.35*	*4.64*	*-15.81*	*2.87*	*-17.06*	*4.94*	-30.63	7.05	-44.47	14.26	-15.11	8.94	-45.57	5.03	-20.39	11.17
epr1997	66.77	10.64	*64.21*	*7.94*	*70.15*	*6.62*	*65.22*	*6.19*	62.61	4.52	55.86	6.60	68.06	8.58	55.00	7.73	75.79	10.17
cpr2003	69.22	9.02	*67.31*	*5.86*	*73.00*	*3.98*	*64.42*	*6.45*	63.96	6.08	55.96	7.37	66.26	8.32	55.15	7.76	75.12	9.93
labeq (std.)	0.68	0.77	*0.11*	*0.37*	*0.70*	*0.46*	*0.45*	*0.32*	-0.58	0.27	-1.29	0.85	0.65	0.59	-1.32	0.41	0.73	0.72
chldl1997	0.06	0.15	*0.19*	*0.55*	*0.00*	*0.00*	*1.03*	*3.65*	3.58	4.05	6.64	8.64	5.83	7.48	11.99	9.42	34.68	8.91
chldl2003	0.05	0.13	*0.10*	*0.29*	*0.00*	*0.00*	*0.67*	*2.50*	2.72	3.56	5.19	7.36	4.50	6.66	9.90	9.07	32.08	8.82
wrkpr1997	0.00	0.00	*0.00*	*0.00*	*0.00*	*0.00*	*1.41*	*3.45*	9.04	7.43	11.82	17.57	16.79	14.57	21.37	24.95	59.91	20.52
wrkpr2003	0.00	0.00	*0.00*	*0.00*	*0.00*	*0.00*	*0.38*	*1.10*	11.45	10.72	11.70	18.00	14.99	14.42	20.67	24.23	58.94	22.79
aveinc1999	25,628	2,308	*22,756*	*4,112*	*26,198*	*4,255*	*11,674*	*5,740*	8,573	3,981	9,364	5,994	3,086	1,644	4,190	2,298	1,262	968
aveinc2003	30,744	3,944	*26,955*	*4,680*	*31,659*	*5,975*	*14,469*	*6,446*	9,424	4,133	10,716	6,694	3,747	2,051	5,600	4,379	1,447	1,076
labpov (std.)	-1.20	0.10	*-1.09*	*0.15*	*-1.23*	*0.16*	*-0.67*	*0.25*	-0.34	0.28	-0.27	0.62	-0.02	0.40	0.18	0.58	1.49	0.43

Note: Data in italic were not used in the analysis.

Factor analyses were conducted by using a principal component method, and the reliability of the score was measured by Cronbach's alpha. Factor scores were constructed with the regression method. Using this factor score, we conducted a series of hierarchical cluster analyses to generate clusters of countries. This was achieved by using Ward's method of measuring squared Euclidean distance (L2squared in Figures 2–4). For descriptive analyses with health outcomes, we downloaded health variables from the WHOSIS (WHO Statistics Information System) website (www.who.int/whosis/en) and used the mean values for 2000–2005. All analyses were conducted with STATA version 10.0.

RESULTS

Originally our dataset included a total of 210 countries, which consisted of 38 core, 61 semi-peripheral, and 111 peripheral countries. Due to missing data points, we finally categorized 134 of these countries into labor market clusters (21 core, 42 semi-peripheral, and 71 peripheral countries). A complete list of the countries is given in Table 3.

Descriptive Analyses

The descriptive statistics of explanatory variables are shown in Table 2. Mean values of variables that were used to generate labor market inequality scores (labeq) were similar in semi-peripheral and peripheral countries. However, variables used to generate labor market poverty factor scores (labpov), such as percentage of child labor, percentage of working poor, and average income, show large discrepancies between these two positions in the world-system. The percentage of GNP generated through the informal sector is similar in the two groups of countries.

Construction of Factor Scores and Association
with Health Indicators

We present Cronbach's alpha values for measuring the reliability of factors and loadings of each variable in Table 4. All indicators used to construct factor scores show high factor loadings, and thus high Cronbach's alpha scores: 0.93 and 0.91 for labeq and labpov, respectively.

Clusters of Countries

Figures 2, 3, and 4 show the results of our hierarchical cluster analyses. We present the final three-by-three cluster of labor markets in Table 3. Figure 5 shows the regional distribution: core countries are in Western and Southern Europe; semi-peripheral countries are mostly East Asian, Eastern European, and

Table 3

Clusters of labor markets by position in the world-system

	More equal ⟵	Labor market ⟶	Less equal
Core	*Social democratic labor institutions* Belgium, Denmark, Finland, Italy, Norway, Sweden	*Corporatist conservative labor institutions* Austria, France, Germany, Greece, Japan, Netherlands, Portugal, Spain	*Liberal labor institutions* Australia, Canada, Ireland, New Zealand, Switzerland, United Kingdom, United States
Semi-periphery	*Residual labor institutions* The Bahamas, Croatia, Czech Rep., Hong Kong, Hungary, Jamaica, Korea Rep., Latvia, Lithuania, Poland, Russian Fed., Singapore, Slovak Rep., Slovenia, Thailand, Uruguay	*Emerging labor institutions* Argentina, Brazil, Chile, Colombia, Costa Rica, Ecuador, Fiji, Kuwait, Malaysia, Mexico, Panama, Paraguay, Peru, South Africa, Trinidad and Tobago, Venezuela	*Informal labor markets* Bahrain, Belize, Botswana, El Salvador, Lebanon, Oman, Saudi Arabia, Tunisia, Turkey
Periphery	*Post-communist labor markets* Albania, Armenia, Belarus, Bolivia, Bulgaria, Cambodia, China, Ghana, Indonesia, Moldova, Mongolia, Papua New Guinea, Philippines, Romania, Tajikistan, Ukraine, Uzbekistan, Vietnam	*Less successful informal labor markets* Algeria, Cape Verde, Côte d'Ivoire, Dominican Rep., Egypt, Equatorial Guinea, Guatemala, Guyana, Honduras, India, Iran, Jordan, Mauritania, Morocco, Nicaragua, Nigeria, Pakistan, Sri Lanka, Sudan, Swaziland, Syrian Arab Rep., Yemen Rep.	*Insecure labor markets* Bangladesh, Benin, Burkina Faso, Burundi, Cameroon, Central African Rep., Chad, Comoros, Congo Dem. Rep., Congo Rep., Eritrea, Ethiopia, Gambia, Guinea, Guinea-Bissau, Haiti, Kenya, Lao PDR, Madagascar, Malawi, Mali, Mozambique, Namibia, Nepal, Niger, Rwanda, Senegal, Tanzania, Togo, Uganda, Zambia, Zimbabwe

Table 4

Labor market factor scores, constituting variables, loadings, and reliability coefficient (Cronbach's alpha)

Factor	Variables		Factor loadings	Cronbach's alpha
labeq (labor market inequality factor score)	stincr99	Estimated earned income ratio between male and female workers, year 1999 (standardized)	0.889	0.934
	stincr03	Estimated earning income ratio between male and female workers, year 2003 (standardized)	0.877	
	stlfp97	Labor force participation gap between female and male workers, year 1997 (standardized)	0.937	
	stlfp03	Labor force participation gap between female and male workers, year 2003 (standardized)	0.912	
	stepr97	Employment-to-population ratio, year 1997 (standardized)	0.810	
	stepr03	Employment-to-population ratio, year 2003 (standardized)	0.787	
labpov (labor market poverty factor score)	stchldl97	% child labor, year 1997 (standardized)	0.926	0.913
	stschldl03	% child labor, year 2003 (standardized)	0.930	
	stwrkpr97	% working poor, year 1997 (standardized)	0.893	
	stwrkpr03	% working poor, year 2003 (standardized)	0.884	
	staveinc99	Average income level, year 1999 (standardized)	-0.794	
	staveinc03	Average income level, year 2003 (standardized)	-0.771	

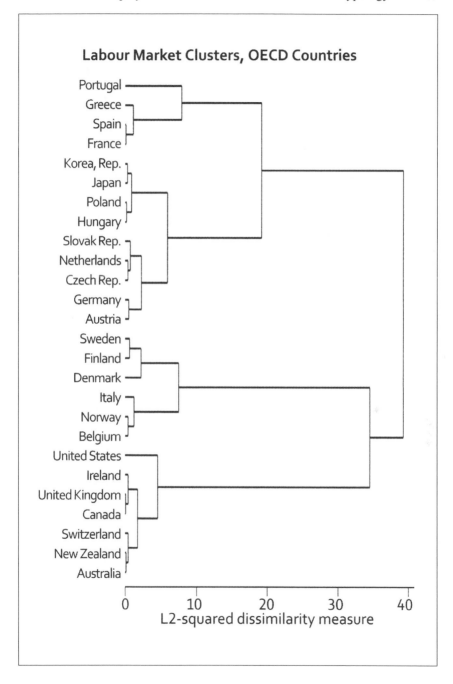

Figure 2. Results from the hierarchical cluster analysis of core countries.

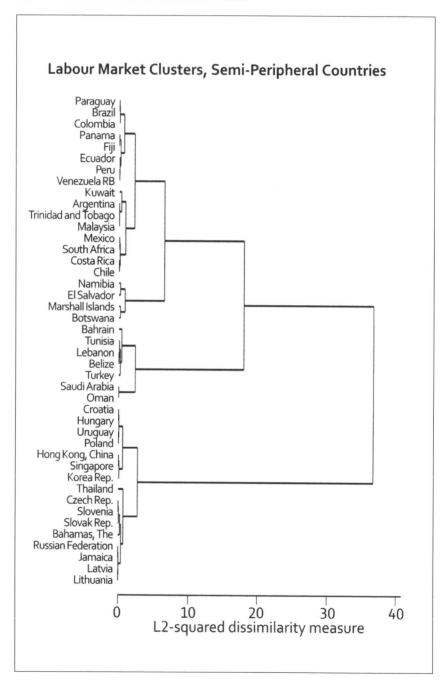

Figure 3. Results from the hierarchical cluster analysis of semi-peripheral countries.

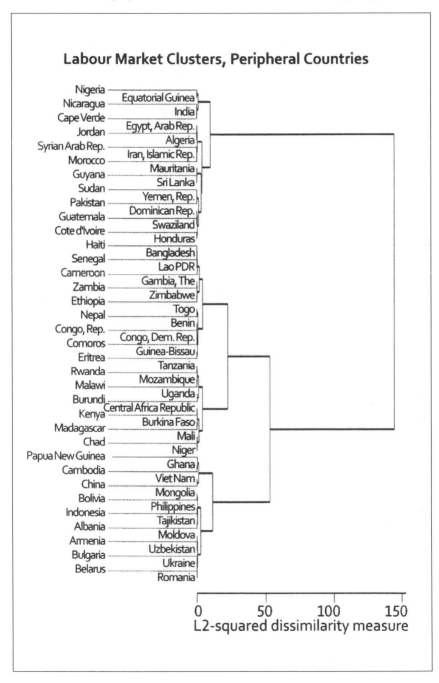

Figure 4. Results from the hierarchical cluster analysis of peripheral countries.

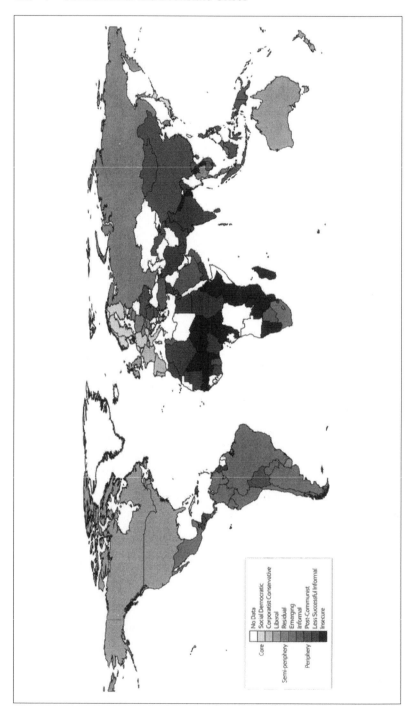

Figure 5. Clusters of labor market institutions by position in the world-system.

Latin American countries, with a couple of African countries; and peripheral countries are predominantly African and Southeast Asian countries, with some Caribbean nations.

Core Countries. The resulting clusters of core countries are, first, Belgium, Denmark, Finland, Italy, Norway, and Sweden; second, Austria, France, Germany, Greece, Japan, Netherlands, Portugal, and Spain; and third, Australia, Canada, Ireland, New Zealand, Switzerland, United Kingdom, and United States. These clusters approximate the three worlds of welfare capitalism (7). We named our categories, based on the widely accepted typology, as "social democratic labor institutions," "corporatist conservative labor institutions," and "liberal labor institutions." Among countries usually categorized as corporate conservative, we categorized Belgium in the social democratic labor institutions and Switzerland in the liberal labor institutions. Japan and the Southern European countries (Portugal and Spain) were categorized as corporatist conservative labor institutions, whereas Italy was grouped with the Nordic countries as liberal labor institutions. As observed in Table 2, the social democratic labor institutions show high average union density (62.28%) combined with medium EPL for both regular (2.05) and temporary (2.17) workers. Corporatist conservative labor institutions show low union density (22.01%) with high EPL for both regular (2.83) and temporary (2.55) workers. Liberal labor institution countries, on average, show low union density (24.78%) with very low EPL for both regular (1.22) and temporary (0.63) workers.

Semi-peripheral Countries. Cluster analyses of the labor market inequality and poverty factor scores resulted in three clusters each in the semi-peripheral and peripheral countries (see Table 3). The first cluster of semi-peripheral countries consists mostly of East Asian and Eastern European countries. Both of these regions are marked by an emphasis on industrialization and thus incorporation of rural workers into urban industrial centers (26, 27). Mass growth in urban working populations necessitated the development of labor contracts, but not as regulated as in core countries. The relationship among workers, companies, and governments is often partially democratic, embedded in labor institutions, but at the same time is more authoritarian than in core countries. For this reason, we named this cluster the "residual labor institutions."

The second cluster includes mostly middle-income (e.g., Argentina, Chile, Mexico) and more stable (e.g., Costa Rica) Latin American countries, South Africa, and Kuwait. These countries underwent limited industrialization with stagnated economic development, so countries in this cluster did not go through as extensive an urbanization as those in the first cluster (26, 27). Nevertheless, the jobs available in urban centers attract immigrants from rural areas and adjacent countries into cities, producing massive urban slums and large informal sectors. Therefore, we call this cluster the "emerging labor institutions."

The last cluster of semi-peripheral countries includes countries with lagged industrialization due to civil wars and other crises, a majority of national income derived from oil exports, and/or authoritarian rule of law. Labor markets in these countries are largely composed of the informal sector, and thus informal contracts. Therefore, we named them the "informal labor market." We used labor "market" instead of labor "institution" here to signify the informal nature of or the absence of labor contracts in these countries.

Peripheral Countries. The first cluster of peripheral countries consists mostly of the former communist countries, as in the case of the semi-peripheral countries. The developmentalist and universalistic tendencies (26, 28) of the ex-communist countries have enabled them to distinguish themselves from the rest of the peripheral region through industrialization and relatively low poverty.

The third cluster of peripheral countries is composed of the poorest countries of the world. This cluster is marked by a significantly higher labor poverty score when compared with the rest of the peripheral region. These countries suffer from long-term wars, natural disasters, and epidemics, so the nation-state cannot function. We named this cluster "insecure labor markets."

As a result, the second cluster of peripheral countries includes relatively diverse countries in the peripheral region that are not as homogeneous as the post-communist labor markets, but not as devastated as the insecure labor market type. We named this cluster "less successful informal labor markets," following the "informal labor market" label used for the semi-peripheral countries.

Labor Market Institutions and Health Outcomes

In Figures 6 through 9 we present box plots of population health indicators by labor market clusters. More egalitarian labor market clusters tend to exhibit better health outcomes compared with their counterparts in the same position of the world-system. The outstanding exception is years of life lost to non-communicable diseases (Figure 9), which shows a positive relationship with labor market equality—that is, more labor market equality results in more years of life lost due to communicable diseases.

DISCUSSION

In this study, we developed a global labor market typology that is associated with population indicators. The most widely used typologies in the political economy of health correspond to welfare state regime types (7), but their application is limited to wealthy countries. Recently, the study of welfare state regime types in middle- and low-income countries has been gathering momentum (27). We adopted a similar global perspective, focusing on one of the pillars of the welfare regime, the labor market, and chose indicators that might be relevant for health (e.g., precarious employment, gender inequity). However, the welfare states of middle-income countries and their relationship with population health, as well as the production of population health status through the labor market, have not been analyzed. In this context, we present a first global typology of labor markets and population health.

The labor market clusters in core countries largely correspond with established welfare state typologies (i.e., social democratic, conservative, liberal). This is consistent with the political and policy research literatures. Studies in the gender and welfare state literature show that the dual-earner type of welfare state in Scandinavian countries encourages women's labor market participation, whereas male-breadwinner-based welfare state institutions in Western and Southern European countries have fostered the development of stay-at-home mothers, and hence a dual labor market (7, 10).

In our analysis, larger flexibility in the labor market is inversely correlated with many child health indicators, such as neonatal, infant, and under-five mortality rates. This conforms to findings from previous research in wealthy countries (29, 30), indicating that maternal child health indicators are particularly sensitive to political and policy variables. Union density, which is the ultimate measure of workers' bargaining power, is additionally correlated with the low-birth-weight rate, also confirming previous findings in which the low-birth-weight rate was the most affected by political and policy conditions (29, 30). The low-birth-weight rate tends to correlate with wider social determinants other than economic development, such as income inequality measured with the Gini coefficient and strength of pro-egalitarian political power measured by the percentage of votes gathered by left parties (29). In our analysis, low-birth-weight rate was associated with union density, showing its close relationship with pro-egalitarian political power and, consequently, labor market and social policies.

There are many limitations to our study; it is mostly of an exploratory nature, aimed at generating new research. Although our interpretation adopts a "top-down" rather than "bottom-up" approach to labor market effects on individual health, which is consistent with the social and health policy literatures, it is also true that bottom-up effects in terms of community or labor organizing could have an impact on macro-structural changes (e.g., changes in union density, voting for a political force that adopts labor rights). Therefore, the social mechanisms are implicitly nonrecursive (reciprocal), although they were not tested in these analyses. A focus on employed or working-age populations would have given greater strength to the suggestion that labor market types affect population health, at least among the OECD countries. Confounding by different types of health systems, which might correlate with different types of labor markets, is also possible. However, we know that at the individual level, access to health care does not explain the variation in population health due to social circumstances, as opposed to previous ecological analyses (29, 30). Furthermore, data from a limited period, 2000–2004, cannot be a strong test of a causal hypothesis

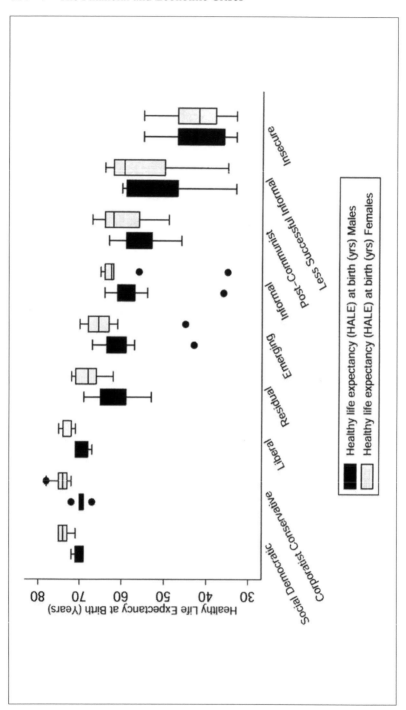

Figure 6. Health outcomes by labor market clusters: healthy life expectancy at birth, males and females.

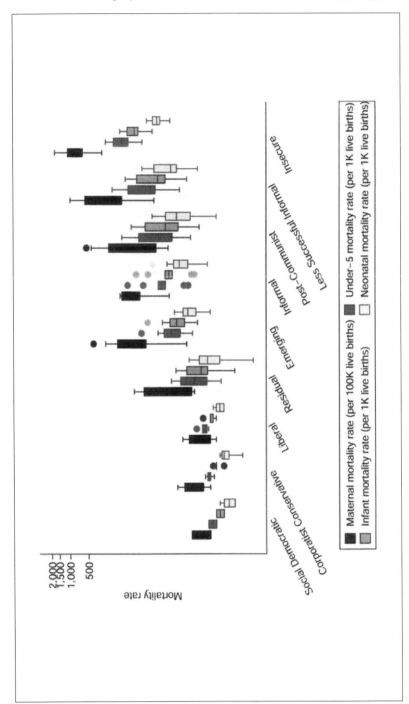

Figure 7. Health outcomes by labor market clusters: maternal and child health indicators (K indicates thousand).

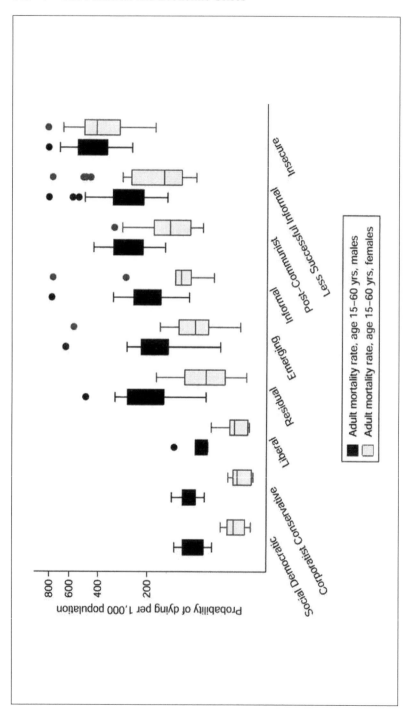

Figure 8. Health outcomes by labor market clusters: adult mortality rates, males and females.

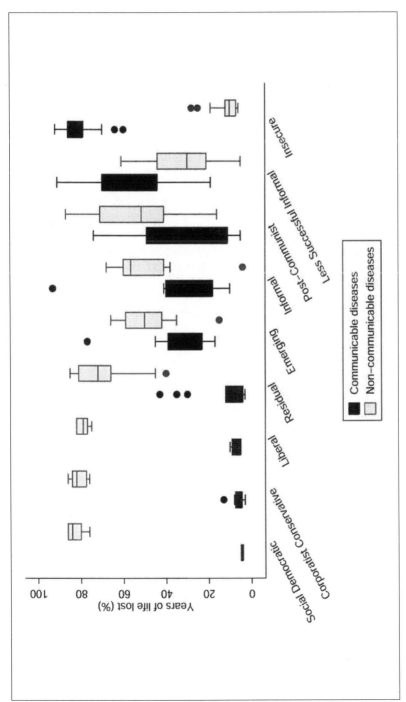

Figure 9. Health outcomes by labor market clusters: years of life lost to communicable and non-communicable diseases.

(employment policies take time to affect health and are thus time-dependent). In that sense, our observations should be interpreted as a proxy for long-term labor market effects and as heuristic.

Country clusters based on labor market characteristics differ greatly between those on the periphery and semi-periphery, on the one hand, and OECD countries on the other. The labor markets of semi-peripheral countries are characterized by growing informality, but do maintain some degree of stability and rule of law, approximating them to the labor markets of the wealthier OECD countries. Some, such as Chile, have even developed their own forms of emerging welfare state institutions and often generate labor movements to challenge globalization (31). Countries of the global periphery, however, represent another level of labor market instability altogether. Plagued by a heavy reliance on informal work, they face severe insecurity in their labor markets. In these countries, war, political instability, authoritarian regimes, and foreign interventions threaten the rule of law and the protection of workers, and only aggravate the problem (32).

Our categorization of countries reveals two very important distinctions. First, it highlights the difference between labor institutions and informal labor markets. Labor institutions are closely related to the strength of the welfare state (8)— that is, labor institutions are the ways in which the state regulates the labor market (e.g., provisions for collective bargaining). Informal labor markets are what emerges in the absence of state regulation of the labor market. They both serve to bring order to an otherwise unregulated marketplace, yet their outcomes are very different. The equality of the labor market typically increases as state intervention erodes the de facto authority of the informal labor market, replacing it with a formally regulated, legitimate authority. In the labor markets of peripheral countries, however, this process is difficult, as the majority of workers labor in the informal sector (33). Unregulated low wages may force workers to sell their labor for less than subsistence income (34). Moreover, insufficient wages for parents force children to venture into the labor market at a very young age (34). The result is a vast proportion of the population that not only is underpaid but also is excluded from social security measures. The hazardous working conditions that this implies were corroborated by our empirical findings.

A second conclusion pertains to the labor market in semi-peripheral countries. Union density and coverage are still important in those countries, as some have emergent or residual welfare states (e.g., the Eastern bloc countries), but their effects could not be analyzed, given the small sample size. The example of East Asia and Eastern Europe illustrates that similar labor market outcomes can be reached through different developmental strategies. Eastern European countries still spend more on welfare than do East Asian countries, even with lower national incomes (35). As seen in the wealthy countries, partially because of the high popularity of welfare services, a welfare state, once established, is hard to dismantle (8). For this reason, population health gains achieved through economic growth might be faster to decline than those obtained through the expansion of the welfare state. For example, after the late 1990s' Asian crisis, a fast increase in precarious employment and unemployment, as well as growing competition to enter the core labor force in a dual labor market, led South Korea to the highest suicide rate among OECD countries (36). Finally, the labor institutions of wealthy countries confirm the findings of previous studies (29, 30). Labor institutions, measured through union density and collective bargaining coverage, correlate closely with welfare state regime type in wealthy countries. The integration of flexicurity labor market initiatives in Scandinavian countries and the "varieties of capitalism" (37) approach could yield more refined labor institution typologies in future studies. For the time being, our effort suggests that world labor markets and their health effects can be described systematically with a combination of world-systems and labor market policy approaches. We hope that this first attempt will provide a positive heuristic in global health policy research.

REFERENCES

1. Commission on Social Determinants of Health. *Closing the Gap in a Generation: Health Equity through Action on the Social Determinants of Health.* World Health Organization, Geneva, 2008.
2. Louie, A. M., et al. Empirical study of employment arrangements and precariousness in Australia. *Relat. Ind.* 61:465–489, 2006.
3. Employment Conditions Knowledge Network (EMCONET). *Employment Conditions and Health Inequalities: Final Report to the WHO Commission on Social Determinants of Health.* World Health Organization, Geneva, 2007.
4. Benach, J., and Muntaner, C. Precarious employment and health: Developing a research agenda. *J. Epidemiol. Community Health* 61(4):276–277, 2007.
5. Chung, H. Health Services Research in the Era of New Welfare State Theories— Political, Welfare State, and Health Care Determinants of Population Health in Wealthy Countries. Ph.D. dissertation, Department of Health Policy and Management, Johns Hopkins University, Baltimore, 2006.
6. Esping-Andersen, G. *Politics against Markets.* Princeton University Press, Princeton, NJ, 1985.
7. Esping-Andersen, G. *The Three Worlds of Welfare Capitalism.* Princeton University Press, Princeton, NJ, 1990.
8. Huber, E., and Stephens, J. D. *Development and Crisis of the Welfare State: Parties and Policies in Global Markets.* University of Chicago Press, Chicago, 2001.
9. Hicks, A. M. *Social Democracy and Welfare Capitalism.* Cornell University Press, Ithaca, NY, 1999.
10. Korpi, W. *The Democratic Class Struggle.* Routledge and Kegan Paul, London, 1983.
11. Stephens, J. D. *The Transition from Capitalism to Socialism.* Macmillan, London, 1979.
12. Levinson, H. *Determining Forces in Collective Wage Bargaining.* John Wiley, New York, 1966.
13. Craypo, C. The decline in union bargaining power. In *New Directions in Labor Economics and Industrial Relations,* ed. M. Carter and W. Leahy. Notre Dame Press, South Bend, IN, 1981.

14. Craypo, C. The sources of union bargaining strength. In *The Economics of Collective Bargaining: Case Studies in the Private Sector*. Bureau of National Affairs, Washington, DC, 1986.
15. Mishel, L. The structural determinants of union bargaining power. *Ind. Labor Relat. Rev.* 40:90–104, 1986.
16. Mishel, L. Unions, monopolies and the Marshallian rules: An institutionalist appraisal. In *Advances in Industrial Relations*, ed. D. Lipsky. JAI Press, Greenwich, CT, 1985.
17. Scherer, F. M. *Industrial Structure and Performance*. Rand McNally, Chicago, 1980.
18. Reynolds, L. G. The impact of collective bargaining on the wage structure in the United States. In *The Theory of Wage Determination*, ed. J. T. Dunlop. St. Martin's Press, New York, 1964.
19. Kwoka, J. E., Jr. Monopoly, plant and union effects on worker wages. *Ind. Labor Relat. Rev.* 36:251–257, 1983.
20. Dalton, J. A., and Ford, E. J. J. Concentration and labor earning in manufacturing and utilities. *Ind. Labor Relat. Rev.* 1:45–60, 1977.
21. Wilthagen, T., and Tros, F. The concept of "flexicurity": A new approach to regulating employment and labour markets. *Transfer* 2:166, 2004.
22. Wilthagen, T., and Rogowski, R. Legal regulation of transitional labour markets. In *The Dynamics of Full Employment: Social Integration through Transitional Labour Markets*, ed. G. Schmid and B. Gazier, pp. 233–273. Edward Elgar, Cheltenham, UK, 2002.
23. European Central Bank. *Labour Market Mismatches in Euro Area Countries*. Frankfurt, 2002.
24. Organization for Economic Cooperation and Development. Employment protection and labour market performances. In *OECD Employment Outlook*, Chap. 2, p. 50. Paris, 1999.
25. Babones, S. J. The country-level income structure of the world-economy. *J. World Syst. Res.* 11:29–55, 2005.
26. Cook, L. J. *Postcommunist Welfare States: Reform Politics in Russia and Eastern Europe*. Ithaca, NY, Cornell University Press, 2007.
27. Haggard, S., and Kaufman, R. R. *Development, Democracy, and Welfare States: Latin America, East Asia, and Eastern Europe*. Princeton University Press, Princeton, NJ, 2008.
28. Rosenstein Rodan, P. N. Problems of industrialization of Eastern and South-Eastern Europe. In *The Economics of Underdevelopment*, ed. A. N. Agarwala and S. P. Singh. Oxford University Press, Bombay 1958 [1943].
29. Chung, H., and Muntaner, C. Welfare state matters: A typological multilevel analysis of wealthy countries. *Health Policy* 80(2):328–339, 2007.
30. Chung, H., and Muntaner, C. Political and welfare state determinants of infant and child health indicators: An analysis of wealthy countries. *Soc. Sci. Med.* 63(3):829–842, 2006.
31. Sandbrook, R., et al. *Social Democracy in the Periphery*. Cambridge University Press, Cambridge, 2007.
32. Gough, I., and Wood, G. *Insecurity and Welfare Regimes in Asia, Africa, and Latin America*. Cambridge University Press, Cambridge, 2004.

33. Portes, A., Castells, M., and Benton, L.A. *The Informal Economy*. Johns Hopkins University Press, Baltimore, 1991.
34. Rudra, N. *Globalization and the Race to the Bottom in Developing Countries*. Cambridge University Press, Cambridge, 2008.
35. Cook, L. J. *Postcommunist Welfare Sates*. Cornell University Press, Ithaca, NY, 2007.
36. Organization for Economic Cooperation and Development. *Society at a Glance*. 2009 OECD Social Indicators. Paris, 2009. www.oecd.org/home (accessed December 23, 2009).
37. Hall, P., and Soskice, D. *Varieties of Capitalism: The Institutional Foundations of Comparative Advantage*. Oxford University Press, New York, 2001.

CHAPTER 8

The Impact of Public Employment on Health and Health Inequalities: Evidence from China

Wei Zhang

Because the public and private sectors often operate with different goals, individuals employed by the two sectors may receive different levels of welfare. This can potentially lead to different health status. As such, employment sector offers an important perspective for understanding labor market outcomes. Using micro-level data from a recent Chinese household survey, this study empirically evaluated the impact of employment sector on health and within-sector health inequalities. It found that public sector employment generated better health outcomes than private sector employment, controlling for individual characteristics. The provision of more job security explained an important part of the association between public sector employment and better health. The study also found less health inequality by social class within the public sector. These findings suggest that policymakers should think critically about the "conventional wisdom" that private ownership is almost always superior, and should adjust their labor market policies accordingly.

*****

The public and private sectors often operate with different goals. While the private sector primarily exists to make a profit, the public sector is, to a great extent, motivated by social and political purposes, such as the eradication of poverty, unemployment, and inequalities. As a result, individuals working in the two sectors can be exposed to different environments that could generate different health status. Understanding the impact of employment sector on health is thus an important avenue to comprehending the outcomes of labor market policies. It also adds a unique perspective to evaluations of the welfare consequences of neoliberal policies that promote privatization and labor market deregulation.

The association between employment sector (public vs. private) and health has not been adequately explored. In the literature of labor economics, for example, empirical research involving the role of employment sector has mostly been done on earnings (1–6), union density (7), job security (8, 9), job satisfaction (10, 11), health care utilization (12, 13), and working conditions (14–17). But few studies have gone one step further, to investigate whether employment sector has any ultimate impact on health—one of the most essential measurements of human well-being.

On the other hand, within the employment-related epidemiological and public health literature, growing evidence suggests that particular employment and working conditions generate adverse health outcomes. Included among these are unemployment (18–24), informal employment (25–28), nonpermanent employment (29–33), hazardous environment (34–39), and declining bargaining power (40–42). Nevertheless, relatively few studies have contributed to understanding the health importance of employment sector. There are exceptions, but they examine developed countries only (29, 43, 44). The health effects of employment sector remain largely unknown for transitional and developing countries. Another weakness of the existing literature is the lack of a global/integrated framework, without which it becomes difficult to fully comprehend the often complex and multidimensional mechanisms linking employment and health (45, 46).

A recent effort by the Employment Conditions Network (EMCONET) under the World Health Organization's Commission on Social Determinants of Health is constructive toward these ends. It provides a platform to situate the role of employment sector in a broader socio-structural framework. In the *International Journal of Health Services* has devoted a special section to EMCONET's work on employment relations, employment conditions, and working conditions, and how these influence workers' health and health inequalities worldwide (45, 47–56). In the glossary (45), *employment relations* refer to the power relations between an individual seller of labor (or a collective of sellers of labor) and an employer; *employment conditions* are conditions or circumstances—whether bound by an explicit contract or not—in which an employee sells her labor to an employer; and *working conditions* refer to the physical, chemical, biological, and psychological conditions of work. In sequential order, employment relations (or power relations) in general, at the top, directly influence employment conditions, employment conditions directly influence working conditions, and working conditions influence health and health inequalities.

Within this analytical framework, employment sector (public vs. private) can serve as a useful indicator of employment relations, because ownership type would, to some extent, reflect the level of class exploitation in the workplace (44, 57). Also, employment sector can be embedded in the framework as an important indicator of employment conditions (and hence also of working conditions). This is because a public sector job (or a government job) is more likely to be a full-time permanent job, a formal job, a secure job, or a job with decent pay and safety protections. This is especially so for transitional and developing countries, where the quality of jobs in the two sectors differs more significantly.

Given the relevance of employment to health, this study aims to empirically evaluate the impact of employment sector on health and health inequalities in the case of China.

Hypothesis, Method, and Data

Since the 1980s, the private sector in China has grown rapidly and played an increasingly important role in the economy. To the contrary, China's public sector has declined, not only in quantity but also in quality. Following the tide of global austerity, especially after the mid-1990s, the public sector started to emulate private sector practices at an accelerated pace, making working conditions less pleasant. Nevertheless, evidence shows that working conditions in the public sector still compare favorably with those in the private sector in many ways. For example, Chen and Chan (14, 58) show that state-owned and state-holding enterprises have more complete occupational health systems than private enterprises. Su (59) finds that public enterprises are more likely to provide personal protective equipment and periodic health examinations for workers frequently exposed to occupational hazards. Chan and Zhu (60) find that, in the private sector, monetary penalties charged for the violation of workplace policies are more prevalent, and even the frequency of toilet use during work time is more restrictive among private enterprises. Chen and Hou (61) show that public enterprise employees have a higher contract signing rate and renewal rate than private enterprise employees, a pattern that also holds true for rural migrant workers on the lowest rung of the social ladder. Taken together, these findings indicate that it is reasonable to hypothesize that public sector employees enjoy better and probably more equal health outcomes.

For this study, the hypothesis was empirically tested on a sample drawn from the most recent wave (2006) of the China Health and Nutrition Survey (CHNS), which used a multistage, random cluster process to collect data in nine provinces that vary in geography and economic development. Detailed discussions of the design and scope of CHNS are available on its official website (www.cpc.unc.edu/projects/china). In this study, health outcome was measured by self-rated health (SRH); logistic regressions were used to assess the health impact of employment sector, controlling for potential confounding and mediating factors. The study used two exclusion criteria to yield the analytic sample. First, the sample under scrutiny was restricted to subjects who indicated their health status during the face-to-face interview. In the original survey, SRH was categorized as excellent, good, fair, or poor. Following prior convention (62–66), the four categories were dichotomized, with 1 for excellent or good SRH, and 0 for fair or poor SRH. Second, given the theme of this study, peasant farmers, family workers, self-employed independent operators with no employees, and the unemployed were not included; the analyses were confined to subjects who worked in either the public or the private sector. The public sector comprised government departments, state institutes, and public enterprises (state-owned and collective-owned) at the federal or local level; the private sector comprised privately owned domestic, foreign, and joint ventures.

The final sample included 2,245 subjects: 1,185 from the public sector and 1,060 from the private sector. Overall, 71.0 percent of the sample (72.6% of public employees and 69.3% of private employees) rated their health as good or excellent. Table 1 presents descriptive statistics. Variables accounting for demographic characteristics included age, gender, education, and geographic location; variables accounting for employment characteristics included employment sector (public vs. private), occupation, size of employer, job tenure, insurance status, and income received from employment.

Demographic Characteristics

Age. On average, public employees were older: about 60 percent of public employees were 40 years or older, with less than 40 percent of private employees in this age range.

Gender. The gender composition was similar in the two sectors: approximately 60 percent male and 40 percent female employees.

Education. Public employees were, on average, more educated: more than 70 percent had senior high school education or higher, compared with less than 35 percent of private employees.

Residential location. About 54 percent of public employees and 38 percent of private employees resided in urban areas (urban or suburban), and the rest in rural areas (county, town, or village).

Employment Characteristics

Occupation. Approximately 60 percent of public employees were white-collar workers—managers, officers, senior/junior professionals, and office staff. In contrast, more than 80 percent of private employees were engaged in blue-collar work: about 18 percent as skilled workers, 36 percent as low-skilled workers, and 29 percent as service workers.

Size of employer. One-third of the subjects were employed by small employers (<20 employees, as defined in the survey), one-third by medium-size employers (20–100 employees), and the remaining one-third by large employers (>100 employees). But proportions were not evenly distributed across the sectors. In the public sector, less than 20 percent were working for small employers, 40 percent for medium-size employers, and about 42 percent for large employers. Nearly half of private employees were employed by small employers, 27 percent by medium-size employers, and the remaining 24 percent by large employers.

Table 1

Descriptive statistics: public versus private

Factors	Total		Public		Private	
	N	%ᵃ	N	%ᵃ	N	%ᵃ
Total	2,245	100.0	1,185	100.0	1,060	100.0
Demographic characteristics						
Age, years						
<30	430	19.2	170	14.4	260	24.6
30–40	638	28.4	303	25.6	335	31.6
40–50	708	31.6	419	35.4	289	27.3
<50	468	20.9	293	24.7	175	16.5
Gender						
Male	1,342	59.8	719	60.7	623	58.8
Female	903	40.2	466	39.3	437	41.2
Education						
No school/primary incomplete	98	4.4	31	2.6	67	6.3
Primary	201	9.0	62	5.2	139	13.1
Lower middle	724	32.3	236	19.9	488	46.0
Upper middle/vocational	813	36.2	519	43.8	294	27.7
College or higher	408	18.2	336	28.4	72	6.8
Urban/rural strata						
Urban	1,036	46.2	634	53.5	402	37.9
Rural	1,209	53.9	551	46.5	658	62.1

Employment characteristics

Occupation						
Manager/officer	9.2	206	13.9	165	41	3.9
Senior professional	9.3	208	15.7	186	22	2.1
Junior professional	8.6	193	14.2	168	25	2.4
Office staff	11.3	254	18.2	216	38	3.6
Skilled worker	13.8	309	10.5	124	185	17.5
Low-skilled worker	24.0	539	13.3	157	382	36.1
Service worker	19.2	430	10.7	127	303	28.6
Other	4.6	104	3.5	41	63	6.0
Scale of working unit, no. of employees						
<20	32.2	693	17.4	200	493	49.4
20–100	33.8	728	40.1	462	266	26.6
>100	33.9	730	42.5	490	240	24.0
Annual income from current employment, mean ¥ [b]						
Wage (coeff. of variation)	(55.2)	11,496	(49.5)	12,422	10,106	(63.2)
Wage & bonus (coeff. of variation)	(61.0)	12,648	(56.2)	14,062	10,525	(65.7)
Tenure						
Nonpermanent	38.4	863	20.7	245	618	58.3
Permanent	61.6	1,382	79.3	940	442	41.7
Insured						
No	36.4	818	22.4	265	553	52.2
Yes	63.6	1,427	77.6	920	507	47.8

[a] As a column percentage of each category in each variable. The sum of each category may not add to 100 percent, due to missing values.

[b] The top 1 percent and bottom 1 percent are excluded to avoid the influence of extreme values on the analysis. Missing values for wage are imputed when possible. For imputation method and other information, consult CHNS documentation on individual income variable construction on the CHNS website.

Income. The raw data showed that public employees enjoyed an earning premium of more than 20 percent. The average annual basic wage was about ¥12,422 for public employees, compared with ¥10,106 for private employees; when bonus was also counted, average income was ¥14,062 for public employees and ¥10,525 for private employees. On examination of the coefficients of variation, income was more equally distributed within the public sector.[1]

Job tenure. Approximately 80 percent of public employees held permanent positions, whereas only 42 percent of private employees had permanent jobs.

Health insurance status. More than 36 percent of private employees were not covered by any form of insurance; in contrast, 78 percent of public employees had some form of health insurance.

RESULTS

Impact of Public Employment on Health

The differences between sectors in demographic and employment characteristics point to the need for multiple regression analysis. The results are given in Table 2 (pp. 130–135). Throughout all regression models, the results consistently show that public sector employment contributes to better health. For example, as shown in model 1, public employees were more likely to report good/excellent health than private employees, adjusting for age, education, and gender (OR = 1.22, $p < 0.1$). Age is negatively associated with SRH, education is for the most part positively associated with SRH, and women generally were less likely to report good/excellent health. In model 2, the inclusion of employment characteristics—occupation and employer size—increases the impact of public employment on health in both magnitude and statistical significance (OR = 1.30, 95% CI 1.02–1.65). The administrator/officer group at the top of the occupational ladder has the highest rate of good/excellent SRH. For other occupations farther down the social ladder, however, no health gradient is evident.

Model 3 also controls for province and urban-rural strata to take account of geographic diversity. This exercise further enhances the positive association between public employment and SRH (OR = 1.36, 95% CI 1.03–1.81). Living in the rural sector is associated with better SRH than urban/suburban residency, a pattern observed previously for China and elsewhere (67, 68).[2] The impact of

---

[1] Coefficient of variation is defined as the ratio of standard deviation to the mean. It is often used to compare dispersions of two groups with different units or means. The larger the coefficient of variation, the larger the dispersion.

[2] The rural-urban gaps in China are well-known; most rural residents have less access to stable income and good living conditions. However, all rural people included in the present analysis had a non-farming job and, compared with the most disadvantaged rural residents, including farmers and the rural unemployed, were probably less likely to be affected by the underdevelopment of China's rural sector.

education is nevertheless reduced. In addition, employer size is negatively associated with SRH. This finding bridges, to some extent, the previous findings of a negative association between employer size and job satisfaction (69–71) and a positive association between job satisfaction and SRH (for a meta-analysis review, see 72).

Model 4 takes into account the role of income. Annual wage income is strongly associated with good/excellent SRH. An important finding is that the positive association between public sector employment and health persists (OR = 1.38, 95% CI 1.04–1.83), suggesting that the public sector wage premium does not explain the contribution of public employment to better health. Further analysis shows that the public sector wage premium is mostly a reflection of the economic returns to individual characteristics, such as education, age, occupation, and geographic location. In fact, once these factors are controlled for, the public sector pay premium disappears (for regression results, see Appendix Table 1, p. 146). Model 5 differs slightly from model 4 in that bonuses received from employment were also counted. The estimated parameter of public sector employment, again, remains statistically significant (OR = 1.36, 95% CI 1.03–1.80).

Model 6 incorporates an additional explanatory factor characterizing employment security—job tenure, an important determinant of physical and psychological health (for literature reviews, see 30, 73). The result shows that permanent tenure is significantly associated with good/excellent SRH (OR = 1.38, 95% CI 1.05–1.83). Compared with model 5, the inclusion of employment contract type attenuates part of the association between public employment and SRH (OR = 1.27, 95% CI 0.96–1.69), suggesting that the public sector's higher level of job security mediates much of the sector's contribution to better SRH. Finally, with further control of insurance status, model 7 shows an even stronger association between public sector employment and good/excellent SRH (OR = 1.37, 95% CI 1.02–1.83). It seems that being insured is associated with a lower probability of reporting good/excellent health. This finding, also reported by several other studies conducted on the CHNS data (74, 75), is somewhat unexpected and is addressed in the discussion section.

*Impact of Public Employment on Within-Sector
Health Inequalities*

Now let's turn to the question of whether employment sector has any impact on within-sector health inequalities. Socioeconomic status (SES) is often used to indicate an individual's economic and social position relative to others, typically measured by categorized income, wealth, education, occupation, or political power. The relationship between SES and health has been extensively documented in the literature (76–78). There is ample research showing that higher SES tends to generate better health, and vice versa. Other studies suggest that the SES-health profile varies across factors, such as gender (79, 80), race (81),

Table 2

Logistic analysis of the impact of employment sector on good/excellent self-rated health

Variables	Model 1 OR (95% CI)	Model 2 OR (95% CI)	Model 3 OR (95% CI)
Employment sector (vs. private)			
Public	1.22 (0.99–1.51) *	1.30 (1.02–1.65) **	1.36 (1.03–1.81) **
Demographic characteristics			
Age (vs. <30)			
30–40	0.87 (0.65–1.17)	0.86 (0.63–1.17)	0.76 (0.52–1.10)
40–50	0.62 (0.47–0.82) ***	0.57 (0.42–0.76) *	0.44 (0.31–0.63) ***
>50	0.39 (0.29–0.54) ***	0.37 (0.27–0.52) ***	0.26 (0.17–0.38) ***
Gender (vs. male)			
Female	0.72 (0.59–0.87) ***	0.77 (0.63–0.94) **	0.73 (0.58–0.92) ***
Education (vs. < primary)			
Primary	1.06 (0.64–1.76)	1.09 (0.64–1.83)	0.83 (0.43–1.59)
Lower middle	1.48 (0.95–2.32) *	1.52 (0.95–2.43) *	1.51 (0.84–2.73)
Upper middle/vocational	1.59 (1.01–2.51) **	1.66 (1.02–2.71) **	1.53 (0.83–2.81)
College or higher	1.53 (0.94–2.49)*	1.62 (0.93–2.81) *	1.50 (0.77–2.93)
Urban/rural			
Rural			1.37 (1.07–1.74) **

	n = 2,243	n = 2,147	n = 1,798
Employment characteristics			
Occupation (vs. manager/officer)			
Senior professional		0.62 (0.40–0.98) **	0.62 (0.38–1.01) *
Junior professional		0.68 (0.42–1.09)	0.62 (0.37–1.03) *
Office staff		0.67 (0.43–1.04) *	0.60 (0.37–0.97) **
Skilled worker		0.69 (0.44–1.09)	0.60 (0.36–0.99) **
Low-skilled worker		0.78 (0.51–1.21)	0.75 (0.46–1.23)
Service worker		0.67 (0.44–1.04) *	0.81 (0.49–1.33)
Other		0.82 (0.45–1.49)	1.12 (0.51–2.46)
Total employees (vs. <20)			
20–100		1.00 (0.78–1.27)	0.84 (0.63–1.14)
>100		0.83 (0.65–1.08)	0.70 (0.52–0.95) **
Annual income from employment			
Wage			
Wage & bonus			
Tenure (vs. nonpermanent employee)			
Permanent			
Insurance status (vs. uninsured)			
Insured			
Obs.	n = 2,243	n = 2,147	n = 1,798

Table 2 (Cont'd.)

Variables	Model 4 OR (95% CI)	Model 5 OR (95% CI)
Employment sector (vs. private)		
Public	1.38 (1.04–1.83) **	1.36 (1.03–1.80) **
Demographic characteristics		
Age (vs. <30)		
30–40	0.72 (0.49–1.04) *	0.72 (0.50–1.05) *
40–50	0.42 (0.29–0.60) ***	0.42 (0.30–0.61) ***
>50	0.24 (0.16–0.36) ***	0.24 (0.16–0.36) ***
Gender (vs. male)		
Female	0.78 (0.61–0.99) **	0.77 (0.61–0.98) **
Education (vs. < primary)		
Primary	0.78 (0.41–1.50)	0.78 (0.41–1.50)
Lower middle	1.36 (0.74–2.47)	1.37 (0.76–2.50)
Upper middle/vocational	1.33 (0.72–2.46)	1.35 (0.73–2.50)
College or higher	1.21 (0.61–2.40)	1.24 (0.63–2.47)
Urban/rural		
Rural	1.41 (1.11–1.80) ***	1.41 (1.11–1.80) ***

Employment characteristics

Occupation (vs. manager/officer)		
Senior professional	0.60 (0.37–0.99) **	0.59 (0.36–0.98) **
Junior professional	0.63 (0.38–1.06) *	0.63 (0.38–1.05) *
Office staff	0.62 (0.38–1.00) *	0.61 (0.38–0.99) **
Skilled worker	0.64 (0.38–1.05) *	0.63 (0.38–1.04) *
Low-skilled worker	0.85 (0.51–1.41)	0.84 (0.51–1.39)
Service worker	0.92 (0.56–1.53)	0.91 (0.55–1.50)
Other	1.20 (0.55–2.63)	1.18 (0.54–2.60)
Total employees (vs. <20)		
20–100	0.80 (0.59–1.08)	0.81 (0.60–1.09)
>100	0.66 (0.48–0.89) ***	0.66 (0.48–0.90) ***
Annual income from employment		
Wage		
Wage & bonus	1.44 (1.13–1.82) ***	1.34 (1.07–1.68) **
Tenure (vs. nonpermanent employee)		
Permanent		
Insurance status (vs. uninsured)		
Insured		
Obs.	n = 1,798	n = 1,798

Table 2 (Cont'd.)

Variables	Model 6 OR (95% CI)	Model 7 OR (95% CI)
Employment sector (vs. private)		
Public	1.27 (0.96–1.69) *	1.37 (1.02–1.83) **
Demographic characteristics		
Age (vs. <30)		
30–40	0.70 (0.48–1.02)	0.73 (0.50–1.06)
40–50	0.41 (0.29–0.59) ***	0.44 (0.30–0.62) ***
>50	0.24 (0.16–0.35) ***	0.25 (0.17–0.38) ***
Gender (vs. male)		
Female	0.77 (0.60–0.98) **	0.78 (0.61–0.99) **
Education (vs. < primary)		
Primary	0.79 (0.41–1.51)	0.82 (0.43–1.55)
Lower middle	1.37 (0.76–2.48)	1.41 (0.78–2.54)
Upper middle/vocational	1.34 (0.73–2.47)	1.41 (0.76–2.59)
College or higher	1.22 (0.62–2.42)	1.31 (0.66–2.59)
Urban/rural		
Rural	1.41 (1.10–1.80) ***	1.39 (1.09–1.78) ***

Employment characteristics

Occupation (vs. manager/officer)		
Senior professional	0.60 (0.36–0.98) **	0.60 (0.37–0.99) **
Junior professional	0.63 (0.38–1.05) *	0.65 (0.39–1.08) *
Office staff	0.61 (0.38–0.99) **	0.63 (0.39–1.02) *
Skilled worker	0.65 (0.40–1.08) *	0.66 (0.40–1.10)
Low-skilled worker	0.91 (0.55–1.52)	0.93 (0.56–1.56)
Service worker	1.01 (0.60–1.69)	0.99 (0.59–1.66)
Other	1.27 (0.58–2.78)	1.29 (0.59–2.79)
Total employees (vs. <20)		
20–100	0.80 (0.59–1.08)	0.83 (0.61–1.12)
>100	0.64 (0.47–0.88) ***	0.66 (0.48–0.90) **
Annual income from employment		
Wage	1.29 (1.02–1.63) **	1.36 (1.07–1.73) **
Wage & bonus		
Tenure (vs. nonpermanent employee)		
Permanent	1.38 (1.05–1.83) **	1.41 (1.06–1.87) **
Insurance status (vs. uninsured)		
Insured		0.62 (0.48–0.82) ***
Obs.	n = 1,798	n = 1,798

Note: Models 3 through 7 also controlled for province (results not shown, to save space). To ensure the comparability with models 4 through 7, the analysis of model 3 was restricted to individuals whose income data were available.

*Significant at 10% level; **significant at 5% level; ***significant at 1% level.

wealth index (82), rural versus urban locality (83), and social development stage (84). However, the SES-health analysis has rarely been conducted across employment sector (public vs. private). We have very limited knowledge on whether the classical SES-health gradient can be identified in either of the two sectors, and whether the pattern makes any difference across the two sectors. The following analyses attempt to fill this gap.

Within-Sector Health Gradient by Education. Education is a frequently used indicator of SES in the study of social determinants of health. The strength of education as a proxy for SES rests on its being most commonly available, relatively stable, and comparable between genders, and preceding other indicators, such as income and occupation (85). Table 3 shows the education-health profile in the private and public sectors. The education-health gradient appears in both sectors, but the gradient is much steeper in the private sector. For instance, private employees with upper-middle-school education or the equivalent had about twice the odds of reporting good/excellent health compared with people who did not finish primary school (OR = 1.96–2.52, $p < 0.05$). In contrast, the health-education profile within the public sector is much smaller and not statistically significant.

Note that for both sectors, there is, more or less, a turning point at the upper end of the educational ladder. For instance, the most educated group in both sectors did not seem to feel healthier than those one grade lower. This is not all that surprising, however, given that China is undergoing a drastic economic and demographic transition. Such a transition can expose individuals with high SES to certain diseases (such as obesity, diabetes, or cardiovascular diseases) or unhealthy behaviors (such as a high-fat diet or a sedentary lifestyle). Historical evidence shows that the correlation between SES and health can change and evolve over time (86–92). For instance, Kaplan and Keil's literature review (92) finds that, during the 1930s and 1940s, the rates of coronary heart disease were *positively* associated with SES in both the United States and United Kingdom; not until two to three decades later did coronary disease in the United Kingdom become more prevalent among people of the low occupational classes (92, p. 1983).

Within-Sector Health Gradient by Income. Table 4 presents the within-sector SES-health profile, for which SES was measured by annual income from employment (basic wage plus bonus). Similar to the findings for education, a steep health gradient occurs in the private sector, moving along the income hierarchy: the health gap between the middle income groups (the middle 60%) and the bottom income quintile is notable, after controlling for confounders (OR = 1.78, 95% CI 1.21–2.63), and the gap between the top quintile and the bottom quintile is even greater (OR = 2.19, 95% CI 1.14–4.21). In contrast, the health gradient in the

Table 3

Within-sector health gradient by education: public versus private

Highest education attained or equivalent	Private sector					Public sector				
	N	OR^a	(95% CI)	OR^b	(95% CI)	N	OR^a	(95% CI)	OR^b	(95% CI)
Less than primary school	67	1.00	—	1.00	—	31	1.00	—	1.00	—
Primary school	139	1.18	(0.65–2.15)	1.54	(0.81–2.95)	62	0.90	(0.37–2.22)	0.93	(0.36–2.39)
Lower middle	488	1.72	(1.00–2.95) **	2.04	(1.14–3.64) **	236	1.23	(0.55–2.73)	1.34	(0.57–3.19)
Upper middle/vocational	294	1.96	(1.11–3.47) **	2.52	(1.36–4.68) ***	519	1.25	(0.58–2.71)	1.38	(0.58–3.29)
College or higher	72	1.68	(0.81–3.51)	2.22	(0.90–5.49) *	336	1.23	(0.56–2.71)	1.32	(0.53–3.27)

^{a}Odds ratio adjusted for age and gender.
^{b}Odds ratio adjusted for age, gender, occupation, and geographic location.
*Significant at 10% level; **significant at 5% level; ***significant at 1% level.

Table 4

Within-sector health gradient by income: public versus private

Income group	Private sector					Public sector				
	N	OR^a	(95% CI)	OR^b	(95% CI)	N	OR^a	(95% CI)	OR^b	(95% CI)
Lowest quintile (<¥ 6,500)	209	1.00	—	1.00	—	165	1.00	—	1.00	—
Middle quintiles (¥ 6,500–18,000)	441	1.64	(1.14–2.37) ***	1.78	(1.21–2.63) ***	678	1.06	(0.71–1.57)	0.98	(0.64–1.49)
Highest quintile (>¥ 18,000)	93	2.17	(1.17–4.04) **	2.19	(1.14–4.21) **	277	1.53	(0.94–2.49) *	1.44	(0.84–2.45)

^{a}Odds ratio adjusted for age, education, and gender.
^{b}Odds ratio adjusted for age, education, gender, occupation, and geographic location.
*Significant at 10% level; **significant at 5% level; ***significant at 1% level.

public sector between the top and bottom quintiles is much smaller in both magnitude and statistical significance, and the health gap between the middle income groups and the bottom quintile is absent.

Within-Sector Health Gradient by Age for Manual Workers. In general, an adult's health status tends to decline with age. But the steepness of the age-health profile depends on one's socioeconomic environment. A good working environment can help cushion the adverse effects of aging on health, while an unpleasant environment can accelerate the aging process. Here, the focus is on whether the age-health profile for manual workers differs in the public and private sectors. "Manual workers" here refers to skilled and low-skilled workers whose work is more physically demanding. As discussed previously, because China's public sector is more likely than the private sector to comply with government laws and regulations and provides better working conditions, including more workplace safety protection, shorter working hours, and less strenuous workloads, it is reasonable to hypothesize that manual workers in the public sector would suffer less wear and tear on their health and hence a more moderate age-health gradient.

This hypothesis is confirmed by the results presented in Table 5. In the private sector, the probability of reporting good/excellent health declined continuously at a notable rate in older age brackets. For instance, private sector manual workers between 40 and 50 years old were much less likely to report good/excellent health than workers under 30 years (OR = 0.50, 95% CI 0.29–0.89), and the gap between subjects over 50 and under 30 is even greater (OR = 0.36, 95% CI 0.18–0.69). Such a pattern, however, is not found in the public sector; actually, only subjects older than 50 years seemed to have a lower probability of reporting optimal health, but the difference is not statistically significant. Also note that, for the youngest group (age <30 years), the private sector shows a slightly higher rate of good/better SRH than the public sector (78.5% vs. 75%), but for all other older groups, that rate is consistently higher in the public sector. This may suggest, to some extent, that manual workers in the private sector, while starting from comparable or even better initial health status, were exposed to a working environment that would grind down health more aggressively over time.

No such gradational pattern across age groups is observed for other occupations that involve less physical wear and tear than manual jobs. The absence may reflect that, in the past, Chinese society was built on a more or less egalitarian base, but various inequalities, including inequalities in health, have arisen in recent years and might take time to show up for less strenuous jobs.

DISCUSSION

This study qualitatively evaluated the impact of employment sector on health and within-sector health inequalities by social class. The findings complement

Table 5

Age-health gradient for manual workers: public versus private

Age group	Private sector						Public sector					
	N	Good, %	OR^a	(95% CI)	OR^b	(95% CI)	N	Good, %	OR^a	(95% CI)	OR^b	(95% CI)
<30	121	78.5	1.00	—	1.00	—	48	75.0	1.00	—	1.00	—
30–40	190	69.5	0.66	(0.39–1.12)	0.66	(0.39–1.14)	79	74.7	1.08	(0.46–2.54)	1.15	(0.47–2.85)
40–50	166	66.3	0.56	(0.32–0.96) **	0.50	(0.29–0.89) **	94	75.5	1.09	(0.48–2.49)	1.05	(0.43–2.58)
>50	90	56.7	0.45	(0.24–0.86) **	0.36	(0.18–0.69) ***	60	63.3	0.67	(0.26–1.73)	0.59	(0.21–1.66)

Note: N = total number of people in each age-sector category.

^{a}Odds ratio adjusted for education and gender.

^{b}Odds ratio adjusted for education, gender, and geographic location.

*Significant at 10% level; **significant at 5% level; ***significant at 1% level.

and extend previous research showing that the public sector in China provides better working conditions. Before my concluding remarks, a few technical issues warrant clarification.

First, the negative correlation between having insurance and health is somewhat against expectation and needs careful interpretation. The presence of adverse selection can be suspected—that is, that an individual with worse health conditions may opt for health insurance, hence raising the issue of endogeneity. If this were the case, however, it should not change the basic conclusion of the study that public sector employment contributes to better health. Given that the public sector is more likely to offer insurance, should there be any endogeneity, the true health benefits of public sector employment will have been underestimated.

On the other hand, another explanation, suggested by some prior evidence, is that the negative relationship between insurance and health reflects the malfunctioning of China's market-oriented health care system, including health insurance. In the literature, there have been some curious findings on the performance of China's health insurance. For example, some evidence shows that health insurance in China has led to a *reduction* in health care utilization, partly due to the difficulty of getting reimbursement (13, 93),[3] and also an *increase* in out-of-pocket medical spending due to overtreatment (94).[4] These findings imply that health insurance in China has, on the one hand, dissuaded use and reduced much of the demand for necessary medical care while, on the other hand, inducing unnecessary care and the diagnosis of pseudo-diseases; both scenarios are detrimental to physical health and can further negatively affect the self-perception of health. In April 2009, in response to mounting public frustration with the failing health care system, the Chinese government finally released a profound health care reform plan, pledging substantive government involvement. The

[3] Henderson and colleagues (13), using the 1989 CHNS, found a puzzling pattern that insured individuals were significantly *less* likely than the uninsured to use medical services when sick ($p < 0.05$). A similar finding was reported in a later study of two additional waves of the CHNS (93). The authors emphasized that their estimation ruled out the possibility of endogeneity, and they suspected that the puzzle was partly due to employers' frequent failure to reimburse medical bills, which discouraged the insured from seeking medical care (93, pp. 1966–1968).

[4] Wagstaff and Lindelow (94) explored three Chinese surveys—the CHNS, the Gansu Survey of Family and Children, and the China Health VIII Project Baseline Survey. These surveys universally showed that health insurance tended to *increase*, rather than reduce, out-of-pocket spending and the risk of catastrophic medical expenses. The authors believed that their estimation ruled out the problem of endogeneity—that is, the possibility of "people with unobserved characteristics that predispose them to high spending being more likely to opt for health insurance." Rather, the explanation for the "curious case" was that being insured had triggered overtreatment and unnecessary medical care. In other words, China's medical care providers tended to prescribe for the insured more, and more costly, tests, drugs, and other medical interventions (94, pp. 1002–1003).

performance of China's health insurance and how it affects health will be an interesting topic for future research.

A second technical issue is non-random selection between health and employment sector. The cross-sectional design of this study limits inferences about causality of events. Longitudinal analyses can be helpful in observing how health status for the same cohort has been evolving over time and the change of employment sector; such information, however, is not adequately available due to significant attrition of the effective sample size. Nevertheless, I am unaware of any prior evidence showing that, in China, people who enter one specific sector (private or public) systematically have better or worse initial health than people who enter the other sector. That is, we have no reason to hypothesize that healthier workers are systematically more likely to enter the public sector than the less healthy. If anything, it is practically easier for the private sector to deny the entry of less healthy workers, since government supervision is less effective in this sector. In addition, propensity score can, to some degree, help ease this concern when treatment assignment may not be random. Introduced by Rosenbaum and Rubin (95), propensity score is defined as the conditional probability of an observation being assigned to a particular treatment, given a set of covariates. In terms of the present study, it refers to a subject's probability of entering the public sector given a set of demographic and employment characteristics. The score is predicted through a logistic model, with employment sector as the explained variable and a set of potential confounders that are closely related to both employment sector and health as the explanatory variables. One way to utilize the constructed score is to include it in the original regression model as a covariate. The results from this exercise are given in Appendix Table 2 (p. 148). The estimates of effect of public employment on health did not change after adjusting for propensity scores, lending support to the robustness of the relationship between public employment and better SRH.

Another limitation of this study, due to data availability, is the difficulty in pinpointing the exact factor(s) that influence health and health inequalities. As demonstrated in the EMCONET frameworks, employment-related health factors—in the categories of employment relations, employment conditions, or working conditions—are many; quite often, they are intertwined. The present study suggests that public and permanent jobs are beneficial to health and health equality, but we do not know exactly whether it is because these jobs provided better safety protection or allowed more worker participation and democracy in the production process, or because their unions were more powerful, or because government supervision was more effective in the public sector. It is also not clear whether the factor(s) worked through physical, biological, or psychological channels. Data employed in this study do not include this information. More work and data are required for a more precise understanding of this issue.

CONCLUSIONS AND POLICY IMPLICATIONS

This study estimated the impact of employment sector on workers' health and within-sector health inequality, using survey data collected in nine provinces of China in 2006. Several important findings emerge from the analyses. After controlling for demographic and employment characteristics, public sector employment is found to significantly contribute to better self-rated health. Part of the health premium is attributable to the fact that the public sector provides jobs with more security. Further, the private sector is found to have a steep SES-health gradient, whereas in the public sector, such a gradient is more moderate or even negligible. There is also some evidence that private sector employment aggravates the rate of depreciation of health with age.

Two policy implications follow. First, public sector employment is comparatively good for health and health equity, whereas further privatization of public enterprises and government functions would jeopardize health and health equity. When choosing between the public sector and the private sector to generate jobs, policymakers should think critically about the claim that private ownership is always superior to public ownership and should take into account the potential health outcomes. Second, job security is critical for health; any decent job, be it in the public or private sector, should guarantee a sense of security. Proposals for less regulation and more flexibility in the labor market are flawed.

At present, it is difficult to predict how the health gap between the two sectors will evolve in China. The extent to which the working conditions of the private sector can be elevated to a level close to that of the public sector is unclear. Although the government has, in the past few years, promulgated several laws and regulations defending labor rights, including the Labor Contract Law and the Law on Mediation and Arbitration of Labor Disputes, their effects have been limited. The nationwide minimum wage increase in the early summer of 2010 was more a result of the recent wave of workers' strikes and protests (96, 97) than a consequence of those laws and regulations. Besides weak implementation and supervision, the laws and regulations lack real enforcement power. For example, to enhance job security and protect workers from arbitrary dismissal, the Labor Contract Law stipulates that "when the employer plans to lay off more than twenty workers or more than ten percent of all workers, the employer shall *inform* the union or the workers thirty days in advance, *solicit* their opinion and *report* to the local labor administrative department" (Article 41, emphasis added). The problem here is that the law lacks language defining what legal or administrative actions the government or the trade union could take if private employers, as the owners, are determined to reduce the labor force.

Meanwhile, the continuing deterioration of the quality of public sector jobs deserves equal attention. The term "iron-rice bowl" is often used to characterize the comprehensive benefits received by public employees through employment under China's planned economy. The benefits—including, but not limited to, lifetime job security, an egalitarian wage structure, free medical care, free child-care, and free housing—are essential to health. But since the market-oriented reforms, especially after the mid-1990s, public sector employment has suffered not only in quantity but also in quality. If the austerity measures that the Chinese government has been pressing for in the public sector continue, we may soon observe that the health gaps between the two sectors fade away.

Acknowledgments — This research used data from the China Health and Nutrition Survey. The author thanks the Carolina Population Center, University of North Carolina at Chapel Hill, and other involved institutions for the CHNS data collection and analysis files.

REFERENCES

1. Hyder, A., and Reilly, B. The public and private sector pay gap in Pakistan: A quantile regression analysis. *Pakistan Dev. Rev.* 44:271–306, 2005.
2. Disney, R., and Gosling, A. Does it pay to work in the public sector? *Fiscal Stud.* 19:347–374, 1998.
3. Borland, J., Hirschberg, J., and Lye, J. Earnings of public sector and private sector employees in Australia: Is there a difference? *Econ. Record* 74:36–53, 1998.
4. Postel-Vinay, F., and Turon, H. The public pay gap in Britain: Small differences that (don't?) matter. *Econ. J.* 117:1460–1503, 2007.
5. Lucifora, C., and Meurs, D. The public sector pay gap in France, Great Britain and Italy. *Rev. Income Wealth* 52:43–59, 2006.
6. Gornick, J. C., and Jacobs, J. A. Gender, the welfare state, and public employment: A comparative study of seven industrialized countries. *Am. Sociol. Rev.* 63:688–710, 1998.
7. Freeman, R. B. Contraction and expansion: The divergence of private sector and public sector unionism in the United States. *J. Econ. Perspect.* 2:63–88, 1988.
8. Bloch, F. E., and Smith, S. P. Human capital and labor market employment: Errata and extension. *J. Hum. Resour.* 14:267–269, 1979.
9. Hall, R. E., Gordon, A., and Holt, C. Turnover in the labor force. *Brookings Papers on Economic Activity* 3:709–764, 1972.
10. DeSantis, V. S., and Durst, S. L. Comparing job satisfaction among public- and private-sector employees. *Am. Rev. Public Adm.* 26:327–343, 1996.
11. Demoussis, M., and Giannakopoulos, N. Exploring job satisfaction in private and public employment: Empirical evidence from Greece. *Labour* 21:333–359, 2007.
12. Jiménez-Martín, S., Labeaga, J. M., and Martínez-Granado, M. An empirical analysis of the demand for physician services across the European Union. *Eur. J. Health Econ.* 5:150–165, 2004.
13. Henderson, G., et al. Equity and the utilization of health services: Report of an eight-province survey in China. *Soc. Sci. Med.* 39:687–699, 1994.
14. Chen, M., and Chan, A. Occupational health and safety in China: The case of state-managed enterprises. *Int. J. Health Serv.* 40:43–60, 2010.
15. Solinger, D. J. Job categories and employment channels among the "floating population." In *Adjusting to Capitalism: Chinese Workers and the State*, ed. G. O'Leary, pp. 3–47. M. E. Sharpe, Armonk, NY, 1998.

16. Weston, T. B., and Jensen, L. M. (eds.). *China beyond the Headlines.* Rowman & Littlefield, Lanham, MD, 2000.
17. Tsui, A. S., Bian, Y., and Cheng, L. (eds). *China's Domestic Private Firms: Multidisciplinary Perspectives on Management and Performance.* M. E. Sharpe, Armonk, NY, 2006.
18. Brenner, M. H., and Mooney, A. Unemployment and health in the context of economic change. *Soc. Sci. Med.* 17:1125–1138, 1983.
19. Ruhm, C. J. Healthy living in hard times. *J. Health Econ.* 24:341–363, 2005.
20. Hammarström, A., and Janlert, U. An agenda for unemployment research: A challenge for public health. *Int. J. Health Serv.* 35:765–777, 2005.
21. Scheid, T. L. An investigation of work and unemployment among psychiatric clients. *Int. J. Health Serv.* 23:763–782, 1993.
22. Jin, R. L., Shah, C. P., and Svoboda, T. J. The impact of unemployment on health: A review of the evidence. *CMAJ* 153:529–540, 1995.
23. Schmitz, H. Why are the unemployed in worse health? The causal effect of unemployment on health. *Labour Econ.* 18:71–78, 2010.
24. Blakely, T. Unemployment and mortality: Learning from the past in times of resurging unemployment. *J. Epidemiol. Community Health* 64:3–4, 2010.
25. Giatti, L., Barreto, S. M., and César, C. C. Household context and self-rated health: The effect of unemployment and informal work. *J. Epidemiol. Community Health* 62:1079–1085, 2008.
26. Ludermir, A. B., and Lewis, G. Informal work and common mental disorders. *Soc. Psychiatry Psychiatr. Epidemiol.* 38:485–489, 2003.
27. Santana, V. S., and Loomis, D. Informal jobs and non-fatal occupational injuries. *Ann. Occup. Hyg.* 48:147–157, 2004.
28. Giatti, L., Barreto, S. M., and César, C. C. Household context and self-rated health: The effect of unemployment and informal work. *BMJ* 62:1079–1085, 2008.
29. Virtanen, P., et al. The working conditions and health of non-permanent employees: Are there differences between private and public labour markets? *Econ. Ind. Democracy* 27:39–65, 2006.
30. Virtanen, M., et al. Temporary employment and health: A review. *Int. J. Epidemiol.* 34:610–622, 2005.
31. Benach, J., et al. A new occupational health agenda for a new work environment. *Scand. J. Work Environ. Health* 28:191–196, 2002.
32. Silla, I., Gracia, F. J., and Peiró, J. M. Job insecurity and health-related outcomes among different types of temporary workers. *Econ. Ind. Democracy* 26:89–117, 2005.
33. Guest, D. Flexible employment contracts, the psychological contract and employee outcomes: An analysis and review of the evidence. *Int. J. Manage. Rev.* 5:1–19, 2004.
34. Richardson, D., et al. Fatal agricultural injuries in North Carolina by race and occupation, 1977–1991. *Am. J. Ind. Med.* 31:452–458, 1997.
35. Loomis, D. P., and Wolf, S. H. Mortality of workers at a nuclear materials production plant at Oak Ridge, Tennessee, 1947–1990. *Am. J. Ind. Med.* 29:131–141, 1996.
36. Robinson, J. C. Trends in racial inequality and exposure to work-related hazards, 1968–1986. *Milbank Q.* 65:404–420, 1987.

References *continue on p. 150*

Appendix Table 1

Ordinary least squares analysis of the determinants of income (log) from employment, N = 1,798

Variables	Model 1	Model 2	Model 3	Model 4
Public employment	-0.06 (0.03) **	-0.05 (0.03)	-0.03 (0.03)	-0.00 (0.03)
Age (vs. <30)				
30-40	0.19 (0.04) ***	0.16 (0.03) ***	0.19 (0.04) ***	0.16 (0.04) ***
40-50	0.18 (0.03) ***	0.17 (0.03) ***	0.17 (0.04) ***	0.15 (0.04) ***
<50	0.22 (0.04) ***	0.17 (0.04) ***	0.20 (0.04) ***	0.15 (0.04) ***
Gender (vs. male)				
Female	-0.18 (0.02) ***	-0.20 (0.02) ***	-0.19 (0.02) ***	-0.20 (0.02) ***
Education (vs. < primary)				
Primary	0.14 (0.08) *	0.16 (0.08) **	0.16 (0.08) **	0.19 (0.08) **
Lower middle	0.30 (0.07) ***	0.32 (0.07) ***	0.31 (0.07) ***	0.34 (0.07) ***
Upper middle/vocational	0.40 (0.07) ***	0.41 (0.07) ***	0.42 (0.07) ***	0.44 (0.07) ***
College or higher	0.62 (0.07) ***	0.60 (0.07) ***	0.66 (0.07) ***	0.64 (0.07) ***

	Model 1	Model 2	Model 3	Model 4
Occupation (vs. manager/officer)				
Senior professional	0.05 (0.05)	0.06 (0.05)	0.12 (0.05) **	0.12 (0.05) **
Junior professional	-0.13 (0.05) **	-0.10 (0.05) **	-0.13 (0.05) **	-0.09 (0.05) *
Office staff	-0.09 (0.05) *	-0.10 (0.05) **	-0.08 (0.05)	-0.09 (0.05) *
Skilled worker	-0.16 (0.05) ***	-0.15 (0.05) ***	-0.17 (0.05) ***	-0.16 (0.05) ***
Low-skilled worker	-0.35 (0.05) ***	-0.35 (0.05) ***	-0.38 (0.05) ***	-0.38 (0.05) ***
Service worker	-0.32 (0.05) ***	-0.33 (0.05) ***	-0.34 (0.06) ***	-0.35 (0.06) ***
Other	-0.20 (0.08) **	-0.18 (0.08) **	-0.19 (0.09) **	-0.18 (0.08) **
Total employees (vs. <20)				
20–100	0.14 (0.03) ***	0.13 (0.03) ***	0.15 (0.03) ***	0.14 (0.03) ***
>100	0.20 (0.03) ***	0.19 (0.03) ***	0.24 (0.03) ***	0.22 (0.03) ***
Urban (vs. rural)				
Rural		-0.08 (0.02) ***		-0.11 (0.02) ***
Constant	8.83 (0.09) ***	8.89 (0.10) ***	8.85 (0.09) ***	8.86 (0.10) ***

Note: Standard errors of coefficient estimates are in parentheses. Values are based on White's heteroskedasticity-consistent covariance matrix. The dependent variable in model 1 and model 2 refers to annual wage; in model 3 and model 4, it refers to annual basic wage plus bonuses. In both cases, it is in logarithm form. Model 2 and model 4 also controlled for province (results not shown, to save space).
*Significant at 10% level; **significant at 5% level; ***significant at 1% level.

Appendix Table 2

Logistic analysis of the association between public employment and good/excellent self-rated health, adjusted for propensity scores, N = 1,798

Variables	Model 1 OR (95% CI)	Model 2 OR (95% CI)	Model 3 OR (95% CI)
Employment sector (vs. private)			
Public	1.35 (1.01–1.80) **	1.34 (1.00–1.80) **	1.34 (1.00–1.79) **
Demographic characteristics			
Age (vs. <30)			
30–40	0.75 (0.50–1.11)	0.71 (0.48–1.05) *	0.79 (0.53–1.18)
40–50	0.43 (0.29–0.64) ***	0.41 (0.28–0.61) ***	0.48 (0.32–0.73) ***
<50	0.25 (0.16–0.39) ***	0.24 (0.15–0.37) ***	0.29 (0.18–0.46) ***
Gender (vs. male)			
Female	0.73 (0.58–0.93) **	0.78 (0.61–0.99) **	0.75 (0.58–0.95) **
Education (vs. < primary)			
Primary	0.83 (0.44–1.59)	0.79 (0.41–1.51)	0.79 (0.41–1.50)
Lower middle	1.52 (0.84–2.75)	1.38 (0.76–2.52)	1.31 (0.72–2.38)
Upper middle/vocational	1.51 (0.82–2.79)	1.34 (0.72–2.48)	1.45 (0.78–2.68)
College or higher	1.49 (0.76–2.91)	1.23 (0.62–2.45)	1.30 (0.65–2.57)
Urban/rural			
Rural	1.37 (1.07–1.74) **	1.42 (1.11–1.81) ***	1.39 (1.09–1.78) ***

Employment characteristics

	Model 1	Model 2	Model 3
Occupation (vs. manager/officer)			
Senior professional	0.62 (0.38–1.02) *	0.60 (0.36–0.98) **	0.59 (0.36–0.97) **
Junior professional	0.61 (0.37–1.02) *	0.63 (0.37–1.05) *	0.66 (0.39–1.10)
Office staff	0.60 (0.37–0.96) **	0.61 (0.38–0.99) **	0.62 (0.38–1.00) **
Skilled worker	0.63 (0.34–1.14)	0.66 (0.36–1.20)	0.48 (0.25–0.92)
Low-skilled worker	0.79 (0.41–1.50)	0.88 (0.46–1.69)	0.64 (0.32–1.28)
Service worker	0.85 (0.46–1.55)	0.95 (0.51–1.75)	0.76 (0.41–1.43)
Other	1.14 (0.51–2.55)	1.21 (0.54–2.70)	1.11 (0.50–2.48)
Total employees (vs. <20)			
20–100	0.83 (0.59–1.16)	0.79 (0.56–1.11)	0.94 (0.65–1.34)
>100	0.68 (0.46–1.01) *	0.64 (0.43–0.94) **	0.82 (0.53–1.27)
Annual income from employment			
Wage & bonus		1.34 (1.07–1.68) **	1.26 (1.00–1.60) **
Tenure (vs. nonpermanent employee)			
Permanent			1.66 (1.15–2.41) ***

Note: The regressions also controlled for province (results not shown, to save space).
*Significant at 10% level; **significant at 5% level; ***significant at 1% level.

37. Quinlan, M., Mayhew, C., and Bohle, P. The global expansion of precarious employment, work disorganization, and consequences for occupational health: A review of recent research. *Int. J. Health Serv.* 31:335–414, 2001.
38. Benach, J., and Muntaner, C. Precarious employment and health: Developing a research agenda. *BMJ* 61:276–277, 2007.
39. Sverke, M., Hellgren, J., and Näswall, K. No security: A meta-analysis and review of job insecurity and its consequences. *J. Occup. Health Psychol.* 7:242–264, 2002.
40. Robinson, J. C. The rising long-term trend in occupational injury rates. *Am. J. Public Health* 78:276–281, 1988.
41. Loomis, D., et al. Political economy of US states and rates of fatal occupational injury. *Am. J. Public Health* 99:1400–1408, 2009.
42. Morse, T., et al. The relationship of unions to prevalence and claim filing for work-related upper-extremity musculoskeletal disorders. *Am. J. Ind. Med.* 44:83–93, 2003.
43. Trinkoff, A. M., et al. Staffing and worker injury in nursing homes. *Am. J. Public Health* 95:1220–1225, 2005.
44. Muntaner, C., et al. Work or place? Assessing the concurrent effects of workplace exploitation and area-of-residence economic inequality on individual health. *Int. J. Health Serv.* 41:27–50, 2011.
45. Benach, J., et al. Introduction to the WHO Commission on Social Determinants of Health Employment Conditions Network (EMCONET) study, with a glossary on employment relations. *Int. J. Health Serv.* 40:195–207, 2010.
46. Lipscomb, H. J., et al. A conceptual model of work and health disparities in the United States. *Int. J. Health Serv.* 36:25–50, 2006.
47. Benach, J., et al. Methods for the study of employment relations and health inequalities in a global context. *Int. J. Health Serv.* 40:209–213, 2010.
48. Muntaner, C., et al. A macro-level model of employment relations and health inequalities. *Int. J. Health Serv.* 40:215–221, 2010.
49. Benach, J., et al. A micro-level model of employment relations and health inequalities. *Int. J. Health Serv.* 40:223–227, 2010.
50. Chung, H., Muntaner, C., and Benach, J. Employment relations and global health: A typological study of world labor markets. *Int. J. Health Serv.* 40:229–253, 2010.
51. Kim, I. H., et al. Case studies on employment-related health inequalities in countries representing different types of labor markets. *Int. J. Health Serv.* 40:255–267, 2010.
52. Benach, J., et al. Six employment conditions and health inequalities: A descriptive overview. *Int. J. Health Serv.* 40:269–280, 2010.
53. Muntaner, C., et al. Unemployment, informal work, precarious employment, child labor, slavery, and health inequalities: Pathways and mechanisms. *Int. J. Health Serv.* 40:281–295, 2010.
54. Quinlan, M., et al. Policies and interventions on employment relations and health inequalities. *Int. J. Health Serv.* 40:297–307, 2010.
55. Muntaner, C., et al. The solution space: Developing research and policy agendas to eliminate employment-related health inequalities. *Int. J. Health Serv.* 40:309–314, 2010.
56. Benach, J., et al. Conclusions and recommendations for the study of employment relations and health inequalities. *Int. J. Health Serv.* 40:315–322, 2010.
57. Wright, E. O. *Classes.* Verso, London, 1985.

58. Chen, M., and Chan, A. Employee and union inputs into occupational health and safety measures in Chinese factories. *Soc. Sci. Med.* 58:1231–1245, 2004.
59. Su, Z. Occupational health and safety legislation and implementation in China. *Int. J. Occup. Environ. Health* 9:302–308, 2003.
60. Chan, A., and Zhu, X. Disciplinary labor regimes in Chinese factories. *Crit. Asian Stud.* 35:559–584, 2003.
61. Chen, L., and Hou, B. The employment flexibility and security under the context of globalization in China. In *Globalization and Changes in Employment Conditions in Asia and the Pacific*, ed. S. Lee and J. Hur, pp. 217–272. Korea Labor Institute, Seoul, 2007.
62. Kaplan, G. A., and Camacho, T. Perceived health and mortality: A nine-year follow-up of the human population laboratory cohort. *Am. J. Epidemiol.* 117:292–304, 1983.
63. Strawbridge, W. J., and Wallhagen, M. I. Self-rated health and mortality over three decades: Results from a time-dependent covariate analysis. *Res. Aging* 21:402–416, 1999.
64. Jylhä, M., Volpato, S., and Guralnik, J. M. Self-rated health showed a graded association with frequently used biomarkers in a large population sample. *J. Clin. Epidemiol.* 59:465–471, 2006.
65. Cummins, S., et al. Neighbourhood environment and its association with self rated health: Evidence from Scotland and England. *J. Epidemiol. Community Health* 59:207–213, 2005.
66. Cummings, J. R., Rice, T., and Hanoch, Y. Who thinks that part D is too complicated? Survey results on the Medicare prescription drug benefit. *Med. Care Res. Rev.* 66:97–115, 2009.
67. Luo, Y., and Wen, M. Can we afford better health? A study of the health differentials in China. *Health* 6:471–500, 2002.
68. House, J. S., et al. Excess mortality among urban residents: How much, for whom, and why? *Am. J. Public Health* 90:1898–1904, 2000.
69. Heywood, J. S., and Green, C. *Performance Pay, Sorting, and the Dimensions of Job Satisfaction.* Working Papers No. 4731. Lancaster University Management School, Economics Department, Lancaster, UK, 2007.
70. Forth, J., Bewley H., and Bryson A. *Small and Medium-Sized Enterprises: Findings from the 2004 Workplace Employee Relations Survey.* Report to the Department of Trade and Industry. London, 2006.
71. Tsai, C. J., Sengupta, S., and Edwards, P. When and why is small beautiful? The experience of work in the small firm. *Hum. Relations* 60:1779–1807, 2007.
72. Faragher, E. B., Cass, M., and Cooper, C. L. The relationship between job satisfaction and health: A meta-analysis. *Occup. Environ. Med.* 62:105–112, 2005.
73. De Witte, H. Job insecurity and psychological well-being: Review of the literature and exploration of some unresolved issues. *Eur. J. Work Organ. Psychol.* 8:155–177, 1999.
74. Zhao, Z. Health demand and health determinants in China. *J. Chinese Econ. Business Stud.* 6:77–98, 2008.
75. Liang, K. Rural-Urban Differences in the Shape of the Socioeconomic Gradients in Health in China. Paper presented at the American Sociological Association Annual Meeting, Boston, 2008.
76. Navarro, V. Inequalities are unhealthy. *Monthly Rev.* 56:26–30, 2004.
77. Marmot, M. G. *The Status Syndrome: How Social Standing Affects Our Health and Longevity.* Times Books/Henry Holt, New York, 2004.

78. Kawachi, I., Kennedy, B. P., and Wilkinson, R. G. *The Society and Population Health Reader: Income Inequality and Health.* New Press, New York, 1999.
79. Tang, M., Chen, Y., and Krewski, D. Gender-related differences in the association between socioeconomic status and self-reported diabetes. *Int. J. Epidemiol.* 32:381–385, 2003.
80. Rathmann, W., et al. Sex differences in the associations of socioeconomic status with undiagnosed diabetes mellitus and impaired glucose tolerance in the elderly population: The KORA Survey 2000. *Eur. J. Public Health* 15:627–633, 2005.
81. Mutchler, J. E., and Burr, J. A. Racial differences in health and health care service utilization in later life: The effect of socioeconomic status. *J. Health Soc. Behav.* 32:342–356, 1991.
82. Vukoviæ, D., Bjegoviæ, V., and Vukoviæ, G. Prevalence of chronic diseases according to socioeconomic status measured by wealth index: Health survey in Serbia. *Croat. Med. J.* 49:832–841, 2008.
83. Zimmer, Z., and Kwong, J. Socioeconomic status and health among older adults in rural and urban China. *J. Aging Health* 16:44–70, 2004.
84. Zimmer, Z., et al. How indicators of socioeconomic status relate to physical functioning of older adults in three Asian societies. *Res. Aging* 26:224–258, 2004.
85. Santos, A. C., Ebrahim, S., and Barros, H. Gender, socio-economic status and metabolic syndrome in middle-aged and old adults. *BMC Public Health* 8:62, 2008.
86. Wang, Y. Cross-national comparison of childhood obesity: The epidemic and the relationship between obesity and socioeconomic status. *Int. J. Epidemiol.* 30: 1129–1136, 2001.
87. Subramanian, S. V., and Smith, G. D. Patterns, distribution, and determinants of under- and overnutrition: A population-based study of women in India. *Am. J. Clin. Nutr.* 84:633–640, 2006.
88. Fernald, L. C. H. Socio-economic status and body mass index in low-income Mexican adults. *Soc. Sci. Med.* 64:2030–2042, 2007.
89. Monteiro, C. A., et al. Obesity and inequities in health in the developing world. *Int. J. Obes.* 28:1181–1186, 2004.
90. Fernald, L., and Adler, N. Blood pressure and socioeconomic status in low-income women in Mexico: A reverse gradient? *J. Epidemiol. Community Health* 62:e8, 2008.
91. Braveman, P. A., et al. Socioeconomic status in health research: One size does not fit all. *JAMA* 294:2879–2888, 2005.
92. Kaplan, G. A., and Keil, J. E. Socioeconomic factors and cardiovascular disease: A review of the literature. *Circulation* 88:1973–1998, 1993.
93. Henderson, G., et al. Trends in health services utilization in eight provinces in China, 1989–1993. *Soc. Sci. Med.* 47:1957–1971, 1998.
94. Wagstaff, A., and Lindelow, M. Can insurance increase financial risk?: The curious case of health insurance in China. *J. Health Econ.* 27:990–1005, 2008.
95. Rosenbaum, P. R., and Rubin, D. B. The central role of the propensity score in observational studies for causal effects. *Biometrika* 70:41–55, 1983.
96. Sun, U. No cheap labor? China increases minimum wages. *China Daily*, July 2, 2010, www.chinadaily.com.cn/china/2010-07/02/content_10053553.htm (accessed July 15, 2010).
97. Reuters. Why Labor Unrest is Good for China and the World. June 2, 2010. www.reuters.com/article/idUSTRE6511TT20100602 (accessed July 15, 2010).

CHAPTER 9

Ensuring a Healthy and Productive Workforce: Comparing the Generosity of Paid Sick Day and Sick Leave Policies in 22 Countries

Jody Heymann, Hye Jin Rho, John Schmitt, and Alison Earle

National paid sick day and paid sick leave policies are compared in 22 countries ranked highly in terms of economic and human development. The authors calculate the financial support available to workers facing two different kinds of health problems: a case of the flu that requires missing 5 days of work, and a cancer treatment that requires 50 days of absence. Only 3 countries—the United States, Canada, and Japan—have no national policy requiring employers to provide paid sick days for workers who need to miss 5 days of work to recover from the flu. Eleven countries guarantee workers earning the national median wage full pay for all 5 days. In Ireland and the United Kingdom, the full-time equivalent benefits are more generous for low-wage workers than for workers earning the national median. The United States is the only country that does not provide paid sick leave for a worker undergoing a 50-day cancer treatment. Luxembourg and Norway provide 50 full-time equivalent working days of leave, while New Zealand provides the least, at 5 days. In 6 countries, paid sick leave benefits are more generous for low-wage workers than for median-wage workers.

*****

INTRODUCTION

Why Paid Sick Days and Paid Sick Leave Matter
to the Health of Workers and Their Families

When policies for taking paid time off from work in case of illness are lacking, many workers continue to go to work even when they are sick (1), jeopardizing their own recovery and health. In this section we review research that demonstrates that the availability of paid sick days for short-term illnesses and paid sick leave for longer-term health issues contributes to a variety of important health outcomes for workers and their family members (1, 2).

If working adults are able to stay home when they are sick, they are less likely to spread infectious diseases to coworkers (1, 3). This risk has been broadly recognized; as just one example, the spread of infectious disease at the workplace is the reason that the U.S. Centers for Disease Control and Prevention recommended that Americans with influenza—a disease that leads to 200,000 hospitalizations and over 36,000 deaths in an average year (4)—stay home when they are sick (5). Conservatively estimated, at least 20 million Americans go to work sick because they are not entitled to sick leave.[1] With the recent outbreak of H1N1 influenza, public health officials are again recommending that adults stay home from work and children stay home from school if they have symptoms. The ability to follow these recommendations is dramatically affected by whether the infected adult or the sick child's parent has paid sick days.

Paid sick day policies affect the ability of working adults to meet the health needs of their children (8). Parents with paid sick days are five times more likely to be able to care for sick children at home than similar parents without paid sick days (9). Sick children have shorter recovery periods, better vital signs, and fewer symptoms when their parents share in their care (8). Parents with paid sick days are also more likely to provide preventive health care (9). Without paid sick days, parents, especially resource-poor parents, may have little choice but to miss needed doctors' appointments or to leave sick children home alone, where they risk missing or improperly managing medications and may not be able to obtain emergency help. Lack of paid sick days puts not only the health of a worker's own children at risk, but that of other children as well (8).

---

[1] National data show a 15 percentage-point gap in the number of workers who go to work sick between those who reported that their company provided paid sick leave and those who did not; those entitled to paid sick days were less likely to go to work when ill. However, many Americans whose companies provide paid sick days are nevertheless financially penalized at work, and thus are more likely to work when sick. In the same national survey, 11 percent of respondents reported job loss because of taking time off for illness, and 11 percent confirmed that they or a family member have been "fired, suspended or otherwise penalized for taking time off for illness" (6). A two-state survey in Florida and Ohio directly asked employed adults whether they had ever gone to work sick because of fears of financial penalties. Nearly half said yes. If these figures hold for the national population, it would mean that over 70 million Americans whose sick leave could be covered by social insurance and 57 million Americans who could be covered by an employer mandate are going to work sick (7).

When parents lack paid sick days, they are far more likely to send their sick children to child care or school (10). Children sent to daycare when they are sick with contagious diseases exacerbate the higher than average rate of observed infections in daycare centers, including higher rates of respiratory and gastrointestinal infections (8).

Paid sick days and sick leave also enable workers to care for their aging parents. When sick adults receive support from family members, they have substantially better health outcomes from conditions such as heart attacks (11, 12) and strokes (13). Elderly individuals also live longer with family support (14, 15).

Finally, in health care and service settings, providing paid sick days to employees also helps to protect the health of patients and customers. For example, nursing homes that provide their employees with paid sick days experience lower rates of respiratory and gastrointestinal illness among the patients they serve (16).

Why Paid Sick Days and Sick Leave Matter
for the Health of the Economy

Paid sick days and sick leave have an equally substantial impact on the finances of working adults and their families as on their health. Lacking the right to take paid leave from work when sick, working adults are placed at risk financially when they take time off to care for their own health or that of family members (8). An immediate effect is wage loss; many households, already economically unstable, cannot afford the 1 to 2 weeks of wage loss that typically occur in a given year due to illness of the wage earner and immediate family members. Long-term effects include the risk of job loss due to absence.

While companies incur some costs from providing paid sick days and supporting paid leave, they also accrue financial benefits. Firms that provide paid sick days and sick leave tend to have lower job turnover rates, lower recruitment and training costs, lower unnecessary absenteeism, and a higher level of productivity than firms that do not offer these benefits (17, 18). This occurs because individuals who are ill cannot work at full capacity, and thus output and production are reduced (19). When workers do not take time off to address illnesses at their onset, they often end up taking longer absences as conditions worsen (20). Moreover, when employees come to work with contagious illnesses, they spread them to coworkers, thereby increasing the pool of absent or low-productivity workers.

While the value of paid sick days and sick leave is clear, how universally available they are has been less well documented. This study analyzes paid sick day and paid sick leave policies in 22 countries that are highly ranked according to the United Nations Human Development Index (HDI).

METHODS

Study Sample

Our sample consists of the top 22 countries as ranked by the 2008 HDI, an index that summarizes a nation's progress in terms of standard of living, calculated using GDP (gross domestic product) per capita; health, measured in terms of life expectancy; and human development, quantified using literacy and enrollment rates (21). The HDI is calculated yearly by the United Nations for 177 countries and areas with sufficient data, and is reported in their annual "Human Development Reports." The top 22 countries in the 2008 report, with an HDI of at least 0.94, are: Australia, Austria, Belgium, Canada, Denmark, Finland, France, Germany, Greece, Iceland, Ireland, Italy, Japan, Luxembourg, Netherlands, New Zealand, Norway, Spain, Sweden, Switzerland, the United Kingdom, and the United States (22).

Data Sources

To assess each country's current paid sick day and paid sick leave policies, we reviewed a range of primary and, where necessary, secondary sources. Our primary sources were original labor codes and other labor-related legislation. The vast majority of the legislation reviewed was accessed through NATLEX, a global database of labor, social security, and human rights legislation maintained by the International Labor Organization (ILO). We also reviewed legislation, labor codes, and official summaries of the main features of leave laws located on national government websites, as well as summaries posted by well-respected international organizations including the ILO, the Organization for Economic Cooperation and Development (OECD), the European Union, and the United States Social Security Administration (which produces the "Social Security Systems Throughout the World" country reports). We also consulted a small number of academic studies. To the best of our knowledge, the policies described here are those in effect in each country at the beginning of 2009. Further information on sources and details is available upon request and in our earlier publication (23).

In most cases, we assessed national paid sick day and paid sick leave policies. In the few countries where no national policy exists, either because the country has not passed national paid sick days or leave legislation or because labor policy is under provincial or state jurisdiction, we examined policies in place at the relevant subnational level. As with national policies, our primary source was original labor-related legislation. Furthermore, our dataset includes only nationally or subnationally guaranteed sick day and sick leave provisions, and excludes voluntary employer policies and collectively bargained agreements covering paid sick days and sick leave.

Definitions

We use the term "paid sick days" to refer to short-term leave for health care appointments, short-term illnesses and injuries, and periodic short-term health needs related to chronic health conditions. The term "paid sick leave" is used to refer to longer-term medical leave needed to address serious health conditions that require lengthier treatment and recovery periods. We use the term "paid sick days and leave" to refer to both of these policies together.

Policies covering short-term illnesses are complex and differ widely across the countries we examine. To simplify our presentation of national laws and to allow an assessment of the adequacy of each nation's policy to address a range of health issues a worker might face, we concentrate on how national paid sick day and paid sick leave policies affect workers in two distinct situations. We first look at the support available to a worker suffering from the flu who must miss 5 days of work, and then what is available to a worker with a more serious illness, such as cancer, who must undergo a treatment that requires a 50-day absence from work.

Standardized Paid Sick Days and Leave

In order to enable accurate comparisons of the benefits available to workers across countries with different numbers of days, weeks, or months of paid time off, as well as different wage replacement rates during this time, we standardize leave duration by calculating the full-time equivalent (FTE) number of days available to workers in each country. In short, the amount of full-time equivalent paid sick days and leave is calculated as the number of days of paid time off multiplied by the wage replacement rate, or the percentage of total wage or salary that the worker is paid during his or her absence from work. For example, if a country requires employers to compensate sick workers with full pay for 5 days, the full-time equivalent duration of leave would be 5 days. If a country withholds payment for the first day, but mandates that the following 4 days be compensated at 100 percent, then the full-time equivalent duration would be 4 days. If 70 percent of pay is guaranteed for 5 days, then the number of FTE sick days would be 3.5.

To facilitate the discussion of leave duration, leave in each country is standardized to a single time unit of "working days." We assume that there are 5 working days per week except when legislation specifies otherwise. In countries where a social insurance fund provides sickness benefits on a calendar-day basis, we convert the benefits into working days. For example, if a worker is paid a daily sickness benefit of $100 per day for a calendar week, the worker would receive a total of $700 in sickness benefits per week. Accordingly, when determining full-time equivalent paid sick days, we calculate that the worker receives $140 of sickness benefits per working day ($700 divided by 5 working days).

Some countries provide paid sick days and paid sick leave at the same rate to all workers, while others seek to save money by capping payments for sick days and leave. In these countries, lower paid workers receive a greater percentage of their earnings than higher paid workers, and thus a greater FTE duration of paid leave. To represent these policies and provide a more complete picture of the generosity of benefits for a greater range of workers, we estimate and display the number of paid sick days that an average worker with median earnings and a low-wage worker with half of median earnings would receive.

When calculating FTE paid sick days for workers whose earnings are at the national median, we made a few decisions to simplify and standardize our calculations. In the absence of internationally comparable recent data on median national earnings, we use internationally comparable data from the OECD on mean wages for 2005 (24), which we adjust in two ways. We increase the mean wage by the wage growth rate from 2005 to 2008 in each country, using OECD data (25, Annex Table 11). We then multiply these estimated 2008 mean wage rates by 0.85 to create estimated 2008 median national earnings levels in national currencies (26).

If benefits provided through a social insurance program are paid only after a waiting period and take effect after an initial employer-financed leave, we assume that the waiting period for social insurance benefits occurs during the initial employer-mandated period.

We estimate FTE paid sick days for a worker with the following characteristics that sometimes determine the level of benefits available: the worker has been with the same employer for 6 months, as eligibility and/or benefit levels sometimes depend on employment history or tenure with the current employer; he or she works full-time, as in some cases benefits vary according to the number of hours worked; his or her workplace has 25 or more employees, as regulations may vary according to company size; and the worker has two dependents, as there are cases in which benefit levels increase with the number of dependents.

RESULTS

Models of Sick Day and Sick Leave Provision

The 22 countries studied use various means to support employed adults while they are unable to work. Some require employers to provide pay while their workers are out sick (Australia, Netherlands, New Zealand, Switzerland, and the United Kingdom); others operate social insurance systems whereby the government covers sick pay using tax revenues (Canada, France, Ireland, Italy, and Japan). Most countries use a combination of employer mandates and social insurance (Austria, Belgium, Denmark, Finland, Germany, Greece, Iceland, Luxembourg, Norway, Spain, and Sweden). Some national systems include an initial waiting period of unpaid leave, ranging from 1 to 14 days, before mandatory employer or government-insured paid sick days or paid sick leave take effect. The share of usual earnings that are replaced during paid sick days and leave also varies substantially among countries. Table 1 (pp. 160–162) outlines the main features of national systems, and Table 2 (pp. 164–166) summarizes the financial support provided to workers during their absence from work.

*Comparison of Generosity of Sick Days
and Sick Leave Benefits*

Five-Day Flu. We first analyze the total full-time equivalent pay the median-wage worker receives if he or she is out of work for 5 days with the flu. Figure 1 (page 167) shows the portion of a median-wage worker's earnings that is replaced by the national paid sick day system in each country over a 5-day absence.

National Policies. U.S. federal law provides no financial support for a worker with a 5-day flu. Canada and Japan are the only other countries of the 22 analyzed here that have no mandated support for workers at the national level. Japanese law provides paid sick days for "serious" illnesses (lasting up to 18 months), but Figure 1 assumes that many cases of the 5-day flu would not meet the serious illness standard. In Canada, decisions regarding job protection for short-term sick leave are made at a provincial level, though long-term illness insurance is provided nationally and described below (27).

Eleven countries—Australia, Austria, Belgium, Denmark, Finland, Germany, Iceland, Luxembourg, New Zealand, Norway, and Switzerland—provide the median-wage worker with full pay while recovering from a 5-day illness. In Greece and the Netherlands, workers receive the full-time equivalent of 3.5 days of pay when they are out sick for 5 consecutive days; in the Netherlands, workers receive 70 percent of pay from the first day of illness, while in Greece, workers receive 50 percent of pay for the first 3 days and full pay for the last 2 days. In Sweden, paid sick days cover 3.2 FTE days of pay during a 5-day illness; workers are entitled to receive 80 percent of wages, but there is no legal guarantee of payment for the first sick day.

Workers are guaranteed fewer FTE sick days in the rest of the countries: Spain provides 1.2 FTE days out of 5, France provides 1, Ireland guarantees 0.7, and the United Kingdom provides 0.4 FTE sick days. Benefits are less generous in these countries primarily because they provide no legal guarantees of pay during the first 3 days of illness-related absences. However, as Figure 2 (page 168) shows, for low-wage workers earning half the median national earnings, the full-time equivalent benefits are more generous in Ireland (rising from 0.7 to 1.5 paid FTE days) and the United Kingdom (increasing from 0.4 to 0.8 FTE days).

Table 1

Main features of national paid sick day and paid sick leave systems in 22 high-HDI countries

Country	Source of payment		Minimum job tenure requirement			Benefit variations[a]
	5-day flu	50-day cancer treatment	5-day flu	50-day cancer treatment		
Australia	E	E	None	None		None
Austria	E	E & SI	None	None		Payment amount depends on job tenure after 5 yrs of service
Belgium	E (white-collar)	E & SI	None	120 hrs in 6 months immediately prior to illness (SI)		None
Canada	None	SI	N.A.	600 hrs work in the last 52 wks or since last claim		None
Denmark	E (private sector); SI if not E	E & SI	72 hrs during 8 wks of service (private sector)	120 hrs in 13 wks immediately prior to illness		None
Finland	E	E & SI		1 month		50% if less than 1 month tenure (E); amount of SI benefits varies by income
France	SI	SI		800 hrs in preceding 12 months (200 hrs of which in first 3 months)		If employed for less than 12 months (200 hrs in the preceding 3 months), benefits paid for 6 months

Germany	E	E & SI		4 wks of service	None
Greece	E-SI (50:50)	E & SI		1 yr of service	If less than 1 yr tenure 100% pay for 2 wks only; duration of benefits thereafter depends on insurance contributions[b]
Iceland	E	E & SI	1 month	1 month (E); 2 months (SI)	Duration of payment depends on job tenure
Ireland	SI	SI		104 wks of insurance contributions	Duration of payment depends on insurance contributions; amount of payment depends on income
Italy	SI	SI	None	None	None
Japan	None	SI	N.A.	2 months of service	None
Luxembourg	E (SI refunds 80%)	E (SI refunds 80%)	None	None	None
Netherlands	E	E	None	None	None
New Zealand	E	E		6 months of service	None
Norway	E	E & SI		4 wks of service	None
Spain	E (SI refunds)	SI	None	None	None

Table continues

Table 1 (Cont'd.)

Country	Source of payment		Minimum job tenure requirement		Benefit variations[a]
	5-day flu	50-day cancer treatment	5-day flu	50-day cancer treatment	
Sweden	E	SI	1 month of service or 14 consecutive days of work before illness		None
Switzerland	E	E	3 months of service		Payment amount depends on job tenure
United Kingdom	E	E	None		SI benefit amounts depend on phase of sickness assessment and age
United States	None	None	N.A.	N.A.	None

Source: See Rho et al. (23) for specific sources of data for each country.

Note: HDI, Human Development Index; E, employer-sponsored paid sick days; SI, social insurance.

[a] See Rho et al. (23) for more details on benefit variations for each country.

[b] Insurance contribution and tenure requirements are two separate cases. A worker with 1 month of employment with the same employer, for example, may have more than 1 month of insurance contributions due to prior employment.

Subnational Policies. Of the three countries with no national paid sick day or paid sick leave policy—Japan, the United States, and Canada—only Canada provides job protection for most citizens at the subnational level.[2]

In the United States, while labor policy can be passed at both federal and state levels, there are no paid sick days mandated at either level. Sick day guarantees exist at the municipal level in only three U.S. cities: Milwaukee, San Francisco, and Washington, DC. For a 5-day flu, our representative worker, with 6 months of job experience in a firm of 25 employees, would receive full pay in Milwaukee and San Francisco. Since Washington, DC, requires that a worker have 1 year of tenure with the same employer, a worker with only 6 months of tenure would not be eligible for paid sick days under the Washington, DC, legislation.[3]

In Canada, decisions regarding job protection are made at a provincial level due to the federal division of powers; the only federal sick leave policy provides insurance for long-term, serious illnesses. No provinces or territories guarantee paid short-term leave for personal health needs. Most jurisdictions guarantee unpaid job-protected leave. Saskatchewan, Quebec, and federally regulated industries guarantee job protection for sick leave for over 12 days. In Ontario, employees in companies with 50 or more employees are guaranteed up to 10 days of unpaid, job-protected leave. Newfoundland and Labrador provide 7 days of job protection, New Brunswick and the Northwest Territories provide 5 days, and Prince Edward Island and Manitoba provide 3 days. In Alberta, British Columbia, Nova Scotia, and Nunavut, no job-protected sick days are guaranteed (27).

Fifty-Day Cancer Treatment

National Policies. In our second policy experiment, we tally the full-time equivalent pay the same worker receives if he or she is out of work for 50 days while undergoing treatment for an illness such as cancer. The full-time equivalent benefits paid to a worker who is absent from work for 50 working days are summarized in Figure 1. In this case, the United States is the only country that has no guaranteed paid sick leave. Luxembourg and Norway provide full pay

---

[2] Japan has a unitary, not a federal system, with labor policy generally being made at the national level.

[3] Employees must have worked one full year and at least 1,000 hours during the 12-month period prior to illness before being eligible for paid sick days. In addition, the Washington, DC, law explicitly excludes "health care workers who choose to participate in a premium program" and "restaurant wait staff and bartenders who work for a combination of wages and tips" (28). The accrual rate and the annual maximum paid sick days also vary by firm size, with small employers required to provide fewer paid sick days than larger employers. Businesses with fewer than 25 employees are required to provide 3 paid sick days; those with 25 to 99 employees, 5 days; and those with 100 or more employees, 7 days.

Table 2

Financial supports in national paid sick days and paid sick leave systems in 22 high-HDI countries

Country	Sickness pay	Social insurance benefit ceiling	Waiting period (calendar days)
Australia	10 days (100%, E)	None	0
Austria	6 wks (100%, E), additional 4 wks (50%, E) (25%, SI); SI benefits continue for 52 wks (50%, 60% after 6 wks)	€3,930 per month	0 (E); 3 (SI)
Belgium	1 month for white-collar workers (100%, E), 7 days for manual workers (100%, E) up to 2 wks (60% plus supplemental, E); if still ill, up to 1 yr (60%, SI)	€112.87 per day	0 (E); 1 (SI)
Canada	12 wks of job protection (unpaid); 15 wks (55%, SI)	CAD $42,300 per yr	14 (SI)
Denmark	2 wks for private sector (100%, E) reimbursed by SI for 2 more wks); if still ill, 52 wks in an 18-month period (61.7%, SI)	DKK 3,515 per a 37-hr work week	0
Finland	First 9 days (100%, E); if still ill, 300 days in a 2-yr period, excluding Sundays (92.7%, SI)	70% × 1/300 earnings for low earners; €66.27 plus 40% × 1/300 earnings for median earners	0
France	12 months in a 3-yr period (50%, SI)	€47.65 per day	3 (SI)
Germany	6 wks (100%, E); if still ill, 78 wks in a 3-yr period (70%, SI)	Up to 90% of net salary	0

Country			
Greece	2 wks (100%, E & SI) (50%, E during waiting period); if still ill, from 180 to 720 days (50.5%, SI)	€15.68 per day for first 15 days, €28.81 thereafter	0 (E); 3 (SI)
Iceland	12 days per yr (100%, E); from 15th day (if illness lasted >20 days), up to 52 wks in a 2-yr period (ISK 1,000 plus twice the 270 for 2 dependents, 13.5%, SI)	Flat rate of ISK 1,000 per day	0 (E); 14 (SI)
Ireland	Up to 52 wks (36.6%, SI)	Flat rate of €204.30 per wk	3 (SI)
Italy	First 20 days (50%, SI); from 21st day, up to 180 days (66.7%, SI)	None	3 (SI)
Japan	Up to 18 months (60%, SI, serious illness only)	None	3 (SI)
Luxembourg	First 77 days (100%, E (80% reimbursed by SI)) until the end of the month during which the 77th day occurs	None	0
Netherlands	2 yrs (70%, E), min. wage not guaranteed in the 2nd yr	None	0
New Zealand	5 days in a 12-month period (100%, E)	None	0
Norway	16 calendar days (100%, E); if still ill, up to 52 wks (100%, SI)	None	0
Spain	First 16 days (60%, SI refunds E); from 16th to 20th day (60%, SI); 21st day up to 12 months (75%, SI), extension up to 18 months	75% of earnings up to €3,074.10 per month	3 (SI)

Table *continues*

Table 2 (Cont'd.)

Country	Sickness pay	Social insurance benefit ceiling	Waiting period (calendar days)
Sweden	First 14 days (80%, E); if still ill, up to 364 days over a 15-month period (80%, SI); extension possible up to 550 days (75%, SI); for more serious illness, no formal max. (70%, SI)	SEK 321,000 per yr	1 (E); 0 (SI)
Switzerland	3 wks (100%, E)	None	0
United Kingdom	Up to 28 wks (£75.40, 20.3%, E); if still ill, 13 wks of assessment phase and additional periods of main phase (SI)	Flat rate of £75.40 per wk for 28 wks	3 (E); 3 (SI)
United States	None	N.A.	N.A.

Source: See Rho et al. (23) for specific sources of data for each country.

Note: Data are for full-time worker with 6 months or more job tenure and national median earnings (and, where relevant, with two dependents). Per-year basis if not noted otherwise. For Denmark, Finland, Greece, and Iceland, we use the 2005 average worker earnings; for Ireland, average production worker earnings, as specified by OECD (24, p. 185); for United Kingdom, 2008 weekly median wage (retrieved from U.K. Office for National Statistics) to calculate full-time equivalent wage replacement rate. In Australia, Finland, France, Greece, Ireland, Switzerland, and United Kingdom, amounts of benefits vary by job tenure, insurance contributions, income, or age. See Table 1. HDI, Human Development Index; E, employer-sponsored paid sick days; SI, social insurance.

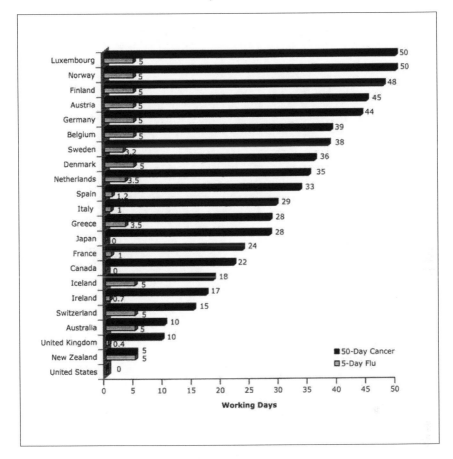

Figure 1. Paid sick days and sick leave in 22 countries, worker at median earnings, full-time equivalent working days. For full-time worker with 6 months or more job tenure, earning the national median, and, where relevant, with two dependents. *Sources:* See Methods section for more information on calculating FTE paid sick days. See Rho et al. (23) for specific sources of data for each country. (*Note:* "50-Day Cancer" indicates days of treatment.)

for the 50 missed days. Three countries mandate more than 40 FTE days of paid leave: Finland, Austria, and Germany. Ten countries guarantee between 20 and 40 days of full-time equivalent leave: Belgium, Sweden, Denmark, the Netherlands, Spain, Italy, Greece, Japan, France, and Canada. The rest mandate at least 5 days: Iceland, Ireland, Switzerland, Australia, the United Kingdom, and New Zealand. In most countries, the costs of paid long-term sick leave are covered by government social insurance programs rather than employer mandates

(23). In Canada, under the National Employment Insurance, employees who have worked for 600 hours in the last year receive up to 15 weeks of benefits after a 2-week unpaid waiting period, paid at 55 percent of earnings up to a weekly maximum.

In 6 countries, paid sick leave available to low-wage workers is even more generous than that available to the median-wage worker (see Figure 2). A low-wage worker earning half of the national median and facing a 50-day absence

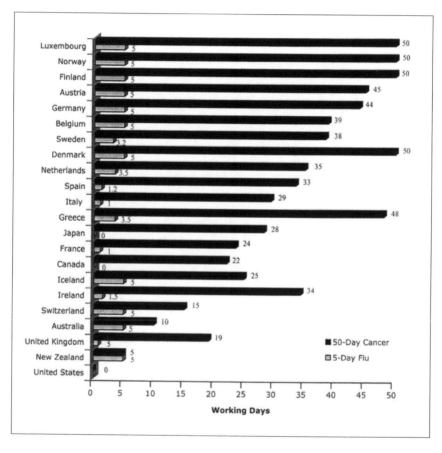

Figure 2. Paid sick days and sick leave in 22 countries, worker at half the median earnings, full-time equivalent working days. For full-time worker with 6 months or more job tenure, earning half the national median, and, where relevant, with two dependents. *Sources:* See Methods section for more information on calculating FTE paid sick days. See Rho et al. (23) for specific sources of data for each country. (*Note:* "50-Day Cancer" indicates days of treatment.)

from work receives 50 FTE days of paid leave in Greece and Denmark, while the median-wage worker receives 28 FTE days in Greece and 36 in Denmark. In Ireland, a low-wage worker is entitled to 34 FTE days of leave, compared with 17 for a worker with median earnings; in Iceland, a low-wage worker receives 25 FTE days, compared with 18 for the median-wage worker; in the United Kingdom, 19 days are available to low-wage workers, compared with 10 for workers at the median wage level. In Finland, though benefits are high for all workers, low-wage workers still have a small advantage (50 FTE days compared with 48).

Subnational Policies. In the only country with no federal paid sick leave policy for a 50-day cancer treatment, the United States, subnational legislation is also limited. Forty-five of the 50 states have passed no statewide sick leave legislation and the 5 states that have done so passed temporary disability legislation that ensures pay during absences only for long-term illnesses. Benefits are paid at varying wage replacement rates for 26 weeks in Hawaii, New Jersey, and New York, 30 weeks in Rhode Island, and 52 weeks in California, each with a 7-day waiting period. Except for Rhode Island, wages are replaced at between 50 and 67 percent of wages, up to a ceiling. Three of these states provide approximately 6 weeks of full-time equivalent pay for a worker who misses 50 days of work due to illness: New Jersey (31 FTE days), California (29 FTE days), and Hawaii (28 FTE days). New York provides almost 11 days of full-time equivalent pay for a 50-day absence. Rhode Island's system grants 30 weeks of coverage, but at much lower benefit rates.[4] As a result, the state's system covers only about 3 days of full-time equivalent earnings over a 50-work-day illness.

DISCUSSION

Everyone is vulnerable to illness and injury. Unlike most of the world's successful nations, the United States does not guarantee that workers receive paid sick days or paid sick leave. The only other wealthy countries that do not provide paid sick days for workers who need to miss work for 5 days to recover from a minor illness are Canada and Japan; in Canada, where labor policy is made at the provincial level, most provinces provide job-protected leave for short-term illnesses. Moreover, the United States stands alone as the only country that does not guarantee paid sick leave for a worker undergoing a 50-day treatment for a more serious illness. Fifteen countries provide at least 20 full-time equivalent days of leave in this case, and 2 of these countries, Luxembourg and Norway, provide

---

[4] In Rhode Island, workers receive 4.62 percent of their wages in their highest quarter, up to 85 percent of the state's average weekly wage in the preceding calendar year, plus the greater of $10 or 7 percent of benefit rate for each dependent up to 5 in all. The wage amount replaced per week ranges between $69 and $671.

full pay for the entire 50-day duration of leave. Even New Zealand and Australia, often highlighted for their limited policies, provide 5 and 10 FTE days, respectively. A number of countries are more generous toward low-wage workers than median-wage workers in terms of leave policy.

While the rest of the world's affluent countries have taken a legislative approach to ensuring paid sick days and leave, the United States relies on voluntary employer policies to provide paid sick days to employees with short-term illnesses. As a result, at least 40 percent of the formal private sector workforce in the United States does not have paid sick days or leave.[5] In addition to these 49 million private sector workers without coverage, some public employees, many agricultural workers, nearly all household employees, and most of the self-employed lack paid sick days and leave. If these groups were to be included in estimates of American workers lacking coverage, these estimates would clearly increase significantly.

Low-wage and part-time workers, who are disproportionately women, are especially likely to lack paid sick days and leave. For example, fewer than a quarter (23%) of private sector workers in the bottom 10 percent of the wage distribution for their occupation have access to paid sick days or leave, compared with more than 83 percent of workers in the top 10 percent of their occupational wage distribution. Only 27 percent of part-time private sector workers have paid sick days or leave, compared with 71 percent of full-timers. Private sector workers in small establishments are also less likely than workers in larger establishments to have paid sick days or leave. At companies with fewer than 50 employees, for example, only about half of workers have paid sick days or leave, compared with 78 percent at companies with 500 or more employees (1, 30–33).

In short, the existing patchwork of employer policies and state and local legislation in the United States leaves many working adults without paid sick days or leave, whether they need time to recover from a short-term, viral illness or from a heart attack. As a result, each year, tens of millions of American workers either go to work sick, lowering their own productivity and that of their coworkers and potentially spreading illness to their coworkers and

---

[5] According to the most recent available data from the Bureau of Labor Statistics' National Compensation Survey (NCS) (covering March 2008), 39 percent of private sector workers in the United States have no paid sick days or leave (29). These estimates, however, almost certainly understate the fraction of private sector workers without paid sick days, because they do not take into account that some workers in jobs that technically receive paid sick days have not worked for the employer long enough to meet the tenure requirement for eligibility. If the coverage estimates are adjusted downward based on Lovell's parallel calculation using 2006 data (30), coverage is reduced by about 4 percentage points. If we add these 4 percentage points to the 39 percent noncoverage rate from the raw NCS data, the share of private sector workers without paid sick days rises to 43 percent.

customers, or stay home, risking pay and job loss. Governments in virtually all other wealthy nations have spared their citizens this choice, and the United States can do the same.

With the proven health benefits of paid sick days and leave and the enormous fraction of the population lacking access to it, why has there been resistance to legislation guaranteeing paid sick days in the United States? Concerns have focused on the cost and economic feasibility of such a policy. However, with the exception of the United States and South Korea, all of the 20 most competitive countries as ranked by the World Economic Forum guarantee paid sick days, and the overwhelming majority provide 31 days or more annually, far more than the 5 to 9 days often proposed in U.S. legislation. In our recent research, we used global data on more than 100 nations to examine whether there was any relationship between the availability of paid sick leave policies and national unemployment rates, as well as economic competitiveness, and we found none (2). Our study examining the duration of paid sick days and leave and national unemployment rates in the same 22 countries discussed in this chapter also found no statistically significant relationship between them (34).

While the evidence suggests that guaranteeing paid sick days and leave is economically feasible, it is valuable for policymakers to consider the advantages of particular approaches to financing and delivering this leave. As shown in Table 2, the approaches taken to providing paid sick leave for working families vary widely, ranging from a solely employer-based payment and administration model to a social security system that provides compensation during time off from work due to illness. Some countries use a combination of these approaches, using social security benefits to either supplement or follow employer-sponsored benefits. In the case of a 50-day absence from work, most countries cover the cost of long-term paid leave through government social insurance programs rather than employer mandates (23).

A two-stage model, whereby employers are required to pay wages for a short initial period of leave, after which time a social insurance system takes responsibility for payment if the worker is still ill or disabled, has several advantages. Keeping the employer-liability period reasonably short, at 7 to 10 days, minimizes the administrative cost of short-term leave and allows employers to reimburse wages at a higher rate. If long-term leave is required, a social insurance program, funded by contributions from workers, employers, and the government, spreads the larger costs of leave across society and ensures that benefits can cover a longer period of time.

While nearly all countries offer more paid sick days than the United States, those with waiting periods before payments begin remain at risk of increased disease spread. Workers are likely to be reluctant to stay home when sick if there are unpaid waiting periods before compensation begins. Providing adequate paid sick days to address short-term contagious illnesses is a low-cost way to improve health and decrease disease spread. Improvements should be considered particularly by Canada, France, Ireland, Italy, Japan, Spain, and the United Kingdom, all of which offer less than 2 days of pay for a 5-day flu.

Finally, long-term illnesses present a serious financial threat to individuals and families who do not have access to paid sick leave, and this is a leading cause of bankruptcy, home loss, and destitution. While the situation is worst in the United States because of the complete lack of paid sick leave legislation, individuals and families are also threatened in the handful of other countries with very limited sick leave. Though the majority of high-income countries provide substantial paid leave for serious illnesses and have demonstrated its economic feasibility, others still lag behind. It is important that paid leave be extended in nations such as Australia, New Zealand, Switzerland, and the United Kingdom in order to adequately protect workers suffering from serious illnesses that require longer-term absences from work.

REFERENCES

1. Lovell, V. *No Time to Be Sick: Why Everyone Suffers When Workers Don't Have Paid Sick Leave.* IWPR Publication No. B242. Institute for Women's Policy Research, Washington, DC, 2004. www.iwpr.org/pdf/B242.pdf.
2. Earle, A., and Heymann, J. A comparative analysis of paid leave for the health needs of workers and their families around the world. *J. Comp. Policy Anal.* 8(3):241–257, 2006.
3. Skatun, J. D. Take some days off, why don't you? Endogenous sick leave and pay. *J. Health Econ.* 22(3):379–402, 2003.
4. Centers for Disease Control and Prevention. Key Facts about Influenza and the Influenza Vaccine. 2006. www.cdc.gov/flu/keyfacts.htm.
5. Centers for Disease Control and Prevention. Good Health Habits for Preventing the Flu. 2006. www.cdc.gov/flu/protect/habits.htm.
6. Smith, T. W. *Paid Sick Days: A Basic Labor Standard for the 21st Century.* Public Welfare Foundation, Washington, DC, 2008.
7. Silberner, J. Why do sick people go to work? Unhealthy fear. *Morning Edition,* National Public Radio, June 28, 2008. www.npr.org/templates/story/story.php?storyId=92762761.
8. Heymann, S. J. *The Widening Gap: Why American Families Are in Jeopardy and What Can Be Done about It.* Basic Books, New York, 2000.
9. Heymann S. J., Toomey, S., and Furstenberg, F. Working parents: What factors are involved in their ability to take time off from work when their children are sick? *Arch. Pediatr. Adolesc. Med.* 153(8):870–874, 1999.
10. Heymann, S. J., Vo, P. H., and Bergstrom, C. A. Child care providers' experiences caring for sick children: Implications for public policy. *Early Child Dev. Care* 172(1):1–8, 2002.
11. Bennet, S. J. Relationships among selected antecedent variables and coping effectiveness in postmyocardial infarction patients. *Res. Nurs. Health* 16:131–139, 1993.
12. Gorkin, L., et al. Psychosocial predictors of mortality in the Cardiac Arrhythmia Suppression Trial-1 (CAST-1). *Am. J. Cardiol.* 71:263–267, 1993.

13. Tsouna-Hadjis, E., et al. First-stroke recovery process: The role of family support. *Arch. Phys. Med. Rehabil.* 81:881–887, 2000.
14. Berkman, L. F. The role of social relations in health promotion. *Psychosom. Med.* 57:245–254, 1995.
15. Seeman, T. E. Health promoting effects of friends and family on health outcomes in older adults. *Am. J. Health Promot.* 14:362–370, 2000.
16. Li, J., et al. Impact of institution size, staffing patterns, and infection control practices on communicable disease outbreaks in New York State nursing homes. *Am. J. Epidemiol.* 143:1042–1049, 1996.
17. Levin-Epstein, J. *Responsive Workplaces: The Business Case for Employment That Values Fairness and Families.* Center for Law and Social Policy, Washington, DC, 2007. www.nationalpartnership.org/site/DocServer/CLASP_Responsive_Workplaces.pdf?docID=2082.
18. Lovell, V. *Valuing Good Health: An Estimate of Costs and Savings for the Healthy Families Act.* Institute for Women's Policy Research, Washington, DC, 2005. www.iwpr.org/pdf/B248.pdf.
19. CCH Incorporated. Unscheduled employee absenteeism hits lowest point in CCH survey history. *Hum. Resources Manage. Trends. Spec. Issue* 569(Oct.):155-164, 2003.
20. Grinyer, A., and Singleton, V. Sickness absence as risk-taking behavior: A study of organizational and cultural factors in the public sector. *Health Risk Society* 2:7–21, 2000.
21. U.N. Development Programme, Human Development Reports. *What Is Human Development Index (HDI)?* Human Development Report Office, New York, n.d. http://hdr.undp.org/en/statistics/faq/question,68,en.html.
22. U.N. Development Programme, Human Development Reports. *Human Development Indices: A Statistical Update 2008.* Human Development Report Office, New York, 2008. http://hdr.undp.org/en/media/HDI_2008_EN_Complete.pdf.
23. Rho, H. J., et al. *A Review of Sickness-Related Leave in 22 High Human Development Index Countries.* Center for Economic and Policy Research Briefing Paper. CEPR, Washington, DC, 2009.
24. Organization for Economic Co-operation and Development. *Benefits and Wages 2007: OECD Indicators.* Paris, 2007.
25. Organization for Economic Co-operation and Development. *OECD Economic Outlook*, Vol. 2, No. 84. Paris, December 2008.
26. Center for Economic and Policy Research. *Extracts of Current Population Survey Outgoing Rotation Group*, Version 1.4. Washington, DC, 2009. www.ceprdata.org/cps/org_index.phpl.
27. Chaussard, M., Gerecke, M., and Heymann, J. *The Work Equity Canada Index: Where the Provinces Stand.* Institute for Health and Social Policy, McGill University, Montreal, 2008.
28. Council of the District of Columbia. Accrued safe and sick leave. In *District of Columbia Register*, Vol. 55, No. 51. Department of Employment Services, Washington, DC, 2008. http://does.dc.gov/does/frames.asp?doc=/does/lib/does/Accrued_Sick_and_Safe_Notice_of_Proposed_Rulemaking.pdf.
29. Kramer, N., and Zilberman, A. New Definitions of Employee Access to Paid Sick Leave and Retirement Benefits in the National Compensation Survey. 2008. www.bls.gov/opub/cwc/cm20081219ar01p1.htm (accessed March 25, 2009).

30. Hartmann, H. I. The Healthy Families Act: Impacts on Workers, Businesses, the Economy, and Public Health. Testimony before the U.S. Senate Committee on Health, Education, Labor, and Pensions, February 13, 2007. www.iwpr.org/pdf/Hartmann_HFA_testimony021307.pdf.

31. Clemans-Cope, L., et al. Access to and use of paid sick leave among low-income families with children. *Pediatrics* 122(2):480–486, 2008.

32. National Partnership for Women and Families. *Get Well Soon: Americans Can't Afford to Be Sick.* Washington, DC, June 2004. www.nationalpartnership.org/site/DocServer/GetWellSoonReport.pdf?docID=342.

33. Phillips, K. R. *Getting Time Off: Access to Leave among Working Parents.* New Federalism Series B, No. B-57. Urban Institute, Washington, DC, April 2004.

34. Schmitt, J., et al. *Paid Sick Days Doesn't Cause Unemployment.* Center for Economic and Policy Research Briefing Paper. CEPR, Washington, DC, June 2009.

CHAPTER 10

Overstretched and Unreciprocated Commitment: Reviewing Research on the Occupational Health and Safety Effects of Downsizing and Job Insecurity

Michael Quinlan and Philip Bohle

Over the past two decades, a leading business practice has been often-repeated rounds of downsizing and restructuring (also referred to as reorganization, re-engineering, and a host of other euphemistic terms) by large private and public sector employers. Frequently associated with other practices such as outsourcing, privatization, and the increased use of temporary workers, downsizing/restructuring has increased the level of job insecurity among workers and led to changes in work processes (including work intensification and multi-tasking) and management behavior. How have downsizing/ restructuring and increased job insecurity affected the occupational health, safety, and well-being of workers, and what measures have employers, unions, and governments taken to address any adverse effects? The authors reviewed international studies of the occupational health and safety (OHS) effects of downsizing/restructuring and increased job insecurity undertaken over the past 20 years. After imposing quality filters, they obtained 86 studies. Analysis revealed that 73 (85%) of the studies found poorer OHS outcomes (using a range of measures). Studies were examined to see whether they provided clues as to the reasons for negative outcomes.

*****

Since the early 1970s there have been major changes in employer practices affecting the organization of work in both developed and developing countries. One of these changes has been often-repeated rounds of downsizing and restructuring (also referred to as reorganization, re-engineering, and a host of other euphemistic terms) by large private and public sector employers. Frequently associated with other practices such as outsourcing, privatization, and the increased use of temporary workers, downsizing/restructuring has increased the level of job insecurity among workers and led to changes in work processes (including work intensification and multi-tasking) and in management behavior. Although organizational restructuring is not a new phenomenon, unlike subcontracting and home-based work it was not historically linked to occupational health and safety (OHS) problems. The objective of this chapter is to review and evaluate international research into the OHS effects of downsizing and job insecurity undertaken in the past 20 years. The chapter does not consider how policymakers and regulators have responded to mounting evidence on the adverse OHS effects of downsizing and job insecurity. The social costs of ignoring work quality in favor of untrammeled labor market flexibility remain unabated. At best, regulatory regimes address a few symptoms of these problems (1). This disarticulation between evidence and policy requires urgent attention.

The OHS effects of downsizing and job insecurity need to be viewed within a broader debate about the global health impacts of precarious employment. There is now a substantial and growing body of research on the OHS effects of downsizing/job insecurity and contingent work arrangements (such as the use of temporary workers). Almost eight years ago (2), we undertook a review of this research both in aggregate terms and according to a number of categories (downsizing/job insecurity, temporary employment, subcontracting/home-based work, part-time work, and small business). We found that more than 80 percent of the 93 studies identified found adverse effects on OHS, with these findings carrying over to all categories, apart from temporary employment (for which the weight of adverse results was less pronounced) and part-time work (for which the small number of studies largely revealed positive results). A review of job insecurity research published shortly after our own review found broadly similar results (2a).

The present study seeks to extend our understanding of the OHS effects of downsizing and job insecurity and add to a subsequent review of research into subcontracting and home-based work (3). The current review is not simply an update of the 2001 report. In this review we imposed quality and double-counting filters so that the reviewed studies were robust and we did not count the same data source twice.

METHODS

To systematically review the available evidence, we compiled a database of published research on the OHS effects of contingent work and job insecurity. At the time of this review, the database contained more than 190 studies published between 1966 and 2007. The studies were identified through searches of online bibliographic databases and citation indexes (such as Medline, the Social Science Citation Index, and the Science Citation Index), manual searches of relevant journals, and tracking of cited references, including references from an early review by Platt and coauthors (4). The vast majority of the studies that we identified appeared in refereed journals, but some were published as chapters in scholarly books or as research reports.

The dataset of published research from which this review is drawn is not simply an updated version of the original dataset (including both more recent studies and earlier studies missed in the original review) but incorporates several other differences. First, and most notably, unlike the first review we filtered studies on the basis of their methodological quality (the paper must have been refereed, and must have used clearly identifiable data and robust research methods) and adopted the conservative approach of counting studies based on the same dataset only once. When assessing research design and methodology, we applied criteria appropriate to the nature of the research conducted. Thus, for quantitative studies, the sample size, sampling method, and adequacy of controls or benchmark data were examined, while for longitudinal studies, the participant attrition rate or sampling consistency across waves of data collection was also considered. For qualitative studies, we examined the apparent rigor of data collection and interpretation and also the depth to which issues related to contingent work or job insecurity were investigated. For all studies, we required that the methods employed be described in sufficient detail to allow us to decide whether the above criteria were met. The original review (1) identified 41 studies of downsizing and job insecurity; this review contains 86 studies (not counting 25 repeat studies included in the Appendix). The revised set includes only 21 studies from the 2001 review (not counting repeat studies included in 2001). In short, there is a substantial difference in the datasets between the 2001 and this review.

Second, we used a more discriminate approach to evaluate study findings in the current report than was used in the 2001 review. Study results were classified into three categories ("positive," "negative," or "mixed"), focusing exclusively on OHS-related outcome variables. Social, organizational, and other categories of outcomes were not evaluated. The results of a study were classified as "positive" if all findings indicated positive effects on OHS, "negative" if all findings indicated negative effects on OHS, and "mixed" if a combination of positive and negative effects was reported.

Third, for the purpose of this review, we examined only studies dealing with downsizing/restructuring and job insecurity. Downsizing and job insecurity were grouped together because there is a considerable overlap in the research literature in this regard, as well as a clear linkage in practice. "Downsizing" refers to the process in which an organization reduces the size of its workforce through a variety of processes, including voluntary and enforced redundancy, closure of worksites, and outsourcing activities. The term "downsizing" quickly acquired such negative connotations that a series of more euphemistic terms soon developed, such as "rightsizing," "reorganization," or a decision by an organization to focus on its "core activities." Other business practices such as "business process re-engineering" and the restructuring of organizations following, for example, takeovers, mergers, or private equity buyouts have invariably entailed cost-cutting measures, including staffing reductions/redeployments, new pay/ performance regimes, and increased workloads. While organizational restructuring need not necessarily entail a cut in the workforce, this was most often the case. Downsizing almost always entailed changes in work organization and work processes, as remaining staff took on bigger workloads or a wider variety of tasks (multi-tasking). The performance pressure and climate of uncertainty created by such changes have clearly contributed to job insecurity among workers, changes in worker-worker and worker-management relations, and changes in workplace behavior (including an increased focus on production/service delivery relative to other activities, such as OHS, and presenteeism). What is interesting is that, despite the overriding economic rationale for such practices (exemplified by stock market responses to such measures, CEO reward systems, and governments imposing "productivity" bonuses on their departments), some studies have indicated that, for the majority of organizations undertaking it, downsizing has not resulted in a measurable increase in productivity or financial performance—indeed, for many it has had the reverse effect (5–7).

Our review of studies of downsizing/job insecurity, temporary employment, and subcontracting/home-based work yielded 217 studies, 111 of which dealt with the OHS effects of downsizing and job insecurity (see Appendix and references 8–124). This number was further reduced to 86 studies of downsizing and job insecurity, once multiple publications based on the same dataset were excluded.

The 86 studies were conducted across a wide variety of contexts and employed a range of methodologies. As a number of studies were undertaken in multiple industries and countries, or used more than one method or indicator, the breakdowns we cite here often do not total 86. Twenty-three were conducted in the United States, 15 in Sweden, 11 in Canada, 9 in the United Kingdom, 5 in Australia, 4 in Germany, 3 each in Belgium, the Netherlands, and Norway, 2 each in Denmark and Finland, and 1 each in China, France, Japan, Israel, Italy, Poland, Spain, South Africa, Switzerland, and Taiwan. Thirty studies used population data or sampled across multiple industries. Of the industry-specific studies, 20 were in manufacturing; 15 in health care; 8 in the public sector; 4 in retail and hospitality; 4 in postal services, telecommunications, and the media; 3 in financial and personal services; 2 in transport; 1 in power generation and distribution; 1 in education; and 1 in the mining and petrochemical industry. In 4 studies the industry focus could not be identified. Six studies analyzed secondary data (3 from population data and 3 from health records in manufacturing and health care). Of those based on primary data, 42 used quantitative longitudinal designs, 33 used quantitative cross-sectional designs, and 6 used qualitative methodologies. Sixty-eight studies used subjective health measures, 24 used objective health measures, 2 used injury measures, 1 used an OHS knowledge/ compliance measure, and 3 used other measures (3 examined occupational violence, 1 examined work-life conflict). It is noteworthy that 22 (25.5%) of the studies used more than one category of outcome variable, usually a combination of subjective and objective health measures.

REVIEW OF FINDINGS AND DISCUSSION

The evidence regarding job insecurity and downsizing was remarkably consistent, with 73 studies (85%) identifying negative OHS effects, 7 (8%) finding mixed effects, 5 (5.8%) finding no effect, and only 1 (1.2%) finding a positive effect. In sum, there is now a substantial—even compelling—body of international evidence that downsizing and job insecurity have significant adverse effects on workers' health and well-being. The high proportion of negative findings carries greater weight when we consider the diversity of national jurisdictions, industry sectors, research methods, and OHS indicators encompassed by the studies. Also noteworthy is the unusual robustness of many of the research designs. Twenty-five studies were based on very large samples (>2,000), of which 15 employed longitudinal designs. Overall, just over half of the studies were longitudinal (most based on primary data).

There are other strengths in the body of research on downsizing and job insecurity. A significant number of the studies we reviewed examined gender effects. Work-family balance and relationship effects and links to burnout, as well as age-related effects, are also attracting increased attention. Existing studies have pointed to both gender and age differences in terms of the impact of downsizing (36, 61). A Swedish study (54) of repeated downsizing in the retailing industry found that older workers were more likely to experience adverse effects and long-term symptoms of distress. Other studies suggest that highly committed workers faced with restructuring/job insecurity are more likely to report distress and negative attitudes (82, 95).

Research has also begun to explore a more diverse array of health indicators and health behaviors. The review revealed few studies of impacts on infections (79)—something warranting further research given the potential for presenteeism to exacerbate risks by encouraging workers to turn up when sick. On the other hand, a still small but growing number of studies have explored the association of downsizing and job insecurity with drug and alcohol use (66, 125, 126). Although management research has linked downsizing to bullying behavior by managers (127), the implications of this for workers' health and well-being have seldom been explored.

Notwithstanding the strengths mentioned above, a number of gaps and methodological limitations are apparent. One limitation is the relatively few studies of mechanisms associated with downsizing that could adversely affect health and well-being—namely, longer hours/presenteeism and work-nonwork conflicts. More recent studies suggest this gap may be filled over time, although not enough consideration has been given to the impact of downsizing/restructuring not only on the length of working hours but also on issues of timing and predictability of shifts that can affect health and well-being.

Another limitation is the lack of attention given to outcome indices other than health. Only eight studies (less than 10% of the total) measured injury (five studies), occupational violence (three studies), or OHS knowledge/compliance (one study dealing with risk-taking) outcomes. Nor is there evidence that this deficiency is being addressed by more recent studies. This makes it difficult to draw conclusions about the effects on injuries, violence, and OHS management and regulatory regimes. There is reason to expect downsizing to have negative effects in the area of occupational violence and injury, due to understaffing, work intensification, multi-skilling and job reassignment, and accompanying management problems (128). Similar pressures may constrain OHS training, diminish OHS knowledge in the workforce, and reduce compliance. The experience of OHS regulators has caused them to express concerns about the safety impacts of downsizing as well as its effect on occupational violence/bullying. By way of contrast, there has been a greater focus on injury outcomes in research on contingent work arrangements (notably self-employment, home-based work, and temporary work) and associated business practices (notably outsourcing). However, like downsizing, these areas have received relatively few studies measuring effects on occupational violence/bullying and (to a lesser extent) compliance with safety rules and regulation. In sum, further systematic investigation of the safety effects of downsizing is required, as well as more general attention to the effects of precarious employment on occupational violence/bullying (including sexual harassment) and OHS management systems and regulations.

Research on downsizing and job insecurity has also been dominated by quantitative methods (only four studies focused on using qualitative data, while several other studies used qualitative data as an additional source). More qualitative studies would be useful, as they are more likely to bring to light subtle processes by which downsizing and organizational change influence workers' attitudes, behavior, work practices, and health and safety. Further, research to date has focused disproportionately on manufacturing, health care, and the public sector, and more work is now required in other industry sectors, particularly transport, construction, mining, and the rapidly growing service sector.

There is also limited knowledge about the organizational sources of job insecurity. For example, it would be valuable to know more about the effects of downsizing on the employment contracts of workers who are retained and whether these contracts increase or decrease job security. More detailed description of the organizational processes associated with different forms of downsizing and restructuring might identify differential effects on variables such as work intensity and job insecurity. At present, it is unclear to what extent the samples in many job insecurity studies include temporary employees, as temporary jobs may replace permanent ones during downsizing. Job insecurity among permanent workers may also be increased by various mechanisms, such as repeated cycles of downsizing, informal and ambiguous forms of restructuring, outsourcing, privatization, or competitive tendering, and combinations of these processes.

Further, despite the high proportion of studies using longitudinal designs, few have assessed the potential "healthy worker effect" associated with downsizing. Redundancy programs may remove workers, particularly older workers, with preexisting illness or injury or those who seem to have suffered most from previous downsizing cycles. A particularly robust group of survivors may be created, disguising negative effects on workers who retain their jobs and inflating differences with those who are laid off (although removing older workers from a workforce may also affect the association between job strain and ischemic disease; 129). This effect may be compounded by "presenteeism" among surviving workers, when they fear that reporting illness or taking sick leave could increase the likelihood of being targeted for future redundancy. To satisfactorily evaluate this effect, it is necessary to collect baseline data before individual workers are notified of redundancy, and then compare the health and injury profiles of those who lose their jobs with those who retain them. Very few of the longitudinal studies published to date have addressed this effect directly or provided sufficient data for others to reliably evaluate it. A Swedish longitudinal study by Hellgren and Sverke (52) evaluated the hypotheses that job insecurity leads to health complaints and that health complaints lead to job insecurity, finding support for the former but no significant cross-lagged effect with regard to the latter. They concluded that prior levels of health should be considered when seeking to explain the relative effect of job insecurity on the physical and mental health of workers.

Consistent with the above discussion, when trying to assess OHS effects, future research needs to recognize interactions with other changes in business practices (such as outsourcing, privatization, and increased use of temporary workers). The latter can compound the insecurity of downsizing "survivors" and increase their workload through spillover effects (such as additional training, administrative, and supervisory tasks, as well as pressures to work longer hours). On the other hand, those undertaking research into the OHS effects of temporary employment or subcontracting need to account for these spillover effects and to recognize that even workers holding nominally permanent jobs may feel insecure as a consequence of repeated rounds of downsizing/restructuring in the organizations where they work. In short, in drawing comparisons between permanent and nonpermanent workers, researchers need to take into account that the shift to labor market flexibility has devalued the benchmark or "gold" standard of permanent work over time. The issue of spillover effects raises a further point about overlapping impacts on public health. As noted in our recent review (3), there is, for example, extensive international research linking reduced health care staffing levels (and associated changes in hours of work and patient mix, and the increased use of less-qualified staff) to adverse health outcomes, including increased error and infection rates in hospitals and a weakening of reporting and surveillance systems. Unfortunately, despite the clear policy implications flowing from such "double-edged" evidence, there seems to be little discourse between this research and that exploring the adverse OHS effects of downsizing for workers, even though our review demonstrates that a number of studies have focused on the health care sector. This and other dual OHS and public health effects of downsizing and restructuring demand more recognition on the part of researchers.

A fundamental question requiring exploration is, How do downsizing, restructuring, and job insecurity damage workers' health? Overall, most studies that we reviewed do not explore the reasons for or mechanisms behind these adverse effects in detail, although the psychological impact of job insecurity is commonly viewed as a key determinant and several studies used Karasek's demand-control or job strain model (with some showing synergistic effects; 34, 107). Siegrist's effort-reward model was also used by some studies (30, 82). In certain respects downsizing can be seen as the archetypal breach in the norm of social reciprocity (in terms of effort and rewards) embedded in the work contract, because workers are asked to remain committed to (if not to work harder for) an organization that, by its actions, has failed to make any commensurate commitment to their ongoing employment (130). For our part, we have proposed a three-factor model—economic/reward pressures, disorganization, and regulatory failure—to explain how precarious employment undermines OHS (1, 128). Although specific testing of this model is presently confined to subcontracting and temporary workers, we would suggest that the model can be applied to downsizing/ restructuring and, indeed, is consistent with the findings of a number of recent studies included in this review.

The first factor in our model, economic and reward pressure, clearly entails job insecurity (and has parallels with Clarke and colleagues' employment strain model; 131), although it also incorporates payment/reward systems and work intensification (in terms of greater task load or longer hours). Several studies (e.g., 53, 93) pointed to an association between downsizing and greater workload intensity, longer hours/presenteeism, or unrewarded efforts. Presenteeism can entail the fatigue of additional hours (and the family/nonwork imbalance problems this may cause), and the consequences of working while ill, and it may also be viewed as an involuntary and often unpaid form of overtime (for a study of the health effects of the latter, see 132). A study by Probst (97) found an association between risk-taking behavior and the threat of layoff. This is consistent with the notion that downsizing may be conducive to cutting corners on safety as managers and workers strive to boost production/service delivery in an effort to safeguard their jobs. However, systematic research is required to test this hypothesis.

The second factor, disorganization, encompasses a weakening of induction, training, and supervisory regimens and a fracturing of formal and informal information flows among workers as well as OHS management systems. Few if any studies we reviewed explored this directly, although some studies did have findings generally consistent with the disorganization hypothesis. A Swedish study of downsizing in health care (53) found the change was associated with mistrust, anger, and lack of collaboration between doctors and nurses (although the traditional doctor/nurse hierarchy also contributed to this). Increasing work demands was also found to decrease the time to plan tasks (93). The negative effects of downsizing on worker commitment (133, 134) may also have implications for OHS, but this has not been researched. Further, another Swedish study (122, 123) found that both expansion and downsizing were associated with adverse effects on workers' health. In other words, organizational instability—even when it was not linked to job insecurity—had negative consequences for health. Critical factors here may be the degree to which changes affect the centralization of management control (downsizing is most often associated with centralization), workloads (including informal administrative, supervisory, and training requirements), and demand-control imbalance (84, 135). Again, further research is needed to investigate how downsizing affects work organization and OHS management, what aspects of this, in turn, affect health and safety outcomes, and which of these effects are symptomatic of both downsizing and expansion or other types of work reorganization (136).

The third dimension of the model, regulatory failure, captures the difficulty of maintaining minimum labor standards, allocating employer responsibility, and monitoring and enforcing legislative requirements. The regulatory framework went largely unmentioned in the studies we reviewed, reflecting in part a disciplinary boundary that health researchers seldom cross, as well as the ambiguity of legislative coverage and limited enforcement in relation to these issues (1).

Research into how downsizing and job insecurity adversely affect OHS, while offering a number of insights, is still very much in the pioneering phase. Overall, the review findings provide substantial evidence that downsizing and job insecurity have had significant adverse effects on OHS. The findings suggest by default, that existing country-specific regulatory and institutional arrangements have been bypassed or can, at best, only moderate the impacts. In short, new types of policy interventions may be required to address these problems.

CONCLUSION

The objectives of this chapter were to review published evidence on downsizing/restructuring and job insecurity. Our review covered international studies of the occupational health and safety effects of downsizing/restructuring and job insecurity undertaken over the past 40 years. After imposing quality and double-counting filters, we obtained 86 studies. Analysis revealed that 85 percent of these studies found adverse OHS outcomes, 8 percent found mixed effects, 5.8 percent found no effect, and only one study (1.2%) found a positive effect. Studies were examined to see whether they provided clues as to the reasons for such negative outcomes. We also identified a range of complexities and spillover effects.

The review revealed a number of critical gaps requiring further research attention. At the same time, there is far more extensive research into OHS effects for downsizing/restructuring than is the case for neoliberal business and work practices, including subcontracting, home-based work, permanent part-time work, and temporary employment. Even for the latter (but more especially for practices such as self-employment, subcontracting, and part-time work) there seems to be a more rapid accretion of research into downsizing and job insecurity, so this gap shows no sign of narrowing. Put in context, there is an urgent need for more research in these areas, including more differentiated studies (comparing a range of different work arrangements rather than just two or three) and longitudinal studies that provide further insights into causal factors and spillover effects. Researchers need to give serious attention to this if the full effects of precarious employment on health are to be better understood.

Setting the last point aside, some substantial challenges remain with regard to downsizing, particularly the need for more research on its effects on safety and occupational violence, work-family and spillover effects, and developing a better understanding of how these changes affect health. In our previous studies we identified three contributory factors associated with these work arrangements as warranting further investigation: economic and reward pressures; disorganization (demonstrated by poor induction/training and supervision, inadequate communication between workers, fracturing of management systems, and a reduced capacity to collectively voice concerns); and regulatory failure.

Acknowledgments — The authors thank Liz Bluff, Richard Johnstone, Wayne Lewchuk, Katherine Lippel, and Annie Thebaud-Mony for invaluable comments on earlier versions of this chapter. The chapter was written, in part, while Philip Bohle was Visiting Professor in Work and Organisation Studies at the University of Sydney. The research was supported by an Australian Research Council Large Grant (A00103185).

REFERENCES

1. Quinlan, M. Organisational restructuring/downsizing, OHS regulation and worker health and wellbeing. *Int. J. Law Psychiatr.* 30:385–399, 2007.
2. Quinlan, M., Mayhew, C., and Bohle, P. The global expansion of precarious employment, work disorganization, and consequences for occupational health: A review of recent research. *Int. J. Health Serv.* 31(2):335–414, 2001.
2a. Sverke, M., Hellgren, J., and Naswall, K. No security: A meta-analysis and review of job insecurity and its consequences. *J. Occup. Health Psychol.* 7:242–264, 2002.
3. Quinlan, M., and Bohle, P. Under pressure, out of control, or home alone? Reviewing research and policy debates on the OHS effects of outsourcing and home-based work. *Int. J. Health Serv.* 38(3):489–525, 2008.

4. Platt, S., Pavis, S., and Akram, G. *Changing Labour Market Conditions and Health: A Systematic Literature Review (1993–98)*. Report to European Foundation for the Improvement in Living and Working Conditions, Dublin, 1998.
5. Cascio, W., Young, C., and Morris, J. Financial consequences of employment-change decisions in major US corporations. *Acad. Manage. J.* 40:1175–1189, 1997.
6. Said, T., Louarn, J., and Tremblay, M. The performance effects of major workforce reductions: Longitudinal evidence from North America. *Int J. Hum. Resourc. Manage.* 18(12):2075–2094, 2007.
7. Gilson, C., Hurd, F., and Wagar, T. Creating a concession climate: The case of serial downsizers. *Int. J. Hum. Resourc. Manage.* 15(6):1056–1068, 2004.
8. Amick, B., et al. Relationship of job strain and iso-strain to health status in a cohort of women in the United States. *Scand. J. Work Environ. Health* 24(1):54–61, 1998.
9. Amick, B., et al. Relationship between all-cause mortality and cumulative working life course psychosocial and physical exposures in the United States labour market from 1968 to 1992. *Psychosom. Med.* 64:370–381, 2002.
10. Ariens, G., Bongers, P., and Hoogendoom, W. High physical and psychological load at work and sickness absence due to neck pain. *Scand. J. Work Environ. Health* 28(4):222–231, 2002.
11. Arnetz, B., et al. Neuroendocrine and immunologic effects of unemployment and job insecurity. *Psychother. Psychosom.* 55:76–80, 1991.
12. Barling, J., and Kelloway, E. Job insecurity and health: The moderating role of workplace control. *Stress Med.* 12:253–259, 1996.
13. Bartley, M., Sacker, A., and Clarke, P. Employment status, employment conditions, and limiting illness: Prospective evidence from the British household panel survey 1991–2001. *J. Epidemiol. Community Health* 58:501–506, 2004.
14. Beale, N., and Nethercott, S. Job-loss and family morbidity: A study of a factory closure. *J. R. Coll. Gen. Pract.* 35:510–514, 1985.
15. Beale, N., and Nethercott, S. Certified sickness absence in industrial employees threatened with redundancy. *BMJ* 296:1508–1510, 1988.
16. Berth, H., Foster, P., and Brahler, E. Unemployment, job insecurity and life satisfaction: Results of a study with young adults in the new German states. *Soz. Preventivmed.* 50:361–369, 2005.
17. Borg, V., Kristensen, T., and Burr, H. Work environment and changes in self-rated health: A five year follow-up study. *Stress Med.* 16:37–47, 2000.
18. Bourbonnais, R., et al. Psychosocial work environment and certified leave among nurses during organisational changes and downsizing. *Relations Industrielles* 60(3):483–509, 2005.
19. Broom, D., et al. The lesser evil: Bad jobs or unemployment? A survey of middle-aged Australians. *Soc. Sci. Med.* 63:575–586, 2006.
20. Burke, R. Job insecurity in recent business school graduates: Antecedents and consequences. *Int. J. Stress Manage.* 5(2):113–119, 1998.
21. Burke, R., and Greenglass, E. Work-family conflict, spouse support, and nursing staff well-being during organizational restructuring. *J. Occup. Health Psychol.* 4(4):327–336, 1999.
22. Bussing, A. Can control at work and social support moderate psychological consequences of job insecurity? Results from a quasi-experimental study in the steel industry. *Eur. J. Work Org. Psychol.* 8(2):219–242, 1999.

References *continue on p. 212*

APPENDIX

Studies of Job Insecurity/Downsizing and Occupational Health and Safety (OHS)

Author(s) and year (reference)	Location of study	Precarious employment category identified or study focus	Method	OHS indices	Link between OHS and precarious employment?	Remarks
Amick et al., 1998 (8)	U.S.	Job insecurity: organizational restructuring (health care industry—all women)	Cross-sectional survey, 1992 (n = 33,689)	Karasek job strain and MOS (Medical Outcomes Study) SF-36 health status questionnaires	Yes; job insecurity linked to lower health status	Job security protective on various indices of physical and mental health. Earlier study (1990) didn't find effects as before labor market instability.
Amick et al., 2002 (9)	U.S.	Job insecurity	Longitudinal cohort study using U.S. Panel Study Data 1968–92 (1968, n = 5,000)	Mortality and imputed psychosocial and physical working conditions	No; no association between risk of death and job insecurity	Study notes that changes in meaning of work and period effects for job insecurity not measured.
Ariens et al., 2002 (10)	Netherlands	Job insecurity	Prospective cohort study (1994–98) using job content questionnaire (n = 758)	Sickness absence due to neck pain	Yes; low job security risk factor for absence	—
Arnetz et al., 1991 (11)	Sweden	Job insecurity (blue-collar men and women)	Prospective longitudinal (n = 354)	Psychological well-being, cardiovascular and physiological risk factors	Yes; anticipated and early unemployment had marked negative effects on physiological risk factors and psychological well-being	Most changes short-term, except cardiovascular risk factors (observed at least 2 yrs after job loss).

Barling and Kelloway, 1996 (12)	South Africa	Job insecurity; downsizing (gold mining)	Surveyed 187 black miners (questionnaire and blood pressure [BP] measured)	Self-reported mood and psychosomatic health plus BP	Yes; job insecurity associated with higher BP and turnover intentions; effects moderated by high perceived workplace control	Study notes finding of workplace control effect consistent with Karasek model.
Bartley, Sacker, and Clarke, 2004 (13)	U.K.	Job insecurity	Examined data on working-age men (n = 2,690) and women (n = 2,629) in good health from British household panel survey, 1991–2001	Limiting illness that affected work activity	Yes; job insecurity linked to higher rate of limiting illness, while secure employment and good working conditions also aided recovery from illness	—
Beale and Nethercott, 1985 (14)	U.K.	Job insecurity: factory closure (manufacturing)	Longitudinal controlled study of families of workers (80 men and 49 women) made redundant by closure	Morbidity—health care center consultation and referrals, attendance at hospital outpatient depts.	Yes; decline in health for workers and families; effects began 2 years before when managers intimated closure	Older workers able to take early retirement were excluded. Significant unexpected finding: job threat stress at least equal to actual job loss.
Beale and Nethercott, 1988 (15)	U.K.	Job insecurity: downsizing threat (manufacturing)	Longitudinal controlled study of mass redundancy and eventual closure of factory	Absence/sick leave records	Yes; workers fearing job loss reported more illness and took longer absence, esp. men and those with history of little consultation with general practitioners	Absence rate dropped for younger workers (i.e., below 40 yrs). Authors argue this is due to greater fear of job loss.

APPENDIX (Cont'd.)

Author(s) and year (reference)	Location of study	Precarious employment category identified or study focus	Method	OHS indices	Link between OHS and precarious employment?	Remarks
Berth, Foster, and Brahler, 2005 (16)	Germany	Job insecurity	Surveyed 419 young people (n = 193 men and 226 women), mean age 30.5 yrs (part of 17th Saxon Longitudinal study in 2003)	Self-rated health	Yes; those who had experienced unemployment several times more dissatisfied with income, housing, and health	Two-thirds had experienced unemployment. Rare study of younger workers noted effects spilled over to family and others.
Borg, Kristensen, and Burr, 2000 (17)	Denmark	Job insecurity	Prospective longitudinal (5 yr) controlled study using telephone questionnaire (1990, n = 5,828; 1995, n = 5,001)	Self-reported health (SRH) problems/ rating	Yes; high job insecurity 1 of 5 work factors significantly associated with lower SRH	Robust study based on large and representative sample of adult Danish population.
Bourbonnais et al., 2005 (18)	Canada	Job insecurity; downsizing (health care workers in 13 facilities—nurses)	Examined sickness absence data from 1,454 files and telephone interviews	Sickness absence records	Yes; sickness absence leave increased during restructuring, esp. for mental health problems	Identified psychosocial work factors that could be modified.
Broom et al., 2006 (19)[a]	Australia	Job insecurity and job quality	Surveyed 2,497 Australians aged 40–44 yrs (then classified according to strain, job insecurity, and marketability)	Depression, physical health, self-rated health, and general practitioner visits	Yes; found unemployed had worse health, but those with poor-quality jobs (characterized by insecurity, low marketability, and job strain) linked to worse health than those with fewer or no stressors	Concluded poor-quality jobs could be as bad for health as being unemployed.

Study	Country	Variables	Method	Outcome	Effect	Comments
Burke, 1998 (20)	Canada	Job insecurity (business graduates)	Surveyed 217 male and female recent business school graduates	Self-reported psychological mood and job satisfaction	Yes; perceived threats to job security had indirect effects on mood	Study notes prior research mostly of long-tenure workers, so seems no group immune to effects.
Burke and Greenglass, 1999 (21)	Canada	Job insecurity; downsizing/restructuring (hospital)	Survey of 686 hospital-based nurses (97% female)	Work-nonwork conflict	Yes; nurses reported significantly more work-family conflict	Downsizing/organizational restructuring variables predicted work-family but not family-work conflict.
Bussing, 1999 (22)	Germany	Job insecurity; anticipated job loss (steel industry)	Cross-sectional comparison of matched secure workers (n = 75) and insecure workers (n = 48) in two firms	Irritation, strain, and psychosomatic complaints	No; effect on health not significant	Study showed moderating effects of social support and job control. Workers were aware of imminent job losses, but not who was to lose job. Insecurity had significant negative effect on job satisfaction.
Catalano, Rook, and Dooley, 1986 (23)	U.S.	Job insecurity	Longitudinal 4 yr study (n = 3,850)	Consideration and likelihood of seeking help for psychological problems	Yes; results suggest job insecurity increased likelihood of getting or considering help	—
Catalano and Serxner, 1992 (24)	U.S.	Job insecurity	Quasi-experimental interrupted time series; low birth weight data California, 1974–79	Child birth weight; effect of legislative change on perceived job security	Yes; effect gender-specific (2 groups of males had elevated risk of low birth weight child)	Study looked at Spanish and non-Spanish birth names.

APPENDIX (Cont'd.)

Author(s) and year (reference)	Location of study	Precarious employment category identified or study focus	Method	OHS indices	Link between OHS and precarious employment?	Remarks
Cheng et al., 2005 (25)	Taiwan	Job insecurity	Data from national representational survey of employees, 25–65 yrs (n = 8,705 men and 5,986 women)	Self-reported health using Taiwan version of SF-36 along with somatic symptoms and musculoskeletal discomfort	Yes; job insecurity associated with poor health (adjusted for age, job control, and social support); stronger effect in men, managerial/prof. women, those in larger companies	Study found high overall prevalence of job insecurity (50%), esp. in low-educated, blue-collar, older women and those in small business.
De Witte, 1999 (26)	Belgium	Job insecurity (metal manufacturing)	Data from 336 metal workers (male and female) plus sample of short-term unemployed	Self-reported psychological distress (GHQ [General Health Questionnaire]-12)	Yes; significant increase in distress among insecure men but not women	GHQ similar to short-term unemployed sample, suggesting effects equally harmful.
Dekker and Schaufeli, 1995 (27)	Australia	Job insecurity; downsizing (public sector/ rail transport)	Longitudinal controlled study of state rail organization 1990–91 (n1 = 105 and n2 = 95)	Self-reported psychological health/distress	Yes; job insecurity led to psychological stress symptoms (less for "ax fell" group than where uncertainty continued)	No evidence that colleague, management, and union support reduced impact. Study used quasi-experimental design, but only short timeframe (2 months for assessment).
Domenighetti, D'Avanzo, and Bisig, 2000 (28)	Switzerland	Job insecurity	Cross-sectional random survey (n = 2,024) of general population	Self-reported physical and psychological health	Yes; job insecurity had negative effect on health indicators	Fear of unemployment had stronger health effect on more-educated workers.

Citation	Country	Focus	Study design/sample	Outcome measures	Findings	Comments
Dooley, Rook, and Catalano, 1987 (29)	U.S.	Job insecurity	Repeated surveys (16) of at least 500, 1978–82 (total n = 8,376); used 3 methods to analyze data	Self-reported psychological health symptoms (using PERI scales)	Yes; symptoms higher for perceived job insecurity; found social support moderators weak/absent	Used objective and subjective measures of job security. Age and sex were main moderators.
Dragano, Verde, and Siegrist, 2005 (30)	Germany	Job insecurity: downsizing	Surveyed 12,240 men and 10,319 women aged 16–59 yrs, 1998–99	Musculoskeletal pain, sleep disorders, depression, skin irritation, and psychosomatic conditions	Yes; compared to ref. group those exposed to downsizing and work stress had more health symptoms, and higher than those exposed to one or other	21% of men and 31% of women of effect size of combined exposure attributable to synergistic interaction.
D'Souza et al., 2003 (31)	Australia	Job insecurity	Cross-sectional survey of managers, professionals aged 40–44 (n = 1,188) from electoral rolls for two cities (55% male)	Self-reports of anxiety and depression, physical health, and overall health	Yes; job insecurity associated with poorer health when demographic, personality, organizational, social variables controlled	Well-sampled, but limited age (40–44 yrs) and occupational (managers, professionals) ranges.
Earnshaw, Amundson, and Borgen, 1990 (32)	Canada	Job insecurity; psychological experience of professional women	Qualitative study of 20 professional women	Reports of negative emotions and cognitions, emotional and physical health	Yes; high work and performance pressure in insecure jobs (both contract and temporary); insecurity linked to stress and other negative psychological effects	Cross-sectional study, with categories of negative effects and incidence derived from interviews. Examined effects on career aspirations/perceptions.

APPENDIX (Cont'd.)

Author(s) and year (reference)	Location of study	Precarious employment category identified or study focus	Method	OHS indices	Link between OHS and precarious employment?	Remarks
Fenwick and Tausig, 1994 (33)	U.S.	Job insecurity	Longitudinal national probability survey (n = 830)	Self-reported stress measure	Yes; high industry unemployment rates linked to high job demands, reduced decision latitude, and led to higher stress	Note: Measured effects were longitudinal and cross-sectional. Data used were old (1973 and 1977), but robust methodology.
Ferrie et al., 1995 (34)	U.K.	Job insecurity; organizational change/privatization (government workers)	Longitudinal controlled cohort study (compared 660 against rest of cohort, included males and females)	Self-reported health and health-related behavior	Yes; job insecurity had no significant effect on health behavior but negative effects on health status	Anticipation of job loss affects health before change in job status. Part of Whitehall II study series.
Ferrie et al., 1998 (35)[b]	U.K.	Job insecurity; organizational change/job transfer (government workers)	Longitudinal (5 yr) case-controlled study using questionnaire and clinical examination (n = 7,149)	Self-reported physical symptoms and GHQ, health behavior, BP, chronic illness, and sleep disruption	Yes; men transferred or anticipating insecurity had higher GHQ, poorer overall health rating, illness, adverse sleep and BP	Women in both exposed groups reported small increases in morbidity and most clinical measures. Robust study; part of Whitehall II series.
Ferrie et al., 1998 (36)[b]	U.K.	Job insecurity: organizational change (government workers)	Longitudinal (5 yr) controlled cohort study (n = 10,308, 500 in dept. under threat)	Self-reported physical symptoms and GHQ, health behavior	Yes; for men and women, increase in body mass and sleep more than 9 hrs, and small increase in blood cholesterol and ischemia; increase in BP for women	Robust study; part of Whitehall II series.

Ferrie et al., 2001 (37)[b]	U.K.	Job insecurity: organizational change/privatization (government workers)	Controlled longitudinal cohort study (Whitehall II) 1985–88, 1989–90, and 1992–93; Study 1: executive agencies; and Study 2: Property Services Agency	Self-reported physical symptoms and GHQ, health behavior, body mass index (BMI) and BP	Yes; threats to job security had modest adverse effects on health outcomes (GHQ and BMI); chronic job insecurity linked to increased BP	No significant effects on health behavior, such as alcohol use.
Ferrie et al., 2001 (38)[b]	U.K.	Job insecurity: organizational change/privatization (government workers)	Longitudinal study (n = 666) of government dept. before and 18 months after privatization	Psychiatric morbidity and general practitioner consultations	Yes; both anticipation phase and chronic job insecurity had modest adverse effect on self-reported physical and mental health and BMI for men and women	Health outcomes for permanent unemployed resembled those for secure re-employed, but more long-term illness.
Ferrie et al., 2002 (39)[b]	U.K.	Job insecurity: chronic (white-collar government workers)	Prospective cohort study (n = 931 women and 2,429 men)	Self-rated health over last year, GHQ, drug use, BP, cholesterol, BMI	Yes; job insecurity had adverse effects on self-reported health and psychiatric morbidity	Effects highest among those with chronic job insecurity.
Ferrie et al., 2005 (40)[b]	U.K.	Job insecurity: chronic (white-collar government workers)	Longitudinal study (n = 960 women and 2,360 men)	Self-rated health over last year and GHQ	Yes; job insecurity link to poor health; pessimism, social/job satisfaction, and financial/housing problems explain much	Combination of pessimism, heightened vigilance, difficulty paying bills, problems with housing, financial security, social and job satisfaction, explained much of association. Some gender differences.

APPENDIX (Cont'd.)

Author(s) and year (reference)	Location of study	Precarious employment category identified or study focus	Method	OHS indices	Link between OHS and precarious employment?	Remarks
Ferrie et al., 2007 (41)	Sweden	Downsizing and workplace expansion	Measured changes in workforce against Swedish Work Environment Survey subset, 1991, 1993, and 1995	Self-reported psycho-social work environment and physical hazards	Mixed; moderate change benefits outweigh adverse effects in public not private; major change—greater physical hazard	Major downsize—better work environments, private sector men. Major expansion worse for public sector women and private sector men.
Flannery et al., 1997 (42)	U.S.	Job insecurity: downsizing (health care)	Longitudinal study of state hospital downsizing/closure in 22 month period	Occupational violence/staff assault by patients	No; assault frequency declined by 63%	Differences with Snyder study (105) partly explained by pattern of ward closure, patient load, overcrowding, and assault program.
Gillespie et al., 2001 (44)	Australia	Job insecurity: downsizing (university staff)	23 focus groups from a sample of 178 staff from 15 universities	Self-reported sources of stress	Yes; job insecurity identified as 1 of top 5 causes of stress; 2/3 of groups reported stress resulted from redundancy cycles	—
Godin, Desmarez, and Kittel, 2006 (45)	Belgium	Job insecurity and threats from the global economy (insurance, health care, telecommunications)	90 semi-structured interviews (twice over 1 yr period) in 4 firms with contrasting job instability and survey of 1,986 workers	Job strain using Karasek model	Yes; found workers perceiving job insecurity more stressed (high strain category), and same result for those perceiving threat from globalization	Value in using both job insecurity and global threats measures. Older workers more threatened by globalization.

Study	Country	Focus	Design/Method	Measure	Effect found	Comments
Grunberg, Moore, and Greenberg, 2001 (46)	U.S.	Job insecurity: downsizing (manufacturing)	Longitudinal panel study using company records, interviews, focus groups, and questionnaire (n = 2,279)	Self-reported work injuries and illness; poor health index, alcohol problems, depression, and health behavior change	Yes; contact with layoff linked to more symptoms of poor health, depression; being laid-off and rehired linked to more injuries, illnesses, and absence	First findings of large panel study. Points to effects on job security of repeated bouts in cyclical industries.
Hamilton et al., 1990 (47)	U.S.	Job insecurity: plant closures (automobile manufacturing)	Quasi-experimental design (4 closing plants, n = 831; and 12 nonclosing, n = 766)	Mental health symptoms from Hopkins Symptom checklist	Mixed; but partial and varied according to demographic variables (black and white)	Unemployment had clear adverse effects on health. Anticipated job loss effects were more subtle.
Harenstam et al., 2004 (48)	Sweden	Downsizing and organizational change	Managers and workers interviewed at 72 worksites (MOA [Modern Working and Living Conditions for Men and Women] project)	Self-reported and expert-assessed psychosocial and ergonomic/physical working conditions	Yes; organizations that had not undergone change had best work conditions; organizational change had more negative effects for public than private sector	—
Heaney, Israel, and House, 1994 (49)	U.S.	Job insecurity (automobile industry)	Longitudinal survey (n = 207), 1986–87	Physical symptoms	Yes; job insecurity increased physical symptoms	Job insecurity a chronic stressor, increased effect with long exposure. Platt et al. (4) note some methodological limitations.
Hellgren, Sverke, and Isaksson, 1999 (50)	Sweden	Job insecurity: downsizing (retailing)	Longitudinal study in a single organization (n = 375)	Self-reported psychological well-being	Yes; quantitative insecurity (re: continued existence of job) negatively affected well-being after controlling for affectivity	Study differentiated quantitative insecurity and qualitative insecurity (job features). It argues previous cross-sectional studies overstate effect.

APPENDIX (Cont'd.)

Author(s) and year (reference)	Location of study	Precarious employment category identified or study focus	Method	OHS indices	Link between OHS and precarious employment?	Remarks
Hellgren and Chirumbolo, 2003 (51)	Italy, Netherlands, and Sweden	Job insecurity	Surveyed unionized workers in Italy (n = 476, Netherlands (panel survey n = 799), and Sweden (n = 1,923)	Distress (GHQ)— mental health complaints	Yes; results indicated job insecurity associated with mental health complaints in all 3 countries; union support did not reduce effects of job insecurity on mental health complaints	One of the few studies that tried to assess impact of union support, but didn't consider union campaigns in this regard.
Hellgren and Sverke, 2003 (52)	Sweden	Job insecurity: downsizing (retail/ wholesale firm)	Two surveys of 786 survivors, mean age 48 yrs (53% female), 1995 (n = 493) and 1996 (n = 395)	Distress (GHQ)— mental health complaints and physical health complaints (10 item inventory of psychosomatic conditions, e.g., muscular tensions, headaches)	Yes; job insecurity associated with mental health complaints, and regression indicates job insecurity causes mental health effects, not vice versa	—
Hertting et al., 2004 (53)[c]	Sweden	Job insecurity: downsizing (health care)	Longitudinal qualitative study of nurses in hospital (n = 14) interviewed in 1997, 1998, and 2001	Psychosocial stressors	Yes; ever-growing demands and effort unrewarded provoked employer distrust; waste and competence drain provoked anger; unfulfilled collaboration with doctors was stressor	Study indicated downsizing linked to mistrust, anger, and lack of collaboration (though other factor here was doctor/ nurse hierarchy).

Study	Country	Type	Design/sample	Outcome measures	Findings	Comments
Isaksson, Hellgren, and Pettersson, 2000 (54)	Sweden	Job insecurity: repeated downsizing/organizational restructuring (retail)	Longitudinal; 2 surveys (T1, n = 555; and T2, n = 395) of "surviving" employees in retailing company	Distress (GHQ) and health complaints	Yes; job insecurity most significant explanation of distress for T1 and T2; negative symptoms remain, and older employees most vulnerable	Study of repeated downsizing highlights potential limits of one-off studies for capturing negative health effects.
Iversen and Sabroe, 1988 (55)	Denmark	Job insecurity: downsizing (manufacturing)	Longitudinal 3 yr study—shipyard closure (n = 1,153) with control group (n = 441)	Psychological well-being (GHQ)	Yes; employed in fear of unemployment had reduced psychological well-being	Study stressed health effects of both unemployment and job insecurity.
Jenkins et al., 1982 (56)	U.K.	Job insecurity: anticipated redundancy (newspaper)	Prospective 6 month longitudinal study (n1 = 162; n2 and n3 = 111)	Psychological well-being (GHQ-30 item), alcohol consumption	Yes; significantly reduced symptoms after redundancy notices withdrawn	Prolonged industrial dispute prior to study. Also examined effects on job satisfaction.
Kinnunen et al., 2000 (58)	Finland	Job insecurity (paper mill, bank, and municipal social/health care dept.)	Longitudinal study 1995–97 (n = 109) in 3 workplaces	Reported occupational well-being	Yes; perceived probability of negative job change led to reduced well-being	Other measure of job insecurity (global worry about job continuity) did not affect well-being.
Kivimaki et al., 1997 (60)	Finland	Job insecurity: downsizing/organizational restructuring (local government)	Longitudinal (5 yr) study using medically certified sickness absence and survey data (n = 763)	Sickness absence and self-reported health	Yes; work characteristics predicted sickness absence	Study controlled for prior absence, lifestyle and demographic differences.

APPENDIX (Cont'd.)

Author(s) and year (reference)	Location of study	Precarious employment category identified or study focus	Method	OHS indices	Link between OHS and precarious employment?	Remarks
Kivimaki et al., 1998 (61)[d]	Finland	Job insecurity: downsizing (local government)	Longitudinal study; analyzed medically certified sickness absence over 5 yr period and surveyed hostility (n = 866)	Sickness absence, psychosocial stressors, and hostility	Yes; stressor exposure increased absence risk; for men, hostility increased only when stressor was trauma, but, for women, stressors included downsizing	Results controlled for baseline levels of sickness absence. Found vulnerability through hostility more evident in women.
Kivimaki et al., 2000 (62)[d]	Finland	Job insecurity: downsizing (local government)	Longitudinal (5 yr) cohort study using survey (n = 764) and absence records	Self-reported health-related behavior and medically certified absence records	Yes; sickness absence rate 2.17 times higher after major downsizing than minor downsizing	Outcomes moderated by effects on physical demands, job control, and security.
Kivimaki et al., 2001 (63)[d]	Finland	Job insecurity: downsizing (local government)	Longitudinal cohort study (n = 764)	Self-reported musculoskeletal pain and certified absence	Yes; 2 measures showed increased risk of musculo-skeletal problems	—
Kivimaki et al., 2001 (64)[d]	Finland	Job insecurity: downsizing (local government)	7 yr longitudinal study (n = 550)	Self-rated health, mediating effects of changes in work and interpersonal relationships	Yes; downsizing pre-dicted long-term health decline; key factors were decreased job control, high insecurity, and physical demands; social conflicts did not affect mediation	—

	Country	Exposure	Study design (sample)	Outcome measures	Effect found	Comments
Kivimaki et al., 2003 (65)[d]	Finland	Job insecurity: downsizing (local government)	Longitudinal cohort study (n = 886)	Self-rated health, distress (GHQ), musculoskeletal symptoms and sickness absence	Yes; deterioration in health most likely in survivors of major down-sizing and among those who become unemployed; health risks among re-employed leavers lower than even minor/no downsizing group	Study notes important age and preexisting health effects in terms of re-employment prospects.
Kivimaki et al., 2007 (66)[d]	Finland	Job insecurity: downsizing (local government)	Prospective cohort study, 1993–2000 (1993, 4,271 lost jobs, 4,783 kept jobs in downsized units, and 17,599 didn't experience downsizing)	Psychotropic drug prescriptions (anti-depressants, anxiolytics, and hypnotics), 1994–2000, from national registers	Yes; those exposed to downsizing but keeping their job at higher risk of being prescribed psycho-tropic drugs than those not exposed; increased risk also for those who lost their jobs	Association strongest for men and hypnotics, and anxiolytics for women. Study argues this drug use managerial strategy may pose mental health risk.
Lau and Knardahl, 2008 (67)	Norway	Job insecurity	Longitudinal study (T1 = 5,163 and T2 = 1,946) (Oslo Health Study)	Self-reported general health, subjective mental health (Hopkins Symptoms checklist) and back pain	Yes; job insecurity asso-ciated with health, stronger for mental distress and self-reported health but weaker for back pain	—
Layton, 1987 (68)	U.K.	Job insecurity	Prospective longitudinal survey of male workers in 4 firms (n = 101)	State anxiety	Yes; anxiety levels of men facing job loss same as when later lost job; anxiety dropped when re-employed	Anxiety levels of those who lost jobs and those who did not were the same when anticipating job loss.

APPENDIX (Cont'd.)

Author(s) and year (reference)	Location of study	Precarious employment category identified or study focus	Method	OHS indices	Link between OHS and precarious employment?	Remarks
Lee et al., 2003 (69)	U.S.	Job insecurity (health care—nurses)	Prospective cohort study, 1992–96 female nurses, 46–71 yrs, from 11 states (n = 36,910)	Coronary heart disease (CHD)	Yes; study indicated job insecurity may increase short-term risk of nonfatal myocardial infarction	Study adjusted for array of confounders (no diagnosed CHD, stroke, or cancer at baseline).
Lipscomb et al., 2004 (70)	U.S.	Downsizing/restructuring—reduced staffing levels (health care)	Cross-sectional survey of 1,163 nurses	Self-reported musculoskeletal disorders	Yes; link between neck, shoulder, and back disorders and organizational change, including workload (physical and psychological)	Controlled for demographics, work characteristics, and job demands.
Mak and Mueller, 2000 (71)	Australia	Job insecurity: downsizing/job insecurity (public sector)	Cross-sectional survey of 222 workers in 2 depts. being restructured/downsized	Self-reported vocational, psychological, physical, and interpersonal strain	Yes; perceived job insecurity linked to greater psychological, physical, and vocational strain	Found personal coping resources have only small effect on strain.
Mantler et al., 2005 (72)	Canada	Job insecurity (high-tech workers)	Surveyed employed (n = 140) and laid-off (n = 206) workers (68% men and 32% women)	Perceived stress	Yes; when employment uncertainty taken into account, no significant variances in stress by employment status	Use of emotional-avoidance coping strategy moderated effect of employment uncertainty.

Study	Country	Focus	Design/Sample	Outcome measure	Finding	Comments
Marchand, Demers, and Durand, 2006 (73)	Canada	Job insecurity	Subset of National Population Health Survey (n = 6,611 15–59 yrs) from 471 occupations, 1994–2001	Psychological distress (using Composite International Diagnostic Interview)	Yes; job insecurity contributes to distress	Measure of job insecurity asked if job permanent or not.
Mattiasson et al., 1990 (74)	Sweden	Job insecurity (industrial shipyard workers)	Longitudinal study (n = 715) with control group (n = 261); followed up after mean of 6.2 yrs	Cardiovascular risk factors and sleep quality	Yes; elevated lipids, sleep disturbance, depression, and anxiety in response to threat of unemployment	Methodologically strong study using multiple measures.
Mauno and Kinnunen, 1999 (75)[e]	Finland	Job insecurity (paper mill, bank, supermarket, municipal social/ health care dept.)	Longitudinal study (n = 219) male and female workers in 4 organizations	Self-reported job exhaustion, overall well-being (somatic symptoms) and family well-being	Yes; for women, job insecurity increased job exhaustion and negative spillover into parenthood	Found job insecurity and well-being both relatively stable in follow-up period.
Mauno and Kinnunen, 1999 (76)[e]	Finland	Job insecurity (paper mill, bank, supermarket, municipal social/ health care dept.)	Questionnaire survey of 215 dual-earner partners in 4 organizations (part of larger study)	Self-reported job exhaustion, psychosomatic symptoms, and marital satisfaction	Yes; job insecurity linked to marital satisfaction via job exhaustion and psychosomatic health	Found job stressors of one partner not transmitted to other as marital dissatisfaction.
McDonough, 2000 (77)	Canada	Job insecurity	Analyzed data from 1994 national probability adult sample	Self-rated health, distress, use of medications and alcohol	Yes; insecurity leading to lower health, increased distress/medication use, not alcohol	—
McHugh, 1998 (78)	Sweden	Job insecurity: organizational restructuring/ rationalization (public sector)	Survey of workers in a social insurance organization (n = 246)	Self-reported anxiety and symptoms of being worn out	Yes; rationalization process linked to anxiety and symptoms of being worn out	Argued public sector organizations needed to take account of effects when planning change.

APPENDIX (Cont'd.)

Author(s) and year (reference)	Location of study	Precarious employment category identified or study focus	Method	OHS indices	Link between OHS and precarious employment?	Remarks
Mohren et al., 2003 (79)	Netherlands	Job insecurity	Cross-sectional and longitudinal study using Maastricht Cohort Study (n = 12,140) data	Self-reported infections and health complaints	Yes; cross-sectional study found job insecurity associated with common infections and complaints; longitudinal, largest effect was flu-like illness and general health complaints	Study corrected for health behavior, long-standing illness, and work-related demands.
Muntaner et al., 1998 (80)	U.S.	Job insecurity	Examined 10,801 men and women at risk of atherosclerosis (black and white)	Measurement of carotid artery wall thickness	No; when controlled for all established risk factors	—
Naswall, Sverke, and Hellgren, 2005 (81)	Sweden	Job insecurity (acute care hospital nurses)	Surveyed acute care nurses (n = 512; 71% response rate and 91% female)	Distress (GHQ) and job-induced tension	Yes; found job insecurity was job stressor even after controlling for personality disposition	—
Niedhammer et al., 2006 (82)	France	Downsizing/ restructuring (publication distributing firm)	Surveyed 504 men and 176 women	Distress (GHQ) and depressive symptoms (CES-D)	Yes; job strain, low decision latitude, effort/ reward imbalance, and job instability associated with depressive symptoms/ disorders among men	Over-commitment risk factor for men and women. Social support reduced depressive symptoms for women.

Study	Country	Topic	Method/Sample	Outcome measure	Findings	Comments
Orpen, 1994 (83)	Australia	Job insecurity (manufacturing)	Survey of manufacturing company workers (n = 129)	Psychological well-being	Yes; job insecurity predictive, but high self-esteem and internal locus of control have positive moderating effect	Strength of relationship between insecurity and well-being unreported. Level of actual job losses in firm are unclear.
Osthus, 2007 (84)	Norway	Downsizing and internal reorganization	Surveyed 1,944 employees (from Norwegian Survey of Living Conditions, 2003)	Work-related musculoskeletal pain	Mixed; downsizing more related to job insecurity than reorganization, but latter more related to high demand, low satisfaction, health-related problems	Study sought to distinguish effect of downsizing from reorganization.
Owen, 1966 (85)	U.K.	Job insecurity: threatened redundancy (railway workshops/transport)	Examined sickness absence records for closing workshop (n = 668) and control (n = 475)	Sickness absence data	Yes; sick leave more frequent and longer duration for men threatened with job loss	Service length effect—stable group absence highest among those with several years service. Little disparity for threatened group.
Park and Butler, 2001 (86)	U.S.	Job insecurity: downsizing	Survey of Minnesota firms (n = 121) matched with 5,125 comp. claims covering years 1990–98	Compensation claims duration and frequency	Mixed; recent downsizing increased claim duration but not frequency	—
Parker, Chmiel, and Wall, 1997 (87)	U.K.	Job insecurity: downsizing (manufacturing)	Longitudinal survey of single plant (n = 139)	Well-being (anxiety/depression)	No; improved work characteristics (control, clarity, participation) offset higher work demands	Methodologically robust, with interesting work organization interventions accompanying downsizing.

APPENDIX (Cont'd.)

Author(s) and year (reference)	Location of study	Precarious employment category identified or study focus	Method	OHS indices	Link between OHS and precarious employment?	Remarks
Pelfrene et al., 2003 (88)	Belgium	Job insecurity and world market competition	Analyzed Belstress sample (n = 16,335 men and 5,084 women) aged 35–59 yrs recruited in 25 firms, 1994–98	Health-related behaviors and cardiovascular risk factors	Mixed; job insecurity and world market competition associated with job strain and some health indicators, but no consistent association with cardiovascular risk factors or health behaviors	—
Pepper, 2000 (89); Campbell and Pepper, 2002 (91)	U.S.	Job insecurity: downsizing (nuclear energy)	Questionnaire surveys of workers at 5 plants (n = 5,850) plus injury, absence records; focus groups and interviews	Sickness absence, injury, psychological well-being, physical health, job characteristics	Yes; those with most direct experience of downsizing had poorer mental health and (4 sites) more medical symptoms	Large multi-method study. Noted other effects: at 2 sites, exposure to harassment linked to G11 mental health or medical symptoms. Extensive NIOSH report (89).
Pepper et al., 2003 (90)[f]	U.S.	Job insecurity: downsizing (nuclear energy)	Surveyed workers at 5 sites (n = 5,889; 55% response rate) in 1997	Physical health symptoms (SF-12) and mental health	Yes; those who believed process fair and communication open, as well as those less affected, reported fewer medical symptoms	—

Study	Country	Type	Study design	Outcome measures	Results	Notes
Pettersson and Arnetz, 1998 (92)	Sweden	Job insecurity: downsizing (health care)	Prospective study of structured interventions in large regional hospital (1994–95) (n = 3,506 in first phase, 2,617 in follow-up)	Self-reported health and well-being	Yes; overall worsening in most measures, but "attenuated" in depts. with active employee and organizational interventions	Worsening "most likely due to a notice of 20% staff reduction prior to follow up assessment."
Pettersson et al., 2005 (93)[c]	Sweden	Job insecurity: downsizing (health care)	Prospective study of structured interventions in large regional hospital (1994–2001)	Self-reported health and well-being	Yes; downward trend in mental health and upward trend in long-term sick leave	Increasing work demands linked to mental health, and less time to plan linked to sick leave. Stable short-term sick leave related to lack of support.
Pollard, 2001 (94)	U.K.	Job insecurity: organizational restructuring (local government)	Longitudinal study, 1995–97, of sample of workers (98 women and 86 men)	Cholesterol levels, systolic and diastolic BP, self-reported psychological well-being	Yes; reorganization caused significant increase in distress and systolic BP	—
Probst, 2000 (95)	U.S.	Job insecurity: organizational restructuring (public sector)	Survey (n = 283) of public sector workers experiencing reorganization	Self-reported health problems, job attitudes, and psychological distress	Yes; workers with high job involvement report more negative health problems and attitudes to insecurity	—
Probst and Brubaker, 2001 (96)	U.S.	Job insecurity (food processing/manufacturing)	Two cross-sectional structural equation modeling analyses and 1 longitudinal regression analysis of 237 workers	Workplace injuries and accidents, safety motivation and compliance	Yes; workers perceiving higher insecurity exhibited less safety motivation and compliance and had higher levels of injury	—

APPENDIX (Cont'd.)

Author(s) and year (reference)	Location of study	Precarious employment category identified or study focus	Method	OHS indices	Link between OHS and precarious employment?	Remarks
Probst, 2002 (97)	U.S.	Job insecurity	Laboratory experiment involving 37 students (15 male and 22 female) at nontraditional university	Risk-taking behavior assessed in relation to tasks when threat of layoff	Yes; students faced with threat of layoff more productive, but violated safety rules and produced lower-quality output compared with control participants	90% of students worked full- or part-time (60% in supervisory positions), average age 30 yrs, and 16% had been laid off.
Rosenman et al., 2000 (98)	U.S.	Job insecurity	Survey (n = 1,598) using standardized questionnaire by phone	Workers' comp. claims for musculoskeletal injury	Yes; only 25% filed claims; those with shorter employment less likely to file; part-time/full-time status had no effect on claims	—
Roskies and Louis-Guerin, 1990 (99)	Canada	Job insecurity (manufacturing/information technology)	Surveyed 1,291 managers (none facing layoff but half in firms who laid off managers in past 5 yrs)	Psychological well-being (GHQ) and need to consult physicians/use medication	Yes; insecure managers showed poorer health, and level of distress rose proportionately with degree of insecurity	Subjective perception of insecurity explained 10% of the variance in mental health.
Saksvik, 1996 (100)	Norway	Job insecurity: organizational restructuring (telecommunications industry)	Two surveys of the same workers in a single organization 1 year apart (n = 401 for first, (n = 301 for second)	Self-reported work conditions, attendance pressure, and sick absenteeism	Yes; working conditions worsened, pressure not to report increased, and those absent more vulnerable	Short period of study (1 year), but points to limits of simple absence measures.

Source	Country	Topic	Study design	Measure	Effect	Comments
Schnall et al., 1992 (101)	U.S.	Job insecurity: downsizing (financial services/ stock brokerage)	Longitudinal screened sample 1986, 1989, 1990 (n1 = 870 and n2 = 369 [139 not] still with firm, 230 not]) and questionaire survey	BP and psychological distress	Yes; elevated psychological distress; no overall increase in BP, but increased diastolic pressure noted in clerical jobs and in 1 dept. on day it was sold	Clerical group had high workload/low control—link to Karasek model.
Schweiger and DeNisi, 1991 (102)	U.S.	Job insecurity: merger/ organizational restructuring (light manufacturing)	Controlled longitudinal field study of two plants (surveyed employees at experimental and control plants at 3 points)	Stress and absenteeism	Yes; increased stress, absenteeism, and uncertainty	Also found lower job satisfaction, honesty, trust, and caring ratings. "Realistic" merger preview moderated negative effects.
Shannon et al., 2001 (103)	Canada	Job insecurity: organizational restructuring/ downsizing (health care)	Longitudinal study (surveys in 1995, 1996, and 1997, n = 712) of large hospital workforce	Self-reported work conditions, psychological well-being, back and neck pain	Yes; significant decline in general health and significant increase in neck and back pain over time of change	Large female sample, and study considered spillover demands of work and family roles.
Siegrist, 1996 (104)	Germany and China	Job insecurity/ extended working hours (industrial/ manufacturing)	5 yr prospective/ longitudinal study with multiple samples (n China = 1,100; n Germany = 4,000)	Cardiovascular risk factors and events (myocardial infarction, death, strokes, BP, and CHD); mix of clinical and survey measures	Yes; job insecurity and work pressure predicted clusters of coronary events, CHD, or stroke; extended hours, job cuts, and insecurity linked to high BP and serum cholesterol	Well-controlled study (age, smoking, BP, etc.). Findings interesting, comparing developed and developing country. Also found heart rate and BP linked to worsening job conditions.
Snyder, 1994 (105)	U.S.	Job insecurity: downsizing (hospitals)	Hospital census of assaults in Baltimore area 1980–89	Occupational violence/patient assaults on staff	Yes; 4-fold increase in assaults as hospital census halved	Findings not confirmed by later Flannery et al. (42), who identify reasons for this.

APPENDIX (Cont'd.)

Author(s) and year (reference)	Location of study	Precarious employment category identified or study focus	Method	OHS indices	Link between OHS and precarious employment?	Remarks
Stechmiller and Yarandi, 1993 (106)	U.S.	Job insecurity (female health care workers)	Cross-sectional survey (n = 300)	Emotional exhaustion and job stress	Yes; job security had modest effect on emotional exhaustion and stress	Pay inversely related to job stress, but authors did not relate this to job insecurity.
Strazdins et al., 2004 (107)[a]	Australia	Job insecurity	Cross-sectional survey (n = 1,188) of middle-aged managers and professionals	Reported mental and physical health problems	Yes; those reporting job strain and job insecurity had markedly higher odds for mental and physical health problems	Like a number of other studies, this looked at a combination of job strain and job insecurity.
Swaen et al., 2004 (108)[g]	Netherlands	Job insecurity/ closure (government agency)	Prospective cohort study (part of Maastricht Cohort Fatigue Study) 1998, 1999, and 2000 (n = 574)	Fatigue and psychological distress	Yes; increased distress among those threatened with workplace closure and highest for those reporting job insecurity	Study notes stronger effect on less-educated may reflect less favorable labor market prospects, while gender differences due to ongoing dominance of males as family wage-earners.
Szubert, Sobala, and Zyci'nska, 1997 (109)	Poland	Job insecurity: downsizing (manufacturing)	Health records at industrial plant 1989–94 (n = 8,588)	Sickness absenteeism	Yes; 20% increase in absenteeism over downsizing period	Like Vahtera et al. (115), this found main cause of absence was musculoskeletal.

Study	Country	Type	Sample/Method	Measure	Results	Comments
Theorell et al., 2003 (110)	Sweden	Job insecurity: downsizing	Examined 5,720 employees, 18–65 yrs, from WOLF cardio risk study, Stockholm, 1992–95	Sickness absence	No; women's sickness absence fell in year after downsizing (esp. high cardiovascular scores); men—no relationship	Suggests impacts on women may relate to greater precariousness in the labor market—presenteeism?
Torkelson and Muhonen, 2003 (111)	Sweden	Job insecurity: downsizing (local government)	Surveyed 98 female and male administrators	Perceived stress and self-reported health symptoms (9 of 25 Hopkins Symptoms checklist)	1/3 of respondents' health symptom score indicated in need of professional help	Small study, primarily concerned with assessing coping strategies.
Tsutsumi et al., 2001 (113)	Japan	Job insecurity: downsizing (manufacturing)	Cross-sectional survey of 190 men and women in 1 plant	Self-reported stress (using demand/control and effort/reward model)	Yes; more depressive symptoms among employees targeted for downsizing	Study confirmed that 2 job stress models identify different aspects.
Vahtera, Kivimaki, and Pentti, 1998 (114)[d]	Finland	Job insecurity: downsizing (local government)	Employer health records of workers 1991–95 (n = 981)	Sick leave data	Yes; significant association between downsizing and sick leave (long-term)	Found effects on long-term absence; most pronounced for older workers.
Vahtera et al., 2000 (115)	Finland	Job insecurity: downsizing (local government)	Longitudinal analysis of employer health records 1991–97 (n = 530)	Sickness absence data	Yes; adverse effects on health, esp. for those in worst psychosocial environment before change	Seven year follow-up study.
Vahtera et al., 2004 (116)[d]	Finland	Job insecurity: downsizing (local government)	Prospective cohort study of 5,909 male and 16,521 female local government employees, 19–62 yrs, who kept their jobs	Sickness absence data and all-cause mortality data from national mortality register	Yes; major downsizing associated with increase in sickness absence for permanent but not temporary employees, and associated with cardiovascular deaths but not others	Concludes downsizing may increase sickness absence and risk of death from cardiovascular disease among those keeping jobs.

APPENDIX (Cont'd.)

Author(s) and year (reference)	Location of study	Precarious employment category identified or study focus	Method	OHS indices	Link between OHS and precarious employment?	Remarks
Vahtera et al., 2005 (117)[d]	Finland	Job insecurity: downsizing (local government)	Prospective cohort study of 19,273 local government employees, 21–54 yrs	Full disability pension data	Yes; 1.81 higher risk of disability retirement after major downsizing than no downsizing	Points to need to offset any financial advantage of downsizing with additional costs to employees and society.
Vicitez, Carica, and Rodriguez, 2000 (118)	Spain	Job insecurity: technological change (auto manufacturing)	Cross-sectional survey of 148 workers in 2 depts. of car components firm	Depression, state–trait anxiety and stress	Yes; perceived threat to security affected psychological well-being	Perceived threats most pronounced in least automated dept. and among less-educated and lower-level occupations.
Viitasara, Sverke, and Menckel, 2003 (119)	Sweden	Downsizing (health care)	Cross-sectional survey of stratified sample (n = 2,391; 80% response rate) of municipal health and welfare	Occupational violence	Yes; downsizing associated with risk of occupational violence	Age, organizational tenure, and high work-load also associated with exposure to violence.
Walthers, McDonough, and Strohschein, 2002 (120)	Canada	Job insecurity (gender differences in health)	Cross-sectional study from 1994 Canadian National Population Health Survey (n = 11,241)	Psychological distress, migraine, arthritis/rheumatism	Mixed; job insecurity significantly related to distress and migraine (not to arthritis/ rheumatism); no gender difference in job insecurity	Study principally focuses on gender differences in health due to work and household structure.

Westman, Etzion, and Danon, 2001 (121)	Israel	Job insecurity: downsizing (manufacturing)	Surveyed 98 married couples in organization	Burnout (i.e., psychological strain causing emotional exhaustion, depersonalization, crossover between partners	Mixed; burnout associated with job insecurity and crossover of burnout from husbands to wives, but not vice versa	Authors suggest a significant gender difference was lower jobs occupied by women and family responsibilities.
Westerlund et al., 2004 (122)[h]	Sweden	Job insecurity: downsizing and rapid expansion	Analyzed medically certified sickness absence and hospital admission in 1997–99 for 24,036 participants in Swedish Work Environment Surveys 1989–99	Sickness absence and hospital admission	Yes; downsizing associated with increased sickness absence, while rapid expansion linked to increased sickness absence and hospital admission	Women in public sector most affected by expansion. Authors say effect may be connected to centralization of functions. Study suggests rapid change in either direction may have adverse effects.
Westerlund, Theorell, and Alfredsson, 2004 (123)	Sweden	Job insecurity: white-collar employees in large firms and entrepreneurs in small firms	Survey and medical screening of 3,904 white-collar workers in 15 large companies (part of WOLF study) and entrepreneurs in small firms	Examined job strain and cardiovascular risk factors (e.g., cholesterol) in organizations rated as stable or unstable	Yes; instability—expansion and downsize—linked to higher job strain and psychophysiology; small-firm effects also with elevated risks	Finding that organizational instability has effects, not just downsizing, warrants further investigation. Small firm aspect also valuable.
Woodward et al., 1999 (124)	Canada	Job insecurity: organizational restructuring, reengineering (health care)	Longitudinal 2 yr study (n = 900) of large hospital	Emotional distress (depression, anxiety, and emotional exhaustion)	Yes; significant increase in depression, anxiety, and exhaustion	Also noted long-term effects on quality of patient care.

Note: The following were not counted: [a] same project as D'Souza et al., 2003 (31); [b] same project as Ferrie et al., 1995 (34); [c] same project as Petterson and Arnetz, 1998 (92); [d] same project as Kivimaki et al., 1997 (60); [e] same project as Kinnunen et al., 2000 (58); [f] same project as Pepper, 2000 (89); [g] same project as Mohren et al., 2003 (79); [h] same project as Theorell et al., 2003 (110).

23. Catalano, R., Rook, K., and Dooley, D. Labor markets and help-seeking: A test of the employment security hypothesis. *J. Health Soc. Behav.* 27:277–287, 1986.
24. Catalano, R., and Serxner, S. The effect of ambient threats to employment on low birthweight. *J. Health Soc. Behav.* 33:363–377, 1992.
25. Cheng, Y., et al. Job insecurity and its association with health among employees in the Taiwanese general population. *Soc. Sci. Med.* 61:41–52, 2005.
26. De Witte, H. Job insecurity and psychological well-being: Review of the literature and exploration of some unresolved issues. *Eur. J. Work Org. Psychol.* 8(2):155–177, 1999.
27. Dekker, S., and Schaufeli, W. The effects of job insecurity on psychological health and withdrawal: A longitudinal study. *Aust. Psychol.* 30(1):57–63, 1995.
28. Domenighetti, G., D'Avanzo, B., and Bisig, B. Health effects of job insecurity among employees in the Swiss general population. *Int. J. Health Serv.* 30(3): 477–490, 2000.
29. Dooley, D., Rook, K., and Catalano, R. Job and non-job stressors and their moderators. *J. Occup. Psychol.* 60:115–132, 1987.
30. Dragano, N., Verde, P., and Siegrist, J. Organisational downsizing and work stress: Testing synergistic health effects in employed men and women. *J. Epidemiol. Community Health* 59:694–699, 2005.
31. D'Souza, R., et al. Work and health in a contemporary society: Demands, control and insecurity. *J. Epidemiol. Community Health* 57:849–854, 2003.
32. Earnshaw, A., Amundson, N., and Borgen, W. The experience of job insecurity for professional women. *J. Employ. Couns.* 27:2–18, 1990.
33. Fenwick, R., and Tausig, M. The macroeconomic context of job stress. *J. Health Soc. Behav.* 35:266–282, 1994.
34. Ferrie, J., et al. Health effects of anticipation of job change and non-employment: Longitudinal data from the Whitehall II study. *BMJ* 311(7015):311–320, 1995.
35. Ferrie, J., et al. The health effects of major organisational change and job insecurity. *Soc. Sci. Med.* 46(2):243–254, 1998.
36. Ferrie, J., et al. An uncertain future: The health effects of threats to employment security in white collar men and women. *Am. J. Public Health* 88(7):1030–1036, 1998.
37. Ferrie, J., et al. Job insecurity in white collar workers: Towards an explanation of associations with health. *J. Occup. Health Psychol.* 6(1):26–42, 2001.
38. Ferrie, J., et al. Employment status and health after privatization in white collar civil servants: Prospective cohort study. *BMJ* 322:1–7, 2001.
39. Ferrie, J., et al. Effects of chronic job insecurity and changes in job security on self reported health, minor psychiatric morbidity, physiological measures, and health related behaviours in British civil servants: The Whitehall II study. *J. Epidemiol. Community Health* 56(6):450–454, 2002.
40. Ferrie, J., et al. Self-reported job insecurity and health in the Whitehall II study: Potential explanations of the relationship. *Soc. Sci. Med.* 60(7):1593–1602, 2005.
41. Ferrie, J., et al. The impact of moderate and major workplace expansion and down-sizing on the psychosocial and physical work environment and income in Sweden. *Scand. J. Public Health* 35(1):62–69, 2007.
42. Flannery, R., et al. Hospital downsizing and patients' assaults on staff. *Psychiatr. Q.* 68(1):67–76, 1997.

43. Gallo, W., et al. Involuntary job loss as a risk factor for subsequent myocardial infarction and stroke: Findings from the health and retirement survey. *Am. J. Ind. Med.* 45:408–416, 2004.
44. Gillespie, N., et al. Occupational stress in universities: Staff perceptions of the causes, consequences and moderators of stress. *Work Stress* 15(1):53–72, 2001.
45. Godin, I., Desmarez, P., and Kittel, F. Work stress and instability of employment: Complementary contribution of different data sources. *Stress Health* 22(1):51–58, 2006.
46. Grunberg, L., Moore, S., and Greenberg, E. Differences in psychological and physical health amongst layoff survivors: The effect of layoff contact. *J. Occup. Health Psychol.* 6(1):15–25, 2001.
47. Hamilton, V., et al. Hard times and vulnerable people: Initial effects of plant closing on autoworkers' mental health. *J. Health Soc. Behav.* 31:123–140, 1990.
48. Harenstam, A., et al. Multilevel analyses of organisational change and working conditions in public and private sector. *J. Work Org. Psychol.* 13(3):305–343, 2004.
49. Heaney, C., Israel, B., and House, J. Chronic job insecurity among automobile workers: Effects on job satisfaction and health. *Soc. Sci. Med.* 38(10):1431–1437, 1994.
50. Hellgren, J., Sverke, M., and Isaksson, K. A two-dimensional approach to job insecurity: Consequences for employee attitudes and well-being. *Eur. J. Work Org. Psychol.* 8(2):179–195, 1999.
51. Hellgren, J., and Chirumbolo, A. Can union support reduce the negative effects of job insecurity on wellbeing? *Econ. Ind. Democr.* 24(2):271–289, 2003.
52. Hellgren, J., and Sverke, M. Does job insecurity lead to impaired well-being or vice versa? Estimation of cross-lagged effects using latent variable modelling. *J. Org. Behav.* 24(2):215–236, 2003.
53. Hertting, A., et al. Downsizing and reorganisation: Demands, challenges and ambiguity for registered nurses. *J. Adv. Nurs.* 45(2):145–154, 2004.
54. Isaksson, K., Hellgren, J., and Pettersson, P. Repeated downsizing: Attitudes and well-being of surviving personnel in a Swedish retail company. In *Health Effects of the New Labour Market*, ed. K. Isaksson et al., pp. 85–101. Kluwer/Plenum, New York, 2000.
55. Iversen, L., and Sabroe, S. Psychological well-being among unemployed and employed people after a company closedown: A longitudinal study. *J. Soc. Iss.* 44:141–152, 1988.
56. Jenkins, R., et al. Minor psychiatric morbidity and the threat of redundancy in a professional group. *Psychol. Med.* 12:799–807, 1982.
57. Kalimo, R., Taris, T., and Schaufeli, W. The effects of past and anticipated future downsizing on survivor wellbeing: An equity perspective. *J. Occup. Health Psychol.* 8(2):91–109, 2003.
58. Kinnunen, U., et al. Perceived job insecurity: A longitudinal study among Finnish employees. *Eur. J. Work Org. Psychol.* 8(2):243–260, 2000.
59. Kristensen, T., Borg, V., and Hannerz, H. Socioeconomic status and psychosocial work environment: Results from a Danish national study. *Scand. J. Public Health* 30(Suppl. 59):41–48, 2002.
60. Kivimaki, M., et al. Psychological factors predicting employee sickness absence during economic decline. *J. Appl. Psychol.* 82(6):858–872, 1997.

61. Kivimaki, M., et al. Response of hostile individuals to stressful changes in their working lives: Test of a psychological vulnerability model. *Psychol. Med.* 28(4):903–913, 1998.

62. Kivimaki, M., et al. Factors underlying the effect of organisational downsizing on the health of employees: Longitudinal cohort study. *BMJ* 320:971–975, 2000.

63. Kivimaki, M., et al. Organisational downsizing and musculoskeletal problems in employees: A prospective study. *Occup. Environ. Med.* 58(12):811–817, 2001.

64. Kivimaki, M., et al. Downsizing, changes in work, and self-rated health of employees: A 7-year 3 wave panel study. *Anxiety Stress Coping* 14(1):59–73, 2001.

65. Kivimaki, M., et al. Human costs of organisational downsizing: Comparing health trends between leavers and stayers. *Am. J. Community Psychol.* 32(1-2):57–67, 2003.

66. Kivimaki, M., et al. Organisational downsizing and increased use of psychotropic drugs among employees who remain in employment. *J. Epidemiol. Community Health* 61:154–158, 2007.

67. Lau, B., and Knardahl, S. Perceived job insecurity, job predictability, personality and health. *J. Occup. Environ. Med.* 50:172–181, 2008.

68. Layton, C. Levels of state anxiety for males facing redundancy and subsequent reporting to be employed or unemployed. *Percept. Mot. Skills* 65:53–54, 1987.

69. Lee, S., et al. Prospective study of job insecurity and coronary heart disease in US women. *Ann. Epidemiol.* 14:24–30, 2003.

70. Lipscomb, J., et al. Health care system change and reported musculoskeletal disorders amongst registered nurses. *Am. J. Public Health* 94(8):1431–1435, 2004.

71. Mak, A., and Mueller, J. Job insecurity, coping resources and personality dispositions in occupational strain. *Work Stress* 14(4):312–328, 2000.

72. Mantler, J., et al. Coping with employment uncertainty: A comparison of employed and unemployed workers. *J. Occup. Health Psychol.* 10(3):200–209, 2005.

73. Marchand, A., Demers, A., and Durand, P. Social structures, agent personality and workers' mental health: A longitudinal analysis of the specific role of occupation and of workplace constraints-resources on psychological distress in the Canadian workforce. *Hum. Relat.* 59(7):875–901, 2006.

74. Mattiasson, I., et al. Threat of unemployment and cardiovascular risk factors: Longitudinal study of quality of sleep and serum cholesterol concentrations in men threatened with redundancy. *BMJ* 301:141–146, 1990.

75. Mauno, S., and Kinnunen, U. Job insecurity and well-being: A longitudinal study among male and female employees in Finland. *Community Work Fam.* 2(2):147–171, 1999.

76. Mauno, S., and Kinnunen, U. The effects of job stressors on marital satisfaction in Finnish dual earner couples. *J. Org. Behav.* 20:879–895, 1999.

77. McDonough, P. Job insecurity and health. *Int. J. Health Serv.* 30(2):453–476, 2000.

78. McHugh, M. Rationalisation as a key stressor for public sector employees: An organisational case study. *Occup. Med.* 48(2):103–112, 1998.

79. Mohren, D., et al. Job insecurity as a risk factor for common infections and health complaints. *J. Occup. Environ. Med.* 45(2):123–129, 2003.

80. Muntaner, C., et al. Work organization and atherosclerosis: Findings from the ARIC study. *Am. J. Prev. Med.* 14(1):9–18, 1998.

81. Naswall, K., Sverke, M., and Hellgren, J. The moderating role of personality characteristics on the relationship between job insecurity and strain. *Work Stress* 19(1):37–49, 2005.
82. Niedhammer, I., et al. Psychosocial work environment and mental health: Job-strain and effort-reward imbalance models in a context of major organisational changes. *Int. J. Occup. Environ. Health* 12(2):111–119, 2006.
83. Orpen, C. The effects of self-esteem and personal control on the relationship between job-insecurity and psychological well-being. *Soc. Behav. Pers.* 22(1):53–55, 1994.
84. Osthus, S. For better or worse? Workplace change and the health and wellbeing of Norwegian workers. *Work Employ. Soc.* 21(4):731–750, 2007.
85. Owen, A. Sick leave among railwaymen threatened by redundancy: A pilot study. *Occup. Psychol.* 40:43–52, 1966.
86. Park, Y., and Butler, R. The safety costs of contingent work: Evidence from Minnesota. *J. Labor Res.* 12(4):831–849, 2001.
87. Parker, S., Chmiel, N., and Wall, T. Work characteristics and employee well-being within the context of strategic downsizing. *J. Occup. Health Psychol.* 2(4):289–303, 1997.
88. Pelfrene, E., et al. Perceptions of job insecurity and the impact of world market competition as health risks: Results from BELSTRESS. *J. Occup. Org. Psychol.* 76:411–425, 2003.
89. Pepper, L. *The Health Effects of Downsizing in the Nuclear Industry.* National Institute of Occupational Health, Cincinnati, 2000.
90. Pepper, L., et al. Downsizing and health in the United States Department of Energy. *Am. J. Ind. Med.* 44:481–491, 2003.
91. Campbell, R., and Pepper, L. Organizational downsizing: Implications for the health of survivors. *New Solutions* 12(2):177–194, 2002.
92. Petterson, I., and Arnetz, B. Psychosocial stressors and well-being in health care workers: The impact of an intervention program. *Soc. Sci. Med.* 47(11):1763–1772, 1998.
93. Petterson, I., et al. Are trends in work and health conditions interrelated? A study of Swedish hospital employees in the 1990s. *J. Occup. Health Psychol.* 10(2):110–120, 2005.
94. Pollard, T. Changes in mental well-being, blood pressure and total cholesterol levels during workplace reorganization: The impact of uncertainty. *Work Stress* 15(1):14–28, 2001.
95. Probst, T. Wedded to the job: Moderating effects of job involvement on the consequences of job insecurity. *J. Occup. Health Psychol.* 5(1):63–73, 2000.
96. Probst, T., and Brubaker, T. The effects of job insecurity on employee safety outcomes: Cross-sectional and longitudinal explorations. *J. Occup. Health Psychol.* 6(2):139–159, 2001.
97. Probst, T. Layoffs and tradeoffs: Production, quality and safety demands under the threat of job loss. *J. Occup. Health Psychol.* 7(3):211–220, 2002.
98. Rosenman, K., et al, Why most workers with occupational repetitive trauma do not file for workers' compensation. *J. Occup. Environ. Med.* 42(1):25–34, 2000.
99. Roskies, E., and Louis-Guerin, C. Job insecurity in managers: Antecedents and consequences. *J. Org. Behav.* 11(5):345–359, 1990.

100. Saksvik, P. Attendance pressure during organisational change. *Int. J. Stress Manage.* 3(1):47–59, 1996.
101. Schnall, P., et al. The impact of anticipation of job loss on psychological distress and worksite blood-pressure. *Am. J. Ind. Med.* 21(3):417–432, 1992.
102. Schweiger, D., and DeNisi, A. Communication with employees following a merger—a longitudinal field experiment. *Acad. Manage. J.* 34(1):110–135, 1991.
103. Shannon, H., et al. Change in general health and musculoskeletal outcomes in the workforce of a hospital undergoing rapid change: A longitudinal study. *J. Occup. Health Psychol.* 6(1):3–14, 2001.
104. Siegrist, J. Adverse health effects of high-effort/low-reward conditions. *J. Occup. Health Psychol.* 1(1):27–41, 1996.
105. Snyder, W. Hospital downsizing and increased frequency of assaults on staff. *Hosp. Community Psychiatr.* 45(4):378–380, 1994.
106. Stechmiller, J., and Yarandi, H. Predictors of burnout in critical care nurses. *Heart Lung* 22(6):534–541, 1993.
107. Strazdins, L., et al. Job strain, job insecurity, and health: Rethinking the relationship. *J. Occup. Health Psychol.* 9(4):296–305, 2004.
108. Swaen, G., et al. Effects of job insecurity from a workplace closure threat on fatigue and psychological distress. *J. Occup. Environ. Med.* 46(5):443–449, 2004.
109. Szubert, Z., Sobala, W., and Zyci'nska, Z. The effect of system restructuring on absenteeism due to sickness in the workplace. *Medycyna Pracy* 48(5):543–551, 1997.
110. Theorell, T., et al. Downsizing of staff is associated with lowered medically certified sick leave in female employees. *Occup. Environ. Med.* 60(9), 2003. doi: 10.1136/oem.60.9.e9.
111. Torkelson, E., and Muhonen, T. Coping strategies and health symptoms among women and men in a downsizing organisation. *Psychol. Rep.* 92:899–907, 2003.
112. Trinkoff, A., et al. Staffing and worker injury in nursing homes. *Am. J. Public Health* 95(7):1220–1225, 2005.
113. Tsutsumi, A., et al. Association between job stress and depression among Japanese employees threatened by job loss in a comparison of two complementary job-stress models. *Scand. J. Work Environ. Health* 27(2):146–153, 2001.
114. Vahtera, J., Kivimaki, M., and Pentti, J. Effects of organisational downsizing on health of employees. *Lancet* 350:1124–1128, 1998.
115. Vahtera, J., et al. Effect of change in the psychosocial work environment on sickness absence: A seven year follow-up of initially healthy employees. *J. Epidemiol. Community Health* 54:484–493, 2000.
116. Vahtera, J., et al. Organisational downsizing, sickness absence, and mortality: 10-town prospective cohort study. *BMJ* online, 2004. doi: 10.1136/bmj.37972.496262.0D.
117. Vahtera, J., et al. Organisational downsizing as a predictor of disability pension: The 10-town prospective cohort study. *J. Epidemiol. Community Health* 59:238–242, 2005.
118. Vieitez, J., Carica, A., and Rodriguez, M. Perception of job security in a process of technological change: Its influence on psychological well-being. *Behav. Inf. Technol.* 20(3):213–223, 2000.

119. Viitasara, E., Sverke, M., and Menckel, E. Multiple risk factors for violence to seven occupational groups in the Swedish caring sector. *Relations Industrielles* 58(2):202–231, 2003.
120. Walters, V., McDonough, P., and Strohschein, L. The influence of work, household structure, and social, personal and material resources on gender differences in health: An analysis of the 1994 Canadian National Population Health Survey. *Soc. Sci. Med.* 54(5):677–692, 2002
121. Westman, M., Etzion, D., and Danon, E. Job insecurity and crossover of burnout in married couples. *J. Org. Behav.* 22:467–481, 2001.
122. Westerlund, H., et al. Workplace expansion, long-term sickness absence and hospital admission. *Lancet* 363:1193–1197, 2004.
123. Westerlund, H., Theorell, T., and Alfredsson, L. Organisational instability and cardiovascular risk factors in white collar employees. *Eur. J. Public Health* 14(1):37–42, 2004.
124. Woodward, C., et al. The impact of re-engineering and other cost reduction strategies on the staff of a large teaching hospital: A longitudinal study. *Med. Care* 37:556–569, 1999.
125. Pelfrene, E., et al. Use of benzodiazepine drugs and perceived job stress in a cohort of working men and women in Belgium: Results from the BELSTRESS study. *Soc. Sci. Med.* 59:433–442, 2004.
126. Sikora, P., et al. Downsizing and alcohol use: A cross-lagged longitudinal examination of the spillover hypothesis. *Work Stress* 22(1):51–68, 2008.
127. Folger, R., and Skarlicki, D. When tough times makes tough bosses: Managerial distancing as a function of layoff blame. *Acad. Manage. J.* 41(1):79–87, 1998.
128. Quinlan, M., and Bohle, P. Contingent work and occupational safety. In *The Psychology of Workplace Safety*, ed. J. Barling and M. Frone, pp. 81–106. American Psychological Association, Washington, DC, 2004.
129. Kivimaki, M., et al. Job strain and ischaemic disease: Does the inclusion of older employees in the cohort dilute the association? The WOLD Stockholm Study. *J. Epidemiol. Community Health* 62:372–374, 2008.
130. Siegrist, J. Social reciprocity and health: New scientific evidence and policy implications. *Psychoneuroendocrinology* 30:1033–1038, 2005.
131. Clarke, M., et al. "This just isn't sustainable": Precarious employment, stress and workers' health. *Int. J. Law Psychiatr.* 30(4-5):311–326, 2007.
132. Beckers, D. G. J., et al. Voluntary or involuntary? Control over overtime and rewards for overtime in relation to fatigue and work satisfaction. *Work Stress* 22(1):33–50, 2008.
133. Knudsen, K., et al. Downsizing survival: The experience of work and organizational commitment. *Sociol. Inq.* 73(2):265–283, 2003.
134. Brennan, A., and Skarlicki, D. Personality and perceived justice as predictors of survivors' reactions following downsizing. *J. Appl. Soc. Psychol.* 34(6):1306–1328, 2004.
135. Bambra, C., et al. The psychosocial and health effects of workplace reorganization: 2. A systematic review of task restructuring interventions. *J. Epidemiol. Community Health* 61:1028–1037, 2007.
136. Leroyer, A., et al. Prospective evaluation of the impact of a change in the organization of work on perceived stress and health in assembly-line workers in an automobile plant. *Rev. Epidemiol. Sante Publ.* 54:15–25, 2006.

CHAPTER 11

Employer-Sponsored Health Insurance Erosion Accelerates in the Recession

Elise Gould

From 2000 to 009, the share of non-elderly Americans covered by employer-sponsored health insurance (ESI) fell 9.4 percentage points. Although the economy was already in a recession in 2008, it continued to dramatically deteriorate in 2009. From 2008 to 2009, the unemployment rate rose 3.5 percentage points, the largest one-year increase on record. As most Americans under age 65 rely on health insurance obtained through the workplace, it is no surprise that ESI fell sharply from 2008 to 2009 at a rate three times as high as in the first year of the recession. Over the 2000s, no demographic or socioeconomic group has been spared from the erosion of job-based insurance. Both genders and people of all ages, races, education, and income levels have suffered declines in coverage. Workers across the wage distribution, in small and large firms alike, and even those working full-time and in white-collar jobs have experienced losses. Along with sharp declines in ESI, the share of those under age 65 without any insurance increased 3.3 percentage points from 2000 to 2009. Increasing public insurance coverage, particularly among children, is the only reason the uninsured rate did not rise one-for-one with losses in ESI.

*****

The share of Americans under age 65 covered by employer-sponsored health insurance (ESI) eroded for the ninth year in a row, falling from 61.9 percent in 2008 to 58.9 percent in 2009. While the country was already in a recession in 2008, the economy sharply deteriorated in 2009. The unemployment rate increased from 5.8 percent to 9.3 percent between 2008 and 2009, the largest one-year increase on record. As most Americans, particularly those under age 65, rely on health insurance obtained through the workplace, it is no surprise that ESI fell from 2008 to 2009 at a rate three times as high as in the first year of the recession.

While ESI remains the predominant source of coverage for Americans under age 65, in 2009 ESI covered nearly 10 percent fewer Americans under age 65 than in 2000. As many as 25 million more people under age 65 would have had ESI in 2009 if the coverage rate had remained at the 2000 level. No demographic or socioeconomic group has been spared from the erosion of job-based insurance over the 2000s. Both genders and people of all ages, races, education, and income levels have suffered declines in coverage. Workers across the wage distribution, in small and large firms alike, and even those working full-time and in white-collar jobs have experienced coverage losses.

Along with sharp declines in ESI, the percentage of those under age 65 without any insurance also has increased over the 2000s, from 15.5 percent in 2000 to 18.8 percent in 2009. The number of Americans under age 65 without health insurance coverage rose from 45.7 million in 2008 to 50.0 million in 2009, an increase of 4.3 million. Since 2000, the number of uninsured has grown by 11.8 million.

Increasing *public* insurance coverage, particularly among children, is the only reason the uninsured rate did not rise one-for-one with losses in ESI. Children saw larger declines in ESI than adults over the 2000s (10.1 percentage points), but actually experienced an *increase* in total coverage rates as the share with public coverage rose 12.4 percentage points. Non-elderly adults regained about half their losses in ESI from other sources as ESI fell 9.1 percentage points, but the percentage of uninsured rose by only 5.1 percentage points over the 2000s. Medicaid, the Children's Health Insurance Program (CHIP), and Medicare have served as a safety net for non-elderly adults and have insured millions as employment-based benefits were lost. Provisions in the American Recovery and Reinvestment Act (ARRA) of 2009 further mitigated the damage by subsidizing COBRA, the common abbreviation for the Con-solidated Omnibus Budget Reconciliation Act, and helping to shore up Medicaid funding.

The current recession highlights Americans' dependence on a healthy labor market for all facets of economic security, including access to health care. While the largest increase in the unemployment rate for this recession is probably behind us, the unemployment rate is forecasted to increase to 9.7 percent in 2010 and 9.9 percent in 2011. Given these projections, ESI coverage could be expected to drop another 0.5 percentage points by 2011 and the number of non-elderly uninsured could increase by another one-half million.

This report's central findings include:

- In 2009, 50.0 million people under age 65 were uninsured, up 4.3 million since 2008. The number of non-elderly uninsured Americans is more than 11.8 million higher than in 2000.
- The share of non-elderly Americans with ESI declined for the ninth year in a row, from 61.9 percent in 2008 to 58.9 percent in 2009, and dropped a

total of 9.4 percentage points since 2000. In 2009, 11.4 million fewer non-elderly persons had employer-sponsored coverage than in 2000.

- As many as 25 million more people under age 65 would have had ESI in 2009 if the coverage rate had remained at the 2000 level.
- Workers ages 18 to 64 experienced losses in job-based coverage, from 70.1 percent in 2008 to 68.1 percent in 2009. Among strongly attached workers (i.e., working at least 20 hours per week and 26 weeks per year), service-sector workers had the lowest rates of coverage from their own jobs and experienced the largest declines.
- Workers were 25 percent more likely to be uninsured in 2009 than in 2000. Uninsured workers are disproportionately young, Hispanic, less educated, and lower-income. Part-time workers were 27.6 percent more likely to be uninsured than full-time workers in 2000, but 58.8 percent more likely to be uninsured in 2009.
- Children's employer-sponsored insurance coverage fell 10.1 percentage points over the 2000s, and the gap in ESI access by income widened substantially over this period.
- Public health insurance—and the boost it received as part of the Recovery Act—is responsible for keeping millions from becoming uninsured as job-based coverage sharply declined over the 2000s. Public insurance covered 20.3 million more people in 2009 than in 2000.
- The decline in ESI coverage through the 2000s was felt nationwide, with a statistically significant decrease in non-elderly coverage in 44 states. No state had a statistically significant increase in coverage over this period.
- Although the Patient Protection and Affordable Care Act (PPACA), informally known as health reform, will substantially insure more Americans, especially as the 2014 insurance exchange provisions take effect, rising unemployment likely will lead to further ESI losses in the near future.

OVERALL HEALTH INSURANCE TRENDS

ESI remains the primary form of coverage for non-elderly Americans, at 58.9 percent (Figure 1). However, this has eroded each year since 2000, a total of 9.4 percentage points. ESI coverage fell 5.4 percentage points even over the previous full business cycle, peak to peak from 2000 to 2007. Declines continued even after the recession ended in 2001 and the economy expanded. Losses in ESI moderated considerably as the economy finally began adding jobs in 2003, but losses continued unabated nonetheless. These relatively small declines in coverage increased as the recession took hold in 2008 and accelerated as the unemployment rate soared in 2009.

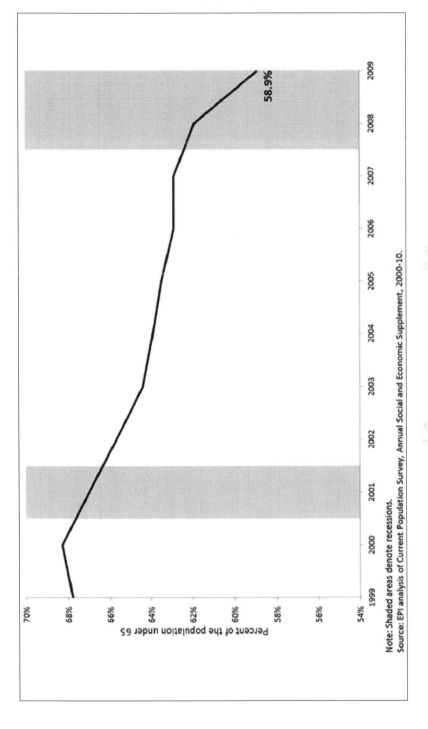

Figure 1. Share of the population under age 65 with employer-sponsored insurance, 1999–2009.

While for many Americans, a loss of ESI translates into a loss of any kind of coverage, rates of overall coverage did not fall as much as ESI losses (Figure 2). In 2009, the uninsured rate of those under age 65 rose to 18.8 percent, an increase of 1.7 percentage points since the recession began and a total increase of 3.3 percentage points since 2000.

While the data do not track individuals over time to see what happens to specific people as they lose ESI, it is clear that overall coverage rates would have fallen further had there not been increases in public coverage, including Medicaid, CHIP, and Medicare. Public coverage increased 2.9 percentage points since 2007 and 6.5 percentage points since 2000, partially offsetting losses in ESI. Non-group or direct purchase insurance remained relatively flat over the entire period, failing to compensate for ESI losses.

DECLINES IN EMPLOYER-SPONSORED COVERAGE

Although ESI coverage losses for those under age 65 slowed in response to economic growth in the mid-2000s, the declines accelerated with the 2008 recession. Coverage fell by 1 percentage point in 2008, followed by a sharp decline of 3 percentage points in 2009 (Table 1). This resulted in a total loss of 9.4 percentage points over the 2000s. About 6.6 million fewer people had ESI in 2009 than in 2008; compared with 2000, 11.4 million fewer people had this coverage. These figures fail to show the true extent of the erosion because they ignore population growth over the 2000s. As many as 25 million more people under age 65 would have had ESI in 2009 if the coverage rate had remained at the 2000 level.

Coverage losses occurred across all age groups, but young adults consistently have the lowest rates of coverage. Less than half of this group finds health insurance through the workplace. The PPACA allows young adults up to age 26 to remain on their parents' ESI plans. While this provision will improve the low coverage rates for this population, coverage for young adults through this avenue is dependent on parental coverage, which fell over the 2000s and is more likely to be secured by higher incomes.

The greatest declines in ESI were among working-age adults (25 to 54 years old), which declined a total of 10.5 percentage points since 2000. Children's losses were close behind, falling 10.1 percentage points. Coverage declined for males and females alike and across racial and ethnic classifications. As shown in Figure 3, racial and ethnic disparities in coverage persist over time, with white non-Hispanics experiencing rates of ESI coverage 80 percent higher than Hispanics and 45 percent higher than blacks. ESI coverage among the native-born is 38 percent higher than that of foreign-born, though the native-born experienced larger losses since the recession began and over the 2000s as a whole.

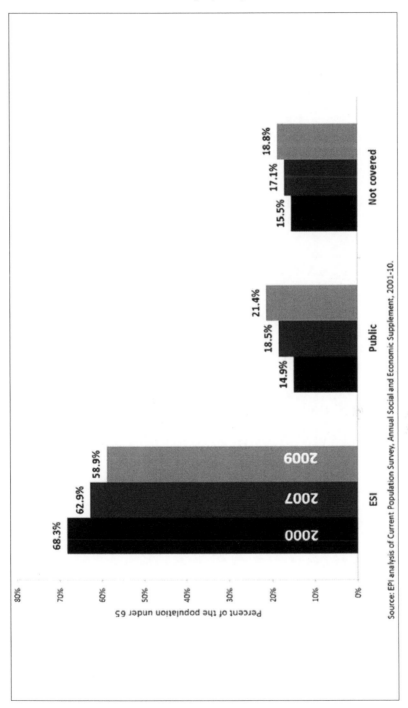

Figure 2. Sources of health insurance coverage for population under age 65.

Table 1

Employer-sponsored health insurance coverage by age, gender, race, nativity, education, and income quintile, 2000–2009

	2000	2007	2008	2009	Percentage-point change			
					2000–2007	2007–2008	2008–2009	2000–2009
Under 65 population	68.3%	62.9%	61.9%	58.9%	–5.4	–1.0	–3.0	–9.4
Age								
0–17	65.9%	59.5%	58.9%	55.8%	–6.5	–0.6	–3.1	–10.1
18–24	53.5%	48.4%	46.9%	43.7%	–5.1	–1.5	–3.2	–9.8
25–54	72.9%	66.8%	65.7%	62.4%	–6.1	–1.1	–3.3	–10.5
55–64	68.1%	67.8%	66.8%	65.7%	–0.3	–1.0	–1.1	–2.4
Gender								
Male	68.2%	62.5%	61.4%	58.2%	–5.7	–1.1	–3.1	–10.0
Female	68.3%	63.2%	62.3%	59.6%	–5.1	–0.9	–2.7	–8.7
Race								
White, non-Hispanic	75.6%	70.8%	69.8%	67.4%	–4.8	–1.0	–2.4	–8.2
Black	56.1%	51.6%	50.2%	46.6%	–4.5	–1.4	–3.6	–9.5
Hispanic	45.8%	41.4%	41.4%	37.5%	–4.4	–0.1	–3.9	–8.4
Other	64.3%	61.7%	60.8%	58.6%	–2.6	–1.0	–2.2	–5.7

Nativity								
Native	70.4%	65.1%	63.9%	61.0%	-5.3	-1.2	-2.9	-9.4
Foreign-born	52.2%	47.4%	47.1%	44.2%	-4.8	-0.2	-3.0	-8.0
Education[a]								
Less than high school	39.0%	30.1%	29.7%	26.9%	-8.9	-0.4	-2.8	-12.1
High school	65.6%	56.4%	55.2%	51.2%	-9.2	-1.3	-3.9	-14.4
Some college	73.3%	67.0%	64.8%	61.9%	-6.3	-2.2	-2.9	-11.4
College	83.5%	80.0%	79.6%	77.2%	-3.6	-0.3	-2.4	-6.3
Post-college	87.6%	85.8%	86.2%	84.6%	-1.9	0.4	-1.6	-3.0
Household income fifth								
Lowest	28.7%	21.9%	19.9%	16.3%	-6.8	-2.0	-3.5	-12.4
Second	61.7%	53.6%	50.4%	46.4%	-8.1	-3.2	-4.0	-15.3
Middle	77.4%	71.6%	71.0%	67.4%	-5.7	-0.6	-3.6	-9.9
Fourth	85.6%	81.9%	81.6%	79.6%	-3.7	-0.3	-2.0	-6.1
Highest	88.4%	86.4%	86.4%	84.9%	-1.9	-0.1	-1.4	-3.4

[a]Education reflects own education for individuals 18 and over and reflects family head's education for children under 18.

Source: Author's analysis of the March Current Population Survey, 2001–2010.

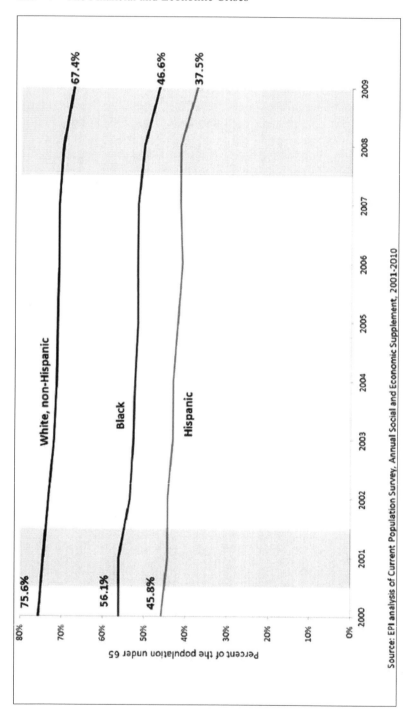

Source: EPI analysis of Current Population Survey, Annual Social and Economic Supplement, 2001-2010.

Figure 3. Share of the population under age 65 with ESI by race, 2000–2009.

Educational attainment is a strong predictor of incidence of insurance. Those with advanced degrees are more than three times more likely to have ESI than those with less than a high school education.[1] Just over half (51.2%) of those with only a high school degree have job-based coverage compared with more than three-fourths (77.2%) of college graduates.

Similar to education, higher household incomes are strongly associated with an increased likelihood of having employment-based coverage. In 2009, only 16.3 percent of those in the bottom income fifth had ESI compared with 84.9 percent of those in the top fifth, a five-fold difference in the likelihood of being insured through work. Each income group experienced losses over the 2000s; however, the declines were much greater for those at the bottom. Those in the second fifth were hit the worst in the recession, experiencing a two-year loss of 7.2 percentage points and a total decline of 15.3 percentage points since 2000.

DECLINING COVERAGE FOR WORKERS

Employer-Sponsored Health Insurance

Unsurprisingly, employer-sponsored health insurance coverage is higher among workers (ages 18 to 64) than the general population under age 65: 68.1 percent in 2009 compared with 58.9 percent for the overall non-elderly. Workers' declines in coverage also have been smaller: 2.0 percentage points from 2008 to 2009 and 6.6 percentage points since 2000 (Table 2). Neither trend is surprising given that ESI is found via work, so when one loses employment, one often loses the benefits that go with it (unless one keeps insurance as a retiree or through a spouse or never had coverage in the first place).

While declines in coverage briefly abated as the economy expanded from 2006 to 2007, coverage fell 3.7 percentage points from peak to peak, 2000 to 2007. The 2.9 percentage-point declines since the peak can be partially attributed to the start of the recession in December 2007 and partially to the overall trend in declining coverage.

Male workers have lower rates of coverage than female (66.3% vs. 70.2%) and have experienced larger declines over the 2000s. The larger declines in coverage for working men and men in general in the recession are not surprising given their higher unemployment rates, leading to not only fewer men employed, but also lower wage growth (1).

Similar to the overall population, large disparities exist in ESI coverage for workers by race and ethnicity. Nearly three-fourths of white non-Hispanic workers are covered, compared to less than half of Hispanic workers. Racial

---

[1] The results under the education heading assign each child the education level of their family head, as children under 18 rarely complete their education by that time.

Table 2

Employer-sponsored health insurance coverage for workers 18–64 years old by gender, race, nativity, education, wage quintile, and work status, 2000–2009

| | 2000 | 2007 | 2008 | 2009 | Percentage-point change | | | |
					2000–2007	2007–2008	2008–2009	2000–2009
All workers	74.8%	71.0%	70.1%	68.1%	-3.7	-0.9	-2.0	-6.6
Gender								
Male	73.9%	69.4%	68.4%	66.3%	-4.5	-0.9	-2.1	-7.6
Female	75.8%	72.9%	72.1%	70.2%	-2.8	-0.8	-1.9	-5.6
Race								
White, non-Hispanic	79.6%	76.4%	75.5%	73.7%	-3.2	-0.9	-1.8	-5.9
Black	68.3%	65.6%	64.4%	62.0%	-3.7	-1.3	-2.4	-6.4
Hispanic	53.4%	50.0%	49.8%	46.3%	-3.4	-0.2	-3.4	-7.1
Other	70.6%	69.5%	68.8%	68.1%	-1.0	-0.8	-0.7	-2.5
Nativity								
Native	77.4%	74.1%	73.1%	71.2%	-3.2	-1.0	-1.9	-6.2
Foreign-born	58.7%	54.0%	53.9%	51.5%	-4.7	-0.1	-2.4	-7.1

Education							
High school	71.8%	65.5%	64.4%	61.3%	−6.3	−1.1	−3.1	−10.5
College	85.3%	82.7%	82.1%	80.2%	−2.6	−0.6	−1.9	−5.2
Wage quintiles[a]							
Lowest	49.3%	45.0%	42.7%	39.8%	−2.3	−2.3	−2.9	−9.5
Second	69.0%	62.5%	61.8%	59.3%	−6.5	−0.7	−2.5	−9.7
Middle	80.6%	77.6%	76.6%	74.8%	−3.0	−1.0	−1.8	−5.8
Fourth	86.9%	84.6%	84.3%	82.4%	−2.4	−0.3	−1.9	−4.5
Highest	88.6%	85.9%	85.8%	85.0%	−2.6	−0.1	−0.8	−3.6
Work time							
Full-time	77.6%	74.3%	74.2%	72.9%	−3.3	−0.1	−1.4	−4.7
Part-time	60.4%	54.6%	51.7%	48.6%	−5.9	−2.9	−3.1	−11.8

[a]For methodology in construction of wage quintiles, see Gould (2010).

Source: Author's analysis of the March Current Population Survey, 2001–2010.

disparities in coverage widened in 2009 with declines of 1.8 percentage points for white non-Hispanic workers contrasted with 2.4 percentage points for black workers and 3.4 percentage points for Hispanic workers, again mimicking their different job market experiences in this recession.

College graduates have far higher rates of employment-based coverage than high school graduates, at 80.2 percent and 61.3 percent, respectively. In addition, high school graduates experienced declines more than twice as large as college graduates since 2000, at 10.5 percentage points versus 5.2 percentage points.

Workers earning lower hourly wages are significantly less likely to have employer-sponsored health insurance than those earning higher wages; however, even those at the high end of the wage scale experienced declines in coverage over the 2000s.[2] Only 39.8 percent of those in the lowest fifth, making less than $9.38 an hour, had ESI while 85.0 percent of those in the top fifth, with hourly earnings above $29.81, had the coverage. Losses for the lowest wage fifth in the two years since the recession began were greater than losses for the top 40th percentile since 2000. Widening disparities in coverage by wage levels over the 2000s are apparent as those in the top wage fifth were 80 percent more likely to be covered than those in the bottom fifth in 2000, but more than 110 percent more likely by 2009.

Nearly three-quarters of full-time workers have ESI compared with less than half of part-timers. Furthermore, part-time workers experienced a sharper decline in coverage since the start of the recession, a fall of 6.0 percentage points from 2007–2009. Since 2000, their coverage has fallen 11.8 percentage points.

An important group of workers to examine more closely are those who are strongly attached to the private-sector labor force, that is, working at least 20 hours per week and 26 weeks per year. Table 3 displays coverage through their own jobs (that is, not as dependents) for these strongly attached workers from 2000 to 2009 by selected job characteristics. After an increase in coverage in 2006 and 2007, coverage for these workers fell 0.2 percentage points in 2008 and 1.6 percentage points in 2009. Only 53.6 percent of these steady workers receive health insurance from their employers, down 5.3 percentage points since 2000.

Service-sector workers are insured through their own jobs at half the rate of both white-collar and blue-collar workers and experienced the largest drop in coverage, 3.4 percentage points, since 2007. Workers in larger firms are more likely to receive health insurance from their employers than workers in smaller firms. Only 31.6 percent of workers in small firms (less than 25 employees) had ESI from their jobs compared with 55.3 percent in firms with 25 to

---

[2] See Gould (2010) for a discussion of wage quintile analysis and balancing fifths (2).

499 employees and 65.1 percent in firms with more than 500 employees. Coverage losses in 2009 and over the 2000s were greatest among workers in mid-size firms.

Low coverage rates among workers in small firms are a result of many factors that make insurance much more expensive for small businesses than for larger firms, including an inability to offer attractive risk pools to potential insurers, high administrative and loading costs, and little competition in insurer markets (3). With the passage of PPACA, very small, low-wage firms can see considerable reductions in their premiums with the use of new tax credits. Furthermore, in 2014, all small firms will be able to purchase insurance through new insurance exchanges, which will make insurance costs more stable and predictable, even if one or more of their workers requires medical care or their workforce size or composition changes from year to year.

Coverage rates in 2009 differ dramatically according to what sector of the economy workers were employed in, but nearly all experienced declines since 2002.[3] The highest rates of coverage are found in mining, manufacturing, and information sectors and the lowest in agriculture, arts, and other services sectors. Previous research has shown that certain industries, such as public administration, mining, and manufacturing, are more likely to be sources of dependent coverage for workers' spouses or children, whereas arts and professional services fall short (4). The likelihood of getting dependent coverage is higher among industries with higher rates of coverage to their workers.

Uninsured Workers

Among workers, declines in ESI tend to translate into lower overall coverage rates. Uninsured workers are increasingly common in the U.S. economy; nearly one-fifth of the workforce is uninsured (Table 4). The rate of workers uninsured grew equally peak to peak, 2000–2007, as it did in the recession that began in December 2007, a total of 4.2 percentage points since 2000.

Older workers are more likely to have coverage, and working men are more likely to be uninsured than working women. White non-Hispanic workers are less likely to be uninsured than black and Hispanic workers, and the disparities have only widened in the 2000s.

Nearly half of workers without a high school degree are uninsured compared with about one-quarter of high school graduates and one-tenth of college graduates. While the levels illustrate clear inequities, the gap in coverage rates among workers of different education levels grew substantially over the 2000s. Those without a high school degree and high school graduates experienced

---

[3] Changes in industry classification make it impossible to compare 2009 with years earlier than 2002.

Table 3

Employer-sponsored health insurance[a] coverage for private-sector workers[b] by occupation, firm size, and industry, 2000–2009

					Percentage-point change			
	2000	2007	2008	2009	2000–2007	2007–2008	2008–2009	2000–2009
All workers	58.9%	55.4%	55.2%	53.6%	-3.4	-0.2	-1.6	-5.3
Occupations								
White-collar	65.0%	61.9%	61.8%	60.3%	-3.0	-0.1	-1.5	-4.6
Blue-collar	59.0%	53.9%	54.1%	52.7%	-5.0	0.2	-1.5	-6.3
Service	33.9%	29.5%	28.2%	26.1%	-4.4	-1.3	-2.1	-7.8
Firm size								
24 or fewer	36.2%	32.1%	32.1%	31.6%	-4.0	0.0	-0.6	-4.6
499 or fewer	61.0%	57.8%	58.1%	55.3%	-3.2	0.2	-2.8	-5.7
500 or more	69.6%	67.1%	66.7%	65.1%	-2.4	-0.4	-1.5	-4.4

Industry[c]

Agriculture, forestry, fishing, hunting	37.1%	27.1%	24.6%	26.2%	-10.0	-2.5	1.6	-10.9
Arts, entertainment, recreation, accommodation	32.5%	31.9%	28.7%	26.3%	-0.6	-3.2	-2.3	-6.1
Construction	47.5%	44.1%	45.3%	44.0%	-3.4	1.2	-1.3	-3.5
Education, health, social services	59.4%	60.2%	59.4%	57.1%	0.7	-0.8	-2.3	-2.3
Finance, insurance, real estate	65.8%	65.1%	66.0%	66.0%	-0.7	0.9	0.1	0.3
Information	73.0%	72.7%	70.9%	69.5%	-0.3	-1.9	-1.3	-3.4
Manufacturing	72.7%	70.2%	70.8%	69.6%	-2.5	0.7	-1.3	-3.1
Mining	78.4%	73.9%	75.7%	75.8%	-4.5	1.8	0.1	-2.6
Other services (except public administration)	40.1%	37.4%	37.6%	35.0%	-2.7	0.2	-2.6	-5.1
Professional, scientific, management, administration	57.4%	56.0%	56.2%	55.1%	-1.4	0.2	-1.1	-2.2
Transportation, communication	66.9%	63.0%	63.6%	62.0%	-3.9	0.6	-1.6	-4.9
Wholesale trade	53.9%	51.6%	51.6%	50.5%	-2.2	0.0	-1.1	-3.3

[a]Worker received employer-sponsored health insurance through his or her own job and employer had to pay at least part of the insurance premiums to qualify as employer-sponsored insurance coverage.

[b]Private-sector, wage and salary workers, ages 18 to 64, who worked at least 20 hours per week and 26 weeks per year.

[c]Industry classification changes make it impossible to compare 2009 with years earlier than 2002.

Source: Author's analysis of the March Current Population Survey, 2001–2010.

Table 4

Uninsured workers by age, gender, race, nativity, education, wage quintile, and work status, 2000–2009

	2000	2007	2008	2009	Percentage-point change			
					2000–2007	2007–2008	2008–2009	2000–2009
All workers	15.9%	18.1%	18.7%	20.2%	2.1	0.6	1.4	4.2
Age								
18–24	25.4%	27.5%	28.5%	29.7%	2.1	0.9	1.3	4.3
25–34	19.7%	23.2%	24.1%	26.3%	3.5	0.9	2.2	6.6
35–44	14.0%	16.9%	17.7%	19.3%	2.9	0.8	1.7	5.3
45–54	10.6%	13.8%	14.1%	15.4%	3.1	0.3	1.3	4.7
55–64	10.8%	10.7%	11.1%	12.2%	-0.1	0.4	1.0	1.4
Gender								
Male	17.8%	20.5%	21.4%	22.7%	2.8	0.8	1.3	4.9
Female	13.9%	15.3%	15.7%	17.3%	1.4	0.5	1.6	3.4
Race								
White, non-Hispanic	11.2%	12.7%	13.4%	14.6%	1.5	0.7	1.3	3.4
Black	21.2%	23.0%	23.8%	25.0%	1.8	0.8	1.2	3.8
Hispanic	37.8%	39.8%	39.5%	42.9%	2.0	-0.2	3.4	5.1
Other	20.0%	19.0%	20.1%	19.4%	-1.0	1.1	-0.7	-0.6

Nativity								
Native	13.2%	14.9%	15.6%	17.0%	1.7	0.7	1.4	3.8
Foreign-born	33.2%	35.5%	35.7%	37.2%	2.3	0.1	1.5	4.0
Education								
Less than high school	39.3%	45.7%	45.6%	47.9%	6.4	−0.1	2.3	8.6
High school	19.1%	23.7%	24.4%	26.6%	4.6	0.7	2.2	7.6
Some college	12.7%	14.9%	16.3%	17.6%	2.2	1.4	1.4	4.9
College	7.3%	8.5%	9.0%	10.4%	1.2	0.5	1.4	3.1
Post-college	3.9%	4.7%	4.6%	5.4%	0.8	−0.1	0.7	1.4
Wage quintiles								
Lowest	32.7%	35.2%	36.5%	38.9%	2.5	1.3	2.4	6.2
Second	21.0%	25.3%	25.8%	27.3%	4.4	0.5	1.5	6.3
Middle	12.6%	14.3%	15.2%	16.4%	1.8	0.9	1.2	3.8
Fourth	7.7%	8.8%	8.9%	10.4%	1.2	0.1	1.5	2.7
Highest	5.6%	6.5%	6.9%	7.5%	0.9	0.4	0.6	1.9
Work time								
Full-time	15.2%	17.0%	17.2%	18.1%	1.8	0.2	0.9	2.8
Part-time	19.4%	23.4%	25.4%	28.7%	3.9	2.0	3.3	9.3

[a]For methodology in construction of wage quintiles, see Gould (2010).
Source: Author's analysis of the March Current Population Survey, 2001–2010.

larger drops in coverage (8.6 and 7.6 percentage points, respectively) than those with a college degree or post-college education (3.1 and 1.4 percentage points, respectively). One-third of all workers in the lowest 40 percent of the wage distribution are uninsured compared with just one-eleventh of workers in the top 40 percent of the wage distribution.

Part-time workers are more likely to be uninsured than full-time workers, a gap in coverage that has grown over time. Part-time workers were 27.6 percent more likely to be uninsured in 2000, but 58.8 percent more likely to be uninsured in 2009. The introduction of insurance exchanges and their accompanying subsidies as part of health reform in 2014 should provide an alternative to workers, particularly part-time workers, who do not have health insurance through their jobs.

Table 5 examines the uninsured workforce side-by-side with the workforce as a whole in 2009. Uninsured workers are disproportionately young. Workers ages 18 to 34 make up 36.2 percent of the total workforce yet nearly half of the uninsured workforce. Working men are more likely to be uninsured than working women. Disparities among the working uninsured are stark by race and ethnicity. Whereas Hispanics make up only 14.5 percent of the workforce, they represent 30.9 percent of the uninsured workforce. A similar trend is found by nativity. The foreign-born are more than twice as likely to be uninsured compared with the native-born.

Insurance coverage among workers rises consistently with increased educational attainment. Workers with a high school education or less represent 38.2 percent of the workforce, yet they make up 60.1 percent of uninsured workers. Those with a college degree or higher represent nearly one-third of the workforce, yet only one-seventh of those uninsured.

The starkest disparities occur at different points in the wage distribution. When the workforce is equally divided by wage into fifths (see Gould [2010] for methodology), it is clear that those at the bottom end of the distribution are far more likely to be uninsured than those at the top. Workers in the bottom two-fifths by definition represent 40 percent of the workforce, but represent a full two-thirds of the uninsured. By contrast, the top two-fifths, again 40 percent of workers, contain about 18 percent of the uninsured.

DECLINING COVERAGE FOR CHILDREN

Except for young adults (ages 18 to 24), children under age 18 have the lowest rates of ESI coverage of the U.S. population under age 65, at 55.8 percent (Table 6). Coverage fell for children every year since 2000 for a total of 10.1 percentage points. Nearly 5.8 million fewer children had ESI in 2009 than in 2000, without even taking into account the growth of the population under age 18 throughout this period. As many as 7.6 million more

Table 5

Characteristics of all workers versus uninsured workers, 2009

	All workers	Uninsured workers
Age		
18–24	13.1%	19.3%
25–34	23.1%	30.1%
35–44	22.8%	21.9%
45–54	24.6%	18.8%
55–64	16.4%	9.9%
Gender		
Male	52.8%	59.4%
Female	47.2%	40.6%
Race		
White, non-Hispanic	68.2%	49.4%
Black	10.8%	13.3%
Hispanic	14.5%	30.9%
Other	6.6%	6.3%
Nativity		
Native	84.4%	71.3%
Foreign-born	15.6%	28.7%
Education		
Less than high school	9.2%	21.8%
High school	29.0%	38.3%
Some college	30.0%	26.2%
College	21.2%	10.9%
Post-college	10.7%	2.8%
Wage quintiles[a]		
Lowest	20.00%	38.9%
Second	20.00%	27.3%
Middle	20.00%	16.4%
Fourth	20.00%	10.4%
Highest	20.00%	7.5%
Work time		
Full-time	80.5%	72.2%
Part-time	19.6%	27.8%

[a]For methodology in construction of wage quintiles, see Gould (2010).
Source: Author's analysis of the March Current Population Survey, 2001–2010.

Table 6

Employer-sponsored health insurance coverage for children under 18 years by race, nativity, education, and family income quintile, 2000–2009

	2000	2007	2008	2009	Percentage-point change			
					2000–2007	2007–2008	2008–2009	2000–2009
All under 18	65.9%	59.5%	58.9%	55.8%	-6.5	-0.6	-3.1	-10.1
Race								
White, non-Hispanic	76.3%	71.0%	70.6%	68.3%	-0.3	-0.3	-2.4	-8.0
Black	51.3%	45.6%	44.3%	41.0%	-1.3	-1.3	-3.3	-10.3
Hispanic	42.8%	37.9%	38.1%	34.3%	-0.3	0.3	-3.8	-8.5
Other	64.4%	60.8%	60.6%	58.0%	-0.1	-0.1	-2.6	-6.4
Nativity								
Native	66.9%	60.3%	59.6%	56.6%	-6.6	-0.7	-3.1	-10.3
Foreign-born	44.5%	39.3%	38.2%	36.4%	-5.2	-1.1	-1.7	-8.0

Education of family head							
Less than high school	34.3%	23.1%	22.7%	20.0%	-11.2	-0.4	-2.7	-14.3
High school	63.5%	51.9%	50.7%	46.1%	-11.7	-1.2	-4.6	-17.4
Some college	73.6%	65.8%	62.7%	60.2%	-7.8	-3.1	-2.5	-13.4
College	85.9%	82.0%	82.5%	80.5%	-3.9	0.4	-2.0	-5.4
Post-college	87.7%	86.2%	89.0%	86.7%	-1.5	2.8	-2.3	-1.1
Family income fifth							
Lowest	24.9%	17.4%	16.4%	13.9%	-7.5	-0.9	-2.5	-11.0
Second	54.6%	42.1%	40.4%	36.2%	-12.5	-1.7	-4.2	-18.4
Middle	74.9%	68.2%	67.3%	63.5%	-6.7	-0.9	-3.8	-11.4
Fourth	86.3%	82.2%	82.3%	79.6%	-4.1	0.1	-2.7	-6.7
Highest	89.0%	87.6%	88.1%	85.9%	-1.5	0.5	-2.2	-3.1

Source: Author's analysis of the March Current Population Survey, 2001–2010.

children would have had ESI in 2009 if the coverage rate had remained at the 2000 level.

As with the general population under age 65, there are stark disparities in coverage for children. White non-Hispanic children have coverage rates as high as workers (68.3%) and twice the rate of Hispanic children. Black children have experienced the largest losses since 2007 (–4.6 percentage points) and since 2000 (–10.3 percentage points). Native-born children experienced greater losses than foreign-born children over the 2000s, yet their coverage rates are still far higher (56.6% vs. 36.4%).

Children's coverage is highly correlated with the education of the family head. Less than half of children of high school-educated parents have ESI compared with four-fifths of children with college-educated parents. Similarly, access to ESI is closely tied to family income (Figure 4). While children across the economic spectrum experienced losses in coverage over the 2000s, disparities have widened. The gap between the top fifth and bottom fifth grew 7.9 percentage points since 2000, while the gap between the second and fourth fifths grew by 11.7 percentage points.

PUBLICLY PROVIDED HEALTH INSURANCE STEMMED LARGER LOSSES IN OVERALL COVERAGE

While losses in ESI since 2000 were greater among children than non-elderly adults, as shown in Figure 5, the percentage of children without any coverage actually fell. The uninsured rate for children dropped 1.6 percentage points while the percent of uninsured non-elderly adults rose 5.1 percentage points from 2000 to 2009. Given that privately purchased, or non-group, insurance coverage was relatively flat over this period (not shown), differences in the overall coverage rates are caused by differences in the incidence of public insurance for these groups.

The percentage of children with public coverage grew 12.4 percentage points since 2000 compared with only 4.4 percentage points for the overall non-elderly population. While both increases lessened the impact of ESI losses on overall coverage, only the increase in public coverage for children was large enough to be fully offsetting. Children have greater access to public insurance through CHIP, but eligibility for public insurance for non-elderly adults is mostly limited to Medicaid or Medicare.

Some claim that losses in ESI actually were driven by increases in public coverage eligibility or generosity, a phenomenon known as crowd-out. However, given the declining economy, it is likely that an increasing number of children became eligible for public insurance rather than public coverage replacing private coverage. The fact that ESI coverage rates for adults fell without the same counterbalancing rise in public coverage further reinforces this fact. Regardless

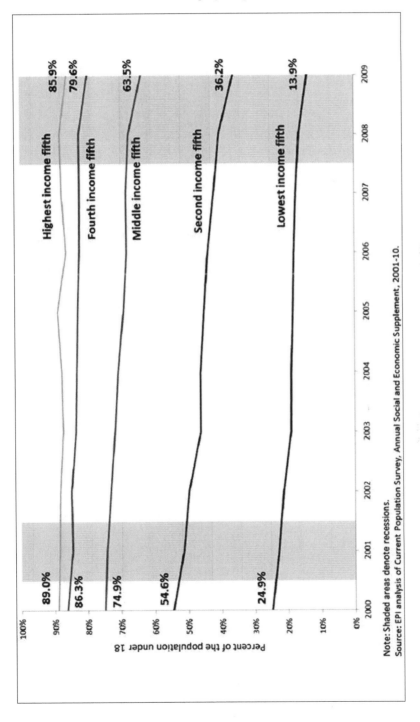

Figure 4. Share of children under 18 with ESI by income fifth, 2000–2009.

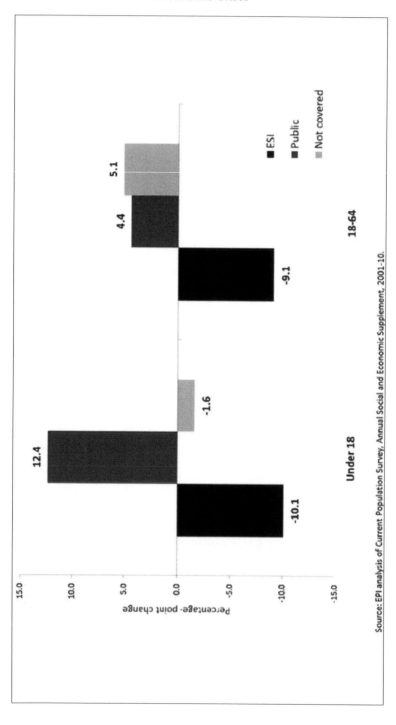

Source: EPI analysis of Current Population Survey, Annual Social and Economic Supplement, 2001-10.

Figure 5. Percentage-point change in ESI coverage rate, public coverage rate, and uninsured rate for under 18 and 18–64 populations, 2000–2009.

of the cause, it is clear that if not for public insurance, the overall coverage rate among children would have fallen.

ESI ACROSS THE STATES

The non-elderly population across the country relies on ESI as its primary form of coverage; however, the incidence of coverage varies widely from state to state. Table 7 compares ESI coverage rates for those under age 65 across states between 2000–2001 and 2008–2009. New Hampshire has the highest rate of ESI coverage at 73.7 percent in 2008–2009. This rate is followed by Massachusetts (72.5%), Connecticut (70.7%), Utah (70.1%), and Maryland (70.0%). Less than half (48.1%) of New Mexico's non-elderly population has ESI. Mississippi and Texas also have relatively low rates of coverage at 50.4 percent and 50.9 percent, respectively.

Across the country, on average, ESI coverage for those under age 65 fell 7.2 percentage points from 2000–2001 to 2008–2009. The largest declines in coverage occurred in Indiana, Michigan, Delaware, Arizona, and Mississippi with losses of at least 10.0 percentage points over the 2000s. Forty-four states had statistically significant losses in coverage for their populations under age 65, while no state had a statistically significant rise in coverage over that period.

The highest rates of ESI coverage for workers are found in Massachusetts and Hawaii, with coverage rates of 80.8 percent and 78.8 percent, respectively (Table 8). It is not surprising that Massachusetts and Hawaii have the highest ESI coverage rates, as both states have employer mandates requiring minimal insurance coverage to workers. The lowest rate of worker coverage is in New Mexico at 58.6 percent, followed by Texas at 60.4 percent. The largest declines in job-based coverage among workers occurred in Tennessee, Delaware, Georgia, and Michigan, each with losses in excess of 7.5 percentage points, far above the national average of 5.3 percentage points.

Similar to the population under age 65 as a whole, New Hampshire boasts the highest rates of ESI coverage for its children at 74.2 percent (Table 9). Utah and Massachusetts follow behind at 72.1 percent and 70.9 percent, respectively. At the other end of the spectrum, less than half of all children in New Mexico, Mississippi, Arkansas, Texas, Arizona, and Washington, D.C., are covered by employment-based health insurance.

As with the national numbers, losses in coverage across the states are greatest among children. Eleven states experienced declines in excess of 10 percentage points from 2000–2001 to 2008–2009. Indiana experienced losses in children's ESI coverage of 15.6 percentage points—twice the national rate. Overall, 38 states had statistically significant declines in children's ESI coverage rates. No state had a statistically significant increase.

Table 7

Employer-sponsored health insurance coverage by state, population under 65 years old, 2000–2001 to 2008–2009

State	Health insurance coverage (%)			Health insurance coverage (#)		
	2000–2001	2008–2009	Percentage-point change	2000–2001	2008–2009	Change
Nationwide[a]	67.6%	60.4%	**-7.2**	167,174,509	159,831,000	**-7,343,509**
Alabama	68.1%	62.2%	**-5.9**	2,624,942	2,489,000	**-135,942**
Alaska	61.9%	57.6%	**-4.3**	365,250	360,500	-4,750
Arizona	62.7%	52.5%	**-10.2**	2,923,423	3,026,500	103,077
Arkansas	61.0%	52.8%	**-8.3**	1,378,922	1,294,000	**-84,922**
California	59.7%	54.3%	**-5.4**	18,464,539	17,719,000	**-745,539**
Colorado	70.1%	62.4%	**-7.8**	2,778,936	2,752,000	-26,936
Connecticut	77.1%	70.7%	**-6.5**	2,229,371	2,119,000	**-110,371**
Delaware	76.5%	66.3%	**-10.3**	525,285	495,000	**-30,285**
District of Columbia	63.2%	59.9%	-3.3	307,732	317,000	9,268
Florida	62.2%	54.3%	**-8.0**	8,411,569	8,202,500	**-209,069**
Georgia	67.6%	59.1%	**-8.6**	5,028,958	5,155,000	**126,042**
Hawaii	70.7%	68.9%	-1.9	745,019	726,500	-18,519
Idaho	65.9%	61.7%	**-4.2**	762,520	823,500	**60,981**
Illinois	70.8%	63.8%	**-7.0**	7,735,097	7,204,000	**-531,097**
Indiana	75.7%	64.3%	**-11.4**	3,947,123	3,527,500	**-419,623**
Iowa	76.9%	68.6%	**-8.4**	1,892,738	1,796,500	**-96,238**
Kansas	70.4%	63.8%	**-6.6**	1,585,578	1,535,500	-50,078
Kentucky	67.9%	58.9%	**-9.1**	2,392,443	2,185,000	**-207,443**

Louisiana	59.9%	56.2%	-3.8	2,315,377	2,161,500	-153,877
Maine	69.5%	61.3%	-8.2	746,312	674,000	-72,312
Maryland	77.9%	70.0%	-7.9	3,622,648	3,466,000	-156,648
Massachusetts	73.3%	72.5%	-0.8	4,035,587	4,044,000	8,414
Michigan	76.4%	66.1%	-10.4	6,646,874	5,659,500	-987,374
Minnesota	77.2%	68.8%	-8.4	3,437,862	3,086,500	-351,362
Mississippi	60.4%	50.4%	-10.0	1,489,990	1,258,500	-231,490
Missouri	72.5%	62.7%	-9.8	3,537,550	3,222,000	-315,550
Montana	59.2%	56.1%	-3.2	454,047	464,500	10,454
Nebraska	69.7%	66.4%	-3.3	1,034,433	1,033,500	-933
Nevada	70.5%	63.0%	-7.5	1,312,779	1,456,000	143,222
New Hampshire	79.1%	73.7%	-5.4	850,302	842,500	-7,703
New Jersey	75.6%	68.8%	-6.8	5,482,343	5,178,000	-304,343
New Mexico	53.0%	48.1%	-5.0	835,302	828,000	-7,302
New York	64.1%	59.3%	-4.9	10,502,864	9,913,500	-589,364
North Carolina	66.7%	57.9%	-8.9	4,730,174	4,699,000	-31,174
North Dakota	66.8%	66.0%	-0.9	358,459	362,500	4,042
Ohio	74.1%	65.3%	-8.8	7,218,433	6,468,000	-750,433
Oklahoma	59.2%	58.9%	-0.4	1,741,147	1,817,000	75,853
Oregon	66.4%	61.7%	-4.7	2,027,243	2,033,500	6,257
Pennsylvania	75.9%	67.6%	-8.4	7,929,984	7,053,500	-876,484
Rhode Island	73.9%	64.6%	-9.3	646,222	581,000	-65,222
South Carolina	69.2%	60.1%	-9.1	2,412,344	2,306,500	-105,844
South Dakota	69.5%	62.1%	-7.4	437,580	426,500	-11,080
Tennessee	65.7%	55.9%	-9.8	3,304,791	2,995,000	-309,791
Texas	59.7%	50.9%	-8.8	11,224,385	11,180,000	-44,385
Utah	73.6%	70.1%	-3.5	1,528,425	1,776,500	248,076

Table 7 (Cont'd.)

State	Health insurance coverage (%)			Health insurance coverage (#)		
	2000–2001	2008–2009	Percentage-point change	2000–2001	2008–2009	Change
Vermont	70.4%	65.6%	**-4.9**	374,075	348,000	**-26,075**
Virginia	72.1%	66.7%	**-5.4**	4,490,036	4,562,500	72,465
Washington	66.9%	63.0%	**-4.0**	3,482,606	3,688,500	**205,894**
West Virginia	64.3%	61.1%	**-3.2**	961,495	917,000	**-44,495**
Wisconsin	78.1%	68.9%	**-9.2**	3,621,595	3,303,500	**-318,095**
Wyoming	65.8%	63.2%	-2.6	281,914	295,000	13,087

[a]Nationwide numbers in this table should be used only to benchmark against state numbers, which require two-year merged data averages for adequate sample size for analysis. Single-year national numbers are best for national-level comparisons and can be found in preceding tables.

Note: Bolded numbers are statistically significant at the 5 percent level.

Source: Author's analysis of the March Current Population Survey, 2001–2010.

LOOKING TO THE FUTURE

One of the clearest indicators of the deepening recession and the most relevant aggregate economic indicator for ESI is the unemployment rate. In 2007, the most recent peak year, the unemployment rate was 4.6 percent. Average unemployment rose modestly to 5.8 percent in 2008, then jumped 3.5 percentage points to 9.3 percent in 2009. While the largest increase in the unemployment rate for this recession already has been felt, the unemployment rate is forecasted to increase to 9.7 percent in 2010 and 9.9 percent in 2011 (5).

While employer-sponsored health insurance remains the predominant form of health coverage for those under age 65, it is often the case that when people lose their jobs, they lose access to their health insurance. Therefore, it can be expected that ESI coverage could drop another 0.5 percentage points by 2011 to nearly 58.4 percent.[4]

While not one-for-one, a drop in ESI coverage is strongly associated with a rise in the number of uninsured Americans, lessened only by increases in public coverage (particularly among children). By 2011, it is likely that the number of non-elderly uninsured will increase by another half million.[5]

RECOVERY ACT OF 2009

There is emerging evidence that the ARRA helped to stem the tide of the uninsured from the current recession. One factor that may have slowed the erosion of health insurance coverage even with such a high unemployment rate is COBRA. COBRA coverage, which allows workers to keep their employer-sponsored health insurance from their previous job for 18 to 36 months as long as they pay their premiums, was expanded as part of the ARRA. Previously, people who participated in COBRA had to pay up to 102 percent of the premium costs. Under ARRA, workers received a subsidy for 65 percent of the premiums if they lost their jobs between September 2008 and December 2009.

Although data on COBRA eligibility and uptake are difficult to measure, early reports suggest that uptake increased significantly with the help of the subsidy. The Commonwealth Fund, using data from Hewitt Associates, estimates the COBRA take-up doubled under ARRA from 19 percent before the subsidy to 38 percent after (8). That finding is on par with a report from the U.S. Treasury Department that looked at people receiving unemployment benefits in New Jersey. That report found the take-up rate to be anywhere from 29 to 32 percent among eligible unemployment insurance recipients (9).

[4] Using methodology from Holahan and Garrett (2009) (6).
[5] Using methodology from Gruber and Levitt (2002) (7).

Table 8

Employer-sponsored health insurance coverage by state, 2000–2001 to 2008–2009, percent of all workers 18–64 years old insured

| | Health insurance coverage (%) | | | Health insurance coverage (#) | | |
State	2000–2001	2008–2009	Percentage-point change	2000–2001	2008–2009	Change
Nationwide[a]	74.4%	69.1%	**-5.3**	106,055,229	101,526,733	**-4,528,496**
Alabama	77.3%	73.3%	**-4.0**	1,623,968	1,561,319	-62,649
Alaska	66.9%	64.8%	-2.0	226,815	235,803	8,988
Arizona	69.8%	63.3%	**-6.5**	1,765,058	1,881,796	**116,738**
Arkansas	70.6%	64.6%	**-6.0**	868,966	836,955	-32,011
California	67.1%	62.8%	-4.2	11,339,309	11,079,011	-260,298
Colorado	75.0%	68.3%	**-6.7**	1,785,068	1,776,376	-8,692
Connecticut	81.3%	76.5%	**-4.8**	1,415,773	1,350,882	-64,890
Delaware	81.6%	73.6%	**-8.0**	333,425	307,688	**-25,737**
District of Columbia	74.3%	73.3%	-1.0	222,900	239,361	16,461
Florida	69.5%	63.5%	**-6.1**	5,360,570	5,286,003	-74,567
Georgia	75.4%	67.6%	**-7.8**	3,098,219	3,108,705	10,486
Hawaii	78.9%	78.8%	-0.1	491,076	471,616	-19,459
Idaho	70.3%	67.7%	-2.6	469,229	498,287	29,058
Illinois	76.4%	72.3%	-4.2	4,921,326	4,548,885	**-372,441**
Indiana	80.8%	75.4%	-5.4	2,528,263	2,238,007	**-290,256**
Iowa	78.8%	73.9%	-4.9	1,223,383	1,227,040	3,657
Kansas	75.3%	71.8%	-3.5	1,024,561	1,013,673	-10,889
Kentucky	77.1%	69.8%	**-7.3**	1,540,472	1,415,900	**-124,572**

Louisiana	68.8%	67.0%	-1.8	1,356,078	1,307,808	-48,271
Maine	75.4%	68.8%	-6.6	509,834	455,194	-54,640
Maryland	81.4%	76.0%	-5.4	2,246,477	2,208,901	-37,576
Massachusetts	79.8%	80.8%	1.0	2,767,696	2,656,436	-111,260
Michigan	81.6%	73.9%	-7.7	4,167,341	3,439,358	-727,983
Minnesota	78.9%	73.8%	-5.1	2,321,896	2,052,465	-269,431
Mississippi	71.0%	66.0%	-5.0	935,444	796,736	-138,709
Missouri	77.8%	70.9%	-6.9	2,290,636	2,069,272	-221,365
Montana	63.9%	63.2%	-0.7	294,706	313,433	18,727
Nebraska	73.3%	72.7%	-0.6	689,664	684,085	-5,579
Nevada	75.4%	70.2%	-5.2	811,973	887,947	75,974
New Hampshire	82.2%	77.8%	-4.4	564,299	558,420	-5,879
New Jersey	80.8%	75.6%	-5.2	3,513,609	3,181,318	-332,291
New Mexico	60.7%	58.6%	-2.0	511,912	517,953	6,041
New York	72.5%	68.8%	-3.7	6,633,773	6,407,879	-225,894
North Carolina	74.2%	67.7%	-6.5	3,044,516	2,997,840	-46,676
North Dakota	71.6%	69.9%	-1.7	255,345	250,751	-4,594
Ohio	79.7%	73.7%	-6.0	4,674,477	4,109,351	-565,125
Oklahoma	66.8%	68.4%	1.6	1,126,733	1,176,413	49,681
Oregon	71.8%	69.5%	-2.3	1,308,021	1,347,057	39,036
Pennsylvania	82.5%	76.2%	-6.3	5,192,396	4,544,430	-647,966
Rhode Island	80.3%	72.9%	-7.4	428,751	392,537	-36,214
South Carolina	77.5%	70.3%	-7.1	1,504,223	1,425,965	-78,258
South Dakota	72.3%	68.9%	-3.4	292,351	291,302	-1,049
Tennessee	74.0%	65.4%	-8.6	2,129,813	1,932,031	-197,782
Texas	67.6%	60.4%	-7.2	6,895,379	6,974,878	79,499
Utah	76.1%	74.4%	-1.7	868,115	974,393	106,278

Table 8 (Cont'd.)

State	Health insurance coverage (%)		Percentage-point change	Health insurance coverage (#)		Change
	2000–2001	2008–2009		2000–2001	2008–2009	
Vermont	74.5%	71.9%	-2.6	256,816	249,352	-7,463
Virginia	78.2%	72.5%	**-5.7**	2,848,842	2,877,637	28,796
Washington	73.1%	70.3%	**-2.8**	2,209,531	2,442,406	**232,875**
West Virginia	74.2%	73.3%	-0.9	602,427	551,064	**-51,363**
Wisconsin	81.1%	74.8%	**-6.4**	2,382,198	2,183,196	**-199,002**
Wyoming	68.8%	67.9%	-0.9	181,577	191,617	10,041

[a]Nationwide numbers in this table should be used only to benchmark against state numbers, which require two-year merged data averages for adequate sample size for analysis. Single-year national numbers are best for national-level comparisons and can be found in preceding tables.

Note: Bolded numbers are statistically significant at the 5 percent level.

Source: Author's analysis of the March Current Population Survey, 2001–2010.

ARRA also included about US$140 billion in aid to states to lessen the need for states to make cuts to services, cuts in spending, or increases in state and local taxes. The consequences of these budget gaps can be severe, with many states reducing services to residents. Federal assistance, in the form of the stimulus, did lessen the extent to which states had to make cuts and reduce services to balance their budgets. A large percentage of the funds that went to states was in the form of increased Medicaid funding to reduce the extent and severity of cuts to that program.

The Center on Budget and Policy Priorities provides specific examples of how major cuts to public insurance were avoided in many states (10). For instance, in New York, major cuts that had been proposed before stimulus funding was made available were never enacted. In Virginia, the fiscal assistance was used to reverse a planned cut in Medicaid payments to hospitals, as well as other program cuts that had been proposed before the availability of stimulus funds. In California, the state reversed a planned requirement that would have forced Medi-Cal beneficiaries to renew their eligibility more frequently, a requirement that would have caused many children to lose coverage. In South Carolina, the state government reversed cuts that had restricted residents' eligibility and access to Medicaid services to qualify for enhanced levels of federal Medicaid assistance, made available in ARRA. The state also did not go through with a plan to impose stricter income requirements for beneficiaries, which would have resulted in the loss of coverage for thousands of elderly and disabled people.

While it is impossible to know what would have occurred had states not received Recovery Act funds, it is clear that those funds did help maintain and increase Medicaid coverage.

CONCLUSION

Employer-sponsored health insurance is increasingly failing American families. If the coverage rate had not fallen 9.4 percentage points as it did from 2000 to 2009, as many as 25 million more people under age 65 would have had ESI in 2009. Public insurance, primarily in the form of Medicaid and CHIP, has been working to counteract this trend. However, many Americans, particularly working-age Americans, are falling through the cracks each day.

Passage of the PPACA, particularly the provisions establishing health insurance exchanges and accompanying subsidies, will make it easier and more affordable for Americans to secure and maintain health insurance coverage. However, the continued poor labor market likely will lead to further losses in insurance coverage before major relief from health reform takes effect.

Table 9

Employer-sponsored health insurance coverage for children under 18 by state, 2000–2001 to 2008–2009, percent of all children insured

State	Health insurance coverage (%)			Health insurance coverage (#)		
	2000–2001	2008–2009	Percentage-point change	2000–2001	2008–2009	Change
Nationwide[a]	65.2%	57.4%	**-7.8**	47,220,271	42,882,791	**-4,337,479**
Alabama	65.3%	56.6%	**-8.7**	742,610	627,064	**-115,546**
Alaska	58.9%	53.2%	-5.7	112,781	97,934	-14,847
Arizona	59.3%	47.3%	**-12.0**	879,454	815,907	-63,547
Arkansas	57.5%	45.8%	**-11.8**	398,691	324,477	**-74,214**
California	56.9%	51.4%	**-5.5**	5,519,658	4,863,695	**-655,963**
Colorado	68.5%	60.7%	**-7.8**	794,865	746,154	-48,710
Connecticut	77.4%	69.9%	**-7.5**	636,777	571,174	**-65,603**
Delaware	73.9%	64.3%	**-9.5**	147,016	135,345	-11,670
District of Columbia	53.6%	48.5%	-5.1	59,546	54,312	-5,234
Florida	58.3%	51.8%	**-6.5**	2,236,149	2,092,162	**-143,986**
Georgia	65.4%	56.9%	**-8.5**	1,488,932	1,460,758	-28,173
Hawaii	65.5%	60.5%	-5.0	199,586	177,186	-22,400
Idaho	63.9%	60.3%	-3.6	242,382	253,369	10,987
Illinois	69.4%	60.2%	**-9.3**	2,163,296	1,922,498	**-240,798**
Indiana	74.2%	58.6%	**-15.6**	1,102,245	947,318	**-154,926**
Iowa	78.8%	66.8%	**-12.0**	569,863	477,844	**-92,019**
Kansas	68.2%	58.5%	**-9.7**	448,335	415,216	-33,119
Kentucky	63.2%	54.2%	**-9.0**	632,458	552,185	**-80,273**

Louisiana	57.5%	52.3%	-5.3	710,060	597,868	**-112,192**
Maine	67.7%	59.9%	-7.8	187,010	163,973	-23,037
Maryland	78.3%	68.3%	-10.0	1,099,500	919,429	**-180,070**
Massachusetts	70.6%	70.9%	0.3	992,610	1,032,055	39,445
Michigan	76.5%	66.8%	-9.7	1,878,051	1,583,870	**-294,180**
Minnesota	78.0%	67.4%	-10.5	932,975	836,230	**-96,745**
Mississippi	54.4%	43.8%	-10.6	426,323	344,162	**-82,161**
Missouri	71.4%	62.0%	-9.4	1,009,339	882,559	**-126,780**
Montana	58.5%	55.2%	-3.4	130,811	120,437	-10,373
Nebraska	66.5%	62.8%	-3.7	292,191	286,560	-5,631
Nevada	69.9%	61.6%	-8.3	397,674	413,345	15,671
New Hampshire	79.5%	74.2%	-5.3	232,251	216,114	-16,137
New Jersey	76.2%	68.0%	-8.2	1,476,387	1,400,507	-75,880
New Mexico	48.2%	42.5%	-5.7	241,215	217,754	-23,461
New York	62.0%	56.6%	-5.4	2,843,277	2,500,116	**-343,160**
North Carolina	63.3%	53.8%	-9.5	1,305,229	1,252,113	-53,116
North Dakota	63.1%	67.6%	4.5	86,987	98,104	11,118
Ohio	72.0%	63.5%	-8.5	1,958,639	1,736,812	**-221,827**
Oklahoma	53.6%	52.2%	-1.4	467,813	478,865	11,052
Oregon	65.0%	58.4%	-6.6	565,044	509,025	-56,018
Pennsylvania	74.3%	64.8%	-9.6	2,072,948	1,812,549	**-260,399**
Rhode Island	72.2%	60.9%	-11.3	177,167	140,742	**-36,425**
South Carolina	66.6%	57.8%	-8.8	675,846	630,674	-45,172
South Dakota	71.1%	59.4%	-11.6	130,868	119,244	-11,624
Tennessee	63.9%	53.3%	-10.6	899,319	790,352	**-108,967**
Texas	55.5%	45.8%	-9.7	3,410,451	3,150,063	**-260,387**
Utah	74.7%	72.1%	-2.6	542,892	629,275	**86,383**

Table 9 (Cont'd.)

State	Health insurance coverage (%)		Percentage-point change	Health insurance coverage (#)		Change
	2000–2001	2008–2009		2000–2001	2008–2009	
Vermont	71.1%	61.2%	**-9.9**	94,841	77,578	**-17,263**
Virginia	69.6%	67.4%	-2.2	1,266,956	1,277,896	10,940
Washington	64.0%	57.9%	**-6.1**	971,306	902,885	-68,421
West Virginia	61.9%	58.0%	-3.9	242,298	225,804	-16,493
Wisconsin	79.9%	69.7%	**-10.2**	1,045,539	917,389	**-128,150**
Wyoming	65.9%	62.4%	-3.5	81,824	83,846	2,022

[a]Nationwide numbers in this table should be used only to benchmark against state numbers, which require two-year merged data averages for adequate sample size for analysis. Single-year national numbers are best for national-level comparisons and can be found in preceding tables.

Note: Bolded numbers are statistically significant at the 5 percent level.

Source: Author's analysis of the March Current Population Survey, 2001–2010.

Acknowledgments — The author thanks Jin Dai, Kathryn Edwards, Andrew Green, and Rebecca Thiess for their valuable research assistance. The Economic Policy Institute is grateful to the Charles Stewart Mott Foundation, Ford Foundation, and Open Society Institute for providing support for the research and publication of this report.

Note — An earlier version of this chapter was published as Economic Policy Institute Briefing Paper No. 283: "Employer-Sponsored Health Insurance Erosion Accelerates in the Recession: Public Safety Net Catches Kids but Fails to Adequately Insure Adults."

REFERENCES

1. Mishel, L., and Shierholz, H. *Recession Hits Workers' Paychecks: Wage Growth Has Collapsed*. Economic Policy Institute Briefing Paper No. 277. EPI, Washington, D.C., 2010.
2. Gould, E. Employer-sponsored insurance erosion continues in 2008 and is expected to worsen. *Int. J. Health Serv.* 40(4):743–776, 2010.
3. Gould, E., and Hertel-Fernandez, A. *Senate Health Bill Scores Big for Small Business: Bill Would Help Provide Affordable, Stable Health Coverage*. Economic Policy Institute Issue Brief No. 268. EPI, Washington, D.C., 2009.
4. Bivens, J., Gould, E., and Hertel-Fernandez, A. *The Health Care Free Ride: Reform Should Help Distribute Responsibility For Coverage More Evenly Between Industries*. Economic Policy Institute Issue Brief No. 259. Economic Policy Institute, Washington, D.C., 2009.
5. Moody's Analytics. *U.S. Macro Outlook, 2010*. www.economy.com (accessed on October 21, 2010).
6. Holahan, J., and Garrett, A. B. *Rising Unemployment, Medicaid, and the Uninsured*. Kaiser Family Foundation, Washington, D.C., 2009.
7. Gruber, J., and Levitt, L. *Rising Unemployment and the Uninsured*. Kaiser Family Foundation, Washington, D.C., 2002.
8. Bovbjerg, R., et al. *COBRA Subsidies for Laid-Off Workers: An Initial Report Card*. The Commonwealth Fund, Publication No. 1358, Vol. 75. Washington, D.C., 2009.
9. U.S. Treasury Department. *COBRA Insurance Coverage Since the Recovery Act: Results from New Survey Data*. Office of Economic Policy, 2010. www.ustreas.gov/offices/economic-policy/cobra%20final%20report.pdf.
10. Oliff, P., Shure, J., and Johnson, N. *Federal Fiscal Relief is Working as Intended*. Center on Budget and Policy Priorities, Washington, D.C., June 29, 2009. www.cbpp.org/cms/index.cfm?fa=view&id=2831.

CHAPTER 12

How Do Macro-Level Contexts and Policies Affect the Employment Chances of Chronically Ill and Disabled People? The Impact of Recession and Deindustrialization

Paula Holland, Bo Burström, Margaret Whitehead,
Finn Diderichsen, Espen Dahl, Ben Barr, Lotta Nylén,
Wen-Hao Chen, Karsten Thielen, Kjetil A. van der Wel,
Stephen Clayton, and Sharanjit Uppal

Low employment rates of chronically ill and disabled people are of serious concern. Being out of work increases the risk of poverty and social exclusion, which may further damage the health of these groups, exacerbating health inequalities. Macro-level policies have a potentially tremendous impact on their employment chances, and these influences urgently need to be understood as the current economic crisis intensifies. The authors examine employment trends for people who report a chronic illness or disability, by gender and educational level, in Canada, Denmark, Norway, Sweden, and the United Kingdom in the context of economic booms and busts and deindustrialization. People with the double burden of chronic illness and low education have become increasingly marginalized from the labor market. Deindustrialization may have played a part in this process. In addition, periods of high unemployment have sparked a downward trend in employment for already marginalized groups who did not feel the benefits when the economy improved. Norway and Sweden have been better able to protect the employment of these groups than the United Kingdom and Canada. These contextual differences suggest that other macro-level factors, such as active and passive labor market polices, may be important.

*****

In many high-income countries, the number of chronically ill and disabled people outside the labor market and in receipt of long-term welfare benefits has increased dramatically in recent decades. The United Kingdom and Sweden, for example, have witnessed a trebling of the proportion of the population receiving sickness or incapacity benefits during the past 30 years (1, 2). Higher rates of chronic illness and disability have been observed among people with low levels of education (3, 4) or employed in low-skilled occupations (5–8)— groups whose employment is likely to become increasingly vulnerable during periods of adverse macroeconomic change.

In this chapter we investigate the influence of macro-level contexts and policies on the employment chances of chronically ill and disabled people in five OECD (Organization for Economic Cooperation and Development) countries. We explore two hypotheses concerned with the impact of economic booms and busts and the trend toward deindustrialization.

Taking an equity perspective, our particular concern is with how these macro-level contexts and policies affect people who are already in the weakest position in the labor market: those with chronic illness and disability and those with low education or few skills. Previous studies have documented social inequalities in employment rates among individuals with limiting longstanding illness (5, 6, 9), ischemic heart disease (10), musculoskeletal disorders (11), epilepsy (12), and mental illness (13). The low rates of employment of working-age people with chronic illness or disability, which decline even further with decreasing education and skills, increase the risk of poverty and social exclusion, and this in turn may damage their health still further and exacerbate health inequalities (14). The current economic crisis intensifies the need to understand what helps or hinders chronically ill and disabled people in the labor market, with a view to identifying how their position might be protected and improved.

Hypothesis 1 (on the economic cycle). There will be widening employment-related polarization between healthy and ill people during economic downturns, as employment entry and exit processes are likely to be more health selective under these conditions. Conversely, inequalities in employment between healthy and ill groups will narrow during economic recovery.

There is growing concern about whether the current economic crisis and resulting rise in unemployment will damage population health (15, 16) and lower the employment rates of the most vulnerable groups. Several studies have noted that economic recession is associated with negative health outcomes. Recession has resulted in excess admissions to psychiatric hospitals in Sweden (17), and increases in suicides and homicides among working-age men and women have been observed during periods of large and rapid rises in unemployment in 26 countries in the European Union (16). Other studies have observed widening health inequalities during recessions as a result of worsening health among the unemployed and improving health among the employed (possibly because they report less sickness in an attempt to prevent job loss) (18, 19). Recessions also have consequences for the employment of people with chronic illness, who suffer from higher rates of unemployment even during economic booms (20, 21). Employers may respond to recessions and the increased need for efficiency and profitability by decreasing the size of their workforce and demanding higher standards in terms of health, skills, and qualifications when recruiting new staff. A 1990s U.K. study of employment trends revealed that health selection into jobs during recessions was particularly pronounced among manual occupations (22).

Hypothesis 2 (on deindustrialization). The growing trend toward deindustrialization will make people with less education or poor health more vulnerable to labor market exclusion, because they are less able to meet the demands and requirements characteristic of service economies. The employment of those suffering from the double burden of low education and chronic illness will be hardest hit, declining during economic downturns and failing to recover during subsequent economic booms.

The economies of many high-income countries have shifted from being based on heavy industry and manufacture to becoming predominantly focused on the provision of services and education, a process that began in the 1950s but increased considerably from the mid-1970s (23). In 1970, between 31 and 45 percent of the labor force in Canada, Denmark, Norway, Sweden, and the United Kingdom were employed in industry, whereas currently only one-fifth of the labor force in each country is employed in this sector (24). While demand for unskilled manual labor has declined, there has been a parallel expansion of professional and technical occupations requiring educated, well-qualified, highly skilled workers, with greater emphasis on flexibility, capacity, and productivity. Manual workers have come under increasing pressure to adapt to the new regime. Gallie (25) observed that although skill requirements increased among all categories of workers in the United Kingdom during the 1980s, four times as many manual workers reported increases in skill requirements in their jobs compared with workers in professional and administrative categories. As demand for up-skilling has increased, so has the requirement for higher qualifications, particularly in unskilled jobs. In Canada during the 1980s and 1990s, the requirement of having a post-secondary education increased by 60 percent in unskilled manual occupations, compared with an increase of 6 percent in professional occupations (26).

The process of deindustrialization, fueled by increasing emphasis on maintaining economic growth in an environment of sharp global competition, may increasingly favor healthy employees in employers' pursuit of efficiency. These processes have been put forward as plausible forces driving increasing educational and health-related inequalities in employment rates observed over the past several decades (21, 22).

In this chapter we examine trends in employment rates from the early 1980s onward among men and women in different educational groups who are healthy or who have a limiting longstanding illness, in the United Kingdom, Denmark, Norway, Sweden, and Canada. We restricted our study to these five countries for comparability reasons. All five countries have substantial numbers of chronically ill and disabled people outside the labor market and therefore are a cause of national concern. All five have advanced social welfare systems and universal health care, so the policy contexts for disabled people are sufficiently similar for cross-country policy learning, and all have experimented with different ways of tackling the common problem while experiencing contrasting macroeconomic trends. In addition, high-quality, individual-level data are available for the five countries, allowing us to carry out robust analyses of the experiences of different subgroups in the national populations.

DATA SOURCES AND METHODS

Datasets

For Denmark, Norway, Sweden, and the United Kingdom, analyses were based on individual-level data from national surveys representative of their populations; for Canada, analyses were conducted on the five-yearly population censuses. Each dataset was chosen for its detailed individual-level data on participation in the labor market, health status, and socioeconomic circumstances. In each country, analyses were based on men and women aged 25–59 years.

The U.K. data were drawn from the Labour Force Survey (LFS), a large-scale survey with 60,000 households taking part each quarter. The LFS is carried out under an E.U. directive and uses internationally agreed upon concepts and definitions, which have stayed fairly constant, in questions relating to health and economic activity. LFS data for the survey years 1984–85 to 2005–6 were aggregated into three-year time periods.

Swedish analyses were based on the Survey of Living Conditions (Undersökning av levnadsförhållanden, ULF), an annual survey that was modeled on the British General Household Survey. The survey started in 1975, initially with a sample of approximately 12,000 individuals; more recently, since the end of the 1980s, the sample size has reduced to approximately 6,000. Response rates average around 80 percent. Survey years were aggregated into three-year time periods.

For Denmark, analyses were based on the Health and Morbidity Survey (Sundheds- og sygelighedsundersøgelse) for the years 1994, 2000, and 2005. This survey is similar to the British General Household Survey and the Swedish Survey of Living Conditions, but it is not conducted annually. The sample for interviews has increased from 4,670 in 1994 to 21,800 in 2005, and the non-response rate has grown from 22 to 33.3 percent.

Norwegian analyses were based on the Norwegian Survey of Living Conditions (Levekårsundersøkelsen). This survey was conducted in 1973, 1980, 1983, 1987, 1991, and 1995, and then, from 1996, annually. Survey years were aggregated to increase sample size in the following way: the 1980 and 1983 surveys, giving a sample size of 4,695 men and women aged 25–59; 1987 and 1991 surveys (n = 4,521); 1995 and 1998 surveys (n = 6,851); and 2002 and 2005 surveys (n = 8,590).

The Canadian analyses were based on the population censuses for the years 1986, 1991, 1996, and 2001. The Canadian data were drawn specifically from responses to the Census Long Form 2B, a detailed questionnaire administered to one-fifth of all private households in Canada (a shorter questionnaire is completed by the remainder of the population). The question on limiting illness changed in the 2001 census, meaning that comparisons cannot be drawn between employment rates in the previous censuses.

Methods

In each dataset, individuals were defined as having limiting longstanding illness ("chronic illness") if they reported a longstanding health problem that restricted their work or daily activities. Individuals who reported a longstanding condition that did not restrict their work or daily activities were classified as being free from limiting longstanding illness (for brevity, referred to in this study as "healthy").

Educational level was grouped into three categories using the OECD ISCED-97 Classifying Educational Programmes (27): low education was defined as ISCED categories 0, 1, and 2 (pre-primary, primary, and lower secondary schooling); intermediate education as ISCED categories 3 and 4 (upper secondary and post-secondary nontertiary schooling); and high education as ISCED categories 5 and 6 (first and second stages of tertiary education).

Employment rates were calculated according to the number of individuals aged 25–59 employed as a proportion of all individuals in this age group and age-standardized to the European Standard Population, with 95 percent confidence intervals (95% CI). It was necessary to standardize for age because limiting illness increases with increasing age and the age structure of the different national populations varies. In each country, age-standardized employment rates were calculated for men and women aged 25–59 who (*a*) were healthy or reported a longstanding illness that was *not* limiting or (*b*) reported a limiting longstanding illness. For both groups, age-standardized employment rates were also calculated for men and women in the highest and lowest groups of education. Statistically significant upward or downward trends in employment rates were tested using linear regression with time fitted as a covariate and employment rates as the dependent variable. Statistically significant results are flagged in the text. All analyses were conducted in SPSS 15.0 for Windows.

RESULTS

Tables 1 to 5 present country trends in employment rates for men and women with and without limiting illness, spanning periods of between 10 and 25 years. All the countries experienced at least one cycle of economic recession and recovery during this period: Canada, Sweden, and the United Kingdom experienced recessions in both the early 1980s and early 1990s, Norway had a recession in the late 1980s, and Denmark in the early 1990s.

There was a marked deterioration in the employment chances of people with both limiting illness and low education even when the countries were experiencing economic recovery (Figure 1). The starkest example of this trend was observed in the *United Kingdom* (Table 1). Employment among healthy British men, in both low and high education groups, followed the macroeconomic fluctuations: increasing in the late 1980s as the country came out of recession, falling back slightly during the early 1990s recession, before improving again from the late 1990s onward as the economy picked up. Healthy British women in both educational groups showed a similar pattern, but their employment did not falter in the 1990s recession as it did for men.

The experiences of men and women with limiting longstanding illness were very different from those of the healthy groups. British men with limiting illness, in both high and low education groups, showed a slight rise in employment in the late 1980s and a substantial fall during the early 1990s recession (much more severe than their healthy counterparts), followed by a further decline in the mid-1990s even as the economy improved. By 2004–6, the high education group of chronically ill men had still not recovered to the employment level achieved in the 1980s. British men with limiting illness and low education did not experience an upturn in their employment (unlike their healthy counterparts), and the relative differential in employment rates between low and high education groups increased continuously from 46 percent in 1987–90 to 58.7 percent in 2004–6.

Like their male counterparts, the employment rates of British women with limiting illness and low education rose slightly in the late 1980s, declined in the early 1990s recession, but then continued to decline throughout the economic recovery of the 1990s and 2000s to a low rate of 18.1 percent by 2004-6. In stark contrast, women with limiting illness in the high education group experienced a continual rise in employment (as did healthy women in both educational groups), culminating in an employment rate of 66.1 percent in 2004–6. These divergent trends resulted in a marked widening of the inequalities in employment between high and low education groups with limiting illness.

In *Sweden*, there was a recession in the early 1990s (Table 2), the effect of which was seen in all groups—healthy and with limiting illness, women and men, high and low education—in terms of substantial drops in employment rates from the period 1988–90 to the period 1991–93. (This contrasts with the United Kingdom, where healthy women and high education women with limiting illness

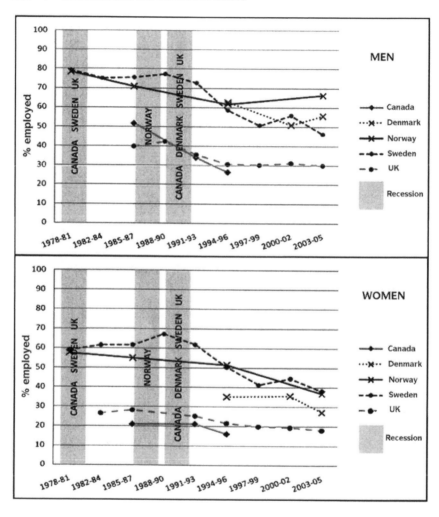

Figure 1. Trends in the proportion of chronically ill men and women aged 25–59 with low education who were in employment, 1978–2005, by country. Vertical gray bars denote periods of recession in the named countries.

did not show a drop in employment with the early 1990s recession.) No group really recovered its pre-1990 level of employment, but the rate for healthy Swedish men and women in the high education groups stabilized at only a slightly lower level for the rest of the 1990s and up to 2005. In the 1970s and early 1980s, the employment rate for healthy Swedish men with low education was very high and slightly higher than their counterparts in the high education group.

Table 1

Trends in age-standardized employment rates for men and women of working age (25–59) by health status: United Kingdom, 1984–2006

	1984–86	1987–90	1991–93	1994–96	1997–99	2000–3	2004–6
	RECOVERY →		*RECESSION* →	*RECOVERY* →			→
Men							
Healthy + low educ. (B)	82.2 (81.8–82.6)	85.4 (85.0–85.7)	82.7 (82.3–83.1)	82.7 (82.3–83.2)	86.0 (85.6–86.4)	86.9 (86.5–87.2)	87.6 (87.2–88.1)
Healthy + high educ. (A)	94.6 (93.0–96.1)	95.5 (94.2–96.8)	93.2 (92.0–94.4)	93.1 (92.0–94.2)	93.7 (92.7–94.7)	94.0 (93.2–94.9)	94.4 (93.3–95.4)
Relative differential (% difference) [(B − A)/A] × 100	−13.1	−10.6	−11.3	−11.2	−8.2	−7.6	−7.2
Limiting illness + low educ. (B)	39.8 (38.4–41.1)	42.3 (41.2–43.4)	35.6 (34.5–36.7)	30.7 (29.7–31.7)	30.3 (29.3–31.4)	31.2 (30.3–32.2)	30.1 (29.0–31.3)
Limiting illness + high educ. (A)	77.2 (74.6–79.9)	78.3 (76.2–80.3)	71.6 (69.6–73.6)	68.6 (66.7–70.4)	68.7 (67.0–70.4)	71.8 (70.4–73.2)	72.8 (71.1–74.4)
Relative differential (% difference) [(B − A)/A] × 100	−48.5	−46.0	−50.3	−55.3	−55.9	−56.6	−58.7
Women							
Healthy + low educ. (B)	57.8 (57.3–58.2)	61.8 (61.4–62.2)	62.4 (61.9–62.8)	62.4 (61.9–62.8)	63.5 (63.0–64.0)	63.5 (63.1–64.0)	62.8 (62.2–63.4)
Healthy + high educ. (A)	75.9 (75.2–76.7)	81.1 (80.5–81.7)	83.1 (82.6–83.6)	84.6 (84.2–85.1)	85.9 (85.5–86.3)	87.3 (87.0–87.7)	87.8 (87.5–88.2)
Relative differential (% difference) [(B − A)/A] × 100	−23.9	−23.8	−24.9	−26.2	−26.1	−27.3	−28.5
Limiting illness + low educ. (B)	26.6 (25.5–27.6)	28.2 (27.3–29.0)	25.3 (24.3–26.2)	21.7 (20.8–22.5)	20.0 (19.1–20.8)	19.5 (18.8–20.3)	18.1 (17.1–19.0)
Limiting illness + high educ. (A)	55.1 (52.0–58.3)	57.3 (54.8–59.8)	57.9 (55.7–60.2)	59.4 (57.5–61.3)	61.8 (60.1–63.5)	63.2 (61.8–64.6)	66.1 (64.5–67.6)
Relative differential (% difference) [(B − A)/A] × 100	−51.7	−50.8	−56.3	−63.5	−67.6	−69.2	−72.6

% aged 25–59 employed (95% CI)

Note: Statistically significant trends: *Men*: healthy/low education $p = 0.05$; limiting illness/low education $p = 0.01$. *Women*: healthy/high education $p = 0.001$; healthy/low education $p = 0.045$; limiting illness/high education $p < 0.001$; limiting illness/low education $p = 0.001$.

Since the recession of the early 1990s, however, rates were higher in the high education than the low education group, and the relative differential grew to (a still modest) 3.7 percent by 2003–5. For Swedish women in the healthy category, employment rates were always lower in the low education group, though the differential fluctuated from 6.0 percent at its narrowest point in 1988–90 to 19.7 percent in 2003–5.

What is most striking about these trends in Sweden is the drastic deterioration in employment for men and women with limiting illness and low education (see Table 2). For men with limiting illness, the rate for the low education group dropped from 77.3 to 72.8 percent during the recession of 1991–93, then dropped markedly during economic recovery to 50.8 percent by the late 1990s. After a rise in the early 2000s, the rate dropped again to 46.3 percent in 2003–5. The result was a substantial widening of inequalities in employment between the low and high education groups with chronic illness: increasing from 6.7 percent at its narrowest point in 1978–81 to 38.7 percent in 2003–5. Swedish women with limiting illness and low education experienced similar falls in employment following the recession of the early 1990s, the rate rising somewhat in 2000–2, before falling again in 2003–5. The relative differential between employment rates of women with limiting illness from high and low education groups, which narrowed throughout the 1980s, started to widen during the 1990s and reached its widest point in 2003–5 at 48.7 percent.

Norway experienced a recession in the late 1980s. Employment rates for healthy men with high education, however, remained high and rose further during the late 1980s and 1990s, peaking at 98.4 percent before falling to 96.0 percent in 2002–5 (Table 3). Conversely, healthy Norwegian men with low education experienced declining employment, by 8.2 percentage points to 88.6 percent, by 2002–5. While employment among men with limiting illness and high education fluctuated between 90.9 and 95.5 percent, their counterparts with low education experienced falling employment (down 16.7 percentage points to 61.8%) during both the recession of the 1980s and economic recovery during the 1990s, before rising to 66.3 percent in 2002–5.

Employment rose among healthy Norwegian women in both educational groups until the late 1990s, before declining slightly for women with low education in 2002–5. A similar trend was observed for chronically ill women with high education, among whom employment rose by 14.6 percentage points to 92.5 percent in 1995–98 but fell sharply to 79.2 percent in 2002–5, almost to the level of the early 1980s. Among chronically ill women with low education, however, employment fell during the recession of the late 1980s and declined steadily thereafter by 20.7 percentage points to 36.9 percent in 2002–5.

In *Denmark* (Table 4), our data only go back to 1994, so we cannot trace what happened during the early 1990s recession. From official statistics, unemployment rates were relatively high in Denmark for a long period in the 1980s and in particular in the years 1989–94, just before the first survey used here. Over the 10-year period 1994–2005, employment rates for healthy Danish men in both high and low education groups remained fairly stable, while the rates for healthy women showed a modest decline. The rates for Danes with limiting illness, however, showed more fluctuation. Diverging employment trends by educational level were evident among men with limiting illness during the 1990s, as employment rates rose from 70.7 to 76.6 percent between 1994 and 2000 for men with high education, yet fell from 62.8 to 50.9 percent for their counterparts with low education. Employment differentials between these groups were attenuated somewhat by 2005. The group with the lowest employment rates in Denmark— women with both limiting illness and low education—experienced a marked decline by 2005, to a rate of 27.3 percent. The relative employment differential between this group and their high education counterparts was large and widened to 63.8 percent in 2005.

In *Canada* (Table 5), only the rates for the first three time periods are comparable, because of a change in the definition of the health variable in the 2001 census. Canada's recession occurred in 1990–91, and there was a striking decline in the employment of men with limiting illness and low education between the 1986 and 1996 censuses, which virtually halved to 26.5 percent. Canadian women with limiting illness and low education exhibited a decline in 1996, to a very low level of 16.1 percent. Their counterparts in the high education group also experienced a decline in employment in 1996 to a low of 55.1 percent. The relative differentials between low and high education groups with limiting illness, both men and women, were very wide: reaching 57.7 percent for men and 70.7 percent for women in 1996—on a par with the size of the inequalities between high and low education groups with limiting illness in the United Kingdom in 2004–6.

DISCUSSION

In this study we explored how healthy and chronically ill men and women in different educational groups have fared in the labor market since the 1980s, a period in which many high-income countries experienced recessions and economic recovery against a backdrop of declining employment in the industrial sectors. As expected, in each country we found the employment rates of men and women with limiting illness were significantly lower than those of their healthy counterparts at every survey or census, indicating their weaker position in the labor market, though the degree of disadvantage varied among the countries.

In relation to *Hypothesis 1*, if the employment chances of chronically ill people were particularly sensitive to the business cycle, then we would expect to see a greater decline in their employment during periods of recession compared with healthy people, resulting in widening inequalities in employment during economic downturns, with a corresponding improvement in employment chances for both the ill and healthy groups during economic recovery. Our findings did *not*

Table 2

Trends in age-standardized employment rates for men and women of working age (25–59) by health status: Sweden, 1978–2005

	1978–81	1982–84	1985–87	1988–90	1991–93	1994–96	1997–99	2000–2	2003–5
		% aged 25–59 employed (95% CI)							
	RECOVERY →	RECESSION →	RECOVERY →		RECESSION →	RECOVERY →			→
Men									
Healthy + low educ. (B)	97.7 (97.2–98.3)	95.9 (94.8–96.9)	95.4 (94.2–96.6)	97.0 (96.0–98.1)	90.7 (88.5–93.0)	89.4 (87.0–91.9)	89.0 (86.1–91.9)	89.8 (86.5–93.1)	87.7 (83.6–91.9)
Healthy + high educ. (A)	96.1 (95.3–96.9)	95.4 (94.3–96.6)	96.3 (95.4–97.2)	96.1 (95.1–97.1)	92.4 (90.9–93.8)	90.0 (88.5–91.5)	91.6 (90.2–93.1)	92.1 (90.8–93.4)	91.1 (89.7–92.5)
Relative differential (% difference) [(B − A)/A] × 100	1.7	0.5	−0.9	0.9	−1.8	−0.7	−2.8	−2.5	−3.7
Limiting illness + low educ. (B)	79.3 (76.5–82.0)	75.1 (70.9–79.3)	75.5 (71.1–80.0)	77.3 (72.3–82.3)	72.8 (66.8–78.8)	58.6 (51.2–66.0)	50.8 (42.8–58.8)	55.9 (47.5–64.2)	46.3 (36.8–55.7)
Limiting illness + high educ. (A)	85.0 (79.1–90.8)	89.9 (84.3–95.6)	86.5 (79.8–93.3)	84.6 (78.0–91.1)	80.0 (74.1–85.8)	80.2 (73.5–86.9)	76.1 (68.9–83.4)	78.3 (71.4–85.2)	75.5 (69.2–81.7)
Relative differential (% difference) [(B − A)/A] × 100	−6.7	−16.5	−12.7	−8.6	−9.0	−26.9	−33.3	−28.6	−38.7

Women

Healthy + low educ. (B)	77.1 (75.7–78.5)	82.5 (80.5–84.4)	86.0 (84.0–88.1)	89.8 (87.6–91.9)	83.7 (80.5–86.9)	77.5 (73.9–81.1)	76.1 (72.2–79.9)	75.4 (70.5–80.2)	72.8 (67.1–78.6)
Healthy + high educ. (A)	91.6 (90.2–93.1)	93.0 (91.4–94.6)	94.8 (93.5–96.1)	95.5 (94.4–96.5)	90.7 (89.1–92.2)	89.5 (88.0–91.1)	88.1 (86.6–89.7)	89.9 (88.5–91.3)	90.6 (89.3–92.0)
Relative differential (% difference) [(B − A)/A] × 100	−15.8	−11.3	−9.3	−6.0	−7.7	−13.4	−13.6	−16.1	−19.7
Limiting illness + low educ. (B)	59.0 (56.0–62.0)	61.5 (57.0–66.1)	61.6 (56.3–66.8)	67.2 (62.2–72.3)	61.9 (55.2–68.5)	50.5 (43.8–57.1)	41.3 (34.0–48.6)	44.6 (36.5–52.7)	38.3 (30.1–46.6)
Limiting illness + high educ. (A)	86.4 (81.1–91.6)	90.9 (85.9–95.9)	86.5 (80.8–92.2)	85.8 (80.8–90.8)	80.4 (74.6–86.1)	76.6 (70.5–82.7)	70.5 (64.1–76.9)	74.4 (69.5–79.4)	74.6 (69.3–79.8)
Relative differential (% difference) [(B − A)/A] × 100	−31.7	−32.3	−28.8	−21.7	−23.0	−34.1	−41.4	−40.1	−48.7

Note: Statistically significant trends: *Men:* healthy/high education $p = 0.006$; healthy/low education $p < 0.001$; limiting illness/high education $p = 0.001$; limiting illness/low education $p < 0.001$. *Women:* healthy/high education $p = 0.001$; healthy/low education $p = 0.006$.

Table 3

Trends in age-standardized employment rates for men and women of working age (25–59) by health status: Norway, 1980–2005

| | % aged 25–59 employed (95% CI) | | | |
| | 1980–83 | 1987–91 | 1995–98 | 2002–5 |
	RECOVERY →	RECESSION →	RECOVERY →	→
Men				
Healthy + low educ. (B)	**96.8 (95.4–98.2)**	**95.0 (93.0–97.1)**	**94.4 (91.8–96.9)**	**88.6 (84.5–92.7)**
Healthy + high educ. (A)	**95.4 (93.5–97.3)**	**98.3 (97.1–99.4)**	**98.4 (97.3–99.5)**	**96.0 (94.8–97.1)**
Relative differential (% difference) [(B – A)/A] × 100	1.5	–3.4	–4.1	–7.7
Limiting illness + low educ. (B)	78.5 (72.9–84.2)	70.9 (62.9–78.8)	61.8 (52.5–71.2)	66.3 (57.3–75.2)
Limiting illness + high educ. (A)	**95.0 (89.3–100.7)**	**93.8 (85.2–102.4)**	**95.5 (90.4–100.6)**	**90.9 (86.5–95.2)**
Relative differential (% difference) [(B – A)/A] × 100	–17.4	–24.4	–35.3	–27.1
Women				
Healthy + low educ. (B)	70.8 (67.3–74.2)	78.8 (75.2–82.4)	80.8 (76.1–85.5)	77.8 (72.3–83.4)
Healthy + high educ. (A)	81.2 (77.0–85.3)	**91.9 (89.2–94.5)**	93.5 (91.3–95.6)	93.3 (87.8–98.8)
Relative differential (% difference) [(B – A)/A] × 100	–12.8	–14.3	–13.6	–16.6
Limiting illness + low educ. (B)	57.6 (52.4–62.9)	55.0 (47.6–62.5)	51.6 (42.8–60.3)	36.9 (25.4–48.5)
Limiting illness + high educ. (A)	77.9 (68.6–87.2)	84.1 (74.1–94.1)	**92.5 (87.0–98.0)**	79.2 (74.4–84.0)
Relative differential (% difference) [(B – A)/A] × 100	–26.1	–34.6	–44.2	–53.4

Note: Figures in bold are not age-standardized, for statistical reasons. No statistically significant trends were observed.

Table 4

Trends in age-standardized employment rates for men and women of working age (25–59) by health status: Denmark, 1994–2005

	% aged 25–59 employed (95% CI)		
	1994	2000	2005
	RECOVERY →		
Men			
Healthy + low educ. (B)	85.6 (80.7–90.5)	86.3 (83.6–88.9)	84.0 (80.3–87.7)
Healthy + high educ. (A)	90.1 (86.5–93.7)	90.0 (88.2–91.7)	89.2 (87.3–91.1)
Relative differential (% difference)			
[(B – A)/A] × 100	–5.0	–4.1	–5.8
Limiting illness + low educ. (B)	62.8 (51.8–73.8)	50.9 (43.7–58.1)	55.6 (47.6–63.6)
Limiting illness + high educ. (A)	70.7 (53.4–88.0)	76.6 (70.0–83.1)	72.5 (63.8–81.1)
Relative differential (% difference)			
[(B – A)/A] × 100	–11.2	–33.6	–23.3
Women			
Healthy + low educ. (B)	73.2 (67.7–87.7)	77.4 (74.0–80.8)	66.8 (61.4–72.2)
Healthy + high educ. (A)	91.4 (87.6–95.2)	87.6 (86.0–89.7)	86.6 (84.8–88.4)
Relative differential (% difference)			
[(B – A)/A] × 100	–19.9	–11.6	–22.9
Limiting illness + low educ. (B)	35.2 (23.4–46.9)	35.7 (29.6–41.8)	27.3 (20.6–33.9)
Limiting illness + high educ. (A)	82.3 (71.3–93.3)	70.8 (64.1–77.4)	75.5 (69.6–81.4)
Relative differential (% difference)			
[(B – A)/A] × 100	–57.2	–49.6	–63.8

Note: No statistically significant trends were observed.

Table 5

Trends in age-standardized employment rates for men and women of working age (25–59) by health status: Canada, 1986–2001

	% aged 25–59 employed (95% CI)			
	1986	1991	1996	2001
	RECOVERY	RECESSION	RECOVERY	RECOVERY
Men				
Healthy + low educ. (B)	83.51 (83.50–83.51)	74.23 (74.23–74.24)	69.60 (69.60–69.60)	72.04 (72.04–72.05)
Healthy + high educ. (A)	91.57 (91.56–91.57)	91.42 (91.42–91.43)	89.61 (89.61–89.62)	89.63 (89.63–89.64)
Relative differential (% difference) [(B – A)/A] × 100	–8.80	–18.80	–22.33	–19.63
Limiting illness + low educ. (B)	51.70 (51.69–51.71)	34.15 (34.14–34.16)	26.50 (26.50–26.51)	38.13 (38.13–38.14)
Limiting illness + high educ. (A)	72.06 (72.05–72.08)	70.31 (70.30–70.33)	62.69 (62.68–62.69)	73.97 (73.97–73.98)
Relative differential (% difference) [(B – A)/A] × 100	–28.25	–51.43	–57.73	–48.45
Women				
Healthy + low educ. (B)	42.42 (42.42–42.42)	45.73 (45.73–45.73)	43.62 (43.62–43.63)	47.92 (47.91–47.92)
Healthy + high educ. (A)	76.20 (76.19–76.20)	80.67 (80.67–80.68)	81.08 (81.08–81.08)	82.06 (82.06–82.06)
Relative differential (% difference) [(B – A)/A] × 100	–44.33	–43.31	–46.20	–41.60
Limiting illness + low educ. (B)	20.99 (20.98–20.99)	21.29 (21.28–21.29)	16.15 (16.14–16.15)	25.09 (25.08–25.09)
Limiting illness + high educ. (A)	59.84 (59.83–59.85)	59.87 (59.86–59.88)	55.15 (55.15–55.16)	67.15 (67.14–67.16)
Relative differential (% difference) [(B – A)/A] × 100	–64.92	–64.44	–70.72	–62.64

Note: Comparisons cannot be drawn between the three earlier years of 1986, 1991, 1996 and the final year of 2001 as the definition of limiting illness in the Canadian census changed in 2001. No statistically significant trends were observed.

support this hypothesis on the economic cycle, however. Rather than revealing increasing inequality between the employment rates of healthy and chronically ill people during economic downturns only, we found increasing inequality *throughout* the 1980s, 1990s, and 2000s, during periods of economic recovery as well as recessions. In most cases, as employment rose in each country as a whole, employment among people with limiting illness and people with low education continued to stagnate or, in some countries, to deteriorate. The employment of chronically ill people with low education was the hardest hit. In contrast, healthy groups saw some improvement in employment with economic recovery, resulting in widening inequalities between ill and healthy groups during economic upturns.

In relation to *Hypothesis 2*, if deindustrialization were having an effect on chronically ill people, we would expect to see growing employment polarization between healthy and ill groups, and between ill groups with high and low education, mainly independent of short-term economic fluctuations. This is basically the pattern we observed. We found growing polarization between the employment rates of healthy and chronically ill individuals over two decades when there were short-term economic fluctuations. We also observed increasing employment-related polarization between individuals with low and high education, among both the healthy and chronically ill. In each of the five countries in the study, men and women with limiting illness and low education had the lowest employment rates, and the gap between them and their healthy counterparts widened over time. This widening inequality, both between the healthy and chronically ill and between people with low and high education, was greatest in Canada and the United Kingdom. In both of these countries, the employment rates for men and women with limiting illness and low education were considerably lower than those observed in Denmark, Norway, or Sweden, as depicted in Figure 1. Previous research has documented how industrial decline in the United Kingdom has led to high levels of labor market detachment and increased claims for disability-related welfare benefits, particularly among men living in industrial and former coalfield areas (28). In our cross-country study, however, the deindustrialization hypothesis is only *partially* supported: although in the United Kingdom and Canada the employment situation for individuals with limiting illness and/or low education was poor, Canada experienced a more limited reduction of industrial employment than the other countries, while the United Kingdom experienced the greatest reduction. Different countries may find themselves in somewhat different phases of deindustrialization, and this may help explain different country patterns. In addition, the impact of deindustrialization may be mitigated by the presence of differing welfare systems and the implementation of active labor market programs within them.

The triggering of a long-term downward trend in employment following recession that we observed among people with limiting illness and people with low education has also been documented among other groups in a weak position in the labor market. In the United Kingdom, for example, not only have unemployment rates risen faster during recession among people of racial/ethnic minority groups compared with the white population, but they have failed to improve during economic recovery, leading to widening racial/ethnic inequalities in unemployment over time (29). Long-term policy initiatives are required to help less powerful groups gain secure employment both during and beyond economic crises, as the employment impact of recessions is long-lasting. The U.K. recessions of the 1970s, 1980s, and 1990s were associated with increases in unemployment that extended well beyond the length of each recession, and unemployment rates did not return to pre-recession levels for many years (30). In Denmark, Norway, Sweden, and the United Kingdom, unemployment rates have failed to return to levels of the early 1970s (24). The exception to this is Canada, where unemployment was higher during this period and resembled rates observed in Sweden and the United Kingdom shortly before the current recession.

People with the double burden of chronic illness and low education have become increasingly marginalized from the labor market in recent decades. Our findings suggest that structural changes concerning deindustrialization experienced in all five study countries may have played a part in this process. In addition, the burden of economic recession has not been shared equally: periods of high unemployment, which increase demand for a streamlined workforce and increased efficiency, have sparked a downward trend in employment for already marginalized groups who are least able to compete in the labor market and who have not felt the benefits when the economy has improved. Some countries, such as Norway and Sweden, have been better able to protect the employment of these groups, while the United Kingdom and Canada have done less well. These contextual differences suggest that other macro-level factors, such as the operation of active and passive labor market polices, may be coming into play. Recent studies demonstrate how investment in active labor market programs can cushion the impact of economic crises on mental health disorders and suicide rates (16, 31).

Acknowledgments — This work was carried out under the auspices of the Public Health Research Consortium (PHRC), which is funded by the English Department of Health's Policy Research Programme. The views expressed in the chapter are those of the authors and not necessarily those of the Department of Health. Ben Barr was on an attachment with the PHRC as part of the Mersey Deanery Postgraduate Public Health Training Programme.

REFERENCES

1. Black, C. (chair). *Working for a Healthier Tomorrow*. Stationery Office, London, 2008.

2. Government Offices of Sweden. *Effective Return to Work: Reforms.* Stockholm, 2008.
3. Jenkins, S. P., and Rigg, J. A. Disability and disadvantage: Selection, onset, and duration effects. *J. Soc. Pol.* 33:479–501, 2004.
4. Avendano, M., Jürges, H., and Mackenbach, J. P. Educational level and changes in health across Europe: Longitudinal results from SHARE. *J. Eur. Soc. Policy* 19(4):301–316, 2009.
5. Burström, B., et al. Inequality in the social consequences of illness: How well do people with long-term illness fare in the British and Swedish labor markets? *Int. J. Health Serv.* 30:435–451, 2000.
6. Burström, B., et al. Winners and losers in flexible labor markets: The fate of women with chronic illness in contrasting policy environments—Sweden and Britain. *Int. J. Health Serv.* 33:209–217, 2003.
7. Bartley, M., and Plewis, I. Accumulated labour market disadvantage and limiting long-term illness: Data from the 1971–1991 Office for National Statistics' Longitudinal study. *Int. J. Epidemiol.* 31:336–341, 2002.
8. Bartley, M., Sacker, A., and Clarke, P. Employment status, employment conditions and limiting illness: Prospective evidence from the British Household Panel Study 1991–2001. *J. Epidemiol. Community Health* 58:501–506, 2004.
9. Lindholm, C., Burström, B., and Diderichsen, F. Class differences in the social consequences of illness? *J. Epidemiol. Community Health* 56:188–192, 2002.
10. Holland, P., et al. Socioeconomic inequalities in the employment impact of ischaemic heart disease: A longitudinal record linkage study in Sweden. *Scand. J. Public Health* 37:450–458, 2009.
11. Holland, P., et al. Gender and socio-economic variations in employment among patients with a diagnosed musculoskeletal disorder: A longitudinal record linkage study in Sweden. *Rheumatology* 45(8):1016–1022, 2006.
12. Holland, P., et al. Labour market participation following onset of seizures and early epilepsy: Findings from a UK cohort. *Epilepsia* 50:1030–1039, 2009.
13. Meltzer, H., et al. *OPCS Surveys of Psychiatric Morbidity in Great Britain, Report 3. Economic Activity and Social Functioning of Adults with Psychiatric Disorders.* Stationery Office, London, 1995.
14. Dahlgren, G., and Whitehead, M. A framework for assessing health systems from the public's perspective: The ALPS approach. *Int. J Health Serv.* 37:363–378, 2007.
15. Dorling, D. Unemployment and health. *BMJ* 338:1091–1092, 2009.
16. Stuckler, D. S., et al. The public health effect of economic crises and alternative policy responses in Europe: An empirical analysis. *Lancet* 374:315–323, 2009.
17. Catalano, R., and Hartig, T. Economic predictors of admissions to inpatient psychiatric treatment in Sweden. *Soc. Psychiatry Psychiatr. Epidemiol.* 39:305–310, 2004.
18. Catalano, R., et al. Job loss and alcohol abuse: A test using data from the Epidemiologic Catchment Area Project. *J. Health Soc. Behav.* 34:215–226, 1993.
19. Åhs, A., and Westerling, R. Self-rated health in relation to employment status during periods of high and of low levels of unemployment. *Eur. J. Public Health* 16:294–304, 2006.
20. Perkins, R., and Rinaldi, M. Unemployment rates among patients with long-term mental health problems. *Psychiatr. Bull.* 26:295–298, 2002.

21. van der Wel, K. A., Dahl, E., and Birkelund, G. E. Employment inequalities through busts and booms: The changing roles of health and education in Norway 1980–2005. *Acta Sociol.* 53(4):355–370, 2010.

22. Bartley, M., and Owen, C. Relation between socioeconomic status, employment, and health during economic change, 1973–93. *BMJ* 313:445–449, 1996.

23. Ostry, A. S. Globalization and the marginalization of unskilled labor: Potential impacts on health in developed nations. *Int. J. Health Serv.* 39:45–57, 2009.

24. Organization for Economic Cooperation and Development. *Annual Labour Force Statistics Summary Tables.* Paris, 2010. http://stats.oecd.org.

25. Gallie, D. The polarization of the labour market and exclusion of vulnerable groups. In *Health Effects of the New Labour Market*, ed. K. Isaksson et al. Plenum, New York, 2000.

26. Holzer, H. J. *What Employers Want: Job Prospects for Less-Educated Workers.* Russell Sage Foundation, New York, 1996.

27. Organization for Economic Cooperation and Development. *Classifying Educational Programmes Manual for ISCED-97 Implementation in OECD Countries.* Paris, 1999.

28. Alcock, P., et al. *Work to Welfare: How Men Become Detached from the Labour Market.* Cambridge University Press, Cambridge, 2003.

29. Leslie, D., Lindley, J., and Thomas, L. Who did worse? A comparison of US and British non-white unemployment 1970–1998. *Appl. Econ.* 34:1041–1053, 2002.

30. Stafford, B., and Duffy, D. *Review of Evidence on the Impact of Economic Downturn on Disadvantaged Groups.* Working Paper No 68. Department for Work and Pensions, London, 2009.

31. Uutela, A. Economic crisis and mental health. *Curr. Opin. Psychiatry* 23:127–130, 2010.

PART IV

Changes in the Welfare States

Edwin Ng

INTRODUCTION

At its core, the modern understanding of the welfare state refers to how state power is used in various ways to modify the impact of market forces. Through a complex of public policies and legislative measures, welfare states provide key services, such as health care and education, and distribute key transfers in the form of unemployment and pension benefits, for example. Given recent global trends in globalization, neoliberalism, and financial instability, the importance of welfare states in structuring social inequalities, which, in turn, affect population health, has gained a renewed sense of purpose and attention. Against this backdrop, there has been a recent surge of research among social epidemiologists and medical sociologists on the comparative impacts of welfare generosity (e.g., national expenditures on health, social services, and education) and welfare regimes (e.g., country clusters based on decommodification, stratification, and private-public partnerships) on population health and health inequalities.

In Part IV we have six studies that advance our current knowledge base on welfare states and health in new and important ways. Fosse (Chapter 13) examines the often theorized link between welfare states and public policies in England, Norway, and the Netherlands, three European nations that represent the liberal, social democratic, and corporatist welfare regimes, respectively. Van der Wel and coauthors (Chapter 14) use a comparative approach to examine the multilevel connections between welfare regimes, limiting longstanding illness, joblessness, and educational levels. Bambra and coauthors (Chapter 15) compare educational inequalities in self-reported health and limiting longstanding illness in six age groups based on decade of birth (1930s–1980s) in 17 countries, categorized into four welfare state regimes (Anglo-Saxon, Bismarckian, Scandinavian, and Southern). Siddiqi and colleagues (Chapter 16) explore whether differences in social policies explain differences in socioeconomic gradients in reading literacy among 15-year-olds across 22 OECD nations. Backhans and coauthors (Chapter 17) investigate trends and clustering of gender policy in 22 OECD countries from 1979 to 2008. And finally, Borrell and colleagues (Chapter 18) describe variations among political traditions in the magnitude of inequalities in self-perceived health by educational level, to determine whether these variations change when contextual welfare state, labor market, wealth, and income inequality variables among European countries are taken into account.

CHAPTER 13

Different Welfare States—Different Policies?
An Analysis of the Substance of
National Health Promotion Policies in
Three European Countries

Elisabeth Fosse

This study examines healthy public policy development in three European countries representing different welfare regimes: England representing the liberal model; Norway, the social democratic model; and the Netherlands, the corporatist model. National policy documents were used for the analysis. In England and Norway, health promotion has a prominent place and there is a political focus on the broader determinants of health. However, while the Norwegian policies have an explicit focus on the social gradient, the English policies have a much clearer focus on disadvantaged groups and geographic areas. In the Netherlands, the main focus is on disease prevention and risk behaviors. In the Netherlands and England there is a strong focus on the free will of the population in changing unhealthy lifestyles. By analyzing the different policies in the light of Esping-Andersen's typology of welfare state regimes, it is possible to better understand the differences among the countries. While all types of regimes seem willing to develop targeted measures, the social democratic regime seems the most willing to also develop structural measures addressing the wider social determinants of health.

*****

This chapter presents an analysis of national health promotion policies to determine to what extent these policies have targeted health equity. The main focus of the Ottawa Charter for Health Promotion (1) is on determinants of health; it describes the fundamental conditions and resources for health as: peace, shelter, education, food, income, a stable ecosystem, sustainable resources, social justice, and equity. The charter outlines five strategies to develop health promotion: building healthy public policy (meaning policy explicitly concerned with health and equity in all areas of the policy and accountability for its health effects), creating supportive environments, strengthening community actions, developing personal skills, and reorienting health services.

The charter states that in building healthy public policy, "Health promotion goes beyond health care. It puts health on the agenda of policy makers in all sectors and at all levels, directing them to be aware of the health consequences of their decisions and to accept their responsibilities for health. Health promotion policy combines diverse but complementary approaches including legislation, fiscal measures, taxation and organizational change. It is coordinated action that leads to health, income and social policies that foster greater equity" (1). This statement shows that to achieve the aims of the Ottawa Charter, it is necessary to focus on the social determinants of health, which requires intersectoral action. However, like many statements from international conferences, this one is quite vague and difficult to use as a tool for action.

Some authors in the field have been trying to operationalize the concept and tie it in with existing literature and traditions in public policy research. There are several definitions of public policy, but the following is useful in the present context: "Public policy is the broad framework of ideas and values within which decisions are taken and action, or inaction, is pursued by governments in relation to some issue or problem" (2, p. 26). Central to this definition is the notion that public policy is more than just government programs, but extends beyond the decisions a government chooses to make. Thus, public policy is a guiding principle as much as an outcome.

De Leeuw and Polman (3) describe healthy public policy as a major prerequisite for health promotion. They define it as making health a legitimate part of policies in all sectors. Health promotion and healthy public policy ideas are summarized by three concepts: intersectoral collaboration, integrated intervention mixes, and participation of the community.

Social equity is thus an overall aim of healthy public policy. Social inequities in health concern systematic differences in health status between different socio-economic groups. Within any country, differences in health can be observed across the population. Mortality studies show that social inequalities in health include, but are not confined to, worse health among the poor. There is a social gradient: mortality rises with decreasing socioeconomic status (4). Three distinguishing features, when combined, turn mere variations or differences in health into social inequities in health: systematic, socially produced (and therefore modifiable), and unfair (5). Systematic patterns of differences in health are not distributed randomly but show a consistent pattern across social groups, and morbidity and mortality increase with declining social position. Social processes produce health differences, and social inequities are differences that are widely considered to be unfair.

Whitehead and Dahlgren (5) emphasize that in the public health community, the phrase "social inequalities in health" alludes to health differences that are unfair and unjust. Some European languages have only one word for the two terms—inequalities and inequities—and there is no distinction between the two when they are translated. In this chapter the terms are used interchangeably and in accordance with the definition of equity outlined above.

The World Health Organization (WHO) Commission on the Social Determinants of Health strongly acknowledges the political aspects of health as having a focus on the "causes of the causes of health and disease": "Strengthening health equity—globally and within countries—means going beyond concentration on the immediate causes of disease. More than any other health endeavour, the Commission focuses on the 'causes of the causes'—the fundamental structures of social hierarchy and the socially determined conditions these create in which people live, work, and age" (6, p. 1153).

Supranational institutions such as the WHO play an important role in formulating goals and objectives in a global strategy to develop healthy public policies. However, nation states have the main responsibility and jurisdiction to develop policies. Despite an increased recognition that the concept of equity is normative and demands political action, this has not always been explicitly stated and problematized within the field of health promotion (7).

Globally, and within the European Union and the wider European context, there are different traditions for redistribution among social groups. Navarro and Shi (8) studied the impact of the major political traditions in the advanced OECD (Organization for Economic Cooperation and Development) countries from 1945 to 1980. Their results indicated that political traditions more committed to redistributive policies (both economic and social) and full-employment policies, such as the social democratic parties, were generally more successful in improving the health of populations. Other authors have also emphasized the significance of macro-politics in understanding why some countries have larger social inequalities than others. Mansyur and colleagues (9) studied how exposures to social and health inequalities probably vary as a consequence of different political cultures. Political systems and structural inequalities are institutionalized manifestations of cultural differences that intervene between dominant cultural dimensions at the societal level and health.

Graham (10, 11) differentiates between policies/strategies aimed at the whole population and strategies targeted at the poorest groups. Policies aimed at the poorest groups may lead to improvements in the social condition and health situation of these groups, but the social gradient—that is, the difference between social groups with the highest and the lowest socioeconomic status—will not have changed. In other words, there are differences between policies aimed at improving the living conditions and the health of the poorest and policies aimed at reducing the social gradient. The latter would require comprehensive intersectoral action affecting all socioeconomic groups. Reducing the social gradient in health would obviously be more controversial than developing interventions aimed at disadvantaged groups, because it requires a certain redistribution among social groups in many areas—tax policies and labor market policies (6).

According to Dahlgren and Whitehead (12), a way of linking healthy public policies to the issue of social inequities in health is to see them as an integrated part of population-based policies and programs for health development. The social dimension of these general policies—just as with age and gender—should always be considered. To be characterized as healthy public policies, health promotion policies need to include aspects of social equity and aim at reducing the social gradient in health.

THEORETICAL APPROACHES

European countries traditionally have different institutional arrangements in place to meet the social needs of their populations. Within social policy research, the study of different welfare state regimes has brought a broader understanding of how historical and political contextual factors have contributed to the different types of welfare states that exist in the Western world. The concept of "welfare state regimes" indicates that different types of welfare states may direct which policies are feasible and legitimate in their particular country. The aim of this study is to examine recent health promotion policies, particularly policies to reduce social inequities in health, in three European countries representing three welfare state regimes (13). Health promotion policies may have different meanings in different countries, and the policy instruments suggested may differ and may also reflect which instruments are considered legitimate in that country. The study analyzes policies in England, the Netherlands, and Norway.

The work of Esping-Andersen in his 1990 book *The Three Worlds of Welfare Capitalism* (13) has been groundbreaking in the study of how different states redistribute resources, particularly to disadvantaged groups. The terms *welfare state* and *welfare state policies* are not unambiguous and have different meanings in different political systems. Esping-Andersen classifies not welfare states but what he calls welfare regimes, according to three types: liberal, corporatist/traditional, and social democratic, each having particular characteristics.

In the *liberal welfare regime*, market forces play a dominant role and the state encourages the market to flourish, either passively, by guaranteeing a minimum of regulation, or actively, by subsidizing private welfare schemes. Public transfers are means-tested, and only modest universal benefits and social insurance plans exist. Examples of this type of welfare state are the United Kingdom, United States, Canada, and Australia. In contrast, in the *corporatist/traditional welfare regime*, the market does not play a predominant role in protecting the health of the population. The ideas of social rights and encompassing social security networks hold a high degree of legitimacy. The basis of these regimes is conservative and built on the upholding of "traditional" family values. Their social security systems are traditionally built around the male breadwinner and are strongly attached to the labor market, hence mostly excluding women not employed outside the home. Among the corporatist regimes are France, Germany, Italy, and even the Netherlands. The *social democratic welfare regime* is characterized by its emphasis on solidarity, universalism, and the redistribution of resources among social groups, mainly through a progressive tax system and entitlements for vulnerable groups. This is a system of emancipation, not only from the market but also of the family. The result is a welfare state with direct transfers to children and one that takes direct responsibility for the care of children, providing the conditions for women with families to engage in paid work. Women are encouraged to work, and the welfare state is dependent on female participation in the labor market. The Scandinavian countries are held as exemplars of the social democratic welfare regime.

Building on Esping-Andersen's classifications, one would expect policies to reduce social inequalities in health to follow the same pattern. The liberal and the conservative countries would be expected to largely apply measures targeted at the poorest groups, while the social democratic countries would apply more structural policy measures. Translated to the health promotion agenda, the social democratic regime would be expected to be most in line with the healthy public policy approach, including comprehensive, intersectoral action to address the social determinants of health. Translated to the social equity agenda, addressing the social gradient would be in line with the aim of redistribution among social groups, which is part of the ideology of social democratic regimes. On the other hand, targeted measures would be expected to be the most important strategy in liberal regimes.

Esping-Andersen's book has raised a lot of debate and has been criticized from several angles. The critiques may be summarized as follows:

- The categorization of welfare states does not capture the main characteristics of the different states included (14).
- A number of studies show that the health of different population groups is not better in the social democratic welfare states, as expected given the comprehensiveness of this type of welfare state regime (15, 16).
- Esping-Andersen is not considering the role of women; the classification is "gender blind" (17).

In later publications, Esping-Andersen (18, 19) explicitly acknowledges the different historical contexts within which different welfare states have developed. He does not put one welfare state above another, but by outlining the present and future challenges in preserving welfare states, he points to the importance of public policies aimed at families, particularly building the foundations for women's participation in the labor market through childcare arrangements and economic transfers.

Even though Esping-Andersen's welfare state typology has been criticized, there is a large body of empirical research that supports the main hypothesis that population health is best in the welfare regimes with the most redistributive and generous welfare arrangements. Bambra and Eikemo (20) studied the relationship between unemployment and increased risk of morbidity and mortality and whether this relationship varies among welfare states with differing levels of social protection for the unemployed. The negative relationship between unemployment and health is consistent across Europe but varies by welfare state regime, suggesting that levels of social protection may indeed have a moderating influence. The especially strong negative relationship for women may well be due to unemployed women being likely to receive lower than average wage-replacement rates.

Lundberg and coauthors (21, 22) report on a project that studied the Nordic welfare states. The conclusion was that the ways in which social policies are designed, as well as their generosity, are important for health because of the increased resources that social policies entail. Hence, social policies are of major importance for how the social determinants of health can be tackled.

An important question is whether countries with more generous welfare policies also have smaller inequalities in health and mortality. Relative health inequalities seem to persist irrespective of social policies and welfare regimes (23). However, absolute inequalities may be linked to the type of welfare policies adopted. The four Nordic countries, which constitute the social democratic welfare regime, form a rather homogeneous welfare state cluster with certain unique institutional features that have proved favorable to social equality (24).

Recent research suggests that generosity as well as the principles and design of social policies matter (25). A common feature of successful programs seems to be that they cover all members of the relevant population. These findings suggest that universal policies rather than means-tested, targeted ones might be better for the poorer segments of societies. Furthermore, any outcome is dependent not only on the redistribution profile but also on the amount being redistributed.

Three countries are included in the present study, each representing one particular type of welfare regime. England represents the liberal regime; Norway, the social democratic regime; and the Netherlands, the corporatist regime. The categorization of the Netherlands has been one of the cases for debate. However, Esping-Andersen concludes that based on the main characteristics of the welfare system, it belongs to the corporatist/traditional regime (13).

This chapter addresses several questions: What is the substance of national health promotion policies in England, Norway, and the Netherlands? How are issues of equity dealt with? Are mainly targeted measures in place or also policies that address the social gradient? And to what extent and in what manner do the policies reflect the welfare state regimes of the three countries?

HISTORICAL AND POLITICAL CONTEXTS

Whitehead has studied the development of policies to reduce social inequalities in health in several European countries, focusing on their historical and political contexts (26). Her findings regarding Britain and the Netherlands are relevant for this study, and the following information is based on her study.

Britain has a tradition of measuring social inequalities in health using occupational class as the social category, dating back to the 19th century. The statistical basis for measuring social inequalities in health has thus been in place for a long time. The issue was raised in the public agenda in the 1970s, when leading researchers pointed to increasing social inequalities in health. In 1980 the Black Report was published, showing large inequalities in health in the United Kingdom. However, during the Thatcher period, the government ignored the problem. Not until the first Blair government came into office in 1997 was the problem fully recognized, and under the Labour governments the reduction of health inequalities was an overall objective.

In the Netherlands, the issue of social inequalities was raised in the 1980s, partly influenced by the Black Report. In 1987, a national conference was arranged on the issue for key policymakers, and the government adopted a broad plan of action and commissioned a five-year research program on health inequalities. In the 1990s the government launched a second five-year research and development program focusing on the causal mechanisms and the evaluation of interventions addressing health inequalities.

Norway was not part of Whitehead's studies. As in Sweden, social inequalities were an overall issue for the labor movement in the 1930s. The Scandinavian postwar welfare states were all built on an ideology of redistribution among social groups. However, from the 1970s the issue of social inequalities received little political attention. Dahl (27) studied how income inequalities in health were defined in national policy documents in the period 1991–2001. In these documents, inequality is mainly perceived in terms of disadvantaged, vulnerable, or marginalized groups and individuals. Inequalities in terms of social stratification or social class are hardly mentioned, and if they are, they are defined as unimportant. The first government white paper on health promotion, issued in 1993, did not address health inequalities (28).

Whitehead (26) has developed a so-called action spectrum, which outlines actions that reflect various degrees of commitment to reducing social inequalities in health. The most committed of these are "comprehensive, coordinated strategies." In the middle of the action spectrum we find the categories "more structured developments" and "isolated initiatives"; at the lower end, the categories "measurement," "awareness raising," and "indifference." Whitehead concluded that in the late 1990s, the Netherlands and the United Kingdom were in the process of developing policies and thus moving in the direction of "more structured developments." Using the action spectrum, Dahl

(27) found that at this time, the Norwegian strategies could be characterized as "indifference."

Whitehead's paper (26) was published in 1998, and there have been some developments in these countries since then, as reported below under Findings.

METHODS

In comparing different countries, it is vital to understand their institutional contexts and to classify institutional differences across countries. Vining and Weimer (29) outline two different types of comparative studies: the study of institutional design itself (first-order policy instruments) and of the policy instruments used as mechanisms of the institutional design (second-order policy instruments). Within political science, the traditions could be divided into studies focusing on policy design, including the content of the policy, and those studying the implementation of policies. Here the focus is on the design of the policies. I chose Esping-Andersen's classification to capture the different institutional contexts in the countries studied. The use of this framework has an exploratory aim, as my intent is to explore whether the framework is useful in studying this particular policy field.

Document analysis is a research strategy within qualitative methods, which can be used in combination with other methods but also as a method in its own right (30–32). When using documents as a data source, it is important to study them in their context and to understand the purpose of the documents. It is also important to critically assess the authenticity, credibility, representativeness, and meaning of the documents (32). This project used as data sources authoritative political documents such as government white papers and government action plans. Political documents usually meet the criteria of authenticity and credibility as they are expressions of formulated government policies. Representativeness in this context is linked to the question of whether the document is typical or atypical. For England, the Netherlands, and Norway, I had access to several documents, and in these countries the policies presented are typical of health promotion documents produced at that time. The issue of meaning will be essential in the analysis. It concerns the explicit and implicit values of the policies presented and is closely linked to the explicit analytical tools chosen for the study.

There are limitations to using political documents as the sole source of data, as they may provide a very specific approach to a political process. They state what a government intends to do and can be accused of presenting wishes and vague plans rather than solid results. Most research shows that in many policies there are discrepancies between intentions and implemented results (33). Nevertheless, policy documents serve as valuable data sources because they are produced by governments and have credibility and authority. They serve as guiding principles and tools for government action and thus reflect government ideology and intentions regarding the choice of policy instruments to deal with policies related to health promotion and health inequalities.

Data

National public health and health promotion policy documents used as a basis for this analysis were accessed using the 2005 data entry into the HP-Source.net database (34). Data entered into HP-Source.net are collected and entered by a designated person or institution in each country. The documents analyzed present national government policies, mostly government white papers and national action plans. In this database, the references of the documents are available with links to the national institutions responsible for publishing them.

The procedure for selecting the documents was the following. First, the relevant countries were classified according to Esping-Andersen's categories. His classification does not cover the former communist countries in Central and Eastern Europe, so these countries were excluded. Only countries that had entered data into the database in 2005 or later were included. The selection of the countries was then based on the quality of the data entered into the database and on whether the countries had health promotion policies in place.

In the document analysis, I first reviewed all abstracts, then read all documents that met the inclusion criteria, looking for policies focusing on health inequalities. When such policies were in place, they were analyzed to assess whether they met the criteria for healthy public policies, and whether they had an explicit or implicit focus on the social gradient or were mainly addressing particular target groups or areas.

Thirty English documents had been entered into the HP-Source.net database (34). Five of the general policy documents were chosen (35–39), all of which outline overall government policies in the field of health promotion. Also included was an action plan focusing particularly on reducing social inequalities in health. The latest status report, published in 2008, was also included in the analysis (40).

From the Netherlands, eight policy documents with relevance to health promotion were entered into the database, seven of which were in English (34). One document met the criteria for inclusion in the study (41). The document outlines public health policy in the Netherlands from 2007 to 2010.

Eleven documents from Norway were entered into the database (34). Three of them met the inclusion criteria for this study (42–44); all were published in English, and all were included in the study.

Limitations of the Methodology

Within the scope of this project, it has not been feasible to fully validate the data. However, cross-checking is performed by the HP-Source team in dialogue with the national researchers. Only documents issued until 2008 are included.

There will always be an issue of language in databases representing many countries, as national policy documents are published in national languages. In this case, all the analyzed documents were published in an English version and were not translated by the national researchers.

FINDINGS

England

In England,[1] health promotion has had a prominent place on the political agenda since 1997, when the Labour government came into office. The United Kingdom was also among the first European countries to place the theme of health inequalities on the political agenda (45). This is also reflected in policies. Several documents have been published over the past few years, all with an explicit focus on reducing social inequalities in health. Furthermore, the U.K. policies recognize the significance of the wider determinants of health and health inequalities, such as income, education, and the environment. The government white paper *Saving Lives: Our Healthier Nation* was launched in 1999 (35). In general terms, it states the broad goals of improving the health of the population in general and the health of the worst off in particular, and of narrowing the health gap.

In 2008, an action program was launched to tackle social inequalities in health (40). The program aimed to reduce health inequalities between different geographic areas, genders, ethnic communities, and social and economic groups, and to tackle the underlying causes of health inequalities. The wider determinants of health inequalities were in focus, such as poverty, poor educational outcomes, unemployment, and poor housing. However, the main aim of the plan was to improve the health of the poorest, and there is no focus on the social gradient. Despite the focus on social determinants of health, no connection is made to the broader aims of social and welfare policies and to the distribution of welfare between social groups. In the white paper *Choosing Health: Making Healthy Choices Easier*, the liberal welfare state ideology resting on individual choice is highlighted: "People want to be able to make their own decisions about choices that impact their health and to have credible and trustworthy information to help them do so. They expect the Government to provide support by helping to create the right environment" (36, p. 3).

Tackling inequalities in health is seen as a priority in these documents. A delivery plan that outlines the key steps, *Delivering Choosing Health*, was published in 2005 (37). The overall focus is to assist people in making healthy choices and to reduce social inequalities in health: "Helping people make more healthy choices is now at the core of mainstream activity by government, the NHS

---

[1] In the HP-Source.net database, the countries in the United Kingdom are separated, but some of the policy documents will still be valid for the United Kingdom.

[National Health Service] and local authorities. . . . Health improvement and tackling health inequalities will become an integral part of the NHS mainstream planning and performance system and will be at the core of its day-to-day business" (37, p. 7). The plan was backed up by two action plans that brought together commitments relating to food, health, and physical activity and set out in further detail the context and next steps for action (38, 39).

The Netherlands

The main national document for health promotion is *Opting for a Healthy Life: Public Health Policy in The Netherlands 2007–2010* (41). With this policy document, the Ministry of Health, Welfare and Sports has set the national priorities for health promotion and disease prevention. The policy document presents a national program with a focus on five main areas: the reduction of smoking, obesity, alcohol misuse, diabetes, and depression.

The first section of the document emphasizes that individuals have the main responsibility for their own health. The main objectives of the policy are stated in the foreword by the Minister of Health, Welfare and Sport: "The title [of the document] deliberately puts the emphasis on the ability to choose. Not only can an individual choose between a healthy and an unhealthy life style—but more than ever before—health care workers can also put more emphasis on promoting the healthy options to their clients" (41). It is further stated that lifestyle issues are the responsibility not only of the individual but also of society, and one of the aims of society is to make healthier choices easier: "People need to be more attracted to the healthy options, but that is not an easy thing to do. . . . By organising society in such a way that the 'healthy and conscious choice' is an easy option, the government can support the public" (41, p. 12).

Several instruments are being suggested to make healthy choices easy, and intersectoral collaboration is also called for: "The government has a number of instruments available for that purpose, such as legislation, information and pricing policy. This calls for (better) cooperation, both inside and outside, nationally and locally. Good cooperation between different government sectors (such as environment, safety, employment, education) will also contribute to this" (41, p. 12).

In the policy, socioeconomic status is mentioned several times, as are the relations between risk-related health behaviors and socioeconomic status. However, there are no explicit aims to reduce social inequalities in health.

Norway

In Norway, health promotion has had a prominent place on the political agenda for many years. Over the past few years, two government papers have been released that focus on public health and health promotion. There has been an increasing focus on social inequalities in health. In 2003, a government white paper on public health was released, *Prescriptions for a Healthier Norway* (42). The overall strategies aim at more healthy life years for the population and the reduction of health inequalities between social groups, ethnic groups, and genders: "The Government seeks to strengthen public health work in all social sectors through active partnerships which places responsibility, bind and inspire action" (42, p. 6).

The white paper was followed up by several action plans. *The Challenge of the Gradient* (43) explicitly outlines measures to reduce social inequalities in health and reduce the social gradient: "Working to reduce social inequalities in health means making efforts to ensure that all social groups can achieve the same life expectancy and be equally healthy. Differences in health not only affect specific occupational groups or the poorest people or those with least education. On the contrary, research indicates that we will not address the relation between socioeconomic position and health if we base our activities on strategies that focus on 'the poor' as an isolated target group" (43, p. 9).

A government white paper on social inequalities in health was released in February 2007. *National Strategy to Reduce Social Inequalities in Health* (44) has a 10-year perspective for developing policies and strategies to reduce health inequities. Both structural and targeted measures are viewed as important strategies. One main point of the white paper is that "equity is good public health policy": "A fair distribution of resources is good public health policy. The primary goal of future public health work is not to further improve the health of the people that already enjoy good health. The challenge now is to bring the rest of the population up to the same level as the people who have the best health—levelling up. Public health work entails initiatives to ensure a more even social distribution of the factors that affect health" (44, p. 1).

The overall strategy for the Norwegian policy covers four areas: to reduce social inequalities that contribute to health differences, to reduce social inequalities in health behavior and use of health services, to create targeted efforts for social inclusion, and to develop increased knowledge and tools for cross-sectoral collaboration and planning.

Table 1 summarizes the situation in the three countries.

DISCUSSION

The substance of health promotion policies varies among the three countries examined in this study. In England and Norway, health promotion has a prominent place, and several documents on this topic have been released over the past few years. There are some similarities between England and Norway: in both countries the focus is on the broader determinants of health, and the overall aim is to reduce social inequalities in health. A strong political commitment seems to exist in both countries, in the sense that policy documents are followed by

Table 1

National health promotion policy strategies in England,
the Netherlands, and Norway

	Goals	Strategies	Personal responsibility?	Targeted?	Gradient addressed?
England	Reduce health inequalities	Intersectoral action	Explicitly stated	Main strategy	No
Netherlands	Improve population health	Healthy lifestyles	Explicitly stated	Main strategy	No
Norway	Reduce health inequalities	Intersectoral action	Society's responsibility explicitly stated	Combined with gradient perspective	Explicitly addressed

action plans with concrete targets, deadlines, and responsibilities. In both countries, there is a recognition that health promotion demands intersectoral collaboration between national government bodies, between different administrative levels of government, and with actors outside government.

Both England and Norway have policies that recognize the significance of the wider determinants of health. However, there are some clear differences in policy aims, target groups, and underlying analysis. The Norwegian policies have an explicit focus on the social gradient, and structural measures are viewed as central. The policies include measures aimed at the whole population as well as measures aimed at disadvantaged groups. The English policies have a more explicit focus on disadvantaged groups and geographic areas, and the suggested measures to reduce social inequalities in health are mainly targeted at these groups. Another difference between England and Norway is that the Norwegian policies are clearly linked to universal welfare policies in the fields of education and work life. In England, the policies to reduce social inequalities in health reflect the narrower focus of the English policy.

In the Netherlands, healthy public policies seem to have a weaker position than in Norway and England as there is no clear focus on the social determinants of health. Individual behavioral changes to reduce risk seem to be the prioritized strategies for action. There are some similarities in the political approaches of the Netherlands and England. Both countries put a strong focus on the free will and responsibility of individuals in terms of changing unhealthy lifestyles. The role of the government is depicted as facilitating and supporting these efforts.

Developments in the three countries can be traced by using Whitehead's action spectrum (26) to analyze the situation. England and Norway may be characterized as having comprehensive, coordinated policies in place. The Netherlands, on the other hand, seems not to have developed in the same direction, and its policies still seem to be in the category "isolated initiatives."

The findings show many common characteristics between English and Norwegian policies, but some significant differences. By analyzing the different policies in the light of Esping-Andersen's typology of welfare state regimes (13), it is possible to understand these differences more clearly: they seem to reflect differences between the liberal and the social democratic welfare state regimes described by Esping-Andersen. England (or the United Kingdom) is classified as a liberal welfare state regime. In principle, the role of government should be a facilitating rather than an active and intervening one. The rhetoric concerning the role of the welfare state especially reflects this, putting the emphasis on the free will of the people and the facilitating role of government.

The Netherlands is a corporatist/conservative type of welfare state regime. As in the liberal type, the ideology of corporatist regimes prescribes that the state should not interfere strongly in the private sphere—and the present Dutch policy seems to reflect this type of regime, with its strong emphasis on health education and personal responsibility. In Norway, the ideology of recent policy documents is in line with a social democratic welfare state regime. Social inequalities in health are being defined in terms of the social gradient.

CONCLUSION

Developing healthy public policies to reduce health inequities will require comprehensive policies in many areas of health services, social services, the labor market, and education, meaning that welfare state arrangements need to be in place (1, 6). Graham (11) argues that targeted approaches are unlikely to reduce health inequalities; on the contrary, such approaches may result in a loss of political commitment to health equity. In the Netherlands, it seems that the issue of health inequalities has been losing political momentum since Whitehead's action spectrum was developed. As shown in this chapter, the countries within the liberal and conservative traditions mostly develop policies targeted at disadvantaged groups, while the social democratic welfare state emphasizes, to a larger extent, structural measures to address the social gradient. Sweden is also characterized as having a social democratic welfare regime, and the Norwegian and Swedish welfare systems have much in common. A study comparing Britain and Sweden showed large differences in living conditions for single mothers between the two countries (46). There was far more poverty among single mothers in the United Kingdom than in Sweden, and the level of general public transfers in

Sweden reduced the number of poor single mothers significantly. As Lundberg and coauthors (21, 22) showed, the ways in which social policies are designed, as well as their generosity, are important for health because of the increased resources that social policies entail. Hence, social policies are of major importance for how we can tackle the social determinants of health.

The policies adopted are, of course, connected to the policy instruments considered legitimate in countries with different welfare state regimes. The states representing the social democratic welfare regimes have a tradition of redistribution through government policies and strong legitimacy for active government policy even in the private sphere. In the liberal welfare state regimes, legitimacy sets narrower borders for how far a government may intervene in the private lives of its citizens.

Based on data from the Eurothine project, Mackenbach and colleagues (33) conclude that there is a gap between policymakers' intentions and the actual delivery of policy, and very few countries have experience in delivering policies that aim to reduce health inequalities. One of the reasons for this may be a lack of political will and consensus about the importance of the issue.

Health policy is seldom discussed in political terms (7). However, health policy is part of a broader public policy agenda whose practical aspects are inextricably linked with power and politics. Connections with the macro-political causes of the major economic and social health inequalities, such as macro-economic policy, trade policy, defense policy, foreign policy, and international development, are seldom made. Addressing structural determinants in the area of health equity at the national, European, and global levels will challenge economic forces that are outside the immediate control of the political sphere but within which all welfare state regimes are embedded.

Thus, there seem to be several dilemmas in the development of healthy public policies. Government cross-sector policies aimed at redistribution among social groups seem to be a condition for increasing equity. However, within the countries representing different welfare state regimes, the necessary policy instruments to achieve this may not be considered legitimate.

This chapter is a first attempt at applying Esping-Andersen's framework to this field of study, and the results indicate that the framework is useful when comparing national policies on health promotion, particularly regarding health inequalities. Further research is needed, both on policy design and to follow up on the implementation of such policies.

REFERENCES

1. World Health Organization. *The Ottawa Charter for Health Promotion.* First International Conference on Health Promotion. Ottawa, 1986.
2. O'Neill, M., and Pederson, A. Building a methods bridge between policy analysis and healthy public policy. *Can. J. Public Health* 83(Suppl. 1):25–30, 1992.

3. De Leeuw, E., and Polman, L. Health policy making: The Dutch experience. *Soc. Sci. Med.* 40(3):331–338, 1993.
4. Marmot, M. Achieving health equity: From root causes to fair outcomes. *Lancet* 370:1153–1163, 2007. doi: 10.1016/S0140-6736(07)61385-3.
5. Whitehead, M., and Dahlgren, G. *Levelling Up (Part 1): A Discussion Paper on Concepts and Principles for Tackling Social Inequities in Health.* Studies on Economic Determinants of Population Health No. 3. WHO Collaborating Centre for Policy Research on Social Determinants of Health, University of Liverpool, Liverpool, 2006.
6. World Health Organization Commission on the Social Determinants of Health. *Closing the Gap in a Generation: Health Equity through Action on the Social Determinants of Health.* Final Report. Geneva, 2008.
7. Bambra, C., Fox, D., and Scott-Samuel, A. Towards a politics of health. *Health Promot. Int.* 20(2):187–193, 2005.
8. Navarro V., and Shi, L. The political context of social inequalities and health. *Soc. Sci. Med.* 52:481–491, 2001.
9. Mansyur, C. L., et al. Culture and the social context of health inequalities. *Int. J. Health Serv.* 39(1):85–106, 2009, doi:10.2190/HS39.1.d.
10. Graham, H. Social determinants and their unequal distribution: Clarifying policy understandings. *Milbank Q.* 82:101–124, 2004.
11. Graham, H. Tackling inequalities in health in England: Remedying health disadvantages, narrowing health gaps or reducing health gradients? *J. Soc. Policy* 33(1):115–131, 2004. doi: 10.1017/S0047279403007220.
12. Dahlgren, G., and Whitehead, M. *Levelling Up (Part 2): A Discussion Paper on European Strategies for Tackling Social Inequities in Health.* Studies on Economic Determinants of Population Health No. 3. WHO Collaborative Centre for Policy Research on Social Determinants of Health, University of Liverpool, Liverpool, 2006.
13. Esping-Andersen, G. *The Three Worlds of Welfare Capitalism.* Polity Press, Cambridge, UK, 1990.
14. Ferrera, M. The "Southern model" of welfare state in social Europe. *J. Eur. Soc. Policy* 6(17):17–37, 1996. doi: 10.1177/095892879600600102.
15. Bambra, C. Going beyond the three worlds of welfare capitalism: Regime theory and public health research. *J. Epidemiol. Community Health* 61:1098–1102, 2007, doi: 10.1136/jech.2007.064295.
16. Bambra, C., et al. Gender, health inequalities and welfare state regimes: A cross-national study of 13 European countries. *J. Epidemiol. Community Health* 63:38–44, 2008. doi: 10.1136/jech.2007.070292.
17. Leitner, S. Varieties of familialism: The caring function of the family in comparative perspective. *Eur. Soc.* 5(4):353–375, 2003, doi: 10.1080/1461669032000127642.
18. Esping-Andersen, G. *Social Foundations of Post Industrial Economies.* Oxford University Press, Oxford, 1999.
19. Esping-Andersen, G. The sustainability of welfare states into the twenty-first century. *Int. J. Health Serv.* 30(1):1–12, 2000.
20. Bambra, C., and Eikemo, T. A. Welfare state regimes, unemployment and health: A comparative study of the relationship between unemployment and self-reported health in 23 European countries. *J. Epidemiol. Community Health* 63:92–98, 2009. doi: 10/1136/jech.2008.077354.

21. Lundberg, O., et al., for NEWS Nordic Expert Group. The role of welfare state principles and generosity in social policy programmes for public health: An international comparative study. *Lancet* 372:1633–1640, 2008.
22. Lundberg, O., et al. *The Nordic Experience: Welfare States and Public Health (NEWS)*. Health Equity Studies No. 12. Centre for Health Equity Studies, Stockholm University/Karolinska Institutet, Stockholm, 2008.
23. Mackenbach, J. P. Socioeconomic inequalities in morbidity and mortality in Western Europe. *Lancet* 349:1955–1959, 1997.
24. Dahl, E., et al. Welfare state regimes and health inequalities. In *Social Inequalities in Health*, ed. J. Siegrist, M. Marmot, and J. Mackenbach. Oxford University Press, Oxford, 2006.
25. Lundberg, O. How do welfare policies contribute to the reduction of health inequalities? *Eurohealth* 15(3):24–27, 2009.
26. Whitehead, M. Diffusion of ideas on social inequalities in health: A European perspective. *Milbank Q.* 76(3):469–492, 1998.
27. Dahl, E. Health inequalities and health policy: The Norwegian case. *Norsk Epidemiol.* 12(1):69–75, 2002.
28. Ministry of Health and Social Affairs, Norway. *Challenges in Health Promotion and Disease Prevention: Report to the Storting No. 37 (1992–93)*. St. meld. 37 (1992–93) Utfordringer i helsefremmende og forebyggende arbeid. Sosial- og helsedepartementet, Oslo, 1993.
29. Vining, R. A., and Weimer, D. L. Informing institutional design: Strategies for comparative cumulation. *J. Comp. Policy Anal. Res. Pract.* 9:39–60, 1999.
30. Yin, R. K. *Case Study Research, Design, and Methods*. Sage, Newbury Park, UK, 1989.
31. Denscombe, M. *The Good Research Guide*. Open University Press, Buckingham, UK, 1998.
32. Flick, U. *An Introduction to Qualitative Research*, Ed. 4. Sage, London, 2009.
33. Mackenbach, J., et al. *Strategies to Reduce Socio-economic Inequalities in Health in Europe: Lessons from the Eurothine Project—Tackling Health Inequalities in Europe: An Integrated Approach*. Final Report from the Eurothine Project. Department of Public Health, University Medical Centre, Rotterdam, 2007.
34. Comprehensive Database of Health Promotion Policies, Infrastructures, and Practices. www.hp-source.net (accessed April 13, 2010).
35. Department of Health, England. *Saving Lives: Our Healthier Nation.* Government White Paper. London, 1999. www.hp-source.net (accessed April 13, 2010).
36. Department of Health, England. *Choosing Health: Making Healthy Choices Easier.* Government White Paper, Executive Summary. London, 2004. www.hp-source.net (accessed April 13, 2010).
37. Department of Health, England. *Delivering Choosing Health: Making Healthy Choices Easier.* London, 2005. www.hp-source.net (accessed April 13, 2010).
38. Department of Health, England. *Choosing a Better Diet: A Food and Health Action Plan*. London, 2005. www.hp-source.net (accessed April 13, 2010).
39. Department of Health, England. *Choosing Activity: A Physical Activity Action Plan.* London, 2005. www.hp-source.net (accessed April 13, 2010).
40. Department of Health, The Netherlands. *Tackling Health Inequalities: 2007 Status Report on the Programme for Action.* The Hague, 2008. www.hp-source.net (accessed April 13, 2010).

41. Ministry of Health, Welfare and Sports, The Netherlands. *Opting for a Healthy Life: Public Health Policy in The Netherlands 2007–2010.* The Hague, 2006. www.hp-source.net (accessed April 13, 2010).

42. Ministry of Health and Care Services, Norway. *Prescription for a Healthier Norway.* Report No. 16 (2002–2003) to the Storting. Oslo, 2003. www.hp-source.net (accessed April 13, 2010).

43. Directorate of Health and Social Affairs, Norway. *The Challenge of the Gradient: Action Plan against Social Inequalities in Health.* Oslo, 2005. www.hp-source.net (accessed April 13, 2010).

44. Ministry of Health and Care Services, Norway. *National Strategy to Reduce Social Inequalities in Health.* Report No. 20 (2006–2007) to the Storting. Oslo, 2007. www.hp-source.net (accessed April 13, 2010).

45. Benzeval, M. National experiences, England. In *Reducing Inequalities in Health: A European Perspective*, ed. J. Mackenbach and M. Bakker. Routledge, London, 2002.

46. Whitehead, M., Burström, B., and Diderichsen, F. Social policy and the pathways to inequalities in health: A comparative analysis of lone mothers in Britain and Sweden. *Soc. Sci. Med.* 50:255–270, 2000.

CHAPTER 14

Social Inequalities in "Sickness": Does Welfare State Regime Type Make a Difference? A Multilevel Analysis of Men and Women in 26 European Countries

Kjetil A. van der Wel, Espen Dahl,
and Karsten Thielen

In comparative studies of health inequalities, public health researchers have usually studied only disease and illness. Recent studies have also examined the sickness dimension of health, that is, the extent to which ill health is accompanied by joblessness, and how this association varies by education within different welfare contexts. This research has used either a limited number of countries or quantitative welfare state measures in studies of many countries. In this study, the authors expand on this knowledge by investigating whether a regime approach to the welfare state produces consistent results. They analyze data from the European Union Statistics on Income and Living Conditions (EU-SILC); health was measured by limiting longstanding illness (LLSI). Results show that for both men and women reporting LLSI in combination with low educational level, the probabilities of non-employment were particularly high in the Anglo-Saxon and Eastern welfare regimes, and lowest in the Scandinavian regime. For men, absolute and relative social inequalities in sickness were lowest in the Southern regime; for women, inequalities were lowest in the Scandinavian regime. The authors conclude that the Scandinavian welfare regime is more able than other regimes to protect against non-employment in the face of illness, especially for individuals with low educational level.

*****

Previous studies have found considerable variation in the magnitude of health inequalities in European countries (1). To an increasing degree, researchers have adopted the idea of welfare state regimes in comparative studies of health inequalities (2–5). This research has been concerned with two of three health dimensions inherent in the sociological concept of health (6), namely, disease and illness. In this chapter we investigate the third, "sickness" aspect of health, that is, how ill health (disease, illness) translates into sickness-non-employment among people with chronic illness (7, 8). These three dimensions of health are related and overlapping, yet separate. While illness and disease relate to an individual's subjective and objective health, respectively, sickness is defined within the social sphere. Therefore, variation in sickness need not be linked to the social and structural context in the same way as illness and disease. The welfare state, constituting an important social context, institutionalizes social norms through eligibility criteria and income replacement programs that are likely to affect sickness in society. Furthermore, welfare states differ in the degree to which they support sick people with resources that may affect sickness behavior, as well as the duration of sickness periods, including the effects of welfare resources on illness and disease (2, 9, 10). This implies that social inequalities in illness, disease, and sickness may differ in size and trends between countries and welfare regimes. In a previous study, using a policy variable approach, we found lower levels of sickness and smaller absolute and relative sickness inequalities in countries that have generous public benefits and are high spenders on active labor market policies (11). Also, employment protection and income equality seemed to be favorable to disadvantaged groups in society. As we will argue here, these findings may be different if one employs a *welfare regime approach*, and may also differ for men and women. Hence, the purpose of the present study is to further investigate this topic and to expand current knowledge on welfare states and health by assessing welfare state regime differences in sickness and the associated levels of social inequalities, separately for men and women.

THE WELFARE STATE AND SICKNESS: DISINCENTIVES OR SOCIAL INVESTMENT?

What we here refer to as "social inequalities in sickness" has previously been documented in a number of national studies. Bartley and Owen (12) found that individuals in low-skilled groups who reported limiting longstanding illness (LLSI) were increasingly—and to a much larger extent than ill people in the professional/ managerial group—found outside the labor market. Other studies support this picture (13–15). Longitudinal studies have found similar associations (16–18). But how are these associations affected by the welfare state?

Key demarcation lines between "worlds of welfare" are related to the availability of social protection, universalism, and the level of decommodification—that is, the extent to which welfare provision is detached from the labor market (19). At least two competing expectations exist concerning the role of these traits in the employment of people with illnesses (sickness). First, a main hypothesis, within a "welfare skepticism approach" (11), is that because individuals have a preference for leisure, generous benefits that are broadly available may represent disincentives to work (20), especially among those who have both few monetary and few non-monetary rewards from labor (21). This disincentive effect is assumed to gain strength over time, because social norms and work ethic will erode as living off public benefits becomes increasingly common and less stigmatized (22, 23). Comparative evidence from a wide range of countries in the World Value Study supports the disincentive hypothesis. Heinemann (22) found, in a study of "benefit morale," that growth in social expenditure was associated with a decline in individuals' view of whether it was justifiable to make illegitimate claims to government benefits. Another study found that in countries with generous social benefits, parents were less inclined to teach their children to "work hard" (23). It should be noted, however, that other studies show small or even opposite effects of generous benefits and comprehensive coverage on work orientation, employment rates, and economic growth (11, 24–26). An issue here is that studies of attitudes may not be highly valid for hypotheses on employment, as in this study. If valid, however, this mainstream economic approach implies that non-employment rates, especially among disadvantaged groups (21), should be higher in the more generous Scandinavian regime than in less generous regime types.

An alternative hypothesis is derived from the welfare resource/social investment perspective (9, 10, 27). The argument is that the transfer of resources, financial and non-financial, to marginal groups in society through universal benefits and active reintegration policies would enhance labor market participation in general, and especially among disadvantaged groups (28). In addition to the counter-literature mentioned above, a few comparative public health studies of the impact of welfare state on sickness indicate that this way of thinking receives some empirical support. Studies comparing the social democratic case of Sweden with the liberal case of Britain have found that non-employment rates, as well as the social distribution of non-employment among different socioeconomic groups and between groups with and without chronic illness, are higher in the latter case (29, 30). Studies comparing three Scandinavian countries (Denmark, Norway, and Sweden) with two countries in the liberal regime type (Canada and the United Kingdom) support this general finding (28, 31, 32). These comparative studies support the welfare resources perspective, as they ascribe the more fortunate situation in the Scandinavian countries, compared with the liberal countries, to the more activating and comprehensive social policies in the Scandinavian countries. However, these studies are based on comparisons of only a few countries within a few regimes, and do not allow a formal distinction between different aspects of the countries included. A recent paper (11) studied sickness and sickness inequalities and how they are affected by policy indicators, using European Union Statistics on Income and Living Conditions (EU-SILC) data for 26 countries in a multilevel analysis, controlling for gross domestic product (GDP) and business cycle. The same data and general strategies are used in the present study. The earlier results strongly favored the social investment hypothesis regarding the effects of welfare generosity and active labor market policies, while somewhat weaker support was found for employment protection and income inequality.

Another difference among welfare regime types is their ability to also include women in the labor force. Dual-earner family policies, pursued by the Nordic countries, are related to higher female labor market participation, when compared with other family policy models (33). Studies of family policies and female labor force participation, using large comparative datasets and multilevel modeling, support this general finding (34) and report smaller educational inequalities in employment in countries with more family-friendly policies (35). These findings are in line with the conclusions from studies of cross-national differences in the employment of women with chronic illness, based on small numbers of countries belonging to different welfare regimes (30–32). Such studies generally find higher employment rates and lower levels of inequality in the Scandinavian countries. A crucial point is that welfare regimes tend to overlap with family policy models, thus probably multiplying the effect of welfare regime on women's sickness patterns (33, p. 121). Hence, previous studies (e.g., 11) not performing separate analyses of men and women may overestimate effects among men and underestimate effects among women.

Although there is much virtue in pursuing a welfare component approach, looking at the specific effects of selected policy variables (11), here we acknowledge the possible impact on sickness of distinct configurations of the state, the market, and the family, captured by the idea of welfare regimes. This combined welfare state effect may not be captured using single policy indicators. Another reason for this approach is that among disadvantaged groups, labor market inclusion may be sensitive to the transfer of social resources accumulated over the life course and in different areas of life (9). Such an approach would be more appropriately captured by theoretical categories such as welfare regimes, rather than single policy indicators. Furthermore, the potential effects and normative decay predicted by the disincentive perspective are hypothesized to evolve within more persistent social structures (23), again possibly better reflected by the regime approach.

Against this backdrop, this study contributes to the understanding of sickness by adopting a comparative welfare state perspective, analyzing men and women separately, applying an appropriate method (multilevel modeling), and utilizing a powerful survey material (EU-SILC). Our purpose is thus to investigate the two opposing views on sickness by looking at how rates of non-employment in Europe among men and women with poor health and/or low educational level are affected by different welfare state regimes (19). We build on previous studies by looking at the associations between social position, health, and employment within a full welfare state typology (36, 37). Our main focus of attention is on the fate of the least advantaged—that is, those who have both poor health and low qualifications—within different welfare regimes, as well as on the range of social inequality in sickness associated with the regimes. We have particular interest in the Scandinavian and Anglo-Saxon/liberal regimes, as these regimes constitute contrasting cases suitable to test the social investment perspective against the disincentive hypothesis.

DATA AND METHODS

We use data from EU-SILC 2005 (38), which are organized by Eurostat and collected by national teams in all EU-25 countries except Malta, as well as in Iceland and Norway; hence the data comprise information from 26 countries. Respondents of prime working age (25–59 years) were selected for the analyses, 102,594 men and 110,991 women, making up a powerful dataset that allows for gender-specific analysis. Iceland had the lowest number of participants, with 1,797 individuals, and Italy had the highest number, with 28,114. Household response rates averaged 71 percent, ranging from 30 percent (the Netherlands, which is an outlier) to 92 percent (Slovakia). The EU-SILC survey is based on a regulation (EC 1177/2003) adopted by the European Parliament and the council of the European Union, and is in accordance with the opinion of the Committee on Statistical Confidentiality.

Individual-Level Variables

The dependent variable in our analysis is non-employment, adapted from the self-reported current socioeconomic status variable; unemployed, early retirement/given up business, permanently disabled and/or unfit to work, fulfilling domestic tasks and care responsibility, and other inactivity were coded 1, and working full-/part-time, pupil/student, and military service were coded 0. The education variable—perceived as a crude measure of socioeconomic position—was re-coded into three levels of education, according to ISCED 97 (International Standard Classification of Education) (39); categories 0 to 2 form the primary education group, categories 3 and 4 form the secondary education group, and categories 5 and 6 form the tertiary education group. (In Table 3, tertiary education and the Scandinavian regime were chosen as reference categories in the categorical variables.) We chose this approach in order to secure comparability with previous research. Health was measured by LLSI, indicated by answering yes to the question "Do you suffer from any chronic (longstanding) illness or condition (yes, no)?" and reporting that the illness "limited" or "strongly limited" activities. The regression analysis uses a centered age variable for control.

Country-Level Variables

The main variable of interest is the welfare regime variable (see classification in Table 1), with each country classified and adapted according to the welfare regime typology used in previous studies (36). The different welfare state regimes and their relevance to public health are discussed elsewhere (37, 40). GDP per capita and a business cycle variable, constructed as the country-specific deviation in 2005 from the nine-year average unemployment rate, were included as contextual control variables. For the business cycle variable, data for Iceland were obtained from Statistics Iceland (www.statice.is). Otherwise, both variables were obtained from the Eurostat database (41) and centered on their means.

Analytical Approach

For the main analysis we used multilevel random intercept logistic regression, conducted separately for men and women, using the xtlogit command in STATA version 9. The multilevel analysis treats the data as hierarchical, with individuals (level 1 units) nested within countries (level 2 units). To investigate whether the associations of LLSI and educational level with non-employment differed among welfare state regimes, we included cross-level interaction terms between welfare state regime and these variables in the regression model. We also included individual-level interaction terms for educational level and LLSI. To compare the combined effects of the variables of interest, we present predicted probabilities of non-employment in the different welfare state regimes, based on the regression coefficients (42).

RESULTS

Table 1 shows rates of non-employment in each country, grouped by welfare state regime type, and non-employment rates for subgroups according to gender, LLSI status, and educational level. The highest overall rate of non-employment was found in the Southern welfare regime type. The largest non-employment rate among people reporting LLSI was found in the Anglo-Saxon welfare regime type (56.7%), 18 percent above the Scandinavian regime type, which had the lowest rates within all groups.

Table 2 shows the gender-stratified findings from the multilevel analyses, with model A including only main effects of the welfare state regimes variable, as well as control variables, and model B including all interaction terms. For both men and women, inclusion of the interaction term significantly improves the model $(-2LL_A-(-2LL_B)) > 36.42$. The intraclass correlation terms show that a significant amount of variation is attributable to the country level in all models, although it is rather modest (0.037). In the A models, all individual-level variables are positive and statistically significant, except for the interactions between educational level and LLSI, which are significant only among men. For both men and women, the welfare regime type increases the logged odds of non-employment compared with the Scandinavian regime type, and more so for women. GDP is statistically insignificant in all models, and business cycle affects only women's risk of non-employment.

Table 1

Non-employment in 26 European countries in total, and by gender, age, limiting
longstanding illness (LLSI), and educational level, grouped by welfare regime, percent

	Total	Gender		LLSI		Education		
		Men	Women	Healthy	Ill	Prim.	Sec.	Tert.
Scandinavian								
Denmark	14.1	11.1	17.3	9.6	43.3	26.7	9.9	10.8
Finland	19.2	19.1	19.3	13.6	36.7	35.4	19.6	10.8
Iceland	9.5	6.4	12.8	3.7	34.9	16.1	8.9	3.4
Norway	14.6	11.7	17.8	7.8	45.1	37.4	16.3	5.7
Sweden	12.6	10.3	15.1	6.9	37.2	26.3	12.4	8.3
Group mean	*14.0*	*11.7*	*16.5*	*8.3*	*39.4*	*28.4*	*13.4*	*7.8*
Bismarckian								
Austria	21.6	10.8	32.4	18.8	41.4	40.1	19.2	12.8
Belgium	27.6	18.7	36.4	22.9	56.8	49.7	25.5	13.9
France	20.9	14.4	27.3	17.7	45.4	32.8	18.4	12.3
Germany	25.8	14.2	36.6	22.0	42.4	48.4	27.6	18.7
Luxembourg	22.1	9.1	35.7	19.8	42.9	30.7	21.7	11.2
Netherlands	24.6	13.0	36.8	18.8	54.1	43.2	23.2	13.8
Group mean	*23.8*	*13.4*	*34.2*	*20.0*	*47.2*	*40.8*	*22.6*	*13.8*
Anglo-Saxon								
Ireland	27.3	18.0	36.2	21.7	63.9	42.0	24.5	11.4
United Kingdom	20.5	13.6	26.7	14.4	49.5	41.8	19.2	12.3
Group mean	*23.9*	*15.8*	*31.5*	*18.1*	*56.7*	*41.9*	*21.9*	*11.9*
Southern								
Cyprus	19.9	7.8	31.6	16.7	41.0	31.7	18.6	10.8
Greece	27.2	12.0	42.4	25.2	54.7	37.1	25.3	14.7
Italy	31.2	17.5	44.9	29.3	54.5	42.3	23.1	15.8
Portugal	21.5	14.5	28.4	16.8	46.9	26.3	10.8	8.1
Spain	27.1	13.1	41.5	24.0	58.1	38.6	20.6	13.9
Group mean	*25.4*	*13.0*	*37.8*	*22.4*	*51.0*	*35.2*	*19.7*	*12.7*
Eastern								
Czech Republic	24.9	14.5	34.3	19.9	52.1	55.3	23.6	12.6
Estonia	19.9	17.4	22.2	14.9	36.4	41.0	19.9	13.4
Hungary	24.2	22.2	26.0	14.4	54.5	44.7	21.4	7.7
Latvia	22.2	19.3	24.8	18.4	38.8	36.4	21.8	12.6
Lithuania	22.4	19.9	24.7	16.5	53.1	43.0	25.2	8.3
Poland	37.2	31.0	43.3	31.7	82.8	61.7	38.2	14.0
Slovakia	21.4	15.2	27.1	17.2	50.4	52.0	21.7	9.0
Slovenia	24.8	21.4	28.3	19.6	56.3	47.6	21.1	6.7
Group mean	*24.6*	*20.1*	*28.8*	*19.1*	*53.1*	*47.7*	*24.1*	*10.5*

Source: EU-SILC, 2005 (38), weighted analysis.

Table 2

Results from multilevel logistic regression analysis of non-employment, educational level, limiting longstanding illness (LLSI) status, and welfare regime type, stratified by gender (102,594 men and 110,991 women in 26 countries), B (p-value)

	Men		Women	
	Model A	Model B	Model A	Model B
Age (centered)	0.034 (0.000)	0.034 (0.000)	0.019 (0.000)	0.018 (0.000)
LLSI	1.547 (0.000)	1.657 (0.000)	0.952 (0.000)	1.298 (0.000)
Primary	1.146 (0.000)	1.098 (0.000)	1.561 (0.000)	1.006 (0.000)
Secondary	0.488 (0.000)	0.477 (0.000)	0.734 (0.000)	0.425 (0.000)
Primary*LLSI	0.194 (0.005)	0.182 (0.013)	0.048 (0.390)	0.191 (0.001)
Secondary*LLSI	0.197 (0.003)	0.159 (0.023)	0.067 (0.203)	0.028 (0.603)
Welfare regime (ref. Scandinavian)				
Bismarckian	0.513 (0.024)	0.620 (0.011)	1.097 (0.000)	1.075 (0.000)
Anglo-Saxon	0.652 (0.036)	0.528 (0.106)	1.080 (0.000)	0.952 (0.000)
Southern	0.472 (0.039)	0.910 (0.000)	1.280 (0.000)	1.135 (0.000)
Eastern	1.101 (0.001)	0.572 (0.100)	1.101 (0.000)	0.622 (0.032)

Cross-level interaction (ref. Scandinavian)				
Bismarckian*LLSI	—	-0.224 (0.010)	—	-0.659 (0.000)
Anglo-Saxon*LLSI	—	0.482 (0.000)	—	-0.152 (0.079)
Southern*LLSI	—	-0.257 (0.004)	—	-0.712 (0.000)
Eastern*LLSI	—	-0.025 (0.764)	—	-0.091 (0.195)
Bismarckian*Primary	—	-0.036 (0.773)	—	0.339 (0.000)
Anglo-Saxon*Primary	—	0.126 (0.392)	—	0.399 (0.000)
Southern*Primary	—	-0.422 (0.001)	—	0.606 (0.000)
Eastern*Primary	—	0.778 (0.000)	—	0.845 (0.000)
Bismarckian*Secondary	—	-0.059 (0.593)	—	0.224 (0.004)
Anglo-Saxon*Secondary	—	-0.209 (0.133)	—	0.235 (0.010)
Southern*Secondary	—	-0.326 (0.005)	—	0.272 (0.001)
Eastern*Secondary	—	0.537 (0.000)	—	0.617 (0.000)
Contextual control				
GDP per capita[a] (centered)	-0.003 (0.738)	-0.003 (0.707)	0.004 (0.572)	0.004 (0.566)
Business cycle	0.058 (0.129)	0.062 (0.106)	0.068 (0.036)	0.073 (0.025)
Intercept	-3.370 (0.000)	-3.381 (0.000)	-2.785 (0.000)	-2.618 (0.000)
Intraclass correlation[b] (SE)	0.038 (0.011)	0.037 (0.010)	0.027 (0.007)	0.027 (0.008)
-2LL		311.868		381.168

Source: UE-SILC, 2005 (38).

[a]GDP measured in thousands.

[b]In a model with only the individual main effects variables included, the intraclass correlation coefficient was 0.072 among men and 0.061 among women.

Among men in model B, the interaction term between welfare state regimes and LLSI shows that in the Anglo-Saxon regime type, respondents with LLSI have higher rates of non-employment compared with the Scandinavian regime type, while in the Southern and Bismarckian regimes, employment differences between ill and healthy men are smaller. There is no significant difference in the association between LLSI and non-employment for men in the Eastern welfare regime type compared with the Scandinavian type. For women, we find smaller differences (negative coefficients) by health in non-employment, compared with the Scandinavian regime, for the Bismarckian, Southern, and Anglo-Saxon regimes—the latter with borderline statistical significance ($p = 0.079$). Again, in the Eastern regime, the health difference in the logged odds of non-employment did not differ from that in the Scandinavian case. For men, there are smaller inequalities between the tertiary education group and the primary education group in countries belonging to the Southern regime type, as compared with the Scandinavian regime type, while there is a larger difference in the Eastern welfare regime type. Among men, the interaction terms between educational level and the Bismarckian and Anglo-Saxon welfare regimes were statistically insignificant. For women, the picture is more clear-cut. In all welfare regimes, educational inequalities among women are larger when compared with the Scandinavian model, and especially so in the Southern and Eastern welfare regimes.

To give a more intuitive presentation of the employment of men and women in different welfare regimes, we estimated predicted probabilities of non-employment for different educational groups with and without LLSI, based on the B models in the regression analysis. These results are presented in Figure 1. Both men and women residing in countries belonging to the Scandinavian regime type have the lowest probabilities of non-employment in Europe. As is evident from the upper section of the figure, there is great variation among welfare regimes as to whether respondents with LLSI are also "sick," that is, are not employed. For men, the highest probabilities of non-employment are found in the Eastern and Anglo-Saxon welfare regimes, with the Bismarckian and Southern regimes in a middle position. There is considerable difference in the probability of non-employment associated with being ill rather than "healthy." Except in the Scandinavian case, this difference is less pronounced in women. By subtracting the predicted probabilities of the Scandinavian regime from the predicted probabilities in each of the other regimes, we can measure the combined "effect" of welfare regimes within each subgroup. These effects are shown in Table 3. In the upper left of the table, we see particularly large differences for the Anglo-Saxon and Eastern regime types. For example, in the Anglo-Saxon case, within all educational groups among men reporting LLSI, the elevated probability of non-employment, compared with the same groups in the Scandinavian regime, approximates or is larger than the individual-level effects of LLSI (0.20, estimated in a model without regimes or interaction terms, for a middle-aged man with secondary education). In the Eastern case, this effect is even stronger in

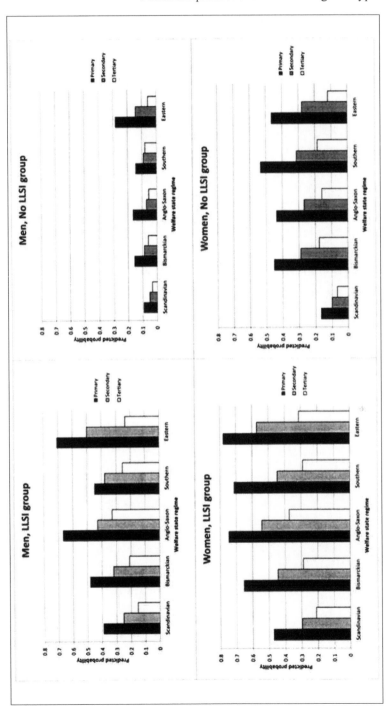

Figure 1. Predicted probabilities of non-employment by educational level (primary, secondary, tertiary) and limiting longstanding illness (LLSI) status in different welfare regime types, for men and women. Based on model B in Table 2.

Table 3

Combined regime "effects" on non-employment compared with the Scandinavian regime, by limiting longstanding illness (LLSI) and educational level (primary, secondary, tertiary), for men and women, based on predicted probabilities and estimated from model B in Table 2

	Men				Women			
	Bismarckian	Anglo-Saxon	Southern	Eastern	Bismarckian	Anglo-Saxon	Southern	Eastern
LLSI								
Primary	0.09	0.28	0.06	0.32	0.18	0.28	0.24	0.31
Secondary	0.07	0.18	0.13	0.25	0.15	0.25	0.15	0.27
Tertiary	0.06	0.18	0.10	0.08	0.08	0.16	0.08	0.10
No LLSI								
Primary	0.06	0.07	0.05	0.19	0.28	0.27	0.37	0.30
Secondary	0.04	0.02	0.04	0.09	0.19	0.17	0.21	0.18
Tertiary	0.03	0.02	0.05	0.02	0.11	0.09	0.12	0.05

Note: The "effects" were estimated by subtracting the predicted probabilities of the Scandinavian regime from the predicted probabilities in each of the other regimes within each subgroup.

the lower educational groups. Among healthy men (lower left of Table 3), the differences from the Scandinavian regime are more modest and uniform across regimes, except for the Eastern case. Among women, both ill and healthy, large differences from the Scandinavian regime are found, especially among the low educational groups.

What is striking in both men and women, as shown in Figure 1, is the highly elevated risk of non-employment faced by respondents incorporating the double labor market disadvantage of LLSI and only primary education. It becomes clear from the figure that not only do we find large between-regime differences in the overall levels of non-employment, but the level of educational inequality in non-employment varies across welfare regimes. This was also evident in Table 3, as the regime effects were not constant across educational groups. Figure 2 presents absolute and relative educational inequalities within each welfare regime in both the ill and the healthy populations. The absolute inequalities are simply the differentials in the predicted probabilities for the highest and lowest educational groups, while the relative inequalities are shown as odds ratios estimated from the predicted logged odds ($\exp(\text{predicted logit}_{\text{primary}})/\exp(\text{predicted logit}_{\text{tertiary}})$). The educational inequalities in non-employment are uniformly larger among the ill population. The absolute inequalities among ill men compared with healthy men are particularly distinct. For men, the absolute inequalities in sickness—that is, non-employment among those reporting LLSI—are largest in the Eastern and Anglo-Saxon regimes and lowest in the Southern and Scandinavian regimes. In terms of relative inequalities in sickness, the Eastern regime again demonstrates the highest level of inequality, while the Southern regime has the lowest level. Here, the three other regimes show intermediate levels of inequality. For women, the Scandinavian regime has the smallest educational inequalities in sickness, in both absolute and relative terms. The Bismarckian and Anglo-Saxon regimes have intermediate levels, while the Southern and Eastern regimes have the highest levels of inequality.

DISCUSSION

This multilevel analysis shows great variation in rates of non-employment—that is, in the sickness dimension of health—in countries belonging to different welfare state regimes, even after controlling for GDP and business cycle. A main finding is that the welfare regime context is a significant moderator of the employment effects associated with traditional labor market disadvantage: low education and poor health. The probabilities of non-employment were consistently lower in the Scandinavian welfare regime type, and the protective effect of the welfare state in terms of reducing the risk of non-employment in the population reporting LLSI and low educational level was largest in the Scandinavian regime. The strength of this protective effect was far from trivial. For a person with less than tertiary education and with poor health, the difference in the probability

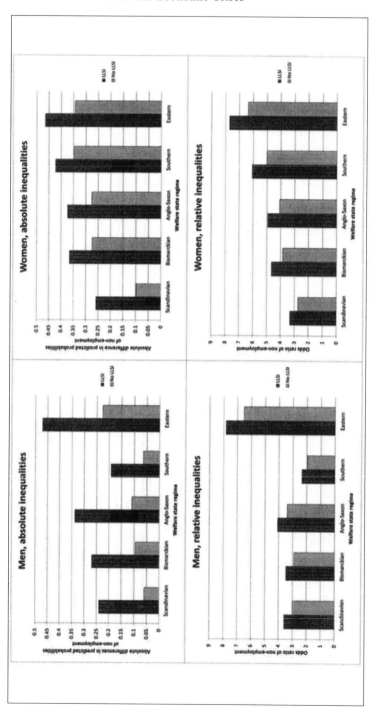

Figure 2. Absolute educational inequalities (differentials in the predicted probabilities for the highest and lowest educational groups) and relative educational inequalities (odds ratios estimated from the predicted logged odds, $\exp(\text{predicted logit}_{\text{primary}})/(\text{predicted logit}_{\text{tertiary}})$) in sickness, by gender. LLSI: limiting longstanding illness.

of non-employment associated with living in the Scandinavian versus the Anglo-Saxon welfare regime ($p = 0.18$–0.28) approximated or was stronger than the individual labor market disadvantage generally associated with having LLSI ($p = 0.20$, estimated in a model without regimes). For women, the regime effects were even more pronounced, probably mirroring the effects of the dual-earner family policy model pursued in the Scandinavian regime type (33–35). These findings are in line with previous research (11, 28–32), and support a social investment perspective on the association between welfare resources, health, and employment over a disincentive perspective.

A further important finding is that the magnitude of *social inequalities in sickness* varies significantly among regimes. For men, both absolute and relative inequalities were lowest in the Southern regime, although absolute inequalities in the Scandinavian regime were also quite low, and among women they were clearly smallest in the Scandinavian regime. The Anglo-Saxon regime has fairly high levels of social inequalities in sickness among men, but the Eastern regime consistently has the largest inequalities. Among men, these somewhat mixed findings, including that egalitarian countries do not necessarily perform best, resemble previous research on the disease and illness dimensions of health (1, 4, 5). Among women, however, the results are clearer: the Scandinavian regime has, decidedly, the lowest sickness inequalities, in absolute as well as in relative terms. The inequality pattern for men (and for women, for that matter), however, should be assessed in light of the fact that sickness levels, as described above, are consistently lower in the Scandinavian regime cluster than in the other types. One illustration of this is that a man with low educational level who is suffering from LLSI in a Scandinavian country has an employment rate comparable to that of a man with secondary education and LLSI in the Southern regime (Figure 1).

This regime approach is also relevant for interpretation of the consistent effect of regime types on sickness patterns among women. The Scandinavian regime model not only provides resources for economic activity but also furnishes resources—in cash and in kind—to individuals and families that emancipate people (read: women) to participate in the labor market. This "dual-earner family policy model" describes the Scandinavian countries (33, p. 121). Social investment programs in Scandinavian countries are thus designed to promote work activity and to reconcile work, family, and care obligations. These "enabling" policies may help explain the particularly strong employment effect on disadvantaged women in the Scandinavian cluster.

In medical sociology and public health research, the regime approach is quite new and somewhat controversial. Among other things, it has been criticized for being unspecific and for concealing significant country differentials within clusters (43). This is true, but there are also advantages to this approach. Studying 26 countries does not, of course, permit in-depth or qualitative probing of each country's social policies. Regimes are ideal types, not empirical facts expected to be found "out there" in reality. The regime approach acknowledges that welfare arrangements come in "packages" and have systemic properties: welfare institutions are interlinked and interact with other social institutions (the market and the family) in ways that follow their own internal logic (44, 45). The regime approach also implies a continuity of matters. A regime has stability and permanence over time, a trait that does not necessarily apply to specific policymaking and political reforms. This is captured by the concept of "path dependency": social policy reforms tend to take systematically different forms in different regimes (46). A drawback of the regime approach is that it cannot identify the concrete policies and interventions that are operating (for example, active labor market policies, access to advanced medical treatment, and rehabilitation services) and how these might influence social inequalities in sickness.

Strengths and Limitations of the Study

The sickness concept, as applied in this chapter, deviates from the literature on the sick role and illness behavior (e.g., 47). Even so, the use of non-employment among the ill as a measure of sickness is supported by the literature (8, p. 12). A weakness of this measure is that we cannot distinguish between, on the one hand, those who occupy the *sick role*, who are legally excepted from standard expectations of self-provision, as in the case of sickness absence or disability pension, and, on the other hand, those who occupy the *social position of sickness*, being both ill and non-employed, which may have several causes. Consequently, we do not know whether people are outside the labor market receiving medically justified public benefits, or are outside because they are not able to work but are not eligible for social benefits (for instance, if considered sick by household members or others providing for them, while the sickness is unrecognized by authorities) or because they cannot find work (employers define them as sick), or their non-employment is completely unrelated to health. While acknowledging these limitations, we find there are also some advantages to studying sickness as a social position.

First, this allows us to study sickness comparatively, with the use of standard indicators available in comparative datasets, which again allows us to assess the extent to which different societies have different levels of sickness. Second, our way of analyzing sickness broadens the concept beyond the narrow case of sickness absence, which is often applied in quantitative studies (e.g., 48). Medically justified sickness represents only a limited part of sickness in society, as welfare bureaucrats (granting, for instance, social assistance benefits), family members, colleagues, or employers may define someone as "sick" even if the sickness has not been medically designated. Also, it is inherently difficult to measure medically justified sickness comparatively, because practices and rules differ widely between countries.

Our measure of health, LLSI, may in some respects be regarded as somewhat tautological in relation to sickness, because "limiting" refers to experiences of difficulties in performing daily tasks caused by the illness. However, as our findings show large variation among countries and welfare regimes in the extent to which people reporting LLSI are employed, the association is obviously also affected by external factors. A related issue is that reporting of limitations may be heavily influenced by the demands of daily life, demands that are substantially different for someone who is employed than for someone who is not working (assuming the two individuals have equal "objective" health). This issue may have led to an underestimation of the individual-level association between health and non-employment. On the other hand, non-employed individuals may over-report illness in order to justify their economic inactivity. Nevertheless, as a measure of health, LLSI is found to reflect severe chronic diseases more strongly than minor conditions (49). Hence, the measure should be appropriate in our setting and may be less heterogeneous than the alternatives in EU-SILC—general self-reported health and longstanding illness. Concerning cross-national validity, however, little is known for LLSI, but it seems reasonable that the urge for caution by Jylhä and coauthors (50) regarding the use of cross-cultural comparisons of self-reported health measures also applies here. In comparative analyses, the cross-country reliability of survey questions is always an issue (51). Certainly, this also applies to our educational measure, even though it is based on the international standard ISCED 97. The value of education in the labor market (52) and its indication of broader social positions (53) may vary across countries. Also, the actual classification of individuals may vary, even within country, for different surveys (39).

Non-employment, as measured here, is a rather broad category, including a variety of social positions outside the labor market. This deliberate choice, rather than choosing to look at the unemployed or people classified as disabled, was intended to mitigate the influence of cross-country differences in welfare provision for people who are not working, which may otherwise have led to low cross-country reliability. Employment as measured in EU-SILC seems to be in agreement with other sources, as the rank-order correlation coefficient between Eurostat statistics (based on the E.U. Labour Force Study) was 0.80 (our analysis).

Finally, the response rates in EU-SILC seem to be sufficient, with the exceptions of the Netherlands (30%) and possibly Belgium (60%), Hungary (62%), and Austria (63%) (38). However, frequencies and cross-tabulations reported here were weighted, and any bias from skewed non-response in the multivariate analyses is not likely to be dramatic.

CONCLUSION

The Scandinavian welfare regime, to a larger degree than, particularly, the Anglo-Saxon and Eastern regimes, facilitates the inclusion of individuals with LLSI and lower educational levels in the labor market, resulting in comparatively low levels of sickness. This general finding was even more pronounced among women, who in Scandinavian countries, in contrast to the other regimes, have employment patterns more similar to those of men. Also, in terms of educational inequalities in sickness, the Scandinavian regime seems to perform well, especially for women, while for men, the Southern regime displayed the lowest absolute and relative inequalities.

Earlier in this chapter we outlined two hypotheses. The disincentive hypothesis predicts poorer economic performance among disadvantaged groups in Scandinavia than elsewhere—that is, high levels of sickness. The social investment, or welfare resource, hypothesis asserts the opposite: that rates of sickness should be lower in Scandinavia than in other welfare regimes. Hence, the present study supports a social investment perspective over the disincentive hypothesis inherent in the welfare skepticism approach.

Acknowledgments — This work was supported by the Norwegian Research Council (grant No. 175303) and the Nordic Council (grant No. 411040-91333). We acknowledge the value of the inspiring discussions we have had in the research network "Helping Chronically Ill and Disabled People Back into Work," headed by Professor Margaret Whitehead, University of Liverpool, replaced by the project "Inequalities in Social Consequences of Ill-Health: Does the Nordic Model Make a Difference?" headed by Professor Bo Burström, Karolinska Institutet. We also thank Thore Egeland for providing skillful statistical advice. All results and conclusions in this chapter are solely those of the authors and are not those of Eurostat, the European Commission, or any of the national authorities whose data were used.

REFERENCES

1. Mackenbach, J. P., et al. Socioeconomic inequalities in health in 22 European countries. *N. Engl. J. Med.* 358:2468–2481, 2008.
2. Dahl, E., et al. Welfare state regimes and health inequalities. In *Social Inequalities in Health: New Evidence and Policy Implications*, ed. M. G. Marmot and J. Siegrist, pp. 193–222. Oxford University Press, Oxford, 2006.
3. Eikemo, T. A., et al. Welfare state regimes and income-related health inequalities: A comparison of 23 European countries. *Eur. J. Public Health* 18(6):593–599, 2008.
4. Eikemo, T. A., et al. Welfare state regimes and differences in self-perceived health in Europe: A multilevel analysis. *Soc. Sci. Med.* 66(11):2281–2295, 2008.
5. Eikemo, T. A., et al. Health inequalities according to educational level in different welfare regimes: A comparison of 23 European countries. *Sociol. Health Illn.* 30(4): 565–582, 2008.
6. Parsons, T. *The Social System.* Routledge, London, 1991.
7. Twaddle, A. C., and Hessler, R. M. *A Sociology of Health.* Macmillan, New York, 1987.
8. Twaddle, A. C. Disease, illness and sickness revisited. In *Disease. Illness, and Sickness: Three Central Concepts in the Theory of Health,* ed. A. C. Twaddle and

L. Nordenfelt, pp. 1–18. Studies on Health and Society 18. Linkoping University, Linkoping, 1994.

9. Lundberg, O. How do welfare policies contribute to the reduction of health inequalities? *Eurohealth* 15(3), 2008.

10. Lundberg, O., et al. The role of welfare state principles and generosity in social policy programmes for public health: An international comparative study. *Lancet* 372(9650):1633–1640, 2008.

11. van der Wel, K. A., Dahl, E., and Thielen, K. Social inequalities in "sickness": European welfare states and non-employment among the chronically ill. *Soc. Sci. Med.* 73:1608–1617, 2011.

12. Bartley, M., and Owen, C. Relation between socioeconomic status, employment, and health during economic change, 1973–93. *BMJ* 313(7055):445–449, 1996.

13. Dahl, E., and Birkelund, G. E. Sysselsetting, klasse og helse 1980–1995: En analyse av fem norske levekarsundersøkelser [Employment, class, and health, 1980–1995: An analysis of five Norwegian surveys). *Tidsskr. Samfunnsforsk.* 40(1):3–32, 1999.

14. Kristensen, P., and Bjerkedal, T. Trender i deltakelse i arbeidslivet—betydningen av kronisk sykdom som barn og utdanningsniva [Employment trends—the impact of chronic disease in childhood and low educational level]. *Tidsskr. Nor. Laegeforen.* 124(22):2879–2883, 2004.

15. van der Wel, K. A., Dahl, E., and Birkelund, G. E. Employment inequalities through busts and booms: The changing roles of health and education in Norway 1980–2005. *Acta Social.* 53(4):355–370, 2010.

16. Lindholm, C., Burström, B., and Diderichsen, F. Class differences in the social consequences of illness? *J. Epidemiol. Community Health* 56(3):188–192, 2002.

17. Van de Mheen, H., et al. The influence of adult ill health on occupational class mobility and mobility out of and into employment in the Netherlands. *Soc. Sci. Med.* 49(4):509–518, 1999.

18. van der Wel, K. A. Long-term effects of poor health on employment: The significance of life stage and educational level. *Sociol. Health Illn.* 33(7):1096–1111, 2011.

19. Esping-Andersen, G. *The Three Worlds of Welfare Capitalism.* Polity Press, Cambridge, 1990.

20. Lindbeck, A. Hazardous welfare-state dynamics. *Am. Econ. Rev.* 85(2):9–15, 1995.

21. van den Noord, P., Girouard, N., and André, C. *Social Safety Nets and Structural Adjustment.* Organisation for Economic Co-operation and Development, Economic Department, Paris, 2006.

22. Heinemann, F. Is the welfare state self-destructive? A study of government benefit morale. *Kyklos* 61(2):237–257, 2008.

23. Lindbeck, A., and Nyberg, S. Raising children to work hard: Altruism, work norms, and social insurance. *Q. J. Econ.* 121(4):1473–1503, 2006.

24. Esser, I. Why Work? Comparative Studies on Welfare Regimes and Individuals' Work Orientation. Doctoral dissertation, Department of Sociology, University of Stockholm, Stockholm, 2005.

25. Lindert, P. H. The welfare state is the wrong target: A reply to Berg. *Econ. J. Watch* 3(2):236–250, 2006.

26. Garfinkel, I., Rainwater, L., and Smeeding, T. *Wealth and Welfare States: Is America a Laggard or Leader?* Oxford University Press, Oxford, 2010.

27. Fritzell, I., and Lundberg, O. (eds.). *Health Inequalities and Welfare Resources: Continuity and Change in Sweden.* Policy Press, Bristol, 2007.
28. Whitehead, M., et al. Helping Chronically Ill or Disabled People into Work: What Can We Learn from International Comparative Analyses? Final Report to the Public Health Research Programme. Department of Health, London, 2009. www.york.ac.uk/phre/papers.
29. Burström, B., et al. Inequality in the social consequences of illness: How well do people with long-term illness fare in the British and Swedish labor markets? *Int. J. Health Serv.* 30(3):435–451, 2000.
30. Burström, B., et al. Winners and losers in flexible labor markets: The fate of women with chronic illness in contrasting policy environments—Sweden and Britain. *Int. J. Health Serv.* 33(2):199–217, 2003.
31. Holland, P., et al. How do macro-level contexts and policies affect the employment chances of chronically ill and disabled people? Part I: The impact of recession and deindustrialization. *Int. J. Health Serv.* 41(3):395–413, 2011.
32. Holland, P., et al. How do macro-level contexts and policies affect the employment chances of chronically ill and disabled people? Part II: The impact of active and passive labor market policies. *Int. J. Health Serv.* 41(3):415–430, 2011.
33. Lundberg, O., et al. *The Nordic Experience: Welfare States and Public Health (NEWS).* Centre for Health Equity Studies (CHESS), Stockholm, 2008.
34. Mikucka, M. Variation in women's employment across European countries: The impact of child care policy solutions. *Int. J. Sociol.* 38(1):12–37, 2008.
35. Van Lancker, W., and Ghysels, J. *Female Employment, Institutions, and the Role of Reference Groups: A Multilevel Analysis of 22 European Countries.* University of Antwerp, Antwerp, 2010.
36. Bambra, C., and Eikemo, T. A. Welfare state regimes, unemployment and health: A comparative study of the relationship between unemployment and self-reported health in 23 European countries. *J. Epidemiol. Community Health* 63(2):92–98, 2009.
37. Eikemo, T. A., and Bambra, C. The welfare state: A glossary for public health. *J. Epidemiol. Community Health* 62(1):3–6, 2008.
38. Eurostat. Comparative Final EU Quality Report 2005. Version 2 Brussels, September 2008.
39. Schneider, S., and Müller, W. *Measurement of Education in EU-SILC: Preliminary Evaluation of Measurement Quality.* Equalsoc, 2009.
40. Bambra, C. Going beyond the three worlds of welfare capitalism: Regime theory and public health research. *J. Epidemiol. Community Health* 61(12):1098–1102, 2007.
41. Eurostat. Database. 2010. http://epp.eurostat.ec.europa.eu/portal/page/portal/statistics/search_database (accessed December 13, 2010).
42. Pampel, F. C. *Logistic Regression: A Primer.* Sage, Thousand Oaks, CA, 2000.
43. Kasza, G. J. The illusion of welfare "regimes." *J. Soc. Policy* 31:271–287, 2002.
44. Esping-Andersen, G. *Social Foundations of Postindustrial Economies.* Oxford University Press, Oxford, 1999.
45. Moene, K., et al. *Den skandinaviske modellen og ekonomisk ulikhet* [The Scandinavian model and economic inequality]. NOD 2009:10 Fordelingsutvalget (Vedlegg). Finansdepartementet, Oslo, 2009.

46. Hemerijck, A. The self-transformation of the European social models. In *Why We Need a New Welfare State,* ed. G. Esping-Andersen et al., pp. 173–213. Oxford University Press, Oxford, 2002.
47. Young, J. T. Illness behaviour: A selective review and synthesis. *Sociol. Health Illn.* 26(1):1–31, 2004.
48. Wikman, A., Marklund, S., and Alexanderson, K. Illness, disease, and sickness absence: An empirical test of differences between concepts of ill health. *J. Epidemiol. Community Health* 59(6):450–454, 2005.
49. Manor, O., Matthews, S., and Power, C. Self-rated health and limiting long-standing illness: Inter-relationships with morbidity in early adulthood. *J. Epidemiol. Community Health* 30(3):600–607, 2001.
50. Jylhä, M., et al. Is self-rated health comparable across cultures and genders? *J. Gerontol. B Psychol. Sci. Soc. Sci.* 53B(3):S144–152, 1998.
51. Mortelmans, D. Comparative research in sociology of health and illness with multilevel models: Issues and promises. *Salute e Societa* 9(Suppl. 2):35–64, 2010.
52. Becker, G. S. *Human Capital: A Theoretical and Empirical Analysis, with Special Reference to Education.* National Bureau of Economic Research, New York, 1964.
53. Bourdieu, P. *Distinction: A Social Critique of the Judgement of Taste.* Routledge & Kegan Paul, London, 1984.

CHAPTER 15

Welfare State Regime Life Courses: The Development of Western European Welfare State Regimes and Age-Related Patterns of Educational Inequalities in Self-Reported Health

Clare Bambra, Gopalakrishnan Netuveli,
and Terje A. Eikemo

This chapter uses data from three waves of the European Social Survey (2002, 2004, 2006) to compare educational inequalities in self-reported health (good vs. bad) and limiting longstanding illness in six age groups based on decade of birth (1930s–1980s) in 17 countries, categorized into four welfare state regimes (Anglo-Saxon, Bismarckian, Scandinavian, Southern). The authors hypothesized that health inequalities in these age groups would vary because of their different welfare state experiences—welfare state regime life courses—both temporally, in terms of different phases of welfare state development (inequalities smaller among older people), and spatially, in terms of welfare state regime type (inequalities smaller among older Scandinavians). The findings are that inequalities in health tended to increase, not decrease, with age. Similarly, inequalities in health were not smallest in the Scandinavian regime or among the older Scandinavian cohorts. In keeping with the rest of the literature, the Bismarckian and Southern regimes had smaller educational inequalities in health. Longitudinal analysis that integrates wider public health factors or makes smaller comparisons may be a more productive way of analyzing cross-national variations in health inequalities and their relationship to welfare state life courses.

*****

Recently, there has been a surge in comparative social epidemiology and public health policy research, and a sizeable amount of this has examined the relationship among different types of welfare states (welfare state regimes) and population health (1). Initially, attention was placed on differences by welfare state regime in terms of overall population health (e.g., infant mortality rates, life expectancy at birth, or self-reported health) (2–6). These studies consistently found that population health is enhanced by the Scandinavian welfare state regime, which offers universalism, comparatively generous replacement rates, and extensive welfare services (7). For example, Navarro and colleagues (4) found that countries that have had long periods of government by redistributive political parties (most notably the Scandinavian countries) have experienced lower infant mortality rates. These findings were reinforced by Chung and Muntaner's multilevel longitudinal analysis of welfare state regimes (8), which showed that about 20 percent of the difference in infant mortality rates among countries, and 10 percent of the difference in low birth weight, could be explained by the type of welfare state, with the Scandinavian welfare states outperforming the others. Similarly, a multilevel study of morbidity by welfare state regime found that the Scandinavian welfare states fared better, with lower rates of limiting longstanding illness and poor self-reported health (6).

More recently, and especially since publication of the results of the Tackling Health Inequalities in Europe project (www.eurothine.org), empirical attention has shifted to examining differences by welfare state regime in terms of socioeconomic inequalities in health (9–14). There was a clear expectation, not least because of their comparatively strong performance in terms of overall population health, that market-generated health inequalities would be smaller in the more generous and egalitarian Scandinavian welfare states. However, with the exception of one study (9), recent comparative research on health inequalities by welfare state regime has found that inequalities in self-reported health are smallest in the Bismarckian welfare states, not the Scandinavian ones (11, 12, 14). Similarly, for mortality, no evidence of systematically smaller inequalities was found in the Scandinavian welfare states—indeed, the inequalities were smallest in the Southern regime countries (10). This has been a contentious finding, given the egalitarian ethos and redistributive policies of the Scandinavian countries (especially when contrasted to the status-maintaining approach of the Bismarckian welfare states) (7). Subsequently, there has been much debate on this topic, and various explanations have been put forward for the counterintuitive findings, ranging from artifact (15), to health behaviors (10), to relative deprivation (16, 17) (for an overview, see 18). These explanations, however, are rather unconvincing, and one possible issue that may have explanatory power, or at least contextual relevance, is whether the findings are consistent in terms of age-related welfare state experience—what we refer to in this chapter as *welfare state regime life course*. This is important not just in terms of establishing whether the earlier findings are consistent when examined by age group, but also because it provides a possible way of gaining insight into how patterns of health inequalities across Europe are related to the development of welfare states and welfare state regimes.

Welfare states are by no means static entities; in fact, they have experienced numerous changes since their initial establishment in the early postwar period (19). In the social policy literature it is possible to identify at least four phases in the development of the majority of postwar Western welfare states: first, pre-welfare state; second, the "golden age" of the Fordist welfare state; third, crisis and restructuring; and fourth, the emergence of post-Fordist workfare states (20). Welfare state experiences will therefore differ by people's age, both within and between countries. For example, the welfare state experienced by older people in the Scandinavian countries will differ considerably from that experienced by younger people in the Anglo-Saxon countries.

Similarly, following life course epidemiology, health status reflects not just an individual's current position but also his or her accumulation of (welfare state) experiences over time (21). The life course perspective highlights the importance of critical periods and pathways of causation that allow us to understand the effect of the lived experience of different welfare state regimes on health inequalities (22). Yet, even though an understanding of the differential impact by socioeconomic status of welfare state regimes on life course trajectories can illuminate the role of public policies, there is a paucity of studies that use life course perspectives on welfare state regimes and health inequalities. This is due, to some extent, to a lack of suitable data. A way out of this impasse is provided by the fact that life course in Western societies is partly age-structured (23). To a certain extent, the life course is thus (age) standardized by common welfare state institutions (24). For certain aspects of the life course, such as education, this age structuring is more substantial than for others. Examining health inequalities by age group therefore enables us to consider the effects of welfare state regime life courses: it provides an opportunity to look at patterns of health inequalities within the development of European welfare states.

WELFARE STATE REGIMES

In his seminal work *The Three Worlds of Welfare Capitalism*, Esping-Andersen presented a three-fold classification of Western welfare states (liberal, conservative, social democratic) (7). His typology was based on the operationalization of three principles: decommodification (the extent to which an individual's welfare is reliant on the market), social stratification (the role of welfare states in maintaining or breaking down social stratification), and the private-public mix (the relative roles of the state, the family, and the market in welfare provision). There have been numerous critiques of the *Three Worlds* typology: in terms of the range of countries and regimes, the absence of a consideration of gender, the methodology, and/or the focus on cash benefits (for an overview, see 1). As a result of this criticism, modified or alternative typologies have been proposed, most of which place emphasis on those characteristics of welfare states not extensively examined by Esping-Andersen and which tweak the number of regimes and/or specific country classifications (25). Although none of these alternative categorizations has been generally accepted as the new standard typology of welfare regimes, Ferrera's typology (26) has been highlighted as one of the most empirically accurate. The Ferrera typology classifies countries on the basis of service coverage, poverty rates, and income replacement rates. It results in a fourfold typology of European welfare state regimes: Scandinavian (social democratic), Anglo-Saxon (liberal), Bismarckian (conservative), and Southern (see Box 1). In this chapter, as with our previous research on welfare state regimes and health outcomes (6, 12–14, 27), we use the Ferrera typology.

BOX 1
WELFARE STATE REGIMES

Scandinavian. The Scandinavian regime type (Denmark, Finland, Norway, Sweden) is characterized by universalism, comparatively generous social transfers, a commitment to full employment and income protection, and a strongly interventionist state. The state is used to promote social equality through a redistributive social security system. Unlike the other welfare state regimes, the Scandinavian regime type promotes an equality of the highest standards, not an equality of minimal needs, and it provides highly decommodifying programs.

Anglo-Saxon. In the welfare states of the Anglo-Saxon regime (United Kingdom, Ireland), state provision of welfare is minimal, social transfers are modest and often attract strict entitlement criteria, and recipients are usually means-tested and stigmatized. In this model, the dominance of the market is encouraged both passively, by guaranteeing only a minimum, and actively, by subsidizing private welfare schemes. The Anglo-Saxon welfare state regime thereby minimizes the decommodification effects of the welfare state, and a stark division exists between those—largely the poor—who rely on state aid and those who are able to afford private provision.

Bismarckian. The Bismarckian welfare state regime (Austria, Belgium, France, Germany, Luxembourg, Netherlands, Switzerland) is distinguished by its "status differentiating" welfare programs, in which benefits are often earnings-related, administered through the employer, and geared toward maintaining existing social patterns. The role of the family and the voluntary sector (especially the Church) is also emphasized, and the redistributive impact is minimal. However, the role of the market is marginalized.

Southern. In Ferrera's typology, the Southern European *welfare states* (Italy, Greece, Portugal, and Spain) comprise a distinctive, southern, *welfare state regime*. The southern *welfare states* are described as "rudimentary" because they are characterized by their fragmented system of welfare provision, which consists of diverse income maintenance schemes that range from the meager to the generous, and welfare services, particularly the health care system, that provide only limited and partial coverage. Reliance on the family and voluntary sector is also a prominent feature.

Source: Adapted from Eikemo and Bambra (29).

WELFARE STATE REGIME DEVELOPMENT

The historical development of postwar welfare provision across Western Europe, as noted above, can be divided into four distinctive periods: pre–welfare state, the golden age of the welfare state, crisis and restructuring, and the emergence of post-Fordist workfare states. To some extent, the timing of these periods of welfare state development varies by country and by welfare state regime. For example, the Southern regime countries (except Italy) experienced dictatorships until the mid-1970s, with highly regressive fiscal policies (4); nor is the timing of developments universal in other regimes—for example, Finland's welfare state developed later than that of the other Scandinavian countries. This historical overview is therefore only able to capture the broad thematic changes in the development of European welfare states.

Pre–Welfare State

For most of the 19th century, there was minimal state welfare within Europe beyond very basic "poor relief"—the provision of basic food rations and shelter (often provided through institutions such as the English workhouse system). Beyond these provisions, welfare came from family members or charity (particularly the Church). This began to change in the early 20th century with the introduction of rudimentary, highly selective (non-workers, which included most women, were typically excluded), state-organized welfare systems, which provided basic pensions, unemployment benefits, and sickness benefits funded through social insurance payments (e.g., the 1911 National Insurance Act in the United Kingdom and the Bismarckian welfare reforms of 1880s Germany).

Golden Age of Welfare

It was not until after World War II (1945) that what is now referred to as the Fordist welfare state was established. There are competing explanations as to why the welfare state emerged at this point, between modernization theory, the power resources model, and the requirements of capital thesis (for a detailed overview, see 20). To a greater or lesser extent (see Box 1), the golden age's Fordist welfare state was characterized by centralism, universalism, Keynesian demand-management, full (male) employment and high public expenditure, and the promotion of mass consumption through a redistributive welfare system and social wage (28). There was also a mainstream political consensus in favor of the welfare state. In the golden age of welfare state expansion (1940s to 1960s), Western Europe experienced significant improvements in public housing, health care, and the other main social determinants of health (29).

Crisis and Restructuring

The golden age of welfare state expansion effectively ended with the economic crisis of the 1970s (high inflation, slow economic growth, the end of full employment), during which there was a general loss of confidence in the ability of Fordist welfare state capitalism to adequately maintain profitability and safeguard capitalist reproduction (initially in the United Kingdom and then across continental Europe). Besides these internal constraints, there were also external challenges such as globalization (30). The political consensus of the early postwar years was also broken, and governments started to dismantle and restructure the welfare state. Reforms (which largely occurred in the 1980s and 1990s) were characterized by the privatization and marketization of welfare services, entitlement restrictions and increased qualifying conditions for benefits, and a shift toward targeting and means-testing; cuts or limited increases in the actual cash values of benefits; modified funding arrangements (with a shift away from business taxation); and an increased emphasis on an active rather than a passive welfare system (29).

Post-Fordist Workfare States

The restructuring of the welfare state has been analyzed by some commentators as a shift from the Fordist system of Keynesian welfare state capitalism, which could afford and required a high level of public welfare expenditure, to a post-Fordist system of Schumpeterian workfare state capitalism in which high welfare expenditure is incompatible with the continuing needs of capital accumulation (20). Post-Fordist workfare states are characterized by decentralization and welfare pluralism, the promotion of labor market flexibility, supply-side economics, the subordination of social policy to the demands of the market, and a desire to minimize social expenditure (20, 28). As in the Fordist welfare states, there are variants on the post-Fordist model reflecting welfare state regimes and their differing policy responses to common challenges (28, 31).

RESEARCH HYPOTHESES

During these different phases of development, the welfare states of Europe have acted as greater (during the golden age) or lesser (during the pre–welfare state and post-Fordist periods) mediators of the impact of social determinants on health and health inequalities. We therefore suggest that educational inequalities in self-reported health will vary by welfare state experience (welfare state life course) both temporally, in terms of the different phases of welfare state development, and spatially, in terms of welfare state regime type. Specifically, we examine two interrelated hypotheses:

1. Patterns of educational inequalities in health will vary by age within welfare state regimes, being smaller among older people.
2. Patterns of educational inequalities in health will vary by age among welfare state regimes, being smallest among the older Scandinavian cohorts.

METHODS

The data are from the European Social Survey (ESS), from which we used the merged version of three waves (2002, 2004, and 2006) for 17 Western European countries. Data and extensive documentation from the ESS are freely available for downloading at the Norwegian Social Science Data Services website (www.nsd.uib.no). We included 85,514 individuals divided into six age groups (people born in the 1930s, 1940s, 1950s, 1960s, 1970s and 1980s, representing different welfare state life courses; see Table 1), after listwise deletion of cases from all applied variables. (See Table 2 for sample sizes and response rates within each country for all three years.)

We used two indicators of morbidity available in the ESS: self-reported general health (SRH) and limiting longstanding illness (LLI). Self-reported general health was constructed from a variable asking: "How is your health in general?" Eligible responses were "very good," "good," "fair," "bad," and "very bad." We dichotomized the variable into "very good or good" health versus "less than good" health ("fair," "bad," and "very bad"). For limiting longstanding illness, people

Table 1

Welfare state life course

| Decade of birth | Age range of sample during periods of welfare state development, years | | | |
	Pre-welfare (1930s, 1940s)	Golden age (1950s, 1960, 1970s)	Reform (1980s, 1990s)	Post-Fordist (2000s)
1930s	0–19	11–49	41–69	61+
1940s	0–9	1–39	31–59	51+
1950s	—	0–29	21–49	41+
1960s	—	0–19	11–39	31+
1970s	—	0–9	1–29	21+
1980s	—	—	0–9	11+

Table 2

Country statistics (N = 85,514)

Welfare regime	Country	Sample size (response rate, %)			Included sample (% missing)[a]	Years of education, average yrs (S.D.)	
		2002	2004	2006		Men	Women
Scandinavian	Denmark	1,506 (67.7)	1,487 (64.3)	1,505 (50.8)	**4,056** (7.8)	13.46 (3.90)	13.20 (3.99)
	Finland	2,000 (73.2)	2,022 (70.7)	1,896 (64.4)	**5,347** (9.2)	12.32 (3.67)	12.88 (3.86)
	Norway	2,036 (65.0)	1,760 (66.2)	1,750 (64.4)	**5,108** (7.5)	13.47 (3.43)	13.52 (3.59)
	Sweden	1,999 (69.5)	1,948 (65.9)	1,927 (65.5)	**5,298** (9.4)	12.46 (3.30)	12.69 (3.36)
Anglo-Saxon	Ireland	2,046 (64.5)	2,286 (59.7)	1,800 (N.A.)	**5,377** (10.1)	12.83 (3.36)	13.05 (3.24)
	U.K.	2,052 (55.5)	1,897 (54.6)	2,394 (52.1)	**5,705** (9.0)	13.11 (3.39)	12.98 (3.19)
Bismarckian	Austria	2,257 (60.4)	2,256 (62.4)	2,405 (N.A.)	**6,285** (7.6)	12.58 (2.98)	12.22 (2.77)
	Belgium	1,899 (59.2)	1,778 (61.2)	1,798 (61.2)	**4,914** (9.4)	12.45 (3.70)	12.30 (3.62)
	France	1,503 (43.1)	1,806 (43.6)	1,986 (46.0)	**4,778** (8.2)	12.25 (3.88)	12.26 (3.85)
	Germany	2,919 (55.7)	2,870 (51.0)	2,916 (52.9)	**7,808** (8.7)	13.54 (3.36)	12.75 (3.13)
	Luxembourg	1,552 (43.9)	1,635 (50.1)	N.A. (N.A.)	**2,911** (6.0)	12.22 (4.08)	11.83 (4.07)
	Netherlands	2,364 (67.9)	1,881 (65.1)	1,889 (59.8)	**5,692** (6.2)	13.36 (3.83)	12.55 (3.61)
	Switzerland	2,040 (33.5)	2,141 (48.6)	1,804 (50.0)	**5,494** (7.8)	11.67 (3.65)	11.35 (3.33)
Southern	Greece	2,566 (80.0)	2,406 (78.8)	N.A. (N.A.)	**4,532** (8.7)	10.90 (4.43)	9.7 (4.40)
	Italy	1,207 (43.7)	1,529 (59.3)	N.A. (N.A.)	**2,500** (6.4)	11.51 (4.34)	10.95 (4.44)
	Portugal	1,511 (68.8)	2,052 (71.2)	2,222 (72.7)	**5,216** (9.1)	8.14 (4.47)	7.37 (4.72)
	Spain	1,729 (53.2)	1,663 (59.7)	1,876 (66.2)	**4,494** (9.4)	11.66 (5.20)	11.33 (5.29)

Note: N.A., not available.

[a]Some cases are excluded from the analysis because they lie outside the chosen age-cohorts. These are not included in the "missing" indication.

were asked whether they were hampered in daily activities in any way by any longstanding illness or disability, infirmity, or mental health problem. Eligible responses were "yes a lot," "yes to some extent," and "no." We dichotomized this variable into "yes" (regardless of whether to some extent or a lot) and "no." Table 3 shows the sample size and prevalence of ill health for each age cohort within each welfare regime.

Education is a widely used indicator of socioeconomic position within the social sciences. It avoids interpretation problems, because it is less volatile than income and occupation (which are more influenced by health-related social mobility later in life) and social mobility. The association between socioeconomic position and poor health is well established, and education has additional specific influences through increasing knowledge and skills that may affect cognitive function, make individuals more receptive to health education messages, and/or make them more able to communicate with and access health services (32). In meritocratic societies, education is a fundamental indicator of people's position in society, because it is an important contributor to later occupation and income (33, 34).

The measure of education was based on a variable describing full-time education in years. However, as Table 2 shows, average years of education varies among European countries and is especially low in the Southern countries. In comparative studies, it is thus important to take into account the extent of variation of reported years of education in different countries. We did this by applying a *total impact* measure of education. First, for each country separately, we standardized the continuous variables of educational attainment such that the national average was equal to 0 and the standard deviation equal to 1 year of education (0.2% of the respondents with 26 to 40 years of education were excluded from the analysis). This was done separately for each age cohort within each country, for men and women separately. Second, we inverted this variable by multiplying it by −1, such that higher values correspond to lower educational levels. Next, the standardized variable was introduced as an independent variable in a logistic regression analysis, controlled for age and ESS-round, with health variables as the dependent variable. Finally, odds ratios (ORs) were computed as the antilogarithm of the estimated logistic regression coefficients. The OR should be interpreted as the health difference between people with average years of education and those with years of education one standard deviation below the national average. ORs of poor self-rated health and limiting longstanding illness are presented for men and women in six age groups within each of the four welfare state regimes.

A weight was applied in all analyses to correct for design effects due to sampling design in countries where not all individuals in the population have an identical selection probability. All analyses were done for men and women separately.

Table 3

Sample size (N) and prevalence of poor self-rated health (SRH) and limiting
longstanding illness (LLI) in four welfare regimes and six age cohorts
for men and women separately (N = 85,514)

Age group, decade of birth	Welfare regime	Men			Women		
		N	SRH	LLI	N	SRH	LLI
1930s	Scandinavian	1,118	41.1	38.6	1,155	51.0	41.3
	Anglo-Saxon	620	31.9	34.5	612	37.4	33.3
	Southern	1,103	57.9	29.6	1,287	72.6	41.7
	Bismarckian	1,983	41.8	36.1	2,060	51.4	40.2
1940s	Scandinavian	1,854	34.7	32.5	1,838	38.8	35.5
	Anglo-Saxon	899	31.0	29.1	992	28.1	28.5
	Southern	1,111	43.0	16.5	1,429	59.2	26.8
	Bismarckian	2,936	35.3	28.7	3,007	39.1	30.4
1950s	Scandinavian	1,894	24.9	23.0	1,865	26.5	29.8
	Anglo-Saxon	903	20.2	20.4	1,118	20.6	18.9
	Southern	1,296	33.5	11.8	1,671	43.3	15.4
	Bismarckian	3,618	26.8	21.4	3,929	29.7	23.9
1960s	Scandinavian	2,021	17.5	18.9	1,966	17.1	21.6
	Anglo-Saxon	1,006	15.2	14.2	1,262	15.1	13.1
	Southern	1,373	20.7	7.3	1,874	31.1	10.4
	Bismarckian	3,822	19.6	14.9	4,787	21.5	15.8
1970s	Scandinavian	1,716	13.7	14.2	1,648	12.2	15.8
	Anglo-Saxon	845	12.3	9.7	992	12.5	10.8
	Southern	2,764	14.8	4.6	1,652	22.0	6.0
	Bismarckian	1,931	14.2	10.4	3,019	18.1	12.1
1980s	Scandinavian	1,411	12.0	13.3	1,323	13.9	17.0
	Anglo-Saxon	876	13.1	8.3	955	8.7	6.2
	Southern	1,287	11.9	3.8	1,204	13.9	4.5
	Bismarckian	3,057	11.8	9.5	2,900	15.7	10.1

RESULTS

Figure 1 presents odds ratios (y axes) for reporting poor self-assessed health and limiting longstanding illness according to educational attainment in four welfare state regimes. Odds ratios are given for men and women separately within six different age groups (x axes). Exact ORs are given in Appendix Tables I and II (pp. 333–334). The results are presented in line with our two research hypotheses.

Our first research hypothesis, that patterns of educational inequalities in health will vary by age within welfare state regimes, being smaller among older people, does not seem to be supported by the results shown in Figure 1. The ORs seem to decrease in all regimes by age (from left to right), and they are smallest among the youngest age cohort (those born in the 1980s). However, to further clarify these findings, we have also estimated correlation coefficients (by correlating ORs with one unit increase of age groups) for all regimes (see Table 4). Negative associations are evident in all regimes for men and women for both health indicators, although far from all are significant. The summary measure of Table 4 shows that the associations of ORs and age are strongest in the Southern regime ($r = -0.72$), intermediate in the Bismarckian ($r = -0.48$) and Scandinavian ($r = -0.45$), and weakest in the Anglo-Saxon ($r = -0.23$). We should add, however, that some of the observed lines in Figure 1 (e.g., for ORs of LLI in Scandinavian and Anglo-Saxon regimes) seem to be curvilinear, increasing from the left and then decreasing again (even more) to the right. In any case, the overall picture seems to be that health inequalities increase by age group.

The second research hypothesis, that patterns of educational inequalities in health will vary by age between welfare state regimes, being smallest among the older Scandinavian cohort, is correct in the first part. There is some patterning of educational inequalities by welfare state regime: inequalities in SRH and LLI tend to be smallest in either the Southern or Bismarckian regimes (with the exception of the 1940s cohorts) and highest in the Scandinavian (with the exception of LLI for the 1940s male cohort and the 1930s and 1940s female cohort). The second part of the hypothesis, that ORs will be smallest among the older Scandinavian cohort, is not supported by our results; on the contrary, health inequalities are relatively large within this group, both for men ($OR_{LLI} = 1.30$, $OR_{SRH} = 1.35$) and women ($OR_{LLI} = 1.19$, $OR_{SRH} = 1.48$). The group with the smallest inequalities in SRH is the youngest (1980s) Southern regime cohort (men, OR = 1.04; women, OR = 0.97), and for LLI they are smallest among the 1980s female cohort in the Southern regime (OR = 0.90) and the 1980s male cohort in the Bismarckian regime (OR = 1.00). The ORs among older Scandinavians are therefore not consistently lower than those for younger Scandinavian age groups, nor are they lower than in other European age groups.

DISCUSSION

The results do not entirely support our two research hypotheses. For the first hypothesis, although patterns of educational inequalities in health did vary a little by age within welfare state regimes, they were not smaller among older people. The extent of age-related differences in the magnitude of health inequalities varied by welfare state regime, as, for example, age was more associated with patterns of health inequalities in the Southern regime than in the others. There were particularly notable decreases in inequalities in health among the younger groups in the Southern countries—perhaps reflecting the beneficial effects of the shift away from dictatorship (4). Overall, however, health inequalities tended to increase with age—not decrease as predicted by our hypothesis. This is counterintuitive from a welfare state development perspective, as the older cohorts experienced stronger and more redistributive welfare state contexts (with the exception of those in Southern regime countries). However, the finding is in keeping with those of a recent longitudinal study of self-rated health, which found that social inequalities in health widened with age in all four welfare states under study (United States, Britain, Germany, and Denmark) (19). That study also noted that educational health inequalities were not apparent until people were over 25 years of age, which is similar to our finding that health inequalities are smallest among the youngest age group (born in the 1980s). This may be because ill health is a rarer event in all social classes at younger ages. Furthermore, the higher levels of decommodification provided by the older welfare states would have affected income inequalities through redistribution, but this may not affect inequalities in health in the same way—as Dahl and coauthors (16) comment, it is more difficult to redistribute health than income. Finally, the older groups experienced the better welfare state provision in earlier periods of their lives, whereas now (when health outcomes are being measured), perhaps when these older people are most in need, they experience the reformed, less generous, welfare state provision.

Similarly, with our second hypothesis, although patterns of educational inequalities in health varied by age among welfare state regimes, they were not smallest for the Scandinavian regime or among the older Scandinavian cohorts. This hypothesis was developed by a desire to assess the consistency, across different age groups, of the finding that health inequalities are not lowest in the Scandinavian countries. In this respect, our findings are in keeping with the broader literature, as the Bismarckian and Southern regimes fairly consistently exhibited smaller educational inequalities in health across most age groups and among both men and women. Various studies of self-rated health and mortality have come to the same conclusion (10–12, 14). Our results, therefore, like those in earlier studies, are very challenging in terms of theorizing the relationship between welfare state inputs and health inequalities outputs. Speculative reasons for the relative underperformance of the Scandinavian model in the area of

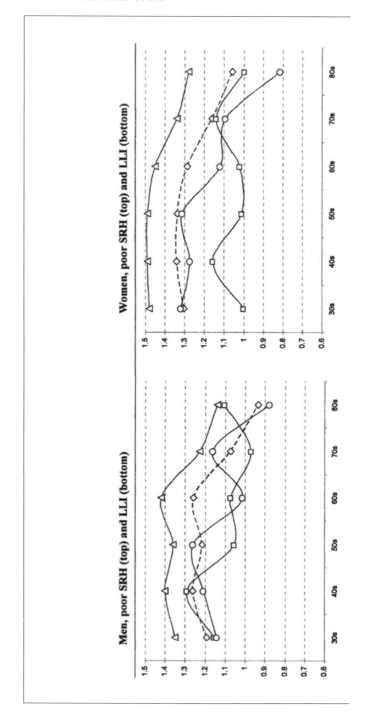

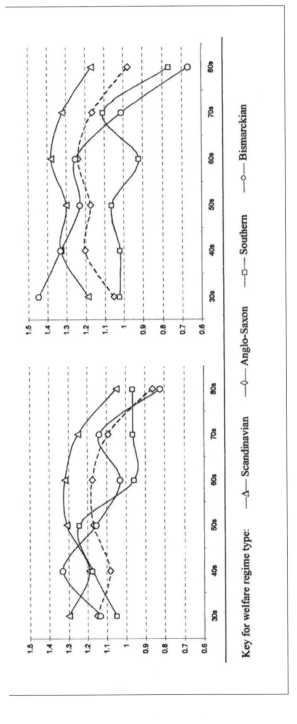

Figure 1. Odds ratios (y axes) and age groups (x axes) for men and women reporting poor self-rated health (SRH) and limiting longstanding illness (LLI) according to education, in Scandinavian, Anglo-Saxon, Southern, and Bismarckian welfare regimes.

Table 4

Correlations between odds ratios of poor self-rated health (SRH) and
limiting longstanding illness (LLI) and (one unit increase of) age groups,
for men and women separately

| Welfare regime | Correlation coefficients (Pearson's r) | | | | |
| | Poor SRH | | LLI | | Summary by regime |
	Men	Women	Men	Women	
Scandinavian	−0.74*	−0.89**	−0.55	−0.33	−0.45**
Anglo-Saxon	−0.52	−0.29	−0.39	−0.29	−0.23
Southern	−0.58	−0.92***	−0.49	−0.92***	−0.72***
Bismarckian	−0.51	−0.57	−0.73*	−0.17	−0.48**

Note: Age cohorts are given values from 1 (born in the 1930s) to 6 (born in the 1980s) in the correlation analyses.
***$p < 0.01$; **$p < 0.05$; *$p < 0.10$.

health inequalities (as opposed to overall population health) have been suggested elsewhere (18, 34–36). These include artifact (the results are not real but due to the measures used in the studies), health selection (the social consequences of ill health are greater in the Scandinavian countries), health behaviors (socioeconomic inequalities in smoking are much higher in the Scandinavian countries than in other welfare state regimes), health care services (tentative evidence suggests that inequalities in mortality as a result of diseases amenable to medical intervention are higher in the Scandinavian countries), or relative deprivation (the health effects of relative deprivation may be more extensive in the Scandinavian welfare states, because these regimes generate, but do not meet, high levels of expectation of upward social mobility and prosperity) (18, 34–37).

These explanations, coupled with our results, suggest that there is a need to integrate details about other, more conventionally analyzed, public health influences (such as smoking rates, health care provision) into the welfare state regime approach—termed elsewhere "public health regimes" (38, 39). The welfare state regime concept has many uses in untangling the complexities of comparing different countries and systems. However, it is perhaps rather limited for getting down to the minute details of how and why inequalities in health are generated (18). Thus there is a need to make more precise comparisons among the different welfare state life courses of groups in particular welfare states (and welfare state regimes) (15). For example, a detailed case study could be made that compares the average welfare state life course experiences of different educational and age groups in the United Kingdom with those of the same groups in Sweden. Finally, there is a clear need for better—longitudinal—data to comprehensively assess our hypotheses.

Limitations of the Study

1. Longitudinal data suitable for studying the effects of welfare state regime life courses on health inequalities are now being collected (e.g., the Survey of Health, Ageing and Retirement in Europe, wave 3), but they are not yet available. We attempted to overcome this lack of data by examining health inequalities in different age cohorts, using cross-sectional cross-national data. We are justified in this approach by the age-structuring of the life course, especially pertaining to education (23). However, the study is subject to the usual limitations of this study design, and longitudinal data would be much preferred.

2. Although a growing number of studies have shown that the measure of self-assessed health is strongly correlated with more objective measures such as mortality (40, 41), we cannot exclude the possibility of a substantial, additional effect of cultural differences.

3. The European Social Survey presents an outstanding opportunity to investigate cross-national patterns of health inequality among age groups, as the survey asks the same questions in all countries. But we acknowledge that many issues may affect the comparability of multi-country studies, such as non-response (see Table 2), modes of data collection, translations, and conduct of the study. This applies especially to the first wave in Switzerland, which had a response rate of only 33.5 percent. If non-response is related to health and education, then this would produce biased inequality measures. Another methodological issue is that our sample comes from three sweeps of the ESS.

4. As noted earlier, the concept of welfare state regimes and their development is itself rather limiting, as it places very generalized and broad parameters around how welfare states evolve over time. The four phases and associated time periods used in our study are therefore very approximate, and there are clear differences both between and within regimes in terms of the time periods when welfare states developed. For example, Sweden did not do any restructuring until the 1990s recession, whereas the reform period in the United Kingdom started in the early 1980s. The Southern regime countries (with the exception of Italy) also had a different developmental trajectory, with dictatorships that lasted until the 1970s. Similarly, there are within-regime differences, as Finland's welfare state developed much later than that of the other Scandinavian countries.

5. The choice of welfare state typology may well have influenced the results. There are various welfare state typologies in circulation, which configure the composition of the regimes in different ways. Most notably for this study, the Navarro and Shi typology (42) has a more concisely defined Southern (late democracy) welfare state regime, which excludes Italy. If a different welfare state typology were used, our results might have been different. However, the Ferrera

typology (26) is well-tested in health research and has been assessed as the most empirically accurate.

6. We have used education as our measure of socioeconomic inequalities. This was done because education is seen as a less volatile measure than income or occupation (32). However, as many epidemiological studies have shown, the extent of health inequalities can sometimes depend on how they are measured (32). This has also been demonstrated in studies of health inequalities by welfare state regime that use income as the indicator of inequality, which produce slightly different country and welfare state regime patterning than the education measure (12, 14). We therefore acknowledge that a different indicator of socioeconomic status might change our results.

CONCLUSION

This is the first study to examine health inequalities by age and welfare state regime across Western Europe. Like many previous studies of health inequalities by welfare state regime, the findings are in contrast to theoretical expectations, as the Scandinavian countries did not have the smallest inequalities. This may be because the welfare state regime concept is too broad, or because it ignores the influence on health inequalities of other important public health factors (such as health care provision and smoking rates). Public health regimes may therefore be a more productive way forward in terms of analyzing cross-national variations in health inequalities. The chapter has also outlined a new concept— that of welfare state life courses—and this is something that can be further developed theoretically and examined in more detail empirically. This, perhaps, could best be done by looking in more detail at how institutional settings shape the life course and health outcomes in the welfare states of just one welfare state regime type, preferably using longitudinal data. To develop the concept and assess its value for public health research, more precise empirical comparisons are needed than can be offered by this exploratory ecological overview.

REFERENCES

1. Bambra, C. Going beyond the Three Worlds of Welfare Capitalism: Regime theory and public health research. *J. Epidemiol. Community Health* 61:1098–1102, 2007.
2. Bambra, C. Health status and the worlds of welfare. *Soc. Policy Society* 5:53–62, 2006.
3. Coburn, D. Beyond the income inequality hypothesis: Class, neo-liberalism, and health inequalities. *Soc. Sci. Med.* 58(1):41–56, 2004.
4. Navarro, V., et al. The importance of the political and the social in explaining mortality differentials among the countries of the OECD, 1950–1998. *Int. J. Health Serv.* 33:419–494, 2003.
5. Navarro, V., et al. Politics and health outcomes. *Lancet* 368:1033–1037, 2006.
6. Eikemo, T., et al. Welfare state regimes and differences in self-perceived health in Europe: A multi-level analysis. *Soc. Sci. Med.* 66:2281–2295, 2008.

References *continue on p. 335*

APPENDIX TABLE I

Odds ratios (95% confidence interval) of reporting poor self-rated health
according to education within four welfare regimes and six age groups,
for men and women separately (N = 85,514)

Age group, decade of birth	Welfare regime	Men	Women
1930s	Scandinavian	**1.35 (1.19–1.53)**	**1.48 (1.30–1.68)**
	Anglo-Saxon	**1.40 (1.16–1.69)**	**1.19 (1.00–1.41)**
	Southern	**1.29 (1.14–1.46)**	**1.49 (1.32–1.68)**
	Bismarckian	**1.28 (1.16–1.40)**	**1.28 (1.17–1.40)**
1940s	Scandinavian	**1.40 (1.26–1.55)**	**1.49 (1.34–1.65)**
	Anglo-Saxon	**1.52 (1.29–1.78)**	**1.35 (1.16–1.57)**
	Southern	**1.37 (1.21–1.55)**	**1.42 (1.27–1.59)**
	Bismarckian	**1.28 (1.18–1.38)**	**1.22 (1.13–1.31)**
1950s	Scandinavian	**1.36 (1.22–1.51)**	**1.49 (1.34–1.67)**
	Anglo-Saxon	**1.25 (1.06–1.48)**	**1.17 (1.01–1.36)**
	Southern	**1.43 (1.26–1.62)**	**1.46 (1.31–1.62)**
	Bismarckian	**1.25 (1.16–1.35)**	**1.33 (1.23–1.43)**
1960s	Scandinavian	**1.42 (1.26–1.61)**	**1.45 (1.29–1.64)**
	Anglo-Saxon	**1.29 (1.07–1.55)**	**1.20 (1.02–1.40)**
	Southern	**1.16 (1.01–1.33)**	**1.24 (1.12–1.38)**
	Bismarckian	**1.32 (1.21–1.43)**	**1.33 (1.23–1.43)**
1970s	Scandinavian	**1.23 (1.07–1.41)**	**1.34 (1.16–1.54)**
	Anglo-Saxon	1.20 (0.97–1.48)	1.39 (1.14–1.68)
	Southern	**1.35 (1.16–1.57)**	**1.23 (1.10–1.39)**
	Bismarckian	**1.32 (1.18–1.47)**	**1.23 (1.12–1.35)**
1980s	Scandinavian	1.14 (0.93–1.39)	1.28 (1.06–1.54)
	Anglo-Saxon	**1.36 (1.10–1.69)**	**1.26 (1.00–1.58)**
	Southern	1.04 (0.88–1.23)	0.97 (0.81–1.15)
	Bismarckian	1.05 (0.92–1.18)	1.05 (0.93–1.18)

Note: Bold indicates significant differences by education ($p < 0.05$).

APPENDIX TABLE II

Odds ratios (95% confidence interval) of reporting limiting longstanding illness
according to education within four welfare regimes and six age groups,
for men and women separately (N = 85,514)

Age group, decade of birth	Welfare regime	Men	Women
1930s	Scandinavian	**1.30 (1.15–1.48)**	**1.19 (1.05–1.35)**
	Anglo-Saxon	**1.25 (1.05–1.49)**	**1.22 (1.02–1.46)**
	Southern	**1.31 (1.13–1.50)**	**1.65 (1.45–1.89)**
	Bismarckian	**1.19 (1.08–1.30)**	**1.16 (1.06–1.27)**
1940s	Scandinavian	**1.19 (1.08–1.32)**	**1.33 (1.20–1.47)**
	Anglo-Saxon	**1.37 (1.17–1.61)**	**1.18 (1.02–1.36)**
	Southern	**1.61 (1.33–1.95)**	**1.54 (1.33–1.77)**
	Bismarckian	**1.27 (1.16–1.38)**	**1.10 (1.01–1.19)**
1950s	Scandinavian	**1.31 (1.17–1.46)**	**1.30 (1.17–1.44)**
	Anglo-Saxon	**1.48 (1.24–1.76)**	**1.24 (1.06–1.45)**
	Southern	**1.39 (1.15–1.68)**	**1.43 (1.23–1.66)**
	Bismarckian	**1.30 (1.19–1.41)**	**1.25 (1.16–1.35)**
1960s	Scandinavian	**1.32 (1.17–1.48)**	**1.38 (1.24–1.54)**
	Anglo-Saxon	1.15 (0.96–1.38)	1.09 (0.92–1.29)
	Southern	**1.27 (1.03–1.58)**	**1.47 (1.25–1.73)**
	Bismarckian	**1.16 (1.06–1.27)**	**1.22 (1.12–1.32)**
1970s	Scandinavian	**1.25 (1.09–1.43)**	**1.32 (1.16–1.51)**
	Anglo-Saxon	1.22 (0.96–1.54)	**1.36 (1.11–1.67)**
	Southern	**1.47 (1.14–1.89)**	**1.24 (1.01–1.52)**
	Bismarckian	**1.15 (1.02–1.30)**	**1.20 (1.08–1.34)**
1980s	Scandinavian	1.05 (0.86–1.29)	1.17 (0.98–1.40)
	Anglo-Saxon	1.23 (0.96–1.57)	1.01 (0.76–1.35)
	Southern	1.10 (0.82–1.46)	0.90 (0.67–1.21)
	Bismarckian	1.00 (0.87–1.15)	1.06 (0.93–1.22)

Note: Bold indicates significant differences by education ($p < 0.05$).

7. Esping-Andersen, G. *The Three Worlds of Welfare Capitalism*. Polity, London, 1990.
8. Chung, H., and Muntaner, C. Welfare state matters: A typological multilevel analysis of wealthy countries. *Health Policy* 80:328–339, 2007.
9. Borrell, C., et al. Explaining variations between political traditions in the magnitude of socio-economic inequalities in self-perceived health. In *Tackling Health Inequalities in Europe: Eurothine*, pp. 213–229. Erasmus Medical Center, Rotterdam, 2007.
10. Mackenbach, J., et al. Socioeconomic inequalities in health in 22 European countries. *N. Engl. J. Med.* 358:2468–2481, 2008.
11. Espelt, A., et al. Inequalities in health by social class dimensions in European countries of different political traditions. *Int. J. Epidemiol.* 37:1095–1105, 2008.
12. Eikemo, T. A., et al. Health inequalities according to educational level under different welfare regimes: A comparison of 23 European countries. *Sociol. Health Illn.* 30:565–582, 2008.
13. Bambra, C., et al. Gender, health inequality and welfare state regimes: A cross-national study of twelve European countries. *J. Epidemiol. Community Health* 63:38–44, 2009.
14. Eikemo, T., et al. Welfare state regimes and income related health inequalities: A comparison of 23 European countries. *Eur. J. Public Health* 18:593–599, 2008.
15. Lundberg, O. Commentary: Politics and public health—some conceptual considerations concerning welfare state characteristics and public health outcomes. *Int. J. Epidemiol.* 37:1105–1108, 2008.
16. Dahl, E., et al. Welfare state regimes and health inequalities. In *Social Inequalities in Health*, ed. J. Siegrist and M. Marmot, pp. 193–222. Oxford University Press, Oxford, 2006.
17. Yngwe, M., et al. Exploring relative deprivation: Is social comparison a mechanism in the relation between income and health? *Soc. Sci. Med.* 57:1463–1473, 2003.
18. Bambra, C. Social inequalities in health. In *Changing Equality: The Nordic Welfare Model in the 21st Century*, ed. J. Kvist et al. Policy Press, Bristol, 2012.
19. Sacker, A., Worts, D., and McDonough, P. Social influences on trajectories of self-rated health: Evidence from Britain, Germany, Denmark and the United States. *J. Epidemiol. Community Health*, 2009. doi: 10.1136/jech.2009.091199.
20. Bambra, C. Welfare state regimes and the political economy of health. *Hum. Society* 33:99–117, 2009.
21. Bartley, M. *Health Inequality: An Introduction to Theories, Concepts, and Methods*. Polity Press, Cambridge, 2004.
22. Blane, D., Netuveli, G., and Stone, J. The development of life course epidemiology. *Rev. Epidemiol. Sante Publ.* 55:31–38, 2007.
23. Settersten, R. A. Age structuring and the rhythm of the life course. In *Handbook of the Life Course*, ed. J. T. Mortimer and M. J. Shanahan, pp. 81–98. Springer, New York, 2003.
24. Kruger, H. The life-course regime: Ambiguities between interrelatedness and individualization. In *Social Dynamics of the Life Course: Transitions, Institutions, and Interrelations*, ed. W. R. Heinz and V. W. Marshall, pp. 33–56. Aldine De Gruyter, New York, 2003.
25. Bambra, C. Sifting the wheat from the chaff: A two-dimensional discriminant analysis of welfare state regime theory. *Soc. Policy Adm.* 41:1–28, 2007.

26. Ferrera, M. The southern model of welfare in social Europe. *J. Eur. Soc. Policy* 6:17–37, 1996.

27. Bambra, C., and Eikemo, T. Welfare state regimes, unemployment and health: A comparative study of the relationship between unemployment and self-reported health in 23 European countries. *J. Epidemiol. Community Health* 63:92–98, 2009.

28. Jessop, B. Post-Fordism and the state. In *Post-Fordism: A Reader*, ed. A. Amin, pp. 251–279. Blackwell, Oxford, 1994.

29. Eikemo, T. A., and Bambra, C. The welfare state: A glossary for public health. *J. Epidemiol. Community Health* 62:3–6, 2008.

30. Rhodes, M. The welfare state: Internal challenges, external constraint. In *Developments in Western European Politics*, ed. M. Rhodes and A. Vincent. Macmillan, London, 1997.

31. Esping-Andersen, G. *Social Foundations of Post-industrial Economies.* Oxford University Press, Oxford, 1999.

32. Galobardes, B., Lynch, J., and Davey Smith, G. Measuring socioeconomic position in health research. *Br. Med. Bull.*, 2007. doi: 10.1093/bmb/ldm001:1-17.

33. Lahelma, E. Health and social stratification. In *The Blackwell Companion to Medical Sociology*, ed. W. C. Cockerham, pp. 64–93. Blackwell, Oxford, 2001.

34. Ross, C. E., and Wu, C. The links between education and health. *Am. Sociol. Rev.* 60:719–745, 1995.

35. Lundberg, O., et al. *The Nordic Experience: Welfare States and Public Health (NEWS).* Contract No. 12. Centre for Heath Equity Studies, Stockholm, 2008.

36. Huijts, T., and Eikemo, T. A. Causality, selectivity or artefacts? Why socioeconomic inequalities in health are not smallest in the Nordic countries. *Eur. J. Public Health*, 2009.

37. Eikemo, T. A., Skalická, V., and Avendano, M. Variations in relative health inequalities: Are they a mathematical artefact? *Int. J. Equity Health* 8:32, 2009.

38. Asthana, S., and Halliday, J. *What Works in Tackling Health Inequalities? Pathways, Policies, and Practice through the Lifecourse.* Policy Press, Bristol, 2006.

39. Abdul Karim, S., Eikemo, T. A., and Bambra, C. Welfare state regimes and population health: Integrating the East Asian welfare states. *Health Policy* 94:45–53, 2010.

40. Heistaro, S., et al. Self rated health and mortality: A long term prospective study in eastern Finland. *J. Epidemiol. Community Health* 55(4):227–232, 2001.

41. Idler, E. L., and Benyamini, Y. Self-rated health and mortality: A review of twenty-seven community studies. *J. Health Soc. Behav.* 38(1):21–37, 1997.

42. Navarro, V., and Shi, L. The political context of social inequalities and health. *Int. J. Health Serv.* 31:1–21, 2001.

CHAPTER 16

Variation of Socioeconomic Gradients in Children's Developmental Health Across Advanced Capitalist Societies: Analysis of 22 OECD Nations

Arjumand Siddiqi, Ichiro Kawachi, Lisa Berkman, S. V. Subramanian, and Clyde Hertzman

Within societies, there is a well-established relation between socioeconomic position and a wide range of outcomes related to well-being, and this relation is known to vary in magnitude across countries. Using a large sample of nations, the authors explored whether differences in social policies explain differences in socioeconomic gradients across nations. Analyses were conducted on reading literacy in 15-year-olds, as an outcome related to cognitive development and to a host of factors that contribute to future well-being, including educational attainment and health. The results show a systematic variation in socioeconomic gradients and average scores across countries. Scores were favorable in countries with a long history of welfare state regimes, but countries where institutional change unfolded more recently and rapidly, or where welfare states are less well developed, clustered at the bottom of the rankings. Strong support was found for the "flattening up" hypothesis, which suggests that nations with higher average scores have less socioeconomic inequality in scores (or flatter gradients). Potential explanations for the observed patterns include differences between nations in the extent and distribution of income and social goods important for children's development.

*****

This study examines cross-national patterns of socioeconomic gradients in children's developmental health among advanced capitalist nations. The intent is twofold. We begin by describing variation in the *within-nation* relation between parents' socioeconomic position (SEP) and children's developmental health, using one of the largest samples of wealthy countries assembled thus far. Second, we use a comparative political economy approach to propose explanations for the patterns observed, including a test of the influence of national-level income inequality on differences in socioeconomic gradients across nations.

Many studies on adult health have demonstrated (using three primary indicators of SEP: income, occupation, and education) that in wealthy societies, socioeconomic gradients exist for a broad range (perhaps even a majority) of health outcomes (1–11). The implication of the evidence for socioeconomic gradients in health is that there are successive increases in health status from lower to higher socioeconomic levels in society. The gradient effect, then, can be conceptualized as a linear relationship. Gradients are in contrast to threshold effects, which imply that the effects of SEP are continuous up to a given point, but that after this point, changes in SEP do not result in changes in health status. The most common threshold effect is the dichotomous relation wherein it is assumed that one level of health is associated with being "rich" and another with being "poor." The gradient effect instead suggests that there are *degrees* of change in health associated with degrees of change in SEP (12).

With the exception of infant mortality (which shows gradients similar to those observed for adult health outcomes), evidence of socioeconomic gradients for "clinical" health outcomes in children has been inconsistent (13). These studies have largely relied on child morbidity and mortality-related health outcomes, which are relatively rare in wealthier societies. However, developmental outcomes for children have shown gradient patterns similar to those for adult health.

Brooks-Gunn and colleagues (14) provide a summary of risks and outcomes that show socioeconomic gradients in childhood. These include an increased risk of low birthweight (itself associated with a host of developmental difficulties later in life), decreased odds of preventive and other forms of health care, difficulties with behavior and socialization, deficits in self-esteem and self-efficacy, an increased likelihood of disengagement from school, and higher teenage pregnancy rates. In addition, a recent review also suggests that low SEP is associated with growth retardation and incomplete in utero neural development (e.g., less vigorous movement, and less neural integration between cardiac and motor functions) and, after birth, a risk of injuries and of dental caries (15, 16). Most of these findings are based on studies conducted in the United States and Canada. Other within-nation studies have also found strong associations between SEP and a variety of outcomes in the cognitive domain (17–19). Across countries, using data from the International Adult Literacy Survey, Willms (20) demonstrated that, in late adolescence and early adulthood, both the slope of socioeconomic gradients in reading literacy and the range of levels of achievement varied considerably among seven wealthy countries.

Despite the range and consistency of these empirical findings, socioeconomic differences in children's development are routinely underemphasized, particularly compared with emphasis on national average outcomes. However, there are several grounds on which equality of children's development deserves consideration equal to that given to average development (21).

Rawls (22) provides support for the pursuit of reducing inequalities in general, suggesting that the essence of justice is to decrease inequalities or to decrease inequalities in access to opportunities that provide socioeconomic goods. In turn, Sen (23, 24) suggests that it is a societal imperative to consider whether individuals are afforded equality of opportunity to develop their *capabilities,* a term that refers to what "people can do or be." Further, he proposes that the provision of these opportunities can be viewed as a type of freedom (or perhaps even a right) and, as such, should be provided in an egalitarian manner. That is, as societies, we must provide for all children the life conditions (or exposures) to allow each child an equal chance of healthy development (25).

In addition, a myriad of studies now underscore the importance of development outcomes, health outcomes, and socioeconomic circumstances during the childhood years as determinants of health in adulthood (13, 26). This life course perspective suggests that, in addition to the fundamental value of the childhood years themselves, their contribution to adult health status gives added fortitude to the value of improving the life conditions of children.

Many mechanisms have been explored to understand the association between socioeconomic conditions and exposures and resultant developmental outcomes (27). The primary contexts in which mechanisms have been considered are the home/family environment (27, 28), the school environment (20, 29, 30), and neighborhoods (31, 32). However, the national context that conditions socioeconomic-related variation in these more micro-environments has been understudied.

Some general (related) themes that have emerged from the literature on socioeconomic gradients provide guidance on this matter. First, among wealthy nations, those with the highest average health status also tend to have the shallowest socioeconomic gradients, or the least extent of socioeconomic inequality in health status. That is, high average health seems to be supported by less inequality in health. Second, if one looks at the pattern of socioeconomic gradients across these nations, a "flattening up" of gradients is observed as the average level increases (33).[1] In other words, in societies with low socioeconomic inequality, the levels of health of the wealthiest remain equivalent to (or even better than) those of the wealthiest in high-inequality societies; between-society

---

[1] There have been some departures from this perspective. Mackenbach et al. (11) found that country rankings for Western Europe of the size of socioeconomic inequalities in morbidity and mortality varied with the measure of SEP. Further, the same team has found a North–South gradient in inequalities in Western Europe, and the United States lies in the middle of the pack (10, 11, 34). These findings do not necessarily correspond to what we know about the rankings of these countries in terms of their health status.

variation in health decreases as one moves higher up the socioeconomic ladder (35). One major implication of the "flattening up" pattern is that gains in health at the lower end of the socioeconomic spectrum are not offset by losses in health at the higher ends.

This chapter furthers our understanding about these emergent properties of socioeconomic gradients, focusing on the developmental health of children. In so doing, this study draws on an assessment, conducted by the Organization for Economic Cooperation and Development (OECD), on one aspect of developmental health—reading literacy. The observed cross-national pattern of socioeconomic gradients is interpreted using a comparative political economy approach.

Some studies of the OECD nations have begun to examine health using a political economy or sociopolitical perspective. Navarro and colleagues (36) found that infant mortality was inversely associated with the proportion of the population voting for left-leaning (pro-redistribution) parties. The association of distribution (and redistribution) with infant mortality was also confirmed in a study using the Theil measure of wage inequality (37). In addition to infant mortality, Muntaner and colleagues (38) found that a host of variables associated with the "welfare state" were associated with a variety of infants' and children's health outcomes.

The term "welfare state" is defined as the complex and interwoven nature of the economic, social, and political institutions of the advanced capitalist (market-based) democracies, as it relates to the provision of income and social goods for members of society (39). The intention of this study is to further our understanding of the contribution of the welfare state in moderating the extent and effect of SEP on reading literacy. The role of income inequality (often considered to be a key indicator of the extent of equality in social provision) in explaining differences in socioeconomic gradients across countries is also tested.

METHODS

Data Source

This study uses data from the Program for International Student Assessment (PISA), conducted by the OECD. Administered in 2000, PISA was a study of 265,000 15-year-old students in 32 countries (the 28 member nations of the OECD and 4 non-member nations) that "assesses how far students near the end of compulsory education have acquired some of the knowledge and skills that are essential for full participation in society" (40). Specifically, PISA's emphasis was on understanding students' *functional* abilities, rather than focusing on curricular competencies per se. Further discussion of the measures investigated by PISA is provided below.

The sampling frame for the study differed slightly by country, but in general consisted of all 15-year-old students attending educational institutions. To obtain a representative sample, a two-staged sampling strategy was employed in each country, in which schools were first sampled, then children within schools. School sampling used a stratified probability proportional to size strategy. Stratification incorporated both explicit and implicit strata. Explicit strata were generally based on factors such as states/territories/other large geographic units, school type, and urban versus rural location. Implicitly, this also sorted schools by smaller geographic units, such as metropolitan areas, public versus private designation, and a small variety of other stratifying variables. Thirty-five 15-year-old students were randomly selected from each school. For schools with fewer than 35 such students, a census was obtained. The coding of each student in the PISA study to his or her respective school and country provides a rich resource for analysis of environmental effects on children. For the present study, it enables the comparison of within-nation socioeconomic gradients in reading literacy.

Because our primary hypothesis is concerned with the world's advanced capitalist societies, all non-OECD nations were excluded from the analysis. (Inclusion in the OECD was considered as the benchmark for an advanced welfare state regime.) Further, the Netherlands was excluded because of unreliability of the test data; Japan was excluded because the socioeconomic data for children indicated that all children in the sample were of the same status (this was likely due to a glitch in the data, but could not be resolved). Exclusions were also made based on inconsistencies in the information on SEP (a full explanation is given below). Finally, Iceland was excluded owing to lack of data on income inequality. The final sample consisted of 118,966 children in 22 countries.

Main Outcome Measure

The outcome of interest for this study is reading literacy. To assess the functional aspect of children's cognitive capabilities, PISA measured *literacy* in the areas of reading, mathematics, and science. In the educational literature, PISA has undergone some criticism, owing to the notion that literacy, as distinct from curricular competency, arises from many spheres of a child's life (e.g., family or neighborhood contexts) and cannot be attributed solely to schooling (41). However, this feature confers two benefits on the present study.

First, it provides a measure of cognition that, by contrast to a more school-based outcome (such as one focusing on curricular competencies), is perhaps a better measure of children's developmental health. A developmental health perspective views the acquisition of cognitive skills as providing children with the basis for functioning in their environments in a manner that contributes to their general well-being (42). This functionality dimension of cognitive development is directly captured by reading literacy, rather than indirectly tapped through a measure of curricular competency. Functional capacity in reading assists children to interact appropriately in a variety of environments, including at school, in other time spent with peers, at home (in reading and communicating with family members), and while engaging with the broader society (through reading and interpreting newspapers and other sources of information)—all of which contribute to children's general sense of well-being. Cognitive ability in children has also been shown to be an important input for future health, both for adults' ability to interact with their environments (which enhances adult well-being) and through its likely influence on ability to garner resources, such as education, income, and satisfying employment—all of which contribute to health status (43). It follows that, as the functional dimension of cognitive capacity, reading literacy would have similar influence on adult health, though this is an area deserving of further inquiry.

Second, if literacy measures a capacity that is obtained and developed from a wide range of environments, this further enables a broad interpretation of the results, suggesting that differences in socioeconomic gradients in children's reading literacy across countries can be attributed to variations in the characteristics of many spheres of society affecting children (themselves patterned by national political economy factors, as the hypothesis suggests), not just the school environment.

PISA assessed reading literacy with a 141 item paper-and-pencil test. The development of the test occurred over multiple stages and was supervised by a team with substantive knowledge in the area. To provide cross-cultural and cross-linguistic representation, an initial pool of items was collected by most participating countries, consistent with the framework for assessment of reading literacy developed by field experts. (Materials for reading were contributed by 19 nations.) A field trial was conducted in many of the participating countries, to select the final set of items from this larger pool (44). Items ranged from basic comprehension tasks to rather sophisticated tasks, which required "deep and multiple levels of understanding" (45). Item format included multiple-choice, short-answer, and extended-response formats. A more detailed description of the test development process is available from Wu (44) and Turner (45).

A primary objective of PISA was to report test scores "in terms of proficiency scales that are based on scientific theory, and that are interpretable in policy terms" (45). The reading proficiency scale was constructed in several steps. First, field experts identified possible subscales, based on the initial framework developed for assessing the domain of reading. The subscales considered were based on groupings of the five major "aspects" of reading (retrieving information, forming a broad understanding, developing an interpretation, reflecting on content, and reflecting on the form of a text). Next, each item on the test was assigned to a subscale, by consultation with field experts and through factor analyses of item scores from the field trial. This process resulted in the creation of three reading literacy subscales: *retrieving information, interpreting texts,* and *reflection and evaluation.*

Retrieving information is related primarily to the process of *locating,* in which the objective of the test items is to find and retrieve information in a text, based on the instructions provided by the items. The interpreting texts subscale contains items that assess a student's ability to identify a theme or main idea (at the simpler end), and to "understand relationships within the text that are an inherent part of its organization and meaning such as cause and effect, problem and solution, claim and evidence" and the like (at the more difficult end). At this latter end of the spectrum, tasks are generally of two types: those that require construing meaning given the context, and analogical reasoning that requires comparing, contrasting, or categorizing ideas. Finally, the reflection and evaluation subscale contains five related processes: *connecting,* or making a basic link between the text and outside knowledge; *explaining,* or giving reasons for the presence or purpose of information provided in the text; *comparing,* or finding similarities (or differences) between something in and something outside the text; *hypothesizing,* or offering explanations for text-based information that are based on the evidence presented, but go beyond it; and *evaluating,* or making judgments about the text (45).

The correlations between the subscales range from 0.89 (between retrieving information and reflection and evaluation) to 0.97 (between retrieving information and interpreting texts) (46). From these three subscales, a combined reading literacy scale was created, which is used in the present analysis. The combined scale has a minimum score of 0 and a maximum possible score of 800. The scale scores are divided into six levels of reading competency. Table 1 provides a description of the six levels and their respective cut-off points. The scale has a mean of 500 and a standard deviation (SD) of 100.

Measuring Socioeconomic Position

Mother's education, as opposed to father's education, income, or occupation, was used as a measure of SEP. Previous studies involving cross-national samples have found the comparability of education to be favorable, compared with other measures such as occupation (9). Income data were not available. In a review of studies from multiple nations, mother's education was found to have twice the influence of father's education on a variety of child health indicators, including infant mortality, child mortality, and nutritional status (47). Further, in a study of data pooled from three OECD nations (Germany, the United States, and the Netherlands), mother's education had a significant influence on children's educational attainment, net of father's educational status (48).

Data on mother's education were obtained from a questionnaire filled out by the children in the sample. Data on validation of students' reports of mother's education could not be located, nor could prior literature on children's reports of family SEP. However, given the age of the children (15 years), it is reasonable to assume a fairly high accuracy rate for their responses. Two questions were asked: (*a*) the level of education obtained by the mother—less than primary, primary, or secondary education; and (*b*) whether or not the mother had obtained tertiary education. Cases with an obvious inconsistency in responses to the two questions

Table 1

The combined reading literacy scale

Boundary	Cut-off point on PISA scale	Level	Distinguishing features of tasks at each level
		5	"The reader must: sequence or combine several pieces of deeply embedded information, possibly drawing on information from outside the main body of the text . . . make evaluative judgments or hypotheses . . . make inferences to determine which of the text is relevant, and to deal with . . . competing information."
Level 4/level 5	625.6	4	"The reader must: locate, sequence, or combine several pieces of embedded information; infer the meaning of a section of text by considering the text as a whole . . . hypothesize about or critically evaluate a text using formal or public knowledge . . . draw on an accurate understanding of long or complex text."
Level 3/level 4	552.9	3	"The reader must: recognize the links between pieces of information that have to meet multiple criteria; integrate several parts of a text to identify a main idea . . . make connections and comparisons . . . often the required information is not prominent but implicit in the text or obscured by similar information."
Level 2//level 3	480.2	2	"The reader must: locate one or more pieces of information that may be needed to meet multiple criteria; identify the main idea . . . make connections or comparisons between the text and everyday outside knowledge."
Level 1/level 2	407.5	1	"The reader must: locate one or more independent pieces of explicitly stated information according to a single criterion . . . make a simple connection between information in the text and common everyday knowledge . . . there is little, if any competing information."
Below level 1	334.8	Below level 1	"There is insufficient information to describe features of tasks at this level."

Source: Turner, 2002 (45). All quoted material is from this source.

(where a student responded that the mother had not been to primary school, or had only been to primary school, or had only been to secondary school, and also responded that the mother had received tertiary education) were excluded from the final sample.

Measuring Income Inequality

For all countries, income inequality was measured using the Gini coefficient, based on post-tax and post-transfer household income. Lower values equate to narrower income distributions. Data were primarily obtained from the Luxembourg Income Study (LIS) website. Since data were not available for every country for any one year, we chose a base year, 1994, as the year in which the most complete information was available. For countries with no data for 1994, the closest year possible was used (in most cases, between 1992 and 1996). For a few countries (Greece, Korea, New Zealand, and Spain), either data were not available from the LIS, or the year for which Gini coefficient data were available fell outside the range of the other countries in the sample. For these nations, we used figures for 1990 from the U.N. World Institute for Development Economics Research World Income Inequality Database.

Per Capita Gross Domestic Product as a Covariate

Per capita gross domestic product (GDP) was included as a covariate, to adjust for absolute differences in between-country wealth, thereby further isolating the effects of income inequality. We used data from 2000, in current international dollars and adjusted for purchasing power parity.

Data Analysis

To examine cross-national differences in socioeconomic gradients in reading literacy, a *relative index of inequality* (RII) score was derived for each country (9). The RII is preferable to an assessment of socioeconomic gradients based on raw data on education, because it enables the inclusion of all educational levels and can be used without regard to the number of available levels, provided that the educational categories are hierarchically arranged. The RII also captures only those differences in reading literacy that can be attributed to differences in the *hierarchical arrangement* of parental educational status, rather than all differences in reading literacy that are associated with parental educational status in absolute terms. So, by combining inequalities in levels of education, and the effects of mother's education on children's reading literacy, the index measures the total difference in reading literacy that can be attributed to inequality in mothers' education. Details of the full methodology are available from Kunst and coauthors (9). An abbreviated version is provided here; this was repeated for each country.

Step 1. The SEP of each educational group, relative to other educational groups, was determined. This variable (the *midpoint*) is calculated as the proportion with greater educational attainment. For example, in a country where the highest educational group comprises 10 percent of the population, the relative position of this group (its SEP) lies between 0 and 0.1, or 0.05 on average.

Step 2. The association between SEP and reading literacy was determined by random slopes regression analysis, which provides maximum likelihood parameter estimation, using an iterative generalized least-squares algorithm. This is a departure from previous work on the RII, as well as most other prior research on socioeconomic gradients in health, which generally employ ordinary least-squares regression techniques and analyze each country sample in separate models. In this study, the hypothesis suggests that there is a common factor that binds these countries—that they are advanced, capitalist nations. As such, the sample of children in each country can be conceptualized as being derived from an overall population of children in countries with similar characteristics. Based on this fact, before analysis, it is reasonable to expect similar parameter estimates for each child and each country.[2] This is often referred to as an assumption of exchangeability. Random slopes modeling allows a way to account for this assumption, by including the overall sample in a single model, from which country-specific estimates can be derived. In a random slopes model, the estimates obtained for each country are a function of both the country and the overall cross-country average. Therefore, there is a *shrinkage* of the estimates in random slopes modeling, such that they are pulled toward the mean estimate value (49).

A detailed explanation of the theoretical and mathematical basis for this modeling strategy can be obtained from Goldstein (50). Briefly, in a random slopes model, the slope of the relation between lower-level predictors (level 1) and the outcome is allowed to vary at a higher geographic level (level 2). In the present analysis, the value for the *midpoint* was allowed to vary at the country level, and thus country-specific RII scores could be obtained. The equation for the regression analysis is as follows:

$$Y_{ij} = \beta_0 X_{0ij} + \beta_1 X_{1ij} + \varepsilon_{0ij} + \mu_{0j} + \mu_{ij}$$

where:

Y_{ij} = reading literacy index score of child (i) in country (j)

β_0 = average reading literacy score across all countries when $X_{1ij} = 0$

---

[2] Though this is the theoretical case, as the earlier studies using ordinary least-squares regression have found between-country differences in slope estimates.

X_{0ij} = constant term
β_1 = average RII score across all countries
X_{1ij} = *midpoint*
ε_{0ij} = child-specific differential in reading score
μ_{0j} = country-specific differential in average reading score
μ_{1j} = country-specific differential in RII score

The regression coefficient (β_1) represents the average RII of all the countries in the analysis. Put differently, it is the average slope of the relation between reading literacy and SEP across the full sample of children, irrespective of country. Country-specific RII scores are obtained by adding (subtracting) the value of the slope differential (μ_{1j}) for each country. These RII scores then represent the *country-specific* magnitude of the difference in reading literacy associated with socioeconomic (i.e., educational) inequality in each country. Comparing the RII scores of different countries provides an indication of the relative influence of SEP between nations. For instance, a higher RII score indicates larger differences in reading literacy between children of mothers with primary schooling compared with children whose mothers attended university. In interpreting the RII, it is also important to recognize that the size of the socioeconomic inequality may be due to multiple factors: (*a*) inequalities in the educational attainment of mothers in each country; (*b*) differences in the level of schooling for a given maternal education level; or (*c*) the level of competence of a child, given maternal education level (notwithstanding years of schooling), which in turn could be due to the differential effects of a given amount of schooling or to differential levels of "developmental advantage" for a given level of maternal education.

Comparison of the country-specific RII scores provides a basis for descriptive assessment of factors operating at the national level, which might explain differences in the effect of SEP or reading literacy. However, it does not provide an empirical assessment of any such factors. Our analysis tests the influence of income inequality, one of the hallmark indicators of extent and type of welfare state provisions. To do so, the Gini coefficient of income inequality was added as a fixed effect to the model described above. The equation for the regression analysis is as follows:

$$Y_{ij} = \beta_0 X_{0ij} + \beta_1 X_{1ij} + \beta_2 X_{2j} + \beta_3 X_{3j} + \varepsilon_{0ij} + \mu_j + \mu_{ij}$$

where:
β_2 = the slope of the relation between reading literacy and income inequality
X_{2j} = the country-specific value of the Gini coefficient
X_{3j} = the country-specific value of per capita GDP

A significant decrease in the variance term (Ω_μ) would indicate that variation in RII scores can be attributed partly to cross-national differences in income inequality.

RESULTS

As Table 2 shows, sample size varied by country, though most nations accounted for between 2 and 4 percent of the sample. The countries with the lowest proportion of children in the sample were Luxembourg, accounting for 2.05 percent of the sample (n = 2,442), and the United States, accounting for 2.18 percent (n = 2,590). The United Kingdom had a slightly larger sample, with

Table 2

Sample size, average reading literacy score, and relative index of inequality score (RII) in 22 OECD nations

Country	n (%)	Average reading literacy score (SD)	RII score
Australia	4,748 (3.99)	532.42 (99.27)	80.54
Austria	4,057 (3.41)	515.65 (90.72)	67.18
Belgium	5,646 (4.75)	525.99 (98.02)	81.56
Canada	27,768 (23.34)	535.29 (94.46)	66.21
Czech Republic	5,248 (4.41)	481.65 (93.13)	116.78
Denmark	3,311 (2.78)	509.96 (92.14)	87.33
Finland	4,355 (3.66)	561.76 (87.68)	55.31
France	4,047 (3.40)	508.9 (89.20)	86.95
Germany	3,845 (3.23)	506.99 (95.17)	96.88
Greece	4,399 (3.70)	469.30 (96.22)	97.35
Ireland	3,593 (3.02)	541.43 (90.43)	62.45
Italy	4,771 (4.01)	500.10 (89.11)	69.15
Korea	4,859 (4.08)	540.16 (72.02)	45.54
Luxembourg	2,442 (2.05)	457.24 (99.25)	89.11
New Zealand	2,699 (2.27)	548.18 (100.15)	70.24
Norway	3,531 (2.97)	524.75 (100.46)	60.23
Portugal	4,262 (3.58)	474.04 (92.63)	104.47
Spain	5,502 (4.62)	500.08 (82.86)	82.89
Sweden	3,919 (3.29)	544.14 (89.39)	40.44
Switzerland	5,408 (4.55)	488.47 (96.11)	112.13
United Kingdom	7,967 (6.70)	534.02 (96.22)	81.88
United States	2,590 (2.18)	519.34 (99.49)	69.66
Total or average	118,966	514.54	78.38

7,967 children, accounting for 6.70 percent of the total sample. The largest proportion of the sample was made up of Canada, which had 27,768 children, or 23.34 percent.

The proportion of mothers with less than a primary school education was low in all countries, ranging from 0.32 percent (n = 14) in Finland, to a high of 3.25 percent (n = 136) in France. The average across the OECD nations was 1.84 percent (n = 2,467). The proportion of mothers with only a primary education varied much more, with an OECD average of 28.78 percent (n = 34,243). At 5.66 percent the Czech Republic had the lowest proportion (n = 298), and Portugal had the highest, with 71.81 percent (n = 3,121). There was also a considerable difference in the number of mothers with only a secondary school education, ranging from 13.53 percent (n = 588) in Portugal to 79.4 percent (n = 769) in the Czech Republic. The average across the OECD nations was 47.80 percent (n = 56,878). As expected, on average, the proportion of mothers with a tertiary education was lower than the proportion with a primary or secondary school education, though the average across nations was similar to that for primary education, 22.56 percent (n = 26,839). The country with the lowest proportion of college- or university-educated women was Switzerland, with 9.31 percent (n = 512); Canada had the highest proportion, with 47.24 percent (n = 13,272).

Table 2 provides a summary of the average reading literacy scores. The average OECD score was 514.54, with substantial variation among countries. The minimum average score was 457.24, for Luxembourg, and the maximum was 561.76, for Finland. Though there were exceptions, the nations falling in the top half tended to be clustered in northern and western Europe, and also included North America and the Pacific nations of Australia and New Zealand. Several western European nations fell in the bottom half (including Denmark, France, and Germany); however, their scores were very close to the OECD mean score.[3] The Mediterranean nations, as well as the central European nations, were grouped at the bottom of the distribution of averages.

Also shown in Table 2 are the RII scores for each nation. (Table 3 provides the full random slopes model for the fixed and overall random components.) Sweden had the lowest RII score of 40.44, indicating the smallest average difference in reading literacy between children of the lowest SEP and children of the highest SEP. The highest RII score belonged to the Czech Republic (116.78). The RII score across all of the OECD nations was 78.38. In general, the regional pattern of average reading literacy scores was maintained in the distribution of RII scores, with lower RII scores observed in northern and western Europe, and higher RII scores in southern and central Europe.

---

[3] The exception is Switzerland, with an average score (488.47) well below the OECD average.

Table 3

Results of multilevel regression analyses

Variables	Model 1 (null)	Model 2 (add midpoint)	Model 3 (add income inequality and GDP per capita)
Constant	506.40 (5.01)	463.44 (7.13)	487.92 (20.38)
Country-level:			
Midpoint		83.72 (4.92)	83.70 (4.92)
Income inequality			−0.80 (0.63)
GDP per capita			0.00 (0.01)
Variance parameters:			
Country-level (μ_{0j})	624.36 (177.06)	1,261.88 (359.86)	1,141.17 (325.22)
Country-level (μ_{1j})		573.13 (171.27)	572.54 (171.06)
Country-level covariance		−719.79 (229.15)	−677.08 (216.84)
Student-level	8,629.46 (33.77)	8,207.29 (32.12)	8,207.29 (32.12)

Figure 1 (depicting country-specific gradients), Table 4 (listing the rankings of averages and RII scores—higher ranks indicating higher average score and lower inequality), and Figure 2 (a scatter plot of the average reading literacy–RII score relation) provide strong support for the "flattening up" hypothesis, suggesting that, in fact, countries with higher average reading literacy scores tended to be those with a smaller degree of socioeconomic inequality. The correlation coefficient for the relationship is −0.77 (Figure 2). Supportive evidence comes from the rankings of countries such as Finland, Sweden, and Korea, which held the highest position (in the case of Finland) or relatively high positions with respect to average score, and had low levels of inequality based on their RII scores. Countries with mid-range averages also held similar ranks for RII scores (see Table 4); these included France, Belgium, Germany, and Italy. Nations with lower averages also tended to have the highest degree of inequality; these included Greece, Portugal, the Czech Republic, and Switzerland.

Table 5 shows the slope differentials for each country and their standard deviations. Five countries had significant slope differentials (Czech Republic, Finland, Korea, Sweden, and Switzerland) and 17 did not. This indicates that the RII scores of these five countries were significantly different from the average RII score across all countries. In practical terms, this measures whether the RII score of each country is significantly different from modal countries such as Belgium, Spain, and the United Kingdom. It is worth noting that this does not suggest the "lack" of a gradient in the remaining 17 nations—which could be the conclusion if the comparison was to a slope of zero rather than to the average slope.

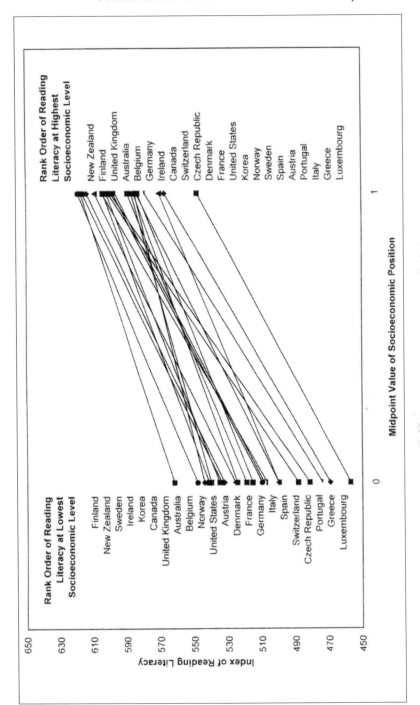

Figure 1. Socioeconomic gradients in children's reading literacy scores in 22 OECD nations.

Table 4

Country rankings for average reading literacy and relative index
of inequality (RII) scores

Average reading literacy score rank	Country	RII score rank	Country
1	Finland	1	Sweden
2	New Zealand	2	Korea
3	Sweden	3	Finland
4	Ireland	4	Norway
5	Korea	5	Ireland
6	Canada	6	Canada
7	United Kingdom	7	Austria
8	Australia	8	United States
9	Belgium	9	Italy
10	Norway	10	New Zealand
11	United States	11	Australia
12	Austria	12	United Kingdom
13	Denmark	13	Belgium
14	France	14	Spain
15	Germany	15	France
16	Italy	16	Denmark
17	Spain	17	Luxembourg
18	Switzerland	18	Germany
19	Czech Republic	19	Greece
20	Portugal	20	Portugal
21	Greece	21	Switzerland
22	Luxembourg	22	Czech Republic

Note: Higher ranking indicates larger average score and lower RII score (i.e., less socioeconomic inequality).

To understand this evidence in terms of the "flattening up" hypothesis, it is useful to examine the country positions along different points of the socioeconomic spectrum. In doing so, we can see that the differences in reading scores between countries are not equivalent at all points along the socioeconomic gradient. At the upper end of the SEP spectrum, the difference between the highest-scoring country (New Zealand, 618.90) and the lowest-scoring (Luxembourg, 548.00) is approximately 71 points. At the lower end of the SEP spectrum, the difference between the highest score (Finland, 561.76) and the lowest-score (Luxembourg, 457.24) is 105 points. Consistent with earlier findings that used other developmental outcomes, this suggests greater between-nation inequality in reading

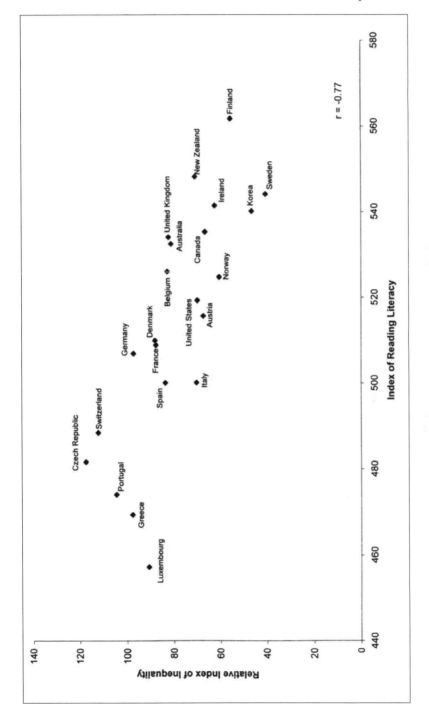

Figure 2. Relation between average reading literacy and relative index of inequality in 22 OECD nations.

Table 5

Random slope differentials and standard deviations (SD) for the relation between index of reading literacy and socioeconomic position

Country	Slope differential	SD
Australia	−2.66	13.1
Austria	−16.32	13.45
Belgium	−1.07	12.66
Canada	−16.96	10.32
Czech Republic	33.13	15.24*
Denmark	3.98	14.03
Finland	−28.56	13.23*
France	3.86	13.65
Germany	13.32	14.49
Greece	13.88	13.28
Ireland	−21.29	13.83
Italy	−13.44	13.27
Korea	−37.19	13.11*
Luxembourg	6.93	15.98
New Zealand	−12.77	15.44
Norway	−23.13	13.62
Portugal	20.67	14.72
Spain	−0.21	13.12
Sweden	−43.03	13.65*
Switzerland	28.51	12.83*
United Kingdom	−1.37	11.86
Unites States	−13.74	15.15

*Significant slope: slope differential ≥ 1.96 × SD. This corresponds to a slope differential significantly different from a differential of zero. In other words, it measures whether the total slope value (averages slope + country-specific slope differential) is significantly different from the average slope among the nations.

literacy scores at lower levels of SEP, compared with higher levels of SEP (20). Another consequence of this pattern is that average scores are driven by the extent of inequality between children of high and low SEP. The extent of inequality, in turn, is mitigated by improvements in the performance of low-SEP children, rather than reduction in the performance of high-SEP children. In other words, there is a "flattening up" of socioeconomic gradients.

Some notable exceptions are apparent. New Zealand is striking in this respect, with an average reading literacy score that ranked second (548.18) and an RII that ranked tenth (70.24). In other words, the data from New Zealand, contrary to the "flattening up" hypothesis, suggest that the average reading literacy score in this country is far higher than one would expect, given that socioeconomic inequality is also quite large. Similarly, the United Kingdom, Switzerland, and the Czech Republic also ranked substantially higher in their average reading literacy score than in their RII score.

There were also exceptions in the reverse direction. In contrast to Norway's rather mediocre average ranking of tenth on average reading literacy score (524.75), this nation moved up to fourth place in the RII rankings (60.23). Italy had a similarly large discrepancy between its low-ranking average reading literacy score (16th, at 500.10), and its higher RII score rank (9th, at 69.15). Such results suggest that these nations, although their average scores were not strong, had a relatively small difference in scores between children of lower SEP and children of higher SEP.

Finally, we tested the association of income inequality with differences in socioeconomic gradients (see Table 3). The results indicated that distribution of income within nations, as measured by the Gini coefficient (when modeled either independently or with per capita GDP), is not a significant predictor of variation in socioeconomic slopes across nations, Ω_μ before adding Gini, 573.13 (173.27); Ω_μ after adding Gini, 572.54 (171.06).

DISCUSSION

Some general themes emerge from the results of this study. First, in terms of both average reading literacy score and socioeconomic differences in reading literacy (based on the RII score), a clear regional pattern can be discerned. The nations of western Europe, North America, and the Pacific had the highest reading literacy scores and the greatest socioeconomic equality in reading scores, while the central and southern European countries lagged behind in their average scores and also had the greatest differentials in reading literacy between socioeconomic groups. Clustering of the central and southern European nations in the present study should be interpreted with caution, because this grouping includes countries with diverse historical foundations (e.g., Greece and the Czech Republic are both in this category). However, their common relative position in the hierarchy of countries is striking.

One of the major differences between the high-average literacy score, low-inequality nations and their low-average, high-inequality counterparts is the length of time that they have had established welfare state regimes and related political institutions. This is not to say that it is the historical time frame that is of greatest significance, but rather to point out that for some countries there has been a long and *gradual* implementation of capitalism and political transformation, while in the poor-performing regions, the introduction of markets was much more abrupt—though there are within-region variations in this respect. Prior work on eastern European nations is instructive in this regard.

In a rather extreme case, Poland implemented many of its market-related institutions as the result of "shock therapy" reforms (51). In this country, as well as several others in central and eastern Europe (e.g., Czech Republic), during the period of transition from communism to capitalist-democracies, the distribution of income markedly widened. Further, the prevailing social order of mutual obligation between the individual and the state that had existed under a communist regime was dismantled by the rapid evolution of market-based transactions, in which the poorest and most vulnerable members of society had neither the protection of the state, which no longer felt responsibility toward them, nor the means to compete for resources under the new system (52, 53). These circumstances have conspired to produce economic and social insecurity for families, which can greatly affect familial relations and the ability to provide effective parenting. Further, the surrounding environment and institutions are profoundly affected by such sudden changes. All of these factors have a powerful influence on children's developmental health (13).

Another observation that arises from our findings is that for reading literacy, there is strong support for the "flattening up" hypothesis among the long-standing welfare state regimes. That is to say, our results confirm that nations (e.g., Finland, Sweden, and Korea) with the highest average reading literacy scores also had the greatest equality of scores between lower and higher SEP.

If one compares the nations with high average scores and high socioeconomic equality with a country such as the United States, which (compared with other long-standing welfare states) has both a low reading literacy average and low levels of equality, one finds a systematic variation in the type and extent of welfare state regime. The use of market forces in the distribution of resources (such as education and health care) that are fundamental to children's well-being is much stronger (a phenomenon sometimes referred to as "neoliberalism") in the United States than in the high-average literacy, high-equality nations. In the United States, these goods are largely tied to employment and housing markets, whereas among the high performers they are considered rights of citizenship and thus their distribution is not left to the invisible hand of the market, but rather is orchestrated by state and federal governments (39).

Egalitarian provision of social goods (as well as provision of income subsidies) implies, indeed necessitates, the transfer of income from wealthier members of society to people at the poorer end of the socioeconomic spectrum. Past literature shows, in fact, that the strongest association of income inequality with health is seen for children's outcomes (54). It is thus curious that the results of our study indicate no significant effect of income inequality on socioeconomic gradients. There are several possible explanations for this apparent discrepancy. Prior studies have focused on the effects of distribution of income on average health outcomes, rather than socioeconomic inequality in health outcomes. And as Lynch and colleagues (54) point out, the effects of income inequality may be outcome-sensitive; the studies that have found associations include those based on mortality and morbidity outcomes, rather than on developmental outcomes (37, 55–57).

There are several other reasons that might explain the apparent lack of association. The first has to do with the comparability of data across countries and time points. Though every effort was taken to ensure that Gini coefficients were based on the same definition of income, there may be variations that were unaccounted for. Second, it is possible that inequality in the distribution of household income is not as important as the distribution of income at other levels of societal aggregation, such as the neighborhood or municipality. This null finding notwithstanding, the present results suggest that providing resources to people at the lower end of the socioeconomic spectrum does not weaken the outcomes of the subsidizers (33). Put differently, there seem to be diminishing marginal returns of parental SEP to children's development (35).

The discussion turns now to the nations that do not conform to the "flattening up" pattern. Based on the data, it seems that, compared with neoliberal economies such as New Zealand and the United Kingdom, Norway (a high-equality country) produces stronger or similar scores for children of lower SEP. However, its average is pulled below those of the neoliberal countries as a result of worse performance among children of higher SEP. What might be some reasons for the better performance of children of wealthier families in societies with stronger market penetration? Why would the developmental health outcomes of wealthier children in the United Kingdom be better than those of wealthier children in Norway? It is possible that, in these nations, the benefits of cross-subsidization that accrue to children of lower SEP are offset by losses to children of higher SEP. However, some other explanations must also be considered.

One strong possibility relates to differences in the environment to which children of lower and higher SEP are exposed in different nations. For instance, levels of economic-based residential segregation in the United Kingdom are quite high (58). As a result, exposures to factors that adversely affect developmental health—such as poverty, unemployment, unsafe neighborhoods, and the like—are concentrated among children of lower-income strata. Conversely, children of higher SEP are more likely to live around others such as themselves and are more insulated from these exposures. These spatial divisions, and concomitant difference in exposures, are less likely to occur in more egalitarian societies, which tend to be less segregated. Therefore, in nations such as Norway, children's exposures to determinants of developmental health (both those that are helpful and those that are harmful) are more equally distributed among socioeconomic groups. In countries such as the United Kingdom, however, rich and poor children have differential exposure to these determinants, with helpful factors concentrated among richer children and harmful ones among children of poorer families.

Another explanation, arising from observations made in earlier research, suggests the potential for selection bias in the PISA study and other national and international research on children's developmental health. Among the advanced capitalist societies, there seems to be a systematic variation in school completion rates, such that in more neoliberal economies such as the United Kingdom, completion of lower and upper secondary schooling lags behind that in the more egalitarian countries (59). Further, within nations, evidence has begun to surface that students from poorer families are more likely to have left school or to have a much weaker attachment to school. Evidence from Winnipeg, Canada, found a marked underestimation in the steepness of the socioeconomic gradient among children who took a standardized language arts test, compared with those who should have taken the test.[4] This difference is due to a commensurate socioeconomic gradient of children who did not take the test, due to factors such as absence, being excused from the test, or being lost in the school system (e.g., due to transiency) (60). These data were for children in grade 3, and, intuitively, one can imagine that the gradients in school-leaving will increase for older children, though this latter proposition deserves formal testing.

There are several limitations to the present study. Although the methodology provides a useful comparative approach, within-nation specificity may be sacrificed in the process (39). In other words, to facilitate comparisons, this approach favors broad generalizations about the welfare state institutions of countries. However, the degree of allocation of social goods by market forces versus legislated universal access may vary greatly by sector. For example, in the United States, though their quality may be unequal, primary and secondary schooling are provided as a universal right of citizenship. By contrast, no such provision is made for health care. Many factors contribute to the disparities in governmental commitment to these two sectors, including a long history of political and legislative battles (e.g., the difficulties encountered in incorporating universal health care into President Johnson's War on Poverty). This example suggests that to understand welfare state institutions and their effects on health more fully, further research should also consider a detailed, historical, case-study approach, in addition to quantitative methodologies. In addition, our ability to generalize the study results to each country is conditioned by the size (and thus representativeness) of the sample for each. The United States, for example, had a small sample size relative to its total population. Despite the study's sampling strategy, providing adequate representation with so few children is difficult. With these caveats, however, it seems that countries with high average reading literacy scores also have greater levels of equality. These nations are marked by stronger welfare provisions and less market penetration in the distribution of social goods.

---

[4] The children who "should have" taken the test were scored by linking their medical plan numbers to their neighborhoods, and then to the school test average for their income quartile (C. Hertzman, personal communication, September 13, 2004).

REFERENCES

1. Antonovsky, A. Social class, life expectancy and overall mortality. *Milbank Mem. Fund Q.* 44:31–73, 1967.
2. Marmot, M. G., Kogevinas, M., and Elston, M. A. Social/economic status and disease. *Ann. Rev. Public Health* 8:111–135, 1987.
3. Vagero, D., and Lundberg, O. Health inequalities in Britain and Sweden. *Lancet* 2:35–36, 1989.
4. Marmot, M. G., et al. Health inequalities among British civil servants: The Whitehall II study. *Lancet* 337:1387–1393, 1991.
5. Kunst, A. E., and Mackenbach, J. P. The size of mortality differences associated with educational level in nine industrialized countries. *Am. J. Public Health* 84:932–937, 1994.
6. Kunst, A. E., and Mackenbach, J. P. International variation in the size of mortality differences associated with occupational status. *Int. J. Epidemiol.* 23:742–750, 1994.
7. Lahelma, E., et al. A comparison of inequalities in health: Evidence from national surveys in Finland, Norway, and Sweden. *Soc. Sci. Med.* 38:517–524, 1994.
8. Adler, N. E., et al. Socioeconomic status and health: The challenge of the gradient. *Am. Psychologist* 49(1):15–24, 1994.
9. Kunst, A. E., Geurts, J. J. M., and van den Berg, J. International variation in socio-economic inequalities in self reported health. *J. Epidemiol. Community Health* 49:117–123, 1995.
10. Kunst, A. E., et al., and the E.U. Working Group on Socioeconomic Inequalities in Health. Occupational class and cause specific mortality in middle aged men in 11 European countries: Comparison of population based studies. *BMJ* 316:1636–1641, 1998.
11. Mackenbach, J. P., et al., and the E. U. Working Group on Socioeconomic Inequalities in Health. Socioeconomic inequalities in cardiovascular disease mortality. *Eur. Heart J.* 21:1141–1151, 2000.
12. Marmot, M. G. Understanding social inequalities in health. *Perspect. Biol. Med.* 46(3):S9–S23, 2003.
13. Hertzman, C., and Power, C. Health and human development: Understandings from life-course research. *Dev. Neuropsychol.* 24:719–744, 2003.
14. Brooks-Gunn, J., Duncan, G. J., and Maritato, N. Poor families, poor outcomes: The well-being of children and youth. In *Consequences of Growing Up Poor*, ed. G. J. Duncan and J. Brooks-Gunn. Russell Sage Foundation, New York, 1997.
15. Bradley, R. H., and Corwyn, R. F. Socioeconomic status and child development. *Ann. Rev. Psychol.* 53:371–399, 2002.
16. DiPietro, J. A., et al. Effects of socioeconomic status and psychosocial stress on the development of the fetus. *Ann. N. Y. Acad. Sci.* 896:356–358, 1999.
17. White, K. R. The relation between socioeconomic status and academic achievement. *Psychol. Bull.* 91:461–481, 1982.
18. Heath, A. Class inequalities in education in the twentieth century. *J. R. Stat. Soc. Ser. A* 153(1):1–16, 1990.
19. Raudenbush, S., and Kasim, R. Cognitive skill and economic inequality: Findings from the National Adult Literacy Survey. *Harvard Educ. Rev.* 68:33–79, 1998.
20. Willms, J. D. Quality and inequality in children's literacy: The effects of families, schools, and communities. In *Developmental Health and the Wealth of Nations:*

Social, Biological, and Educational Dynamics, ed. D. P. Keating and C. Hertzman. Guilford Press, New York, 1999.

21. Subramanian, S. V., Belli, P., and Kawachi, I. The macroeconomic determinants of health. *Ann. Rev. Public Health* 23:287–302, 2002.
22. Rawls, J. *A Theory of Justice.* Harvard University Press, Cambridge, 1971.
23. Sen, A. *Commodities and Capabilities.* Oxford University Press, New York, 1999.
24. Sen, A. *Inequality Reexamined.* Harvard University Press, Cambridge, 1992,
25. Josephson, J. J. 2001. Liberal justice and the political economy of children's well-being. *New Polit. Sci.* 23:389–406, 2001.
26. Kuh, D., and Ben-Shlomo, Y. *A Life Course Approach to Chronic Disease Epidemiology,* Ed. 2. Oxford University Press, Oxford, 2004.
27. National Research Council and Institute of Medicine. *From Neurons to Neighborhoods: The Science of Early Childhood Development.* Committee on Integrating the Science of Early Childhood Development, Board on Children, Youth, and Families, Commission on Behavioral and Social Sciences and Education. National Academy Press, Washington, DC, 2000.
28. Duncan, G. J., and Brooks-Gunn, J. (eds.). *Consequences of Growing Up Poor.* Russell Sage Foundation, New York, 1997.
29. Eccles, J. S., and Roeser, R. W. Schools as developmental contexts. In *Blackwell Handbook of Adolescence,* ed. G. R. Adams and M. D. Berzonsky. Blackwell, Malden, MA, 2003.
30. Orr, A. J. Black-white differences in achievement: The importance of wealth. *Sociol. Educ.* 76:281–302, 2003.
31. Leventhal, T., and Brooks-Gunn, J. The neighborhoods they live in: The effects of neighborhood residence on child and adolescent outcomes. *Psychol. Bull.* 126: 309–337, 2000.
32. Kohen, D. E., et al. Neighbourhood income and physical and social disorder in Canada: Associations with young children's competencies. *Child Dev.* 73:1844–1860, 2002.
33. Hertzman, C. Health and human society. *American Scientist* 89:538–545, 2001.
34. Mackenbach, J. P., et al., and the E.U. Working Group on Socioeconomic Inequalities in Health. Socioeconomic inequalities in morbidity and mortality in western Europe. *Lancet* 349:1655–1659, 1997.
35. Willms, D. *Ten Hypotheses about Socioeconomic Gradients and Community Differences in Children's Developmental Outcomes.* Report no. SP-560-01-03E. Human Resources Development Canada, Toronto, 2003.
36. Navarro, V., et al. The importance of the political and the social in explaining mortality differentials among the countries of the OECD, 1950–1998. In *The Political and Social Contexts of Health,* ed. V. Navarro. Baywood, Amityville, NY, 2004.
37. Macinko, J. A., Shi, L., and Starfield, B. Wage inequality, the health system, and infant mortality in wealthy industrialized countries, 1970–1996. *Soc. Sci. Med.* 58:279–292, 2004.
38. Muntaner, C., et al. Economic inequality, working-class power, social capital, and cause-specific mortality in wealthy countries. *Int. J. Health Serv.* 32:629–656, 2002.
39. Esping-Andersen, G. *The Three Worlds of Welfare Capitalism.* Princeton University Press, Princeton, NJ, 1990.
40. Adams, R. Scaling PISA cognitive data. In *PISA 2000 Technical Report,* ed. R. Adams and M. Wu. OECD, Paris, 2002.

41. Goldstein, H. International comparisons of student attainment: Some issues arising from the PISA study. *Assess. Educ. Principles Policy Pract.* 11:319–330, 2004.
42. Keating, D. P., and Hertzman, C. Modernity's paradox. In *Developmental Health and the Wealth of Nations: Social, Biological, and Educational Dynamics*, ed. D. P. Keating and C. Hertzman. Guilford Press, New York, 1999.
43. Richards, M., and Wadsworth, M. E. Long term effects of early adversity on cognitive function. *Arch. Dis. Child.* 89:922–927, 2004.
44. Wu, M. Test design and test development. In *PISA 2000 Technical Report,* ed. R. Adams and M. Wu. OECD, Paris, 2002.
45. Turner, R. Proficiency scales and construction. In *PISA 2000 Technical Report,* ed. R. Adams and M. Wu. OECD, Paris, 2002.
46. Adams, R., and Carstensen, C. Scaling outcomes. In *PISA 2000 Technical Report,* ed. R. Adams and M. Wu. OECD, Paris, 2002.
47. Cochrane, S. H., Leslie, J., and O'Hara, D. J. Parental education and child health: Intracountry evidence. *Health Policy Educ.* 2:213–250, 1982.
48. Korupp, S. E., Ganzeboom, H. B. G., and Van Der Lippe, T. Do mothers matter? A comparison of models of the influence of mothers' and fathers' educational and occupational status on children's educational attainment. *Quality and Quantity* 36(1):17–42, 2002.
49. Greenland, S. Principles of multilevel modelling. *Int. J. Epidemiol.* 29:158–167, 2000.
50. Goldstein, H. *Kendall's Library of Statistics 2: Multilevel Statistical Models,* Ed. 3. Arnold, London, 2003.
51. Sachs, J. D. Russia's struggle with stabilization: Conceptual issues and evidence. In *Proceedings of the World Bank Annual Conference on Development Economics.* World Bank, Washington, DC, 1994.
52. Hertzman, C., and Siddiqi, A. Health and rapid economic change in the late twentieth century. *Soc. Sci. Med.* 51:809–819, 2000.
53. Hertzman, C., Siddiqi, A., and Bobak, M. The population health context for gender, stress, and cardiovascular disease in central and eastern Europe. In *Heart Disease: Environment. Stress and Gender,* ed. G. Weidner et al. IOS Press, Amsterdam, 2002.
54. Lynch, J., et al. Is income inequality a determinant of population health? Part 1: A systematic review. *Milbank Q.* 82:5–99, 2004.
55. Chiang, T. L. Economic transition and changing relation between income inequality and mortality in Taiwan: Regression analysis. *BMJ* 319:1162–1165, 1999.
56. Lobmayer, P., and Wilkinson, R. Income inequality and mortality in 14 developed countries. *Sociol. Health Illness* 22:401–414, 2000.
57. Lynch, J., et al. Income inequality, the psychosocial environment, and health: Comparisons of wealthy nations. *Lancet* 358:194–200, 2001.
58. Byrne, D. Deindustrialisation and dispossession: An examination of social division in the industrial city. *Sociology* 29:95–115, 1995.
59. Organization for Economic Cooperation and Development. *Education at a Glance.* Paris, 2004.
60. Manitoba Centre for Health Policy. *Manitoba Child Health Atlas.* Winnipeg, 2004.

CHAPTER 17

Gender Policy Developments and Policy Regimes in 22 OECD Countries, 1979–2008

Mona C. Backhans, Bo Burström,
and Staffan Marklund

This study investigates trends and clustering of gender policy in 22 OECD (Organization for Economic Cooperation and Development) countries during 1979–2008. The starting point was Sainsbury's gender policy regime framework, and the study included indicators reflecting the male breadwinner, individual earner-carer, and separate gender roles regimes. The indicators were followed over seven time points for mean, range, and distribution. Cluster analyses were performed for the years 1979, 1989, 1999, and 2004. In accordance with previous studies, the authors found a Nordic cluster of earner-carer countries, while several Southern European countries and the United States were marked by their low generosity and high pension requirements. Though aspects of the separate gender roles regime have become more widespread, no country could be classified as fully belonging to this regime type. The two aspects of the model—compensatory measures in the pension system, and benefits for caring activities—were never present simultaneously.

*****

INTRODUCTION

This study investigates gender policy developments in OECD (Organization for Economic Cooperation and Development) countries over time, within a "gender policy regimes" framework. The gender-focused typologies first emerged as a response to Esping-Andersen's welfare regime typology (1), and have become highly influential in welfare research. They emphasize the importance of achieving commodification (access to paid work and to services that facilitate employment) as a prerequisite for decommodification (relative economic autonomy from the market). Research within this framework has investigated the degree of individualization of social rights and stratification based on gender, with a focus on the sexual division of labor (2–6).

Our study was primarily based on Sainsbury's gender policy regimes framework (5, 7, 8). One advantage of her model is that it is a pure policy typology; it does not mix policy and possible outcomes. It is an alternative to rather than an extension of Esping-Andersen's welfare regime typology and thus allows an examination of the interaction between gender policy and mainstream welfare state dimensions. Moreover, Sainsbury has proposed emerging aspects of a separate gender policy model, representing a "different but equal" strategy— policies that we were eager to explore.

Gender Policy and Gender Regimes

Esping-Andersen's original approach focused on three salient characteristics of welfare states: social rights in terms of their capacity for decommodification, the redistributive effect of welfare states, and state-market relations in welfare production and distribution (1). His theoretical framework and the resulting three-world typology, while highly influential, have been criticized for the number of countries studied, the clustering of countries, the dimensions included, and the method of analysis (9–16). Early feminist critiques remarked that the welfare regime approach lacked a gender dimension: that decommodification for women is likely to lead to unpaid work, that gender should be incorporated as a form of social stratification, and that the crucial relationship for women is that between paid work, unpaid work, and welfare (2, 5). Esping-Andersen, in response to this critique, has incorporated the family as welfare producer and examined the degree of "defamilization": how much of social services is produced within the family (17). In his more recent writings there has been a clear shift from the gender-blind to the gender-sensitive (18). The main thrust of his welfare typology, however, is unchanged, with a focus on class-based inequalities.

Lewis (2, 19; see also 20) was among the first to criticize Esping-Andersen from a gender perspective, and her ideas have been highly influential. She makes a distinction between strong, modified, and weak breadwinner states and emphasizes the gendered relationship between paid work, unpaid work, and welfare. Lewis has studied labor market position, social security and tax position, and provision of childcare, and her typology rests on measures of both policy and outcome (Figure 1). Both O'Connor and Orloff have added gender relations to Esping-Andersen's typology (3, 4, 21, 22). One key aspect is an expansion of the term "decommodification" to "personal autonomy" or "the capacity to form an autonomous household." Another important dimension is the significance of political, civil, and social rights, including reproductive "body rights" and a broadening of the political to include social movements, client representative groups, and the exercise of power through "femocrats" (23, 24). Korpi (6) has investigated gendered policy institutions, with a focus on the degree to which policies support women's labor force participation, as participation in the labor

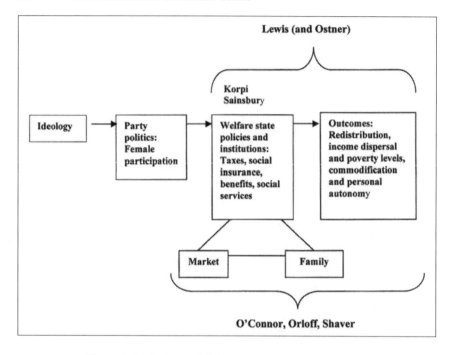

Figure 1. Main focus of different gender regime typologies.

force both forms the basis for material inequality and is likely to affect a person's self-perception, identity, and bargaining position within the family. He distinguishes between countries characterized by dual-earner support, where the welfare state encourages women's labor force participation and the redistribution of care work, and countries characterized by general family support, which encompasses both more neutral family support *and* support for the traditional male-breadwinner model. A third type of welfare state (market-oriented) is characterized by a lack of any kind of support.

Sainsbury defines the concept of gender policy regime as "a given organization of gender relations associated with a policy logic . . . ideologies that describe actual or preferred relations between women and men, principles of entitlement, and policy construction" (8). Distinguishing the different regimes is whether rights are attached to the individual or based on family relationships and marital status, the scope of state responsibility for caring tasks, degree of equality of access to paid work, and degree of gender differentiation in entitlements.

Sainsbury originally proposed two ideal types: the *male breadwinner* and the *individual earner-carer* (hereafter abbreviated to *earner-carer*) regimes (5). The male breadwinner regime is characterized by a gender ideology of male privilege based on a gendered division of labor (Table 1). As family providers, men have entitlements that stem from the principle of maintenance. Women receive derived rights as wives and are obliged to care for husband and children through unpaid work. In the earner-carer regime, the preferred relations between women and men are shared roles and obligations, leading to equal rights; there is strong state involvement in the care of children, the sick, and the elderly through services that facilitate employment for all, while temporary caring activities are remunerated. In later writings, Sainsbury (8) claimed that the policies of specific countries were moving toward a separate gender roles regime, with social rights attached to the role as either male family provider or female caregiver. Korpi's and Sainsbury's models are rather similar, the main difference being Sainsbury's addition of the separate gender roles model, and Korpi's conflation of general family support with support directed at the male breadwinner.

Some later feminist writings on the welfare state have criticized these attempts and have suggested an expansion of institutions and aspects to be studied. Shaver (25), for example, called attention to important but neglected domains of welfare state activity such as child welfare policies, women's shelters, crime and public safety, education, and health care. Others have argued against the "working mother" as the privileged subject of gendered welfare state studies (26). There are also other types of typologies, emphasizing the importance of cultural norms in explaining a particular society's "gender arrangements" (27, 28). Although Sainsbury explicitly incorporates gender ideology (clearly a cultural concept) in her framework, it is not measured but rather seen as a political basis for the current regime type.

Previous Empirical Studies

Esping-Andersen's framework has been expanded and adjusted (9–12, 14), as well as explicitly tested (15, 29), but this has been less pronounced in the gender regime literature, which tends to deal with a limited number of countries in the form of case studies (7, 22, 30–34). Here we include only studies comparable to the present one, with a larger sample and quantitative analyses.

Gornick and colleagues (35) used LIS (Luxembourg Income Study) data to classify 14 OECD countries according to level of employment-supporting policies for mothers. They investigated childcare, parental leave, and school schedules in 1984–1987. The study found different clusters depending on the index used, but the top performers (Denmark, Sweden, Belgium, France) and bottom performers (Australia, United Kingdom, United States) were the same across indices. Anttonen and Sipilä (36) examined social care services (measured as uptake of services) in the mid-1980s in 14 European countries and found two extreme groups of either abundant (Scandinavian, excluding Norway) or scarce (Southern European) social services and two with different profiles, with services directed either to the elderly (most evident in the Netherlands) or to children (Belgium, France).

Table 1

Sainsbury's gender policy regimes

	Male breadwinner	Separate gender roles	Individual earner-carer
Ideology	Male privilege	Different but equal	Shared roles and obligations
Ideology	Strict division of labor Husband = earner Wife = carer	Strict division of labor Husband = earner Wife = carer	Father = earner-carer Mother = earner-carer
Entitlement	Unequal among spouses	Differentiated by gender role	Equal
Basis of entitlement	Breadwinner/dependent	Maintenance or care	Earner/carer/citizen
Recipient of benefits	Head of household Supplements for dependents	Men as family providers Women as caregivers	Individual
Taxation	Joint taxation Deductions for dependents	Joint taxation Deductions for dependents for both spouses	Separate taxation Equal tax relief (if any)
Employment and wage policies	Priority to men	Priority to men	Aimed at both sexes
Sphere of care	Primarily private	Primarily private	Strong state involvement
Caring work	Unpaid	Paid component to caregivers in the home	Paid component to caregivers in and outside the home

Source: Sainsbury (8, p. 78).

Bettio and Plantenga (37) mixed practice and policy data in an investigation of informal and formal care arrangements in E.U. countries around 1995. Their analysis resulted in five groups of countries, again with the Nordic cluster at one end and the Southern European countries at the other. The three middle clusters consisted of only two countries each, and they differed in how well they catered to carers when it came to time off, financial provisions, and services.

Korpi (6) classified countries by using indicators from 1985–1990 on child allowances, family tax benefits, day care, parental leave, and services directed to the elderly. All Nordic countries were classified as dual-earner support, the English-speaking countries, with the exception of Ireland and with the inclusion of Switzerland and Japan, as market-oriented, and the rest as having a general family support model. Ferrarini (38) studied parental leave generosity during the child's first year in 18 OECD countries between 1950 and 2000 within Korpi's framework. His analysis mainly supported Korpi's classification of countries, although he also found a movement toward a "contradictory" family policy model in some countries with both dual-earner and general family support. Here, Ferrarini mentioned several Nordic countries, Austria, France, Belgium, and Canada. He also found that, over time, parental leave generosity, while expanding in most countries, has become more divergent as the increased generosity in dual-earner countries clearly exceeded that of the other models.

Bambra (39) investigated an index of defamilization (measured as female/male labor force participation rate, gender wage gap, and maternity leave compensation and duration) against an index of decommodification for 18 OECD countries in 1997. Using the same method as in Esping-Andersen's original work,[1] the study found that four countries moved from one group to another, depending on what index was used: as three of these countries are liberal, this meant that half of the liberal countries changed groups—Canada, Ireland, and the United Kingdom joined the medium performers. In a later study using hierarchical cluster analysis, Bambra (40) found five clusters based on the same defamilization indicators, except for relative wage. The five-cluster solution consisted of one large cluster of mainly European continental countries, three clusters of just two countries apiece (Norway and Sweden, Australia and the United States, Italy and Japan), and one cluster of three (Canada, Finland, and the United Kingdom). Several countries were set aside as "unclear cases."

Thus far, most studies have investigated social services and parental leave, and few have looked at male breadwinner support or policies that support carers in the home; this calls for inclusion of such factors. Further, though country clustering is always dependent on the indicators used, certain top and bottom performers can be discerned. No study has investigated clustering over time.

---

[1] This method always results in three clusters.

Aim and Research Questions

The aim of this study is to investigate country clustering over time within a "gender policy regimes" framework. More specifically, we wish to answer the following questions: Can the 22 countries included in the study be classified into male breadwinner, earner-carer, and separate gender roles regimes? And how stable is the clustering of countries over time? Underlying our interest is a concern for developing knowledge for research that looks into the long-term effects of gender policy on the health of the population (41).

MATERIAL AND METHODS

Data Sources

Our study used material collected for 22 OECD countries in 1979–2008. The main data source was the International Social Security Association's publication *Social Security Programs Throughout the World* (SSPTW), with information on pensions, disability and sickness, maternity, unemployment, and family allowances. For data on social services (1980–2005), we used the OECD's Social Expenditure Database. Information on the marriage subsidy was taken from the Social Citizenship Indicator Program (SCIP) database. These data were complemented by the OECD's *Taxing Wages* (42) for countries that were not included in SCIP and for the most recent time points (2005 and 2008).

For parental leave, additional sources were Moss and Deven (43) and Moss and Korintus (44), and for pension rights, Gilbert (45) and Leitner (46). For the Nordic countries, SSPTW was complemented with information from the Nordic Social Statistical Committee's (NOSOSCO) publication *Social Protection in the Nordic Countries.* From 1998 onward, we also used data from the Mutual Information System on Social Protection in the Member States of the European Union (MISSOC). When publications differed, NOSOSCO and MISSOC were preferred because they are more detailed and closer to the sources. We also retrieved additional information directly from specific countries: on parental leave for Portugal (47), on extended leave for Spain (48) and Austria (49), on both parental and extended leave for Germany (50) and Denmark (51), on pension child credits for Germany (52, 53), Spain (48), Austria (54–56), and France (57), and on pension requirements for Belgium (58) and France (57).

Indicators and Measurements

The indicators included in the study were parental leave, social services in kind, taxes, social insurance, pensions, and benefits for caring, to reflect all three policy regimes in Sainsbury's framework (Table 2).

Table 2

Gender policy regimes and policy indicators

Gender policy regime	Logic	Outcome	Indicator	Measurement
Earner-carer	Gender equality friendly	Personal autonomy	Generous parental leave (to mother and father)	1. Maternity score (weeks * replacement rate)
				2. Reserved and paid paternity leave (weeks)
			High access to social services	3. Benefits in kind to families and in old age (expenditure as % of GDP)
			Separate taxation	4. Individuals taxed separately (yes/no)
Male breadwinner	Supports gender asymmetry	Dependency within the family	High monetary support to breadwinner	5. Marriage subsidy (% of couple's take-home pay)
				6. Dependent wife supplement (0–5)
			Pensions strictly tied to contributions	7. Minimum pension requirement (years)
				8. Maximum pension requirement (years)
Separate gender roles	Supports gender dichotomy	Sex segregation	Gendered compensatory measures in pension system	9. Retirement age gender gap (years)
				10. Child care credits (years for two children)
			Paid component to caregiver in the home	11. Extended leave score (weeks * replacement rate)
				12. Benefits for caring (replacement rate)

Parental Leave. An optimal maternity leave in the earner-carer model combines a high replacement rate with a maternity leave period that is adequate yet does not lead to discrimination against women (due to the anticipation of prolonged absences) (59). A *maternity score* was constructed based on duration in weeks multiplied by the replacement rate of an average production worker (APW) (see Table 2). A leave of 52 weeks at 100 percent replacement rate gives a score of 52. All calculations were based on a family with two children.

For fathers, even when part of the leave can be shared between parents, take-up has been low everywhere unless leave is paid and explicitly reserved for the father (44). Reserved and paid *paternity leave* was measured in number of weeks. This type of policy is indicative of the earner-carer model.

Social Services. High social services expenditure is indicative of the earner-carer model and constitutes both an incentive and an opportunity for paid work (60). Data on *social services* were limited to expenditure on social benefits in kind for families and in old age, measured as percentage of GDP (gross domestic product).

Taxation. For married couples, *taxation* can be either separate or joint (or optional; tax systems tend to favor the joint alternative). With joint taxation, the spouses' income is pooled, which puts a tax penalty on the second income, given a proportional tax system. Separate taxation is indicative of the earner-carer model, and joint taxation of the male breadwinner model. The indicator was dichotomous, with 1 indicating separate taxation.

Many tax systems have tax allowances or tax credits directed at a sole earner/head of household. This so-called *marriage subsidy* is indicative of the male breadwinner model. The data were taken from the SCIP database and coded as the difference in take-home pay between a couple without children (calculated as family take-home pay minus child allowances) and a single-person household (measured as percentage of couple take-home pay). The indicator runs from 1970 every fifth year until 2000. For 2005 and 2008, the same indicator was constructed based on the OECD's *Taxing Wages.*[2]

Social Insurance Supplement. As an indicator of the male breadwinner regime, the consistency of *dependent wife supplements* for different social insurance benefits (old age pension, disability pension, sickness, work injury, and unemployment)

---

[2] For some countries, where differences in average tax rates between those with and without children are large, the calculation led to results far from those in SCIP 2000. An alternative calculation was to deduct the tax rate for a couple without children from APW to construct couples' take-home pay. Couples with and without children, regrettably, are not completely comparable in the OECD's *Taxing Wages*, as those with children are single earner families and couples without children have two earners, with the second earner at 33 percent of APW; this calculation is an approximation only.

was included. For a few countries, the supplement is included as a special family supplement outside these systems. The indicator was measured as a discrete variable (0–5).

Pensions. Pension systems with universal pension rights support the earner-carer model, while those that have *minimum pension requirements* of long duration support the male breadwinner model. Systems with long *maximum pension requirements* are also likely to lead to gender differences in pension rights, thus supporting the male breadwinner model, given the different labor market attachment. When this period differed for men and women, the indicator refers to the value for women. When "all years count," 45 years was considered a reasonable score. Where the pension was based on residency rather than contributions, both indicators were set to zero.

Rules that differentiate retirement age for men and women can be seen as a compensation for women by making allowances for their lower labor market attachment. A wide *retirement age gender gap* has also been defended by women's movements (61) and supports a separate gender roles model, especially if combined with low maximum pension requirements for women and with pension *child credits* for periods of caring. Child credits were measured as number of years credited for two children. All pension indicators refer to the years that new policies were introduced.

Benefits for Caring in the Home. Extended childcare leave after the end of maternity leave can support a separate gender roles model, but for this to be true, the replacement rate has to be reasonably high. However, extended leaves tend to have much lower benefit levels than maternity benefits. The indicator *extended leave score* was measured as weeks multiplied by replacement rate.

Benefits for caregiving, apart from childcare leave, could not generally be included as an indicator of separate gender roles, as these were poorly recorded in SSPTW. As a test, we used the available information and coded a summed indicator of *caring* in 2004, consisting of the combined replacement rate for benefits for home care of a disabled person, single-parent supplements, and allowances for a sick or disabled child, all as percentage of family or single-person take-home pay (as appropriate). If high enough, all these benefits have the potential to substitute for paid work.

Missing Data

Of the 1,474 possible observations, 26 were missing (1.5%). For social services expenditure and individual taxation, data for Iceland were missing for 1979 and 1985. For the marriage subsidy, Greece, Portugal, Spain, and Iceland are not included in SCIP. Instead, we used the OECD's *Taxing Wages* to construct the indicator. For Portugal and Iceland, values either varied widely depending on which method of calculation was used (see footnote 2, p. 370), or were implausible (below zero). These countries were therefore excluded for this indicator. For pension child credits, there is no consensus among sources for Italy and Portugal and we coded them only for 1979–1993. For caring benefits (available for 2004), Italy could not be coded due to missing information on benefit amounts.

To include all countries in the cluster analyses, mean scores were imputed for missing values. As a sensitivity test, all cluster analyses were also performed without the countries with the missing values (Iceland and Portugal for all years, Italy in 1999–2004). Countries with imputed data are shown in italic in the cluster solutions (see Figure 2).

Analyses

First, the means, ranges, and distributions of the indicators were described. As a standardized measure of distribution we used the coefficient of variation (CV; the standard deviation divided by the mean). Second, data were clustered at four time points (1979, 1989, 1999, and 2004). Although some of our indicators were available for 1973, 1979 is the first year in which all indicators were present. The choice to use every tenth year was arbitrary, but this should be a time period over which policy change is likely to be substantive. The most recent year for which all indicators were available is 2004.

We used hierarchical cluster analysis. The distance measure was squared Euclidian, and all indicators were first standardized into Z-scores. Three methods were tested: average linkage between clusters (baverage), furthest neighbor, and Ward's method. The first two often resulted in clusters consisting of only one country, and overall, Ward's method gave the most reasonable clusters.

Data at different scaling levels should, ideally, not be combined in the same analysis. To include taxation (bivariate), which was an important indicator, we calculated Gower's general coefficient of (dis)similarity in SAS proc distance before clustering (62). The resulting cluster solutions, however, gave too much weight to this single bivariate indicator, and the clusters did not distinguish well between the other indicators. As an alternative we decided to mix indicators of different levels and evaluate the results based on the dendrogram and on how different the clusters were on all indicators; the latter was assessed using ANOVA. The dendrogram is a tree diagram of the clustering process, in which one can see at what point countries and initial clusters were joined. The distance between clusters is standardized to a 0–25 scale (Figure 3), and the greater the distances before two clusters are joined, the greater the differences between these clusters. The option of making all indicators bivariate was not pursued because few indicators were suitable for dichotomization. Analyses were performed using PASW/SPSS 18.0.

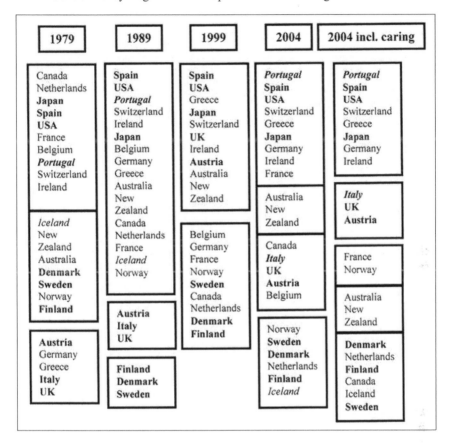

1979	1989	1999	2004	2004 incl. caring
Canada	**Spain**	**Spain**	*Portugal*	*Portugal*
Netherlands	**USA**	**USA**	**Spain**	**Spain**
Japan	*Portugal*	Greece	**USA**	**USA**
Spain	Switzerland	**Japan**	Switzerland	Switzerland
USA	Ireland	Switzerland	Greece	Greece
France	**Japan**	UK	**Japan**	**Japan**
Belgium	Belgium	Ireland	Germany	Germany
Portugal	Germany	**Austria**	Ireland	Ireland
Switzerland	Greece	Australia	France	
Ireland	Australia	New		*Italy*
	New	Zealand	Australia	UK
Iceland	Zealand		New	**Austria**
New	Canada		Zealand	
Zealand	Netherlands	Belgium		
Australia	France	Germany	Canada	France
Denmark	*Iceland*	France	*Italy*	Norway
Sweden	Norway	Norway	UK	
Norway		**Sweden**	**Austria**	
Finland		Canada	Belgium	Australia
	Austria	Netherlands		New
	Italy	**Denmark**		Zealand
Austria	UK	**Finland**	Norway	
Germany			**Sweden**	**Denmark**
Greece			**Denmark**	Netherlands
Italy	**Finland**		Netherlands	**Finland**
UK	**Denmark**		**Finland**	Canada
	Sweden		*Iceland*	Iceland
				Sweden

Figure 2. Cluster solutions in 1979, 1989, 1999, and 2004. Core countries (always in the same cluster) are in bold type (Ireland and Switzerland also belong in this group) countries with missing (imputed) data in italic. Clusters are separated either by a gap (clusters that were joined together late) or by a line (clusters that were joined early).

RESULTS

Descriptive Results

The general picture across indicators was one of unchanging or decreasing variation across countries during the entire period (Table 3). Only three indicators showed increased variation: the marriage subsidy, the dependent wife supplement, and the retirement age gender gap. Indicators reflecting the male breadwinner regime experienced a declining trend, with the exception of pensions, which generally have become less universal. Both earner-carer and separate gender roles indicators have become more common.

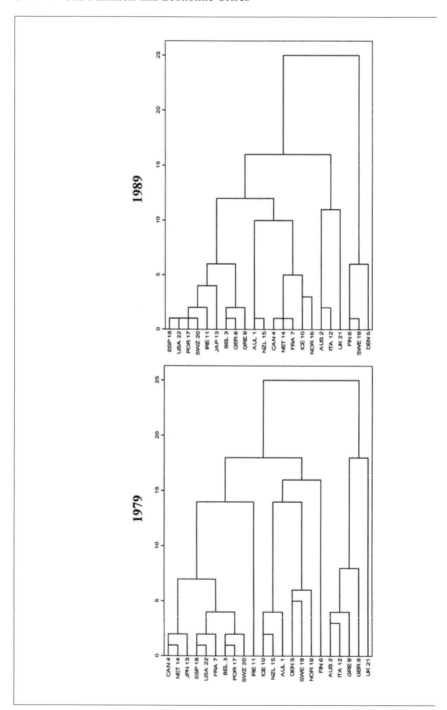

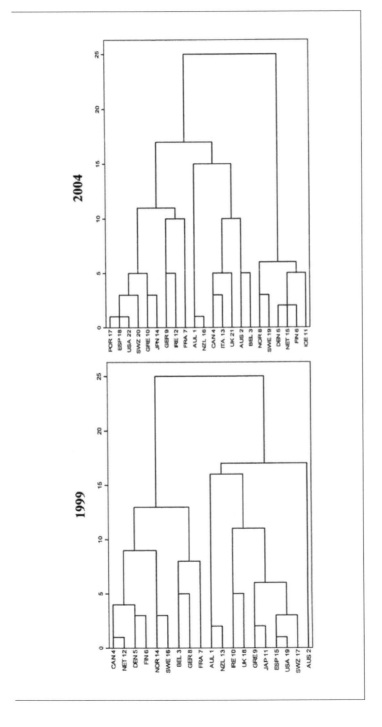

Figure 3. Dendrograms for 1979, 1989, 1999, and 2004, constructed using Ward's method with squared Euclidian distances. The 22 countries are: Canada (CAN), Netherlands (NET), Japan (JPN), Spain (ESP), United States (USA), France (FRA), Belgium (BEL), Portugal (POR), Switzerland (SWZ), Ireland (IRE), Iceland (ICE), New Zealand (NZL), Australia (AUL), Denmark (DEN), Sweden (SWE), Norway (NOR), Finland (FIN), Austria (AUS), Italy (ITA), Greece (GRE), Germany (GER), and United Kingdom (UK).

Table 3

Policy indicators: mean, range, and coefficient of variation (CV), 1979–2007/8, N = 22 (unless shown otherwise)

Indicator	1979	1985	1989	1993	1999	2003–4	2007–8
Earner-carer							
Maternity score, duration * RR							
Mean	11.5	13.0	12.8	14.0	14.2	15.9	17.8
Range	0–32.0	0–34.7	0–34.7	0–46.3	0–41.4	0–39.0	0–48.8
CV	0.80	0.78	0.74	0.82	0.77	0.69	0.67
Paternity leave, weeks							
Mean	0.09	0.29	0.29	0.52	2.5	3.7	3.1
Range	0–2	0–2	0–2	0–4	0–26	0–26	0–14.4
CV	4.7	2.4	2.4	2.2	2.4	1.8	1.5
Social services expenditure, % of GDP[a]							
Mean	0.88	0.90	1.1	1.5	1.8	2.0	—
Range	0.0–4.4	0.0–4.3	0.0–4.4	0–6.0	0.2–5.6	0.2–6.1	—
CV	1.4	1.4	1.3	1.1	0.85	0.81	—
N	21	21	22	22	22	22	—
Individual taxation							
%	52	52	55	59	59	64	—
N	21	21	22	22	22	22	—

Male breadwinner

Marriage subsidy, % of take-home pay[b]							
Mean	5.4	5.8	5.7	5.3	5.1	4.8	4.8
Range	0–12.2	0–13.0	0–13.3	0–12.8	0–17.0	0–15.2	0–15.1
CV	0.56	0.56	0.65	0.73	0.90	0.88	0.87
N	19	20	20	20	20	20	20
Dependent wife supplement (No)							
Mean	2.6	2.4	2.4	2.2	1.8	1.6	1.6
Range	0–5	0–5	0–5	0–5	0–5	0–5	0–5
CV	0.61	0.70	0.70	0.76	0.89	0.92	1.01
Minimum pension requirement, years							
Mean	4.7	4.6	5.8	5.7	5.5	5.5	5.5
Range	0–20	0–15	0–25	0–25	0–25	0–25	0–25
CV	1.3	1.2	1.3	1.3	1.3	1.3	1.3
Maximum pension requirement, years							
Mean	34	34	34	35	35	36	36
Range	0–50	0–50	0–50	0–50	0–50	0–50	0–50
CV	0.46	0.45	0.44	0.43	0.42	0.42	0.42

Table *continues on next page*

Table 3 (Cont'd.)

Indicator	1979	1985	1989	1993	1999	2003–4	2007–8
Separate gender roles							
Extended leave score, duration * RR							
Mean	1.2	0.86	1.0	2.9	5.3	5.4	5.2
Range	0–10.2	0–9.0	0–9.9	0–27.0	0–39.2	0–38.1	0–21.5
CV	2.5	2.9	2.6	2.6	1.8	1.7	1.4
Retirement age gender gap, years							
Mean	2.1	2.1	1.9	1.4	1.2	0.93	0.86
Range	0–5	0–5	0–5	0–5	0–5	0–5	0–5
CV	1.2	1.2	1.3	1.5	1.7	1.9	2.0
Pension child credits, years							
Mean	1.0	1.3	1.6	2.2	4.9	6.3	6.7
Range	0–20	0–19	0–19	0–19	0–20	0–20	0–20
CV	4.2	3.3	2.6	2.1	1.3	1.2	1.1
N	22	22	22	22	20	20	20
Caring benefits, % of take-home pay							
Mean	—	—	—	—	—	12.7	—
Range	—	—	—	—	—	0–54.9	—
CV	—	—	—	—	—	1.1	—
N	—	—	—	—	—	21	—

[a]The 1979 value is for 1980.
[b]The values are for 1980, 1985, 1990, 1995, 2000, 2005, and 2008.

Cluster Solutions

For 1979, the dendrogram supported a two- or three-cluster solution (the same cluster solution was found when Iceland was excluded, rather than missing values being imputed) (Figure 3). In the two-cluster solution, there was a large mixed cluster (N = 17) and a small cluster of five countries characterized by a high maternity score, high minimum and maximum pension requirements, high(er) extended leave score, child credits, and retirement age gender gap (Table 4). The five countries were a mix of continental European, southern, and one liberal country (United Kingdom). These might be called separate gender roles countries, or *compensatory breadwinner* countries, given that the scores on the separate gender roles indicators were rather low.

In the three-cluster solution for 1979, another set of countries (N = 7) was distinguished by higher social services expenditure, individual taxation, universal pensions, and low maximum requirements. These countries scored low on the separate gender roles indicators and had a medium maternity score. They could be called earner-carer, or *universal earner*, countries, as support to carers is not especially high. This cluster consisted of all the Nordic countries, New Zealand, and Australia. The remaining cluster consisted of *male breadwinner* countries (N = 10) characterized by the lowest maternity score, low social services expenditure, infrequent individual taxation, low minimum pension requirements, and low child credits.

In 1989, countries were best distinguished by a three-cluster solution (the same solution was found when countries with missing data were excluded). There was a large *mixed* cluster (N = 16), and two small clusters of three countries apiece. One consisted of Nordic *earner-carer* countries. These had individual taxation and universal pensions, the highest score on all earner-carer indicators, few dependent wife supplements, no retirement age gap, and no pension child credits. The other cluster to emerge was the *compensatory breadwinner* cluster.

For 1999, there were quite large differences between cluster solutions based on all countries and those excluding countries with missing values. With missing-value countries excluded, only a two-cluster solution was meaningful (Figure 3). Here, there was a *mixed earner-carer* cluster (N = 9), with both earner-carer countries and a few that normally belong with the male breadwinner countries, and a *mixed breadwinner* cluster with the remaining countries (N = 10).

For 2004, two analyses were made, one without and one with the indicator *caring*. In the solution without caring, the dendrogram supported either two or four clusters (Figure 3). In the two-cluster solution, all Nordic countries, along with the Netherlands, were found in one *earner-carer* cluster (N = 6). When countries with missing values were excluded, Canada was also part of this cluster. The Netherlands was an outlier in this cluster, and its scores placed it somewhere between the earner-carer and the male breadwinner clusters (the same can be said for Canada). In the four-cluster solution, the *mixed*

Table 4

Cluster characteristics at four time points: 1979, 1989, 1999, and 2004

	N	Maternity score	Paternity leave	Social services	Individual taxation	Min. pension requirements	Max. pension requirements	Marriage subsidy	Dependent wife supplement	Extended leave score	Child credits	Retirement age gender gap	Benefits for caring
1979													
Male breadwinner	10	7.9	0	0.41	30	3.3	40.2	5.4	2.6	1	0.25	1.1	—
Compensatory breadwinner	5	17.5	0	0.51	60	14	41.9	4.2	2.8	3.3	4	5	—
Universal earner	7	12.2	0.29	1.8	86	0	17.1	6.1	3.1	0.11	0	1.4	—
p value		0.160	0.360	0.026	0.076	0.000	0.000	0.536	0.504	0.222	0.213	0.003	—
1989													
Mixed	16	9.6	0.03	0.75	44	5.5	32.4	6.1	2.4	0.19	0.98	1.6	—
Compensatory breadwinner	3	13.7	0	0.62	100	13.3	41.5	4.0	3.7	5.9	6.6	5.0	—
Earner-carer	3	28.9	2	3.5	100	0	36.3	5	1	0.61	0	0	—
p value		0.001	0.000	0.001	0.058	0.074	0.630	0.617	0.140	0.000	0.070	0.017	—

1999													
Mixed earner-carer	9	22.0	3.2	2.8	56	0.69	40.2	6.7	1	10.4	4.4	0.4	—
Mixed breadwinner	10	6.7	2.6	0.60	60	9.4	32.6	3.6	2.9	1.5	5.9	1.7	—
p value		0.002	0.848	0.007	0.855	0.007	0.224	0.154	0.007	0.051	0.622	0.174	—
2004													
Earner-carer	6	28.7	5.7	4.2	83	0	35.8	3.4	0.5	4.9	3.7	0	(19.4)
Universal citizen	2	2.8	0	1.5	100	0	0	2.0	2.5	0	0	0.8	(26.5)
Male breadwinner	9	10.2	0.54	1.2	22	10.1	40.2	6.1	1.6	6.1	7.4	0.22	(8.3)
Compensatory breadwinner	5	16.8	8.5	1.1	100	6.0	41.2	5.2	2.6	7.0	10.1	3.4	(7.1)
p value		0.001	0.108	0.000	0.003	0.029	0.000	0.472	0.080	0.849	0.258	0.001	—
2004 including caring													
Mixed earner-carer	10	22.1	3.6	3.0	80	0.03	29.1	3.5	1.0	6.7	4.2	0.15	20.1
Male breadwinner	8	9.4	0.36	1.0	25	11.4	40.5	6.2	1.6	2.1	7.6	0.25	5.3
Compensatory breadwinner	4	14.1	10.6	1.4	100	7.5	41.9	5.2	3.0	8.7	9.1	4.3	8.9
p value		0.046	0.031	0.015	0.009	0.001	0.178	0.377	0.063	0.433	0.429	0.000	0.062

breadwinner cluster was divided into three. One consisted only of the antipodean countries (Australia and New Zealand). This cluster was distinguished by the lowest maternity score, no paternity leave, individual taxation, pensions based on residency, the lowest marriage subsidy, no extended leave score, and no child credits. These may be called *universal citizen* countries, given their combination of universality and low monetary support. Apart from these, there was, as before, a *compensatory breadwinner* cluster (N = 5) and a *male breadwinner* cluster (N = 9).

When *caring* was included for 2004, the same solution was found whether countries with missing data were excluded or not. The result was either a two- or a five-cluster solution, according to the dendrogram (not shown). In the two-cluster solution, there were two equally large clusters, one of *mixed earner-carer* countries (N = 10) and one of *mixed breadwinner* countries (N = 12). The five-cluster solution consisted of three larger clusters and two small clusters with only two countries. One of the small clusters consisted of the *universal citizen* countries (Australia and New Zealand); these were also distinguished by their high mean benefit level for caring. The other small cluster consisted of France and Norway. Apart from their unusually high caring scores, there were large discrepancies between the two countries in parental leave and social services, extended leave score, and pension child credits. To avoid this cluster, we opted for keeping the mixed earner-carer cluster intact (N = 10) while the mixed breadwinner countries were divided into a *male breadwinner* cluster (N = 8) and a small *compensatory breadwinner* cluster (Figure 2).

Discounting the anomalous 1999 results, core countries—those that always appear in the same cluster (shown in bold type in Figure 2)—were Austria, Italy, and the United Kingdom (compensatory breadwinner), Japan, Spain, Portugal, Ireland, Switzerland, and the United States (male breadwinner), and Denmark, Sweden, and Finland (universal earner/earner-carer). Apart from 1989, Norway was also part of the earner-carer cluster.

The first three core countries noted above, Austria, Italy, and the United Kingdom, seem to have evolved from a compensatory breadwinner model toward a separate gender roles model, but have they crossed the line? One basic condition for this could be that someone who has stayed home to care for two children should be eligible for a basic pension. The United Kingdom has already met this condition by 1979, but Austria never does (and the Italian data for pension child credits are unreliable). Another condition could be that the replacement rate for (more permanent) caring activities should be at least 50 percent of an APW, to achieve real autonomy from a male breadwinner. This was not achieved in any of these countries. The common denominator was thus a high gender gap in retirement age. Although the United Kingdom has matched the retirement age gap with equal differences in maximum pension requirements, the lower statutory pension age for women in the remaining countries has resulted in difficulties for women to reach the maximum pension benefit. The United

Kingdom, on the other hand, has had no extended leave and low replacement rates for caring activities. Thus it does not seem warranted to classify any of these three countries as a separate gender roles model.

The core male breadwinner countries have had (apart from 1979) especially high thresholds for receiving a basic pension, and meager, if any, compensatory measures. Although all but the United States and Switzerland increased their maternity score, other caring benefits were low or nonexistent. Switzerland and Ireland were different because the basic pension requirement was low. In 1995, Switzerland also introduced a very generous child credit to all parents (not just carers). With the exception of Ireland, support to breadwinners has not been especially high in these four countries. Instead, it was their consistently low scores on other measures that set them apart.

Three of the five Nordic countries are among the core earner-carer countries, with Norway left out only in 1989, and Iceland leaving the cluster in 1989 to return in 2004, primarily due to a delayed development of parental leave. More surprising may be the addition of other countries, different for different years. As was shown for the Netherlands in 2004, these countries were often hybrid cases, sharing some but not all policy characteristics with the core earner-carer countries.

As a test of the relevance of the cluster solutions, we plotted the clusters found in 2004 against two measures of gender equality in 2007: the World Economic Forum's gender gap index (63), consisting of the sub-indices economic participation and opportunity, educational attainment, political empowerment, and health and survival, and the U.N. Development Program's Gender Empowerment Measure (64), with the dimensions political and economic participation and decision-making, and power over economic resources based on earned income. As shown in Figure 4, the earner-carer countries were dispersed along the top half, the male breadwinner countries in the lower half, and the compensatory breadwinner countries in the middle, except for one outlier (Italy). The two universal citizen countries were located in the middle to upper half. The same picture emerged for the cluster solution with the factor *caring* included, although with a greater degree of overlap in the middle (not shown). It seems, then, that gender policy regime type in 2004 was related to a large degree to gender-relevant outcomes.

DISCUSSION AND CONCLUSION

The main findings of the cluster analyses of the 22 OECD countries were, first, that the classification does not entirely correspond to Sainsbury's three regime types, and second, that due to rapid policy change, both clusters and country classifications have changed considerably over time.

It is clear that even as policies indicative of the separate gender roles model have become more common, no country has embraced all parts of this model

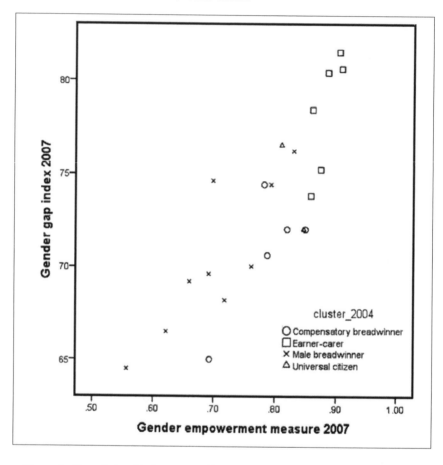

Figure 4. The relationship between welfare state regimes in 2004 and gender equality outcomes in 2007.

(8). Two aspects of the model—compensatory measures in the pension system and benefits for caring activities—were never present simultaneously. The two antipodean countries are interesting as they seem particularly generous to permanent carers. As an example, a single parent could receive almost 70 percent of an APW in New Zealand, family benefits included. Compensatory measures have been nonexistent, but, given that basic pensions are universal and equal for men and women, this is irrelevant. However, monetary support either to the breadwinner or to working parents (mothers) in the presence of a breadwinner was low or nonexistent. This finding partly supports theories claiming that Australia and New Zealand belong to a "fourth world" of radical welfare capitalism, characterized by low expenditure but high benefit equality and redistribution through taxation (10, 65). However, there are some decisive differences between them regarding the universality of the basic pension. While both have an income test, in Australia this is assessed on the joint income of both spouses, which means that women's pension rights are affected by their husband's typically higher income (66).

Our cluster results show several similarities with previous taxonomies. These include the relative consistency of the Nordic/social democratic/dual earner/high defamilization cluster across time and, at the other end, a cluster marked by low generosity, consisting of Southern European countries and the United States (1, 6, 10, 37, 40). These male breadwinner countries were close to Korpi's market-oriented cluster, given their consistently low scores (6), but as in Bambra's study (39), the liberal/English-speaking countries were not grouped together. Whereas the United States and Ireland were usually in the male breadwinner cluster, the United Kingdom was always placed in the compensatory breadwinner cluster. Australia and New Zealand had their own unique profile, and Canada was variously found in the male breadwinner or earner-carer cluster.

Apart from the core countries, about half of the 22 countries tended to fall between clusters. However, disregarding 1999, when the earner-carer countries were not singled out, only the Netherlands moved from the male breadwinner to the earner-carer cluster. As described above, it appeared as a hybrid case. That countries move between groups and regime groupings change over time is partly due to rapid policy change, with a dismantling of dependent wife supplements and the gender gap in retirement age, and with expansion of the parental leave system and development of pension child credits.

Data Limitations

Not all aspects of Sainsbury's model were included in the present study. One reason was the sheer complexity of a many countries–many indicators approach; another was the availability of comparable data. Employment and wage policies (see Table 1) were not included, even though an initial attempt was made to look at antidiscrimination legislation. Inclusion of these would have required a more thorough knowledge of actual praxis.

The quality of data in SSPTW has increased with time as the level of detail in the publication has increased, most notably from 1993 onward. In the OECD's *Taxing Wages*, the family types used for comparison were extended from two to eight in 1996, which improved the possibility of making correct calculations of the marriage subsidy. Since 1998 it has been possible to complement the information in SSPTW with MISSOC. This revealed important discrepancies between the two sources, pointing to the possibility of undiscovered errors prior to 1998. In cases where we could complement the data with information directly from specific countries, potential flaws could be remedied. All efforts were made to enhance the validity of the data, but this also means that comparability over time and between countries may be questioned. However, as data in SSPTW are ultimately dependent on the quality of reporting from individual countries, there is always the question of reliability. The problems we have experienced call attention to the limitations in using internationally collected but not harmonized data.

For most indicators, decisions had to be made on how to interpret and code the information given in various publications. Concerning benefits for caregiving, it was often unclear whether benefits were for caring by a family member in the home or for other expenses, including care by a third party. The period of caring was often undefined, and the specific circumstances were seldom spelled out. We decided to code this indicator only for one year. To delve more deeply into the aspect of paid components for care, additional (national) sources should be used. In such an investigation, it would be beneficial to make a distinction between caring for the aged and for children, as previous studies have shown these policies to be highly divergent (36).

As we elected not to weight indicators in the cluster analysis, a change in one factor can be decisive in the cluster allocation when a country's profile lies between two clusters. The lack of weighting means that all indicators were allowed to influence the solution equally. In countries with coherent policy packages this was less of a problem, but many continental European countries score medium across the board. Social services expenditure is a decisive policy area that could have been given greater weight by inclusion of more indicators. As mentioned earlier, it would also have been valuable if high-quality data on caring benefits had been available.

Conclusion

Incorporating indicators of the separate gender roles model has led to new insights and a somewhat different clustering of countries than in earlier typologies. However, no country could be classified as belonging to this regime type. Instead, some countries are classified as compensatory breadwinner countries, while some give high support to carers in specific situations.

Contrary to many previous studies, but in accordance with Bambra (39), we found that the liberal countries were dispersed across clusters. Rapid policy change implies a "moving target" regarding both the defining feature of clusters and the country classification for about half of all studied nations. Apart from the anomalous 1999, the compensatory breadwinner cluster was present across all time points, with a proper earner-carer cluster first appearing in 1989.

Acknowledgments — This research was funded by the Swedish Research Council, grant no. dnr 521-2008-4317.

REFERENCES

1. Esping-Andersen, G. *The Three Worlds of Welfare Capitalism*. Polity Press, Cambridge, 1990.
2. Lewis, J. Gender and the development of welfare regimes. *J. Eur. Soc. Policy* 2: 159–173, 1992. doi: 10.1177/095892879200200301.
3. O'Connor, J. S. Gender, class and citizenship in the comparative analysis of welfare state regimes: Theoretical and methodological issues. *Br. J. Sociol.* 44: 501–518, 1993.
4. Orloff, A. S. Gender and the social rights of citizenship: The comparative analysis of gender relations and welfare states. *Am. Sociol. Rev.* 58:303–328, 1993.
5. Sainsbury, D. Women's and men's social rights: Gendering dimensions of welfare states. In *Gendering Welfare States*, ed. D. Sainsbury. Sage, London, 1994.
6. Korpi, W. Faces of inequality: Gender, class, and patterns of inequality in different types of welfare states. *Soc. Polit.* 7:127–191, 2000. doi: 10.1093/sp/7.2.127.
7. Sainsbury, D. *Gender, Equality, and Welfare States*. Cambridge University Press, Cambridge, 1996. doi: 10.2277/0521565790.
8. Sainsbury, D. Gender, policy regimes, and politics. In *Gender and Welfare State Regimes*, ed. D. Sainsbury. Oxford University Press, Oxford, 1999. doi: 10.1093/0198294166.001.0001.
9. Leibfried, S. Towards a European welfare state? On integrating poverty regimes into the European Community. In *Social Policy in a Changing Europe*, ed. Z. Ferge and J. E. Kolberg. Campus Verlag, Frankfurt, 1992.
10. Castles, F. G., and Mitchell, D. Worlds of welfare and families of nations. In *Families of Nations: Patterns of Public Policy in Western Democracies*, ed. F. G. Castles. Dartmouth, Aldershot, UK, 1993.
11. Ferrera, M. The "Southern model" of welfare in social Europe. *J. Eur. Soc. Pol.* 6:17–37, 1996. doi: 10.1177/095892879600600102.
12. Korpi, W., and Palme, J. The paradox of redistribution and the strategy of equality: Welfare state institutions, inequality and poverty in the Western countries. *Am. Sociol. Rev.* 63:662–687, 1998.
13. Bonoli, G. Classifying welfare states: A two-dimension approach. *J. Soc. Policy* 26:351–372, 1997. doi: 10.1017/S0047279497005059.
14. Navarro, V., and Shi, L. The political context of social inequalities and health. *Soc. Sci. Med.* 52:481–491, 2001. doi: 10.1016/S0277-9536(00)00197-0.
15. Arts, W., and Gelissen, J. Three worlds of welfare capitalism or more? A state-of-the-art report. *J. Eur. Soc. Pol.* 12:137–158, 2002. doi: 10.1177/0952872002012002114.
16. Bambra, C. Decommodification and the worlds of welfare revisited. *J. Eur. Soc. Policy* 16:73–80, 2006. doi: 10.1177/0952872002012002114.
17. Esping-Andersen, G. *Social Foundations of Postindustrial Economies*. Oxford University Press, Oxford, 1999. doi: 10.1093/0198742002.001.0001.
18. Esping-Andersen, G. A new gender contract. In *Why We Need a New Welfare State*, ed. G. Esping-Andersen. Oxford University Press, Oxford, 2002. doi: 10.1093/0199256438.001.0001.
19. Lewis, J. Gender and welfare regimes: Further thoughts. *Soc. Polit.* 4:160–177, 1997. doi: 10.1093/sp/4.2.160.

20. Ostner, I., and Lewis, J. Gender and the evolution of European social policies. In *European Social Policy: Between Fragmentation and Integration*, ed. S. Liebfried and P. Pierson. Brookings Institution Press, Washington, DC, 1995.

21. O'Connor, J. S. Understanding women in welfare states. *Curr. Sociol.* 44:1–12, 1996. doi: 10.1177/001139296044002002.

22. Orloff, A. S. Comment on Jane Lewis's "Gender and welfare regimes: Further thoughts." *Soc. Polit.* 4:188–202. 1997. doi: 10.1093/sp/4.2.188.

23. O'Connor, J. S., Orloff, A. S., and Shaver, S. *States, Markets, Families: Gender, Liberalism, and Social Policy in Australia, Canada, Great Britain, and the United States*. Cambridge University Press, Cambridge, 1999. doi: 10.2277/0521630924.

24. Shaver, S. Body rights, social rights and the liberal welfare state. *Crit. Soc. Policy* 13:66–93, 1994. doi: 10.1177/026101839401303905 .

25. Shaver, S. Gender, welfare, regimes, and agency. *Soc. Polit.* 9:204–211, 2002. doi: 10.1093/sp/9.2.203.

26. Brush, L. D. Changing the subject: Gender and welfare regime studies. *Soc. Polit.* 9:161–186, 2002. doi: 10.1093/sp/9.2.161.

27. Pfau-Effinger, B. Conclusion. In *Gender, Economy, and Culture in the European Union*, ed. S. Duncan, and B. Pfau-Effinger. Routledge, London, 2000.

28. Pfau-Effinger, B. Culture and welfare state policies: Reflections on a complex inter-relation. *J. Soc. Policy* 34:3–20, 2005. doi: 10.1017/S0047279404008232.

29. Bambra, C. Sifting the wheat from the chaff: A two-dimensional discriminant analysis of welfare state regime theory. *Soc. Policy Adm.* 41:1–28, 2007. doi: 10.1111/j.1467-9515.2007.00536.x.

30. Pfau-Effinger, B. Gender cultures and the gender arrangement: A theoretical frame-work for cross-national gender research. *Innovation* 11:147–166, 1998.

31. Haas, B. The work-care balance: Is it possible to identify typologies for cross-national comparisons? *Curr. Sociol.* 53:487–508, 2005. doi: 10.1177/0011392105051337.

32. Lewis, J. *Work-Family Balance, Gender, and Policy*. Edward Elgar, Cheltenham, UK, 2009.

33. Sümer, S. The Scandinavian gender regimes: Myth or reality? In *European Gender Regimes and Policies: Comparative Perspectives*, ed. S. Sümer. Ashgate, Farnham, UK, 2009.

34. Eichler, M., and Pfau-Effinger, B. The "consumer principle" in the care of elderly people: Free choice and actual choice in the German welfare state. *Soc. Policy Adm.* 43:617–633, 2009. doi: 10.1111/j.1467-9515.2009.00684.x.

35. Gornick, J. C., Meyers, M. K., and Ross, K. E. Supporting the employment of mothers: Policy variation across fourteen welfare states. *J. Eur. Soc. Policy* 7:45–70, 1997, doi: 10.1177/095892879700700103.

36. Anttonen, A., and Sipilä, J. European social care services: Is it possible to identify models? *J. Eur. Soc. Policy* 6:87–100, 1996. doi: 10.1177/095892879600600201.

37. Bettio, F., and Plantenga, J. Comparing care regimes in Europe. *Feminist Econ.* 10:85–113, 2004. doi: 10.1080/1354570042000198245.

38. Ferrarini, T. *Parental Leave Institutions in Eighteen Post-war Welfare States*. Stockholm University, Stockholm, 2003.

39. Bambra, C. The worlds of welfare: Illusory and gender blind? *Soc. Policy Society* 3:201–211, 2004. doi: 10.1017/S147474640400171X.

40. Bambra, C. Defamilisation and welfare state regimes: A cluster analysis. *Int. J. Soc. Welfare* 16:326–338, 2007. doi: 10.1111/j.1468-2397.2007.00486.x.
41. Bambra, C. Going beyond "The Three Worlds of Welfare Capitalism": Regime theory and public health research. *J. Epidemiol. Community Health* 61:1098–1102, 2007. doi: 10.1136/jech.2007.064295.
42. Organization for Economic Cooperation and Development. *Taxing Wages* [earlier title: *The Tax/Benefit Position of Employees*]. Paris, 1982–2009.
43. Moss, P., and Deven, F. *Parental Leave: Progress or Pitfall? Research and Policy Issues in Europe.* NIDI/CBGS Publications, Brussels, 1999.
44. Moss, P., and Korintus, M. *International Review of Leave Policies and Related Research 2008.* Department for Business, Enterprise and Regulatory Reform, London, 2008. www.berr.gov.uk/files/file47247.pdf (accessed January 15, 2009).
45. Gilbert, N. (ed.). *Gender and Social Security Reform: What's Fair for Women?* Transaction Publishers, New Brunswick, NJ, 2006.
46. Leitner, S. Sex and gender discrimination within EU pension systems. *J. Eur. Soc. Policy* 11:99–115, 2001. doi: 10.1177/095892870101100201.
47. Pereira, J. Personal communication, Unidade de Doença Deficiência e Dependência, February 19, 2007.
48. Kiehl, E. Personal communication, Consejería de Trabajo y Asuntos Sociales de las Embajadas de España en Dinamarca, Finlandia, Noruega y Suecia, September 16, 2008.
49. Bundesministerium für soziale Sicherheit GuK. *Sozialschutz in Österreich.* Vienna, 2006.
50. Kukulenz, C. Personal communication, Bundesministerium für Familie, Senioren, Frauen und Jugend, June 23, 2008.
51. Wamsler, J. Personal communication, Familiestyrelsen, January 30, 2007.
52. Deutsche Rentenversicherung. *Kindererziehung: Plus für die Rente.* Berlin, 2006.
53. Fichtner, E. Personal communication, Bundesministerium für Arbeit und Soziales, December 11, 2006.
54. Ruschitzka, E. Personal communication, Pensionsversicherungsanstalt, September 9, 2009.
55. Pensionsversicherungsanstalt. *Versicherungszeiten.* Vienna, 2008.
56. Pensionsversicherungsanstalt. *Die Pensionen der Zukunft: Pensionskonto–Parallelrechnung.* Vienna, 2008.
57. Barbe, B. Personal communication, Caisse nationale d'Assurance vieillesse, Département Réglementation National 961, February 24, 2010.
58. Huygens, C. Personal communication, Rijksdienst voor Pensioenen, September 11, 2008.
59. European Commission. *"Making Work Pay" Debates from a Gender Perspective: A Comparative Review of Some Recent Policy Reforms in Thirty European Countries.* Office for Official Publications of the European Communities, Luxembourg, 2006.
60. Jensen, C. Worlds of welfare services and transfers. *J. Eur. Soc. Policy* 18:151–162, 2008. doi: 10.1177/0958928707087591.
61. Marier, P. Affirming, transforming, or neglecting gender? Conceptualising gender in the pension reform process. *Soc. Polit.* 14:182–211, 2007. doi: 10.1093/sp/jxm011.

62. Romesburg, H. C. Resemblance coefficients for mixtures of quantitative and qualitative attributes. In *Cluster Analysis for Researchers*, ed. H. C. Romesburg. Lulu Press, Raleigh, NC, 2004 (1984).

63. Hausmann, R., Tyson, L. D., and Zahidi, S. *The Global Gender Gap Report 2007*. World Economic Forum, Geneva, 2007. www.weforum.org/issues/global-gender-gap.

64. United Nations Development Program. *Human Development Report 2009: Overcoming Barriers—Human Mobility and Development*. New York, 2009. http://hdr.undp.org/en/media/HDR_2009_EN_Complete.pdf (accessed November 9, 2010).

65. Castles, F. G. A farewell to Australia's welfare state. *Int. J. Health Serv.* 31:537–544, 2001. doi: 10.2190/E6W8-3HYY-EHJ5-7VFK.

66. Simmers, D. Diverging paths: Retirement income policies in Australia and New Zealand. *Soc. Policy J. N. Z.* 4, 1995. www.msd.govt.nz/about-msd-and-our-work/publications-resources/journals-and-magazines/social-policy-journal/spj04/04-retirement-income.html.

CHAPTER 18

Analyzing Differences in the Magnitude of Socioeconomic Inequalities in Self-Perceived Health by Countries of Different Political Tradition in Europe

Carme Borrell, Albert Espelt, Maica Rodríguez-Sanz,
Bo Burström, Carles Muntaner, M. Isabel Pasarín,
Joan Benach, Chiara Marinacci, Albert-Jan Roskam,
Maartje Schaap, Enrique Regidor, Giuseppe Costa,
Paula Santana, Patrick Deboosere, Anton Kunst,
and Vicente Navarro

The objectives of this study are to describe, for European countries, variations among political traditions in the magnitude of inequalities in self-perceived health by educational level and to determine whether these variations change when contextual welfare state, labor market, wealth, and income inequality variables are taken into account. In this cross-sectional study, the authors look at the population aged 25 to 64 in 13 European countries. Individual data were obtained from the Health Interview Surveys of each country. Educational-level inequalities in self-perceived health exist in all countries and in all political traditions, among both women and men. When countries are grouped by political tradition, social democratic countries are found to have the lowest educational-level inequalities.

*****

The scientific literature on social inequalities in health has increased considerably in the field of public health in recent years, but the impact of political factors on health and on social inequalities in health has rarely been studied. Indeed, few studies have analyzed the effects of important political variables on health outcomes (1, 2). Infant mortality is one of the health outcomes most studied (3, 4), mainly because it is sensitive over a short period of time, not needing long lag times to produce results; also, the infant mortality indicator is sensitive to social development and to political and welfare state conditions. These studies have found a relationship between the type of welfare regime and infant mortality, with the social democratic countries having better indicators. Some other health outcomes have also been studied, comparing countries with different political traditions (1, 5–7).

Dahl and colleagues (8), reviewing the empirical evidence from published articles on health inequalities in different countries, assessed whether social class inequalities in health diminished for several welfare state regimes. However, the studies included in their review did not compare health outcomes for different typologies of countries. Dahl and coauthors did not conclude that health inequalities are systematically smaller in social democratic countries than in other European countries with different welfare regimes. Muntaner and colleagues (9) compiled data comparing Sweden, the United Kingdom, and Italy as examples of social democratic, liberal, and Christian democratic traditions, respectively. Their results were similar to those of Dahl and coauthors. Muntaner and colleagues concluded that error in measurement of social class (e.g., manual vs. nonmanual workers) could account for the observed absence of differences.

More recently, Espelt and coworkers (10–12; including a commentary by Lundberg) showed the differences among three political traditions (social democratic, Christian democratic, and late democracies) of self-perceived health inequalities, using Wright's neo-Marxist social class dimensions, in the adult and elderly populations of nine European countries. In this study, health inequalities were larger in the late democracies, and primarily among women, mainly when using the educational level ("skills/credentials") dimension. The inequalities were not so clear when using other dimensions of social class ("ownership" and "supervision"). These results were more important for poor self-perceived health than for long-term illness indicators. Espelt and coauthors' studies, however, included only populations older than 50 years in nine European countries.

The present chapter expands the approaches of the earlier studies. First, it focuses on the conceptual model presented in Figure 1, which explains socio-economic inequalities in self-perceived health through political traditions, welfare state and labor market policies, and income inequalities and wealth. Second, it broadens the age range of the population studied, as well as the number of countries included. Our hypothesis was that countries governed by social democratic parties have a more generous welfare state, full employment policies, and lower income inequalities. All these factors are related to health outcomes and inequalities in health outcomes.

Thus, the two main objectives of this chapter are, first, to describe the variations among political traditions in the magnitude of inequalities in self-perceived health by educational level in men and women in Europe; and second, to determine whether these variations change when contextual variables of welfare state, labor market, and wealth and income inequalities of each country are taken into account.

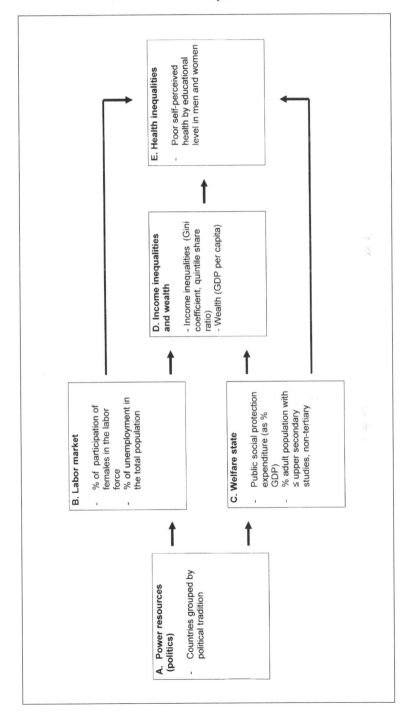

Figure 1. Model showing the relationship between power resources, labor market, welfare state, income inequalities, and self-perceived health inequalities (the variables studied are included). *Source:* Navarro et al. (1).

METHODS

Design, Population Studied, and Sources of Information

Using a cross-sectional design, we studied the population of men and women aged 25 to 64 of Norway (2002), Sweden (2000, 2001), Finland (1994, 1998, 2000, 2002, 2004), Denmark (2000), England (2001), Ireland (1995, 2002), Netherlands (2003, 2004), Belgium (1997, 2001), Germany (1998), France (2004), Italy (1999, 2000), Spain (2001), and Portugal (1998, 1999). Data were obtained from the Health Interview Surveys of each country and were gathered for the EUROTHINE project (13); the overall aim of this project is to facilitate mutual learning by collecting and analyzing information from different European countries that will help policymakers at the European and national levels develop rational strategies for tackling socioeconomic inequalities in health. Overall, we obtained data on 196,280 people, with sample sizes in individual countries ranging from 4,781 for Norway to 77,531 for Italy. Contextual variables were obtained from the Organization for Economic Cooperation and Development (OECD, IRDES: OECD Health Data 2005, Statistics and Indicators for 30 countries), except for income inequality variables, which were obtained from the Luxemburg Income Study.

Variables

Dependent Variable. Self-reported health status was measured through a single question: "Would you say your health is very good, good, fair, poor, or very poor?" A dichotomous outcome variable was created (1 = fair, poor, or very poor; 0 = very good, good). Self-reported health is related to objective health, and it is also a valid predictor of mortality (14).

Individual Independent Variables. Age was categorized into three groups (25–34, 35–44, 45–64). As a measure of socioeconomic position we used educational level, which measures the highest level of education completed by the respondent. It was categorized using the International Standard Classification of Education (ISCED). The categories were: no or only primary education (ISCED 1), lower secondary education (ISCED 2), upper secondary and post-secondary non-tertiary education (ISCED 3–4), and tertiary education (ISCED ≥ 5).

Contextual Country Independent Variables. These include the variables obtained for each country (see Figure 1). We chose the year of the independent variables to obtain a time lag between them and the dependent variable (15). Income inequality variables had to be for 2001 because we could not obtain data for earlier years.

Political Tradition. The countries were grouped according to political tradition into four groups, following the typology of Huber, Ragin, and Stephens (16), further elaborated by Navarro, Schmitt, and Astudillo (17), taking into account the total time (years and months) during which social democratic, Christian democratic, and liberal parties were in government in each country since 1950. We thus obtained four groupings, as follows: social democratic, including Denmark, Finland, Norway, and Sweden; Christian democratic, including Belgium, France, Germany, Italy, and Netherlands; liberal, including England and Ireland; and late democracies, including Portugal and Spain (ex-dictatorship countries).

Welfare state variables:

- Level of education in 1999: Percentage of adult population (25–64 years) with ISCED levels 3–4 (≤ post-secondary education, non-tertiary).
- Public expenditure in 1992: Total public social expenditure as a percentage of gross domestic product (GDP).

Labor market variables:

- Participation of women in the labor force in 1999: Percentage of women employed or looking for a job.
- People unemployed in 2001: Percentage of unemployed persons in relation to the total population.

Income inequality and wealth variables:

- Quintile share ratio in 2001: The ratio of total income received by the 20 percent of the population with the highest incomes (top quintile) to total income received by the 20 percent with the lowest incomes (lowest quintile). Income is understood as equalized disposable income.
- Gini coefficient in 2001: This is a measure of the inequality of a distribution. It is defined as a ratio with values between 0 and 100. The numerator is the area between the Lorenz curve of the distribution and the uniform (perfect) distribution line; the denominator is the area under the uniform distribution line. Zero corresponds to perfect income equality; 100 corresponds to perfect income inequality.
- GDP in 1993: The GDP of a country is defined as the market value of all final goods and services produced within the country in a given period of time. We included the GDP per capita in PPP (purchasing power parity, millions US$).

Data Analysis

We used two types of weights in the analyses: (*a*) weights that take into account the sample design for the countries where this was necessary, and (*b*) weights to obtain the same sample size for each country. The sample size for each country was 2,435 for women and 2,346 for men (these were the minimum sample size of the surveys).

All analyses were carried out for men and women separately, because the perception of health differs by gender, and the association of educational level and self-perceived health can also differ for men and women (18). First, we described all individual and contextual variables. Second, we described self-perceived health by political tradition, age-standardized by the direct method, using the whole sample for the 13 countries as a standard population.

Log-binomial regression models (19) were fitted to show the association between self-perceived health and educational level, adjusting by age group, in the different countries (see Table 1). In these models, for the countries where it was necessary, data were weighted only by the specific weight to take into account the sample design. Moreover, log-binomial regression models were fitted to show the association between self-perceived health and the independent variables: educational level, political tradition, and age group, and the inter-action between educational level and political tradition (see Model I in Tables 3 and 4). Educational level was introduced as a quantitative variable (with four values between 0 and 1, which reflect the educational-level distribution in the population for each political tradition). Therefore, with this model, we obtained the relative index of inequality (RII) of educational level for each political tradition, which can be interpreted as the prevalence ratio of poor perceived health for the two extremes of the educational spectrum (20). As a further step, we fitted eight different log-binomial regression models (Model II to Model IX in Tables 3 and 4) with the same independent variables as Model I, but also including country contextual variables (all the individuals of one country had the same independent variables), to see whether they reduced the RII between self-perceived health and educational level for the different political traditions.

RESULTS

Table 1 shows the cases included in the study for each country and the crude percentages of poor self-perceived health. Poor perceived health status varies among the countries, Portugal having the highest percentages and Netherlands the lowest. Women have worse self-perceived health than men in all countries except Finland and England. The distribution of contextual variables among countries is presented in Table 2. In the late democracies, less than 15 percent

Table 1

Number of people per survey, percentage of population with poor perceived health (less than good), and association between poor perceived health (less than good) and educational level in each country grouped by political tradition, women and men 25–64 years

	Women				Men			
	n	% poor health	RII	95% CI	n	% poor health	RII	95% CI
Social democratic								
Norway	2,346	18.4	3.82	2.70–5.40	2,435	16.1	3.27	2.27–4.70
Sweden	3,922	24.1	2.48	2.00–3.07	3,786	19.8	3.03	2.38–3.85
Finland	9,047	32.3	1.92	1.70–2.17	7,916	36.8	1.76	1.57–1.97
Denmark	5,786	20.5	3.81	3.10–4.69	5,702	19.1	2.82	2.29–3.46
Christian democratic								
Netherlands	5,584	12.3	3.92	2.78–5.52	5,721	9.2	4.53	3.07–6.68
Belgium	6,015	23.8	3.61	2.98–4.37	5,760	19.2	3.94	3.18–4.88
Germany	2,622	17.3	2.48	1.71–3.60	2,627	14.8	3.57	2.42–5.25
France	3,339	23.3	2.70	2.07–3.53	2,554	18.5	2.87	2.02–4.08
Italy	39,342	44.4	1.63	1.56–1.70	38,189	35.4	1.79	1.70–1.88
Liberal								
England	5,803	21.5	3.59	2.92–4.42	4,720	21.7	3.13	2.55–3.83
Ireland	4,671	15.9	6.32	4.07–9.80	4,124	14.7	4.61	2.81–7.59
Late democracy								
Spain	6,675	29.8	2.39	2.02–2.82	6,568	20.0	2.88	2.35–3.52
Portugal	9,492	69.3	2.18	1.99–2.39	5,252	55.3	2.53	2.20–2.91

Note: n = number of cases (non-weighted). RII, relative index of inequality; RII values are age-adjusted.

Table 2

Description of contextual variables in the countries of each political tradition

	Welfare state		Labor market		Income inequalities		Wealth
	Level of education 1999, %[a]	Public expenditure 1992, %[b]	Female labor force 1993, %	Unemployment 2001, %[c]	Quintile share ratio 2001[d]	Gini coefficient 2001	GDP 1993[e]
Social democratic							
Norway	57.4	26.8	45	1.9	3.5	26.1	21,139
Sweden	47.9	35.3	48	2.5	3.4	24.3	19,141
Finland	40.2	33.9	47	4.6	3.7	26.1	17,185
Denmark	53.1	30.7	47	2.2	3.0	22.5	20,125
Christian democratic							
Netherlands	42.1	28.3	41	1.1	4.0	25.1	19,877
Belgium	30.7	28.4	43	2.6	4.0	27.2	19,803
Germany	58.3	26.4	42	3.7	3.6	27.7	19,991
France	40.4	28.0	45	3.9	3.9	27.3	19,888
Italy	34.2	24.3	36	4.0	4.8	34.7	19,157

Liberal						
England	57.2	23.4	44	2.4	5.4	32.6	17,738
Ireland	34.7	20.4	37	1.7	4.5	30.4	14,898
Late democracy						
Spain	14.1	21.4	36	4.6	5.5	32.9	14,433
Portugal	10.1	15.6	45	2.0	6.5	35.6	12,090

[a] Level of education: attainment ISCED 3–4, percentage of adult population (25–64 years).
[b] Public expenditure: total public social expenditure as % GDP.
[c] Unemployment: unemployed as percentage of total population.
[d] Inequality of income distribution (income quintile share ratio): the ratio of total income received by the 20% of the population with the highest income (top quintile) to that received by the 20% of the population with the lowest income (lowest quintile). Income must be understood as equalized disposable income.
[e] Gross domestic product per capita in PPP (million US$, purchasing power parity).

of the adult population has post-secondary education, a much lower percentage than in other countries. The highest percentages of public expenditure and of participation of women in the labor force occur in the social democratic countries. Late democracies and liberal countries have higher income inequalities and lower GDP.

Figure 2 shows that the highest percentage of poor self-perceived health (67.3%) was among women with less education in the late democracies, while the lowest (10.3%) was among women with tertiary education in the liberal countries. Absolute inequalities by educational level were more important in the late democracies. Figure 2 also shows the different distributions of population by educational level among countries with different political traditions, social democracies having the highest levels of education and late democracies the lowest.

The association between poor self-perceived health and educational level (age-adjusted) in each country is also shown in Table 1. In all countries, poor self-perceived health is related to low socioeconomic position. We can observe important discrepancies among countries within the same political tradition. For example, Ireland has a higher RII of poor self-perceived health for women (RII = 6.32; 95% CI, 4.07–9.80) than England (RII = 3.59; 95% CI, 2.92–4.42).

Tables 3 and 4 show, for women and men, the age-adjusted associations between poor self-perceived health, educational level, and the political tradition of the countries. The associations between poor self-perceived health and educational level differ by political tradition (Model I). Among women and men, the RII is lower in social democracies (RII = 2.89; 95% CI, 2.61–3.19 for women and RII = 2.82; 95% CI, 2.55–3.11 for men). The RII of social democracies does not differ from the RII of liberal countries for men.

When the contextual variables of the conceptual model were introduced into Models II to IX, the variations of educational-level inequalities between political traditions were reduced (except in liberal countries), with the exception of the introduction of labor market variables, which did not reduce the variations. The role of the contextual variables was the one hypothesized in the conceptual model: the higher the educational level, public expenditure, and wealth, the lower the percentage of poor health. Conversely, the higher the unemployment, quintile share ratio, and Gini coefficient, the higher the percentage of poor health. The female labor force percentage was related in the opposite direction from that expected: the higher the labor force participation, the higher the percentage of poor health.

In Model IX, which includes all the variables of the conceptual model, the RII of educational level for women varied between 2.31 (95% CI, 2.13–2.51) for late democracies and 4.42 (95% CI, 3.66–5.35) for liberal countries. For men, the RII of educational level varied between 2.32 (95% CI, 2.11–2.56) for social democracies and 3.37 (95% CI, 2.73–4.16) for liberal countries.

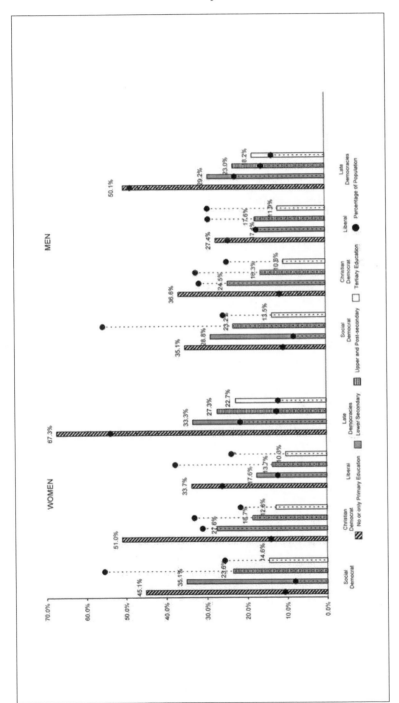

Figure 2. Poor self-perceived health according to educational level (age-standardized percentages) and percentage of population in each educational level, grouped by political tradition, women and men, 25–64 years.

Table 3

Association between poor perceived health (less than good) and independent variables
by political tradition, nine log-binomial models, women 25–64 years

	Model I		Model II		Model III		Model IV	
Individual variables	RII	(95% CI)	RII	(95% CI)	RII	(95% CI)	RII	(95% CI)
Educational level: *RII by political tradition*								
Social democratic	2.89	(2.61–3.19)	2.74	(2.48–3.03)	2.95	(2.67–3.27)	2.88	(2.60–3.18)
Christian democratic	3.74	(3.43–4.07)	3.45	(3.18–3.74)	3.55	(3.26–3.86)	3.90	(3.58–4.24)
Liberal	4.13	(3.40–5.01)	3.77	(3.09–4.59)	4.02	(3.31–4.88)	4.25	(3.50–5.15)
Late democracy	3.51	(3.23–3.82)	3.31	(3.04–3.59)	3.00	(2.76–3.27)	3.10	(2.85–3.38)
p-value[a]<	.001		.001		.001		.001	
Contextual variables			PR	(95% CI)	PR	(95% CI)	PR	(95% CI)
Welfare state								
Level of education 1999[b]			0.982	(0.980–0.984)				
Public expenditure 1992[c]					0.965	(0.960–0.970)		
Labor market								
Female labor force 1993							1.002	(1.016–1.022)
Unemployment 2001[d]								
Income inequality								
Quintile share ratio 2001[e]								
Gini coefficient 2001								
Wealth								
GDP 1993[f]								

Note: All models are age-adjusted. RII, relative index of inequality of the association between educational level and poor perceived health; PR, prevalence ratio; GDP, gross domestic product.

[a]*p*-value of the interaction between educational level and political tradition.

[b]Level of education: attainment ISCED 3–4, percentage of adult population (25–64 years).

[c]Public expenditure: total public social expenditure as % GDP.

[d]Unemployment: unemployed as percentage of total population.

[e]Inequality of income distribution (income quintile share ratio): the ratio of total income received by the 20% of the population with the highest income (top quintile) to that received by the 20% of the population with the lowest income (lowest quintile). Income must be understood as equalized disposable income.

[f]Gross domestic product per capita in PPP (million US$, purchasing power parity).

Table 3 (cont.)

Model V	Model VI	Model VII	Model VIII	Model IX
RII (95% CI)	RII (95% CI)	RII (95% CI)	RII (95% CI)	RII (95% CI)
2.83 (2.57–3.14)	2.87 (2.60–3.17)	2.91 (2.63–3.22)	2.62 (2.37–2.89)	2.67 (2.42–2.95)
3.66 (3.36–3.98)	2.87 (2.64–3.11)	2.56 (2.35–2.79)	3.55 (3.27–3.86)	2.73 (2.51–2.97)
4.16 (3.42–5.05)	4.61 (3.81–5.59)	4.28 (3.53–5.19)	3.75 (3.08–4.57)	4.42 (3.66–5.35)
3.78 (3.46–4.13)	2.21 (2.04–2.40)	2.82 (2.60–3.06)	2.71 (2.50–2.95)	2.31 (2.13–2.51)
.001	.001	.110	.001	.013
PR (95% CI)	PR (95% CI)	PR (95% CI)	PR (95% CI)	PR (95% CI)
				0.991 (0.984–0.999)
1.039 (1.029–1.049)				1.067 (1.054–1.080)
	1.884 (1.828–1.942)			1.752 (1.671–1.838)
		1.108 (1.102–1.112)		
			0.864 (0.854–0.874)	0.949 (0.935–0.964)

Table 4

Association between poor perceived health (less than good) and independent variables by political tradition, nine log-binomial models, men 25–64 years

	Model I		Model II		Model III		Model IV	
Individual variables	RII	(95% CI)	RII	(95% CI)	RII	(95% CI)	RII	(95% CI)
Educational level: RII by political tradition								
Social democratic	2.82	(2.55–3.11)	2.60	(2.36–2.87)	2.94	(2.66–3.25)	2.80	(2.54–3.09)
Christian democratic	4.38	(3.96–4.84)	4.07	(3.69–4.49)	4.24	(3.83–4.69)	4.57	(4.13–5.06)
Liberal	2.86	(2.33–3.51)	2.42	(1.96–2.98)	2.76	(2.25–3.39)	3.10	(2.52–3.80)
Late democracy	4.08	(3.65–4.56)	3.87	(3.47–4.33)	3.66	(3.27–4.11)	3.52	(3.13–3.94)
p-value[a]<	.001		.001		.001		.001	
Contextual variables			PR	(95% CI)	PR	(95% CI)	PR	(95% CI)
Welfare state								
Level of education 1999[b]			0.984	(0.981–0.986)				
Public expenditure 1992[c]					0.975	(0.969–0.980)		
Labor market								
Female labor force 1993							1.024	(1.020–1.029)
Unemployment 2001[d]								
Income inequality								
Quintile share ratio 2001[e]								
Gini coefficient 2001								
Wealth								
GDP 1993[f]								

Note: All models are age-adjusted. RII, relative index of inequality of the association between educational level and poor perceived health; PR, prevalence ratio; GDP, gross domestic product.

[a]p-value of the interaction between educational level and political tradition.

[b]Level of education: attainment ISCED 3–4, percentage of adult population (25–64 years).

[c]Public expenditure: total public social expenditure as % GDP.

[d]Unemployment: unemployed as percentage of total population.

[e]Inequality of income distribution (income quintile share ratio): the ratio of total income received by the 20% of the population with the highest income (top quintile) to that received by the 20% of the population with the lowest income (lowest quintile). Income must be understood as equalized disposable income.

[f]Gross domestic product per capita in PPP (million US$, purchasing power parity).

Table 4 (cont.)

Model V	Model VI	Model VII	Model VIII	Model IX
RII (95% CI)	RII (95% CI)	RII (95% CI)	RII (95% CI)	RII (95% CI)
2.65 (2.40–2.92)	2.69 (2.44–2.97)	2.78 (2.52–3.07)	2.34 (2.13–2.58)	2.32 (2.11–2.56)
4.14 (3.74–4.58)	3.39 (3.07–3.75)	3.00 (2.71–3.33)	4.17 (3.77–4.61)	3.17 (2.86–3.51)
2.93 (2.39–3.60)	3.76 (3.07–4.62)	3.17 (2.58–3.88)	2.31 (1.88–2.86)	3.37 (2.73–4.16)
4.69 (4.16–5.28)	2.59 (2.32–2.88)	3.32 (2.98–3.70)	3.11 (2.78–3.47)	2.74 (2.44–3.06)
.001	.048	.001	.001	.013

PR (95% CI)	PR (95% CI)	PR (95% CI)	PR (95% CI)	PR (95% CI)
				0.992 (0.983–1.001)
1.079(1.065–1.092)				1.087 (1.071–1.103)
	1.990(1.914–2.068)			1.809 (1.711–1.913)
		1.112 (1.106–1.118)		
			0.849(0.837–0.861)	0.932 (0.916–0.948)

DISCUSSION

We found educational-level inequalities in self-perceived health in all the countries examined and in all the political traditions of wealthy countries, for women and men. When countries are grouped by political tradition, we observe that social democracies have the lowest inequalities, while the other political traditions do not differ much. We must take into account, however, the substantial variability among countries within the same political tradition. When contextual variables of welfare state, income inequalities, and wealth were taken into account, educational-level inequalities diminished in all political traditions (except the liberal tradition), and the differences became smaller. Labor market variables did not reduce the differences in educational-level inequalities among political traditions.

The results of this study are in accord with previous findings based on self-perceived health reported by Mackenbach and coauthors (13), also using EUROTHINE data. These authors also acknowledged that self-perceived health inequalities are smaller in Nordic countries, although their article did not compare countries by political tradition.

Data Evaluation

Self-perceived health is a variable that represents a multidimensional concept of health (21), is related to morbidity and mortality (14), and has been used in many European studies on health inequalities (22, 23). The question about self-perceived health had five possible answers in each country, usually two for good health (very good, good) and three for poor health (fair, bad, very bad). But in two countries (Germany and Netherlands), there were three categories of good health (excellent, very good, good) and two of poor health. Taking into account that interviewees chose one of five categories, these different response options may have biased the results. For this reason, we repeated the analysis excluding Germany and Netherlands (Table 5), and we found similar results. Moreover, we changed the categories of the dependent variable ("less than fair" health), finding that, in this case, late democracies showed higher inequalities.

Another fact to be taken into account is that health interview surveys have heterogeneous time periods, and therefore it was not possible to achieve the desired time lags with contextual variables in all cases.

Finally, a larger number of countries for each type of political tradition would be preferable for future studies. Liberal countries should also include the United States, Australia, New Zealand, and Canada. Portugal and Spain should be grouped with Greece.

Table 5

Association between poor perceived health (less than good and less than fair) and educational level by political tradition (excluding Germany and the Netherlands), women and men 25–64 years

	Less than good		Less than fair	
	Women RII (95% CI)	Men RII (95% CI)	Women RII (95% CI)	Men RII (95% CI)
Social democratic	2.89 (2.61–3.19)	2.85 (2.58–3.15)	4.24 (3.37–5.34)	4.17 (3.37–5.15)
Christian democratic	3.18 (2.93–3.44)	3.37 (3.05–3.72)	6.05 (4.58–7.99)	6.45 (4.49–9.27)
Liberal	4.13 (3.40–5.02)	2.89 (2.36–3.55)	5.99 (3.63–9.90)	3.56 (2.39–5.32)
Late democracy	3.51 (3.23–3.82)	4.16 (3.72–4.65)	10.69 (8.37–13.65)	12.03 (8.71–16.62)
p-value[a]	.002	.001	.001	.001

Note: RII, age-adjusted relative index of inequality.
[a]p-value of the interaction between educational level and political tradition.

Poor Self-Perceived Health by Political Tradition

We found differences by political tradition, but we should emphasize that within each political tradition, countries had different profiles. For example, Ireland had higher inequalities than England. The fact that the British Labour Party was in power relatively frequently before 1980 is probably reflected in the indicators of social policy in Britain, mainly in the area of health care (24), and this is a factor that may influence health inequalities.

Few earlier studies have analyzed self-perceived health inequalities by socio-economic position in countries with different political traditions. Two recent studies (10, 25) found higher inequalities by educational level in late democracies, but Christian democratic countries did not show higher inequalities than social democracies. Both studies, however, used other sources of information, different countries, and different age groups than those in our study. As noted in the introduction to this chapter, the study by Espelt and coauthors (10) was based on the population aged over 50 and used Wright's social class dimensions. Eikemo and coauthors (25) used the European Social Survey and analyzed information for 23 countries.

An important issue to take into account in the present study is the different distributions of the population by educational level. In late democracies, the majority of the population has the lowest educational levels; this situation is reversed in other political traditions, particularly in the social democratic countries. This finding is even more evident among women. For this reason, in the late democracies, a large proportion of the population, with low educational level, is being compared with a small proportion, with a high educational level, while in other political traditions the opposite occurs. This low educational level of the population in the late democracies is related to the lower development of public policies in these countries during the second half of the 20th century, and persisting today (7, 26).

In social democratic countries, the population with low educational level is probably a specific group with a higher concentration of poor health than in other types of countries, a fact that may increase the inequalities found in these countries. We should also mention that among men with no education in social democracies, the proportion of those who are unskilled workers is about 40 percent, whereas in other political traditions it is below 30 percent (data not shown).

This study also showed that when contextual variables of welfare state (public expenditure), income inequalities (quintile share ratio and Gini coefficient), and wealth (GDP) are taken into account in the models, the differences between political traditions become smaller. One important consequence of the expansion of the welfare state is that public benefits are high and are universal—available for everyone. Benefits directed to the whole population facilitate access to all public goods (education, health care, social care, maternity leave, home care, etc.). For example, universal free education would increase the overall level of education but also contribute to social mobility by opening up for all, regardless of money, the opportunity to have a university education and thereby climb the social ladder (2, 4, 8). Moreover, the benefits of the welfare state imply being protected in the face of adverse situations such as unemployment or sickness absence, which are related to worse health outcomes. And universalistic health coverage implies better health outcomes and more utilization of preventive and curative health care services (3, 4, 27, 28).

Another aspect of our findings to highlight is the reduction in educational inequalities among welfare state regimes when economic inequalities were taken into account. In this area, it has been reported that redistributive economic policies that imply the existence of lower income inequalities are related to better health outcomes (4, 29, 30). We should point out that in our study, in the models shown in Tables 3 and 4, labor market variables did not diminish the differences in educational-level inequalities between political traditions, probably due to the high percentage of female participation in the labor force in Portugal. For women, it is probably also necessary to consider variables related to household labor (31, 32).

CONCLUSIONS AND RECOMMENDATIONS

This study has shown how inequalities in poor self-perceived health by educational level exist in all political traditions, for women and men, although there are important variations among countries within the same political tradition. These inequalities are reduced when contextual variables of welfare state, income inequalities, and wealth are taken into account. Future studies need to increase the number of countries for each type of political tradition and the number of different health outcomes, in order to better understand the role of political tradition in health inequalities.

Acknowledgments — This study was partially financed by the project Tackling Inequalities in Health in Europe (EUROTHINE), European Union.

REFERENCES

1. Navarro, V., et al. Politics and health outcomes. *Lancet* 368:1033–1037, 2006.
2. Borrell, C., et al. Politics and health (editorial). *J. Epidemiol. Community Health* 61(8):658–659, 2007.
3. Chung, H., and Muntaner, C. Welfare state matters: A typological multilevel analysis of wealthy countries. *Health Policy* 80(2):328–339, 2007.
4. Chung, H., and Muntaner, C. Political and welfare state determinants of infant and child health indicators: An analysis of wealthy countries. *Soc. Sci. Med.* 63(3): 829–842, 2006.
5. Coburn, D. Beyond the income inequality hypothesis: Class, neo-liberalism, and health inequalities. *Soc. Sci. Med.* 58(1):41–56, 2004.
6. Raphael, D., and Bryant, T. The welfare state as a determinant of women's health: Support for women's quality of life in Canada and four comparison nations. *Health Policy* 68:63–79, 2004.
7. Navarro, V., et al. The importance of the political and the social in explaining mortality differentials among the countries of the OECD, 1950–1998. *Int. J. Health. Serv.* 33(3):419–494, 2003.
8. Dahl, E., et al. Welfare state regimes and health inequalities. In *Social Inequalities in Health: New Evidence and Policy Implications*, ed. J. Siegrist and M. Marmot, pp. 193–222. Oxford University Press, Oxford, 2006.
9. Muntaner, C., et al. Social class inequalities in health: Does welfare state regime matter? In *Staying Alive: Critical Perspectives on Health, Illness and Health Care*, ed. D. Raphael, T. Bryant, and M. Rioux, pp. 139–158. Canadian Scholars' Press, Toronto, 2006.
10. Espelt, A., et al. Inequalities in health by social class dimensions in European countries of different political traditions. *Int. J. Epidemiol.* 37(5):1095–1105, 2008.
11. Lundberg, O. Commentary: Politics and public health—some conceptual considerations concerning welfare state characteristics and public health outcomes. *Int. J. Epidemiol.* 37(5):1105–1108, 2008.
12. Espelt, A., et al. Answer to the commentary: Politics and public health—some conceptual considerations concerning welfare state characteristics and public health outcomes. *Int. J. Epidemiol.*, January 8, 2009 [Epub ahead of print].
13. Mackenbach, J. P., et al. European Union Working Group on Socioeconomic Inequalities in Health: Socioeconomic inequalities in health in 22 European countries. *N. Engl. J. Med.* 358(23):2468–2481, 2008.

14. Idler, E. L., and Benyamini, Y. Self-rated health and mortality: A review of twenty-seven community studies. *J. Health Soc. Behav.* 38:21–37, 1997.
15. Blakely, T. A., et al. What is the lag time between income inequality and health status? *J. Epidemiol. Community Health* 54(4):318–319, 2000.
16. Huber, E., Ragin, C., and Stephens, J. *Comparative Welfare States Data Set.* Northwestern University and University of North Carolina, Chapel Hill, 1997.
17. Navarro, V., Schmitt, J., and Astudillo, J. Is globalisation undermining the welfare state. *Camb. J. Econ.* 28:133–152, 2004.
18. Kunkel, S. R., and Atchley, R. C. Why gender matters: Being female is not the same as not being male. *Am. J. Prev. Med.* 12:294–296, 1996.
19. Schiaffino, A., et al. [Odds ratio or prevalence ratio? Their use in cross-sectional studies.] *Gac. Sanit.* 17:70–74, 2003.
20. Mackenbach, J. P., and Kunst, A. E. Measuring the magnitude of socio-economic inequalities in health: An overview of available measures illustrated with two examples from Europe. *Soc. Sci. Med.* 44:757–771, 1997.
21. Simon, J. G., et al. How is your health in general? A qualitative study on self-assessed health. *Eur. J. Public Health* 15(2):200–208, 2005.
22. Mackenbach, J. P., et al. Socioeconomic inequalities in morbidity and mortality in western Europe. The EU Working Group on Socioeconomic Inequalities in Health. *Lancet* 349:1655–1659, 1997.
23. Kunst, A. E., et al. Trends in socioeconomic inequalities in self-assessed health in 10 European countries. *Int. J. Epidemiol.* 34(2):295–305, 2005.
24. Huber, E., and Stephens, J. *Development and Crisis of the Welfare State*, p. 90. University of Chicago Press, Chicago, 2001.
25. Eikemo, T. A., et al. Health inequalities according to educational level in different welfare regimes: A comparison of 23 European countries. *Sociol. Health Illn.* 30(4): 565–582, 2008.
26. Navarro, V., and Quiroga, A. [Welfare state policies for equity.] In *Informe de la Sociedad Española de Salud Pública y Administración Sanitaria (SESPAS) 2004: La salud pública desde la perspectiva de género y clase social*, ed. C. Borrell, M. M. García-Calvente, and J. V. Martí-Boscà. *Gac Sanit.* 18(Suppl. 1):147–157, 2004.
27. Hadley, J. Sicker and poorer. The consequences of being uninsured: A review of the research on the relationship between health insurance, medical care use, health, work, income. *Med. Care Res. Rev.* 60 (Suppl.):3–75S, 2003.
28. Lasser, K. E., Himmelstein, D. U., and Woolhandler, S. Access to care, health status, and health disparities in the United States and Canada: Results of a cross-national population-based survey. *Am. J. Public Health* 96(7):1300–1307, 2006.
29. Lynch, J. W., et al. Income inequality and mortality: Importance to health of individual income, psychosocial environment, or material conditions. *BMJ* 320: 1200–1204, 2000.
30. Wilkinson, R. G., and Pickett, K. E. Income inequality and population health: A review and explanation of the evidence. *Soc. Sci. Med.* 62(7):1768–1784, 2006.
31. Artazcoz, L., et al. Women, family demands and health: The importance of employment status and socio-economic position. *Soc. Sci. Med.* 59(2):263–274, 2004.
32. Borrell, C., et al. Social class and self-reported health status among men and women: What is the role of work organisation, household material standards and household labor? *Soc. Sci. Med.* 58(10):1869–1887, 2004.

PART V

Changes in Class Inequalities

Edwin Ng

INTRODUCTION

The preceding parts of the book have focused on the interconnections between welfare states and regimes, public policies, labor markets, social inequalities, and population health. In Part V we turn our attention to global changes in inequality and finance and their effects on social class and health. The underlying argument is that social class, understood in terms of productive relations, matters in the struggle toward achieving egalitarian outcomes, including population health and health equality. Because social class is a defining feature in capitalist economies, different social classes tend to possess different self-interests and use different resources to materialize these interests (e.g., working classes tend to support labor unions and left political parties to achieve generous wage agreements and job security measures; business classes rely on anti-union laws and right political parties to advance policies based on fiscal conservatism, low wages, and flexible forms of employment).

In recent years, the idea that social class matters to egalitarianism has become more than an academic exercise. Telling examples abound; however, perhaps the most notable example is the mobilization of the Occupy Wall Street movement. The driving forces behind this movement are relevant issues related to social and economic inequality, corporate greed, and political corruption. Guided by the slogan "We are the 99%," the Occupy movement has publicized the growing and intractable gap between the wealthiest 1 percent and the rest of the population. The three studies included in Part V reflect different perspectives on this theme. In Chapter 19, Figueiredo Santos paves new ground on the association between class divisions and health chances within the understudied context of Brazil. In Chapter 20, Nowatzki augments existing studies on income inequality and health by examining the health effects of wealth inequality, which is far greater and conceptually different from income inequality. And in Chapter 21, Zhang offers a much-needed analysis on the unintended health consequences of the "Chinese economic miracle," revealing that improvements in health outcomes and health care systems have slowed in recent years and lag considerably behind economic growth.

CHAPTER 19

Class Divisions and Health Chances
in Brazil

José Alcides Figueiredo Santos

This chapter analyzes the association between class divisions and health chances in the Brazilian population. It uses data from the health supplement of the 2008 National Household Survey. Multiple logistic regression models are estimated to determine the relation between social class and self-rated health status. This empirical investigation of health inequalities combines two modalities for social class comparison, thus benefiting from the potential utility of each. On the one hand, socioeconomic inequalities in health are analyzed with reference to the combination of two main assets, capital and expert knowledge, which generate material and health advantages in Brazil. The results demonstrate that social class measurements for Brazil capture a source of variation in health chances among social groups that is independent of education and family income. On the other hand, the use of theoretically univocal categories for exploring diversified class contrasts offers some explanatory starting points for health inequalities in the Brazilian population.

*****

Socioeconomic asymmetries in the distribution of health and mortality are a well-established fact, based on a wide, rigorous, and cumulative research process. Health inequalities are huge and persist in spite of great progress in general average health levels of populations and improvements in the quality and availability of modern medical services (1–3). There is an invariant pattern of health inequality in contemporary societies: the worse the social position, the worse the health. People in the lower socioeconomic strata tend to be at a disadvantage for a wide set of biomedical, environmental, behavioral, and psychosocial risk factors that mediate the relation between social conditions and disease (4–8).

Distinguishing the cause of variation in individuals' and groups' health chances is crucial for understanding the social determinants of health (9).

Sociology offers a perspective through an "upstream" explanation of disparities in health. It puts proper value on the macro-social factors that shape socioeconomic position and its distribution in society. The sociological approach provides both context and content for researching the trajectories and mechanisms that relate social position to health (10). Social structure has a causal power in the uneven distribution of health chances. Social conditions make up "fundamental causes" for health and disease, as they determine access to important resources that may be used to prevent or minimize the consequences of disease, affect multiple health results through many mechanisms or risk trajectories, and persist under changing circumstances. The flexible and multiply applicable nature of economic and social resources allows for their use in different ways in different situations to promote individuals' welfare. In the context of a dynamic system of changing patterns of illness, treatments, risk factors, and protections, the association between social condition and distribution of health and disease reproduces itself over time, through a transposition of resource advantages from one situation to another and through socially selective processes shaping the substitution of mediating mechanisms that lead to health or illness. People who own such resources as knowledge, money, power, and prestige can use these advantages to increase their well-being, no matter the health risks and protections at play at any given time. Health disparities are fed by the social expansion of different abilities to control one's health conditions. When people use their resource advantages to obtain health benefits, they do so in a structurally unequal system. Given the existing social and economic inequalities, the benefits of this recently developed ability to obtain better health are more successfully appropriated by those segments of the population that have more resources. The combination of information and resource inequalities is fundamental to an understanding of health disparities (11–15).

Social class is a true health determinant, and the effect of social position is closely associated with material conditions. However, social class remains a "black box" of causal factors and mechanisms. Research must dissect the components of class affiliation that are translated into health outcomes (16). The investigation of inequality in health may further benefit from using a theoretically rooted measure of social position and promoting an interpretation of results in accord with this theoretical base. Using indicators without any clear theoretical base, or those that allow multiple, sometime contradictory, theoretical justifications, has hindered researchers' ability to overcome the limitations of mere descriptions of patterns and progress in explaining health inequalities. Inconsistencies between studies arise and persist because of unexamined differences in the conceptual bases of social position measures (17, 18). The concept of social class may uncover important sources of variation in health distribution, and it could help explain the generation and persistence of trajectories leading to health inequalities (19, 20).

This chapter considers how a sociological notion of class can contribute to the observation and interpretation of variations in health chances among social groups. A socioeconomic classification for Brazil, with empirical categories that reflect a neo-Marxist focus on social class, offers a way to observe and interpret the determinants of health inequalities as closely related to property relations, to social powers in the context of work organization, and to the usual nexus of exploitation and exclusion from control over valuable economic resources. This empirical investigation of health inequalities brings together two modalities for social class comparison, making use of the potential benefits of each method. On the one hand, socioeconomic inequality in health is analyzed with reference to the combination of two main assets—capital and expert knowledge—that can generate material and health advantages in Brazil. The study demonstrates that social class measurement for Brazil captures a source of variation of health chances among social groups that is independent of education and family income. On the other hand, the use of theoretically univocal categories for exploring different class contrasts offers some explanatory starting points for understanding health inequalities in the Brazilian population.

METHODS

The study uses micro-data from Brazil's National Household Survey (PNAD) of 2008, with its special supplement that investigates the health characteristics of household inhabitants. The sample in the study consisted of 191,428 valid cases with information for all variables. The PNAD incorporates all the elements that define a complex sample plan: stratification, conglomeration, unequal selection probabilities, and sample-weight adjustment. The statistical models were implemented by using the special capabilities of the Strata program, version 11, for analyzing complex data surveys, incorporated into the SYV command.

The focus of this study is social class discrepancies in the distribution of individual self-rated health (SRH) status, which has the advantage of capturing the medium health of the population. Self-rating of health status is probably the most affordable, comprehensive, and fruitful measure in population studies, capturing health dimensions that are missed in more guided and detailed questions (21, 22). The dependent variable was treated as a binary variable, with the aim of dealing with the asymmetric distribution of answers on SRH status (23). There is evidence of an underestimation of more negative answers on SRH in the PNAD (24). The choice of a binary format for the dependent variable, with a cut-off of "not good" health, overcomes this measurement problem. In this binary variable, "not good" SRH, coded 1, comprises the definitions of very bad (0.4%), bad (2.3%), and fair (19.5%) SRH; the combination of good (56.6%) and very good (21.1%) SRH is coded 0.

The present study applies a notion of social class based on the contributions of Erik Olin Wright in the Marxist tradition of social science. Social class is defined and measured in terms of property relations, that is, individuals' rights and powers in various types of productive assets (25). The nexus between class, assets, exploitation, and domination explains why reward inequalities are generated by asymmetries in rights and powers over productive resources (26). The exploitative relations among these groups can be deduced from the structural properties of social classes (27).

The socioeconomic classification for Brazil (see Table 1) constructs class categories with both theoretical meaning and empirical pertinence for the concrete analysis of a concrete reality (28–30). The theoretical criterion for ownership and deployment of capital assets, with its differentiation of scale and labor division, delimits the positions of *capitalists*, *small employers*, and *self-employed with assets*. The differentiated situation of small-production agriculture—where land control is considered a productive asset, but there is no hiring of waged workers—is described as *agricultural self-employed*. The middle class of privileged locations, either within waged work or as autonomous activity, has the categories of *expert self-employed*, *managers*, and *expert employees*. The classification also delimits the great set of *typical workers*, whose employment relations more clearly entail the asymmetrical interdependencies characteristic of exploitation and dominance processes, and differentiates the ambiguous situations of *skilled workers* and *supervisors*. The classification specifies and qualifies the large aggregate of destitute positions, both in and outside the sphere of waged work, which characterize the Brazilian class structure. A conceptual extension of the principle of exclusion from the control of assets or economic resources, such as capital assets, land, jobs, skills, and labor force, is used to theoretically justify and empirically classify these destitute class positions (30). The *elementary worker* and *domestic worker* categories represent class situations associated with a strong economic depreciation of labor capacity and waged work under hugely asymmetric circumstances. The *precarious self-employed* are, in practice, without capital or skill-related assets, working in the fringes or interstitial spaces of the goods and services markets. The classification portrays *subsistence workers*, with no income, as highly "disconnected" from the economic system that exists in rural areas. *Surplus workers* are part of the unemployed in the broader sense. The job from which a person is excluded is a basic asset or resource for obtaining the means for living above the level of destitution or dependence on state transfers (31).

Age was measured at the interval level, and the sample includes ages from 10 to 104 years, with a mean of 36.8 years and a standard deviation of 13.8 years. *Gender* was included as usual. A binary variable, *health informant*, was created to control for the PNAD's use of an informant other than the surveyed individual ("self") in some cases. Three categories were constructed to measure the variable for *race or color*.[1] The *region* variables were southeast, south, northeast, center-west, and north. *Income* and *education* indicators were constructed using 10 categories each, to minimize the effect of different scales and units in the adjusted estimations. Both variables were also measured as categories considering the nonlinear relation with health (32, 33). Appendix Table 1 (p. 428) shows the distribution of independent control variables and the age-standardized percentage of "not good" health status associated with each category.

The investigation uses the notion of social class as analytically distinct from factors such as education and income, which allows a comparison of the power of this sociological concept with the more conventional markers of social position. Maintaining this analytical separation also allows us to examine the contribution of these factors as links in the causal chain of class effects on a population's health (34). Models of multiple logistic regressions (odds ratios, OR) were estimated to determine the relation of class and "not good" health status. A basic model was estimated as a reference standard, with controls present in each subsequent model, adjusting the effects of class position for age, gender, health informant (self or other), race, and region of residence. The reference group is the combined categories of capitalist and expert self-employed. These correspond to the most privileged class positions in terms of material rewards and health status (see Table 1 and Appendix Table 2, p. 429). Estimations for 2008, based on logistic models controlling for gender, age, race, and region, show there are no statistically significant health differences between these two categories.

All coefficients in the tables are expressed as percentage changes in the odds (OR – 1 * 100). As a comparison strategy between models, the percentage change (reduction) resulting from the addition of new controls is estimated, when the odds estimated by the extended model decrease (35). The reduction in the estimated effects was calculated by the expression: (basic model – extended model)/(basic model) * 100. A calculation using the original OR coefficient would not allow proper evaluation of the magnitude of change. Calculation of the amount of change (reduction) from the original effect should be made with the coefficients already converted in terms of percentage change.[2]

---

[1] The race/color categories in the study, based on those used in Brazil, are: white/yellow, brown/indigenous, and black. Those in the yellow category (Asian) are closer in health advantage to those designated white, and the indigenous are closer in disadvantage to those designated brown (*Pardo*, in Portuguese, meaning mixed-color), as being in rural areas; both, summed, are just 0.9 percent of the total.

[2] When expressed in terms of percentage change, for example, the odds for domestic workers having "not good" health are 393 percent greater than odds for the capitalist category. The extended model decreases these odds 113 percent, as shown in Table 2 (model 2), so the original effect is reduced 71 percent [(393 – 113)/393]. However, the calculation based on OR, [(4.93 – 2.13)/4.93], should indicate a reduction of only 57 percent of the original effect. Making this comparison using information in the original multiplicative form of OR seems unsuitable, because this property will distort every comparison.

Table 1

Percentage distribution of class categories and
health, adjusted by age, Brazil, 2008

Class category	Percent in category	Percent reporting "not good" health
Capitalist and large farmer	0.5	7.2
Expert self-employed	1.0	6.1
Manager	2.5	11.6
Expert employee	3.7	8.5
Small employer	3.5	16.5
Self-employed with assets	5.7	21.2
Agricultural self-employed	4.2	30.5
Skilled worker	6.6	13.8
Supervisor	1.2	14.1
Typical worker	32.1	19.5
Elementary worker	9.9	25.9
Precarious self-employed	8.8	26.8
Domestic worker	6.9	29.3
Subsistence worker	4.0	39.5
Surplus worker	9.4	29.3
Total	100.0	22.2

Source: Special tabulations from the 2008 PNAD.

RESULTS

Considering the age-standardized ratio of people who reported "not good" health according to the class categories, with its corresponding relative weight in the social structure, provides a first approach to the research problem (Table 1). All the privileged categories, in terms of capital assets, expert knowledge, and exerted power/authority, have health advantages over the other categories. At the opposite pole are the destitute class positions, from the elementary to the surplus worker, and the agricultural stratum of non-employer, where the proportion reporting "not good" health is greatly increased. There is a hierarchy in health distribution among those who control resources or exert power, as shown by the health discrepancies associated with the quality or amount of capital, expertise, and authority—as in the example of skilled workers and expert employees. The health status of the typical working class, a large social category, is clearly worse than that of those in privileged positions. The subsistence worker, in turn, occupies a position of extreme disadvantage among the destitute positions.

The focal relation between social class and health chances is next elaborated through the application of logistic models. Such models introduce alternative indicators of social position as independent control variables, with the aim of understanding the major factors and types of resource that antecede, specify, or mediate the causal relation between class categories and health outcomes. Picking model 1 as a base for comparison, which includes the variables for race and region, represented the choice of a more conservative estimation of social class–independent consequences in health outcomes.[3] The subsequent models (2, 3, and 4) introduce one or more "test factors," generating a kind of statistical experiment to assess the force and specify the contributions of these factors in the observed relation. The percentage reduction of the original effect promoted by the added variables expresses the amount of that variable's contribution to the formerly observed patterns. These percentages are comparable because they represent alterations or differences in relation to the same basic model.

Model 1 shows the existence of a sharp class contrast in the relative distribution of health chances (Table 2). The most privileged class combination, capitalist and expert self-employed, shows the best health condition, because the original coefficients for all other categories are larger than 1. In all other class categories, the chance of having "not good" health shows an increase, ranging from 24 percent for the expert employee to 526 percent for the subsistence worker. The class arrangement among proprietors of capital assets is reflected in the health patterns, with "not good" health increasing from the small employer to the self-employed with assets. The large group of typical workers shows a worse indicator than that for skilled workers and supervisors. All the destitute class positions, from the surplus worker to the elementary worker, reveal a much worse picture. Also, among the destitute positions, which as a whole compose a distinctive grouping, there are internal gradations that disfavor the surplus worker (unemployed), more concentrated in urban areas, and the subsistence worker, exclusively rural, both with zero personal income.

Ownership of capital and expert knowledge, the latter when applied to an enterprise, represent the most important assets for both income and health advantages. These characteristics, together in the same group, should be taken into account in analyzing the results, because the estimated coefficients for all other categories in this part of the analysis are related to this contrast. The expert self-employed are at the head of the enterprises, and these may be employers with up to five employees, representing a common thread with the capitalists, though

---

[3] The social class association with race and region could make these controls in the logistic regression remove part of the class effect, since the effects are not totally independent of one another. There is a very strong intersection between class and race, because both divisions presuppose exclusion from access to valuable resources. In turn, the uneven development of capitalism generates an imbalance or variation in the regional distribution of class positions and in the income gaps among these positions (36).

Table 2

Percentage change in the odds of "not good" health by class category, Brazil, 2008

Class category	Model 1 (age, gender, race, region)		Model 2 (+ education)			Model 3 (+ income)			Model 4 (+ education and income)		
	OR	95% CI	OR	95% CI	% reduction	OR	95% CI	% reduction	OR	95% CI	% reduction
Capitalist and expert self-employed	—	—	—	—	—	—	—	—	—	—	—
Expert employee	24**	0.1, 53	32**	7, 63	—	13***	-9, 42	—	21***	-3, 51	—
Manager	66	33, 105	31**	5, 64	53	30**	3, 63	54	15***	-9, 46	—
Small employer	167	121, 221	65	35, 101	61	102	65, 147	39	53	24, 89	68
Self-employed with assets	249	188, 323	96	60, 141	61	119	77, 169	52	62	31, 101	75
Agricultural self-employed	391	302, 499	118	75, 170	70	139	93, 197	64	58	26, 99	85
Skilled worker	99	65, 141	63*	34, 99	36	39	13, 71	61	34*	8, 65	66
Supervisor	144	90, 213	62	24, 110	57	68	29, 121	53	38**	5, 83	74
Typical worker	217	165, 280	80	48, 118	63	86	53, 126	60	42	15, 74	81
Elementary worker	353	276, 445	100	63, 145	72	120	79, 170	66	45	17, 80	87
Precarious self-employed	343	269, 432	117	78, 165	66	136	93, 188	60	65	33, 104	81
Domestic worker	392	305, 497	113	72, 164	71	138	93, 194	64	55	23, 94	86
Subsistence worker	526	415, 560	157	107, 218	70	173	121, 238	67	75	40, 120	86
Surplus worker	383	301, 482	149	103, 205	61	122	81, 173	68	67	35, 108	82
Average value[a]	258	—	96	—	63	106	—	59	54	—	79
Adjusted Wald test	377.94	—	334.47	—	—	277.44	—	—	254.93	—	—

Note: Model 1: adjusted by age, gender, type of informant (self or proxy), race, and geographic regions. Model 2: model 1 plus controlling for education. Model 3: model 1 plus controlling for per capita family income deciles. Model 4: model 1 plus controlling for education and income.
*Significant at 0.05 level; **significant at 0.01 level; ***not significant (>0.05). All other coefficients are significant at 0.001 level or more.
[a] Averags value of statistically significant coefficients when odds ratio is reduced compared with the basic model.

the advantages of the expert self-employed depend more on the "opportunity-hoarding" generated by the command of professional expertise. Comparison with a group that combines both main resources (capital and expertise), though carrying the disadvantage of mixing distinct mechanisms, has the merit of making the comparison more representative and less "biased" by the typical resource mechanisms, since all other categories are compared with this group. It is important to note that if just the capitalist category were used as reference, because its class advantage depends less on expertise and knowledge, differences with other categories would have been less related to the education factor. A full exploration of the analytical potential of having each class category built on a theoretically univocal characterization is developed in the second part of the study, in which various specific class contrasts are estimated.

Model 2 shows that education has an important independent effect on health; its statistical control reduces the class discrepancies in health by, on average, 63 percent. This reduction reflects the role of education as an antecedent variable in the sorting of people among class positions. It also expresses two other factors: differences in educational distribution among and within class categories, and the specific causal potency of education for health. In the comparison between privileged class categories, education has a quite different role. For the expert employee, education works to reduce inequality in relation to the reference group of capitalist and expert self-employed. This is the proper characteristic of a suppression or reduction variable: its control increases the original effect—in other words, the effect would be larger if not for the reduction it imposes on this effect. When controlling for education increases the original effect, this reveals that it compensates for a relative disadvantage or protects the expert employee more than other categories. This is understandable, because both capitalist and expert self-employed command enterprises from which their advantages flow, whereas the expert employee depends more on the "expert knowledge" itself. In a different way, the relative class position of a manager, in terms of its implications for health, seems to depend more on the authority exerted, since controlling for education has a lower reductive effect—below the general medium value—on the difference from the reference group. The most important reductions occur among the destitute class positions, emphasizing the role of the educational discrepancies. However, even among these categories, 28 to 39 percent of the original class effect persists, which is completely independent of education. The educational differences reveal the importance of education for health when they reduce the class effect and when they add a specific effect. The coefficients for the educational categories continue high and statistically significant after controlling for social class (results not shown).

Model 3 controls for inequality of relative income, suppressing the class effect on health that flows through monetary rewards. The general impact of this factor, which reduces the original class effect by, on average, 59 percent, approaches that of the educational control. The health disadvantages of the small employer, when compared with the reference group, are less mediated by income than by education, possibly because this comparison is also made with the expert self-employed. In relation to the skilled worker, the pattern is inverted, since it depends more on income than on education. The class differences in relation to the supervisor and the typical worker are almost equally associated with income as with education. The income variable, like education, contributes to explaining the majority (around 65%) of the health disadvantages of the five destitute class positions.

Model 4 introduces the combined control of education and income. All the privileged class positions would form one block, if not for the educational and income differences between them, because controlling for these factors makes the coefficients statistically nonsignificant. Among the five destitute class positions, the variables education and income contribute in a very high proportion (medium value 84%) to explaining the observed differences. However, in two categories that embody very different explanatory principles, capital assets (small employer) and qualification assets (skilled worker), 32 percent or more of the class effect does not depend on education and income. In general terms, without considering the relative weight of the categories in the social structure, an original class effect of 21 percent persists that is completely independent of education and income.

A socioeconomic classification constructed in a theoretically informed way opens the possibility to explore several types of theoretically and empirically important contrasts that are much more informative than comparisons based on conventional socioeconomic indicators, such as contrasting family income groups. Moreover, as this classification formulated for Brazil does not mix theoretically differentiated social mechanisms, it allows the exploration of different contrasts with a more univocal theoretical content.

Table 3 shows 13 contrasts in health chances between class categories, comparisons of which can reveal the demarcation of meaningful sources of relative advantages and disadvantages in health. Introduction of the expanded models with separate and additional controls for education and income contributes to indicating which of these factors more strongly influence(s) the definition of relative differences. To understand the consequences of the statistical controls, average values of education and family income for the class categories are presented in Appendix Table 2.

The first three contrasts in Table 3 set the capitalist in relation to other categories with distinct class characteristics. Capital assets contribute most to health in terms of income returns, as revealed by comparing manager and capitalist, because the manager's disadvantage becomes statistically nonsignificant with control for family income. The typical worker has a high disadvantage in relation to the capitalist category, which is more affected by family income than by education; this meets the theoretical expectation, since both categories are not characterized properly by controlling for educational credentials. In contrasting

Table 3

Percentage change in the odds of "not good" health for select class contrasts, Brazil, 2008

Class contrasts	Model 1 (age, gender, race, region)		Model 2 (+ education)			Model 3 (+ income)		
	OR	95% CI	OR	95% CI	% reduction	OR	95% CI	% reduction
Manager vs. capitalist	42**	5, 93	41**	4, 92	2	7***	−22, 47	—
Typical worker vs. capitalist	173	106, 261	93	45, 158	46	54*	14, 107	69
Small employer vs. capitalist	129	74, 202	78	34, 136	39	67	24, 124	48
Typical worker vs. manager	92	68, 119	37	20, 57	60	43	25, 64	53
Manager vs. expert employee	34	13, 58	1***	−16, 17	—	14***	−4, 35	—
Typical worker vs. expert employee	157	129, 187	36	19, 55	77	64	45, 84	59
Elementary worker vs. typical worker	43	34, 52	11	5, 18	74	18	11, 26	58
Surplus worker vs. typical worker	52	43, 62	38	30, 47	27	20	12, 27	61
Supervisor vs. skilled worker	22**	4, 45	1***	−17, 18	—	21**	1, 45	4
Self-employed with assets vs. small employer	31	17, 46	19*	6, 33	39	8***	−3, 21	—
Precarious self-employed vs. self-employed with assets	27	17, 37	11**	2, 20	59	8***	−1, 17	—
Subsistence worker vs. agricultural self-employed	27	12, 45	18**	4, 34	33	14**	0.2, 30	48
Domestic worker vs. elementary worker	8**	1, 17	7***	−1, 15	—	8**	0.3, 17	—

Note: Model 1 (basic): adjusted by age, gender, type of informant (self or proxy), race, and geographic regions. Model 2: model 1 plus controlling for education. Model 3: model 1 plus controlling for per capita family income deciles.

*Significant at 0.01 level; **significant at 0.05 level; ***not significant (>0.05). All other coefficients are significant at 0.001 level or more.

the small employer and capitalist, something special gives the capitalist an advantage that surpasses the quantitative association between level of capital and level of income.

The contrast between typical worker and manager is a bit more associated with education than with income. The next two contrasts involve the middle class position of expert employee. Among the salaried, expert knowledge supplants authority in terms of health advantage, but this discrepancy within the middle class is indistinctly associated with either education or income differences between the two categories. This redundant pattern might lead one to suppose that the effect of education is expressed through income, because the effects of both variables are superposed and, after all, education is obtained before taking a job and receiving income. The health disadvantage of the typical worker is very high; however, it is smaller than his disadvantage in relation to the capitalist. Education reduces 77 percent of the discrepancy, which makes theoretical sense because educational credentials are the selection criterion for access to specialist jobs.

The typically exploited worker is compared with two destitute categories. Elementary workers—42 percent of whom are in the agricultural sector—show an important health disadvantage that is much affected by education. On the other hand, the effect of employment exclusion on health, using the same comparison with the typical worker, generates a larger disadvantage for the surplus worker; however, it does not much depend on education, because the two categories have similar educational levels (see Appendix Table 2).

The comparison between supervisor and skilled worker focuses the differentiated effects of authority versus skill inside the range of these ambiguous working-class positions. As in the case of the middle class, skill seems to protect health more than does authority. Controlling for education makes the differences statistically nonsignificant, which is expected because the supervisor has an educational disadvantage. Controlling for family income maintains the coefficient at its original level, reflecting the fact that there are almost no income discrepancies between the two categories (see Appendix Table 2).

Among the autonomous activities, with or without employees, the possession of capital assets, and their amount, makes a difference. The self-employed with assets have a worse health status than small employers. On the other hand, the precarious self-employed, being deprived of capital, have a health disadvantage in relation to the self-employed with assets. Both differences are related to family incomes, because controlling for these makes the differences disappear.

All the non-employer agricultural strata have strong health disadvantages. However, this is not a generic burden associated with the segmentation of economic activity: agricultural capitalists and small employers are not subject to it. Besides, the contrast between agricultural self-employed and subsistence worker indicates that regular access to land can be important, since subsistence workers, lacking command over this asset and personal income, show a worse health condition in all models with several kinds of control.

The isolated household work peculiar to the domestic waged worker reveals a relative disadvantage, even when compared with a category of strong agricultural composition such as the elementary worker. This picture does not change with family income, but is affected by education, because controlling for these removes any statistically significant difference between these categories. Agricultural segmentation works as a suppressor variable of the "real differences," that is, the class differences without this economic segmentation, because their statistical control in a separate model (not shown) increases the difference from 8 to 13 percent. This suggests that some component associated with "domestic" work, such as work conditions, or with the "domestic worker," such as family circumstances, is generating the relative health disadvantage.

DISCUSSION

The first part of this empirical analysis was based on contrasts with the most privileged group in material and health terms, because this comparison indicates a level of health that is biologically feasible under present social conditions. The class divisions captured by the socioeconomic classification show accentuated discrepancies in the distribution of health chances across the Brazilian population. On the one hand, property relationships, position of authority, and control of expert knowledge favor better health status. On the other hand, relative health disadvantage is associated with work subject to exploitative processes and, even more, with all situations of exclusion from control over economic resources. Taking the privileged positions in capital assets and expert knowledge as the reference group, the study finds that more than half (on average, 59%) of the class effects on health are mediated by material factors associated with family income. Education has a more complex role in the causal chain linking social class and health; it can work as an antecedent variable, conditioning access to certain class positions, or as a qualification factor for exercising positional causal power. There are also educational differences between and within class categories that testify to a specific health effect of education. According to the theory on fundamental health causes, a combination of resource inequality and use of information plays a key role in understanding health disparities.

Muntaner and colleagues (37) conducted a review of English-language empirical studies that adopted relational social class indicators in the socio-epidemiological literature. They point out the specific importance of integrating situations of underemployment, nonstandard employment relations, or precarious employment in theory-grounded social class measures. The present study uses a class typology that theoretically delineates and empirically draws a wide set of destitute class positions that characterize the social structure in Brazil (30, 31). This feature has special importance, given that the prime determinant of individual and population health should not be what occurs over the whole of or at any level of socioeconomic distribution (inequality per se) but, in particular, the absolute and relative position of those in the lower groups, that is, the groups below the 40 to 60 percent limit of disadvantage (7, 38, 39).

These results for Brazil should be compared with those from other studies that use a conceptual and relational class approach for analyzing the association between social groups and self-rated health. A recent study applying the new European socioeconomic classification, conceptually based on a neo-Weberian class schema, estimated that the *greatest* class discrepancy in health (rate ratio) in all member states of the European Union, as a whole, is about 100 percent, controlling for country and five-year age group. In Brazil, by contrast, the *average* discrepancy (odds ratio) is 238 percent, with additional controls for race and geographic regions, both of which carry a huge socioeconomic content in Brazil. Health inequality by social class, then, is much sharper in Brazil than in Europe. On the other hand, in Europe, about 30 to 50 percent of class differences persist after controlling for education (three categories only) and income, whereas in Brazil, about 21 percent, on average, of the original effect persists after controlling for education and income (10 categories each), plus race and geographic region (40). These differences in adjusted class discrepancies reflect the fact that the distributions of education and income, as well as their association with social class and health, have very different patterns in Brazil and in Europe as a whole. Part of these differences, however, could be due to the kind of income and education measures used in the European study.[4]

Borrell and coworkers (21) investigated the relation between Wright's measures of social class and poor reported health in a southern European population (Barcelona). The class differences in relative health status were greater among men in Barcelona than for both sexes in Brazil, reaching up to 679 percent for the class contrast between best and worst health status, after controlling for age, marital status, region (Barcelona only), and gender (men only). These health estimates may be subject to sizable random fluctuations, however, since the 95 percent confidence intervals are very large. Brazil presents a clear monotonic, social class hierarchy in health distribution, with "not good" SRH decreasing with the kind, quality, and amount of resources controlled or power exerted. In Barcelona, the social class differentiation is less hierarchical, since the small

---

[4] The educational measure (only three categories) reflected the lack of detailed educational classifications in the European Community Household Panel (ECHP) data, as made available by Eurostat (40, p. 219). Estimates for women were adjusted by income deciles in a linear format (1, 2, 3, . . . 10) plus a quadratic term, and estimates for men were based on quintile categories (41). This can have an important implication for the results for women. The original effect for the typical worker, for instance, is reduced only 31 percent, instead of 60 percent, if I use, for the Brazilian data, this kind of measure based on 10 equal linear intervals as a proxy for overall income distribution. However, I assume that control for both education and income in the model can neutralize part of this income measurement inconsistency for the estimates for women in the European study.

employer class (with capital assets) has worse health than the petit bourgeoisie (with less capital) and semi-skilled workers (without capital assets and with lower skills), when compared with managers and expert supervisors.

Social class measurement for Brazil captures a pattern of health chances that is independent of educational and income distributions and their effects. Maintaining a class concept analytically differentiated from education and income allows incorporation of both socioeconomic indicators in the analysis, with a more appropriate definition of their role in health inequality. The notion of social class based on ownership of assets, guiding the construction of theoretically univocal categories, provides less ambiguous explanatory orientations. This solution allows better judgment and comparisons in studying important social configurations that generate relative health advantages and disadvantages. The consequences of social structure for the unequal distribution of health chances acquire a more specific and clearer meaning. The sharp health disparities, as well as the more nuanced differences, can be socially located and associated with specific determinants of observed outcomes. Progress in the understanding of socioeconomic health inequalities is accomplished precisely when the investigations contribute to a better specification of the valuable, flexible, and multiple-use resources that generate health advantages, as well as to a more appropriate stipulation of the circumstances, dependencies, and exclusions that generate health disadvantages among social groups.

REFERENCES

1. Marmot, M., Kogevinas, M., and Elston, M. A. Social/economic status and disease. *Annu. Rev. Public Health* 8:111–135, 1987.
2. Marmot, M., Bobak, M., and Smith, G. D. Explanations for social inequalities in health. In *Society and Health*, ed. B. C. Emick et al. Oxford University Press, Oxford, 1995.
3. Elo, I. T. Class differentials in health and mortality: Patterns and explanations in comparative perspective. *Annu. Rev. Sociol.* 35:553–572, 2009.
4. House, J. S., et al. Social stratification, age, and health. In *Aging, Health Behaviors, and Health Outcomes*, ed. K. W. Schaie, D. Blazer, and J. S. House. Erlbaum, Hillsdale, NJ, 1992.
5. House, J. S., et al. The social stratification of aging and health. *J. Health Soc. Behav.* 35:213–234, 1994.
6. House, J. S., et al. Continuity and change in the social stratification of aging and health over the life course. *J. Gerontol. Psychol. Sci. Soc. Sci.* 60B(Special Issue 2):15–26, 2005.
7. House, J. S., and Williams, D. R. Understanding and reducing socioeconomic and racial/ethnic disparities in health. In *Promoting Health: Intervention Strategies from Social and Behavioral Research*, ed. B. D. Smedley and S. L. Syme. National Academy Press, Washington, DC, 2000.

References *continue on p. 429*

Appendix Table 1

Relative distribution of categorical variables and percentage of "not good" health, adjusted by age (persons with a class position), Brazil, 2008

Categorical variable	Distribution, %, between categories	"Not good" health, %, adjusted by age, at the category
Health status informant		
Self	57.1	23.1
Other person (ref.)	42.9	20.8
Gender		
Men (ref.)	56.5	20.4
Women	43.5	24.4
Region		
South	15.3	20.7
Southeast (ref.)	43.8	17.7
Center-west	7.6	23.5
North	7.2	29.1
Northeast	26.1	28.4
Race/color		
White and yellow (ref.)	49.2	18.3
Brown and indigenous	43.0	26.2
Black	7.8	24.7
Education		
Illiterate	7.3	36.1
Zero year complete (but literate)	2.2	31.6
1–3 yrs	7.4	31.1
4 yrs	9.3	28.4
5–7 yrs	13.6	26.3
8 yrs (fundamental)	10.3	22.2
9–10 yrs	7.7	22.6
11 yrs (high school complete)	26.7	16.1
College incomplete	6.3	12.2
College complete (ref.)	9.2	9.5
Per capita family income decile		
1	10.00	34.5
2	10.00	31.5
3	10.00	28.3
4	10.00	25.6
5	10.00	23.9
6	10.00	21.9
7	10.00	19.6
8	10.00	17.1
9	10.00	13.9
10 (ref.)	10.00	9.0

Source: Special tabulations from the 2008 PNAD.

Appendix Table 2

Average values for schooling and per capita family income
for all class categories, Brazil, 2008

Class category	Average schooling, yrs[a]	Average per capita monthly family income, reais
Capitalist and large farmer	11.7	3,729
Expert self-employed	14.5	2,828
Manager	12.0	1,665
Expert employee	14.4	2,301
Small employer	9.0	1,470
Self-employed with assets	8.0	833
Agricultural self-employed	3.4	374
Skilled worker	12.1	999
Supervisor	10.2	1,007
Typical worker	8.8	587
Elementary worker	5.2	322
Precarious self-employed	6.3	493
Domestic worker	5.9	370
Subsistence worker	3.1	234
Surplus worker	8.2	255

[a]Average schooling computed using values from 0 to 15 complete years of schooling.

8. Lahelma, E. Health and social stratification. In *The Blackwell Companion to Medical Sociology*, ed. W. Cockerham. Blackwell, Oxford, 2001.

9. Marmot, M. Historical perspective: The social determinants of disease—some blossoms. *Epidemiol. Perspect. Innov.* 2:1–7, 2005. doi: 10.1186/1742-5573-2-2.

10. Robert, S., and House, J. S. Socioeconomic inequalities in health: An enduring sociological problem. In *Handbook of Medical Sociology*, Ed. 5, ed. C. E. Bird, P. Conrad, and A. M. Fremont. Prentice Hall, Upper Saddle River, NJ, 2000.

11. Link, B. G., and Phelan, J. Evaluating the fundamental cause explanation for social disparities in health. In *Handbook of Medical Sociology*, Ed. 5, ed. C. E. Bird, P. Conrad, and A. M. Fremont. Prentice Hall, Upper Saddle River, NJ, 2000.

12. Link, B. G., and Phelan, J. The concept of fundamental causes in explaining social inequities in health. In *Socioeconomic Conditions, Stress, and Mental Disorders*, ed. A. Maney and J. Ramos. Mental Health Statistics Improvement Program, Bethesda, MD, 2003. www.mhsip.org/nimhdoc/socioeconmh_home.htm.

13. Link, B. G., and Phelan, J. Fundamental sources of health inequalities. In *Policy Challenges in Modern Health Care*, ed. D. Mechanic et al. Rutgers University Press, New Brunswick, NJ, 2005.

14. Link, B. G., et al. The resources that matter: Fundamental social causes of health disparities and the challenge of intelligence. *J. Health Soc. Behav.* 49:72–91, 2008.

15. Phelan, J., et al. "Fundamental causes" of social inequalities in mortality: A test of the theory. *J. Health Soc. Behav.* 45:265–285, 2004.

16. Carpiano, R. M., Link, B. G., and Phelan, J. Social inequality and health: Future directions of the fundamental cause explanation. In *Social Class: How Does It Work?* ed. A. Lareau and D. Conley. Russell Sage, New York, 2008.

17. Bartley, M., et al. Understanding social variation in cardiovascular risk factors in women and men: The advantage of theoretically based measures. *Soc. Sci. Med.* 49:831–845, 1999.

18. Bartley, M. *Health Inequality: An Introduction to Theories, Concepts, and Methods.* Polity Press, Cambridge, UK, 2004.

19. Muntaner, C., et al. The associations of social class and social stratification with patterns of general and mental health in a Spanish population. *Int. J. Epidemiol.* 32:950–958, 2003.

20. Krieger, N., Williams, D. R., and Moss, N. E. Measuring social class in US public health research: Concepts, methodologies, and guidelines. *Annu. Rev. Public Health* 18:341–378, 1997.

21. Borrell, C., et al. Social class and self-reported health status among men and women: What is the role of work conditions, household material standards and household labor? *Soc. Sci. Med.* 58:1869–1887, 2004.

22. Jylha, M. What is self-rated health and why does it predict mortality? Towards a unified conceptual model. *Soc. Sci. Med.* 69:307–316, 2009.

23. Miech, R. A., and Hauser, R. M. Socioeconomic status and health at midlife: A comparison of educational attainment with occupational-based indicator. *Ann. Epidemiol.* 11:75–84, 2001.

24. Dachs, J. N. W., and Santos, A. P. R. Auto-avaliação do estado de saúde no Brasil: análise dos dados da PNAD/2003. *Ciência e Saúde Coletiva* 11:887–894, 2006.

25. Wright, E. O. *Class Counts: Comparative Studies in Class Analysis.* Cambridge University Press, Cambridge, 1997.

26. Wright, E. O. Foundations of a neo-Marxist class analysis. In *Approaches to Class Analysis*, ed. E. O. Wright. Cambridge University Press, Cambridge, 2005.

27. Roemer, J. *Free to Lose: An Introduction to Marxist Economic Philosophy.* Harvard University Press, Cambridge, MA, 1988.

28. Figueiredo Santos, J. A. *Estrutura de Posições de Classe no Brasil: Mapeamento, Mudanças e Efeitos na Renda.* Editora UFMG, Belo Horizonte; Iuperj, Rio de Janeiro, 2002.

29. Figueiredo Santos, J. A. A socioeconomic classification for Brazil. *Revista Brasileira de Ciências Sociais* (Special English Edition) 2, 2006. http://socialsciences.scielo.org.

30. Figueiredo Santos, J. A. Comprehending the class structure specificity in Brazil. *S. Afr. Rev. Sociol.* 41:24–43, 2010.

31. Westergaard, J. *Who Gets What? The Hardening of Class Inequality in the Late Twentieth Century.* Polity Press, Cambridge, UK, 1995.

32. Herd, P., Goesling, B., and House, J. S. Socioeconomic position and health: The differential effects of education versus income on the onset versus progression of health problems. *J. Health Soc. Behav.* 48:223–238, 2007.

33. Backlund, E., Sorlie, P., and Johnson, N. A comparison of the relationships of education and income with mortality. *Soc. Sci. Med.* 49:1373–1384, 1999.

34. Rose, D., and Pervalin, D. J. Social class differences in mortality using the National Statistics Socio-economic Classification—too little, too soon: A reply to Chandola. *Soc. Sci. Med.* 51:1121–1127, 2000.
35. Aneshensel, C. S. *Theory-Based Data Analysis for the Social Sciences.* Pine Forge Press, Thousand Oaks, CA, 2002.
36. Figueiredo Santos, J. A. Class effects on racial inequality in Brazil. *Dados–Revista de Ciências Sociais* (Special English Edition) 2, 2006. http://socialsciences.scielo.org.
37. Muntaner, C., et al. Employment relations, social class and health: A review and analysis of conceptual and measurement alternatives. *Soc. Sci. Med.* 71:2130–2140, 2010.
38. Robert, S., and House, J. S. Socioeconomic inequalities in health: An enduring sociological problem. In *Handbook of Medical Sociology*, Ed. 5, ed. C. E. Bird, P. Conrad, and A. M. Fremont. Prentice Hall, Upper Saddle River, NJ, 2000.
39. Robert, S., and House, J. S. Socioeconomic inequalities in health: Integrating individual, community and societal level theory and research. In *Handbook of Social Studies in Health and Medicine*, ed. G. Albrecht, R. Fitzpatrick, and S. C. Scrimshaw. Sage, London, 2000.
40. Kunst, A., and Roskam, A. Using the ESeC to describe socio-economic inequalities in health in Europe. In *Social Class in Europe: An Introduction to the European Socio-economic Classification*, ed. D. Rose and E. Harrison. Routledge, London, 2010.
41. Kunst, A., Roskam, A., and van Agt, H. The European Socioeconomic Classification (ESEC): Exploring Its Potential to Describe Class Differences in Health among Middle-aged Men and Women in 11 European countries. 2005. www.iser.essex.ac.uk/research/esec/ (accessed December 10, 2010).

CHAPTER 20

Wealth Inequality and Health:
A Political Economy Perspective

Nadine R. Nowatzki

Despite a plethora of studies on income inequality and health, researchers have been unable to make any firm conclusions as a result of methodological and theoretical limitations. Within this body of research, there has been a call for studies of wealth inequality and health. Wealth is far more unequally distributed than income and is conceptually unique from income. This chapter discusses the results of bivariate cross-sectional analyses of the relationship between wealth inequality (Gini coefficient) and population health (life expectancy and infant mortality) in 14 wealthy countries. The results confirm that wealth inequality is associated with poor population health. Both unweighted and weighted correlations between wealth inequality and health are strong and significant, even after controlling for a variety of potential aggregate-level confounders, including gross domestic product per capita, and after excluding the United States, the most unequal country. The results are strongest for female life expectancy and infant mortality. The author outlines potential pathways through which wealth inequality might affect health, using specific countries to illustrate. The chapter concludes with policy recommendations that could contribute to a more equitable distribution of wealth and, ultimately, decreased health disparities.

*****

As a result of increasing economic inequality within developed nations, as well as growing health disparities, researchers have been exploring the possibility of a causal relationship between income inequality and population health. Over the past 15 years, research on income inequality and health has exploded, with studies being conducted at different levels of geographical aggregation and with a variety of inequality measures and health indicators. Review articles have pointed to the generally inconsistent findings, as well as the methodological and theoretical limitations of research to date, concluding that the relationship between income inequality and health is unclear (1–3).

Within the income inequality literature, several researchers have suggested that future studies address *wealth* inequality, which is much more extreme than income inequality (4, 5). In rich countries, Gini coefficients for income inequality range from 0.2 to 0.4 (6), while Gini coefficients for *wealth* inequality range from 0.5 to 0.9 (7–9). In the United States, the top 1 percent of households owns 38 to 47 percent of the wealth, depending on the definition of wealth (10–12).

Given this highly unequal distribution of wealth, and the political power and health-promoting resources associated with wealth, a focus on income inequality may be inappropriate for explaining health disparities and may seriously underestimate the health effects of inequality. Despite the strong conceptual and empirical grounds for a study of the relationship between wealth inequality and health, very few researchers have undertaken such a study because of the difficulties associated with measuring wealth and the consequent lack of quality, comparable data on wealth (10).

This chapter discusses the results of an exploratory, cross-sectional study of the relationship between wealth inequality (Gini coefficient) and two commonly used health outcomes: life expectancy and infant mortality. The bivariate, aggregate-level analyses took into consideration some of the methodological concerns raised by income inequality researchers, such as the inclusion of appropriate controls for potential confounding variables that might explain the relationship between inequality and health (13, 14).

WEALTH AND WEALTH INEQUALITY

The literature on inequality and health has focused almost exclusively on income and income inequality. As an indicator of financial well-being, income (what you earn) has limitations because it captures only a short-term, transitory "flow" that affects current consumption and saving. Wealth (what you own) is a much broader and more stable category than income. Components of wealth include bank accounts, investments, real estate, possessions such as vehicles, and non-marketable assets such as pensions (15). Wealth can be pictured as a pool of resources that serves as a source of financial security when there are emergency expenditures such as home or vehicle repairs or unexpected changes in income as a result of ill health, disability, unemployment, or family break-up (12, 16). Thus, wealth better reflects "the capacity of a family to maintain a particular standard of living" (17, p. 497).

On a broader level, wealth is an important determinant of political power (18). Extreme concentrations of wealth are associated with financial, political, and ideological corruption that concentrates power in the hands of a few and undermines democracy (19–21). The wealthy form a highly impermeable elite that has a powerful influence on government and the policy formation process, as well as public opinion (22, 23). This influence is most visible in campaign financing, lobbying, the funding of policy institutes, as well as ownership and control of the mass media (24).

Wealth permits the rich to create social arrangements most likely to sustain and expand their existing bases of power and influence. Wealthy individuals and corporate interests that pay wealth taxes are highly motivated to reduce or abolish them and use their power to put tax cuts or tax repeal on the political agenda (24, 25, p. 191). Progressivity in the federal tax system in the United States is now virtually nonexistent because of reductions in taxes on corporate income, capital gains, and estates, as well as loopholes, deductions, and exceptions (26, 27). Despite anti-government, free-market rhetoric, the U.S. government continues to act on behalf of the wealthy and is "one of the most powerful forces shaping the creation and distribution of wealth" (20, p. 214).

An analysis of wealth inequality is therefore distinct and has some conceptual advantages. It illustrates how economic inequality accumulates over the life course and is perpetuated across generations. Wealth provides a deeper understanding of social inequality and social mobility because it reflects the assets built up by previous generations, the current resource base, plus the prospects for long-term well-being and financial stability (17, 28). As a measure of class, wealth is better able to capture the structural and relational aspects of inequality because it more accurately reflects differences in power. It represents the opportunities and resources available to individuals, households, and corporations, thus uncovering "a qualitatively different pattern of inequality" that is otherwise concealed by traditional measures of status such as income, education, and occupation (29, p. 3).

Despite the advantages of focusing on wealth as an axis of inequality, researchers and policymakers continue to focus on income redistribution. This is unfortunate: "A consideration of wealth in conjunction with income will result in a more accurate empirical portrayal of stratification, provide a better guide for social policy considerations, and enhance greatly our theoretical understanding of the sources and consequences of inequality. Alternative measures of wealth consistently uncover both depths and patterns of inequality that income conceals" (30, p. 147).

At the individual level, the current body of evidence strongly suggests that wealth is just as important, if not more important, than income as a determinant of population health outcomes (31). The mechanisms through which wealth might influence health are numerous and include both psychosocial and material pathways. Wealth is a source of prestige and social status, it provides leisure, luxury, and freedom, it is a major source of economic security and confidence, and it provides those who have it with personal and political power, as well as safe and high-quality living conditions. But does the distribution of wealth within a geographic area, in addition to an individual's own net worth, have an effect on health? Given the highly skewed distribution of wealth, a relationship between wealth inequality and health is highly plausible.

METHOD

Data Sources and Measures

In a recent paper, Davies and colleagues (8) attempted to calculate the global distribution of wealth and, in doing so, compiled wealth data from a large number of developing and developed countries. They provided detailed information on the original data sources, how household balance sheets were constructed in each of the countries, and which assets are covered (8). Wealth inequality (Gini coefficient) and wealth per capita data are available for the year 2000 for 14 OECD (Organization for Economic Cooperation and Development) countries: Australia, Canada, Denmark, Finland, France, Germany, Italy, Japan, Netherlands, New Zealand, Portugal, Spain, United Kingdom, and United States. Consistent with previous research (32, 33), the middle-income and non-OECD countries were excluded from the present study. The goal was to analyze a set of wealthy, democratic, and stable market-based economies to which theoretical and policy-relevant generalizations have been, and continue to be, made.

Health outcomes data for the year 2000 were taken from the OECD (34). They include life expectancy at birth (for total population, and males and females separately) and infant mortality rates. Other variables of interest include public expenditures on health as a percentage of total expenditures on health and percentage of the population ages 15 and older who are daily smokers (total, males, and females).

The OECD (35, 36) also provides data for the following labor and welfare state variables, all for the year 2000 except where indicated:

1. Wage inequality: the ratio of earnings at the 90th percentile of workers to those at the 10th percentile of workers (not available for Portugal)
2. Trade union density: the ratio of active wage- and salary-earning trade union members divided by the total number of wage and salary earners
3. Public social spending as a percentage of gross domestic product (GDP)
4. Public and mandatory private social expenditures on pension (old age and survivor) as a percentage of GDP
5. Net replacement rates (as a percentage of individual pre-retirement earnings net of taxes and contributions), mandatory pension entitlement by earnings level = 1, year 2005
6. Net present value of pension benefits at normal pension age, for men and women, as a percentage of gross earnings of an average production worker, year 2005

One variable, *percentage of total votes for left parties*, was taken from the Comparative Welfare States Data Set (37). Data are not available for Spain or

Portugal. Data on women's participation in government (*percentage of women in the lower or single house*) were taken from the Statistical Archive of "Women in National Parliaments" (38).

Analysis

Tests of normality revealed that many variables of interest were not normally distributed. As a result, Kendall's tau, a non-parametric correlation suitable for small datasets, was chosen (39). Correlation coefficients were calculated for the relationship between the Gini coefficient for wealth inequality and two frequently used health outcomes: life expectancy and infant mortality. The Gini coefficient is by far the most commonly used indicator of inequality, and its use allows for comparisons with income inequality studies. Consistent with Lynch and colleagues (33), sex-specific associations are reported for life expectancy. Because the determinants of health are different for men and women, this disaggregation is warranted.

Previous studies of income inequality and health (40–42) have controlled for GDP per capita using purchasing power parity (PPP) exchange rates. Economic growth has been an important macro-level contributor to reduced mortality rates, and GDP per capita is therefore a potentially significant confounder (43). GDP per capita data were taken from the Penn World Table (44). The analyses were repeated controlling for GDP per capita and median wealth per capita, another indicator of economic prosperity.

The political economy perspective points to indicators of class and gender relations within the labor market and broader society as important health determinants, yet many cross-national studies have not included macro-political indicators as potential explanatory variables. These include indicators of public policy such as spending on health care and social security expressed as a percentage of GDP (13, 40, 45) and rates of trade union membership and political representation by women (33, 42). Each of these indicators was entered into partial correlations as a control variable to see if there were any attenuations of the wealth inequality and health correlations.

It was hypothesized that greater wealth inequality would be associated with lower life expectancy and higher infant mortality. Because there is a clear directionality in these hypotheses, one-tailed tests were used. Previous research (46) has recommended repeating analyses after excluding the United States (consistently the most unequal country with regard to income distribution). One study found that excluding the United States substantially decreased the association between income inequality and child mortality (33). Given that previous research shows the United States to be the most unequal in terms of wealth distribution (9, 11), the analyses also were repeated after excluding the United States, to see if the correlations changed.

Analyses were weighted by population size, and both unweighted and weighted results are presented. The bulk of the analyses were carried out using SPSS. However, it is not possible to compute partial tau-b in SPSS. As a result, weighted tau-b, without controls, was computed in SPSS, and SAS was used to compute unweighted tau-b, with and without controls. It is not possible to weight partial tau-b analyses in SAS. Finally, because the sampling distribution of partial tau-b is unknown, probability values are not available.

RESULTS

In Figures 1 and 2, bivariate scatterplots reveal a clear linear relationship between wealth inequality and health in the 14 OECD countries. Japan, Italy, Spain, and Australia form a loose cluster of low wealth inequality/high life expectancy countries, while the United States and Denmark are at the opposite end of the distribution (Figure 1). The pattern is similar for infant mortality, but Finland is now part of the low inequality/better health cluster (Figure 2). Denmark fares much better than the United States in terms of a lower infant mortality rate.

Table 1 shows that unweighted correlations (Kendall's tau-b) between wealth inequality and both population health outcomes are in the expected direction and are statistically significant at $p < 0.01$ (column 1). The correlations with female life expectancy (tau = -0.58) and with infant mortality (tau = 0.51) are higher than with male life expectancy (tau = -0.43, $p < 0.05$). Consistent with previous studies, the United States is an outlier with respect to its poorer health outcomes and high level of wealth inequality. The bivariate analyses were repeated after excluding the United States (column 2): the correlations are attenuated slightly (by 10 to 12%).

Weighted correlations (Kendall's tau-b) between wealth inequality and population health outcomes are shown in the last two columns of Table 1. The correlations are in the expected direction and are very strong: tau = 0.84 for infant mortality and tau = -0.83 for life expectancy ($p < 0.001$). Again, sex disaggregation reveals that the association is somewhat stronger for females. Excluding the United States attenuates the weighted correlations considerably (by between 21 and 23%); however, the correlations remain strong (tau = 0.66, $p < 0.001$) for both outcomes.

Having found statistically significant unweighted and weighted correlations between wealth inequality and health, it was necessary to explore whether these correlations are attenuated after adjusting for other macro-level health determinants. Overall, the adjustments do not have a large effect on the first order correlations. Controlling for GDP per capita (column 3) makes little difference. In other words, the size of the economy is not an explanatory factor in the wealth inequality and health relationships. Controlling for wealth per capita, union density, wage inequality, female representation in parliament, and welfare state

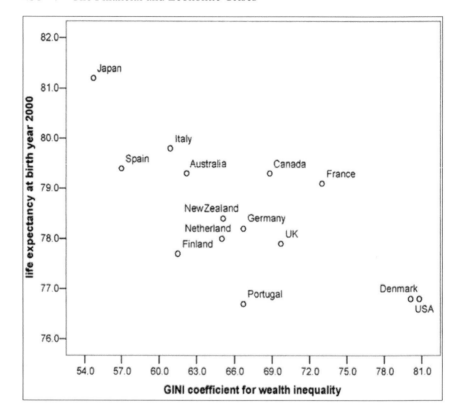

Figure 1. The relationship between wealth inequality and life expectancy at birth (total population) in 14 OECD countries, 2000.

Source: See Davies et al. (8) for sources of wealth inequality data. Life expectancy data are from the OECD (44).

spending (public social expenditures and public expenditures on health care) has very little or no effect on the correlations (results not shown).

Several control variables, however, result in more substantial attenuations. Controlling for the percentage of votes for left parties (column 6) attenuates the correlation with female life expectancy by 14 percent, suggesting that left parties may play a role in both wealth inequality and health. Data for this variable are not available for Spain and Portugal, and given the small sample size, this finding should be interpreted with caution. Controlling for male smoking (column 7) results in an attenuation of the correlations, most noticeably for infant mortality (by 12%).

Although controlling for public expenditures on pensions has no effect on the correlations (results not shown), controlling for the net present value of pensions

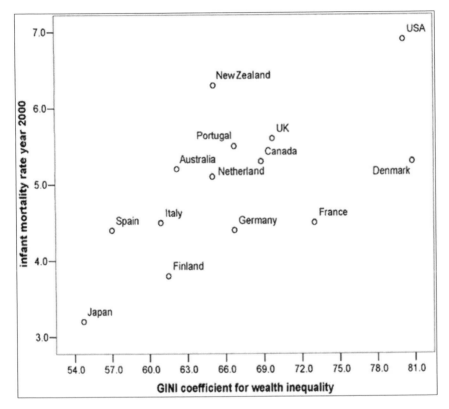

Figure 2. The relationship between wealth inequality and infant mortality rate (total population) in 14 OECD countries, 2000.

Source: See Davies et al. (8) for sources of wealth inequality data. Infant mortality data are from the OECD (44).

(column 4) and pension replacement rates (column 5) results in the largest attenuations of the correlation between wealth inequality and infant mortality (by 27% and 20%, respectively). This suggests that part of the relationship between wealth inequality and infant mortality can be explained by the generosity of pensions. The results for pensions are consistent with previous research, which has argued that it is not *spending* on pensions, but rather the *generosity* of pensions that is important (43). For example, Palme (47) notes that the age structure of the population can affect pension expenditures such that they are not an adequate indicator of pension rights (coverage and adequacy). This may be why there is no attenuation when controlling for pension expenditures, but significant attenuations when controlling for pension replacement rates and the net present value of pensions. Although it is plausible that countries that spend

Table 1

Relationship between wealth inequality (Gini Coefficient) and health outcomes in 14 OECD countries, 2000

	Unweighted tau-b							Weighted tau-b	
	Kendall's Tau-b	exclude US	control: GDP	control: penvalm[a]	control: penrep[a]	control: penrep[a]	control: leftvote[a]	Kendall's Tau-b	exclude US
Infant mortality	0.51**	0.45*	0.49	0.37	0.41	0.50	0.45	0.84***	0.66***
Life expectancy	−0.49**	−0.44**	−0.48	−0.46	−0.49	−0.46	−0.47	−0.83***	−0.66***
Life expectancy male	−0.43**	−0.39*	−0.45	−0.46	−0.46	−0.47	−0.42	−0.80***	−0.62***
Life expectancy female	−0.58**	−0.51**	−0.57	−0.52	−0.55	−0.50	−0.55	−0.85***	−0.65***

Source: See Davies et al. (8) for sources of wealth inequality data. Health outcomes, smoking, and pension data are from the OECD (44–46). Data on the percentage of votes for left parties are from Huber et al. (47). Data on GDP/capita are from Heston et al. (55).
*** $p < 0.001$, ** $p < 0.01$, * $p < 0.05$.
[a]Significance levels not available in SAS for partial tau-b because the sampling distribution of partial tau-b is unknown.

more on pensions are also more likely to provide more generous pensions, direct health effects are more likely to result from the generosity of pensions. Pensions presumably contribute to better material living conditions, as well as a sense of security and overall well-being, which are particularly good for health.

Table 2 (weighted tau-b) shows that pension replacement rates and the net present value of pension benefits are negatively correlated with the Gini for wealth inequality (tau = –0.50 and –0.47, respectively), suggesting that countries with more generous pensions have lower levels of wealth inequality. These results provide further evidence of the potential importance of welfare state policies for both the level of inequality in a society and health outcomes, particularly for the most vulnerable: women and children (42, 48–50).

It may be fruitful to further examine the relationships between political economy variables and wealth inequality. In Table 2, the Gini coefficient for wealth inequality is significantly associated with union density, left votes, and spending on pensions and health, indicating that higher levels of wealth inequality are related to lower levels of welfare state spending and a weaker political presence of the left. Although statistically significant ($p < 0.001$), the coefficients (ranging from 0.27 to 0.37) are generally much lower than those for *wage* inequality (which range from 0.52 to 0.62). The lower coefficients may explain why there is little attenuation in the wealth inequality/health correlations when controlling for these macro-level indicators. Moreover, these results suggest that labor and welfare state variables may have a closer relationship with income inequality than with wealth inequality. If this is the case, other factors may be involved in the wealth inequality/health nexus (see discussion).

Previous studies have reported significant correlations between income inequality and health (40, 48). How does wealth inequality compare with income inequality in its relationship with health outcomes? Although wage inequality is significantly correlated with both infant mortality and female life expectancy (tau = 0.65 and –0.56, respectively, $p < 0.001$), the correlations with wealth inequality are much higher, suggesting that wealth inequality may be an even more important determinant of population health than income inequality.

DISCUSSION

The results of bivariate analyses confirm that wealth inequality is associated with poor population health. Both unweighted and weighted correlations between wealth inequality and health are strong and significant, even after controlling for a variety of macro-level indicators and after excluding the United States, the most unequal country.

It is interesting to see how the relative positioning of the countries with regard to wealth inequality compares to that of income inequality. The position of the United States is not surprising—it is consistent with previous research on income inequality and health. Unlike the case of the United States, however,

Table 2

Relationship between selected inequality, health, labor, and welfare state variables (Kendall's tau-b) in 14 OECD countries, 2000 (weighted)

	Gini	Wage	IM	LEf	Union	Left	Socx	Healthx	Penx	Penrep	Penvalm[a]
Gini (wealth)	1	0.62***	0.84***	-0.85***	-0.37***	-0.32***	-0.27***	-0.65***	-0.34***	-0.50***	-0.47***
90/10 Wage Inequality		1	0.65***	-0.56***	-0.57***	-0.62***	-0.64***	-0.66***	-0.52***	-0.65***	-0.58***
Infant Mortality (IM)			1	-0.84***	-0.31***	-0.49***	-0.44***	-0.81***	-0.36***	-0.49***	-0.56***
Life Expectancy Females (LEf)				1	0.30***	0.34***	0.37***	0.69***	0.41***	0.44***	0.44***
Union Density					1	0.48***	0.47***	0.32***	0.13	0.28***	0.23***
Left Votes						1	0.89***	0.58***	0.41***	0.51***	0.57***
Public Expenditures (Socx)							1	0.53***	0.53***	0.50***	0.55***
Health Expenditures (Healthx)								1	0.35***	0.35***	0.38***
Pension Expenditures (Penx)									1	0.62***	0.58***
Pension Replacement Rate (Penrep)										1	0.92***
Pension Value, Men (Penvalm)[a]											1

Source: See Davies et al. (8) for sources of wealth inequality data. Data for health outcomes, expenditures, wage inequality, union density, and pensions are from the OECD (44–46). Data on the percentage of votes for left parties are from Huber et al. (47).

***$p < 0.001$, **$p < 0.01$, *$p < 0.05$.

[a]Results similar for women.

the position of Denmark is surprising, as the Nordic countries have some of the lowest levels of income inequality and best health outcomes in the world.

A possible explanation is that the Gini data for Denmark are statistically unreliable. Luxembourg Wealth Study (LWS) authors found that Sweden had the highest Gini coefficient in the LWS. To explain this puzzling finding, they suggest that a statistical artifact may result from the very high proportion of Swedish households with zero or negative net worth, as well as tax laws that encourage tax holding (51). This may be what is happening with Denmark, too. In the LWS database, the bottom three deciles in Sweden and the bottom four deciles in Denmark have negative net worth. Davies and colleagues (8) report even more exaggerated trends, with the bottom six deciles in Sweden and the bottom seven deciles in Denmark reporting negative net worth. In both studies, virtually all of the other countries report positive net worth for the bottom deciles.

In most countries, wealth components are valued on a "realization" basis, where respondents estimate the amount that would be obtained if they were sold on that day. In the Nordic countries, however, wealth components are valued on a taxable basis. Wealth tax regulations may assign to some assets, such as real estate, only a fraction of their market value, resulting in gross underestimations. LWS researchers suggest this contributes to the majority of households in Sweden reporting negative net worth. Statistics Norway estimated that in the 1990s, the taxable value of houses was less than one-third of their market value (9, fn. 10).

Components of debt that are not included in other countries (e.g., student loan debt and debts incurred to buy assets, such as consumer durables) are routinely included in the Nordic countries. Moreover, households are defined somewhat differently, with the "inner family" serving as the reference unit. In these cases, young adults (age 18 and older) living at home and economically dependent on their parent(s) (such as students), as well as unmarried cohabiting adults, are counted as separate households (52). This household definition does not take into account economies of scale and boosts the number of wealth-poor units compared to other household definitions in which young adults are considered as part of their original family (53).

These methodological issues likely result in an inflation of the number of household units registering negative net worth in Denmark and increase measured inequality. These issues highlight the need for further development of standardized definitions of wealth, as well as definitions of households. The recent creation of the LWS undoubtedly will lead to better quality and more comparable wealth data. In the meantime, the results for Denmark on wealth inequality should be interpreted with caution.

At the other end of the distribution, the results are quite distinct from the income inequality literature. Previous studies, albeit using older data, have found that Australia, Italy, and Spain have formed a cluster of high inequality/poor health countries for outcomes such as infant mortality (13, 32, 45), life expectancy

(33), and potential years of life lost (32). These three countries tended to cluster with other liberal welfare states, including Canada (33, 45) and the United Kingdom (13).

Since the wealth inequality/health relationship appears to be significantly different from the income inequality/health relationship in these countries, an exploration of potential explanatory factors is called for. One of these potential factors is wealth taxation, which is high in some of the most equal countries. Spain is one of the only OECD countries with capital gains, net wealth, estate, and gift taxes. Moreover, the tax rates are high in cross-national comparison (54). Japan also has a higher tax threshold and much higher taxes on high incomes and wealth than the United States. This includes high corporate income tax rates, with double taxation of dividend income, and high taxes on capital gains compared to other OECD countries (51, 55). In Australia, the Labor government also initiated a capital gains tax and a progressive fringe-benefits tax on business expenses (56). In these three countries, wealth taxation may have a redistributive effect, reducing wealth inequality, increasing investments in social programs, and potentially contributing to better health outcomes.

Home ownership is another potential explanatory factor. Home ownership rates are very high in Australia, Italy, and Spain. Rates are high even among low-income families, and outright ownership is common (57–60). This means that a substantial number of households have a great deal of equity at their disposal. In Australia, the high value of homes allows most Australians to maintain the same living standards in retirement that they had when they were younger (61) and may offset the need for pensions (62). In Japan, previous research has suggested that low levels of wealth inequality may be a result of the extremely large weight that owner-occupied housing has in the household portfolio (Bauer and Mason, in 9).

Another potential factor is regulatory frameworks, which protect families' wealth from changes in housing and credit markets. For example, mortgage and housing markets are well-regulated in Spain (63). Japan has a relatively large down payment ratio (35% in 2000) compared to the United States (64), while Italy has even higher down payment requirements (50% in 2001), stricter borrowing protocols, and a shorter typical loan term of 15 years (compared to 30 years in the United States). In Italy, residential mortgage debt in 2002 was 11.4 percent of GDP (compared to 58% in the United States), and the ratio of home loan to the estimated value of the home was 55 percent (compared to 78% in the United States) (54). The ratio of debt to total assets is also very low (4%), with only 10 percent of Italian households owing debt (8, 51). Because of the down payment requirements, home buyers in Italy start off with less debt and have substantial equity in their homes. This reduces measured inequality compared to countries with lax requirements that result in lower savings, higher debt, and greater vulnerability to the vagaries of the market. Homeowners in southern Europe and Japan are far less likely to be preoccupied with the markets or their ability to keep up with payments. This financial security is an important determinant of health (see 65).

Social cohesion is another potential factor. The concept of family in Southern Europe is much broader and includes the entire set of kinship relationships across generations (57). Close family ties no doubt have both direct and indirect effects on health. The social support provided by the extended family is likely to have a positive and direct effect on health by providing emotional and instrumental support and by buffering the health-damaging effects of stress. Family ties also may have an indirect effect through the transmission of family wealth. Families in Southern Europe often assist newly married couples with the purchase or building of their home. This transmission reduces wealth inequality by providing a majority of families with access to the health-promoting aspects of home ownership. In Japan, excellent health outcomes and low levels of inequality both have been attributed to the psychosocial benefits of cultural values that include loyalty and group commitment, social harmony and solidarity, and reciprocity. Japanese companies are characterized by supportive and participatory work structures that focus on consensus decision making and concern for the personal welfare of all group members (55).

Another potential factor in the relatively more equal countries is pension wealth. Italy, Spain, and to a lesser extent Japan have some of the most generous public pension systems in the world. Expenditures, as a percentage of GDP, are among the highest in the OECD (14.8% in Italy, 8.6% in Spain, and 7.4% in Japan, compared to 5.9% in the United States). Replacement rates are at almost 90% in both Italy and Spain, and the net present value of pension entitlements is also high, at 12.8 in Italy and more than 13 in Spain (the highest of OECD countries) (35). The pension system in Italy provides more than 80 percent of the income of senior households (66). In Japan, average public pension income constitutes more than 96 percent of total pension income (64).

Evidence from these countries suggests that there is some substitutability between private wealth (with the exception of home ownership) and pension wealth. In other words, public pensions "crowd out" or discourage private solutions, reducing the need to save for a rainy day (47, 67, 68). Thus, pensions seem to reduce wealth inequality, as households are more willing to spend wealth rather than save for retirement. Moreover, pensions may contribute to health, as households do not face considerable stress or pressure to save for retirement and can enjoy comfortable material living conditions in the present. Generous public pension benefits in these three countries have been reduced in recent years, which likely will have an impact on wealth inequality, as well as health disparities.

Limitations and Directions for Future Research

One of the major limitations of this exploratory study is the small sample. With only 14 countries, the selection of countries can have an effect on the results.

Larger sample sizes may be needed in order to have the statistical power to more accurately detect the health effects of inequality (2).

Cross-sectional analyses have a number of limitations. First, correlations between variables do not necessarily represent causal relationships (3, 41). We cannot conclude that wealth inequality "causes" poorer health outcomes, only that there is an association. Controlling for a variety of macro-level indicators, however, results in greater confidence that the wealth inequality/health associations are not explained by other factors. Second, cross-sectional analyses do not allow for the inclusion of time lags. Research on income inequality has suggested that inequality may have stronger effects on health after a time lag of 10 to 15 years, compared with contemporaneous inequality (40, 69). Health among adults, for example, may reflect the inequalities of the past, with infant mortality rates reflecting more recent changes in income or wealth distribution (14, 32).

Future studies should apply more rigorous methodological approaches to the study of wealth inequality and health. This will be possible only with better quality, longitudinal data for a larger number of countries. Such data will permit multi-level modeling, fixed effects models, and the inclusion of time lags, revealing a more accurate picture of the relationship between wealth inequality and health.

Future studies should examine other measures of wealth inequality. Given the extreme concentrations of wealth found in many OECD countries, researchers should examine the associations between the share of wealth held by the richest 1 percent and richest 0.5 percent with population health outcomes. In addition, further examination of the political and economic processes that permit the extreme concentration of wealth is needed, particularly in cross-national comparison.

This study was unable to address the concentration of corporate wealth. Quality wealth data have become available only recently at the household level, and even then they suffer from issues of comparability. Corporate-centered globalization has led to an increase in the wealth and power of major corporations and their executives, the health ramifications of which have yet to be well-understood.

Other measures of population health should be tested in future studies. Standard indicators such as life expectancy are frequently used and generally accepted as measures of health status, but are limited in their ability to capture broader definitions of health and well-being that are independent of illness. Living longer is considered to be positive, but life expectancy only illuminates the loss of life and reveals very little about the quality of life of the population (70).

Despite these limitations, this study represents one of the first known studies to examine the aggregate-level relationship between wealth inequality and health. The results have ramifications for how economic inequality is measured cross-nationally. For example, purely income-based comparisons may exaggerate or underestimate the differences between countries. Previous studies have found that the inclusion of wealth in definitions and measures of poverty and inequality produces different results, with large reductions in poverty in Italy and Australia (61, 71, 72). Future studies must consider wealth and wealth inequality in order to have a more nuanced understanding of both poverty and inequality in cross-national comparison.

Policy Implications

The results of this study reveal that wealth inequality is associated with poor population health. This suggests that policies related to wealth redistribution in the more unequal countries may contribute to decreased health disparities and overall improvements in population health.

Hacker and Pierson (26, p. 182) argue that "Any political analysis of rising inequality must be attentive to tax policy." The countries with more equitable wealth distributions and better health outcomes have higher taxes on wealth, suggesting that taxes may be one way in which policymakers can influence the distribution of wealth and tackle health disparities. Traditionally, redistributive policies have been based on income data alone. However, income data "underestimates seriously the extent and perhaps the sources of the problems they attempt to address" (30, p. 130).

A progressive direct tax on wealth is one option, and revenues could be used to finance social (including health care) and environmental programs and infrastructure that could improve population health. Direct wealth taxes exist in some OECD countries, but not in North America (12, 73). More effective and progressive taxation of intergenerational transfers is another appropriate and efficient route toward reduced wealth inequality. Most of the OECD countries have either a gift, estate, or inheritance tax (12, 73). In the United States, the estate tax has gradually been repealed, and critics suggest it should be retained and strengthened (16, 17). A lifetime inheritance quota, which could be applied to all gifts and bequests, is another option (74). A strong case can be made for taxing wealth transfers: they undermine equality of opportunity as well as productivity. Unlike labor market rewards, they are unrelated to a person's efforts or contribution and are contrary to the popular notion of a meritocracy (19, 75).

More equitable wealth distribution, and potentially improved health outcomes, also could be achieved through regulatory frameworks. Shifts in U.S. tax policy came after very intense lobbying by organized interests (26). Rules and regulations regarding campaign financing, lobbying, and the formation of media conglomerates are one upstream measure that could contribute to a more equitable distribution of wealth and potentially better health outcomes in countries such as the United States, via more progressive tax policy.

The countries with more equitable distributions of wealth, and better health outcomes, clearly have stricter financial regulatory frameworks. A central factor in increasing inequality in the United States has been the rise of American finance and the related financial deregulation that allowed gains to be highly concentrated at the top (26). Extensive government interventions designed to ensure the integrity and security of the financial system have gradually been shredded. This deregulation has allowed financial professionals to see their wealth skyrocket, while working families have become vulnerable because of the lack of oversight in mortgages, credit, and investments. Financial regulation therefore has the potential to affect wealth holdings, as well as health, in the more unequal Anglo countries by reducing wealth concentration and by protecting citizens from the harmful health effects of financial insecurity. Higher down payment requirements, stricter borrowing protocols, and regulation of mortgage and credit would go a long way to protect the assets of individuals and families from changes in the market.

Finally, "social" wealth is a direct way of ensuring economic well-being and hence better health (76). Adequate public policies reduce income uncertainty, provide affordable and quality housing, protect the vulnerable from economic shocks, and reduce the need to accumulate wealth to ensure basic economic security. Starfield and Birn (77) argue that tackling income inequality alone may be an inadequate approach to reducing health disparities and suggest that universal social programs are critical to reducing inequities in health. The same argument can be made for wealth inequality. The literature on the relationship between welfare state generosity and health is now well-established: those countries with the most generous social policies have the best health outcomes.

One example of "social wealth" that may have a particularly important role to play in both wealth distribution and population health is public pensions. The significant attenuations that occurred in the associations between wealth inequality and health when controlling for the generosity of public pensions suggest that this is one avenue to reducing wealth inequality and potentially improving the well-being and health of populations. Ensuring income security in retirement would reduce the need to accumulate private wealth and would provide households with sufficient material living conditions, and more confidence and stability, which are likely predictors of good health.

CONCLUSION

The results of this study indicate that wealth inequality is associated with life expectancy and infant mortality in a sample of 14 rich countries. Wealth is an axis of inequality that deserves far more attention from researchers, particularly in relation to population health. Relying on income alone to describe inequality and form public policy is inadequate and inappropriate for understanding and addressing the economic and health circumstances of individuals and families. The inclusion of wealth in studies of health disparities will result in a more accurate picture of social stratification and better informed social policy considerations.

Acknowledgments — The author is indebted to the work of James Davies, Susanna Sandstrom, Anthony Shorrocks, and Edward Wolff, who compiled wealth data from around the world.

The author would like to thank the members of her doctoral advisory committee for their guidance and mentorship: Dr. Alexander Segall (advisor), Dr. Gregg Olsen, Dr. Lori Wilkinson, and Dr. Robert Chernomas. This research would not have been possible without the financial support of the Social Sciences and Humanities Research Council (Canada Graduate Scholarship) and the Manitoba Graduate Scholarship.

REFERENCES

1. Lynch, J., et al. Is income inequality a determinant of population health? Part 1. A systematic review. *Milbank Q.* 82(1):5–99, 2004. doi:10.1111/j.0887-378X.2004.00302.x.

2. Macinko, J. A., et al. Income inequality and health: A critical review of the literature. *Med. Care Res. Rev.* 60(4):407–452, 2003. doi:10.1177/1077558703257169.

3. Subramanian, S. V., and Kawachi, I. Income inequality and health: What have we learned so far? *Epidemiol. Rev.* 26:78–91, 2004. doi: 10.1093/epirev/rnxh003.

4. Braveman, P. A., et al. Socioeconomic status in health research: One size does not fit all. *JAMA* 294:2879–2888, 2005. doi:10.1001/jama.294.22.2879.

5. Lynch, J., and Kaplan, G. A. Socioeconomic position. In *Social Epidemiology,* ed. L. Berkman and I. Kawachi. Oxford University Press, New York, 2000.

6. Gottschalk, P., and Smeeding, T. Empirical evidence on income inequality in industrialized countries. In *Handbook of Income Distribution,* ed. A. B. Atkinson and F. Bourguignon. Elsevier, Amsterdam, 2000.

7. Davies, J. B., et al. *Estimating the Level and Distribution of Global Household Wealth.* Research paper No. 2007/77. UNI-WIDER, Helsinki, 2007. www.wider.unu.edu/publications/working-papers/research-papers/2007/en_GB/rp2007-77 (accessed November 24, 2011).

8. Sierninska, E., Brandolini, A., and Smeeding, T. *Comparing Wealth Distribution Across Rich Countries: First Results from the Luxembourg Wealth Study.* Luxembourg Wealth Study Working Paper Series, No.1. LIS, Luxembourg, 2006. www.lisdatacenter.org/working-papers (accessed November 24, 2011).

9. Wolff, E. International comparisons of wealth inequality. *Rev. Income Wealth* 42:433–451, 1996. doi:10.1111/j.1475-4991.1996.tb00193.x.

10. Keister, L. A., and Moller, S. Wealth inequality in the United States. *Annu. Rev. Sociol.* 26:63–81, 2000. doi:10.1146/annurev.soc.26.1.63.

11. Wolff, E. Recent trends in the size and distribution of household wealth. *J. Econ. Perspect.* 12(3):131–150, 1998.

12. Wolff, E. *Top Heavy: The Increasing Inequality of Wealth in America and What Can Be Done About It,* Ed. 2. The New Press, New York, 2002.

13. Judge, K., Mulligan, J. A., and Benzeval, M. Income inequality and population health. *Soc. Sci. Med.* 46:567–579, 1998. doi:10.1016/S0277-9536(97)00204-9.

14. Wilkinson, R., and Pickett, K. E. Income inequality and population health: A review and explanation of the evidence. *Soc. Sci. Med.* 62:1768–1784, 2006. doi: 10.1016/j.socscimed.2005.08.036.

15. Chawla, R. K. Wealth inequality by province. *Perspect. Labour Income* 5(4):13–20, 2004.
16. Shapiro, T. M. *The Hidden Cost of Being African American: How Wealth Perpetuates Inequality.* Oxford University Press, New York, 2004.
17. Spilerman, S. Wealth and stratification processes. *Annu. Rev. Sociol.* 26:497–524, 2000. doi:10.1146/annurev.soc.26.1.497.
18. McNamee, S. J., and Miller Jr., R. K. Inheritance and stratification. In *Inheritance and Wealth in America,* ed. R. Miller and S. McNamee. Plenum Press, New York, 1998.
19. Brittain, J. A. *Inheritance and the Inequality of Material Wealth.* The Brookings Institution, Washington, D.C., 1978.
20. Phillips, K. *Wealth and Democracy: A Political History of the American Rich.* Broadway Books, New York, 2002.
21. Wright, E. O. Reducing income and wealth inequality: Real utopian proposals. *Contemp. Sociol.* 29:143–156, 2000.
22. Domhoff, G. W. The policy-formation network. In *Who Rules America: Power and Politics in the Year 2000.* Mayfield Publishing, London, 1998.
23. Forcese, D. *The Canadian Class Structure,* Ed. 4. McGraw-Hill Ryerson, Toronto, 1997.
24. Gates Sr., W. H., and Collins, C. *Wealth and Our Commonwealth: Why America Should Tax Accumulated Fortunes.* Beacon Press, Boston, 2004.
25. Collins, C., and Muhammad, D. Tax wealth to broaden wealth. In *The Wealth Inequality Reader,* Ed. 3, ed. Dollars and Sense and United for a Fair Economy. Dollars and Sense and Economic Affairs Bureau, Boston, 2008.
26. Hacker, J. S., and Pierson, P. Winner-take-all politics: Public policy, political organization, and the precipitous rise of top incomes in the United States. *Polit. Soc.* 38:152–204, 2010. doi:10.1177/0032329210365042.
27. Picketty, T., and Saez, E. How progressive is the U.S. federal tax system? A historical and international perspective. *J. Econ. Perspect.* 21:3–24, 2007. doi:http://dx.doi.org/10.1257/089533007780095538.
28. Conley, D. Being black, living in the red: Race, wealth, and social policy in America. In *Wealth and Poverty in America: A Reader,* ed. D. Conley. Blackwell, Malden, MA, 2003.
29. Oliver, M. L., and Shapiro, T. M. *Black Wealth / White Wealth: A New Perspective on Racial Inequality,* Ed. 2. Routledge, New York, 2006.
30. Oliver, M. L., and Shapiro, T. M. Wealth of a nation: A reassessment of asset inequality in America shows at least one third of households are asset-poor. *Am. J. Econ. Sociol.* 49(2):129–151, 1990. doi:10.1111/j.1536-7150.1990.tb02268.x.
31. Pollack, C. E., et al. Should health studies measure wealth? A systematic review. *Am. J. Prev. Med.* 33:250–264, 2007, doi:10.1016/j.amepre.2007.04.033.
32. Lobmayer, P., and Wilkinson, R. Income, inequality and mortality in 14 developed countries. *Sociol. Health Illn.* 22:401–414, 2000. doi:10.1111/1467-9566.00211.
33. Lynch, J., et al. Income inequality, the psychosocial environment, and health: Comparisons of wealthy nations. *The Lancet* 358:194–200, 2001. doi:10.1016/S0140-6736(01)05407-1.
34. Organisation for Economic Co-operation and Development. *OECD Health Data 2009: Frequently Requested Data.* Paris, 2009.

35. Organisation for Economic Co-operation and Development. *Pensions at a Glance: Public Policies across OECD Countries.* Paris, 2005.
36. Organisation for Economic Co-operation and Development. *OECD Stat Extracts.* Paris, 2010. stats.oecd.org/index.aspx (accessed November 24, 2011).
37. Huber, E., et al. *Comparative Welfare States Data Set.* Northwestern University, University of North Carolina, Duke University, and Indiana University, 2004. www.lisdatacenter.org/resources/other-databases (accessed November 24, 2011).
38. Inter-parliamentary Union. *Statistical Archive of Women in National Parliaments, September to December 2000.* Geneva, 2000. www.ipu.org (accessed November 24, 2011).
39. Field, A. *Discovering Statistics Using SPSS,* Ed. 3. Sage, Los Angeles, 2009.
40. Macinko, J. A., Shi, L., and Starfield, B. Wage inequality, the health system, and infant mortality in wealthy industrialized countries, 1970-1996. *Soc. Sci. Med.* 58(2):279–292, 2004. doi:10.1016/S0277-9536(03)00200-4.
41. Mellor, J. M., and Milyo, J. Re-examining the evidence of an ecological association between income inequality and health. *J. Health Polit. Pol. Law* 26:487–522, 2001. doi:10.1215/03616878-26-3-487.
42. Muntaner, C., et al. Economic inequality, working-class power, social capital, and cause-specific mortality in wealthy countries. *Int. J. Health Serv.* 32:629–656, 2002.
43. Lundberg, O., et al. The role of welfare state principles and generosity in social policy programmes for public health: An international comparative study. *The Lancet* 372:1633–1640, 2008. doi:10.1016/80140-6736(08)61686-4.
44. Heston, A., Summers, R., and Aten, B. *Penn World Table Version 6.2.* University of Pennsylvania, Center for International Comparisons of Production, Income and Prices, Pittsburgh, 2006.
45. Wennemo, I. Infant mortality, public policy and inequality: A comparison of 18 industrialized countries 1950-1985. *Social. Health Illn.* 15:429–446, 1993. doi:10.1111/j.1467-9566.l993.tb00354.x.
46. Coburn, D. Beyond the income inequality hypothesis: Class, neo-liberalism, and health inequalities. *Soc. Sci. Med.* 51:41–56, 2004. doi:10.1016/S0277-9536(03)00159-X.
47. Palme, J. *Pension Rights in Welfare Capitalism: The Development of Old Age Pensions in 18 OECD Countries 1930-1985.* Swedish Institute for Social Research, Stockholm, 1990.
48. Chung, H., and Muntaner, C. Political and welfare state determinants of infant and child health indicators: An analysis of wealthy countries. *Soc. Sci. Med.* 63:829–842, 2006. doi:10.1016/j.socscimed.2006.01.030.
49. Conley, D., and Springer, K. Welfare state and infant mortality. *Am. J. Sociol.* 107:768–807, 2001. doi:10.1086/374818.
50. Raphael, D., and Bryant, T. The welfare state as a determinant of women's health: Support for women's quality of life in Canada and four comparison nations. *Health Policy* 68:63–79, 2004. doi:10.1016/j.healthpol.2003.08.003.
51. Jäntti, M., Sierminska, E., and Smeeding, T. *The Joint Distribution of Household Income and Wealth: Evidence from the Luxembourg Wealth Study.* Organisation for Economic Co-operation and Development Social, Employment and Migration Working Papers. OECD, Paris, 2008. www.oecd.org/dataoecd/2/40/40774821.pdf (accessed November 24, 2011).

52. Klevmarken, N. A. *The Distribution of Wealth in Sweden: Trends and Driving Factors.* Paper presented at the conference Steigende Wirtschaftliche ungleichheit bei steigendem Reichtum? Vienna, November 7, 2005. www.nek.uu.se/pdf/wp2006_04.pdf (accessed November 24, 2011).

53. Sierminska, E., Brandolini, A., and Smeeding, T. The Luxembourg Wealth Study: A cross-country comparable database for household wealth research. *J. Econ. Inequal.* 4:375–383, 2006. doi:10.1007/s10888-006-9030-z.

54. Leach, M., et al. Wealth, inheritance, and property. In *The Luxembourg Wealth Study (LWS) Database of Institutions that Build Economic Security and Asset Holdings.* Version I, 2008. LIS, Luxembourg, 2008. www.lisdatacenter.org/resources/other-databases (accessed November 24, 2011).

55. Bezruchka, S., Namekata, T., and Gilson Sistrom, M. Improving economic equality and health: The case of postwar Japan. *Am. J. Public Health* 98:589–594, 2008, doi:10.2105/AJPH.2007.116012.

56. Baker, M. *Restructuring Family Policies: Convergences and Divergences.* University of Toronto Press, Toronto, 2006.

57. Allen, J., et al. *Housing and Welfare in Southern Europe.* Blackwell, Oxford, 2004.

58. Bernardi, F., and Poggio, T. Home ownership and social inequality in Italy. In *Home Ownership and Social Inequality in Comparative Perspective,* ed. K. Kurz and H. P. Blossfeld. Stanford University Press, Stanford, 2004.

59. Kurz, K., and Blossfeld, H. P. Summary and conclusions. In *Home Ownership and Social Inequality in Comparative Perspective,* ed. K. Kurz and H. P. Blossfeld. Stanford University Press, Stanford, 2004.

60. Cabré Pla, A., and Módenes Cabrerizo, J. A. Home ownership and social inequality in Spain. In *Home Ownership and Social Inequality in Comparative Perspective,* ed. K. Kurz and H. P. Blossfeld. Stanford University Press, Stanford, 2004.

61. Bradbury, B., and Yates, J. *Home Ownership as a (Crumbling) Fourth Pillar of Social Insurance in Australia.* Luxembourg Wealth Study Working Paper Series, No. 8. LIS, Luxembourg, 2009. www.lisdatacenter.org/working-papers (accessed November 24, 2011).

62. Pierson, C., and Castles, F. G. Australian antecedents of the Third Way. *Polit. Stud.* 50:683–702, 2002. doi:10.1111/1467-9248.00002.

63. Alvaredo, F., and Saez, E. Income and wealth concentration in Spain from a historical and fiscal perspective. *J. Eur. Econ. Assoc.* 7:1140–1167, 2009. doi:10.1162/JEEA.2009.7.5.1140.

64. Börsch-Supan, A., and Lusardi, A. Saving: A cross-national perspective. In *Life Cycle Savings and Public Policy: A Cross-National Study of Six Countries,* ed. A. Börsch-Supan. Academic Press, San Diego, 2003.

65. Nettleton, S., and Burrows, R. Mortgage debt, insecure home ownership and health: An exploratory analysis. *Sociol. Health Illn.* 20:731–753, 1998. doi:10.1111/1467-9566.00127.

66. Börsch-Supan, A. (ed.). *Life Cycle Savings and Public Policy: A Cross-National Study of Six Countries.* Academic Press, San Diego, 2003.

67. Brugiavini, A., and Padula, M. Household saving behavior and pension policies in Italy. In *Life Cycle Savings and Public Policy: A Cross-National Study of Six Countries,* ed. A. Börsch-Supan. Academic Press, San Diego, 2003.

68. Kitamura, Y., Takayama, N., and Arita, F. Household savings and wealth distribution in Japan. In *Life Cycle Savings and Public Policy: A Cross-National Study of Six Countries,* ed. A. Börsch-Supan. Academic Press, San Diego, 2003.

69. Blakely, T., et al. What is the lag time between income inequality and health status? *J. Epidemiol. Community Health* 54:318–319, 2000. doi:10.1136/jech.54.4.318.

70. Segall, A., and Chappell, N. L. *Health and Health Care in Canada.* Prentice Hall, Toronto, 2000.

71. Ritakallio, V. M. The importance of housing costs in cross-national comparisons of welfare (state) outcomes. *Int. Soc. Sec. Rev.* 56(2):81–101, 2003. doi:10.1111/1468-246X.00159.

72. Smeeding, T., Magri, S., and Brandolini, A. *Asset-Based Measurement of Poverty.* Luxembourg Wealth Study Working Paper Series, No. 10. LIS, Luxembourg, 2010. www.lisdatacenter.org/working-papers (accessed November 24, 2011).

73. Kerstetter, S. *Rags and Riches: Wealth Inequality in Canada.* Canadian Centre for Policy Alternatives, Ottawa, 2003.

74. Haslett, D. W. Distributive justice and inheritance. In *Is Inheritance Legitimate? Ethical and Economic Aspects of Wealth Transfers.* ed. G. Erreygers and T. Vandevelde. Springer, Berlin, 1997.

75. Jackson, A. *Why Charity Isn't Enough: The Case For Raising Taxes On Canada's Rich.* Alternative Federal Budget 2008, Technical Report One. Canadian Centre for Policy Alternatives, Ottawa, 2007.

76. Frank, E. No more savings: The case for social wealth. In *The Wealth Inequality Reader,* Ed. 2, ed. Dollars and Sense and United for a Fair Economy. Dollars and Sense and Economic Affairs Bureau, Boston, 2008.

77. Starfield, B., and Birn, A. E. Income redistribution is not enough: Income inequality, social welfare programs, and achieving equity in health. *J. Epidemiol. Community Health* 61:1038–1041, 2007. doi:10.1136/jech.2006.054627.

CHAPTER 21

The Other Side of the Chinese Economic Miracle

Wei Zhang

Despite the financial crisis still sinking the world economy, China's GDP growth rate in 2010 reached 10 percent, continuing the great momentum maintained since the 1980s. This is often referred to as the Chinese economic miracle. While many marvel at and try to mystify the miracle, the other side of the miracle is less than miraculous. Compared with the period of its planned economy between the 1950s and 1970s, in the ensuing three decades, China has undergone slower progress in major health indicators, and this has been accompanied by an ailing health care system. This report presents a portrait of China's underdevelopment of health and its health care system, with up-to-date statistics. Such information is important for a fuller, more balanced, and more accurate view of the Chinese economic miracle.

*****

Starting in the 1980s, China's growth in per capita GDP (gross domestic product) topped the world by a great margin (Table 1). This is often referred to as the Chinese economic miracle (1–3). In 2010, when the global economy was still struggling to survive the economic crisis, China's GDP, once again, hit a double-digit growth rate, making the "miracle" even more miraculous.

While many marvel at and attempt to interpret China's economic miracle, the other side of the miracle is less than miraculous. Contrary to what one would predict, the health and quality of life of Chinese citizens have not made equal progress. Despite its long-term, fast GDP growth, some of China's health indicators have made only limited progress over the past 30 years; indeed, several indicators have deteriorated. Moreover, the performance of China's health care system has been equally unsatisfactory. Such information needs to be made known before assessing the Chinese economic miracle. The present report serves this purpose by presenting up-to-date statistical information, with some analysis.

I begin by presenting data on several vital health indicators for the Chinese population, and make some comparisons with countries having a wide range of political and economic regimes. I then present data pertaining to the performance of the country's health care system.

Table 1

Average annual GDP growth, 1960–2009, selected countries, percent

Country	1960–1970	1971–1980	1981–1990	1991–2000	2001–2009
China	4.65	6.28	9.35	10.45	10.49
Mexico	6.75	6.71	1.88	3.53	1.39
Cuba	—	4.43	4.27	−1.11	6.13
Venezuela	5.10	2.75	0.92	2.19	3.88
USA	—	3.27	3.25	3.44	1.56
Japan	9.83	4.50	4.64	1.19	0.50
Korea	10.37	7.30	8.74	6.19	3.92
France	5.57	3.71	2.41	1.99	1.17

Source: Author's calculation based on GDP (constant LCU) data from *Database World Development Indicators and Global Development Finance*.

One clarification needs to be made at the outset. When presenting the two sets of statistics—for health outcomes and for health system performance—sequentially, this report does not intend to imply that China's failure to improve many of its health outcome indicators is solely or primarily the result of its dysfunctional health care system. It is not. The health care system is a cause but not necessarily the leading cause or the root cause—there is a set of political and economic factors that more fundamentally shape both health indicators and a nation's health system operation (4–9). This point is further elaborated in the discussion and conclusion.

HEALTH INDICATORS

Life Expectancy

The life expectancy at birth for Chinese men and women improved dramatically between the time when the People's Republic of China was founded and the start of the reform and opening-up process of the 1980s. In the ensuing three decades, however, life expectancy, one of the most important yardsticks for measuring health, rose only slightly, from 66 years to 73 years, presenting a pattern that does not match China's persistent and accelerating economic growth during the same period (Figure 1).

Even if we take into account that it is more difficult to increase life expectancy once it has reached a certain point, China's progress in this indicator should still be considered less than impressive: it took Cuba approximately 14 years

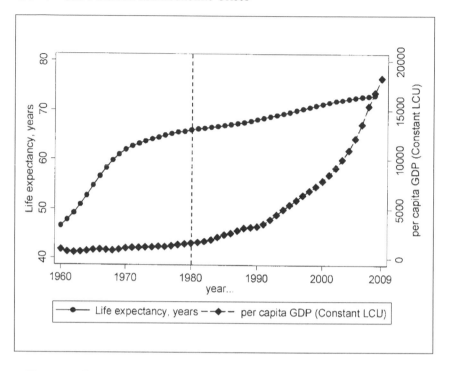

Figure 1. Life expectancy versus per capita GDP, China (1960–2009). *Sources*: Data for GDP per capita (constant LCU) from *World Development Indicators and Global Development Finance*; data for life expectancy from Health Nutrition and Population.

(between 1963 and 1976), and it took Vietnam 12 years (between 1991 and 2002), to raise life expectancy from 66 to 73 years (10).

Indeed, between 1980 and 2008, quite a few countries were more efficient than China in improving life expectancy (Table 2). For example, Albania in 1980 had a higher life expectancy (70 years) than China (66 years), making it theoretically more difficult to increase; by 2008, however, Albania's life expectancy had increased to 77 years, on a par with China's seven-year improvement (to 73 years). Mexico also had a slightly higher life expectancy (67 years) than China in 1980, but between 1980 and 2008, Mexico increased its life expectancy by eight years, one more year of gain than China. Furthermore, Libya and Vietnam both had a lower life expectancy in 1980 (60 and 57 years, respectively) than China, but by 2008, both countries had raised life expectancy to 74 years. These facts become especially striking when we take into account that none of these countries had GDP growth comparable to that of China.

Another noteworthy fact about life expectancy is the large and persistent regional gap in China (Table 3). In 1990, among all administrative regions,

Table 2

Life expectancy, 1980–2008, years

Country	1980	2008	Δ1980–2008	Country	1980	2008	Δ1980–2008
Albania	70	77	7	Korea, Rep.	66	80	14
Australia	74	81	7	Kuwait	70	78	8
Austria	72	80	8	Libya	60	74	14
Bahrain	68	76	8	Macao, China	72	81	9
Belgium	73	80	7	Malaysia	67	74	7
Bermuda	72	79	7	Malta	73	80	7
Chile	69	79	10	Mauritius	66	73	7
China	**66**	**73**	**7**	Mexico	67	75	8
Colombia	65	73	8	New Zealand	73	80	7
Czech Republic	70	77	7	Nicaragua	58	73	15
Dominican Republic	63	73	10	Oman	60	76	16
Ecuador	63	75	12	Peru	60	73	13
France	74	82	8	Portugal	71	79	8
French Polynesia	64	74	10	Qatar	67	76	9
Germany	73	80	7	Saudi Arabia	61	73	12
Grenada	65	75	10	Singapore	71	81	10
Hong Kong, China	75	82	7	Slovenia	70	79	9
Iceland	74	82	8	Switzerland	75	82	7
Ireland	73	80	7	Syrian Arab Republic	63	74	11
Israel	74	81	7	Tunisia	62	74	12
Italy	74	82	8	United Arab Emirates	68	78	10
Japan	76	83	7	Vietnam	57	74	17
Jordan	63	73	10				

Source: World Development Indicators.

Shanghai had the highest life expectancy at 74.9 years, at least 10 years higher than the bottom five regions with the lowest life expectancies. One decade later, in 2000, Shanghai still held the leading position, with a life expectancy of 78.1 years. In fact, four of the top five regions remained in the top five. On the other hand, all the bottom five regions in 1990 remained in the bottom five in 2000, and the gap between them and Shanghai was still more than 10 years.

Infant Mortality Rate

China's infant mortality rate (IMR) has experienced a similar trend (Table 4). In 1970, the infant mortality rate was 83 per 1,000 live births; among all 139 countries for which data are available, China ranked 73rd. After a decade, China managed to reduce its IMR to 46 per 1,000 live births. Because this progress

Table 3

Life expectancy by administrative region, China, 1990–2000

Rank	Region	1990	Region	2000
Top				
1	Shanghai	74.9	Shanghai	78.1
2	Beijing	72.9	Beijing	76.1
3	Guangdong	72.5	Tianjin	74.9
4	Tianjin	72.3	Zhejiang	74.7
5	Zhejiang	71.4	Shandong	73.9
Bottom				
5	Guizhou	64.3	Xinjiang	67.4
4	Xinjiang	63.6	Qinghai	66.0
3	Yunnan	63.5	Guizhou	66.0
2	Qinghai	60.6	Yunnan	65.5
1	Tibet	59.6	Tibet	64.4

Source: Ministry of Health, *China Health Statistical Yearbook 2010.*

Table 4

Infant mortality rate (IMR) and ranking in the world, China, 1970–2009

	1970	1975	1980	1985	1990	1995	2000	2005	2008	2009
IMR, per 1,000 live births	83	64	46	37	37	36	30	22	18	17
World ranking		73	67	58	59	65	72	72	65	64	62

Source: World Bank, *Health Nutrition and Population (HNP) Statistics.*

was faster than the world average level, China's ranking improved to 58th. However, between 1980 and 2000, its world ranking declined. In 2000, although IMR was down to 30 per 1,000 live births, China ranked 72nd for the same cohort of countries. China's ranking did see some improvement after 2000, but, as of 2009, its ranking was 62nd, still worse than in the early 1980s.

Immunization Rates among One-Year-Olds

In the 1980s, China adopted the World Health Organization–recommended Expanded Programme on Immunization as the basis of its national immunization program. Four vaccines for children—Bacille Calmette Guerin (BCG), measles-containing vaccine (MCV), diphtheria, tetanus, and pertussis combined vaccine

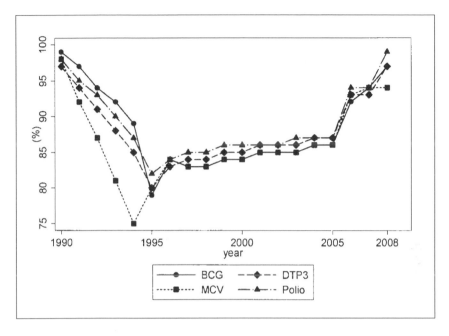

Figure 2. Immunization coverage among 1-year-olds, China (1990–2008). *Source:* World Health Organization, Global Health Observatory database.

(DTP), and oral poliomyelitis vaccine (OPV)—were included (11). In 1990, the immunization rates among 1-year-olds for all four vaccines were above 95 percent. However, the first half of the 1990s saw a continuous decline (Figure 2). In particular, MCV coverage decreased from 99 to 79 percent between 1990 and 1995. After 1995, the rate returned to around 85 percent, thanks to a regulation implemented by the central government that required local governments—at the township (*xiang*) level—to achieve immunization rates of 85 percent by 1995 (12).[1]

The rapid decline in the early 1990s and stagnation in the subsequent decade were directly linked to insufficient government funding, which forced health facilities to either cut off the free immunization services or provide them for a fee; children of migrants are especially vulnerable under these circumstances (13–15). It was not until recent years that we saw some real improvement—after the

[1] The improvement did not go any farther, staying at 85 percent until the mid-2000s. In addition, the same regulation also required immunization coverage to reach 90 percent by 2000; this target was not met.

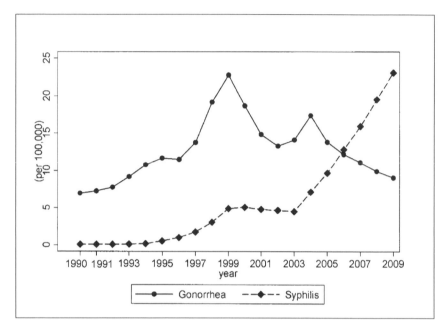

Figure 3. Sexually transmitted diseases incidence, China (1990–2009). *Source*: Ministry of Health, *China Health Statistical Yearbook 2010* (23).

central government reiterated free immunization policies and increased government funding through a series of regulations.[2]

Infectious Diseases: STDs and Tuberculosis

Sexually transmitted diseases (STDs) were virtually eradicated under the leadership of Mao Zedong (18, 19), yet they reemerged after the 1980s (Figure 3). The incidence of gonorrhea peaked in 1999 at 22.8 cases per 100,000 people. The rate has declined since then. The data for syphilis, however, are less than promising. A sharp surge was observed in the early 2000s. As of 2009, syphilis incidence was 23.07 cases per 100,000 people, four to five times the level in 2003. As some observers remarked, "No other country has seen such a precipitous increase in reported syphilis cases in the penicillin era" (20).

The picture for AIDS is equally worrisome. The first case in China was reported in 1982, and the first death from that disease was reported in 1985 (21). During the

---

[2] For example, the State Council issued, in 2005, the Regulations on Vaccine Circulation and Preventive Inoculation (16); and the Ministry of Health issued, in 2007, the Implementation Act of the National Immunization Expansion Plan (17).

first half of the 1990s, the growth of AIDS was relatively moderate: until 1996, AIDS incidence was still considered "rare" in China (18). After that, however, the incidences of both HIV-positive status and AIDS began to grow exponentially (Figure 4). In both 2008 and 2009, AIDS was China's number one infectious disease killer: the official death tolls were 5,389 and 6,596, respectively (22, 23).

In addition to infection through sexual contact or intravenous drug use, a sizable proportion of HIV/AIDS patients in China were infected through commercial plasma donation and transfusion of infected blood and blood products in the mid-1990s. According to UNAIDS, by the end of 2009, 7.8 percent of the 740,000 HIV-positive individuals in China were infected in this way (24). Most of them were low-income rural farmers (25–27).

Following HIV/AIDS, pulmonary tuberculosis (TB) was the second largest cause of death in China from an infectious agent in 2009; it also had the second highest incidence rate (81.09 per 100,000), after viral hepatitis (23). Today, China is considered a country with a high burden of TB and a high burden of multidrug-resistant tuberculosis (MDR-TB) (28). Given the well-established association of TB with socioeconomic impoverishment (29–31), the persistently inefficient control of TB in China is another illustration of the failure in translating China's economic "miracle" into progress on quality of life (Figure 5).

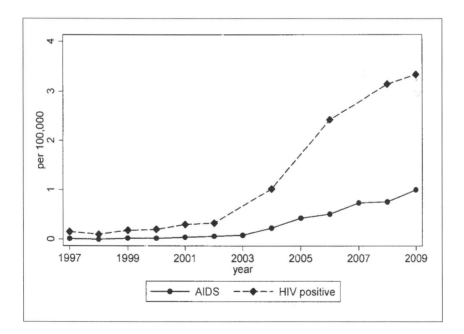

Figure 4.   Incidence of HIV positive and AIDS, China (1997–2009). *Source:* Ministry of Health, *China Health Statistical Yearbook 2010* (23).

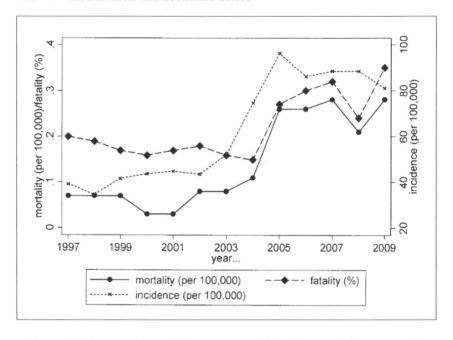

Figure 5. Pulmonary tuberculosis, China (1997–2009). *Source*: Ministry of Health, *China Health Statistical Yearbook 2010* (23).

THE PERFORMANCE OF CHINA'S
HEALTH CARE SYSTEM

In 1980, the Chinese Communist Party, under the leadership of Deng Xiaoping, gradually shifted to a GDP growth–centered development strategy, deviating from the principle of giving top priority to equality (32, 33). Following this deviation, there appeared in China a consistent decline in resources allocated to the health sector.

Government Expenditure on Health

Between 1998 and 2008, China's total expenditure on health never exceeded 5 percent of GDP. This was only marginally higher than in Thailand but lower than in a number of other countries across a wide range of development stages and political regimes, including the United States, France, the United Kingdom, Sweden, Russia, and Cuba (Figure 6).

When out-of-pocket health expenditure is considered, individual citizens' financial burden was significantly heavier in China than in the other countries in this group (Figure 7). For example, between 1998 and 2008, China's

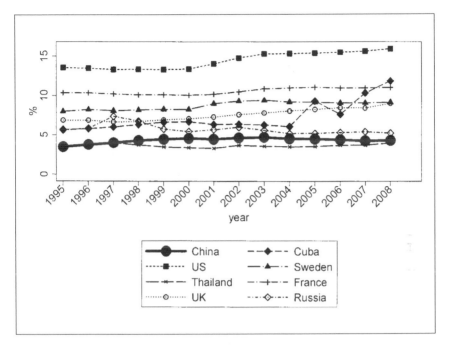

Figure 6. Total health expenditure as % GDP, selected countries (1995–2008). *Source*: World Health Organization, National Health Accounts.

out-of-pocket health expenditure was about 2.4 percent of GDP, whereas all other selected countries held it below 2 percent; Cubans during this period spent about 0.5 percent of GDP on health out-of-pocket.

Between 1995 and 2008, China's annual total expenditure per capita on health surged from $53 to $259 (purchasing power parity, NCU per US$); this was equivalent to an annual growth rate of 13.0 percent—faster than the country's GDP growth. However, public money (government plus social) barely covered half of that increase (Figure 8).

The smaller role played by the Chinese government resembles, to some extent, the situation in the United States: in both countries, more than 50 percent of health spending falls on the private sector. This philosophy of minimal government does not seem to be shared by the other countries in the selected group (Figure 9).

Hospitals and Physicians per 1,000 Persons

Hospital beds per 1,000 and physicians per 1,000 persons were gradually on the rise between 1970 and 1990, but that trend was discontinued between 1990

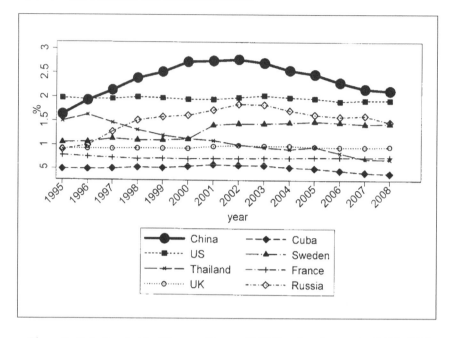

Figure 7. Out-of-pocket health expenditure as % GDP, selected countries (1995–2008). *Source*: Calculations based on data from World Health Organization, National Health Accounts.

and 2003, coinciding with the time when China's market economy began to blossom. During this period, China had, on average, around 1.5 physicians and 2.5 hospital beds per 1,000 persons (Figure 10). That stagnation cannot be considered compatible with the country's double-digit GDP growth within the same time frame. Again, it was not until very recently that we saw some increase in hospital beds and physicians.

Insurance Coverage

Between the mid-1980s and the early 2000s, the majority of Chinese citizens were not covered by any form of medical insurance. In the urban sector, the marketization and privatization of state-owned enterprises made the medical insurance system for urban workers—the Labor Insurance Scheme—dysfunctional (34, 35). In the rural sector, the collapse of the commune system undermined the financial viability of the Rural Cooperative Medical System, as well as the "barefoot doctor" program (36). By 2003, nearly 45 percent of urban and 80 percent of rural dwellers were left uninsured (Table 5).

The notable reduction in the number of uninsured in 2008 was attributable to the rapid expansion of the New Cooperative Medical Scheme (NCMS) in rural

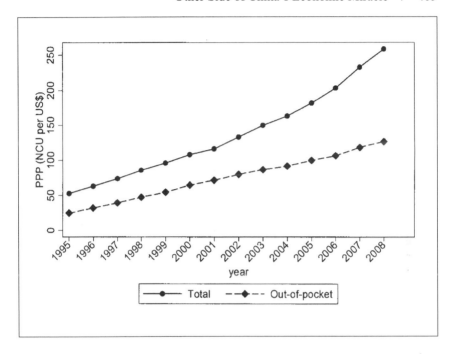

Figure 8. Health expenditure per capita, China (1995–2008). *Source*: Calculations based on data from World Health Organization, National Health Accounts.

China after 2003. The scheme has a small enrollment fee (as low as $1.5 to $3 per person per year) (37, 38), but the downside is that it mainly covers catastrophic hospital services, and the deductibles are relatively high (39–41). Despite its high enrollment rate, the NCMS has delivered limited benefits to rural residents (Table 6): between 2003 and 2008, the biweekly rate of rural residents not seeking care for illness was reduced, but remained quite high (37.8%)—in fact, it was higher than the rate in 1998, when, as shown in Table 5, nearly 90 percent of rural residents were uninsured. In other words, the high enrollment rate of the NCMS does not suffice to ensure progress in real access to health care.

DISCUSSION AND CONCLUSION

This report presents statistics on several vital population health indicators in China and the performance of the country's health care system. Despite its startling economic miracle, since the 1980s, China has shown relatively slow progress in improving its people's health; some health indicators have even worsened. Equally disappointing has been the performance of China's health care system. This information should be kept in mind by anyone interested in

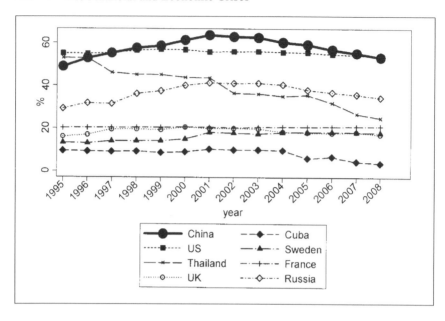

Figure 9. Private as % total health expenditure, selected countries (1995–2008). *Source*: World Health Organization, National Health Accounts.

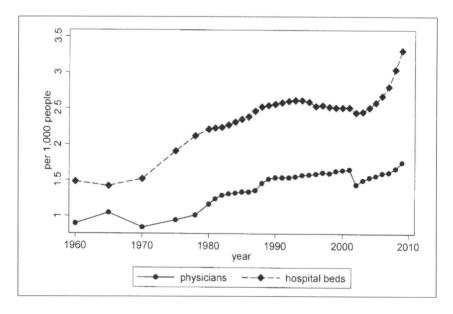

Figure 10. Physicians and hospital beds, China (1960–2009). *Source*: Calculations based on Ministry of Health, *China Health Statistical Yearbook 2010* (23).

Table 5

Rate of uninsured persons, China, percent

	Total	Urban	Rural
1998	76.4	44.1	87.3
2003	70.3	44.8	79.0
2008	12.9	28.1	7.5

Source: Ministry of Health, *China Health Statistical Yearbook 2010.*

Table 6

Biweekly rate of not seeking care for illness, China, percent

	Total	Urban	Rural
1998	38.5	49.9	33.2
2003	48.9	57.0	45.8
2008	37.6	37.3	37.8

Source: Ministry of Health, *China Health Statistical Yearbook 2010.*

demystifying China's economic miracle. Some evidence presented in this report may provoke further reflections on the possibility of China's economic miracle if there were no sacrifices in people's health and the country's health care system.

A few clarifications need to be made. First, as stated earlier, this report does not intend to suggest that China's unsatisfactory health outcomes are mainly the result of its ailing health care system. A country's health care system certainly influences that country's health outcomes, but it cannot be the root determinant. Health outcomes and the health care system are both shaped by the same set of political and economic factors. For example, China's market-oriented reform triggered the dismantling of both the commune system of collectivized agriculture and the "iron rice bowl" system of guaranteed lifetime employment and benefits in state enterprises—two institutions that served as China's safety nets until the late 1970s (36, 42). It was this shift that contributed to the destruction of both China's health care system and its population's health: on the one hand, rural farmers and urban workers immediately lost their health insurance and access to affordable health care—hence the deterioration of the health care system; on the other hand, many of those who became unemployed had to take up informal jobs, leaving them vulnerable to physiological insecurity and substandard working conditions—hence the deterioration of health.[3]

Another clarification is that this report does not imply that good health outcome indicators and a good health care system are equivalent to the betterment of well-being and quality of life. Well-being and quality of life are dependent on a much broader range of social, economic, and political factors that are not necessarily within the field of medicine (4, 44, 45). These factors include, but are not limited to (4):

1. Collective, structural factors in the realms of political participation (such as the absence of barriers to electoral participation and joining unions), labor market participation (such as full employment policies), welfare state (such as public provision of care for children and the elderly), and culture (such as embracing solidarity rather than competition).
2. Individual, lifestyle factors, such as eating healthy and safe foods, being physically active, and being free of drugs.
3. Empowerment factors that link the individual, lifestyle factors and the collective, structural factors, such as a sense of commitment and solidarity.

Without the building of the full set of factors, even good performance in a few health and social indicators would not guarantee real improvement in people's quality of life; people can still feel unfulfilled. Indeed, many of the Middle East and North African countries currently engaged in social revolution stand quite strong in terms of life expectancy, infant mortality, and the Human Development Index (Table 7). But what matters is not just longevity: health and happiness are equally, if not more, important. The national health plan implemented by the social democratic government of Sweden—often referred to as one of the happiest countries on the planet (46, 47)—might be a good example to consider. That plan goes beyond medical interventions and incorporates both individual and structural determinants of health (4).

The last, and important, clarification to make is that this report is not an in-depth exploration of China's political economy in recent decades. That would require another study. The primary purpose of this report is to provide readers—especially those who have been fascinated with China's economic development but have not followed closely the development (or underdevelopment) of its population health and health care system—with updated information, allowing a fuller understanding of the Chinese economic miracle.

---

[3] The deadly coal mine industry in China is a demonstration of how workers suffer from substandard working conditions. In the mid-2000s, when coal mine safety fueled a public outcry nationwide, the government began to take more forceful measures, including nationalization of small coal mines (43). The official death toll was then reduced to below 2,500 in 2010—a substantial improvement, but still a high level by international standards (see Appendix Table 1).

Table 7

Leading African countries in health indicators, 2007

Ranking	Infant mortality rate, per 1,000 live births		Life expectancy, yrs		Human Development Index	
	Country		Country		Country	
1	Seychelles	11.6	Tunisia	74.3	Libya	0.85
2	Mauritius	12.8	Libya	74.2	Seychelles	0.84
3	Libya	16.5	Seychelles	73.2	Mauritius	0.80
4	Tunisia	18.0	Mauritius	72.4	Tunisia	0.77
5	Cape Verde	24.0	Algeria	72.3	Gabon	0.76
6	Egypt	29.9	Morocco	71.1	Algeria	0.75
7	Morocco	32.4	Cape Verde	70.9	Equatorial Guinea	0.72
8	Botswana	32.5	Egypt	70.0	Cape Verde	0.71
9	Algeria	32.8	Sao Tome and Principe	65.4	Egypt	0.70
10	Eritrea	45.6	Comoros	65.1	Botswana	0.69

Source: World Bank, *Africa Development Indicators*.

Appendix Table 1

Coal mine safety, China, 2000–2010

Year	Total accidents	Total deaths
2000	2,863	5,798
2001	3,082	5,670
2002	4,344	6,995
2003	4,143	6,434
2004	3,639	6,027
2005	3,341	5,986
2006	—	4,746
2007	—	3,786
2008	—	3,215
2009	—	2,631
2010	—	2,443

Source: For 2000–2005: *China Labor Bulletin*, www.clb.org.hk/en/node/19316; for 2006: Reuters, www.reuters.com/article/2007/01/11/idUSPEK206148; for 2007: Reuters, http://uk.reuters.com/article/2008/01/12/china-mines-idUKPEK32921920080112; for 2008–2009: Reuters, http://uk.reuters.com/article/2010/02/14/china-coal-deaths-idUKTOE61D00V20100214; for 2010: *China Daily*, www.chinadaily.com/cn/cndy/2011-02/26/content_12081377.htm (all data accessed March 20, 2011).

REFERENCES

1. Lin, J. Y., Cai, F., and Li, Z. *The China Miracle: Development Strategy and Economic Reform.* Chinese University Press, Hong Kong, 2003.
2. Gilboy, G. J. The myth behind China's miracle. *Foreign Aff.* 83:33, 2004.
3. Huang, Y. Private ownership: The real source of China's economic miracle. *McKinsey Q.*, no. 1, 2009, pp. 149–155.
4. Navarro, V. What is a national health policy? *Int. J. Health Serv.* 37:1–14, 2007.
5. Navarro, V. (ed.). *Neoliberalism, Globalization, and Inequalities: Consequences for Health and Quality of Life.* Baywood, Amityville, NY, 2007.
6. Navarro, V., et al. Politics and health outcomes. *Lancet* 368:1033–1037, 2006.
7. Navarro, V. (ed.). *The Political and Social Contexts of Health.* Baywood, Amityville, NY, 2004.
8. Navarro, V., and Muntaner, C. (eds.). *Political and Economic Determinants of Population Health and Well-being: Controversies and Developments.* Baywood, Amityville, NY, 2004.
9. Navarro, V. Why some countries have national health insurance, others have national health services, and the United States has neither. *Int. J. Health Serv.* 19:383–404, 1989.
10. World Databank. *Health Nutrition and Population (HNP) Statistics.* http://data.worldbank.org/data-catalog/health-nutrition-population-statistics.

11. World Health Organization. Expanded Programme on Immunization: Vaccinating China's Children. www.wpro.who.int/China/sites/epi (accessed March 20, 2011).
12. State Council. China Children's Development Outline in the 1990s (in Chinese). 1992. www.people.com.cn/GB/99013/99041/100696/100819/6186091.html (accessed March 20, 2011).
13. Hsiao, W., and Liu, Y. Economic reform and health—lessons from China. *N. Engl. J. Med.* 335:430–432, 1996.
14. Cui, F. Q., and Gofin, R. Immunization coverage and its determinants in children aged 12–23 months in Gansu, China. *Vaccine* 25:664–671, 2007.
15. Sun, M., et al. Immunization status and risk factors of migrant children in densely populated areas of Beijing, China. *Vaccine* 28:1264–1274, 2010.
16. The State Council. Regulations on Vaccine Circulation and Preventive Inoculation. State Council Ordinance no. 434. 2005. www.gov.cn/zwgk/2005-05/23/content_275.htm (accessed March 20, 2011).
17. Ministry of Health, China. Implementation Act of the National Immunization Expansion Plan. December 29, 2007. www.gov.cn/gzdt/2008-02/19/content_893572.htm (accessed March 20, 2011).
18. Cohen, M. S., et al. Successful eradication of sexually transmitted diseases in the People's Republic of China: Implications for the 21st century. *J. Infect. Dis.* 174:S223, 1996.
19. Horn, J. S. *Away with all Pests: An English Surgeon in People's China, 1954–1969.* Monthly Review Press, New York, 1971.
20. Tucker, J. D., Chen, X. S., and Peeling, R. W. Syphilis and social upheaval in China. *N. Engl. J. Med.* 362:1658–1661, 2010.
21. Lu, W., and Ning, W. HIV/AIDS epidemic and the development of comprehensive surveillance system in China with challenges. *Chin. Med. J.* 123:3495–3500, 2010.
22. Ministry of Health, China. *China Health Statistical Yearbook 2009.* Beijing, 2009.
23. Ministry of Health, China. *China Health Statistical Yearbook 2010.* Beijing, 2010.
24. UNAIDS. China's Epidemic and Response. 2010. www.unaids.org.cn/en/index/page.asp?id=197&class=2&classname=China+Epidemic+%26+Response (accessed March 20, 2011).
25. Huang, Y. The politics of HIV/AIDS in China. *Asian Perspect.* 30:95–125, 2006.
26. Wu, Z., et al. Evolution of China's response to HIV/AIDS. *Lancet* 369:679–690, 2007.
27. Zhang, M., et al. Natural history of HIV infection in former plasma donors in rural China. *Front. Med. Chin.* 4:346–350, 2010.
28. World Health Organization. Tuberculosis Country Profiles. www.who.int/tb/country/data/profiles/en/index.html (accessed March 20, 2011).
29. Jackson, S., et al. Poverty and the economic effects of TB in rural China. *Int. J. Tuberc. Lung Dis.* 10:1104–1110, 2006.
30. Holtgrave, D. R., and Crosby, R. A. Social determinants of tuberculosis case rates in the United States. *Am. J. Prev. Med.* 26:159–162, 2004.
31. Lönnroth, K., et al. Drivers of tuberculosis epidemics: The role of risk factors and social determinants. *Soc. Sci. Med.* 68:2240–2246, 2009.
32. Li, M. *The Rise of China and the Demise of the Capitalist World-Economy.* Monthly Review Press, New York, 2008.
33. Harvey, D. *A Brief History of Neoliberalism.* Oxford University Press, New York, 2007.

34. Yip, W., and Hsiao, W. Medical savings accounts: Lessons from China. *Health Aff. (Millwood)* 16:244, 1997.
35. Yip, W., and Hsiao, W. C. The Chinese health system at a crossroads. *Health Aff. (Millwood)* 27:460, 2008.
36. Blumenthal, D., and Hsiao, W. Privatization and its discontents—the evolving Chinese health care system. *N. Engl. J. Med.* 353:1165, 2005.
37. Babiarz, K. S., et al. New evidence on the impact of China's New Rural Cooperative Medical Scheme and its implications for rural primary healthcare: Multivariate difference-in-difference analysis. *BMJ* 341, 2010.
38. Wang, H., et al. Community-based health insurance in poor rural China: The distribution of net benefits. *Health Policy Plann.* 20:366, 2005.
39. You, X., and Kobayashi, Y. The New Cooperative Medical Scheme in China. *Health Policy* 91:1–9, 2009.
40. Wang, H., et al. The impact of rural mutual health care on health status: Evaluation of a social experiment in rural China. *Health Econ.* 18:S65–82, 2009.
41. Shi, W., et al. The influence of the rural health security schemes on health utilization and household impoverishment in rural China: Data from a household survey of western and central China. *Int. J. Equity Health* 9, 2010.
42. Chen, M. S. The great reversal: Transformation of health care in the People's Republic of China. In *The Blackwell Companion to Medical Sociology*, ed. W. C. Cockerham, pp. 456–482. Wiley-Blackwell, Oxford, 2001.
43. Nationalisation rides again. *Economist*, November 12, 2009. www.economist.com/node/14859337?Story_ID=E1_TQRVJPPS (accessed March 20, 2011).
44. Navarro, V. Development and quality of life: A critique of Amartya Sen's development as freedom. *Int. J. Health Serv.* 30:661–674, 2000.
45. Navarro, V. The labor process and health: A historical materialist interpretation. *Int. J. Health Serv.* 12:5–29, 1982.
46. Helman, C. The World's Happiest Countries. January 19, 2011. www.forbes.com/2011/01/19/norway-denmark-finland-business-washington-world-happiest-countr.html (accessed March 20, 2011).
47. Levy, F. The World's Happiest Countries. July 14, 2010. www.forbes.com/2010/07/14/world-happiest-countries-lifestyle-realestate-gallup.html (accessed March 20, 2011).

PART VI

Focus on Solutions

Edwin Ng

INTRODUCTION

An encouraging development in public health research has been the acknowledgment that the discipline needs to shift from being "problem-focused" (e.g., describing health issues, documenting associations, and confirming social gradients) to "solution-focused" (e.g., engaging the policy arena, spearheading social interventions, and evaluating what works for whom and in what contexts) (1). Such an acknowledgment has the potential for reorienting social epidemiologists, for example, from being merely professional or critical scholars who produce theoretical, empirical, and foundational types of knowledge (e.g., documenting and replicating social determinants of health) to being more policy-, popular-, and politically-oriented scholars who generate more concrete and engaged forms of knowledge (e.g., assessing the economic costs and health benefits of policies and interventions and engaging in community-based participatory health research).

Consistent with this reorientation from describing the problem to considering solutions, chapters in this last part of the book speak to how population health and health inequalities can be improved and redressed through action-oriented and politically-oriented strategies. First, in Chapter 22, Muntaner and coauthors provide a critical appraisal of Wilkinson and Pickett's most recent and much-lauded book, *The Spirit Level: Why Equality Is Better for Everyone* (2) and argue that greater attention needs to be paid to the political and economic factors that generate income inequalities in the first place, which in turn, affect population health. Muntaner and colleagues (Chapter 23) then heed the call to not only describe the extent of employment-related health inequalities but provide a useful heuristic that outlines a comprehensive program of research aimed at improving workers' health and ameliorating health inequalities between social classes. Finally, Navarro's contribution (Chapter 24) concludes by reiterating one of this book's central theses: the fundamental drivers of public health are political in nature, and thus, efforts to significantly improve health and reduce inequalities need to be informed by political dimensions.

REFERENCES

1. O'Campo, P., and Dunn, J.R. *Rethinking Social Epidemiology*. New York, Springer, 2012.
2. Wilkinson, R., and Pickett, K. *The Spirit Level: Why Equality is Better for Everyone*. Penguin, London, 2009, revised 2010.

CHAPTER 22

Social Class, Politics, and the Spirit Level: Why Income Inequality Remains Unexplained and Unsolved

Carles Muntaner, Nanky Rai, Edwin Ng,
and Haejoo Chung

Richard Wilkinson and Kate Pickett's latest book, The Spirit Level: Why Equality is Better for Everyone, *has caught the attention of academics and policymakers and stimulated debate across the left-right political spectrum. Interest in income inequality has remained unabated since the publication of Wilkinson's previous volume,* Unhealthy Societies: The Afflictions of Inequality. *While both books detail the negative health effects of income inequality,* The Spirit Level *expands the scope of its argument to also include social issues. The book, however, deals extensively with the explanation of how income inequality affects individual health. Little attention is given to political and economic explanations on how income inequality is generated in the first place. The volume ends with political solutions that carefully avoid state interventions such as limiting the private sector's role in the production of goods and services (e.g., non-profit sector, employee-ownership schemes). Although well-intentioned, these alternatives are insufficient to significantly reduce the health inequalities generated by contemporary capitalism in wealthy countries, let alone around the world.*

*****

Richard Wilkinson and Kate Pickett's latest book, *The Spirit Level: Why Equality is Better for Everyone* (henceforth TSL), (1) has caught the attention of academics and policymakers alike and stimulated debate across the left-right political spectrum. Interest in income inequality has remained unabated since the publication of Wilkinson's previous volume, *Unhealthy Societies: The Afflictions of Inequality* (2). While both books detail the negative health effects of income inequality, TSL expands its income inequality thesis to include negative social consequences (e.g., educational attainment, imprisonment, social mobility, trust and community life, violence, charitable giving) as well as health problems (e.g., infant mortality, self-rated health, life expectancy, teenage pregnancy, obesity, mental health, drug use).

The idea is a familiar one: after the United States and other wealthy countries achieve a certain standard of living (approximately US$25,000 per capita), TSL argues that what most determines population levels of social and health problems is how income is distributed between the rich and poor (income distribution was measured using the 20:20 ratio and Gini coefficient for international country and United States comparisons, respectively). The bulk of TSL (14 out of 16 chapters) is devoted to empirically documenting this link, elucidating the nature of social gradients in health, and demonstrating that income inequality affects not only the poor but even middle- and high-income groups. Findings indicate that more equal societies (e.g., Scandinavian countries, Japan, New Hampshire) experience significant social and health advantages compared to unequal countries and states (e.g., liberal nations such as the United States, United Kingdom, Australia, Louisiana). Explaining these associations involves psychosocial mechanisms that connect the experience and perception of inequality with status differences. It follows that income inequality and its adverse consequences lead to biological reactions such as stress and anxiety, which, in turn, shape and determine poor health outcomes among individuals and populations.

TSL could be labeled "populist" because it aims to be both critical in implicating the negative effects of income inequality *and* politically neutral for its solutions on how to reduce income distributions (calls for "decommodifying" welfare states are carefully avoided).[1] Balancing on this tightrope explains, in part, why TSL has captured the attention of politicians across the ideological spectrum, including the United Kingdom's major political parties, other European countries, and even across the Atlantic, in the United States and Canada (3–6). Remarkably, this book continues to receive critical attention during the current climate of partisan politics and economic uncertainty, which generates greater interest to understand the strength of its claims and its implications for social change.

TSL has garnered unprecedented attention from academics and non-academics alike, ranging from legitimate praise to unfounded criticism. Some have lauded TSL for its wide-ranging theory of social gradients and for noting the limits of economic growth to achieve equality. Others have leveled critiques that challenge TSL's incomplete conceptualization of social stratification, conflation

---

[1] Paraphrasing TSL, "What matters is how much income you have, not how you got it." In a talk in Toronto on December 10, 2010, titled "The Age of Unequals," Richard Wilkinson made clear that he was not advocating for state intervention, was aiming at something "deeper than the welfare state," and was reaching out to the political right and left alike. Indeed, TSL has gotten positive attention from leaders of both the Conservative (David Cameron) and Labor (Ed Milliband) parties in the United Kingdom.

of class and status (7), and biased results resulting from selective sampling of rich countries and choice of outcomes (8). In this chapter, we contribute to this debate by undertaking a critical appraisal of TSL's relative merits and drawbacks. After the publication of *Unhealthy Societies,* Carles Muntaner and colleagues raised a number of critical issues regarding the explanatory power of the "income inequality and social cohesion" hypothesis (9, 10). Given that these issues remain largely unexamined and unresolved, we reiterate the need for a social class perspective and comment on TSL's unclear stance on the role of politics in narrowing income inequalities and the limited value of its recommended strategies for transforming unequal societies into more egalitarian ones.

TO THE SPIRIT LEVEL'S CREDIT

TSL deserves much praise for advancing public health as a whole and social epidemiology in particular by highlighting research on the social nature of population health and health inequalities. The authors' work has captured a wide audience through its powerful claim that income inequality not only affects the poor, but also follows a social gradient that negatively impacts middle- and high-income groups. TSL also was published during an opportune time that coincided with recent and current economic crises in the United States and the European Union (although the crucial role of income inequality in generating the current crisis receives surprisingly little attention). Inevitably, these crises invite greater academic, policy, and public attention to the effects of rising income inequalities (e.g., movements such as Occupy Wall Street and We Are the 99%), for which TSL offers a much-needed public health perspective. Aside from its popularity, we commend TSL for elevating income inequality as a social determinant of health to an international stage and for challenging the idea that pronounced inequality is necessary for contemporary economies.

Advancing Income Inequality
as a Social Determinant of Health

By applying a social determinants of health (SDOH) framework to understand why some people are healthy and others are not, TSL stands out for synthesizing the extant literature on income inequality and presenting this work into a readable and engaging volume. Given that most public health researchers are content with finding statistical associations without much theory, Wilkinson and Pickett have taken an extra step to theorize and present their empirical work to a general audience. Unquestionably, the authors have crafted an effective piece of knowledge transfer that bridges public health research and the need for non-health care interventions.

Since the authors have successfully engaged the broader public with the ethical implications of their research, they also have opened themselves to vitriolic criticism (mostly from the right side of the political spectrum) and allegations of bias by supposedly "value-free" scientists. By design and purpose, social epidemiology is an applied science (11) and not a spectator sport (e.g., producing new knowledge for the sake of knowledge development). For example, social epidemiologists do not examine the link between precarious employment and depression because it represents an interesting line of inquiry. Instead, limited attention and resources are paid because depression causes avoidable human suffering and new knowledge has the potential to inform prevention or treatment strategies. Thus, social epidemiology is not a basic or pure science in the same vein as quantum mechanics. Being fully aware of its applied nature, TSL uses research to test the premise that greater levels of income inequality cause pronounced social and health problems.

From a social justice and health equity perspective, it is difficult to criticize the authors' effort. Wilkinson and Pickett have achieved what few scholars have: summarizing support for the hypothesis that income inequality negatively impacts social and health outcomes, synthesizing extant literatures that map out plausible pathways, and demonstrating the meso- and macro-level consequences of income inequality at the individual level. They achieved this feat despite the fact that income inequality remains a contested idea within academia and politics. Furthermore, we acknowledge that it is far easier to critique a theory of social gradients than to develop an original framework, produce supporting evidence, and defend its merits (12). An excess of criticism shuns creativity, promotes comfortable skepticism, and leads to nihilism, an unconstructive outcome for a technology such as public health whose ultimate goal is the alleviation of human suffering through social change (12).

Challenging the Davis-Moore Thesis

The idea that income inequality has negative effects on health and well-being provides a much-needed counter-narrative to standard economic thinking that inequality is necessary and beneficial.[2] From this viewpoint, income inequality has beneficial consequences for the successful operation and growth of society. According to the Davis-Moore thesis (13), income inequality is universal and necessary because it motivates and rewards the most talented individuals to perform the most important occupational positions. Given that occupational positions vary in required skills and credentials (e.g., some positions do not require specialized skills while others require extensive education and training), a system of differential rewards based on income is necessary, even healthy, because it motivates people to innovate, work harder, and produce more.

---

[2] Yet we could argue that income inequality already is widely accepted as a major social problem. Even President Barack Obama in his January 2012 State of the Union address cited income inequality as the "defining issue of our time."

Conferring large salaries and even bigger bonuses on those who work on Wall Street, for example, is justified and even encouraged because differential rewards are needed to motivate these individuals to engage in the most significant activities possible (e.g., investing capital to produce more capital). Such thinking remains influential because it complements dominant neoliberal ideologies that view each person's income as an appropriate reward for his or her productive activity. Consequently, any attempts to reduce inequality, such as generous welfare state policies, are viewed as disincentives for citizens to be productive.

To its credit, TSL provides an important and compelling rejoinder to this argument. Rather than viewing inequality as natural and necessary, Wilkinson and Pickett broaden the scope to consider the negative consequences of income inequalities. TSL repeats that inequality has its limits and hurts us all. Yet the implicit classless approach to egalitarian change, according to which we *all* suffer from income inequality, is unrealistic (9, 10). The economic benefits reaped by social classes at the top of the income distribution are so huge—compared with a hypothetical egalitarian alternative in which their well-being supposedly would be improved—that it is reasonable to assume they will use their power to maintain the status quo. Although seeing "class struggle" as the only engine of social change is limiting, the social cohesion approach is politically naïve. Income inequality does not have uniform effects across class, gender, ethnicity, and other forms of stratification. Thus, although TSL does provide a thoughtful critique of income inequality by demonstrating its negative consequences, it still overlooks how inequality is generated through interdependent social class relations (9, 10).

THEORETICAL AND POLITICAL LIMITATIONS
OF THE SPIRIT LEVEL

Our critique of TSL reflects fundamental differences in our respective theoretical paradigms, understanding of politics, and preferred solutions. Whereas TSL views income inequality in Durkheimian terms, explains health inequalities through psychosocial mechanisms, and remains apolitical, we counter that income inequality should be viewed through a social class perspective that emphasizes exploitation, class conflict, and power resources as social mechanisms.

SOCIAL FACTS VERSUS SOCIAL CLASSES

Like *Unhealthy Societies*, we find TSL's thesis and supporting arguments to be incomplete, failing to account for the intractable issue of social class. The income inequality hypothesis was developed and tested using empirical data first, using a paradigm of quantitative observational studies, and explained second, using a combination of diverse disciplines such as psychology, sociology, economics, and primatology. From a sociological perspective, TSL and the Durkheimian tradition have much in common in that both view society and its individuals as being comprised of external, objective facts (9). Yet the treatment of income inequality in TSL as a perfectly exogenous construct implies a conflict-free vision of society (e.g., as opposed to class conflict being an inherent feature of capitalist economies) and implicates income inequality as the social fact to be transformed. This reduces income inequality to a distributional conflict over income as opposed to the encompassing conflict over relations of production that social class implies (9, 10).

On one hand, the authors' approach inspires new and testable hypotheses on the effects of income inequality, a welcome addition to social epidemiology's endless stream of studies replicating the association between socioeconomic position (e.g., education, income, occupation) and health without much theorizing about plausible social mechanisms. On the other hand, TSL offers little guidance in taking action on the mechanisms that generate income inequality in the first place. Most of the book's attention is devoted to documenting the negative social and health consequences of income inequality rather than explicating on its political and economic causes (e.g., scant attention is paid to the decline of trade unions, the importance of political parties and class alliances, or the strength of welfare state regimes) and potential policy solutions (e.g., only one chapter is devoted to outlining very broad remedies on how to build a more egalitarian future).

Missing from TSL's conceptualization of income inequalities are the inherent conflict and struggle between social classes over valued resources. Instead of beginning with income inequality, we advocate for a social class approach that acknowledges that the United States and other wealthy countries operate under economic systems in which productive resources are privately owned. Across all capitalist societies (including those discussed in TSL), social classes emerge when a small number of people own productive enterprises (i.e., capitalists) and the vast majority of workers sell their labor for wages. This near-universal economic arrangement leads to inevitable conflict from the productive process itself, not from the process of status differentiation as suggested by the authors. A particularly speculative explanation in TSL is its attribution of Latinos' poor diet in the United States to their desire to match the status of mainstream America by dining at fast food restaurants. Poverty among working-class Latinos and food deserts (i.e., areas where healthy, affordable food is difficult to access) appear to be much more plausible explanations (14). Income inequalities thus constitute only one form of inequality generated by the conflict over the labor process (other conflicts may include hours, schedule, benefits, intensity, effort, and autonomy) between classes with interdependent and antagonistic interests (9, 10, 15).

Given that TSL's main argument is based on observations of income inequality indicators and various outcomes, an unresolved gap remains between observed associations and offered explanations. This leads us to take issue with the way in which income inequality is treated as a cause of social and health problems rather than a potential mediator that results from political and economic factors (9, 10). If income inequality is treated as a proximal mediator, its reduction likely will reduce its negative impact on population health and well-being; however, it will leave intact the political and economic processes that gave rise to income inequality in the first place (declining union strength, growth of the financial sector, decline of manufacturing, stagnant wages for the average worker, weak welfare state, regressive taxation policies). Taking action on income inequality through the market (e.g., increasing wages) or the state (e.g., progressive taxation, redistribution policies) will narrow the gap between the poor and rich; however, significant gradients in health will persist. Although Nordic countries have been more successful in narrowing income inequalities, they have far from eliminated significant inequalities between owners, professionals, managers, workers, and unemployed individuals (15). The fact that class and health inequalities are observed even among more equal societies suggests that both inequalities are properties of a larger structural process. Applying a political economy framework to understand income inequalities allows us to widen our theoretical gaze to include structural determinants of income inequality, including class relations (9, 10).

The argument that what matters for population health is the distribution of income and not the social process through which income inequalities are generated (i.e., through the labor process under capitalist, feudal, slave, primitive, or socialist relations of production) rests on observations from a single country: Japan. The remaining egalitarian countries (mostly Scandinavian) that show good health and social indicators have strong "decommodifying" welfare states (i.e., these states take a substantial part of goods and services provision out of capitalist markets and use the state to provide them instead). Japan, on the other hand, achieves less income inequality via a narrower distribution of wages. Yet, one could have chosen indicators where Japan fares poorly (suicide, homelessness), in which case the conclusion could not have been neutral with regard to capitalism. The data would have favored the strong statist, welfare state model that limits the presence of capitalist production relations in important areas of providing goods and services to its population (16). The appeal of TSL to both ends of the political spectrum, then, would have not been possible either. The point here is to underscore the fragility of TSL's claims that the type of production relations, and thus social class, is not important for population health and well-being.

PSYCHOSOCIAL COMPARISONS VERSUS
CLASS RELATIONS

Although TSL offers some theoretical guidance on how to understand social gradients, its psychological hypotheses are less than parsimonious. For example, the authors resort to attributing negative health effects to narcissist anxiety created by income inequality. Narcissist anxiety is not included in the *Diagnostic and*

Statistical Manual of Mental Disorders, Fourth Edition, and narcissistic personality disorder has a low lifetime prevalence rate. On a related note, the authors appear to prefer subjectivism, as revealed in their argument that obesity is more strongly determined by a person's subjective social status than by their objective status as measured by education or income. One could argue that a person's subjective account of social position is determined by objective conditions and is more valid than a single indicator such as education or income. However, there is no rationale to assume that perceptions of social status cause obesity, but rather that these perceptions are grounded within one's objective and subjective conditions.

TSL's speculative approach to psychological effects of income inequality as the cause of health problems contradicts evidence from the current recession where the poor and the working-class patronize restaurants such as McDonald's for economic reasons. The millions of hungry poor and working-class U.S. citizens also should be acknowledged before claims can be leveled of moving beyond "material" needs. According to Pressman, TSL repeats data from The Heritage Foundation using a U.S. survey known to overstate poverty when compared with other major surveys such as the Current Population Survey (20). In addition, the fact that someone has a motor vehicle or air conditioning (basic necessities in most U.S. states) does not preclude suffering the hazards of poverty (e.g., being hungry, paying substantial interest on past debt, and paying a high proportion of income on taxes, transportation, and childcare) (20).

From a social class perspective, social gradients in health do not reflect negative social comparisons; rather they represent the degree to which workers are exploited and dominated during the labor process. Income inequalities reflect unequal social class relations among those who own means of production (the capitalist class), skills and credentials (the professional middle class), and non-credentialed labor power (the working class). The theoretical advantage of implicating class relations is that it moves beyond focusing on what people have (e.g., income) to examining the conflicts of interest between classes regarding what people do with what they have (e.g., invest capital, hire workers, sell their labor power). By directing attention to the conflicts within production and not simply market outcomes such as income inequality, the inherent interdependence between social classes is singled out for explaining how income and other forms of economic inequality emerge through the labor process (9).

Underlying this class interdependence is the concept of exploitation, which, according to Wright (17), satisfies three criteria: (*a*) the material welfare of exploiters causally depends upon the material deprivations of the exploited; (*b*) the welfare of exploiters and exploited depends upon excluding the exploited from access to productive resources; and (*c*) exclusion generates material advantage to exploiters because it enables them to appropriate the labor effort of the exploited. Rather than viewing inequality as a contextual explanation and social comparisons as mediators, social class and material standards still matter given that exploitation represents a near-universal mechanism through which income inequalities are generated and material standards are determined. We argue that "what matters" are not income inequalities, but the exclusionary rights and powers over productive resources that give rise to economic inequalities through the labor process (9).

APOLITICAL VERSUS POLITICAL

Throughout TSL, it is unclear where Wilkinson and Pickett stand on the role of politics and governments in reducing income inequalities. At times, the authors make it clear that mainstream politics provides no vision or guidance for creating a more egalitarian and healthier society. At other times, the authors make explicit calls for the government to take action on income inequality, listing a host of policy measures that include, but are not limited to, increasing taxes and benefits, implementing minimum wage legislation, and supporting employment retraining schemes (p. 263). On the whole, TSL offers conflicting accounts of whether national and state governments should assume an active or laissez-faire role in reducing income inequalities.

In terms of its political leanings, TSL remains adamantly neutral, avoiding any preference for left-, center, or right-wing ideologies or political parties. Remaining apolitical is troublesome given that TSL advocates a more equal society through income distribution, which requires political action. Advocating for societal change without engaging political processes overlooks the impor-tance of institutionalized systems in distributing power and making decisions to achieve equality and the fundamental differences that exist among political parties. For example, political parties espouse a particular set of values and goals. While the political left tends to be egalitarian, collectivist, and interventionist, all of which are key to reducing income inequalities, the political right favor private enterprise, big business, and free markets. Moreover, Scandinavian countries have achieved their comparatively high levels of equality through an active, and often contentious, engagement with politics through strong labor unions and pro-redistribution political parties (18). Rather than elucidate the political nature of health inequalities, the authors allow the data to speak for themselves, which amounts to being a bystander in the generation and repro-duction of income inequalities.

Despite its apolitical approach, the book has received praise and criticism from all sides of the ideological spectrum (3). Both the left and right concur that inequality is a problem (e.g., politicians of all parties in the United Kingdom made pledges in 2010 before the general election to take action on reducing income inequalities). In this respect, TSL provides a little bit for everyone. Right-minded individuals who justify structural inequalities rooted in property relations identify with explanations based on cultures of envy and breakdowns of social norms. Those on the left who are committed to narrowing social inequalities identify with arguments that lay blame on the increasing earning differentials between chief executive officers and average workers. Yet the right and left differ sharply when it comes to finding solutions (e.g., means-tested versus universal benefits). This is where TSL falls short. Despite calls for various forms of workplace democracy, TSL is largely dismissive of government interventions to reduce income inequality (1, 19).

EMPLOYEE-OWNERSHIP SCHEMES VERSUS WELFARE STATES

Since TSL's argument sets aside politics, it implicitly supports the status quo: social and economic systems based on private property and market competition. Such hierarchical and market relations exist even within cooperatives, not-for-profit firms, employee joint stock ownership plans, and other forms of participatory management that the authors strongly recommend as real alternatives. These recommendations are proposed as egalitarian solutions; however, upon closer scrutiny, these alternatives often are not strong enough in isolation. Past research has shown that cooperatives flourish in contexts where they are institutionally supported by local development banks (21). Employee buy-outs require unique circumstances to originate; in particular, firms must be failing or near closure so that employees can organize to form participatory management schemes. To date, these alternatives have been unable to rouse support for income equality and have offered little to no blueprint on how to advance public health policy.

As Pressman (19) points out, participatory management schemes, which often exclude non-standard forms of employment, can be easily reversed by top management, even more easily reversed than "limited" egalitarian welfare state policies. The quest for a deeper transformation of human nature than welfare state policies is of course commendable[3] but eroding the power of private market relations to provide universal social services might be a good start (22).

The authors' overall skepticism toward politics means that welfare states also receive little attention. This is unfortunate given the importance of welfare states in redistributing income within society; generous welfare policies provide an essential service with universal and targeted policy efforts. Homeless populations, for example, may need not only a society that redistributes income via taxation, but also special services related to housing, job training and placement, and health care. Incidentally, Japan, one of the most equal countries cited in TSL, has a

---

[3] Wilkinson's call for a deeper transformation of human nature, by appealing to both the right and left, echoes some forms of 1960s countercultural movements, young Christian groups, Greens, and other political movements that strongly emphasize interpersonal behavior as a means of social egalitarian change.

troublesome homelessness problem. This is the kind of specific health policy interventions that reduce social inequalities, about which TSL is silent.

Three essential components are missing from TSL: (a) macro-social explanations of how economic inequality is generated (income inequality is not exogenous); (b) pathways linking these macro-social explanations (e.g., economic inequality can be aggravated by austerity policies) to meso- and micro-levels such as institutions (e.g., work organization, including precarious temporary contracts) and individuals (e.g., material poverty affecting diet and insecurity, leading to anxiety disorders or depression); and (c) design of policies, interventions, and evaluations to reduce economic inequality and its consequences on individual health (e.g., "flexicurity" labor market arrangements). TSL falls short on components (a) and (c). Although the book is largely devoted to component (b), the plausible distance between a single macro indicator of income inequality and individual psychopathology is too vast and simple to accept.

CONCLUSION

It may be true that one should aim at a deeper transformation of "human nature" than what has been achieved with social democratic welfare states. Few egalitarians would disagree with that position, yet in a period when welfare states are aggressively under attack, playing down their contribution to human betterment seems irresponsible. As Pressman astutely pointed out (19), TSL's skepticism about government as a means to reduce income inequalities suggests, as an alternative, participatory management methods that are even less under worker control than liberal representative democracies (19). Shared ownership or "responsible capitalism" has broad appeal: it has been favored by the Liberal partner of the current center-right coalition ruling the United Kingdom. Yet there is little evidence that it makes capitalism more egalitarian. For example, shared ownership often puts workers' savings and pensions at risk, as in the well-known case of Enron (23). Employee stock ownership, participatory management, not-for-profits, and even cooperatives can exclude large segments of the workforce. Without comprehensive policy options that would include government policy (e.g., regulate or nationalize the financial sector, public pensions, universal single-payer health care systems, living wages), little will be achieved to reduce economic inequality.

TSL should be praised for raising the moral issue that economic inequality is bad for health and that something needs to be done about it. The opposition to such a simple idea cannot be underestimated in our neoliberal world. TSL constitutes a great advance from *Unhealthy Societies* in terms of its attention to politics in its last chapter and, in particular, its ideas on redistribution policies, corporate ownership, and management reform. However, the generality of its policy recommendations, coupled with its overwhelming emphasis on the correlates of income inequality at the individual level, limits its appeal to public health scholars. Moreover, macro-social explanations of how economic inequality is produced and how it affects health are absent, thus limiting the amount of policy solutions to public health problems that can be implemented and evaluated. One such explanation, based on social class (the labor process) as generating both economic inequality and a pathway to individual illness, has been found to be particularly salient in the evidence linking work to health inequalities (24). Most importantly, TSL would have benefitted from paying more attention to the above-mentioned three issues (macro-social explanations, pathways linking macro- to meso-levels and individuals, and design of policies, interventions, and evaluations in reducing economic inequalities). In this regard, TSL suffers from the typical weaknesses associated with SDOH scholarship (25): an overreliance on descriptive studies that examine the social stratification correlates of health and an absence of explanatory sociological models, policy interventions, and evaluations to reduce health inequalities. The emphasis on explanatory mechanisms is an important one, given that an accurate understanding of the social mechanisms underlying the production of disease is imperative for engendering effective political action. Since *Unhealthy Societies* did not include politics and TSL makes an honest attempt, we can only hope that Wilkinson's next bestseller will address these outstanding issues.

REFERENCES

1. Wilkinson, R., and Pickett, K. *The Spirit Level: Why Equality is Better for Everyone.* Penguin, London, 2009, revised 2010.
2. Wilkinson, R. G. *Unhealthy Societies: The Afflictions of Inequality.* Routledge, New York, 1996.
3. Booth, R. The spirit level: How 'ideas wreckers' turned book into political punchbag. *The Guardian*, August 14, 2010. www.guardian.co.uk/books/2010/aug/14/the-spirit-level-equality-thinktanks (accessed February 2, 2012).
4. The Economist. *The rich and the rest: What to do (and not do) about inequality.* January 20, 2011. http://www.economist.com/node/17959590 (accessed February 2, 2012).
5. The Economist. The joyless and the jobless. Should governments pursue happiness rather than economic growth? November 25, 2010. http://www.economist.com/node/17578888 (accessed February 2, 2012).
6. Bagehot, W. On equality: The lessons of the spirit level for the left, right and the British public. *The Economist.* August 19, 2010. http://www.economist.com/node/16844516 (accessed February 2, 2012).
7. Gordthorpe, J. H. Analysing social inequality: A critique of two recent contributions from economics and epidemiology. *Eur. Sociol. Rev.* 26:731–744, 2010.
8. Snowdon, C. *The Spirit Level Delusion: Fact-Checking the Left's New Theory of Everything.* Democracy Institute/Little Dice, Washington, D.C., and London, 2010.
9. Muntaner, C., and Lynch, J. Income inequality, social cohesion, and class relations: A critique of Wilkinson's neo-Durkheimian research program. *Int. J. Health Serv.* 29(1):59–81, 1999.

10. Muntaner, C., Lynch, J., and Oates, G. L. The social class determinants of income inequality and social cohesion. *Int. J. Health Serv.* 29(4):699–732, 1999.
11. Muntaner, C. Social epidemiology: No way back. A response to Zielhuis and Kiemeney. *Int. J. Epidemiol.* 30:625–626, 2001.
12. Muntaner, C. Commentary: Social capital, social class, and the slow progress of psychosocial epidemiology. *Int. J. Epidemiol.* 33:674–680, 2004.
13. Davis, K., and Moore, W. Some principles of stratification. *Am. Sociol. Rev.* 10: 242–249, 1945.
14. The Economist. Just deserts: Poor access to fresh food is a solvable health problem. October 29, 2011. http://www.economist.com/node/21534806 (accessed February 20, 2012).
15. Cuff, E. C., and Payne, G. C. F. (eds.). *Perspectives in Sociology.* Allen and Unwin, London, 1979.
16. Esping-Andersen, G. *The Three Worlds of Welfare Capitalism.* Princeton University Press, Princeton, NJ, 1990.
17. Wright, E. O. *Class Counts.* Cambridge University Press, Cambridge, 1997.
18. Milner, H. *Sweden: Social Democracy in Practice.* Oxford University Press, Oxford, 1990.
19. Pressman, S. Minding the gap: A review of The Spirit Level by Richard Wilkinson and Kate Pickett. *Dollars & Sense, Real World Economics* 288:27–28, 2010.
20. Pressman, S. How poor are America's poor? *Challenge* 54:109–121, 2011.
21. Gagliardi, F. Banking market structure, creation and activity of firms: Early evidence for cooperatives in the Italian case. *Ann. Public Coop. Econ.* 80(4):575–610, 2009.
22. Navarro, V., et al. Politics and health outcomes. *Lancet* 368:1033–1037, 2006.
23. The Economist. The feeling is mutual: A cuddly model of capitalism has been oversold. January 21, 2012. http://www.economist.com/node/21543161 (accessed February 22, 2012).
24. Benach, J., Muntaner, C., and Santana, V. *Employment Conditions and Health Inequalities: Final Report to the Commission on Social Determinants of Health (CSDOH).* Employment Conditions Network (EMCONET), World Health Organization, Geneva, 2007.
25. O'Campo, P., and Dunn, J. R. *Rethinking Social Epidemiology: Towards a Science of Change.* Springer Verlag, Berlin, 2011.

CHAPTER 23

The Solution Space: Developing Research and Policy Agendas to Eliminate Employment-Related Health Inequalities

Carles Muntaner, Sanjeev Sridharan, Haejoo Chung,
Orielle Solar, Michael Quinlan, Montserrat Vergara,
Joan Benach, and the EMCONET Network

As in many other areas of social determinants of health, policy recommendations on employment conditions and health inequalities need to be implemented and evaluated. Case studies at the country level can provide a flavor of "what works," but they remain essentially subjective. Employment conditions research should provide policies that actually reduce health inequalities among workers. Workplace trials showing some desired effect on the intervention group are insufficient for such a broad policy research area. To provide a positive heuristic, the authors propose a set of new policy research priorities, including placing more focus on "solving" and less on "problematizing" the health effects of employment conditions; developing policy-oriented theoretical frameworks to reduce employment-related inequalities in health; developing research on methods to test the effects of labor market policies; generalizing labor market interventions; engaging, reaching out to, and holding onto workers exposed to multiple forms of unhealthy employment conditions; measuring labor market inequalities in health; planning, early on, for sustainability in labor market interventions; studying intersectoral effects across multiple interventions to reduce health inequalities; and looking for evidence in a global context.

*****

We believe that the EMCONET (Employment Conditions Knowledge Network) final report to the World Health Organization's Commission on Social Determinants of Health (1) was strong in its marshaling of epidemiological evidence on employment conditions, but was weak in its policy recommendations. As in many other areas of social determinants of health (2), policy recommendations were not implemented or evaluated. Case studies at the country level can provide a flavor of "what works," but they remain essentially subjective.

Therefore, a likely implication for future research on employment conditions and health is that it will include policy implementation and evaluation.

Employment conditions research should provide policies that reduce health inequalities among workers. Workplace trials showing some desired effect on the intervention group are insufficient. We argue that the goal of reducing health inequalities in labor markets needs new policy research priorities, which we summarize in this chapter.

More Focus on "Solving" and Less Focus on "Problematizing"
the Health Effects of Employment Conditions

Most research on employment conditions and health has devoted itself to the "problem space"—describing and explaining how labor contracts differentially affect the health of workers. What is now needed is implementation and evaluation on policies that might "solve" these problems. In addition, most research on "solutions" such as labor market policies does not involve evaluations (3).

Policy-Oriented Theoretical Frameworks to Reduce
Employment-Related Inequalities in Health

The employment conditions that produce inequalities—domination, exploitation, low wages, lack of benefits, job insecurity, discrimination—are generally well understood. Yet the interventions needed to reduce health inequalities among workers are less clear (4). The theoretical framework on employment conditions must address why and how a particular labor market intervention could reduce health inequalities among workers (e.g., Does "flexicurity" reduce health inequalities? Which specific workers benefit from "flexicurity" labor markets?). More explicit and pragmatic thinking is necessary to suggest how and why a labor market intervention (e.g., government employment) can reduce health inequalities.

Research on Methods to Test the Effect of
Labor Market Policies

Stronger methods are needed to evaluate the impact on health inequalities of labor market policies. This could include, for example, the analysis of "natural experiments" such as when a government introduces a new labor market policy—such as creating government jobs for unemployed workers (3).

Determining the Generality of the Effect of Labor
Market Policies on Health Inequalities

A "one size fits all" approach to labor market policy interventions to reduce health inequalities is likely to fail (5). This is why we generated a global scheme that classifies countries based on wealth and labor markets. There is limited understanding of how applicable to different labor markets most interventions are (e.g., training). For example, under what conditions would a labor market intervention that is known to work to reduce health inequalities in, let's say, Barcelona be generalizable to Caracas?

Spreading New Labor Market Interventions

How can specific innovations in labor market policies applied to address health inequalities be used in other labor markets? Are there examples of such applications to different labor markets? Have these innovations been successful in reaching the chronically unemployed? An example could be Venezuela's Misión Vuelvan Caras, a program for the unemployed with a strong local participatory-democracy component (Consejos Comunales) (6, 7).

Diverse Mechanisms in Labor Market
Policy Interventions

What exactly is it that makes a labor market policy work to reduce health inequalities? For example, can we unpack "flexicurity" to learn whether stable income, social inclusion, and job security are the mechanisms by which this labor market policy might "work"?

Engaging, Reaching Out, and Holding onto Workers Exposed
to Multiple Forms of Unhealthy Employment Conditions

How can labor market interventions to reduce health inequalities work for hard-to-reach and hard-to-engage workers (e.g., the unemployed homeless; underemployed individuals with serious mental disorders) (8)? Are special sampling techniques being used to reach the hardest-to-reach workforces? What ensures that workers affected by many forms of labor market inequality (immigration status, racial/ethnic discrimination, domination, exploitation) do not drop out of labor market interventions?

Measurement of Labor Market Inequalities in Health

Efforts to overcome the "inverse care law" require that labor market interventions target those workers most in need. An important planning tool for labor market interventions to reduce health inequalities will require inequality metrics weighted to the needs of participants. The monitoring of progress requires a way to ensure that delivery, treatment, and engagement for a small group of precarious workers in need are rewarded, compared with another intervention that treats a considerably larger number with lesser needs—the "worried well."

Early Planning for Sustainability of Labor
Market Interventions

Early in the development of labor market interventions, planning on how to sustain them should be included (9). One implication is that labor market policies should move away from a model in which policy activities occur along a linear sequence of planning, implementation, and sustainability.

Addressing health inequalities in the labor market requires an appreciation of the structural complexity that might shape these inequalities, including gender, age, migration, ethnicity/race, and disability stratifications. Only sustained interventions will be able to address such multiple determinants of labor market inequalities. In addition, there are other reasons for planning for the sustainability of labor market interventions. Most such interventions will experience a "latency period between the beginning of program-related activities and their effects on population health" (10, p. 122); policies that are sustained allow sufficient time for observing health outcomes in the workforce. The "latency period" for health inequality outcomes in the labor market might be even longer. Also, programs that are sustained over a long period allow for long-term program effects, which are especially relevant for complex labor market interventions focused on decreasing health inequalities. Focusing on timelines for the effects of interventions is especially important because of the limited knowledge, as evident in the employment conditions policy research literature, about the timeframes of intervention effects (11), especially for labor market interventions, given their complexity. Workforces with a history of terminated programs may exhibit "disillusionment" and be reluctant to support new policies in the future (10, p. 122).

In the light of all these factors, planning for sustaining labor market interventions should occur early in their development. The received view that intervention programs need to worry about sustainability only when the money is drying out is inadequate. Instead, there is a growing literature on the wisdom of embedding planning for sustainability in the early phases of developing intervention programs (12, 13).

Intersectoral Effects across Multiple Interventions
to Reduce Health Inequalities

Synergies across multiple interventions (health services, social services) can reduce health inequalities among workers. Multiple intersectoral interventions might be necessary to reduce employment-related health inequalities.

Global Evidence

We need research that evaluates actions taken by high-, medium-, and low-income countries to reduce health inequalities caused by employment conditions—for example, Denmark's "flexicurity" (14) and Venezuela's participatory-democracy employment and poverty reduction programs (6, 7).

Overall, the new priorities outlined here would advance the field of employment conditions policy research by making the research more applied, more technical, and with a greater focus on reducing health inequalities.

Acknowledgment — This work was supported by the CIBER Epidemiologia y Salud Pública (CIBERESP), Spain.

Note — EMCONET network members are Bo Burström, Pere Jódar, Katherine Chung-Bridges, Lora E. Fleming, Sarai Vivas, María E. Martínez, Carlos H. Alvarado, Francisco Armada, Leslie Schuld, René Guerra Salazar, Yong Li, Chamberlain Diala, Marcos Rodríguez Fazzone, Marel Gonnet Wainmayer, and Dérgica Sanhueza Cid.

REFERENCES

1. Employment Conditions Knowledge Network (EMCONET). *Employment Conditions and Health Inequalities: Final Report to the WHO Commission on Social Determinants of Health (CSDH).* World Health Organization, Geneva, 2007.
2. World Health Organization Commission on Social Determinants of Health. *Closing the Gap in a Generation: Health Equity through Action on the Social Determinants of Health.* Geneva, 2008.
3. Cahuc, P., and Zylberberg, A. *The Natural Survival of Work: Job Creation and Job Destruction in a Growing Economy.* MIT Press, Cambridge, MA, 2006.
4. Borrell, C., and Artazcoz, L. Policies to reduce health inequalities. *Gac. Sanit.* 22: 465–473, 2009.
5. Chung, H., and Muntaner, C. Welfare state typologies and global health: An emerging challenge. *J. Epidemiol. Community Health* 62:282–283, 2008.
6. Armada, F., et al. Barrio adentro and the reduction of health inequalities in Venezuela: An appraisal of the first years. *Int. J. Health Serv.* 39:161–187, 2009.
7. Muntaner, C., et al. Venezuela's barrio adentro: An alternative to neoliberalism in health care. *Int. J. Health Serv.* 36:803–811, 2006.
8. Sridharan, S., et al. Contemporaneous relationship between substance abuse treatment and poly-substance use: Evidence from the Persistent Effect of Treatment Studies. *J. Subst. Abuse Treat.* 28(Suppl. 1):S83–90, 2005.
9. Sridharan, S., et al. Analysis of strategic plans to assess planning for sustainability of comprehensive community initiatives. *Eval. Program Plann.* 30:105–113, 2007.
10. Pluye, P., et al. Making public health programs last: Conceptualizing sustainability. *Eval. Program Plann.* 27:121–133, 2004.
11. Sridharan, S., et al. Developing a stakeholder-driven timeline of change for evaluations of social programs. *Am. J. Eval.* 27:148–162, 2006.
12. Pluye, P., et al. Program sustainability begins with the first events. *Eval. Program Plann.* 28:123–137, 2005.

13. Johnson, K., et al. Building capacity and sustainable prevention innovations: A sustainability planning model. *Eval. Program Plann.* 27:135–149, 2004.
14. Rugulies, R., et al. Job insecurity, chances on the labour market and decline in self-rated health in a representative sample of the Danish workforce. *J. Epidemiol. Community Health* 62(3):245–50, 2008.

CHAPTER 24

Why We Don't Spend Enough on Public Health: An Alternative View

Vicente Navarro

The primary determinants of public health are political. Comparisons among countries have shown that the importance of public health within public institutions and the priorities given by those institutions depend on the power relations in existence in that society. Authors who attribute the limited influence of public health in the United States to the public's limited understanding of the issues and/or to the supposed anti-government position of the American population miss the roots of the problem.

*****

The enormous growth of medical care expenditures in the United States (and, to a lesser degree, in other developed countries) has raised concerns about whether the country is spending too much on care and getting little in return, given that our health indicators are not good. The United States tends to be at the bottom of the health league among the countries of the Organization for Economic Cooperation and Development (the club of countries with the highest gross national product per capita). This high medical expenditure but low health ranking is the basis for the debate, in some quarters, on whether we should spend less on highly technological, very expensive, specialized medicine and more on public health, often erroneously equated with preventive medicine. Interest in this area has led to the question of "why we don't spend enough on public health" ("we" meaning U.S. society, but the same question could be asked for many other countries as well). An article with this title, written by Professor David Hemenway and published in the *New England Journal of Medicine* on May 6, 2010, is representative of the issues raised in this debate. Before I continue, let me emphasize that Hemenway makes many good observations that I don't disagree with. But his article does not address the root of the problem of why public health gets so little money and attention—or, as the issue is sometimes expressed, "why public health is the least developed area of medicine."

494

Let me say, first of all, that I disagree with the way in which the question is generally posed. Public health is *not* a branch of medicine. Rather, medicine is a branch of public health. There is overwhelming scientific evidence that the public's health depends primarily on political, economic, social, and cultural factors. Medical care, as its name suggests, takes care of people when they are ill or injured, but it does not do much curing. Most morbidity in the United States is chronic—long-term illness and disability. And the strategy in medicine is to take care of this state of morbidity. I am certainly not belittling the importance of medicine. It plays a critical role in improving quality of life for the ill and injured. But it is not the main determinant of the level of health in the population. The constant reference in the popular media and the academic literature to medicine as the primary determinant of the level of health in the population may be well-intentioned, but it is wrong.

With that clarification, let's move on. To answer the question of why we don't spend enough on public health, we must look at the political context of the issue being raised here. Public health is, for the most part, public, meaning that it is part of the state (or, in popular parlance, the government). We cannot understand the status of public health policy without understanding the U.S. state and the influences that shape it. And to assume that the U.S. state is the outcome of people's desires, values, and opinions is remarkably naive. The majority of people in the United States (74% according to the most recent *New York Times* poll) do not believe they have much influence in determining the policies of their government. They have not been polled, specifically, on what they think about the government's public health policies, but the percentage believing they have minimal influence there, too, would most likely be very high.

So, who does influence the U.S. government in its public health policies? There is no single answer. The state (and thus public health) is subject to many different influences, including, among many others, "popular opinion." But popular opinion (shaped largely by the highly controlled media) is not necessarily the most important influence. To find out whose opinions carry the most weight, we would have to look at the many different areas of public health, intervention by intervention. Of course, the scientific community also has influence. What the public health sciences have to say about the causes of health problems and how to solve them carries some weight, but, again, it is not the most important input. The determining factors are specific economic, financial, corporate, and professional interests—the U.S. establishment, also known as Corporate America, which wields enormous power over the state in all of its branches (executive, legislative, and judicial) and over public health. This corporate influence reproduces the power of the dominant class, a term never used in U.S. political and academic discourse even though class is the most important variable for understanding what goes on in our government—including our public health. None other than Martin Luther King, in one of his least-quoted statements, said: "The central struggle in the U.S. about power and control over government is class struggle."

Consider, for example, the huge underdevelopment of occupational health in the United States, which is simply the most dramatic example of how class power shapes priorities in public health. To believe that this is what people (most of whom are working people) want is to indulge in apologetics of the status quo—which is what a lot of academic work in this area does. We see the same thing in the area of public health research, most of which is financed by government heavily influenced by Corporate America and by private sources.

But the clearest illustration of the point I'm making here is the orientation of public health itself. The scientific evidence clearly shows that the most important determinants of health are economic, political, and social interventions. It is not by chance that, in general, the world's healthiest societies are those with the lowest inequality—societies where left-wing forces are strong. (This is not a partisan comment; it is a scientific one.) In both the highly developed and less-developed countries, the stronger the left-wing forces, the better is the health of the population. (For more on this topic, see my article "Has Socialism Failed? An Analysis of Health Indicators under Socialism (1).) The poor health indicators in the United States are a direct result of class (Corporate America) dominance in our political, economic, financial, and media institutions.

Given the huge amount of robust evidence that the most important determinants of health are economic, political, and social, what is the response of the U.S. establishment? Focusing public health on changing individual behavior. With this focus on the individual, collective responsibility disappears. The message created and reproduced by the establishment is that you, the individual, achieve the level of health you choose through your lifestyle and behavior. Meanwhile, Corporate America works to prevent collective interventions, as is made brutally clear by what is happening not just in occupational health but in environmental health. The underdevelopment of environmental protections is rooted in this reality.

The power of Corporate America is enormous. A good indicator is that this article would most likely not be accepted for publication in the *New England of Medicine*, where Hemenway's essay appeared. It would be rejected as too polemical. This is how the establishment defines academic diversity and freedom. To believe that the insufficiency of spending on public health results from the causes described by Hemenway, and by the many other authors who dominate the current debate, rather than from the realities I describe here, is to hold a position of opportunistic innocence.

REFERENCE

1. Navarro, V. Has socialism failed? An analysis of health indicators under socialism. *Int. J. Health Serv.* 22(4):583–601, 1992 (with a modified version in *Sci. Soc.* 57(1): 6–30, 1993).

About the Editors

VICENTE NAVARRO is a professor of health and public policy at the Johns Hopkins University (JHU). He is also an honorary professor at the Pompeu Fabra University (UPF) in Barcelona, in the Department of Political and Social Science, and serves as director of the JHU-UPF Public and Social Policy Program. He has written extensively on the political, economic, and social determinants of health, as well as in the area of health, quality of life, and social well-being. Dr. Navarro has authored twenty-five books, published in several languages. According to the Agency of International Scientific Information of the University of Pennsylvania (Lauder Institute of Management and International Studies), he is one of the most quoted scientists in the international social science literature (including the areas of political science, economics, and sociology, among others). Dr. Navarro has served as an advisor to many international institutions, including the United Nations, World Health Organization, and Pan American Health Organization, as well as to several governments: Chile's Unidad Popular government; the Cuban government, on its work in reforming the national health service; the Swedish social democratic government; the socialist government of Spain; the progressive government of Catalonia; and the U.S. government, where he worked in the White House on the health care reform task force led by Hillary Clinton. A recipient of many awards from various institutions, he holds honorary doctoral degrees from the University of Lleida and the University of Malaga, Spain. Dr. Navarro recently received the Ernest Lyman Stebbins Medal, annually awarded to an outstanding faculty member of the Johns Hopkins Bloomberg School of Public Health. He is the founder and editor-in-chief of the *International Journal of Health Services*.

CARLES MUNTANER, M.D., Ph.D., is a Professor in the Faculty of Nursing, Dalla Lana School of Public Health, and in the Department of Psychiatry, Faculty of Medicine, at the University of Toronto. He is also with the Center of Research in Inner City Health (CRICH) at St Mike's Hospital in Toronto. Since the 1990s, he has conducted research on social inequalities in health in the United States, European Union, Latin America, and Western Africa, integrating the public health fields of occupational health and social epidemiology. Originally from Barcelona, Dr. Muntaner studied at the Lycée Français, University of Barcelona, and Johns Hopkins University. He completed his postdoctoral training at the Laboratory of Socio-Environmental Studies, National Institute of Mental Health, in the United States. His research focuses on the study of work organization in relation to psychiatric disorders, the conceptualization and

497

measurement of social class and racism, comparative politics, welfare state, labor markets, precarious employment and health, and philosophy of epidemiology. Dr. Muntaner has worked with the World Health Organization, Pan American Health Organization, U.S. and Spanish unions, and the Ministries of Health of the Bolivarian Republic of Venezuela and the Republic of Chile. Dr. Muntaner was a co-chair of the Employment Condition's Network of the WHO Commission on Social determinants of Health and a founding member of GREDS/EMCONET at the Pompeu Fabra University. He is the recipient of the Wade Hampton Frost Award from the American Health Association. Dr. Muntaner is also associate editor of the *International Journal of Health Services.*

About the Authors

MONA C. BACKHANS is a doctoral student in the Department of Public Health Sciences, Karolinska Institute, Stockholm. She received an M.Sc. in sociology from Stockholm University (2004). She worked for several years at the National Institute of Public Health, with a focus on public health aspects of the labor market. Her Ph.D. project aims to enhance knowledge on gender policy and gender equality as determinants of health.

CLARE BAMBRA is a lecturer in public health policy in the Department of Geography, Durham University, England. She was formerly a lecturer in public health policy in the School for Health, Durham University; lecturer in sociology and social policy at Sheffield Hallam University. She has a B.Soc.Sc. in political science from the University of Birmingham (1998) and M.A. Econ. in European politics and policy (1999) and Ph.D. (2002) both from the University of Manchester. Bambra's research interests include the influence of welfare state policies and political structures on international variations in public health and health inequalities, and labor markets and the relationships between work, worklessness, and health.

BEN BARR is a research fellow at the University of Liverpool. He studied anthropology at University College London, trained as a nurse, and undertook post-graduate studies in public health and epidemiology at the London School of Hygiene and Tropical Medicine and the National Health Service. He was awarded a National Institute for Health Research doctoral fellowship in 2010 and has a consulting post with NHS Blackburn with Darwen.

SILVIA BELLINI is an epidemiologist at the Epidemiologic Observatory of the Regional Health Service, Grugliasco, Turin, Italy. She has a medical degree from the University "Insubria" of Varese, Italy (2001), and postgraduate degree in public health from the University of Turin 2005). Her publications include, as coauthor, "Inequalities in Female Cancer Screening Rates: A Review of the Impact of Interventions Promoting Participation" and "The Effects of Health Care Reform on Health Inequalities: A Review and Analysis of the European Evidence Base" (both in *Tackling Health Inequalities in Europe (Eurothine), Final Report*, 2007). Bellini's research interests are in the field of social inequalities in health and health care.

JOAN BENACH leads the Health Inequalities Research Group/Employment Conditions Network GREDS/EMCONET) at Pompeu Fabra University in Barcelona. He studied medicine, history, and public health in Barcelona and obtained a Ph.D. at the Johns Hopkins University. Most of his teaching and research have taken place at Pompeu Fabra University. His main fields of scientific research include health inequalities, employment and working conditions, precarious employment, small-area geographic analysis, and health policy— areas in which he has published extensively during the past decade. He has worked with several public health networks around the world and in the WHO Commission on Social Determinants of Health, chairing the Employment Conditions Knowledge Network (EMCONET).

LISA BERKMAN, Ph.D., is the Thomas D. Cabot Professor in Public Policy and Epidemiology at the Harvard School of Public Health, chair of the Department of Society, Human Development and Health, and chair of the Harvard Center for Society and Health. She is an internationally recognized social epidemiologist whose work focuses extensively on social influences and health outcomes. She edited, with Ichiro Kawachi, *Social Epidemiology*, the first systematic account of the field of social determinants of health. Berkman is past president of the Society for Epidemiologic Research and a member of the Institute of Medicine.

PHILIP BOHLE, Ph.D., is a professor and leader of the Work and Health Research Team in the Ageing, Work and Health Research Unit, Faculty of Health Sciences, University of Sydney. For more than 20 years, his research has concentrated principally on occupational health. His key research interests currently include working hours, work–life conflict, and health; the impact of workplace death on victims' families; aging, employment, and occupational health and safety; and the health and safety of precarious employees.

CARME BORRELL is a specialist in family medicine and in preventive medicine and public health, and is head of the Health Information Systems Service of the Agència de Salut Pública de Barcelona, with responsibility for analysis of the health situation of Barcelona city. She received her M.D. and Ph.D. at Universitat Autònoma de Barcelona. Her main field of research is inequalities in health, and she has led many research projects and had many publications in this field. She was editor of the 2004 report of the Spanish Society of Public Health on inequalities in health, and of the two Catalan reports on inequalities in health (2003 and 2005).

BO BURSTRÖM, M.D., Ph.D., is a professor of social medicine in the Department of Public Health Sciences, Karolinska Institute, Stockholm, where he has worked for the past 15 years. His prime research interests are in inequalities in health and health care, and in social and economic consequences of disease. He is engaged in international projects, including comparative studies on the impact of health and social policies on the health of disadvantaged groups in the United Kingdom and Sweden.

WEN-HAO CHEN is an economist at the Organization for Economic Cooperation and Development and a senior researcher at Statistics Canada. He received his Ph.D. in economics from Michigan State University (2004). His research focuses on income inequality, poverty, mobility within and across generations, and social policy evaluation, in particular employment insurance. He has published articles in the *Review of Economics and Statistics, Canadian Journal of Economics, Demography, Review of Income and Wealth, Applied Economics,* and *Research in Labor Economics.*

HAEJOO CHUNG is an assistant professor in health policy at the Korea University College of Health Sciences and a research scientist for the employment relations HUB of the WHO Commission on Social Determinants of Health. She received a master's degree from the Department of Pharmacy, Seoul National University, and a Ph.D. in health and social policy from the Department of Health Policy and Management at the Johns Hopkins University Bloomberg School of Public Health (2006). Chung's research deals with the political economy of health, especially the impact of welfare states on health care systems and population health. Her most recent contributions include an analysis of the effects of welfare state regime type on population health.

STEPHEN CLAYTON is a university teacher and research fellow in the Department of Public Health and Policy at the University of Liverpool. He received his Ph.D. in social policy from the University of Essex (2004). He has conducted qualitative social research in several different settings and has a specific interest in the politics of social policy formulation and implementation. Clayton has recently been involved in comparative studies of the impacts of active labor market policies aimed at people with long-term illnesses and disabilities.

GIUSEPPE COSTA is a professor of public health at Turin University, Italy. He was formerly an epidemiologist at the Epidemiologic Observatory of the Regional Health Service (in the Turin Unit, 1979–93; director of the Grugliasco Unit, 1994–2009). He has a medical degree (1977) and postgraduate degrees in occupational medicine (1980) and public health (1988), all from Turin University. Costa's research interests are in the fields of epidemiology of occupational risks, environmental risks, and social inequalities in health, and in health services research.

ESPEN DAHL is a professor of health and social policy at Oslo University College. He received his Ph.D. from the University of Oslo in 1994. His research focuses on health inequalities, social policy, labor market policy, and social exclusion, and he has published extensively on these topics.

PATRICK DEBOOSERE has been in charge of the unlocking of administrative data for scientific research in Belgium and was project leader in several interuniversity research projects on, among other topics, the future of the Belgian census. He has a master's in political sciences and Ph.D. in sociology from the Vrije Universiteit Brussel. His research focused for some years on the evolution of households and household composition in Belgium. In recent years, his main research interests have moved toward causes and evolution of inequalities in health, mortality, and aging.

FINN DIDERICHSEN, M.D., is a specialist in social medicine. He is a professor in prevention in public health and head of the Social Medicine Section in the Department of Public Health, University of Copenhagen. His research has primarily been in social epidemiology, on mechanisms generating social inequalities in health and health policy issues. He is currently chairing the Danish Review on Social Inequalities in Health.

ALISON EARLE is co-director of the Project on Global Working Families, Harvard School of Public Health, Boston.

TERJE A. EIKEMO is a postdoctoral fellow in the Department of Public Health, Erasmus MC, University Medical Centre Rotterdam, Netherlands. His past positions include researcher at SINTEF Health Services Research, Trondheim, Norway; research fellow in the Department of Sociology and Political Contributors/ 571Science, Norwegian University of Science and Technology, Trondheim; and trainee at the Royal Norwegian Embassy, Prague. He received a bachelor's degree in sociology, Nordic languages, and German at the Norwegian University of Science and Technology (2001), and master's in sociology (2003) and Ph.D. (2008) at the Norwegian University of Science and Technology. His research is in the fields of medical sociology and social epidemiology.

ALBERT ESPELT is a social epidemiologist working in the Public Health Agency of Barcelona and is responsible for the Drug Information System. He is a teaching assistant in epidemiology at the Pompeu Fabra University and professor in econometrics at the Universitat Oberta de Catalunya. Espelt is trained as a statistician and received his M.P.H. at Pompeu Fabra University. His main research area is inequalities in health, especially in diabetes, in self-perceived health, and in the drug field.

DAVID FEENY is senior investigator at the Center for Health Research, Kaiser Permanente Northwest, and was formerly at the University of Alberta and McMaster University. He received his Ph.D. from the University of Wisconsin–Madison in 1976. His publications, with coauthors, include "Multi-Attribute and Single-Attribute Utility Functions for the Health Utilities Index Mark 3 System (*Medical Care*, 2002); "Comparing Directly Measured Standard Gamble Scores to HUI2 and HUI3 Utility Scores: Group- and Individual-Level Comparisons" (*Social Science and Medicine*, 2004); and "Understanding the Determinants of Health for People with Type 2 Diabetes" (*American Journal of Public Health*, 2006). Feeny's research interests are in health-related quality of life and population health.

ELISABETH FOSSE is an associate professor in the Department of Health Promotion and Development, University of Bergen, Norway. Her areas of research are policy analysis, health policies and health promotion policies, and social inequalities in health. Since 2009 she has been work package leader in the European research project GRADIENT (Tackling the Gradient: Applying

Public Health Policies to Effectively Reduce Health Inequalities amongst Families and Children), a project funded by the European Union's 7th Framework program. Fosse has publications (in Norwegian and English) on Norwegian health promotion policies and Norwegian and European policies to reduce social inequalities in health.

ELENA GELORMINO is a public health consultant at the Epidemiologic Observatory of the Regional Health Service, Grugliasco, Turin, Italy. She was formerly an epidemiologist at the Cancer Epidemiologic Centre–Piedmont. She has a medical degree (1995), postgraduate degree in public health (2005), and M.Sc. in health economics and policy (2007), all from Turin University. Gelormino's research interests are in health policy, health economics, and knowledge transfer from the academy to the political arenas.

CLARE GERADA is a general practitioner in south London and has held a number of local and national leadership positions, including director of primary care for the National Clinical Governance Team and senior medical advisor to the Department of Health. She is medical director of the Practitioner Health Programme and serves as the Chair of Council of the Royal College of General Practitioners.

ELISE GOULD, Ph.D., is director of health policy research at the Economic Policy Institute. Her research areas include employer-sponsored health insurance, poverty, the burden of health costs, income inequality and health, the employer tax exclusion, and retiree coverage. She has authored a chapter on health in *The State of Working America* (2008–2009), co-authored a book on health insurance coverage in retirement, and published in academic journals. She holds a master's degree in public affairs from the University of Texas and a Ph.D. in economics from the University of Wisconsin.

CLYDE HERTZMAN has been on the faculty in the Department of Health Care and Epidemiology at the University of British Columbia since 1985. He completed his training in medicine, community medicine, and epidemiology at McMaster University in Hamilton, Ontario, between 1976 and 1985. Through the Canadian Institute for Advanced Research, he has played a central role in developing the conceptual framework for the determinants of health and elucidating the special role of early childhood development as a determinant of health.

JODY HEYMANN is founding director of the Institute for Health and Social Policy, McGill University, Montreal.

PAULA HOLLAND is a lecturer in public health and director of a distance-learning Ph.D. in public health in the Division of Health Research at Lancaster University in England. She received her Ph.D. from the University of Liverpool (2006). Her research focuses on gender and social inequalities in the employment and financial consequences of chronic illness. Holland has published on the employment consequences of epilepsy (*Epilepsia*, 2009), ischemic heart disease (*Scandinavian Journal of Public Health*, 2009), musculoskeletal disorders (*Rheumatology*, 2006), and diabetes (*Diabetic Medicine*, 2006). She is conducting qualitative research on the employment experiences of people with chronic illness in the United Kingdom.

NATHALIE HUGUET, Ph.D., is a research associate at the Center for Public Health Studies, Portland State University, Oregon. She received a Ph.D. in urban studies from Portland State University. Her current studies examine healthy aging and veterans' suicide. Huguet's most recent publication, with coauthors, is "Socioeconomic Status and Health-Related Quality of Life among Elderly People: Results from the Joint Canada/United States Survey of Health" (*Social Science and Medicine*, 2008). Her research interests are in aging and health, health care systems, and chronic care.

MARK S. KAPLAN is a professor of community health at Portland State University, Oregon, and holds adjunct appointments in psychiatry at the Oregon Health & Science University and in epidemiology and community medicine at the University of Ottawa. He received his Dr.P.H. from the University of California, Berkeley, and also has an M.S.W. and M.P.H. His research, funded by the National Institute of Mental Health, National Institute on Aging, and private foundations, focuses on using population-wide data to understand depression and health behavior in elderly populations. As a 2004 Fulbright Scholar, Kaplan studied the Canadian approach to population health.

ICHIRO KAWACHI is a professor of social epidemiology and director of the Harvard Center for Society and Health at the Harvard School of Public Health, in Boston. Kawachi is the author of several recent books, including *The Health of Nations* (with Bruce Kennedy; New Press, 2002); *Neighborhoods and Health* (with Lisa Berkman; Oxford University Press, 2003); and *Globalization and Health* (with Sarah Wamala; Oxford University Press, 2006).

ANTON KUNST is a medical demographer and social epidemiologist (Ph.D.) working as associate professor in the Department of Public Health, Academic Medical Centre, University of Amsterdam. His key research interests are in geographic, socioeconomic, and ethnic inequalities in mortality, ill health, health risks, and health care. Besides his studies on health inequalities in the Netherlands, he has coordinated comparative studies at the European and global levels.

CHIARA MARINACCI works at the Regional Epidemiology Unit of Piemonte, Italy, with a permanent position as a senior statistician (since April 2001). She is a researcher at the International Centre for Birth Defects, and was formerly at the National Institute of Social Medicine (1996–1998) and received a grant from the Agency for Public Health of Lazio region (1998–2001). From 2006 to 2008 she was head of the Epidemiology Unit in the Health Authority of La Spezia. Marinacci receive a degree in statistical sciences and a postgraduate degree in operational research and decision strategy at the University "La Sapienza" of Rome.

STAFFAN MARKLUND is a professor of work and health at the Karolinska Institute, Stockholm. He finished his doctoral degree in sociology at Umeå University in 1975, and became a professor at the National Institute for Working Life in 2000. His main research has been on social welfare, sickness absence, and occupational health. BENTSON H. MCFARLAND is professor of psychiatry, public health, and preventive medicine at Oregon Health & Science University and affiliate investigator at the Kaiser Permanente Center for Health Research in Portland, Oregon, and is a senior scientist at the Oregon Research Institute in Eugene, Oregon. He received his M.D. and Ph.D. in biostatistics from the University of Washington in Seattle. Board-certified in general and geriatric psychiatry, McFarland is nationally known for his research on quality of behavioral health care. In addition to his research, McFarland maintains a clinical practice focused on psychopharmacology.

MARTIN McKEE trained in internal medicine and public health and is a professor of European public health at the London School of Hygiene and Tropical Medicine. He manages a large research team working on health and health policy in countries undergoing political, social, and economic transition to market-based economies.

KENNETH NELSON is a researcher at the Swedish Institute for Social Research, Stockholm University, and teachers comparative social research methodology in the Department of Sociology, Stockholm University. His work has focused on comparative welfare state research, particularly on minimum income benefits and social insurance. He has previously written about income redistribution and power in welfare democracies.

GOPALAKRISHNAN NETUVELI is a research fellow at the International Centre for Life Course Studies in Society and Health, Department of Primary Care and Social Medicine, Imperial College London. His past positions include program director at Jahra School Health Program, Kuwait, and vice dean and professor at S.D.M. College of Dental Sciences, Dharwad, Karnataka, India. Netuveli received a B.Sc. from the University of Kerala (1971); B.D.S. from the Medical College, University of Kerala (1976); M.D.S. from the Postgraduate Institute of Medical Education and Research, Chandigarh (1980); and Ph.D. in epidemiology and public health from University College London (2002).

EDWIN NG earned his BSW and MSW degrees from the Universities of Windsor and Toronto, respectively. He completed his PhD in Social Science and Health in the Dalla Lana School of Public Health, University of Toronto. His research interests include the political dimensions of population health— testing the health effects of welfare generosity and leftist politics; the Neo-Marxian concept of social class—advancing exploitation and domination as relational determinants of health inequalities; and the clustering of welfare states into regimes—exploring interrelationships among global welfare clusters, social inequalities, and population health.

NADINE R. NOWATZKI, Ph.D., recently completed a post-doctoral fellowship with the Centre on Aging at the University of Manitoba in Winnipeg, Canada. She received her doctorate in sociology from the University of Manitoba (2011). Her primary areas of interest are poverty, inequality, and health.

LOTTA NYLÉN is a researcher in the Department of Public Health Sciences, Division of Social Medicine, at the Karolinska Institute, Stockholm. She received her Ph.D. at the Karolinska Institute (2006). Her research focuses on inequalities in the area of work and health. Currently she is involved in studies on social consequences of ill health, especially attachment to the labor market. Nylén has 20 years of research experience at the Swedish National Institute for Working Life, focusing on work environment matters, living conditions, work-home relationships, and their health effects.

M. ISABEL PASARÍN is head of the Community Health Service in the Public Health Agency of Barcelona and associate professor at the Pompeu Fabra University. Her main areas of interest in work and research are analysis of health and its determinants, analysis of inequalities in health, primary health care evaluation, and primary prevention in health, mainly in the adolescent population.

MICHAEL QUINLAN, Ph.D., is a professor of industrial relations at the University of New South Wales, Australia (since 1994), and holds an adjunct post at Middlesex University in the United Kingdom. His research has focused on occupational health and safety, especially its intersection with industrial relations, regulation, and the impact of precarious employment. He has been an expert witness in court/tribunal hearings and has undertaken government inquiries and investigations into occupational health and safety, including changed work arrangements and the Beaconsfield mine rockfall in 2006.

NANKY RAI is a medical student at the University of Toronto. She received her master's degree in public health from the Dalla Lana School of Public Health, University of Toronto, with a specialization in health promotion and global health (2011). Rai's research interests include the political economy of migrant health, history of social medicine, and South-South cooperation models aimed at addressing health inequities. Her most recent contributions include an analysis of Misión Milagro, a counter-hegemonic approach to eliminating avoidable blindness caused by cataracts across the Global South.

ENRIQUE REGIDOR, M.D., Ph.D., is assistant professor of preventive medicine and public health at Complutense University of Madrid. His research is based on the relation between socioeconomic position and health, and he is also interested in measures of social inequalities in health.

LUCY REYNOLDS is a research fellow at the London School of Hygiene and Tropical Medicine. She trained in molecular biology, finance, international development, and public health. She has extensive experience in the private and non-governmental sectors around the world, including work in health care delivery in nine countries. Her doctoral thesis was a case study of the functioning of a competitive market in health care.

HYE JIN RHO is a research assistant at the Center for Economic and Policy Research in Washington, DC.

MAICA RODRÍGUEZ-SANZ is senior statistician in the Health Information Service of the Public Health Observatory at the Agency of Public Health of Barcelona. She has responsibility for the mortality register and the Health Interview Surveys. She received her M.P.H. in 2004. Her field of research is the study of population health and health inequalities, and she has experience in the application of hierarchical models. Rodríguez-Sanz is also a researcher at CIBERESP, the Spanish Research Network on Epidemiology and Public Health.

ALBERT-JAN ROSKAM is a psychologist and epidemiologist working for the Department of Public Health of Erasmus Medical Center, Rotterdam, The Netherlands. He specializes in social inequalities in health, particularly obesity and related diseases and risk factors.

PAULA SANTANA is professor (in-cathedra) of geography and researcher at the University of Coimbra, Portugal. She is broadly interested in urban social geography, but her research centers on determinants of health and well-being, with a focus on social and spatial inequalities and neighborhood influences on health in metropolitan areas. She became associated with the IGU Commission on Health in 1995 and was first elected to the Steering Committee in 2001. In 2007 she was invited to support the Portuguese High Commissioner for Health (Health Ministry), coordinating a multidisciplinary group responsible for National Health Plan monitoring.

JOSÉ ALCIDES FIGUEIREDO SANTOS is a sociologist and associate professor in the Social Sciences Department at the Federal University of Juiz de Fora, Brazil. He is author of the book The Structure of Class Positions in Brazil (2002) and has published articles on class, race, and gender inequalities in the leading social science periodicals in Brazil. His research program is on social inequalities in Brazil, using a class typology.

MAARTJE SCHAAP is a researcher in the Department of Public Health at Erasmus Medical Center, the Netherlands (since 2005), working on her thesis in socioeconomic inequalities in smoking in Europe. She has a master's in public health sciences from Maastricht University.

JOHN SCHMITT is a senior economist at the Center for Economic and Policy Research in Washington, DC.

ARJUMAND SIDDIQI is a doctoral student in the Department of Health and Social Behavior and a research specialist in the Division of Public Health Practice at the Harvard School of Public Health. She completed her training in occupational therapy at McGill University in Montreal, Canada, in 1997, and her M.P.H. with an emphasis on policy and management, at Boston University in 1999. She is interested in socioeconomic determinants of health and the implications of these relationships for public policy.

ORIELLE SOLAR is currently Research Coordinator of Work, Employment and Health Equity Program (TEES) at Flasco–Chile and Professor of the

Dr. Salvador Allende School of Public Health, Universidad de Chile. She was previously a leader in the WHO Commission on Social Determinants of Health, working in Geneva, where she developed the commission's framework, among other activities leading to the report "Closing the Gap in a Generation." She was chief of cabinet of sub-secretary of public health of the Ministry of Health in Chile. At the ministry, she worked on equity-related programs involving participatory democracy and on a national survey on work and health, among other endeavors.

TERESA SPADEA is a senior statistician and epidemiologist at the Epidemiology Unit of ASL TO3 Piedmont Region, Italy. She was formerly a statistician at the Epidemiology Unit of the Regional Health Authority of Lazio. She has a degree in statistical sciences (1986) and postgraduate degree in health statistics, both from University "La Sapienza" of Rome, and M.Phil. in epidemiology from the University of Cambridge (1993). Spadea's main research interests are in the field of social inequalities in health and health care, equity in clinical governance, monitoring immigrants' health; she has been involved in various European networks working on these topics.

SANJEEV SRIDHARAN is a scientist at the Keenan Research Centre of the Li Ka Shing Knowledge Institute and director of the Evaluation Program at the Centre for Research on Inner City Health (CRICH), both at St. Michael's Hospital in Toronto. He is also associate professor in health policy, management, and evaluation at the University of Toronto. He received a B.Tech. in civil engineering from the Indian Institute of Technology in Madras, M.S. in public policy from Purdue University, and Ph.D. in social ecology from the University of California, Irvine.

S. V. SUBRAMANIAN is an assistant professor in the Department of Society, Human Development and Health, School of Public Health, Harvard University, in Boston. He has a Ph.D. in geography with specialization in multilevel statistical methods and a master's degree in development studies from University of Dehli. The main focus of his research is on understanding how different contextual settings influence individual health outcomes and population disparities in health achievements. Subramanian has published more than 85 articles, book chapters, books and working papers. He is assistant editor for *Social Science and Medicine*, editorial consultant to the *Lancet*, member of the editorial board of *Health and Place* and *BMC Public Health*, and book review editor for *Economics and Human Biology*.

KARSTEN THIELEN is an assistant professor in the Department of Public Health at the University of Copenhagen. He previously worked as occupational medical officer at the State Institute of Occupational Safety and Health in Düsseldorf, Germany (1996–2005). He qualified as a physician in Germany (1996) and has an M.P.H. (2004). His current research and teaching are concerned with the effect of working environments on mental health and health/social disparities related to clinical and social rehabilitation. Thielen's most recent publication is "Job Stress and the Use of Antidepressant Medicine" (*Occupational and Environmental Health*, 2011).

SHARANJIT UPPAL is a senior economist with Statistics Canada. He received his Ph.D. in economics from the University of Manitoba (2002). His areas of research include labor economics, economics of aging, and population health. He has published his work in *International Journal of Manpower*, *Social Science and Medicine*, *Journal of World Health and Population*, *Applied Economics*, *Health Reports*, *Perspectives on Labour and Income*, and *Education Matters*.

KJETIL A. VAN DER WEL is a researcher at Oslo and Akershus University College of Applied Sciences, in Oslo, Norway. He has a master's degree in sociology (2005) and has recently submitted his Ph.D. dissertation in sociology. His research interests include long-term trends in social and health-related employment inequalities (published in *Acta Sociologica*, 2010), life-course employment consequences of poor health (forthcoming in *Sociology of Health & Illness*), and comparative analyses on effects of welfare state arrangements on social inequalities in sickness and employment (forthcoming in *Social Science and Medicine*).

MONTSERRAT VERGARA studied statistics and public health in Barcelona, obtaining a Ph.D. at Pompeu Fabra University (2009). She works in the Health Inequalities Research Group/Employment Conditions Network (GREDS/EMCONET). Her main fields of scientific research include health inequalities, employment conditions, small-area geographic analysis, and health policy. Her recent publications are mainly focused on small-geographic analysis of avoidable mortality in Catalonia and Spain. Vergara also collaborates in some international networks, offering technical assistance, including EMCONET and GRAAL, which include some Latin American groups.

MARGARET WHITEHEAD, Ph.D., FFPH, is W. H. Duncan Professor of Public Health at the University of Liverpool, where she is head of the World Health Organization Collaborating Centre for Policy Research on Social Determinants of Health. For more than 20 years, her research interests have focused on social inequalities in health and the most effective ways of tackling them. She is currently senior advisor to the WHO European Review of Health Inequalities and the Health Divide.

STACEY S. WILLIAMS is Farm to School Program Assistant in the Food & Farms Program at the conservation nonprofit Ecotrust in Portland, Oregon, and is editorial assistant for the *International Journal of Men's Health*. She received her B.A. in cultural anthropology from the University of British Columbia in Vancouver in 2002 and her M.P.H. in health promotion from Portland State University in 2008. Her publications include, with M. Kaplan, "Suicide, Environment, and Ecology" (in *Handbook of Suicide Behaviour*, ed. A. Shrivastava; Royal College of Psychiatrists, in press). Williams' research interests are in sustainable food systems and policy, the effects of farm-to-school initiatives on population health, and food equity.

WEI ZHANG, Ph.D., received her doctorate in economics from the University of Massachusetts Amherst. She was a post-doctoral fellow in the School of Public Health at Johns Hopkins University. Her research emphasizes how countries' political economies shape health and health policies. She teaches at the School of Labor and Human Resources at Renmin University of China.